3 groups

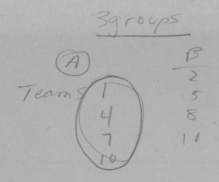

(A)   B   C
      2   3
Teams 1   5   6
       4   8   9
       7   11
       10

Pvs. Q

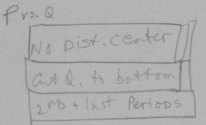

No Dist. center

Cut Q. to bottom

2ND + last Periods

Marketing Management Casebook

Marketing Management Casebook

Edited by

HARPER W. BOYD, Jr., Ph.D.
Sebastian S. Kresge Professor of Marketing and
Director of Continuing Education Programs

and

ROBERT T. DAVIS, D.C.S.
Professor of Marketing and
Director of the Sloan Program

Both of the Graduate School of Business
Stanford University

1971

RICHARD D. IRWIN, INC. *Homewood, Illinois   60430*
IRWIN-DORSEY LIMITED, Georgetown, Ontario

FIRST PRINTING, JULY, 1971
SECOND PRINTING, AUGUST, 1972
THIRD PRINTING, JANUARY, 1973

Library of Congress Catalog Card No. 74-149906
PRINTED IN THE UNITED STATES OF AMERICA

Preface

The authors or editors of any new book need to explain why they feel it should be published. This casebook has several objectives, the most important of which is to make available to teachers of marketing management a selection of cases designed to cover a variety of marketing areas. Thus, of the 45 cases included in this book, 19 deal with consumer goods, 17 with industrial products, and 9 with "services." A breakdown of domestic (U.S.) versus foreign reveals 38 of the former and 7 of the latter. A further feature is that some seven of the cases can or do involve the use of a decision model.

The cases included can be further classified by the subject area in which the "problem" is located. Eight such areas are involved—the role of the marketplace, the development of marketing plans, product and product line, price, channels of distribution, promotion, organization, and control and reappraisal. Hopefully, the cases adequately reflect the range of problems faced by a variety of marketing managers operating in a large number of industries both in the United States and abroad. All cases seek to challenge both the conceptual and analytical skills of the students. All have been tested in the classroom.

The editors are greatly indebted to a large number of individuals. First and foremost, we acknowledge with thanks the contributions made by those firms who made these cases possible. Many marketing executives as well as members of their staffs gave unselfishly of their time to help in developing the needed materials. In many cases, they remain anonymous, because, for a variety of reasons, it was necessary to use fictitious names.

We are immensely grateful to our faculty associates—both past and present—for their help and encouragement, including especially Professors Henry J. Claycamp, George S. Day, Gerald J. Eskin, Joseph W. Newman, David L. Rados, Michael L. Ray, and Alexander A. Robichek. We would like also to thank Jorge J. González Arce, Gonzalo Rivero Torrico, and Klaus Bredemeier who, as former ICAME (International

Center for the Advancement of Management Education, Stanford University) fellows, contributed their services as case writers. Donald M. T. Gibson, Charles P. Iffland, Lee A. Tavis, and Maneck S. Wadia—all former ICAME staff members—also made substantial contributions.

In addition, we should like to thank Bruce Fauman, Richard Fink, and Susan Emmett Rahl who helped in the preparation of many of the cases. They were financed by funds provided by the General Electric Foundation and the school's case development program headed by Paul Johnson. We deeply appreciate the untiring help we received in the preparation of the manuscript from Hilda Hebden and El Vera Fisher.

Stanford, California   HARPER W. BOYD, JR.
July 1971   ROBERT T. DAVIS

Contents

SECTION IV

PRICE

SECTION V

CHANNELS OF DISTRIBUTION

SECTION VI

PERSONAL SELLING AND ADVERTISING

SECTION VII

ORGANIZATION

SECTION VIII

CONTROL AND REAPPRAISAL

SECTION **I**

ROLE OF THE MARKETPLACE

Brewer Company

The Brewer Company, located in a large city in the Southwest, had a 450,000 annual barrel capacity brewery and sold its line of malt beverages in parts of the states of Arizona, New Mexico, and Texas.[1] A family owned business, the company had enjoyed almost continuous success since its founding in the 1880's. Although the company in early 1964 was enjoying an accelerating demand for its line of products the company's vice-president and general manager, Mr. James Brewer, was concerned about what strategies to employ over the next several years.

THE MALT BEVERAGE INDUSTRY

Since the repeal of prohibition, the growth of the malt beverage industry has been subject to ups and downs. But since 1959, sales have moved continuously upward with each year's sales setting a new national all-time high. The following table gives an indication of the growth experienced by the U.S. malt beverage industry:

TABLE 1

Year	Sales in Millions of Barrels
1934	32
1950	83
1955	85
1960	88
1964 (estimated)	98

The future for the brewing industry was considered excellent. Between 1950 and 1960, national sales increased only 6 percent. But between 1960

[1] Capacity was computed at ten times the greatest monthly output in any yearly period. One barrel equals 31 gallons or 14 cases each of 24, 120 containers.

and 1964, sales were expected to increase 11.3 percent (est.). Estimates indicated that industry sales would increase nearly 50 percent over the next ten years.

Malt beverages were served by about two-thirds of the homes in America. The popularity of beer is indicated by the 1963 per capita consumption figures for popular beverages in Table 2.

TABLE   2

	Annual Gallons per Person
Milk	32.1
Coffee	27.6
Beer (all malt beverages)	15.9
Soft drinks	14.2
Tea	7.8
Distilled spirits	1.5
Wine	1.0

Besides the growth in sales, another significant trend in the industry had been the move toward concentration. In 1934, there were 752 breweries. By 1950, the number had dropped to 252, and in 1963 there were less than 200 brewing companies. Most of the decline represented local, small-volume breweries. But growth of the large national brewers, through acquisition of the smaller breweries and internal expansion, had more than compensated for the loss in the number of brewing plants. This trend toward "bigness" was clearly indicated by the fact that the four largest brewers accounted for 80 percent of the sales increases between 1959 and 1963. In the Southwest—despite the above trend—several small regional brewers prospered, and Brewer was in this group.

THE MALT BEVERAGE CONSUMER

While beer drinkers were not restricted to any one particular social or economic group, the bulk—as would be expected—came from the broad middle income class (about 75 percent). Surveys indicated that slightly over 64 percent of all men and approximately 40 percent of all women were beer consumers. However, the quantity consumed by each drinker varied sharply. Over two-thirds (68.7 percent) of all beer sold was consumed by only 14.3 percent of the total population. This 14.3 percent comprised the "prime beer market."

The 21–39 year old age bracket was the top malt beverage consuming group, in terms of both consumer quantity and consumption frequency. Because a major portion of the 21–26 year old age group (the young market) consisted of "World War II babies," this segment was experiencing rapid growth in relation to the rest of the population. The young market was important since it offered a brewer customers with maximum longevity. The older age groups consumed less beer per drinker but, due to increased longevity, were increasing in number.

Approximately 87 percent of the total U.S. beer consumption occurred in urban places and only 13 percent in rural areas. The average male drank more than twice as much beer as his female counterpart. In fact, men accounted for over 80 percent of all beer consumed, even though they represented only some 60 percent of all beer drinkers. Thus, the 21–39 year old male heavy beer drinker (one of the 14.3 percent who drank over two-thirds of the beer sold) was literally worth several light drinkers.

Surveys reported that people drank beer at social gatherings because it was refreshing and relaxing and permitted them to break down social barriers. Beer was also a beverage which could be enjoyed "alone." It could be consumed when a man, or a woman, was reading, watching TV, or working. Most people associated beer drinking with events surrounding the evening meal and after dinner relaxation. This did not mean, however, that most beer was consumed at the evening meal. As a matter of fact, less than 30 percent was consumed at a meal.

In considering when beer was consumed during the week, nearly 75 percent was consumed from Monday through Friday and slightly more than 25 percent on Saturday and Sunday.

Because there had been a pronounced trend toward more beer drinking in the home, there had been a substantial swing toward packaged beer. In 1963, 82 percent of all beer consumed was packaged, versus 18 percent draft. In the early 1950's, this ratio was 74 percent versus 26 percent. Returnable bottles and cans were the most popular containers. And over 75 percent of all packaged beer was bought in container sizes of 12 ounces and under.

Food stores—for the nation as a whole—accounted for over 50 percent of all off-premise beer sales. In such outlets, nearly three out of five shoppers were women. Package liquor stores accounted for between 25 and 30 percent of total beer sales and two out of three customers were men. Taverns and bars represented about 15 percent of all off-premise sales and three out of four customers were men. The past decade had witnessed a substantial trend toward heavier beer purchasing in supermarkets and a decline in purchases made in smaller grocery outlets.

The average order for canned beer and 12 ounce no deposit bottle beer was about the same. Approximately 80 percent of the total volume was sold in six packs.

The Southwest Beer Consumer

The beer drinker in the Southwest was thought to be much the same as the beer drinker nationally. He was visualized as being typically a blue collar worker, male, 21–39 years of age, with an income between $5,000 and $8,000 annually. He was apt to visit on-premise outlets on his way home from work and he or his wife bought additional beer for home consumption. The Southwest had historically been a heavy on-premise beer area; however, in recent years, approximately 50 percent of the beer sold in the Southwest area served by the Brewer Company was consumed on-premise and 50 percent off-premise.

Between 1954 and 1963, the percent of draft versus package beer sold in the company's marketing area was as follows:

TABLE 3

	Draft (Percent)	Package (Percent)
1954	32.0	68.0
1955	28.1	71.9
1956	27.6	72.4
1957	26.6	73.4
1958	27.0	72.0
1959	27.0	72.0
1960	25.0	75.0
1961	24.0	76.0
1962	23.0	77.0
1963	21.0	79.0

These data show that package beer gained 11 percent of the total beer market during this 10 year period and further illustrates the trend towards "at home" consumption.

COMPANY'S PRODUCT LINE

In 1963, the company's product line consisted of the Brewer and the Fargo brands. The latter was a creation of the Brewer Company and was a price beer which did not receive any media advertising support. Special in store displays, however, were made available to distributors.[2]

The Brewer brand was by far the company's biggest selling brand. It was heavily advertised and the company's sales force spent a vast majority of its time promoting this brand. Slightly over 85 percent of the company's volume was sold under the Brewer label. The company estimated that in 1963 the Brewer brand contributed $9.89 per barrel to the gross margin account versus $4.62 for Fargo. If more of the brewery capacity could be employed the contributions would increase substantially. Thus, at full (or near full) capacity the Brewer brand contribution would increase to $15.25 and Fargo to $6.15.

---

[2] Although the aging process was essentially the same for both the Brewer and Fargo brands, the alcoholic content of the Fargo brand was normally less than 3 percent by weight and its production required less. It sold at retail for about 25 percent less.

Past and Present Brewer Market Shares

It was clear that Brewer was enjoying a favorable and accelerating demand for its product. To a considerable extent this could be traced to changes in the beer industry—primarily those within that part of the state of Texas which sold the company's brands. The four leading companies accounted for about 75 percent of total beer sales in that part of the Southwest served by Brewer. In the 1959–1963 period all but Brewer lost market share as follows:

	Market Share (Est.)		
Brand	1959	1963	Gain or Loss
Brand A	24.6	22.9	−1.7
Brewer	19.7	23.8	+4.8
Brand B	16.3	11.2	−5.1
Brand C	10.1	8.5	−1.6

The general manager pointed out that a loss in market share did not necessarily imply a loss in the number of barrels sold since the total number of barrels sold in the area increased by about 100,000. Thus, despite a loss in brand share of 1.7 percentage points, Brand A actually increased its sales during the 1959–1963 period. Brand B, of course, lost heavily. He went on to say that a gain in market share, during a period when total industry sales were increasing rapidly, increased the number of barrels sold substantially, as witness the rise in the Brewer brand sales from 162,473 barrels in 1959 to 220,793 in 1963. Brewer sales increase, therefore, had to be in part a function of such losses. During this same period one national brand (Brand D) picked up in excess of 12,000 barrels and another (Brand E) did almost as well with 10,000 barrels.

During the 1959–1963 period Brewer did a number of things which strengthened its position. This included an improvement in its quality control, a change in labels, the addition of new distributors, and the use of a consistent advertising campaign.

In 1962 a market survey among malt beer drinkers in the company's marketing area indicated the following:

1. That Brewer had made its primary gains at the expense of Brand B. Earlier, this brand (a local one), which had been purchased by a large national brewery, reduced the brand's advertising. The company's push was diverted to their national brand.
2. Brewer had greater loyalty among its customers than did the other brands.
3. Brand A was the brand people said they would buy if Brewer was not available.

4. In response to a question dealing with what was liked about the brand used most often, people replied:

Brand Used Most Often*

Reason	Brand A (Percent)	Brewer (Percent)	Brand B (Percent)
Long habit	17	34	32
Mild, light	65	30	27
Local product	5	28	—
Better flavor	12	11	24
Tangy taste	—	9	4
Stronger taste	—	8	—
Smooth and mellow	5	7	5
Consistent quality	—	5	2
The hops and malt	1	3	—
Refreshing	2	3	2
More body	2	1	—
Good blend	2	—	4

* Many respondents gave several reasons. Percentages based on number of men saying Brand A (or Brewer or Brand B) was the beer they used most often.

5. That, in part, the Brewer success had been based on going in the completely opposite direction from Brand A—letting Brand A have the mild, light story and instead going after and keeping the real beer drinker, the person who wants taste, tang, hops, malt, quality, aging, i.e., the person who wants a quality beer.

6. Individual brand images were reported as follows (among all beer drinkers in the study):

	Brand A (Percent)	Brewer (Percent)	Brand B (Percent)	Brand C (Percent)
Mild	61	25	20	20
Aged	12	23	18	25
Harsh	—	7	2	4
Watery	15	1	1	4
Dependable	16	17	15	10
Well brewed	20	30	20	12
Green	2	4	2	5
Refreshing	28	24	14	14
Light	30	14	11	8
Slow brewed	10	16	14	11
Heavy	—	6	2	4
Good flavor	27	31	26	14
Strong	1	9	2	5
Stimulating	11	10	5	5
Bitter	2	10	5	6
It's the hops	7	2	4	7
Quality	12	9	6	5
Old fashioned	3	4	2	6
Prestige	5	7	5	5
Premium	6	7	5	5
Popular	20	25	9	9

Brewer's Future Market Coverage and Sales

The company's marketing area was expected to experience a good population growth. The increase in 1964 over 1963 was forecasted at 56,000 barrels and similar increases were expected through 1967. The 1963 per capita consumption of beer was 15.1 gallons—up considerably over 1960. The most likely explanations for such an increase were shifting age groups and rising incomes. Even higher per capita beer consumption was forecasted for the future, but the company followed a conservative policy of assuming in its forecast that per capita consumption would remain at 15.1 gallons on an annual basis.

Despite the fact that the trend favored the sale of packaged beer versus draft beer and that the former was more profitable, the company's draft sales (in barrels) were up in all but seven distributor areas. The city in which the company's headquarters and brewery were located had shown the largest drop—800 barrels—in 1963 over 1960, although package beer had increased during this same period by 10,800 barrels.

Mr. Brewer was concerned about a number of matters pertaining to market coverage. He felt that there was a definite limit to the amount of brand share the company should seek in the present marketing area. "After all," he said, "we've got all our eggs in one basket if we concentrate on only our present market. The higher our brand share the more vulnerable we are. Our growth has to be in Texas. That's where the people are. More specifically we should be looking at the Dallas, Fort Worth, and Houston markets. But the competition is fierce there and it would take a lot of money to even try to enter these markets. Besides, we have to demonstrate that we know how to enter, successfully, new markets."

In referring to the company's problems in entering new markets Mr. Brewer was specifically concerned with the company's failure to gain a foothold for his brand in two "new" small Texas metropolitan areas located about 100 and 125 miles from their furthest current penetration. In the closest area, the 1963 advertising budget was over $25,000 and this was increased to $50,000 in 1964. A full time salesman was hired to devote 100 percent of his time to helping the distributor procure distribution. Although Brewer had managed to get good distribution sales had been disappointing. It was estimated that brand share was less than 2 percent. Management was concerned that sales per outlet were so low that consumers might be buying overage beer. The distributor was underfinanced and not considered to be effective. The distributor did sell several thousand barrels of the company's price brands yearly.

In the other market the company had experienced similar difficulties. In 1963, the company spent $15,000 for media advertising and in 1964 had increased this to $20,000. A full time salesman was put into the area to help the distributor who carried two other brands of beer.

Mr. Brewer was also considering what to do with the company's price beer which was distributed in many parts of the company's market. Although price beers were probably less than 5 percent of the market, he wondered if he should make an aggressive introduction of Fargo throughout his marketing area within the next year or so. He thought this move might be successful if Fargo were positioned against Brand A. It would be promoted through point-of-purchase advertising and its "light" label as a mild beer. All Brewer distributors would be asked to carry Fargo—assuming that a "go" decision was made.

In late 1963, the company had hired a price beer manager with the express purpose of increasing the sale of its price beer. Gaining entry to a market was difficult, because most distributors—especially the better ones—already carried a full line of beer. But the company had the advantage of being known as a quality producer and of being fair to deal with. By early 1964, the price beer manager had succeeded in getting a distributor in Dallas to take on Fargo. Mr. Brewer was seriously considering hiring a salesman to work solely in Dallas to help sell Fargo. In addition, the price beer manager had interested six distributors in Texas and Southern California to sell Fargo. It was still too early to tell what barrelage these and other prospective distributors might move in 1964, but it was thought that 10,000–15,000 barrels would be a conservative estimate.

Channels of Distribution and Sales Force

The company distributed its product to a variety of retailers (of which supermarkets were the most important for the sale of packaged beer) through 27 distributors, of which two were company owned. In general, the management was well satisfied with the performance of the distributors, although some 12 were estimated to have a share of less than 10 percent in their areas.

The company's retail prices for the Brewer brand were competitive with other regional beers but below such national brands as Budweiser and Miller. The typical retail price for six-pack cans is given below:

Brewer	$1.17
Fargo	0.89
Budweiser	1.39
Miller's	1.39

The following were typical retailer and distributor margins:

	Retail	Distributor
Brewer	23%	$0.60*
Fargo	22	0.42

* Per case of 24 units (12 ounce can equivalents).

The company's contact with its distributors was largely through its 14 man sales force which reported to an assistant sales manager. The company's sales manager was responsible for both advertising and selling as well as trade relations. The manager of the company's home market distributor reported to the sales manager. The average salesman was paid $620 a month and the use of a car. In addition, a salesman could earn up to $500.00 a year in bonuses. The sales force was mostly comprised of high school graduates and the average age was in the late 30's. They resided in their individual territories but made frequent trips to the brewery to discuss local problems. Over the past several years the company had done little sales training although several sales meetings were held annually at which time salesmen exchanged ideas on ways of meeting difficult problems. Turnover of salesmen was low—less than one a year. Most salesmen had been with the company for over 10 years.

Salesmen were primarily controlled through the submission of call reports. These were analyzed daily by the assistant sales manager, who prepared statistical summaries for the sales manager. Typically, no action was taken unless a salesman's report showed a drop-off in calls. The assistant sales manager and the sales manager tried to spend enough time in the field to travel with each salesman several times a year. In recent years, this had not been accomplished. The assistant sales manager had been bogged down with paper work and, in addition, had not been well. As a result, the sales manager had been forced to spend most of his time in the office.

A salesman had the responsibility of checking all A and B accounts in his territory. The classification of stores into A, B, C, and D categories had been accomplished by the marketing research director with the help of individual distributors. In calling on the package A and B accounts (high volume outlets), the salesman was expected to: check all point-of-purchase displays; install special "new" point-of-purchase displays; check the stock in the back room to determine its adequacy and freshness; rotate and stock coolers; check the number of facings and if possible increase them; make certain that the account carried the complete Brewer package line; handle any questions or complaints; and check all stock for cold beer and rotate present stocks.

In calling on an A or B draft account the salesman was supposed to: check all point-of-purchase displays; install new POS during new promotions; check to make certain the draft equipment was functioning correctly; provide the owner/manager with ideas for promoting the sale of Brewer draft beer; buy non-Brewer drinkers who were present a glass of Brewer beer; check his package stock for rotation.

One problem the company experienced was that many distributors, especially the ones who had been company distributors for many years, frequently went around the sales manager to Mr. Brewer Senior, president of the company. Another problem was that many, if not most, distributors expected the company salesman assigned to their territories to set up displays. Theoretically, the salesmen were responsible only for checking the distributor's driver sales force and for helping the distributor with any problems he had. In practice the salesmen frequently did work that was supposedly that of the distributor.

Each distributor was assigned a quota on Brewer beer. This quota was applied onto all barrels—not by individual package types or sizes. This target was developed only after consideration of the local economy, previous market share, share trends, competitive pressures, and advertising expenditures. They were adjusted quarterly. Before setting quotas the marketing research manager discussed them with the applicable salesman.

Distributors were not expected to spend any of their monies for local advertising or to make any contribution to the Brewer company for regional advertising or POS. They were encouraged to participate in community projects and service groups.

ADVERTISING

The company had always maintained a heavy expenditure in advertising. In 1961 total advertising dollars (including media, point-of-purchase, and production costs) were $407,000; in 1962, $442,000; in 1963, $465,000. In 1964, the budget was $502,000. Almost all of these monies were spent on the Brewer brand. The distribution of the advertising budget by media type for 1957–1964 is shown in Exhibit 1. In analyzing the advertising expenditures it must be kept in mind that media costs had increased. The amount of the increase was not known.

The company's agency had not done any extensive testing of the advertising copy used. Since 1961, the company's advertising theme and copy strategy can be described briefly as follows:

1961. Enjoy The Perfect Beer
    —Since the 1890's we have been developing and refining a perfect blend of brewer's artistry and modern science.
1962. Essentially a continuation of the 1961 strategy.
1963–64. A Refreshing Interlude
        —No other brewery in the Southwest can match Brewer's years of brewing *experience* at blending nature's best ingredients into a refreshing beer.

In 1962, a study of the effectiveness of Brewer advertising versus other leading brands among male beer drinkers was made. The results are shown in Exhibit 2.

Conclusion

Mr. Brewer hoped to develop a plan of action which he could present to his father and the company's board of directors in the early fall 1964.

While he could expect some help from the sales manager, the advertising manager, and the marketing research director he knew that the major burden of preparing the plan would fall on himself. He fully expected that his plan would call for some "investment spending" that would exceed the budget. While he anticipated some questioning of this he felt that the company's strong profit and financial position would enable him to obtain the extra funds provided he had a well integrated plan which demonstrated that they would "pay off" in the long run. The company had never had a written plan of any consequence although it did operate with fairly detailed budgets. Mr. Brewer thought he should present a one year plan for the calendar year 1965 in some detail and a less detailed three-year plan. The latter, he thought, was important because some of the expenditures made in 1965 would not pay off until later.

EXHIBIT 1

Distribution of Advertising and Sales Promotion by Media Type, 1957–1964

Media Type	1957	1958	1959	1960	1961	1962	1963	1964 Budget
Outdoor costs per barrel..........	—	$0.72	$0.70	$0.77	$0.70	$0.69	$0.62	$0.60
TV costs per barrel...............	—	0.87	0.98	1.07	0.97	0.87	0.71	0.78
Newspaper costs per barrel........	—	0.03	0.35	0.09	0.17	0.19	0.15	0.15
Radio costs per barrel............	—	0.46	0.35	0.23	0.25	0.26	0.33	0.21
Misc. publications costs per barrel..	—	0.05	0.06	0.07	0.05	—	0.06	0.05
Point of sale costs per barrel.......	—	0.62	0.82	0.44	0.31	0.34	0.33	0.30
Public relations costs per barrel....	—	0.44	0.51	0.09	0.06	0.07	0.07	0.07
Sales promotion costs per barrel....	—	—	—	0.09	0.10	0.04	0.07	0.07
Total per barrel.................	—	3.42	3.88	2.86	2.64	2.51	2.34	2.24

EXHIBIT 2

Recall of Brand A Advertising and What It Is Trying to Get Across

	Total (Percent)	Brand A (Percent)	Brewer (Percent)	All Other (Percent)
Recall slogan "It's light"	68	62	75	70
"Pure Ingredients"	22	21	15	27
Quality	20	22	20	17
Saw advertising—TV, billboard	11	18	7	9
Good flavor, good taste	10	11	10	9
Made in Arizona	10	13	8	10
Mild, light, smooth	6	10	3	4
Cool, refreshing	6	4	3	10
Horse show	5	9	5	3
Open for tours	5	4	5	4
All other positive	4	4	5	3
All other negative	2	2	6	—
Confused with other brands' advertising	—	—	—	—
Don't know	7	6	11	3

Brand A advertising is pretty much the same as it was in 1957—and it is a good seat to hold onto for more than five years.

We have only to look at this brand's recall picture over the years to see how it has stood up to time.

Recognition of Brand A Advertising 1955–1962

	1962 (Percent)	1957 (Percent)	1956 (Percent)	1955 (Percent)
Recall Brand A advertising	93	94	90	80
Don't recall	7	6	10	20

Observation. The over-all diffusion of most beer advertising in this area in the past has made Brand A's consistency particularly effective. It has become an oasis of familiarity in an everchanging slogan scene.

Yet for all that, it is not, as we have seen, selling beer the way it should. Has it lost its usefulness? Our own feeling would be otherwise. Rather what has happened is that Brand A has not yet learned how to back up the "It's light" story with the kind of strong reason why story, the body copy needed for maximum efficiency and optimum usefulness.

The light story belongs to Brand A. But it needs a new framework; additional underscoring; solid support to push ahead in the new situation.

Brand B Advertising

Brand B has done little or no advertising since late 1959 or early 1960. All the recall picture shows is the rather surprising postfactor benefits of former advertising.

Observation. The fascinating story, here, is that three years after Brand B stopped almost all its advertising, about half of the beer drinkers'

EXHIBIT 2 (Continued)

Recall of Brand B Advertising

	Total (Percent)	Brand B Drinkers (Percent)
Sponsor wrestling	15	23
Singing, yodeling	8	5
Saw ad on billboards, TV	6	24
Old recipe beer	5	9
German type of beer	5	2
Let's have a Brand B	4	7
Sociable, fun, get-together	4	11
Remember German scenes	3	5
Remember little men	2	3
Slow-brewed	2	10
Best quality	2	5
Best flavor, taste	2	2
Light, mild	2	2
All other positive	3	11
Confuse with other brands' advertising	3	2
Don't know	49	31

market is unaware of the change; and less than two out of three of the brand's own drinkers note the change. Yet the question, which in all fairness must be asked, is whether this is a tribute to Brand B's former advertising or the lack of individuality and uniqueness of most of the other beer advertising.

Observation. "Aged" is the best thing going for this brand in its current campaign. Without this, the brand would be in trouble.

The one other factor which has also helped has been the "Made in the Southwest, Local Beer" tag line.

Observation. Over-all the Brewer company's advertising efforts are achieving the same mark as 1957 and are certainly an improvement over the previous efforts.

EXHIBIT 2 (Continued)

Brand C Advertising
Recall of Brand C Advertising

	Total (Percent)	Brand C Drinkers (Percent)
The Beer of the Old Southwest	24	36
Label with Spurs (Red, Silver, Gold)	15	20
Aged	13	25
Local beer—made in the Southwest	11	15
Partying, fun	4	5
Dance time	4	10
Sports	4	—
American beer	4	5
Dislike advertising	3	—
People's beer; workingman's beer	2	5
Outdoor sports	2	—
Old reliable beer	1	10
Less expensive, better buy	1	5
All other positive	3	10
Don't know	40	15

Brewer Advertising Recall

	Total (Percent)	Brewer Drinkers (Percent)	All Others (Percent)
Remember "Made for Over 60 years by Experienced Craftsmen"	15	21	13
Remember "Made locally"	12	21	12
Saw advertising on billboards, TV	10	12	10
Quality, best beer	7	7	7
Show outdoor scenes	5	9	4
Waterfalls	4	7	2
Sponsor sports	4	6	2
"Perfected"	3	3	4
Refreshing, cool	2	2	2
Made from old formula	1	2	—
Good flavor	1	—	2
Man pouring beer from glass	1	2	—
Light, mild	1	1	1
Visit the brewery, tours	3	4	3
Confuse with other brands' advertising	3	1	4
All other positive	1	2	—
All other negative	1	—	2
Don't know	60	39	67

EXHIBIT 2 (Continued)

If we recap the Brewer advertising recall trend, here is what we find:

Recall of Brewer Advertising, 1955–1962

	1962 (Percent)	1957 (Percent)	1956 (Percent)	1955 (Percent)
Recall Brewer Advertising	40	41	30	24
Don't recall	60	59	70	76

Observation. Yet, this is only part of the story. For in actual fact, if we look back at the ad recall table, we find that what is working is not the central advertising theme, but the back-up signature of "The West's Oldest and Most Experienced Brewery" and the local appeal.

Experience and local overtones in the image are good, but the basic quality beer story is not coming through any more than it comes through in the advertising recall.

When we recap the over-all beer advertising recall picture, the need for a basic reevaluation of the company's advertising approach is apparent.

Comparative Recall of Individual Brand's Advertising Efforts among All Beer Drinkers

Brand	Recall Advertising (Percent)	Don't Recall (Percent)
Brand A	93	7
Brand C	60	40
Brand B	51	49
Brewer's	40	60

The evidence speaks for itself.

In addition, beer drinkers appear to be rather consciously aware of the weakness of Brewer's current theme. This is indicated in the next table which shows their responses to the question: "If you had to choose a brand of beer on the basis of advertising, which one brand would you choose?"

Brand Choice on Basis of Advertising

	Total (Percent)	Brewer Drinkers (Percent)
Brand A	39	32
Brand C	10	9
Brand B	8	12
Brewer's	7	13

EXHIBIT 2 (Continued)

Observation. It is a mistake, of course, to try to make advertising experts of consumers. What they do, how they react is the important factor—not what they say.

Yet the low read on Brewer advertising in the total market and among its drinkers must be carefully weighted and considered, for it does bear out and substantiate the weakness of Brewer advertising which we've seen throughout this study.

One step further, before we try to look for further clues on the kind of advertising message which might work best for Brewer. In the following table,

Aided Recall of Brand Slogans

	Percent		*Percent*		*Percent*
Largest Selling				*Does the Most*	
Beer		*Aged*		*Advertising*	
Brand A	37	Brand C	55	Brand A	42
Brewer	14	Brewer	9	Brand C	28
Brand B	14	Brand A	4	Brewer	6
All others	20	Don't know	32	All others	10
Don't know	19				
Slow-Brewed		*People Like It*		*Best Tap Beer*	
Brand B	15	Brand C	48	Brewer	22
Brewer	11	Brewer	8	Brand A	18
All others	20	All others	11	Brand B	10
Don't know	43	Don't know	31	All others	5
				Don't know	35
				The Best Packaged	
Oldest Beer Company		*Pure Pleasure*		*Beer*	
Brewer	40	Brand A	19	Brand A	19
Brand A	13	Brand C	12	Brewer	12
All others	7	Brewer	7	Brand B	9
Dont know	40	All others	10	Brand C	8
		Don't know	30	All others	7
				Don't know	28
The Lady's Beer		*The Sportsman's Beer*			
Brand A	35	Brand A	12		
Brand C	2	Brewer	15		
Brand B	2	Brand B	10		
All others	2	Brand C	8		
Don't know	50	All others	10		
		Don't know	23		

we have shown, slogan by slogan, how each of the brand's individual slogans are related back to the individual brands by the beer drinkers. In this instance, the drinker was reminded of the slogan and then asked to tell us what brand came to mind for each one:

Yet of all of the brands of beer on the shelves, Brewer beer, in actual life, does satisfy the physical beer needs of its users more than any other brand.

The real story for Brewer's advertising lies in the responses of the different

EXHIBIT 2 (Continued)

brand users to the single question: "When does your brand of beer taste best
to you?"

When Brand Tastes Best

	Total (Percent)	Brewer (Percent)	Brand A (Percent)	Brand B (Percent)
When I'm hot	24	33	24	12
When I'm thirsty for a glass of beer	22	35	15	22
After work	35	46	35	22
When I'm tired	14	17	13	17
In the summer	11	8	14	11
With meals	4	4	4	5
Social occasions	9	2	13	7
Any time	3	—	5	4
In the evening, after dinner (watching TV)	22	15	23	25
Outdoors	9	2	14	11
When I'm relaxing	9	7	11	10
All others	9	9	6	8

Observation. Here we see the real dividing line between a mild, light beer
and a real beer. The mild beer is the social beer, the occasional outdoor beer,
the summer beer, even the TV watching beer.

But the real beer—the one with hops and malt, brewed, and aged—with
real ingredients—this is the beer for the moments when the beer need is
greatest—when thirsty, tired, after work—hot—just plain thirsty for a glass
of beer.

This is the Brewer story, which is not now being sold or told. This is the
story which, if properly executed, can help Brewer keep its current customers,
build more loyal users, increase consumption, and extend its present share of
customers.

We will recognize that it is an easier story to unlock than it is to tell—but
it is the story which does need telling. Only then will Brewer advertising pull
its weight and really contribute to the outstanding job being done by Brewer
on other scores.

Brand Associations

A measure of brand image is its association with various types of people
or occupations. The beer drinkers were read a list of occupations and types of
people and asked to associate a beer brand with each. They were also handed
a card listing the brand names that they could refer to at any time.

The groups have been separated into those associated more with Brewer
and those associated more with Brand A.

As might have been expected, Brand A is strongly associated with women
and white-collar workers. It is also connected with drinkers who are not very
knowledgeable about beer (young people) and those who don't drink much
beer (athletes and retired people).

Brewer is a rough, masculine beer—for the heavy beer drinker and the
man who is sports minded.

EXHIBIT 2 (Continued)

Brands Associated with Different Occupations and Types of People

	Brewer (Percent)	Brand A (Percent)	Brand B (Percent)	Brand C (Percent)	Don't Know (Percent)
Associate More with Brewer's					
Men	27	16	9	6	26
Fishermen	21	16	3	8	28
Mechanics	21	12	7	8	36
Truck drivers	18	11	10	11	30
Hunters	18	11	8	11	30
Boaters	15	12	7	7	38
Associate More with Brand A					
Women	7	46	4	2	25
College students	11	36	5	5	30
Young people	10	35	3	5	30
Retired people	7	28	4	1	39
Waiters	8	27	4	3	38
Athletes	9	20	8	3	49
Salesmen	11	15	7	4	40
Doctors	6	14	8	1	40
Farmers	12	13	7	7	44
Military officers	9	11	9	4	44

Brand Identification

In an attempt to determine the importance of various beer characteristics and to evaluate brand image with these characteristics, respondents were presented with sets of paired values on a five point rating scale. The "pairs" consisted of matched antonyms. Negative words were avoided and words connoting similar ideas were rotated, thus minimizing bias.

The respondent was asked in the beginning to designate for each "pairing" where he would rate "what he looks for" in a beer. For example, the respondent was asked to indicate whether he looked for a very light beer, a somewhat light beer, neither a light nor a dark beer, a somewhat dark beer, or a very dark beer. The same procedure was used for five other "pairs" of values. The frequencies for the various traits were averaged to derive comparable means for the different brands and subgroups. The means for "look for" ratings will be referred to, in this report, as the "ideal" beer.

The purpose of this design is to provide a workable benchmark for future reference so that trends can be observed and evaluated. Therefore, statistical variance and standard deviation have been determined for every mean average shown. The size of our sample was such that a difference of .02 percent or more in a total column shall be considered significant. Lowering the sample size increases the variability, therefore, when evaluating the means in the heavy user, moderate-light user, or other subgroups, they must be at least .04 percent from one another to be statistically significant.

The data are first presented in tabular form and then reproduced graphically for easier readability and more comprehensive comparison.

EXHIBIT 2 (Continued)

Mean Averages of Ratings Given "Ideal" Beer
Compared with Ratings Given Various Brands

	Ideal Beer (Percent)	Brand A (Percent)	Brewer (Percent)	Brand B (Percent)	Brand C (Percent)
Light/Dark					
Total beer drinkers............	2.0	1.7	2.2	2.3	2.6
Heavy beer drinkers...........	1.9	1.6	2.2	2.3	2.4
Moderate-light beer drinkers....	2.0	1.7	2.2	2.3	2.7
Smooth/Tangy					
Total beer drinkers............	2.7	2.4	3.4	3.2	3.4
Heavy beer drinkers...........	2.8	2.4	3.5	3.2	3.2
Moderate-light beer drinkers....	2.5	2.3	3.3	3.3	3.5
Bland/Sharp					
Total beer drinkers............	2.9	2.5	3.4	3.2	3.4
Heavy beer drinkers...........	3.0	2.5	3.4	3.1	3.4
Moderate-light beer drinkers....	2.7	2.5	3.4	3.3	3.4
Light Body/Full Body					
Total beer drinkers............	2.9	2.5	3.4	3.4	3.4
Heavy beer drinkers...........	3.1	2.4	3.5	3.3	3.2
Moderate-light beer drinkers....	2.7	2.6	3.3	3.4	3.7
Mild Flavor/Strong Flavor					
Total beer drinkers............	2.3	2.0	3.0	2.9	3.4
Heavy beer drinkers...........	2.4	1.9	3.0	2.7	3.3
Moderate-light beer drinkers....	2.2	2.1	3.1	3.1	3.6
Sweet/Hoppy					
Total beer drinkers............	3.6	3.2	3.8	3.7	3.7
Heavy beer drinkers...........	3.7	3.1	3.8	3.7	3.7
Moderate-light beer drinkers....	3.4	3.2	3.7	3.7	3.7

EXHIBIT 2 (Continued)

"Ideal" Beer Ratings of Various Groups

	Drink Brewer (Percent)	Drink Brand A (Percent)	Drink Brand B (Percent)	Drink Brand C (Percent)	Drink Other Brands (Percent)	Heavy Beer Drinkers (Percent)	Moderate-Light Beer Drinkers (Percent)	Males (Percent)	Females (Percent)
Light/dark	2.1	1.8	1.9	2.0	2.0	1.9	2.0	2.0	1.8
Smooth/tangy	2.9	2.4	3.1	2.0	2.5	2.8	2.5	2.7	2.4
Bland/sharp	3.1	2.7	3.0	2.8	2.7	3.0	2.7	2.9	2.6
Light body/full body	3.3	2.8	2.9	2.7	2.7	3.1	2.7	3.0	2.8
Mild/strong	2.6	2.0	2.3	2.5	2.2	2.4	2.2	2.4	2.0
Sweet/hoppy	3.7	3.4	3.4	3.6	2.4	3.7	3.4	3.7	3.2

EXHIBIT 2 (Continued)

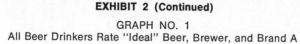

GRAPH NO. 1
All Beer Drinkers Rate "Ideal" Beer, Brewer, and Brand A

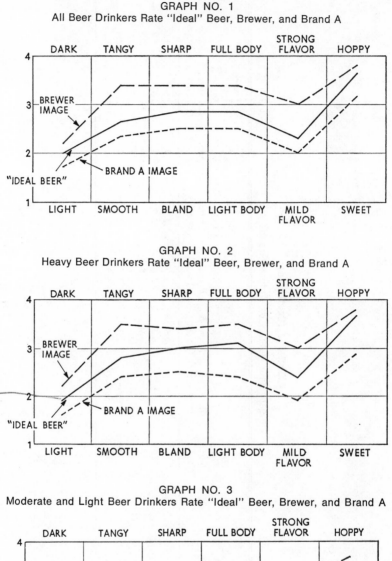

GRAPH NO. 2
Heavy Beer Drinkers Rate "Ideal" Beer, Brewer, and Brand A

GRAPH NO. 3
Moderate and Light Beer Drinkers Rate "Ideal" Beer, Brewer, and Brand A

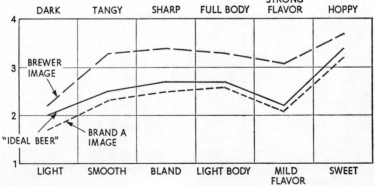

EXHIBIT 2 (Continued)

GRAPH NO. 4
All Beer Drinkers Rate Brewer, Brand C, and Brand B

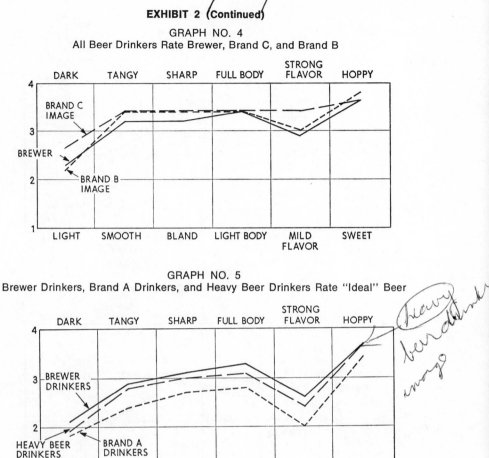

GRAPH NO. 5
Brewer Drinkers, Brand A Drinkers, and Heavy Beer Drinkers Rate "Ideal" Beer

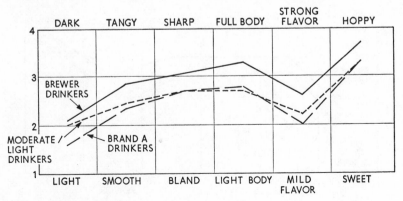

GRAPH NO. 6
Brewer Drinkers, Brand A Drinkers, and Moderate/Light Drinkers Rate "Ideal" Beer

EXHIBIT 2 (Continued)

GRAPH NO. 7
Brewer Drinkers, Males, and Females Rate "Ideal" Beer

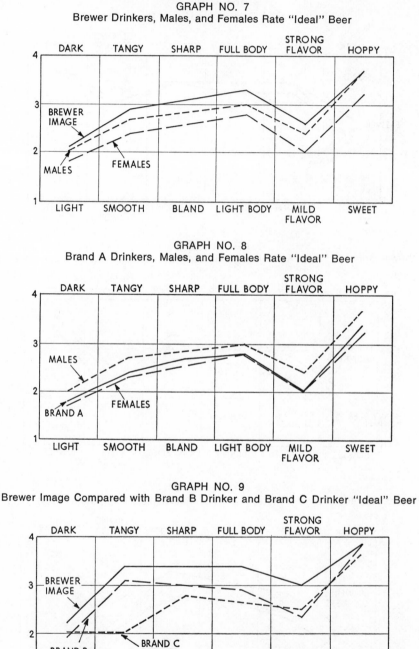

GRAPH NO. 8
Brand A Drinkers, Males, and Females Rate "Ideal" Beer

GRAPH NO. 9
Brewer Image Compared with Brand B Drinker and Brand C Drinker "Ideal" Beer

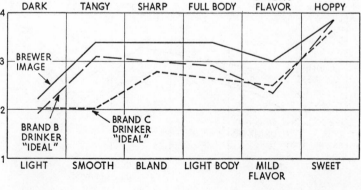

EXHIBIT 2 (Continued)

GRAPH NO. 10
Brewer Image Compared with Heavy Drinkers and Moderate/Light
Drinkers "Ideal" Beer

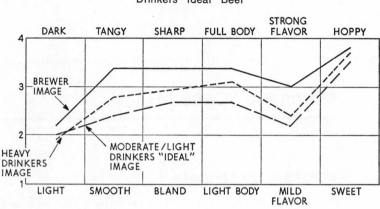

GRAPH NO. 11
Brewer Image Compared with Brewer Drinkers and Brand A Drinkers "Ideal" Beer

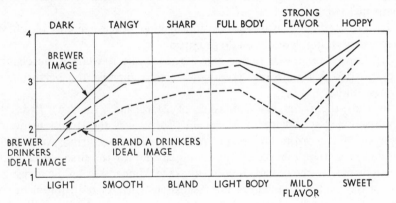

Marchand (Canada) Ltd.

QUESTIONS TO CONSIDER

1. Which influences and developments, inside and outside the company organization, were the most important to the final purchase decision? What are the implications of this analysis to the marketing programs of: the companies involved in this particular situation and all companies selling industrial products?

2. How effective was the decision-making process in this purchase? What, if anything, would you do to improve it?

3. How would you define the duties of the Marchand purchasing department? What criteria would you use to appraise the performance of these duties?

In 1961 the razor blade division of Marchand (Canada) Ltd., the wholly-owned subsidiary of Marchand Corp., was the largest manufacturer of safety razors and razor blades in Canada. During April 1961, division executives completed the arrangements for the first blister package to be used in the Canadian company (see Appendix A). The investigation of this packaging medium and discussions with related equipment and material suppliers had extended over a period of 17 months. The following discussion traces the chronological sequence of events and the process by which the necessary decisions were made within the organization.

COMPANY BACKGROUND

The razor blade division was the largest and most profitable of the four Canadian divisions. The other divisions produced a complex variety of high volume, heavily promoted, consumer durable and nondurable goods. All manufacturing facilities and the head office were located in Windsor, Ontario.

Copyright by the University of Western Ontario. This case was prepared by George S. Day under the direction of Professor David S. R. Leighton. Reproduced by permission.

The company's dominant position in the razor blade market was the result of advanced and sophisticated manufacturing skills and aggressive sales and promotion policies. A major marketing strength was the extremely broad distribution pattern. Wholesale drug distributors, who covered drugstores, tobacconists, and other small stores, provided 75% of the company's sales. The remaining 25% of sales were made direct to chain retailers. In 1960 the company was estimated to have 35% of the total shaving market: electric shavers had 50% of the market, and four other razor blade manufacturers held the remaining 15%. The most severe competition was felt from electric razor manufacturers, who had rapidly expanded their market share between 1948 and 1953.

The division also manufactured and marketed five razor sets, ranging from an inexpensive three-piece model to an expensive gold-plated, one-piece prestige set. All sets were manufactured to extremely high tolerances. Razors had traditionally been a loss item, although as a result of automation some profits were being incurred. A strong justification for the emphasis of razor sets was the high degree of correlation between Marchand razor ownership and the usage of Marchand blades.

PURCHASING DEPARTMENT ORGANIZATION AND RESPONSIBILITIES

In 1956 the rapid growth of the Canadian subsidiary necessitated a major revision of the organization into separate and distinct divisional units (see Exhibit 1). However, the purchasing department, directed by John Reid, continued to serve all divisions. In common with purchasing departments in similar companies, its basic responsibility was to select from among various possible sources of supply. Exceptions to this included the choice of advertising media and salesmen's cars, which were handled in other departments.

The buyers in the purchasing department issued approximately 40 purchase orders each working day. Each order ranged in purchase value from $5.00 to $30,000 with an average of $2,500. Each order was usually the result of three or four separate purchase requisitions issued by other departments. They were grouped either for convenience, or to take advantage of quantity discounts. Bruce Lee, the packaging buyer, issued 20 or more purchase orders each day, since he did the more routine ordering. Lee also did the buying for the purchasing engineer, Jack Hughes. However, most of the activity in the department was nonroutine and related to changes in materials, specifications, and vendors. These changes usually required considerable time and analytic work. Consequently the manager of the purchasing department, John Reid, seldom issued more than two purchase orders per day. The other buyers, Palmer and Myers, might account for 8 or 10 orders per day.

John Reid—Purchasing Department Manager

To elaborate on his department's role, John Reid said,

In our company, over 50% of the sales dollar goes for purchases of raw materials that we process further, and finished products for our own use or resale. In some areas, such as raw materials, we have undisputed decision-making powers, subject to the usual controls by top management concerning large expenditures. In other areas we act as the co-ordinator for the points of view of all the people who are interested in the purchase such as production, industrial engineering, warehousing, and so on. . . . We seem to be in the best position to assess and summarize the pertinent cost factors. Accountants are good on plant costs but don't understand the total cost picture which considers demurrage, damage, returns, and so on. . . . In either kind of purchase, however, the decision almost always becomes apparent once the significant factors have been defined and quantified. The most indeterminate and difficult part is appraising the long-run performance. For example, what is the sacrifice that a cost-cutter makes to get our business? If it's in quality control, what is the cost to us in the final analysis? That's why good working relationships are so important. In case of doubt you go to the company where you know the people, the equipment, the potential, and their weaknesses—and they understand your needs.

Concerning equipment selection specifically, John Reid made the following comment:

The responsibility for specification sometimes falls in a gray zone between our department and engineering, when their specification can only be met by one source. Our attitude is that this is either laziness or expediency. By and large, few pieces of equipment are so special that they can't be reduced to blueprints.

John Reid defined his own job as head of the purchasing department as follows;

Besides some responsibility for major purchases of commodities, such as steel and plastic films, my job is primarily to keep my people fully aware of the long-range implications of their actions. Sometimes they are prone to get carried away with immediate problems and pressures, such as processing requisitions, and neglect to make complete investigations. . . . At all times we're concerned with cost reductions, and I expect my people to initiate many opportunities.

John Reid was regarded by people inside and outside the company as an "enlightened" purchasing agent. A university graduate in science, with 16 years service with Marchand, he was active in a number of community affairs as well as the national executive of the Canadian Association of Purchasing Agents.

He was vitally interested in learning as much as possible about the industry and suppliers he dealt with. To this end he read *The Financial Post* and *Canadian Business* magazine closely and scanned articles of interest in the seven major Canadian and U.S. purchasing, packaging, and plastics magazines. He found direct mail advertising and institutional material such as internal house organs, employee papers, and company trade papers such as Dupont's *Packaging Patter*, to be more meaningful than normal trade magazine advertisements in developing a good supplier image and "keeping their name in front of me."

In 10 years' time John Reid's relations with salesmen had changed substantially as the purchasing department grew from one to five men. Originally, he saw an average of 10 salesmen a day. By 1961, the increasingly technical and longer term nature of his buying decisions meant he saw about two salesmen or groups of salesmen a day, usually by previous appointment or at his request. He preferred technical forums once or twice a year where key supplier people and Marchand technical people met for half a day to review all outstanding problems and plan for the coming period. In this situation he saw his job as ensuring that both parties understood each other completely. For the rest of the time, close telephone and mail contact sufficed.

John Reid was very positive about the key role of the salesman in providing service by communicating information quickly and representing the customer's interest to the supplier. "We're a marketing-oriented company, and the need to get promotions set up and into the market in a matter of days creates a real pressure for speed. The supplier must recognize this fact and do a conscientious job of meeting our needs, following up quickly on problems, and keeping us fully informed of the situation . . . one thing we don't need is a bunch of alibis."

Jack Hughes—Packaging Engineer

For historical and other reasons, within the Canadian subsidiary, the purchasing department also included a packaging engineer (see Exhibit 1), who kept in touch with packaging problems in every division. The packaging engineer, Jack Hughes, was a graduate engineer with seven years experience in industrial engineering and product supervision and three years in his present position.

His view of his job was,

. . . . primarily to co-ordinate the development of new packages for the Canadian company—right from the idea stage to the details of the specifications and the placing of the first order. Some of the ideas I initiate myself to achieve cost reductions. This includes reducing the overlap in our 2,500 different packages. Other ideas stem from marketing innovations or from the production department's desire to change a process. . . . In the future I'm planning to do a lot in getting more uniformity in our suppliers' packages.

Although I pretty well run my own show, I find some real advantages in being part of the purchasing department. It provides a flexibility that our parent, with separate groups, certainly doesn't have. Of course they have more factories, people, and other variables to co-ordinate. It may take them a year to make a change that would only involve us for a month or so.

At present I'm too involved in the actual purchasing process, although Bruce Lee (the packaging buyer) handles the repeat orders, my requests for quotations and does the printing buying. The only way I can cut it down is to give Bruce detailed specifications at an earlier stage. This is difficult to do, because the requirements usually remain in a state of flux for too long.

Bruce also acts as a screen for packaging salesmen, so that I just talk to those whom I've asked in for a specific purpose or who have something new that I can use immediately. Normally when I have a specific requirement I use catalogues and other trade listings to give me leads on possible suppliers. I read all the major U.S. and Canadian packaging and plastics magazines and attend four or five trade shows each year, mainly as a source of new ideas. In these ways I've collected a lot of data, although I'm still finding it hard to keep up to date on all the changes in packaging technology.

Edward Palmer—Purchasing Engineer

Essentially the purchasing engineer's job was to act as the buyer and a screen against salesmen for the engineering and maintenance departments. Ed Palmer, a graduate engineer, was well suited for this job, having spent 12 years as a project engineer in the engineering department before taking his present job in 1958.

Although most of the requirements were defined by the engineering department, Ed Palmer reviewed 10 magazines a month, on topics such as materials handling, design engineering, equipment selection, and purchasing, in search of new ideas or improvements that might be pursued. In describing the process of selecting possible suppliers, he said, "The big trade directories (Fraser for Canada and Thomas for the U.S.) handle about 90% of my problems. In the more difficult situations I'll depend on manufacturer and distributor catalogues and my knowledge of suppliers' capabilities . . . . direct mail is of very little use, since the information is limited and seldom comes when I'm interested in buying something."

Ed Palmer concluded, when he looked at the influence of salesmen on his decisions:

. . . In most cases we could do without them. Ideally the supplier should have a good office that is readily accessible by telephone when I have a problem, will keep me stocked with good literature and prices, and has technically competent salesmen who can advise me in case of problems. . . . In my experience, most salesmen don't know much about technical details, and fewer are of any use in following up orders, keeping us informed about the status of orders, or solving problems quickly.

On some days I will see as many as six or eight men, for visits of 20 minutes to over an hour (if, for example, they've been called in to talk with engineering also). About a third are suppliers who already have good relations with us and are calling to service orders or show new products. Another half are people who have never sold to us and seldom call. Sometimes they have a new product and can't understand why we won't try them out. As far as we're concerned, if the product doesn't have immediate application, then we don't have time to try it. The remainder of my callers are various agents and distributors who sell staples like bolts, ball bearings, etc., and can only offer service. There are a lot of these around; particularly now that they're coming from as far away as Toronto.

Over the long term, Ed Palmer expected to see the scope of his job expand substantially. "It will mean eliminating the routine of ordering, pricing orders, and grouping orders to save money, that any clerk can do, in favor of more special work. . . . I feel I have as much opportunity as anyone in the company to save money, by spending more time on negotiation with suppliers, arranging equipment trials, following new products, and developing Canadian sources of supply."

Sequence of Events

Need for New Package. As early as 1950 Canadian marketing executives had been unhappy with the alternatives for packaging inexpensive razors (those costing between $0.80 and $1.50). The most frequently used package, essentially a formed rigid plexiglass box, was felt to lack eye appeal and consumer interest. Consequently, between 1955 and 1958 the newly-developed techniques of blister and skin packaging (Appendix A) were examined. The chief attraction, in addition to improved product visibility, was the possibility of multiple packaging of blades with razors. During this period these advantages did not appear to overcome the high cost of materials, forming blisters, and sealing blisters to cards.

Initiation of Informal Packaging Project. The first serious investigation of blister packaging was started in December, 1959. Ray Lewis, assistant marketing manager, had seen a new and inexpensive sealing machine[1] demonstrated at the annual Canadian Packaging Show. He returned to Windsor, very enthusiastic about the possibilities for the machine at Marchand. The marketing manager, Bert Crofts, agreed and suggested that the company packaging engineer conduct an informal investigation of blister packs in general.

In the early stages of the investigation Jack Hughes confined himself to collecting a firm quotation on the Melville Engineering sealing machine, seen by Lewis, and competitive quotations from blister and card suppliers. For these latter quotations he used sizes and order volumes typical of most of the existing razor packages. Hughes also submitted the published literature on the Melville Engineering sealing machine to the division industrial engineer for an estimate of the sealing and packing time per razor.

After consultation with the purchasing agent, John Reid, Hughes chose

[1] A Melville Engineering Corporation Model A 10 distributed in Canada by Clement Equipment of Canada. See Appendix A for a summary of the manufacturers' literature.

Multi-Pak Limited of Guelph, and Service Packaging of Toronto, as the best sources of quotes for blisters. Service Packaging was an easy choice; they had done excellent custom packaging work for Marchand for more than 10 years, they were known to be technically competent, and their salesman made a point of calling four or five times a year. As John Reid summarized, "We always think of them in this connection."

Multi-Pak was chosen for different reasons. John Reid had been aware for several years that they were one of the first companies in Canada to attempt skin and blister packaging at a time when the technology was still changing very rapidly. He had also not heard anything unfavourable about other custom packaging jobs they had undertaken. Consequently he thought that they could probably provide a good quality of formed blisters. Rather than depend on hearsay he asked the opinion of a salesman whom he trusted from long previous association. The salesman, John Doyle of Fairmont Chemical, currently the major supplier to Marchand of polyethylene and cellulose acetate packaging films, had developed a strong personal interest in packaging technology in order to sell more packaging film. Doyle was acquainted with Multi-Pak and judged them to be one of the leading companies in blister packaging.

Hewson Printers and K. J. Cowan and Sons were chosen as sources of quotes for printed and coated backing cards. These two printing houses had been doing most of Marchand's printing, and the relatively small requirement precluded asking for quotes from any other suppliers.

On January 25, Jack Hughes asked Bruce Lee, the packaging buyer, to contact the chosen suppliers and request quotations. Since there was no urgency to the request, the letters were not sent until February 19. All replies were received between February 25 and March 12. Jack Hughes summarized the lowest material quotations, the machine quote and the estimated packing time, and asked the divisional controller to ". . . establish and report the cost of this package, so it can be used as a guide to compare with other methods of packaging." Based on these costs[2] and normal depreciation and overhead charges, it appeared there would be a 15% to 25% premium for blister packages.[3]

Crofts and Lewis found these results, "interesting but speculative." No action was taken however, as other more pressing projects had to be given priority. As far as Hughes was concerned the project had died. This situation continued until the middle of June, when John Eadie, the division manager, sent a copy of a recent article on skin and blister packaging to John Reid and asked what the company was doing to evaluate these pack-

---

[2] The sealing machine was quoted as $1,733 plus $150 for the required tooling. The lowest blister quote was $15.80 per thousand for 100,000 units (from Multi-Pak). The lowest card quote was $11.35 per thousand for 100,000 units (Hewson Printers).

[3] This comparison applied to typical volumes and sizes of packages. (Total package cost figures have not been included because of the complexity of the overhead allocation procedure.)

ages. This enquiry was handed on to Jack Hughes. He, in turn, checked with Ray Lewis and found that there had been no concrete thinking on appropriate applications.

It was finally decided that the same two companies should be asked to requote on the costs of blisters, and also on skin packaging, for one of the smaller razor sets. This was done as before by Bruce Lee. The quotes were received from both Multi-Pak and Service Packaging by the end of July. Also, during July, Jack Hughes arranged to have some of the company products blister packed by Clement Equipment during a demonstration of the Melville Engineering heat sealer in Toronto. Several skin packages were also made for the same products.

The new cost information, plus the standard samples, was ready by the end of August. Skin packaging was immediately eliminated from consideration because of poor display appearance. The cost summary did show that blister packaging became appreciably more attractive as the package size diminished.

The razor marketing group responded quickly to the favourable cost summary and on September 5, Ray Lewis wrote to Bert Crofts:

We are writing to recommend that as a further step in our investigation we arrange, if possible, the loan or trial installation of a blister sealing unit from Clement Equipment, and also that we procure samples of blisters and cards for further in-plant investigation of this project. The blister samples and cards will be a standard item available from Clement Equipment at a nominal cost (to be confirmed by Jack Hughes). The trial installation would give us more accurate industrial engineering times for further costing.

May we refer you to the preliminary estimate prepared on March 21 by the cost department. You will note on this study that the blister pack compares favourably with our standard display pack. It is on the basis of this original cost study and our recent confirmation of these costs by Jack that we recommend the procurement, on a trial basis, of the necessary equipment.

Formal Packaging Project T-145

As a consequence of Lewis' letter, Bert Crofts and John Eadie decided that a formal packaging project designed to study specific alternatives was desirable and necessary. The project was to cover two promotional items that were suffering from packaging limitations. One was a projected "deal" combining 15 blades with a safety razor for a dollar. It was further suggested that at least 100 units be packed on the Melville Engineering equipment to gain some operating experience.

As a routine measure, Ray Lewis reported the keen interest in blister packaging to the regular semimonthly meeting of the razor division packaging committee on September 15. This committee, chaired by Jack Hughes, met primarily to keep members informed about current packaging projects, manufacturing and marketing problems, and new products within the division (see Exhibit 1 for the actual committee membership). The meetings usually lasted less than an hour and covered 12 to 20 separate items.

The consequences of Lewis' report to the meeting were immediate and rather unexpected. It transpired that this was the first time the production department had been informed about the interest in the packaging machine and the recommendation for a trial purchase. Jim Murphy, the production superintendent, reacted to the report from his representatives on the packaging committee by immediately calling Bert Crofts. Murphy accused the marketing people of ". . . not consulting or informing the production people . . . making all sorts of unfounded assumptions without establishing a proper need." He concluded by saying that he wouldn't have anything to do with the blister sealer until he knew exactly what the machine would be doing, how it would affect his production rates, and that it was the best available piece of equipment from the standpoint of quality control, maintenance, and flexibility of output.

The reaction of Crofts and Lewis was one of surprise, since their attitude was primarily, ". . . We're not really specifying a piece of equipment, all we want are some costs." Although they did confess to having made a "faux-pas over communications," there was a strongly implied feeling that, "Jim Murphy is somewhat against change in general, because he has everything going so smoothly right now."

According to Ray Lewis, "For the next week, there was a lot of pussyfooting around; no one was quite sure what to do or wanted to take the responsibility for a decision." Finally Crofts got the production and industrial engineering groups to agree to an in-plant trial where a number of samples could be prepared and the necessary equipment evaluations could be made. The trial was conducted soon afterward, and all concerned pronounced themselves well satisfied with the construction and performance of the Melville Engineering equipment.

The successful demonstration convinced Crofts and Lewis that the Melville Engineering sealer was ideally suited to their needs. Furthermore, ". . . we've been looking at this machine for eight months now, why should we delay any longer?" This attitude led to further resistance from the production department, who contended that no specific requirements concerning output, size, and so on had been decided. It also resulted in a negative reaction from the purchasing department. John Reid, who until that time had not been directly concerned, questioned the advisability of an immediate purchase in a memo dated September 27 directed to Bert Crofts (see following). Reid's contention was, "It may be their dollars they're spending, but it's the responsibility of this department to recommend how it should be spent." His memo read:

I am sending this memo as a cautionary note with respect to Project T-145. The memos received to date seem to be strongly oriented towards the purchase of a blister sealing machine without a complete understanding of (*a*) the customer acceptance of our product packaged in blister, and (*b*) a full definition of our requirements. We may well find ourselves with a machine that either we don't need, after a period of a year, or we may find that it has too limited an output. Our basic interest in expediency now may result in buying a machine with much too limited an output, based on actual market acceptance of a blister pack.

We intend to investigate this project from the standpoint of custom packaging which would enable us to test market this package without an investment in equipment, as well as to explore, to a somewhat limited degree, the cost of blister sealing equipment and the cost of blisters from different sources.

If the blister package is completely acceptable to our customers and more than exceeds your honest expectation, it may well be that our strength would lie in having a completely integrated line for blister forming, loading, and blister sealing.

Should not then our main thrust be directed toward custom packaging and test marketing of these packages and, as a secondary objective, canvassing the market for prices of blisters and packaging equipment?"

Formal Packaging Project T-153

The marketing department, faced with these arguments, agreed to redefine packaging project T-145 by prescribing exact requirements and a target date for distribution of January 2, 1961. The new project, number T-153, was issued on October 10, based on an estimated demand per order of 96,000 units of the razor-plus-15-razor-blades deal. This amount was roughly six months' normal demand for the cheapest razor set.

Most of the information needed for the new project had been submitted by Multi-Pak and Service Packaging by October 9 in response to a previous request for quotes. Because of confusion over who would pay die costs, Jack Hughes was unable to compare the suppliers on an equal basis until November 10. His results, as forwarded to the controller's department on November 12, showed:

1) Custom packaging charges of $34.00 per thousand for quantities of 100,000 (based on Multi-Pak supplying backing cards, blisters, equipment time, and packing labor).

2) Material costs of $8.28 per thousand for blisters (from Multi-Pak) and $12.75 per thousand for the coated backing board (from Hewson Printers). Packing times and the machine cost (of $1,883) had been submitted previously to the controller's department. It was then up to the marketing department and the division manager to make the key decision authorizing the blister packed deal by balancing market acceptance against any additional costs. Only after this decision was made did the purchasing department have the authority to select suppliers.

At this time John Eadie, the division manager, was asked about the alternative of custom packaging that had been suggested earlier by the purchasing department to give the whole project more flexibility and avoid an undesirable equipment purchase. According to Eadie, ". . . there are just too many production problems for us to be able to do this. However, it does give us an interesting comparison with our own costs. Production people have always taken a very dim view of work being taken away from their people. And it's hard to explain but people on the line really feel it is a slap in the face. Equally important is the effect on union relations. This issue has never come up, but there is always the possibility."

In early December Ray Lewis queried the controller's department to find out what had happened to the final cost summary, only to find that the cost accountant was overloaded with more urgent projects. Several days later some unexpected price cutting by Marchand's largest competitor demanded the full-time attention of the whole razor blade marketing group. It was decided that it was neither feasible nor desirable to put the new package into the market during January or February.

New Sources of Supply

With his report of November 5, Jack Hughes had no further authority or pressure to go further in his examination of blister packaging for the razor deal. However, he did continue to keep himself informed, in anticipation of the decision to go ahead.

Since he was in close contact with the U.S. head office packaging department on several problems each week and depended on the head office for technical assistance on various packages being developed in Canada, he requested comments on U.S. experience with blister packaging for low price deals. The reply, dated November 15, dealt mainly with technical matters of board quality, blister material, and quality control. The end of the letter, dealing with equipment recommendations and comments on the usefulness of blister packaging, read:

We have an old vacuum-forming machine, known as an Abbott, which we have had at our main plant for probably six or eight years. While this machine is certainly not the greatest piece of equipment, it has done a job for us in adequate style. I would suggest, however, that if you are entertaining the idea of buying a vacuum former you contact someone like the Vacuum Equipment Company at Chicago. I do not know whether they have a Canadian plant, but I do know they are well established along these lines and produce an excellent piece of equipment for almost any vacuum or pressure forming operation you might be interested in.

In answer to your last question, I believe the most used comment on blister packaging that we have is that generally speaking it is quite expensive, and while we have used blister packing on a number of the kinds of items you are interested in, we usually end up with some other package that is less expensive and sooner or later drop the use of the blister.

I do believe the blister package does a good job and is a popular package on today's market. However, as for the product you have suggested, we feel we have not found that the blister has actually added to sales and consequently we find no reason to pay a premium to use a blister package.

Also during November, Jack Hughes followed up on some reports that the purchasing department had received about a Berwin blister sealer. They came from John Mason, a new salesman for Johnson Printers. According to John Reid:

Although Mason has only called on us a few times, and we really haven't had very good experience with his firm in the past, he has a fresh approach that is very worthwhile. Not only is he enthusiastic, but he has developed a strong technical orientation toward blister packaging—apparently as a hobby. He feels that he can ultimately sell printing by first selling the blister pack idea or at least being in a position to offer good technical assistance. One step he has taken is to ally himself with the Berwin people so he can offer a complete system. This is good for Berwin too, since it increases their sales representation. In this particular instance it's not going to work, because the backing-card requirement really isn't big enough to justify quotes from more than two printing houses. However in our eyes he has definitely overcome the past inertia of Johnson Printers and will be well received in the future.

At Mason's request Ken Murray, a manufacturers' agent representing Berwin in the Windsor-London area, submitted literature and a quotation for a blister sealing machine and also offered a 30-day in-plant trial. The machine chosen for quotation was designed to handle smaller volumes than the Melville Engineering sealer and lacked an automatic indexing mechanism to move the blisters in and out of the sealing area. It was priced at $1,050, compared with $1,700 for the Melville Engineering sealer.

Up to this point Jack Hughes had co-ordinated the contacts with the equipment suppliers. This constituted a minor precedent, since the engineering department, by virtue of its responsibility for equipment specification, was usually involved in equipment supplier contact at an early stage in the purchase decision. However, due to the nature of the purchase and a heavy work load, the engineering department had declared that it wasn't interested in participating in setting specifications on equipment that might not be purchased. Had the usual situation been true, Ed Palmer would have handled the supplier contacts for the equipment.

John Mason also supplied the lead on a new adhesive-coated blister being supplied by Remco Industries, a small plastics fabricator in Chicago. This represented a considerable innovation and potential cost-saving, as it meant that the backing board didn't have to be coated. At Mason's request, Remco submitted a quotation that proved competitive with Multi-Pak and also supplied a number of high-quality samples of their work. Jack Hughes commented, "At the moment I don't know anything about them, although since it's not a critical item, I suspect we can take a chance and not get into trouble. If I have time I'm going to try and visit them in

Chicago. . . . The big reservation is that buying from them goes against my principle of using Canadian sources of supply wherever possible."

Top Management Approval of Blister Package

The razor blade marketing department received the necessary cost data from the divisional controller on December 14, 1960. It was used to prepare a formal "Request for Addition to Stock"[4] which was duly approved by Messrs. Eadie and Hilson. In view of the changed circumstances in the market, volume per order was reduced from 96,000 to 72,000 units, and the target date for the completion of the packages and display racks was advanced to March 31, 1961.

On January 10, 1961, Jack Hughes received his copy of the approved "Request for Addition to Stock." This was his authority to obtain a final set of quotes based on the exact quantity required and decided on the source of supply for the blisters and backing cards. The only change from the earlier list of suppliers was the decision to have Johnson Printers' quote on the printed backing board. Simultaneously, the engineering department was authorized to prepare machine specifications for Ed Palmer and thereby initiate the purchase process for this piece of equipment. Ed Palmer anticipated the receipt of the specifications and asked Ken Murray to supply a Berwin sealing machine for an in-plant trial during February.

Ed Palmer reported on February 5 that he hadn't yet received the approved specifications.[5] "When I do, I'll send 'requests for quotations' to four or five suppliers that are listed in Fraser's trade directory. I expect there should be quite a number of suppliers, although I haven't looked yet. Actually I don't have much of a feel for the packaging machine market. We seldom buy this kind of equipment, preferring to build most of it ourselves. Also, I don't know when a packaging equipment salesman has been in to see me. I guess they are just too busy calling on the big buyers who are always in the market for more equipment."

A follow-up by Jack Hughes, after the normal two-week time allowance for projects of this nature, revealed that the assigned engineer had been tied up with other projects, then took sick. The upshot was the decision on February 10 to restrict the consideration of sealing machines to those made by Melville Engineering and Berwin and go with the cheaper Berwin machine if the in-plant trial was satisfactory. Jack Hughes commented, "Because of the pressures of time we won't be able to canvass other manufacturers or find out if any other divisions could use blister packaging. If we choose the Berwin machine we'll probably scrap it or

---

[4] Approval meant that the sale of new product or package was authorized, and purchase orders for necessary supplies and equipment could be initiated.

[5] Specifications included: maximum size of blister, cycle time, air pressure and electrical power requirements, and a limit on the price.

trade it for a bigger machine in one or two years as our requirements become clearer."

In the meantime the quotes on the blisters had been received, and an order placed with Multi-Pak, the low bidder. Jack Hughes said about Remco Industries, "After we get going with the initial order we'll get 150 or 200 of the new coated blisters and test them in the lab. If this blister is as good as it is supposed to be, there will probably be a Canadian company supplying it fairly soon."

The selection of a printed backing card supplier was delayed by a decision to completely revise the art work. It was March 15 before a sample card was finished by the art department and sent out for quotations. Quotes on the original card had been received from the three printing houses before February, so the two lowest were given the opportunity to requote. The lowest by far was Johnson Printers at $9.00 per thousand, although Jack Hughes suspected that they were either sacrificing something to get established with Marchand or had overlooked some costs. The next lowest was Hewson Printers at $12.10 per thousand. This was a large company with a number of printing plants across the country and considerable experience in this type of work. The highest quote was K. J. Cowan and Sons, a smaller local supplier. Their price of $18.00 per thousand reflected their inexperience in printing on this medium and the inconvenience of a small order of this sort. Johnson Printers were still the lowest by a wide margin on the second set of quotes and were awarded the job on April 6.

The Berwin blister sealing machine trial was concluded at the end of February with high marks in output, construction, and durability. A meeting of engineering, production, industrial engineering, and purchasing decided that there was no immediate advantage of speed of output or flexibility of the Melville Engineering sealer, that justified an extra $650. During the period previous to the decision Ed Palmer had one contact with Ken Murray to arrange a demonstration, and had heard nothing from Clement Equipment, the distributor of the Melville Engineering sealer, since the in-plant trial on September 1960.

The blister sealing machine was on hand, and all material deliveries completed by April 28. The sealing and packing operations were finished by May 12, 1961 in time for a June 1 introductory campaign. Further material orders from Johnson Printers and Multi-Pak would be contingent on market acceptance of the blister package.

EXHIBIT 1

Organization Chart

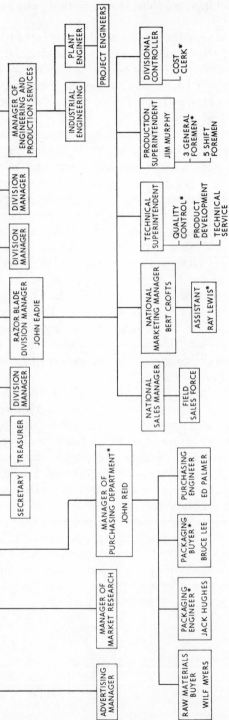

NOTE: Each * represents one member of the razor packaging committee.

SOURCE: Company records and personnel.

EXHIBIT 2

Chronological Summary of Events

1959

December 14	—Ray Lewis attended Canadian Packaging Show in Toronto.

1960

January — Jack Hughes selected five suppliers and requested quotations on blisters, backing cards, and a sealing machine for a representative size of package.·

March 15 — Quotations were summarized and submitted to the divisional controller for cost analysis.

March 30 — Razor blade marketing department received cost comparisons of a representative blister package against the present package.

June 15 — John Eadie queried the status of blister and skin packaging in the company.

June 30 — Backing card and blister suppliers were asked to requote on a small razor set package.

August 28 — Second set of costs, plus sample packages, submitted to the marketing department for consideration.

September 10 — Packaging project T-145 issued.

September 15 — Backing card and blister suppliers were asked to requote on a projected "deal" comprising 15 blades with a safety razor for one dollar.

September 23–25 — In-plant trial of Melville Engineering blister sealing machine.

October 10 — Packaging project T-153 issued, defining exact volume requirements and a target date of January 2, 1961.

November 12 — Quotations, based on requirements of project T-153, were summarized and submitted to the divisional controller.

December 20 — Blister packaging of razor plus razor blades deal approved by top management.

1961

January 10 — Jack Hughes authorized to obtain final blister and backing card quotes based on revised volume requirements, and select a final supplier. Engineering department authorized to establish machine specifications.

February 2 — Multi-Pak chosen as blister supplier.

February 10 — Choice of blister sealing machines limited to Berwin and Melville Engineering due to lack of time.

February 27 — Berwin blister sealing machine chosen after successful in-plant trial.

March 15 — Revised backing card sent out for quotations.

April 6 — Johnson Printers chosen as backing card supplier.

EXHIBIT 2 (Continued)

April 28   —All material deliveries completed, and blister sealing machine installed.

May 12   —Sealing and packing operations completed.

APPENDIX A:—DESCRIPTIVE NOTE ON BLISTER AND SKIN PACKAGING

The following has been extracted from an article entitled "Thermo-formed Plastics" that appeared in the February 1958 *Modern Packaging* magazine, and literature supplied by the Melville Engineering Corporation.

Introduction

To understand thermoforming it is necessary to keep in mind that this process is confined to plastics in sheet or film form. In packaging terminology, sheet plastic is any gauge more than 3 mils in thickness; anything under 3 mils is classed as film. For the purposes of this discussion, "sheet" will be used as covering the entire range of plastics for thermoforming, although many skin packs now use thin film on a backing board.

In the thermoforming equipment, the sheet is softened with heat, while pressure forms it to the contours either of a die or mold, or of the actual product to be contained. Such mechanical assists as plugs, rings, and clamps are often used.

The simplest type of equipment employs atmospheric or vacuum pressure at about 15 lbs. per square inch. This is vacuum forming. Although the method is basically easy, for high speed and accuracy, very complex machines are needed and have been developed. Vacuum forming's forte is versatility in handling different materials, gauges, and forming requirements with minimum cost in dies and change-over time.

Where greater force is needed for higher speed and more precision, air or hydraulic pressures (up to 200 p.s.i.) are used. This is pressure forming.

The Package

These are the distinguishing features of the three basic types of thermo-formed packages:

1. The skin pack uses thin sheet or film which is thermoformed directly about the product and seals it, usually onto a backing—eliminating mold costs and providing the skintight fit which gives the package its name. Skin packaging is done only by vacuum forming.

2. The contour pack is related to the skin pack only in the sense that it conforms closely to the contours of the product. It is preformed, often in multiples, over a mold or die rather than the product itself, and it generally uses heavier, semirigid sheet stock.

3. The blister or dome pack differs from the contour pack in that the blister is a simple curved or angular shape, not conformed to the shape of the product, and hence is applicable to many different products within a given size range.

Contour and blister packages can be made by either vacuum or pressure forming.

Advantages

1. Transparency and sparkle—to display the product and attract sales. Colour, opacity, and printing are available.

2. Conformability—thermoformed sheet plastics are supreme in this characteristic. Few limitations are imposed on size, shape, or detail; the packager has a freedom in blister and contour thermoforming not found in any other type of rigid packaging.

3. Flexural strength—this characteristic is like a built-in muscle. It means that all sorts of working and gripping features can be devised. Thermoformed plastic sheet can be made to hold a product or to provide such dispensing features as slide tracks, snap locks, and hinges.

4. Adaptability—the choice of materials is wide and growing wider. Because of this and the protective properties inherent to plastics, thermoformed packs are among the most versatile packages you can find.

5. Economy—the equipment, the dies (if any), and the process are relatively low in cost. Some blister and skin packs cost as little as two cents apiece. Even elaborate, high-cost thermoformed containers as used for instruments, gifts, and personal products are competitive and economical for their purpose.

6. Sales appeal and dealer convenience. The thermoform neatly combines the features most essential in packaging for today's merchandising requirements. It secures the product so that it cannot be lost or damaged, yet puts it fully on view for close examination by the shopper. The backing card or folder usually used with the thermoform provides a billboard for promotional and informational copy that can be taken in at a glance along with the product itself —and it has the very important advantage to the dealer of giving manageable size to items which would otherwise have to be stowed out of sight in bulk and in bins, to be sold only—and often unprofitably—by clerk service. The latter advantage explains why thermoforms have swept so prominently into hardware stores. Many carded packs are perforated for display on wire racks.

Blister Sealing (extract from Williams Engineering product literature)

Williams Engineering machines can seal one blister in just 1½ seconds and can be handled by a single inexperienced operator. Efficient two-station indexing table rotates automatically as each blister is sealed. Tooling is an inexpensive operation and can be done in your own plant. Changeover from one package size to another can be made in less than five minutes. The sealing area (up to 10″ × 9″ × 3″ deep) is generous enough to accommodate virtually any small product. Each machine comes complete. Simply connect to 50–60 p.s.i. air supply, standard electrical supply, and operate. There's nothing else to buy.

Austin Company

Bergen Equipment Company, a manufacturer of heavy cranes, materials-handling equipment, and earth-moving equipment, developed a special paste solder for use in its own plants to seal joints in air, fuel, and hydraulic lines. Over a period of several years a significant external demand developed, a separate company was formed, and by 1965 it was apparent that major decisions would have to be made on the general sales program.

The new solder had a definite advantage in that it could be applied before a joint was assembled. If heat were applied to the joint after assembly, the solder would make a permanent bond, completely sealing the joint. At the time Bergen developed the solder, the company was manufacturing equipment for the Navy and presented the product to the Navy Department for approval. The Navy liked the item and saw other applications for it. Within a short time, Bergen had received several large orders for its solder. To fill these, it purchased a plant in Austin, Minnesota, and set up a separate division, the Austin Company, to handle production and distribution. In subsequent years Austin started producing a fairly complete line of solid and liquid solders so as not to be dependent on one product. By 1965 the special paste solder accounted for about 40 per cent of all sales. By this time, competitors had developed products comparable to it.

During the Korean War there was no sales problem—demand exceeded supply and distribution was a matter of allocation according to priority. This situation prevailed to some extent until the late 1950's. After that, however, the Austin management began work on a sales and distribution organization, looking forward to the time when the market would be more competitive. But the management of Bergen Equipment, the parent company, refused to allocate funds for the development or expansion of this division. As a result, little was accomplished.

This attitude changed in 1965, after Austin's sales and profits declined from their record high in 1960. The management of Austin was able to convince the parent company that the solder business still had a bright future but that substantial revisions in marketing were needed. In 1965 Austin was given permission to submit an action plan with respect to its selling activities.

At that time Austin had 135 distributors in seventeen sales districts in the United States and also had outlets through the parent company in Europe, South America, and Canada. The districts were the same as those maintained by the parent company. A salesman was maintained in each district to work with the distributors and to solicit business directly from large users. These salesmen were specialists who furnished technical advice both to direct customers and to customers of distributors. They worked out of the Bergen district offices but sold only Austin products.

TABLE 1

Total Industry and Austin Sales of Solder by End Use: 1964
(millions of pounds)

End Use	Total Industry Sales	Austin Sales	Austin Per Cent of Market
Manufacturing			
Industry...............	354	31.9	9.0
Electrical equipment			
and machinery...........	42	7.2	17.2
Fabricated metal			
products................	58	8.4	14.6
Machinery (except			
electrical)...............	96	7.6	8.0
Primary metals............	11	0.7	6.3
Transportation			
equipment..............	103	6.3	6.1
All other.................	44	1.7	3.9
Nonmanufacturing			
Industry................	157	10.6	6.8
Construction..............	39	3.7	9.5
Utilities..................	22	0.6	6.6
Metal working shops........	49	1.2	2.4
Transportation............	25	0.3	1.1
All other.................	22	4.8	21.8
Total Market..........	511	42.5	8.3

From industry publications the sales staff developed data on the total market for solder. These data were compared with their own sales figures, and it was found that Austin's pattern of solder sales by end use varied considerably from the industry (Table 1). The company's market share was higher among manufacturing users than among nonmanufacturing users. Among manufacturers, Austin's sales were highest in the electrical equipment, machinery, and fabricated metal products segments. In the nonmanufacturing markets the company was strong in the construction and "all other" segments.

Total industry sales were broken down geographically and compared with Austin's geographic sales pattern (Table 2). Again it was found that Austin's geographic sales pattern differed substantially from that of the industry. Three of the seventeen Austin sales districts accounted for nearly half the total solder industry market. Part of the variation was the result of shipping to warehouse stocks. Austin maintained a warehouse in each of the four districts—Norfolk, Kansas City, Milwaukee, and Dallas—to

TABLE 2

Austin and Industry Sales by Austin Sales Districts: 1964
(millions of pounds)

	Total Industry Sales	Austin Sales	Austin Per Cent of Market
Detroit....................	87	6.2	7
Pittsburgh.................	74	5.9	5
Chicago...................	64	2.5	4
Boston....................	41	2.7	7
Los Angeles...............	36	2.7	7.5
New York.................	35	0.8	2
Philadelphia...............	26	5.0	19
Kansas City...............	25	1.8*	7.5
Milwaukee.................	20	3.5*	17
St. Louis..................	18	2.0	11
Minneapolis...............	17.5	3.0	17
Seattle....................	17	1.3	8
San Francisco..............	14	2.9	21
Denver....................	11	0.7	6.5
Norfolk...................	10	1.9*	19
Dallas....................	7	0.8*	11
Washington, D.C...........	7	0.5	8
Total†.............	509.5	44.2	8.3

* Includes shipments to warehouse stocks.
† Totals do not agree with those in Table 1 because of different sources and the inclusion of shipments to warehouse stocks.

serve areas where distributors were not really available. Shipments to these warehouses were recorded as sales. The penetration of individual sales districts had been determined primarily by allocation to customers up to 1958. The sales pattern still reflected much of this practice.

Industry data showed that 54 per cent of all sales were made through distributors, while 46 per cent were made direct to end users. Austin's pattern was almost the same, 56 per cent through distributors and 44 per cent direct. Austin's policy was to attempt to sell direct to end users who purchased 50,000 pounds or more annually, even though in many cases this volume was bought from several suppliers. The percentage sold through distributors was exaggerated in those districts where shipments of solder were made to warehouse stocks, because these shipments were recorded as sales to distributors, although much of the warehouse sales were made direct to small users in the area. Actually, the warehouses were essentially sales branches. Sales analysis showed further that 81 per cent of the total tonnage of solder sold direct by Austin went to eighty-nine accounts buying 50,000 pounds or more. These eighty-nine accounts represented only 13 per cent of the total direct accounts. The same pattern existed in sales to distributors where 82 per cent of the company's shipments went to 21 per cent of the distributors, all of whom purchased 100,-000 pounds or more annually. Solder prices averaged about 10 cents a pound, so that a distributor handling less than 100,000 pounds accounted for less than $10,000 in sales. Table 3 shows the direct and distributor sales patterns.

TABLE 3

Austin Shipments Direct and to Distributors by Size of Account: 1964

	Accounts		Shipments	
	No.	Per Cent	Millions of lbs.	Per Cent
Direct Sales				
Under 1,000 lbs.	302	44	0.056	0.3
1,000–1,999	129	19	0.374	2
5,000–9,999	44	6	0.374	2
10,000–19,999	48	7	0.561	3
20,000–49,999	68	10	2.151	11.5
50,000–99,999	42	6	2.618	14
Over 100,000	47	7	12.529	67
Sales to distributors				
Under 20,000 lbs.	122	52	0.714	3
20,000–49,999	42	18	1.666	7
50,000–99,999	22	9	1.904	8
100,000–249,999	24	10	4.403	18.5
250,000–499,999	17	7	7.616	32
Over 500,000	8	3.4	7.378	31

Data on the sales of solder to different types and sizes of firms were obtained from trade publications and from Austin's own sales records. From these data, estimates were made of the potential sales of solder to different types of firms according to their sales volumes. With these estimates and with data on the distribution of manufacturers in the United States from the Census of Manufacturers, the sales staff established sales potentials by district for both direct and distributor sales. All firms with an annual potential of 50,000 pounds or more were classified in the direct-sales group. The others were put in the distributor-sales group. The total was adjusted to make the total potential approximately equal the industry's total sales volume. Table 4 shows the breakdown of potential by sales district and the number of prospects for direct sales in each district.

A survey was made among solder users to determine future trends, but the results brought a different problem to the attention of the company. Although Austin accounted for 8.3 per cent of the total sales of solder,

TABLE 4

Number of Direct Sales Prospects and Potentials for Direct Sales and Distributor Sales by Sales District
(millions of pounds)

Sales District	Number of Direct Sales Prospects	Direct Sales			Distributor Sales		
		Est. Potential	Austin	Austin Per Cent of Potential	Est. Potential	Austin	Austin Per Cent of Potential
New York	127	16.3	0.4	2.4	18.8	0.4	2.1
Boston	195	18.9	1.1	5.8	21.8	1.6	7.3
Los Angeles	211	16.8	2.2	13.1	19.5	0.5	2.6
Detroit	271	40.5	2.3	5.7	46.9	3.9	8.3
Pittsburgh	297	34.1	2.6	7.6	39.4	1.3	3.3
Chicago	150	29.6	1.2	4.1	34.4	1.4	4.1
Minneapolis	86	8.1	1.9	23.5	9.4	1.1	11.7
Dallas	25	3.2	0.2	6.2	3.8	0.6	15.8
San Francisco	36	6.3	2.4	38.1	7.4	0.5	6.8
Seattle	19	7.9	0.1	12.7	9.2	1.2	13.0
St. Louis	33	8.5	1.6	18.8	9.9	0.5	5.1
Philadelphia	85	12.1	1.6	13.2	13.9	3.5	25.2
Milwaukee	28	9.4	0.4	4.2	10.9	3.1	28.4
Washington, D.C.	9	3.2	0.3	9.4	3.7	0.2	5.4
Norfolk	12	4.6	0.2	4.3	5.3	1.7	32.1
Denver	25	5.0	0.3	6.0	5.8	0.4	6.9
Kansas City	33	11.5	…	…	13.3	1.8	13.5
Total U.S.	1,665	236.0	18.8	8.0	273.4	23.7	8.7

the survey showed that only 1.9 per cent of the users expressed a preference for Austin products when asked which brand of solder they preferred. Jansen solder had outstanding preference, with four to six times the percentage preferring it as preferred to the next highest ranking brand. Jansen was the leading brand in the field and probably accounted for one-third of the industry's sales. Table 5 shows the relative preference ratings for all major brands of solder. There were no technical reasons expressed for preferring a particular brand, although each respondent was asked the reasons for his preference. Most respondents gave noncommittal replies, such as, "We've always dealt with them" or "We just like them better."

An executive committee was appointed to evaluate the information given in Table 5 and recommend specific steps to be taken, as follows:

TABLE 5

Brand of Solder Preferred by Users

Jansen	32.3%	Austin	1.9%
A & T	5.1	A. A. Metal	1.6
Harley	4.6	Bondex	1.3
Mueller	4.5	Fastet	0.8
Hobert	3.8	All others	4.0
Permafix	3.5	No preference	10.0
Metal Products	2.3	Don't know	22.2
Solderall	2.2		
Total			100.0%

(1) build Austin product preference, (2) set sales goals and quotas for direct and dealer sales, and (3) realign sales districts. In addition, the committee was to study the future trends of the solder market.

To build Austin product preference, the committee made the following recommendations: (1) distribute the facts of the market situation to the Austin sales organization; (2) give strong support to the sales organization through advertising and publicity; and (3) make a survey of present users to serve as a guide to future product improvement.

Another recommendation was that the company establish a goal in terms of the total tonnage of solder Austin should sell in 1965. Austin's market share was estimated at 8.3 per cent in 1964; 10 per cent was recommended as a reasonable and practical goal. The goal would be distributed among the sales districts in proportion to potential; e.g., if Detroit had 8.7 per cent of the industry potential, it would have 8.7 per cent of the Austin sales goal. The breakdown based on industry sales of 509.4 million pounds is shown in Table 6.

If there were any reason why a sales district should not have a goal relative to its potential, it would be given special consideration. The goal for each district should be divided into two parts, a goal for direct sales and a goal for distributor sales (Table 7). This division was based on the national sales pattern of 54 per cent through distributors and 46 per cent direct. Both these markets were to be developed equally. In many outlying territories large accounts were being sold by distributors. It was recommended that a policy be established for direct solicitation of all prospective customers whose total solder purchases exceeded 50,000 pounds and that smaller accounts be left exclusively to distributors.

Many of the districts would be unable to attain their goals immediately, so each year quotas would be set that would permit them to move at a

TABLE 6

	Sales (Millions of Pounds)	Per Cent
Austin total goal	50.9	100
Detroit	8.7	17
Pittsburgh	7.3	15
Chicago	6.4	13

TABLE 7

	Sales (Millions of Pounds)		
	District Total	Direct	Distributors
Total company	50.9	23.4	27.5
Detroit	8.7	4.0	4.7
Pittsburgh	7.3	3.4	3.9
Chicago	6.4	3.0	3.4

reasonable rate toward their goals. Some districts were already over the 10 per cent goal and would require quotas higher than their goals. An analysis of each individual district would be necessary in setting the quota to determine the district potential, the areas within the district that needed further development, and manpower requirements. The Chicago sales district was analyzed as an example (Table 8).

It was recommended that each area be further analyzed by class of user so that the company could tell more precisely the industries from which additional business should come. The company could provide each district with a detailed list of accounts that should be solicited. The committee further recommended that in the future a refinement of the market analysis be worked out on the basis of type of solder used. It also recommended that the company consider methods of realigning sales districts so that all would be approximately equal. The committee believed that it

TABLE 8
Example of Breakdown of Sales Goals in Chicago District
(millions of pounds)

	Industry Total	Direct Sales			Distributor Sales		
		Industry	Austin Goal	Austin 1956 Shipments	Industry	Austin Goal	Austin 1956 Shipments
Total district	63.9	29.3	2.93	1.2	34.6	3.46	1.36
Chicago	41.9	19.2	1.90	1.1	22.7	2.27	0.83
Gary	7.2	3.3	0.30	0.1	3.9	0.39	0.41
Hammond	3.3	1.5	0.15	...	1.8	0.18	...
Waukegan	3.2	1.5	0.15	...	1.7	0.17	...
Rockford	2.7	1.2	0.12	...	1.5	0.15	0.01
Aurora	2.0	0.9	0.01	...	1.1	0.11	...
Peoria	1.4	0.7	0.07	...	0.7	0.07	0.05
Springfield	0.8	0.4	0.04	...	0.4	0.04	0.01
Elgin	0.7	0.3	0.03	...	0.4	0.04	0.04
Other areas	0.7	0.3	0.03	...	0.4	0.04	0.01

was desirable to divide the sales districts so that each would have a sales goal of between 2 and 3 million pounds annually.

The conclusion was reached that in the long term the demand for solder would remain fairly constant, with possibly a slight downward trend. New materials, such as plastic pipe, and new methods, such as printed circuits in the electric industry, would have a noticeable effect on the solder market, but little change was expected in the next ten years. The demand for solder was closely tied to the demand for durable goods, which was expected to have a long-term upward trend. This trend would offset any loss resulting from new innovations during the next ten years.

Questions

1. Are the committee's recommendations sound?
2. Are the sales goals and quotas valid and useful?

California Office of Consumer Counsel

Mr. Jerry Miner, senior staff member of the Committee for the Assessment of Government Efficiency (CAGE)[1] was reviewing his notes for a report to CAGE on the California Office of Consumer Counsel (COCC). CAGE was a nonpartisan group of concerned citizens whose ongoing examination of the Government of California had been the basis for many changes initiated by both the Governor's Office and the State Legislature. Many of its recommendations had been adopted by several other states as well. It was expected that the CAGE report on the COCC would have an important bearing on the future structure and functioning of this institution.

In 1959 the California legislature created the position of Consumer Counsel in the Office of the Governor and authorized the Governor to appoint such assistants and employees for the Consumer Counsel as he found necessary. Two primary duties were given to the Consumer Counsel: to advise the Governor on "all matters affecting the interests of the people as consumers," and to "recommend to the Governor and the Legislature the enactment of such legislation as he deems necessary to protect and promote the interests of the people as consumers." To fulfill these duties the Consumer Counsel was directed to conduct studies and to report the results of such studies to the people of the state. The law also authorized the Consumer Counsel to "appear before governmental commissions, departments, and agencies to represent and be heard on behalf of consumers' interests," and to "cooperate and contract with public and private agencies" to obtain and publish statistical and economic information as necessary. Finally, "each agency, officer, and employee of the

---

[1] The Committee for the Assessment of Government Efficiency and its staff are fictitious. All other persons and organizations referred to in this case are real.

55

State" was ordered to cooperate with the Consumer Counsel in carrying out these duties. In the first ten years of existence of this law, only two people served as Consumer Counsel, but their respective interpretations of their responsibilities under this legislation reflect quite different approaches to providing consumer protection.

Serving from 1959 to 1967, under Governor Edmund Brown, Mrs. Helen Ewing Nelson was the first Consumer Counsel. In Mrs. Nelson's view: "The consumer is alone. Business likes him that way—alone, impotent, submissive, uninformed. He's easier to deal with that way." Speaking of the legislation creating her position, she said, "The intent of it clearly was that the Consumer Counsel should speak for the consumer." As spokesman for such a hapless constituency, Mrs. Nelson sought to buffer the power and influence of business by aggressively voicing the consumer's position before the Legislature, and the administrative and regulatory agencies: ". . . all the other interest groups have the lawmaker's ear. The pressure should be equalized. Legislators should hear the consumer view put to them often and competently." Her active lobbying for consumer interests created many enemies in the Legislature, but she dismissed this:

Certainly they resented me, and understandably so. My office caused a great deal of embarrassment. Legislators were faced with a dilemma caused by the fact that consumers can't give great blocks of money to finance reelection campaigns—while interest groups can. There were a great many pressures on the legislators not visible in the hearing room.

Mrs. Nelson's vigorous advocacy of consumer interests, often focused (by legislative lobbying or administrative agency hearing) against specific industry representatives, seemed to lead to a characterization of the Office of Consumer Counsel as an adversary of the business community. Having adopted an adversary role, the Office, under Mrs. Nelson, tended to respond to consumer complaints with a legalistic approach. Solutions to consumer problems were either found through encouraging the use of existing legal remedies, or they were sought by proposing and lobbying for new legislation in the area of the complaint. This approach is reflected in several extracts from correspondence from the Office during Mrs. Nelson's incumbency.

The following extracts are from responses to consumers who had written to complain of misleading advertising:

I can certainly understand your concern for the techniques employed. Information such as you have provided is extremely useful to our program and can be used to advise the Governor and the Legislature on specific problems of consumer concern.

The type of problem you describe is a very difficult one to resolve. Unfortunately, there is no government agency with authority to assist you directly. If you can prove that the [product] was misrepresented, you would likely have legal grounds for an adjustment. However, you will need legal advice to make this determination. Therefore, I would suggest that you consult with an attorney on this matter.

California has laws prohibiting false and misleading advertising (Section 17,500 of the California Business and Professions Code). It is the responsibility of the district attorney in each county to interpret these laws. Therefore, you should call this matter to the attention of your local district attorney.

I am forwarding your recent letter and its enclosures to the California Bureau of Weights and Measures. This matter comes under the jurisdiction of that state agency. The Bureau will advise you of its findings.

The matter described in your letter does not come under my jurisdiction. However, I am taking the liberty of forwarding a copy of your letter to the Federal Trade Commission in San Francisco. That Federal Agency is very much interested in the type of situation you describe.

I am sending a copy of your letter to the [X] Corporation and to the [Y] Corporation, because I think that they will be interested to know how their brand names are being used. If their names are registered, as I believe they are, the companies will want to stop this practice.

If you feel you are personally entitled to a refund, I would suggest you consider taking action in the Small Claims Court to recover the amount of money in question. The enclosed brochure explains how to use the Small Claims Court.

During Mrs. Nelson's incumbency, California was swept by a referral selling scheme (customers charged exorbitant prices but promised large cash rebates for providing names of others who subsequently became purchasers) for aluminum house siding. The progress of attempts to halt these operations is revealed in letters which contain, in substance, the following kinds of comments:

Interpreting your contract is a legal matter, and as a state officer I cannot give legal advice. I recommend that you consult an attorney.

Thank you for your letter, which I will add to our file on aluminum siding in preparing support for legislation soon to be proposed.

Copies of pending legislation in regard to aluminum siding are attached for your information.

Your letter has been referred to the Consumer Fraud Unit of the Attorney General's Office for action.

A similar file on usury contains responses of the same type recorded above, enclosing brochures on the cost of credit and the maximum credit charges allowed by California law, and pointing out the California laws regulating pawnbrokers and encouraging consultation with the local district attorney to seek enforcement.

With an aggressive legislative program, an active information program that consisted primarily of the preparation and distribution of reprints and special pamphlets of general interest to the consumer, and a close involvement with other state sponsored programs directed toward specific population groups, the Office staff grew to eight persons and the operating budget rose to $119,000 per year during Mrs. Nelson's term in office.

In 1967, following a two-month study of the Office of Consumer Counsel for the newly elected Governor Ronald Reagan, Mrs. Kay Valory was appointed Consumer Counsel and asked to implement the recommendations of her investigation. One of her first actions was to reduce her staff to one secretary and her budget to $33,000. Mrs. Valory's approach to her position stands in vivid contrast to the activities of the Office of Consumer Counsel under Mrs. Nelson. Summarizing her first two years in office, a report to the Governor contained the following description of the job of Consumer Counsel:

Mrs. Valory views her role as that of educator and catalyst in the consumer-business-government relationship. Working as a clearinghouse for individual consumer complaints, the Consumer Counsel initially channels them to the business or professional association traditionally responsible for maintaining ethical standards in that area of commerce. When necessary, these complaints are referred to the appropriate regulatory and law enforcement agencies. The Consumer Counsel encourages these authorities to act vigorously, but responsibly; bringing to justice those who would defraud the consumer, but bringing to bear the full weight of the law only in cases of criminal activity or when business fails in its responsibility to police itself.

This catalyst's role differs in several important respects from Mrs. Nelson's role as advocate or spokesman. First, it implies neutrality in the consumer-business-government relationship rather than identification with consumer interests in an adversary posture toward business. This neutrality is expressed by Mrs. Valory's opinion that most consumer-business problems reflect misunderstanding; a communication gap between the consumer's wishes and demands and the sizable contributions business is currently making for the consumer's benefit. A national news magazine recently characterized Mrs. Valory's incumbency as follows:

California's Kay Valory, consumer counsel to Governor Ronald Reagan, has not testified in three years before any committee considering consumer legislation. She recently made the extraordinary recommendation that buyers shun the "very narrow" testing reports of Consumers Union in favor of the handbook of the National Association of Manufacturers.

Mrs. Valory contends that her practice of seeking to bridge this gap by bringing consumer complaints directly to the business or industry concerned has been successful in all but a small percentage of cases, which demonstrates that consumers and business need not be considered implacable enemies. Mrs. Valory's neutrality is also manifested by her absence from active lobbying; her conception of her role as a catalyst leads her to research all aspects of a given problem so that her office can be used as a legislative resource rather than an advocate in the legislative process.

Responding to a consumer complaint about confusing billing statements from a finance company, Mrs. Valory writes:

Thank you for your letter concerning the new truth-in-lending law and [X] Company statements. Such letters are extremely helpful to this office as they provide us with firsthand information on consumer concerns.

We are enclosing a brief summary of the law which we thought might be of interest to you. We are also taking the liberty of forwarding a copy of your letter to [X] Company for their comments.

Copies of the letter were sent not only to the [X] Company, but also to the California Retailers Association.

Another consumer wrote directly to the offending company and sent Mrs. Valory a copy of that correspondence along with a further explanation. Her reply:

Although this office does not have regulatory or enforcement authority, we have had some success in enlisting the cooperation of business and industry in solving individual consumer complaints. If you do not receive a satisfactory response to your letter to [X] Company in a reasonable time, please let us know and we will attempt to assist you.

Letters such as yours are extremely helpful to this office for advising the Governor and the Legislature on matters of concern to consumers. Thanks for writing.

Occasionally Mrs. Valory has sought to enlist the assistance of her counterparts in other states, rather than seeking either federal intervention or dealing directly with the firm herself. This is a letter to the Consumers' Council of Massachusetts:

Gentlemen:
Enclosed are copies of correspondence from Mr. [X] concerning a transaction with a Massachusetts firm. Will you please take whatever action you can to assist Mr. [X] with his problem.

The most characteristic method of dealing with consumer complaints has been direct correspondence with the company against whom the complaint has been lodged. A typical letter follows:

Enclosed is a copy of a letter from Mr. [Y] of [Z], California, concerning a complaint against your company.

It is the responsibility of the California Consumer Counsel to advise the Governor and the Legislature on matters of interest to consumers and to recommend any needed legislation or regulation.

In carrying out this responsibility, it is our policy to encourage business to take the initiative in solving consumer problems without further legislation or regulation.

In view of this policy, we would appreciate receiving your comments on the enclosed letter and your advice as to what action Mr. [Y] should take.

If this letter failed to induce a response which satisfies the complaining consumer and/or brings the company's operating practices within the bounds of existing regulations, Mrs. Valory then referred the entire file of correspondence to the state agency or local district attorney with the jurisdiction and authority to further pursue the complaint.

In some aspects the catalytic role is the more active one in the resolution of consumer problems. Mrs. Nelson's adversary position generally led to either: (1) presentation and definition of a disputed problem before a legislative or administrative body, with the responsibility for formulating solutions to the problem remaining with that body; or (2) referral of the problem to an appropriate legal enforcement mechanism for resolution. Mrs. Valory's catalytic role often results in the use of her position to resolve the problem directly through either: (1) bridging an actual communication gap between the businessman and consumer involved; or (2) applying a subtle moral persuasion on the businessman by catching him in an unfavorable position; or (3) presenting an implied threat of governmental intervention if he doesn't get his affairs straightened out.

Perhaps the greatest difference in the approach taken by the two Consumer Counsels involves the question of consumer education. In a speech given July 9, 1969, Mrs. Valory commented:

Acting from my conviction that the best protected consumer is the aware and informed consumer, I have focused my strongest efforts on educating and informing the buying public, for I believe that a thoroughly informed society of consumers is a far more effective and less expensive deterrent to dishonesty, fraud, and misrepresentation than the enactment of sometimes costly, sometimes ineffective new "consumer protection" laws.

Mrs. Valory's legislative research on consumer interest topics is a reflection on this view. Also consistent with this attitude is an active attempt to prepare special consumer education films to be presented on television, and even public service "spot commercials" of consumer advice.

Mrs. Nelson, from her subsequent position with the Illinois Federation of Consumers, has been particularly critical of this portion of Mrs. Valory's program: "There is no excuse for anyone in the Governor's office taking a chiefly educational role." One of the sources of this criticism is undoubtedly a sharp disagreement about the nature of the "consumer revolution." Returning to the origins of this movement, recall that the initial consumer protection measures arose to counteract the impact of the doctrine of *caveat emptor* in a marketplace where the buyer had become incapable of attaining equality of bargaining power with the seller. Miner thought that Mrs. Valory's educational goal seems to tacitly accept *caveat emptor*, but attempts to attain bargaining equality by educating the buyer. Speaking of a federal study describing deception in gasoline and supermarket games, Mrs. Valory observed: "I am not sure it is the government's place to legislate in areas of this sort. I think it may be enough for the government to warn that deceptions may exist." Miner saw Mrs. Nelson's aggressive advocacy of the consumer interest can be seen as an attack on *caveat emptor* itself, accompanied by a conviction that the only practical, sure way to attain bargaining equality for all consumers is not to rely on education of the buyer, but rather to limit or restrict the powers of the seller.

Mr. Miner had also referred to the note on "The History of Government and Consumer Protection." This note, which had been prepared for him by his assistant, Miss Marion Arnold, a law student, appears as Appendix A.

In preparing his report, Miner had discovered that there are many other state agencies that guard the consumer's interests. Most of these agencies had been in existence long before the COCC was formed and many had functions that overlapped those of the COCC, particularly under Mrs. Nelson. Appendix B lists those agencies.

He reflected upon a recent speech about the respective roles of business, government and consumer. The following excerpt was particularly important to Mr. Miner:

Business and government must work together to solve problems posed by the knowledge explosion and the population explosion. But there must be a clear definition of which functions belong to government and which to business.
. . . As it happens there are few major problems that can be solved by government alone without business or by business alone without government. As government and business both respond to the major problems of our day, as each of them enlarges the scope of its responsibilities to the public, they inevitably move into the no-man's-land where functions overlap and boundaries are ill defined, so the real question is which of them should do what.

Miner thought that the relationship between the individual citizen in his role as a consumer in the American marketplace and the businessman who provides the goods and services offered in that marketplace has become one of those areas of overlapping functions and ill defined boundaries. He was concerned about where does government, as a representative of the citizenry as a whole, fit into this relationship between consumer and business?

Before he drafted his report to CAGE, Miner was particularly concerned then with two major issues. First, what ends should the COCC serve; and second, how should it be organized to do so.

APPENDIX A: REPORT ON CONSUMER PROTECTION FOR THE COMMITTEE FOR THE ASSESSMENT OF GOVERNMENT EFFICIENCY

prepared by M. L. Arnold

The Beginnings of Consumer Protection

During the Middle Ages there was a clear answer to the question of consumer protection. In that society the equality of bargaining position between buyer and seller was complete: First, all goods (grain, vegetables, cloth) were displayed on the open market and could be examined thoroughly for defects. Secondly, a man bargained almost exclusively with his neighbors, who cheated him only at the risk of severe social repercussions in the community. Government had no place in this relationship, and the legal doctrine *caveat emptor* (let the buyer beware) evolved.

The expansion of trade, and improved transportation systems which made new markets available to distant producers, eroded the equality of bargaining position by increasing the distance between buyer and seller. Their relationship was no longer marked by personal knowledge and mutual responsibilities in a common community, but by an impersonal marketplace where the buyer had to rely on the assurances of an occasionally irresponsible seller. As this void between buyer and seller began to open, government (and its legal institutions) began to act to protect the trusting buyer from those sellers who sought to exploit their freedom from the informal sanctions of the buyer's community. If a seller had made a definite statement about an article (a warranty), in a case where a defect could not easily be seen, the medieval courts ignored *caveat emptor* and gave the buyer legal recourse against the seller. Similarly, doctrines protecting the buyer from fraud or misrepresentation by the seller were developed and later codified.

In the late nineteenth and early twentieth centuries the pace of government intervention into business activities quickened. Much of this early activity was directed toward protecting the businessmen themselves from their overzealous competitors. But such activities as "trust-busting" (the Sherman and Clayton Acts), prevention of unfair trade practices (formation of the Federal Trade Commission), and regulation of the transportation, utility, communications, and securities industries (creation of the ICC and CAB, FPC, FCC, SEC, etc.) have all produced indirect benefits to consumers by ensuring orderly industrial growth and adequate and fairly priced goods and services in markets relatively free from fraud and deception.

Protection was provided directly to the consumer only in those areas where his health or safety was jeopardized by the seller's products. Publication of Upton Sinclair's *The Jungle* in 1906 shocked the country with its accounts of the unsanitary conditions in Chicago's meat-packing houses, and the government responded with the Food and Drug Act of 1906 and the Meat Inspection Act in 1907. Similar exposés have resulted in such additional governmental action as: expansion and tightening of the food and drug laws in 1938 and 1962; the Flammable Fabrics Act in 1953; and recent developments in automobile safety, gas pipeline safety, control of environmental pollution, further tightening of meat inspection standards, and the extended debate over the health hazards of cigarette smoking.

Consumer Protection in the 1960's

Much of the legislation directed toward consumer protection has been enacted during the decade of the sixties, including the initial efforts to break away from the limitations of health and safety protection. The "truth-in-packaging" and "truth-in-lending" bills, enacted in 1966 and 1967, represent a movement toward economic protection of the consumer, and this move has excited the questioning of the relative roles of business, government, and the consumer.

Critics of this expansion of the boundary of government action argue primarily along two lines. In 1968, 33 federal departments devoted 64,714 employees and nearly a billion dollars to consumer protection activities. Most of the states have bodies which parallel the activities of at least some of these federal departments, further increasing the total tax bill for consumer protection. It is argued that these costs, to support the administrative machinery required to implement consumer legislation, have risen beyond the point where further legislative proliferation can be justified.

The second common line of criticism is that economic protection of the consumer constitutes an interference with our overall economic structure and poses a threat to the capitalistic system on which our country has risen to its present state of economic well-being:

When protecting the consumer is used as a base for launching antibusiness missiles, it does the consumer more harm than good. It undermines the foundation on which our competitive system rests.

. . . . .

The crucial question is: To what extent can the government continue to castigate the business community and deprecate business in the public's eyes without completely undermining public confidence, jeopardizing our free enterprise system, and creating a class society?

Two advocates of further expansion of governmental consumer protection activities respond as follows:

The trouble is not in the precepts of the American economy, but in its practices. No fundamental weakness in capitalism or the profit system has been identified, and none is suggested here. There can be no doubt that this nation's industrial revolution has created the most productive and rewarding economic system in history. But the robber barons who created it handed down as part of their legacy a system and an attitude with monstrous flaws. The ills they inflicted upon the society are such a part of the American scene that some, such as water and air pollution, may already be impossible to eliminate. Others are correctable, but the lengthy and often vicious battles over impure meat, dangerous drugs, or hidden installment costs amply demonstrate how difficult they are to identify, fix, and eliminate.

The modern businessman cannot be blamed for creating the industrial system. Nevertheless, he can be blamed for preserving it in its original form. He defends the status quo with all his strength and warns that any change, any governmental intrusion, any adjustment not of his own making, will lead to disaster. To an extent, he is right. Wanton disregard of the realities of American business could seriously disrupt the nation's economy. Revolutionary schemes such as nationalization or decentralization could very well end in disaster. But such an attack has never been mounted or even intended.

It would not succeed if it were. For all its serious flaws, the system built by the Morgans and the Rockefellers at least has permanence. Indeed, the edifice created by the American industrial revolution has such structural rigidity that it has proved and is still proving to be incredibly resistant to change. But is it change that the consumerists want—not a revolution in economics, but a revolutionary change in the attitude of its practitioners.

The change in attitude these advocates seek would include a willingness on the part of manufacturers, distributors, and sellers to adopt a greater sense of responsibility toward the consumer. They ask that more complete product information be provided to the buyer so that he can make his consumption choices in a marketplace of known qualities and values, and they insist that unnecessarily dangerous, harmful, or deleterious products be kept from the marketplace.

The consumerist advocates argue that these conditions are necessary to facilitate a return of equality of bargaining position to the American marketplace. Since this equality is also believed to be a minimum requirement for attaining the "quality of life" this country assures its citizens, the consumerists insist that, if the business community fails to meet its responsibility here, government intervention is not only appropriate but should be pursued regardless of cost.

Governmental Organization for Consumer Protection

One point should be apparent from this brief account of the history of consumer protection: governmental intervention into the relationship between the consumer and business is a deeply ingrained fact of the American marketplace. It is highly unlikely that this intervention, particularly the protection of the consumer's health and safety, will be discontinued no matter how the conflict described above is resolved. Granting, then, that government will remain involved in consumer protection, three practical problems are posed:

1. What levels of government should be involved?
2. How should the governmental consumer protection efforts be organized?
3. Is there a preferred approach which the principal overseer of governmental consumer protection activities should take?

What Government?

The massive involvement of the federal government has been indicated previously, and it is clear that in many areas the adoption of uniform standards and the need for consistency in regulatory action require formulation and enforcement of laws on a national scale. (Imagine the chaos confronting a national marketer of consumer products if each of the 50 states had its own labelling and packaging laws!) But many of the deceptive or fraudulent activities of unscrupulous operators are outside the reach of federal authority, or they may employ a "hit-and-run" tactic that an often ponderous and slow federal mechanism cannot react to quickly enough. Paul Rand Dixon, Chairman of the Federal Trade Commission (1961–69), has stated: "By stopping such practices before they grow into problems of interstate proportions, the need for federal action will be minimized, and the people most directly affected will have a telling voice in deciding what constitutes unfairness and deception."

The limitations to the effectiveness of national action are not restricted to regulatory or enforcement activities. After seventeen months as the Special Assistant to the President for Consumer Affairs, Mrs. Esther Peterson remarked:

The letters that pour into us, the requests from agencies, indicate that the place where the real consumer protection is needed and where the action is needed is at the state and local level where the people are. One thing has become very sumer must also receive representation at the state level and also at the local clear—consumer representation at the federal level is not enough. The con- level.

What Organization?

The great volume of existing consumer protection legislation has already defined some of the organizational parameters of governmental activity in the field. It seems reasonably clear that the administration and enforcement of the technical requirements of various laws are best left to those executive departments and administrative agencies with special expertise in the subject of the regulation. Thus administration of automobile safety standards is entrusted to the Department of Transportation, the Civil Aeronautics Board and Federal Aviation Administration ensure safe operating practices for the nation's airlines, harmful drugs are kept off the market by the Food and Drug Administration, etc. This pattern of technical agencies responsible for administering consumer legislation is also prevalent at the state and local levels.

Where legislation has established specific standards of compliance or provided for criminal or other sanctions for actions in violation of the laws, responsibility for enforcement is commonly vested in the appropriate prosecutorial agency: the U.S. Department of Justice, state attorney general, or local district attorney. These local bodies also enforce the more general laws against fraud and misrepresentation in their jurisdictions. As the consumer movement has grown, many of these agencies have formed special units to coordinate their enforcement efforts in areas of special consumer interest.

Legislative bodies have, themselves, acknowledged the growth of consumerism by establishing committees and subcommittees to investigate, propose, and screen potential legislation of interest to the consumer. In addition to fulfilling an important legislative function, these committees also provide an invaluable forum for the presentation and discussion of the many different views toward consumer protection.

As these diverse interests and multiple agencies have proliferated, the need for some form of central coordinating group has arisen. There are, however, wide differences of opinion over the form and scope of duties such a group should have. The most common structure has been the special adviser to the chief executive, a form which has been justified on the national level as follows:

To coordinate and catalyze action on the part of the consumer, the simplest and best idea seems to be to have an office in the White House separate from the cabinet empires. This office can act as an executive oversight agency and exert its influence through the President directly and through interdepartmental meetings. . . . The Presidential adviser . . . acts as the cutting edge of the movement, listening to the consumer's complaints and industry's responses, proposing, suggesting, cajoling, and recommending legislation to the President if need be.

More vigorous consumer advocates have proposed a cabinet level Department of Consumer Affairs, contending:

You need a large number of people—lawyers, economists, scientists—to deal with consumer problems in a continuous way. . . . You need cabinet status to give the whole thing the prestige to compete with other government power centers.

These active consumerists seek, at the very least, a formal Office of Consumer Affairs with specified duties and responsibilities, rather than the informal "special adviser" type of organization.

APPENDIX B: STATE OF CALIFORNIA AGENCIES
SAFEGUARDING CONSUMERS

Bureau of Food and Drug Inspection, State Department of Health

Bureau of Meat Inspection, Division of Animal Industry

Deputy Attorney General in Charge, Consumer Fraud Section (Fraud and Deceptive Practices)

Bureau of Weights and Measures

State Insurance Commissioner

Bureau of Air Sanitation, State Department of Public Health

State of California Air Resources Board

State Water Resources Control Board

Bureau of Field Crops and Agricultural Chemicals, State Department of Agriculture (Pesticide Control)

Public Utilities Commission

California Office of Consumer Counsel

Supermercados La Criolla

Mr. Ernesto López was the owner of two supermarkets in Managua, the capital of Nicaragua (estimated population approx. 270,000). At the end of 1963 he came to the conclusion that within twelve to eighteen months the expanding city would be ready for a new supermarket. After surveying the market and its development, he settled upon three sites as possible locations. Mr. López then proceeded to review their respective merits in order to decide which one he should purchase.

THE APPEARANCE OF SUPERMARKETS IN MANAGUA

Managua's first supermarket, *La Colonia*, had been opened in 1956 by Felipe and Carlos Mántica, sons of Mr. Felipe Mántica, who owned one of the largest import and wholesale companies in Nicaragua.[1] In July 1957, Ernesto López, whose family also owned a large import and wholesale company in Managua, returned from the United States, where he had completed his education in business administration. During his absence from Nicaragua he had become acquainted with U.S. retail business and observed the trend toward the integration of wholesale and retail operations. This, and the opening of *La Colonia*, had induced him to reflect on the future of his family's business. Convinced that supermarkets would gradually reduce the volume of wholesale operations in Managua, López decided that the interests of his family's business would best be served by entering the supermarket field. His decision, with which his father agreed, was partly influenced by his preference for the cash basis of supermarket sales, compared to the 60- or 90-day credit basis of the wholesale business.

The Mánticas' store, *La Colonia*, resembled a modern U.S. supermarket. In addition to luxurious appointments, the store was equipped with air

---

[1] The Mánticas' company handled a large variety of goods, ranging from office and household appliances, toys, etc. to canned foods, liquors, and wines. López' operations covered approximately the same assortment of merchandise.

68

conditioning—a seemingly attractive feature in a country where the year-round average temperatures exceed 26.6°C (80°F), and where the humidity reaches 90%.[2] It was situated in an upper-middle-class area in the southwestern part of the city close to the *Estadio Nacional* (National Stadium). The store's location on a main highway, which connected an important out-of-town residential section with the city itself and the downtown business district, attracted additional clientele. Originally the Mánticas had planned to develop the location into a complete shopping center, and they had constructed their building accordingly. Later, however, after finding it impossible to interest enough merchants in leasing stores within the proposed center, the Mánticas remodelled and expanded their market to cover much of the unused land. The shopping area nevertheless included a few other stores, such as a shoe repair shop and a pharmacy, as well as a branch of Banco de América, one of Nicaragua's leading banks. The cost of *La Colonia*, including the remodelling, amounted to around 3.5 million córdobas[3] (without any allowance for working capital).

López' approach to the setting up of a supermarket differed radically from the Mánticas' in that he recognized the novelty of supermarket merchandising to most of the citizens of Managua. Luxurious surroundings, according to López' conception, were undesirable, because they made many lower-class people and even middle-class people (including the servants of the well-to-do) uncomfortable and apprehensive of high prices; thus they tended to avoid such stores. He also decided that air-conditioning should not be used, since many Managuans believed that it induced colds. López preferred, moreover, to establish his supermarket in rented premises rather than to invest in land and an expensive building. He selected a large warehouse in the middle of the central market district where groceries, meat, and other foodstuffs were sold daily in the street market. The supermarket was placed in direct competition with the street market and small grocery stores, called *pulperías* and *tiendas*. The supermarket's main competitive strengths were its lower prices, guarantee of honest weights, and rigorously hygienic merchandise.

The *pulperías* usually dealt in low-priced items such as *plátanos* and other nationally produced foodstuffs (oats, sugar, rice, beans, dairy products, etc.) and a few imported canned foods.[4] Each of them had only one refrigerator, and no frozen food cabinets. The *tiendas*, somewhat larger stores, carried a greater number of imported items. Usually they had one or two refrigerators, as well as a frozen food cabinet. Both types of stores were supplied by wholesalers of domestic products and importers. The

---

[2] Nicaragua has a wet season (winter) from May to January and a dry season (summer) from January to mid-May.

[3] Seven córdobas to one U.S. dollar at the official and only rate of exchange.

[4] *Plátanos* have the same appearance as bananas but are used as vegetables, or cut into fine slices and fried, like potato chips.

pulperías were required to pay cash, while the *tiendas* could obtain up to 60 days credit. The selling prices in the *tiendas* and *pulperías* were usually about 45% over import or wholesale cost.[5] This difference derived from the addition by the intermediate wholesaler or importer of 20% to his own cost, plus a markup by the storeowner of about 20% on his purchase price. López' supermarket further distinguished itself by eliminating the wholesaler and by handling its own imports. Its prices did not exceed 30% over import or wholesale cost. The markup was reduced to 20% and sometimes even 8% on merchandise with rapid turnover, such as meat, vegetables, fruit, rice, beans, cheese, poultry, and other locally produced foodstuffs. As a result, the retail prices were generally 10 to 15% lower than those of the *pulperías* or the *tiendas*. The supermarket did not offer any credit to its customers, however, while its competitors would occasionally grant up to 10 or 15 days credit to their regular clients.

López opened his supermarket in September 1957. He called it *La Criolla* (the country girl), a name which conveyed the idea of service and simplicity, and established an atmosphere in which servants would feel welcome and at ease. It covered some 300 square meters (about 3,250 square feet), and its layout was based on the supermarkets López had visited in the United States. The merchandise was also much the same: meat, vegetables, sugar, flour, rice, oils, vinegars, canned foods, beverages, wines, liquors, household utensils, magazines, books, and cigarettes. The main difference was its extreme simplicity: bare walls, rough metal shelves, etc. A dozen attendants constantly dusted the merchandise, swept the floor, and restocked the shelves, and there were two check-out counters, operated by girls. The supermarket was immediately successful and attracted a rapidly increasing number of customers. Mr. López took great pleasure in operating the store. He enjoyed watching the behavior of the customers and studying their buying habits. He frequently changed the display of the merchandise in order to provoke new reactions. This enabled him to give useful advice to local manufacturers with respect to presentation, product design, advertising media, etc., and also allowed him to make some valuable observations as to which categories of merchandise were purchased by different types of customers.

THE BUYING HABITS OF THE VARIOUS INCOME GROUPS

López made his analysis of Managuan buying habits on the basis of a distinction between (a) goods with a low markup—meat, rice, cereals,

---

[5] These percentages were often misleading. In many instances, the real markups were substantially higher. Several practices were frequently used by the small stores as well as by the street-market vendors to increase the real selling prices well above the stated prices; e.g., mixing high and low qualities while charging for top quality only, and cheating on weights (in some cases, the scales showed as much as 500 gm when the merchandise actually did not weigh more than 400 gm). The small stores further increased their net profits by charging the 2% sales tax, but not remitting this amount to the government.

beans, dairy products, and other items produced domestically for daily consumption, and (*b*) supplies which were generally more expensive and. bore a higher markup—liquors, canned foods, delicatessen, and household items. In general, López thought that his customers could be put into one of the following five income classes:

1. *Upper Class.* Weekly purchases averaged 650 to 700 córdobas per household, of which some 300 córdobas were spent on daily consumption goods from category (*a*), and 350 to 400 córdobas on items from category (*b*). People in this class usually earned a regular income of over 10,000 córdobas per month. Most of them owned their own businesses, plus a farm or a plantation from which they enjoyed substantial additional incomes. Their yearly incomes often exceeded 300,000 córdobas. Typically, they had several children, five or more servants, owned comfortable houses and at least one or two automobiles.

   The shopping in goods from category (*b*) was often done by the lady of the house on her return from social activities in town, or by the male head of the house on his way home from his office. These purchases included expensive liquors, such as imported whisky, brandy, gin, champagne, and quality wines, and substantial amounts of food delicacies.

   During the period from June to October, however, when Nicaragua's weather is least pleasant, such people often travelled to the United States or Europe. Their absence drastically reduced this type of luxury consumption. The servants stayed at home, however, and so the consumption of ordinary foodstuffs during the rainy season declined very little.

   In view of the type of supermarket that *La Criolla* was and had been intended to be, the upper-class customers accounted for less than 5% of the business. The majority of customers came from the lower-income brackets, and a sizable minority from the upper-middle class.

2. *Upper-Middle Class.* The typical upper-middle-class household spent 400 to 450 córdobas weekly: 175 córdobas on foodstuffs for daily consumption from category (*a*), and around 200 to 250 córdobas on items from category (*b*). The goods purchased were usually of the same type as those consumed by the upper-class people, but the quantities purchased were smaller. The head of the household earned a regular income of from 3,500 to 4,000 córdobas per month and was usually self-employed. In some instances, he also owned a small plantation. The average yearly income was therefore in excess of 50,000 córdobas. These families generally had at least five children, three or four servants (depending on the number of children), and owned an automobile. About 30% of *La Criolla's* sales were made to upper-middle-class customers.

3. *Middle-Middle Class.* Their purchases amounted to from 300 to 350 córdobas per week: 150 córdobas for daily consumption goods, and

150 to 200 córdobas for category (*b*) goods. They spent less than the upper-middle-class customers on canned goods and imported food delicacies. They also avoided imported liquors and bought instead the cheaper domestic rum, whisky, gin, or even aguardiente.[6] Middle-middle-class households had an income of some 2,500 to 3,500 córdobas monthly. This was the approximate income of a government employee or of a middle ranking army officer. The families usually had at least five children and employed two or more servants.

Sales to middle-middle-class customers accounted for approximately 40% of *La Criolla's* total sales.

4. *Lower-Middle Class.* Most of these families lived in inexpensive *taquezal* or mud houses with eight, nine, ten, or more children, usually without servants. They earned a monthly income that ranged from 800 to 1,200 córdobas, and their weekly food purchases seldom exceeded 200 córdobas. They spent about 100 córdobas of their total weekly purchases for category (*a*) foods and 65 to 100 córdobas for category (*b*) items, mainly canned foods and aguardiente. The lower-middle class represented 20 to 25% of *La Criolla's* customers.

5. *Lower Classes.* The consumers from the lower classes earned as little as 400 córdobas monthly, and some had no regular income. Although they frequently visited the supermarket, they purchased very little and accounted for only 2 or 3% of *La Criolla's* sales. López believed that their attendance at the supermarket was essential for the success of the venture, on the grounds that other patrons would look upon it as evidence of the competitiveness of the store's prices.

THE MULTIPLICATION OF SUPERMARKETS

In November 1959, the Mánticas ("perhaps stimulated by my success," said López) opened their second supermarket, the *Supermercado Central*, in the downtown area of Managua. At a cost of nearly 3 million córdobas, they set up a store which rivaled any of its kind in any country of the world. After the initial rush was over, however, business fell short of the Mánticas' expectations. Catering to the same clientele as the one served in their first supermarket, *La Colonia*, they noticed that their total sales from both stores showed no marked increase. In effect, the same amount of purchases previously made at *La Colonia* tended to be divided between the two stores. Only one year after its inauguration, the *Supermercado Central* was discontinued. The closing stunned the city and received front-page coverage in the Managuan press. (See Exhibit 1 for a translation of one of the articles that appeared at the time.)

The advent of the Mánticas' second supermarket had no apparent effect

---

[6] A very low-priced brandy made from aniseed or sugar cane.

on *La Criolla's* operations, nor did its failure divert López from his intentions to open his own second supermarket, *La Criolla II*. While Carlos Mántica had attributed the failure of *Supermercado Central* to insufficient consumer demand, López felt it was due mainly to the store's location. In his opinion, this location was badly chosen on two counts. First, no clientele lived in the immediate neighborhood. A school and the military academy lay to the south of the store and a church to the east, while the rest of a six-block radius was taken up by offices or by houses inhabited by middle- or lower-middle-class people, who avoided the supermarket because its elegance made them ill at ease. López knew of instances when a servant had disobeyed specific instructions to buy a particular item at the *Supermercado Central*. She would find out the supermarket's price for the item, then buy it at her customary *tienda*, and, if necessary, pay the difference from her own pocket.

Second, both of the Mánticas supermarkets were located on the same route followed by many upper-class people on their way home from work or from their downtown social activities. Many of those who shopped at the *Supermercado Central* were former customers of *La Colonia*. But *Supermercado Central* was somewhat less accessible from the homeward route of the upper-class patrons than was *La Colonia*. Moreover, it lacked adequate parking space. Consequently, most of those customers who were initially attracted to *Supermercado Central* because of its novelty later reverted to *La Colonia*. This probably accounted to a large extent for the drop of sales per customer to which Carlos Mántica referred. (See Exhibit 1.)

In December 1961, one year after the *Supermercado Central* was closed, López opened *La Criolla II*. The new store, somewhat smaller than the first one, was located in the northwestern part of the downtown area, in the post office square, close to the government offices. Again, as in the case of *La Criolla I*, the store was set up in rented premises, at a relatively low installation cost—about 200,000 córdobas for equipment and furniture. (See Table 1.) The surrounding area was cleaner than that of *La Criolla I*, however, and more parking spaces were available, so that the store drew more customers from the wealthier classes. The prices, generally lower than at *La Colonia*, were the same as at *La Criolla I*, and the quality of the merchandise was identical. *La Criolla II* derived an initial advantage, in that many customers had already acquired the supermarket habit from the previously established stores. For the most part, the customers of *La Criolla II* were middle-middle-class to upper-middle-class families living in the northwestern sector of the city. A number of customers also came from the wealthy outskirts. By López' estimation, around 20% of the sales went to upper-class customers, 35% to upper-middle-class, 30% to middle-middle-class, 15% to lower-middle-class, and a negligible percentage to lower-class customers.

TABLE 1

Some Financial Data on the First Two Stores

I. *La Criolla I:*

Rent.................... 1,800 córdobas per month
Investment in equipment.... 200,000 córdobas per month
Investment in merchandise.... 400,000 córdobas per month

	1958	1959	1960	1961	1962	1963 (*Est.*)
Sales...........	1,200,000	1,800,000	1,450,000	2,100,000	2,300,000	2,600,000
Gross profit........	285,000	380,000	340,000	405,000	430,000	450,000
Net profit........	42,000	N.A.	N.A.	128,000	132,000	150,000

II. *La Criolla II:*

Rent.................... 1,200 córdobas per month
Investment in equipment.... 200,000 córdobas per month
Investment in merchandise.... 300,000 córdobas per month

	1962	1963 (*Est.*)
Sales........	1,100,000	1,500,000
Gross profit........	285,000	325,000
Net profit........	35,000	80,000

THE PROPOSED LA CRIOLLA III

At the end of 1963, the success of *La Criolla II* and the continued population increase of Managua led Ernesto López to think that a third supermarket could be added to the chain of *Criollas*. The population of the city was increasing at a rapid rate through migration from the rural areas[7] as well as from a natural annual growth of 6% (compared with a natural growth of 3.5% a year in the whole of the Republic). Estimated at 200,-000 in 1957, the population exceeded 269,000 in 1963. (See Table 2.)

A number of housing developments had been planned, and in the southern part of the city some were under construction. The new store would cater mainly to the higher-income people who purchased these new homes. It would, therefore, have to be more attractive in its external and internal appearance and would also have to be equipped with air-conditioning. At the same time, however, it would have to avoid extreme

TABLE 2
Some Data on the Nicaraguan Economy

1. *Population*

Years	Nicaragua	(per sq. km)	Dept. of Managua	(per sq. km.)	City of Managua	(per sq. km.)
1950	1,059,000	7.6	162,000	47.0	143,000	238.0
1951	—	—	—	—	—	—
1952	—	—	—	—	—	—
1953	—	—	—	—	—	—
1954	—	—	—	—	176,600	293.0
1955	1,245,000	8.9	206,800	59.9	180,000	300.0
1956	1,288,000	9.2	218,100	63.3	193,000	321.0
1957	1,332,500	9.5	230,000	66.7	200,000	333.0
1958	1,377,500	9.9	242,400	70.2	218,000	363.0
1959	1,423,500	10.2	255,600	74.1	235,000	391.0
1960	1,474,500	10.6	271,800	78.8	249,000	414.0
1961	—	—	—	—	—	—
1962	—	—	—	—	—	—
1963	1,663,000	11.9	—	—	269,000	448.0

2. *Gross Domestic Product*

Years	Total, Millions of Córdobas	Per Capita, Córdobas	Years	Total, Millions of Córdobas	Per Capita, Córdobas
1955	2,180	—	1959	2,294	1,581.5
1956	2,074	—	1960	2,328	1,550.5
1957	2,267	1,672.0	1961	2,526	1,628.2
1958	2,311	1,651.5	1962	2,812	1,754.1

[7] The people who migrated from the rural areas generally remained in agriculture, for Nicaraguan city workers are often seasonal crop pickers. They accounted for most of the population of the eastern sector of Managua, and in 1959, over 15% of the city's total population was comprised of formerly rural people.

TABLE 2 (Continued)

3. *Foreign Trade* (*in millions of córdobas*)

. . . Value of Exports . .

Years	Value of Imports	Total	Cotton	Coffee
1950	—	132.55	9.20	86.65
1951	—	242.75	36.04	121.77
1952	—	279.51	45.14	142.96
1953	—	301.49	55.44	140.78
1954	—	360.49	110.62	165.66
1955	—	474.67	204.47	183.88
1956	481.70	381.24	155.56	152.92
1957	566.40	433.47	152.56	188.17
1958	545.61	436.62	174.23	160.92
1959	467.89	455.06	205.44	97.01
1960	501.86	391.68	102.83	134.55
1961	520.46	424.37	128.11	121.56
1962	681.85	577.04	219.08	108.10

4. *Price Indexes* (1958 = 100)

. . . . . Export . . . . .

Years	Cost of Living	Import	Total	Cotton	Coffee
1950	61	83	83	100	84
1951	73	95	120	220	117
1952	74	94	109	128	117
1953	83	94	109	115	120
1954	90	93	137	122	157
1955	102	94	117	115	129
1956	99	97	124	106	142
1957	95	100	116	101	125
1958	100	100	100	100	100
1959	97	100	89	86	83
1960	95	101	91	94	82
1961	95	103	88	99	77
1962	96	103	88	97	74
March 1963	93	103	90	92	76

Source: *International Financial Statistics*, XVI (October, 1963), 199; supplement to 1965/66 issues, 185, 187.

luxury, to deserve the popular connotation of its name and to attract the lower-income clientele. *La Criolla III* would carry essentially the same lines of merchandise as the *Criollas I and II*.

Because of the absence of adequate rental premises in any of the possible locations, the store would have to be specially constructed. López requested the advice of a group of specialized U.S. architects, who provided him with sample plans for a modern supermarket. It would be surrounded by ample parking space and would cover an overall area of 1,000 square meters (10,778 square feet). He thought it would be necessary to spend about 1 million córdobas for land, construction, furniture, and equipment plus 600,000 córdobas for working capital. The working capital would

people buying habit $'s to spend = potential sales

FIGURE 1
Supermercados La Criolla

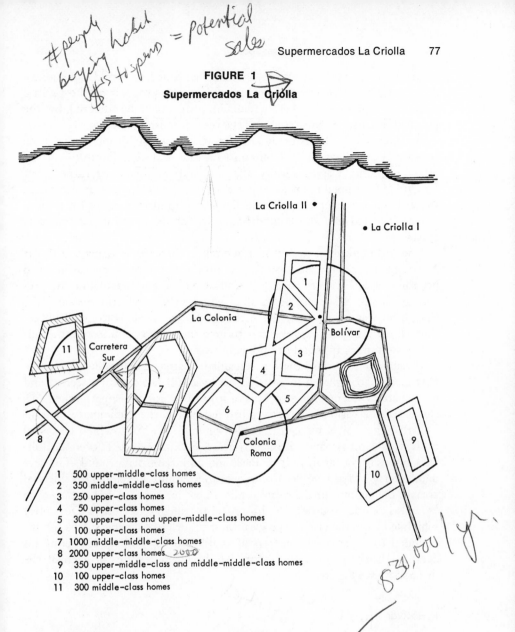

La Criolla II •

• La Criolla I

La Colonia

Bolívar

Carretera
Sur

La Colonia

Colonia
Roma

1   500 upper–middle–class homes
2   350 middle–middle–class homes
3   250 upper–class homes
4   50 upper–class homes
5   300 upper–class and upper–middle–class homes
6   100 upper–class homes
7 1000 middle–middle–class homes
8 2000 upper–class homes 2000
9   350 upper–middle–class and middle–middle–class homes
10 100 upper–class homes
11 300 middle–class homes

$39,000 / yr.

have to provide merchandise for yearly sales of around 1.7 to 2 million
córdobas (120,000 córdobas monthly during the first six to seven months,
increasing later to some 180,000 córdobas per month). Although the operating costs would be higher than at the other two *Criollas*, López expected that prices would not have to be increased, because the higher
operating costs would be offset by the economy of larger purchases.

López realized that the success or the failure of such an undertaking
would depend not only on his skill in selecting the best location, setting up
the supermarket, and managing it, but also on the relative prosperity and
growth of the country's economy. In the foreseeable future, this was de-

pendent to a very large extent on what happened to world commodity prices, especially cotton and coffee, and on the progress of the Central American Common Market, which, in turn, could be affected by the political situation in Nicaragua and the rest of Central America.

In 1960, when the Nicaraguan exports of cotton dropped from the previous year's level of 29.4 million to a low of 15.1 million dollars, the whole economy was drastically affected, and the inventory turnover of *La Criolla I* dropped from six to less than five. In 1963, many Nicaraguans showed concern over a possible decline in world market prices for cotton. It was reported that the United States was about to sell its current surpluses.

López thought that such a drop would be particularly damaging to the Nicaraguan economy because the country's cotton-growing surface had been increased by more than 20% following the good results of the preceding season. Also, the political situation in Central America and the Caribbean was far from stable. Although he was anxious to avoid unreasonable risks, López was reluctant to give these political uncertainties undue weight in his appraisal of opportunities.

Presuming that the situation remained relatively favorable within the next twelve to eighteen months, López was still faced with a second and immediate problem—the selection of a location for the supermarket. His survey of the various alternatives had led him to the preliminary conclusion that three sites were reasonably suitable. The first, which he called *Bolívar*, was on Avenida Primera (la Av. S.O., also called Avenida Bolívar) opposite the small Bolívar Park and children's playground. The second, referred to as *Colonia Roma*, was in a rapidly developing residential area, in the vicinity of the new hospital. The third, designated as *Carretera Sur*, was on the southern highway (also called Carretera a Diriamba) which led from the city to the wealthiest suburb of Managua. This suburb included 10–15 square kilometers of sizable estates. To help in making his decision, López made an inventory of the characteristics of each of the three sites (see Figure 1).

I. Bolívar

(a) *Houses and People within a Six-block Radius.* The customers were by no means expected to come from within a six-block radius only. On the contrary, since the supermarket was surrounded by ample parking space, it was meant to attract people from much greater distances as well. These would come by car and would be able to store as much as one week's supplies in their refrigerators. Taking only the six-block radius into consideration, however, helped to give an idea of the potential market which would exist regardless of transport facilities.

Of the 1,300 homes within this radius, about 250 were large houses, most of them south of the store. Although the majority of these were made of concrete, some were made of brick. The cost of such homes ranged from 300,000 córdobas to over 1,000,000. They had many rooms and spacious gardens. By law, each owner had to buy at least 1,000 square meters (10,778 square feet), at a cost of 60 to 70 córdobas per square meter (5.6 to 6.5 córdobas per square foot), in order to be allowed to build a house. Only upper-class people could afford such homes.

The houses to the east of the store location, about 200 of them, were mainly prefabricated dwellings. Close to the military academy, most of them were occupied by military officers, who could not be considered potential customers. They shopped in commissaries where the goods were exempt from import duties.

North of the proposed store site, toward Lake Managua and downtown, were around 500 older homes. These had at least five bedrooms, plus living room and dining room, all with very high ceilings, and a large patio. The houses were very close to one another, however, and the parking of cars was often a problem. The cost of the houses ranged between 200,000 and 300,000 córdobas, and the owners usually belonged to the upper-middle class.

West of the location were around 350 three- or four-bedroom *taquezal* or mud houses, all adjoining, owned by middle- or lower-middle-class families. The cost of such a home was from 50,000 to 80,000 córdobas.

López expected that approximately 60% of his anticipated sales to people from within the six-block radius would be made to residents of the northern and the western sectors.

(*b*) *Traffic.* The supermarket would be passed by about 600 private cars and 500 taxis daily, according to the traffic count reports López had had made. The cars would come from town through Avenida Roosevelt or Central, a one-way street, turn west on Calle Colón, and head north on another one-way street, Avenida Bolívar. They could stop at the supermarket, then either go downtown via Avenida Bolívar, or return to Calle Colón, Calle 27 de Mayo, or the new bypass (Pista exterior de Circunvalación) by turning around Bolívar Park. Every fifteen minutes a bus stopped at Bolívar Park, on the way to the downtown area or to the Estadio Nacional and Carretera Sur. Many more pedestrians than motorists passed the site, and the store would be within walking distance from downtown.

(*c*) *Future Housing Developments and Outlying Areas.* Possibilities for housing developments were few, if any, in all but the southern sector. A small number of houses in the northern and western sectors might be replaced by newer ones, which would probably raise the average living standards in these areas to some extent. The changes could not be very striking, however, because no space was available for garages, or even street parking.

Families who improved their incomes and changed their habits sufficiently to become potential car owners were apt to leave the city and move to one of the newer developments. These were taking shape, or being planned, south of the city. A new project was due to start in the months to come, west of the new hospital, in the *Colonia Roma* area. The land was easy to buy, and, by official decree, the construction of residential buildings had to start as soon as the land was acquired, an obvious asset from López' point of view. Two other projects that could benefit a super-market at Bolívar were under construction in the outskirts of Managua, on Carretera a Masaya, southeast of Laguna de Tiscapa and the Presidential Palace. One was a government housing development for middle-class peo-ple, and plans included some 350 houses, of which around 100 were near completion. The other one was a private development. A large construc-tion company had bought the land, made the necessary improvements, and was starting to sell the lots to individual owners. The population density of this area promised to increase rapidly, since its elevation was a few meters higher than Managua itself, and its exposure to the winds made living more comfortable. Its average temperature was actually 4 to 4.5°C. (7 to 8° F.) lower than that of downtown Managua.

(*d*) **Existing Shopping Facilities.** The Bolívar location was about eleven blocks from the street market and from *La Criolla I*, far enough away not to divert too many customers from López' first supermarket. A few *pulperías, tiendas*, and small drugstores were close by, in Calle Colón. The inhabitants of the southern sector, which had no stores, patronized *La Colonia* and sometimes, although rarely, *La Criolla II*.

(*e*) **Restaurants, Clubs, Recreation Parks, and Churches in the Area.** López considered such environmental elements important, because they created opportunities for many people to see the supermarket and get ac-quainted with it while going for a walk, going to church, or attending social activities. Bolívar's main asset, from this point of view, was the small park opposite the projected store location; this was one of the most fre-quented children's playgrounds in the city. At a distance of less than two blocks, there was also a fairly good restaurant where it was proper to take ladies (this was far from the case everywhere in Managua). The closest church, however, was at the Instituto Pedagógico, more than four blocks away. Nor was there any club in the vicinity, but two tennis courts were close by.

II. Colonia Roma

(*a*) **Houses and People within a Six-Block Radius.** The Colonia Roma location was in the middle of a future housing development. The six-block radius was consequently of very low population density, especially to the northwest and the west, where, as yet, no buildings or roads existed at all. To the south, the area was occupied by the Country Club, and to the east, the hospital separated the store location from an older and poor quarter, which was beyond reasonable walking distance. The only existing homes which could be taken into consideration were those of a completed housing development in the northeastern sector, an area which held 150 upper-class and upper-middle-class families. The remaining development area would be exhausted within twelve to eighteen months, upon completion of about 150 new homes which were still in the planning or construction stage.

(b) *Traffic.* The Pista exterior de Circunvalación, or bypass, on which the supermarket would be located, was still to be extended from the hospital to the Carretera a Diriamba. This bypass, which would be completed within three to four months, would then be expected to divert and absorb most of the traffic from Calle Colón. This traffic would pass in front of *La Criolla III* instead of the rival *La Colonia.*

The traffic would be substantially greater than at Bolívar, although a numerical comparison obviously could not be made yet.

(c) *Future Housing Developments and Outlying Areas.* The Colonia Roma housing project, northwest and southwest of the supermarket, was scheduled to start within three months. A well-known construction company had bought the land, was in the process of laying out the sewage system and the utilities, and was starting to sell the lots. With a construction time ranging from four to six months, 15 to 20 houses would be built simultaneously. When completed, the development would include around 100 upper-class homes, with extensive garden areas and ample parking space.

To the north, an area of some 50 luxury homes would also be likely to provide a Colonia Roma supermarket with good business.

Twelve blocks to the west of the store, an existing section of over 1,000 homes was made a likely source of customers because of the easy access to the store provided by the new bypass. The owners of these houses were mostly in the middle-middle-class income bracket, and many of them owned cars.

(d) *Existing Shopping Facilities.* The closest stores were a number of *pulperías* in Calle 8a or Calle 9a. The shopping of upper- or middle-class households was mostly done in *La Colonia* and sometimes in *La Criolla II.*

(e) *Restaurants, Clubs, Recreation Parks, and Churches in the Area.* The exclusive Country Club was located four blocks south of the Colonia Roma intersection. Its patrons would drive by the supermarket on their way to and from their homes in the wealthy suburb on Carretera Sur. Also nearby were a recreation park and a few churches (a chapel in the hospital and a small sanctuary in the Casa Nazaret, or girls' orphanage).

III. Carretera Sur

(a) *Houses and People within a Six-Block Radius.* The immediate neighborhood of a supermarket at Carretera Sur was very sparsely inhabited. The closest homes were around four blocks away, at 21a Av. S.O., the boundary of a section of 1,000 middle-class homes.

(*b*) *Traffic.* Carretera Sur, or Carretera a Diriamba, was the most important highway in Nicaragua. It was part of the Interamerican Highway, leading from Managua to the Costa Rican border. It was also the only way to leave Managua for León and the country's Pacific coast ports of San Juan del Sur, Puerto Somoza, and Corinto. Buses departed from Managua every half-hour on this highway. More important still, with respect to the supermarket, the highway was the link between the city and the southwestern outskirts, which included its wealthiest residential district. The completion of the Pista exterior de Circunvalación, or bypass, would divert the traffic from the rival *La Colonia* in favor of *La Criolla III.*

(*c*) *Future Housing Developments and Outlying Areas.* As already mentioned, the southwestern residential suburb would provide the greatest part of the supermarket's customers. This area extended over 15 km. (over 9 miles) of beautiful scenery up to Casa Colorado (elevation: 970 meters, or 2,950 feet) and included around 2,000 magnificent residences. The families who lived there mostly had four or five children whom their parents drove to school, inasmuch as the school bus did not go any farther than 4 km. (2.5 miles) from town. Many of the houses were new, although there were a number of older mansions. The residence of the U.S. ambassador was in the area, as well as the homes of several members of the embassy's staff.

The other outlying area which would provide the store with customers would, of course, be the new development of Colonia Roma. Much closer, a new middle-class housing development of approximately 300 dwellings was also planned west of the Carretera.

(*d*) *Existing Shopping Facilities.* There were no shops in the immediate neighborhood. The people shopped in town, mostly at Mántica's *La Colonia* and sometimes in *La Criolla II.* There was a small general store at Km. 8 of Carretera Sur; its business was limited, however (its inventory did not exceed 100,000 córdobas), and its prices were relatively high.

(*e*) *Restaurants, Clubs, Recreation Parks, and Churches in the Area.* As in the case of Colonia Roma, the passing traffic would be the most effective promotion for the store. There were no clubs, restaurants, or parks in the vicinity. The closest park, very attractive and frequently visited, was at Km. 3 of Carretera Sur, i.e., around 2 km. (1.2 miles) from the supermarket location. A few hundred meters farther out, clustered in a short strip of one or two blocks, were about fifteen bars of low reputation, which attracted a great many people from the city. The residents of the outlying sectors, however, very rarely visited them, and women customers were never seen there.

In López' judgment, the three locations were equally attractive and promising. Bolívar, perhaps, had some immediate advantages, but Colonia Roma and Carretera Sur had their assets too, especially with regard to traffic and proximity to customers who patronized the rival *La Colonia.* He had to make a final choice, however, for his option on the Bolívar site was coming to a close, and the sale of plots had already started in Colonia Roma.

EXHIBIT 1

Newspaper Article on the Closing of Supermercado Central

DARING SUPERMARKET SUSPENDS ITS OPERATIONS

More Customers But Fewer Purchases

The *Supermercado Central*, one of the best of its kind in Central America, will be officially closed on December 31 of this year (1960). On January 1, 1961, the premises will be occupied by the Central Bank of Nicaragua.

The *Supermercado Central*, owned by the Mántica Company, was set up one year ago at a cost of approximately three million córdobas. It opened for business in November 1959.

This commercial center was superior to its twin, *La Colonia*, in layout and elegance and was a source of pride for the commercial section of Managua.

Reason for Closing

"We are closing the *Supermercado Central* in order to obtain the maximum return on capital and effort invested," Mr. Carlos Mántica stated.

Since the capacity of *La Colonia* alone was large enough to cater to the clientele of both stores, the maintenance of both resulted in an unnecessary duplication of costs and efforts. Closing the *Supermercado Central* will increase the capital and sales of *La Colonia*, which will benefit the customers through lower prices, wider selection of products, and better personal attention.

The capital of the *Supermercado Central* will be used to establish various food industries which should make it possible to substitute for products now being imported, particularly *Embutidora Nacional* which inaugurated its new meat-canning operation the very same day that the *Supermercado Central* was closed.

Mr. Carlos Mántica, manager of the supermarket, explained that the decision was made, not because the store was commercially unsound within itself, but because certain financial considerations had clearly shown that the city could not support another large supermarket.

"To have two establishments belonging to the same company is like having two hotels both of which have half their rooms unoccupied," said Mr. Mántica. "In that case, it is better to close one of them and to leave all of the demand to the other.

"When we opened the *Supermercado Central*, we did it because *La Colonia* could not satisfy all of the demand. Since then, things have changed.

"Immediately after the *Supermercado Central* started to operate, it was well accepted. The number of customers gradually increased. Some months ago, 11,000 people were visiting the store monthly; now there are 19,000."

EXHIBIT 1 (Continued)

More Visitors, Smaller Purchases

"The number of people who did their shopping in the *Supermercado Central* increased considerably. But the fact is that they purchased less. Our statistics show that the average purchase dropped noticeably. Initially, a customer purchased an average of around 30 córdobas per day; recently this average had dropped to 19 córdobas. This means that the people are consuming at a minimum.

"The drop in sales is particularly noticeable in imported goods. Previously, 46% of the total demand was concentrated on such goods. Recently, this dropped to only 35%."

The *Supermercado Central*, or rather its construction, cost 1,045,000 córdobas for the furniture and the equipment. These figures demonstrate that such an establishment calls for practically the same investment in construction as in equipment.

The customer who visits a supermarket daily may not be in a position to know about its intricate operation. Nor can he always appreciate the techniques and methods that make such a monster run efficiently. Nevertheless, it may be of interest to note that a supermarket like the *Central* had 18 refrigerating units, costing 3,000 to 4,000 córdobas each, plus a great quantity of other costly equipment.

SECTION II

DEVELOPMENT OF MARKETING PLANS

Institutional Services, Inc.

Institutional Services, Inc. (ISI), a subsidiary of Saga Administrative Corporation (Saga), is headquartered in Menlo Park, California. In early July, 1969, David Reeves, Vice President and General Manager of ISI, was reviewing the progress of this company's first six months of operations. Mr. Reeves was scheduled to report to the Board of Directors at their end of July meeting on progress to date, ISI's prospects for future development, and to recommend, for the Board's approval, a strategy for the company to follow over the next several years.

Saga's Background

In the spring of 1948 the cafeteria at Hobart College in Geneva, New York, went out of business. Three enterprising Hobart students who were supplementing their G.I. bill with various part time jobs presented a proposal to the dean to reopen and operate the dining hall themselves. Permission was granted and success followed quickly. Based on their record, a neighboring girls' college asked them the following year to take over their food service operation on a contract basis. Further growth and expansion brought the firm's annual sales to over $1 million by 1956. The partnership was dissolved and the business incorporated in 1957, with the three original partners serving as the principal officers of the corporation.

As the firm entered the 1960's, diversification was planned in either or both of two directions. Saga had, by this time, gained considerable expertise—as well as reputation—in institutional food service, but had restricted its operations to colleges and universities. Expansion into other institutional markets was thought feasible, and thus, in 1963 a hospital division was started with the objective of coordinating and channeling the firm's food service expertise into hospitals and other health care

---

facilities including retirement homes. Because a successful college food service operation required close familiarity with both college financial administration and changing student attitudes, it was thought that Saga could also enter the college market in fields other than food service. Thus, in 1965 a subsidiary company, Scope, was formed to specialize in the design, construction and operation of off-campus student dormitories and residences. In 1968, Saga provided a food service program for 244 colleges and universities in 41 states, the District of Columbia, Canada, and Puerto Rico. In these schools, Saga served about 200,000 students out of a boarding student potential of about 2.5 million.

In early 1967 a Venture Committee, later set up as a development division, was organized to facilitate the carrying out of expansion opportunities. The first completed project was the formation of Le Fromage, a chain of specialty cheeses and gourmet cooking supplies shops, which opened its first store in October, 1967. In November, 1968, Institutional Services was organized as a subsidiary, followed in April, 1969, by the acquisition of Harding-Williams, a Midwestern food service operator specializing in corporate cafeterias and catering. The Harding-Williams acquisition was to provide the organizational nuclei for a horizontal expansion of Saga's food service expertise into the corporate food market. A preliminary step toward vertical integration of food service was taken by entering into a joint venture agreement with General Foods Corporation to manufacture preprepared frozen food products.

In fiscal 1968 the College Division accounted for 92% of Saga's $89.9 million in sales. Scope Corporation was carried on an equity basis, so its minor losses to that date entered the income statement only at the earnings level and did not contribute to the sales figure. The remaining 8% of sales came from the Hospital Division. Harding-Williams was to be accounted for as a purchase rather than pooling of interests, so the fiscal 1969 results would reflect its contribution only from the April acquisition date through the end of the fiscal year in June. An investment advisory service estimated fiscal 1969 Saga sales at $105 million. Their report also forecasted that fiscal 1970 sales would rise to $135 million, with the Harding-Williams and other acquisitions contributing $20 million of this total (see Exhibits 1 and 2 for 1968 income and asset/liability data).

Formation of ISI

During discussions of diversification possibilities, a consultant to Saga in the fields of materials management and procurement suggested that college purchasing practices were commonly outmoded and inefficient, and were often extremely costly to the institutions in terms of lost opportunities for large savings through modern procurement methods. The consultant argued that better purchasing methods were urgently needed by the institutions Saga served, and the potential savings were great enough to provide a reasonable profit to Saga, as well as to significantly reduce materials costs for the institutions. In preliminary contracts with college financial and purchasing managers, this idea was favorably received, and further discussion and examination of the potential market led to the formation of ISI in October, 1968.

The consultant who initially proposed the idea agreed to devote approximately half of his time to the new company to guide development of its policies and operating plans. The full-time staff was to consist, initially, of a Vice President/General Manager, selected for his knowledge and experience in purchasing management, and a secretary. ISI's initial capital was 1,000 shares of one dollar par value, with Saga holding 85% and the principal officers and Board members holding the remainder. Additional financing was provided by Saga through a line of credit, at one quarter point above the prime rate, for up to $150,000 over the first two years of operation. The corporate charter declared, "the primary business in which this corporation intends to engage is the provision of a service to colleges, universities, hospitals, and other institutions in the area of organized cooperative purchasing."

Beneath these formalities was a simple set of ground rules established for ISI by Saga. ISI was to begin business on November 1, 1968 "as a single product company (consolidated purchasing services) serving two classes of customers: colleges and hospitals." The $150,000 in loan funds could be used over the two-year period to develop that product with either one or both of the customer classes, but ISI was expected to establish a base sufficient to finance operations beyond the two-year period from its own retained earnings. Because of the greater familiarity of the officers with the college market, ISI devoted its initial efforts to this area.

Consolidated Purchasing. Current college purchasing practices suffer from three major problems: lack of standardization, effective negotiation, and size. The standardization problem stems, in part, from the characteristic independence of the academic community and the absence of strong, centralized control over such administrative functions as procurement. For example, each departmental secretary is generally allowed to use the particular mimeograph paper she likes best, while each building superintendent uses the brand of floor wax he considers easiest to apply, etc. A leading purchasing text[1] calls the solution to this problem "simplification" —reducing the number of standard items carried in inventory—and cites the example of a company which saved $67,000 yearly from having standardized the paper towels used throughout its multiplant operations.

Simplification savings come primarily from reduced inventory investment, greater quantity discounts, better competitive prices because of greater unit volume, and reduced clerical and handling costs resulting from the fact that

---

[1] Lamar Lee, Jr., and Donald W. Dobler, *Purchasing and Materials* (New York: McGraw Hill Book Co., 1965).

fewer different items have to be recorded, controlled, received, inspected, and delivered."[2]

If standardization is difficult on a single college campus, the problem would seem hopelessly multiplied in trying to serve a multi-college customer class, but ISI had some hope of resolution. Because brand differences are often minute or nonexistent, brand preference can be attacked in a simplification program by taking samples of "preferred" products, and promising exact duplication under private brand labeling. Actual quality differences must, of course, be recognized, but this can still be done through standardization within each grade level, and through attempting to minimize the number of different levels carried and used. Impetus can be given to this effort by obtaining prices on the desired "standard" products so attractive that the cost differential becomes too great to justify a small quality differential.

The negotiation problem is at least partially due to the inability, or unwillingness, of colleges to pay the salary of really first-rate purchasing personnel. A glance through the classified sections of the *Wall Street Journal* during early 1969 would have revealed salaries offered to purchasing managers of between $15,000–22,000 per year. A survey of 1968–69 college operating practices noted in *College and University Business*[3] reported the average annual salary for purchasing agents in public institutions was $10,604, while private colleges paid only $9,301. Skill in conducting effective negotiations can only be acquired through experience, and negotiating strength is increased by thorough knowledge of the suppliers with whom the bargaining is done. It is only natural to expect that the men with this knowledge and experience will seek the more lucrative industrial positions, resulting too often in a college purchasing manager poorly equipped to do an effective job of negotiating. ISI, with the guidance of its consultant, and with an experienced purchasing manager as its Vice President/General Manager, had, it was thought, the necessary knowledge and experience to offer colleges who participated in the ISI program a savings alternative to "negotiating" skills. Two strategies, in particular, were expected to add greatly to the effectiveness of ISI's negotiations. First, suppliers would be sought who had not previously participated in the college market. ISI could offer such suppliers entrance to a large market with substantially no marketing cost to them. ISI expected to be able to negotiate these marketing cost savings into price reductions for ISI customers. The second approach would be to seek out suppliers with current overcapacity. By operating at full capacity the supplier could allocate his fixed costs over a larger number of units and, therefore, could improve his profits even if he sold the incremental units

[2] *Ibid.*, pp. 58–59.

[3] Dennis W. Binning, "1968–69 College Operating Practices Analysis, Part 2," *College and University Business*, Vol. 44, No. 10 (October, 1968).

at a price which covered less than the full cost. ISI planned to utilize this rationale in negotiating for marginal cost pricing from such suppliers.

The third major problem is size, or lack of sufficient purchasing volume to be able to take advantage of quantity discounts. The small college is by far the dominant type of higher educational institution in the U.S.: in the 1965–66 school year 53.2% of all colleges had enrollments of less than 1,000, and another 24.9% fell in the enrollment range of 1,000 to 2,500.[4] Lack of standardization accentuates this problem of low purchasing volume, and the two factors combined virtually preclude the kind of purchasing "muscle" necessary for establishing a strong negotiating position. Although some larger universities have been relatively successful in overcoming these problems, their purchasing effectiveness could be improved upon through buying in still larger quantities. Thus, purchasing of standardized products by an experienced and capable purchasing staff in the large quantities made possible by consolidation of many schools' demands, combine to provide unusual opportunities for reduction of materials costs.

The mechanism which makes consolidated purchasing possible is master purchasing contracts. As practiced by many of the largest corporations (GE, RCA, IBM, for example), a central corporate purchasing office negotiates a large volume order with a supplier of a single item or class of items. These contracts provide four primary benefits to the purchaser.[5] The supplier will usually agree to keep the materials on hand and available for shipment on request from the buyer, thus reducing the buyer's inventory problems. Second, because the supplier is assured of a sizeable volume of business and knows approximate delivery schedules, he can more efficiently schedule his production and marketing efforts thereby reducing his costs in these areas. Through negotiation and competitive bidding, the buyer benefits from these savings through lower costs. A third advantage can be protection against price increases during the term of the contract. Finally, since contracts are negotiated for longer periods of time than if the purchases were made as needed, the buyer spends less time negotiating separate agreements for recurring requirements. The combination of better service and better price obtained through the master contract is generally so dramatic that even though the individual divisions and subsidiaries are not bound to buy against the master contract, they can find no better deal elsewhere. Thus, the volume promised in the contract can be fulfilled even without centralized control over the purchasing functions of the divisions.

In the corporate setting, the operating costs of the central purchasing organization are simply included in the total corporate overhead. Be-

---

[4] U.S. Department of Health, Education and Welfare, Office of Education, *Digest of Educational Statistics, 1967* (Washington, D.C.: U.S. Government Printing Office, 1968).

[5] Lee and Dobler, *op. cit.*, p. 44.

cause ISI would operate as a financially distinct enterprise from the colleges it served, its master contracts would be drawn up differently; i.e., the colleges would pay a nominal membership fee to become affiliated with ISI, and would thereby become entitled to purchase against the master contracts at the contract price. The master contract would not only provide for the lower price to the ISI affiliated colleges, but also for a payment from the supplier to ISI proportional to the volume actually purchased against the contract.[6]

Competition. The idea of a buyers' co-operative was not a new one; co-ops have been an especially common device for improving the economic leverage of farmers and individual consumers. Generally these co-ops, rather than pass on their purchasing savings through reduced prices, accumulate the benefits from quantity buying and distribute them periodically in a lump-sum rebate proportional to each member's purchases during the period. When such co-operatives become large enough to require full-time management and staff, the savings often disappear into operating overheads and the co-op members receive neither lower prices nor their rebate. In such an organization there is often very little incentive to cut operating costs and manage efficiently, because any excess costs come out of member's rebates and not the manager's pocket. ISI's founders believed that by reducing prices to the customer so that a relatively small margin was left to ISI, the profit incentive would enable them to operate more efficiently than the traditional co-ops.

The major competitor of ISI in the college market was Educational and Institutional Co-op (E & I Co-op), organized as a nonprofit buyer's co-op. Formed by the National Association of Educational Buyers (NAEB), its services were available only to NAEB member schools. The 1968 annual report of E & I Co-op showed that they had processed $18.2 million of purchasing volume for 1,189 member schools, down from $19.5 million in 1967. Their fees had totaled 5.5% of this volume in 1968, and with a staff of approximately 80 (including a ten-man field service staff) their operating costs were nearly 4.4% of total volume. The remaining 1.1% of volume distributed as rebates would, if spread equally among all 1,189 members, total less than $170 per school. This annual report and other sources known to Saga indicated that E & I had several problems. First, the NAEB tend to be dominated by its big school members, who need the services of E & I Co-op least because of their own economic strength. Second, attractiveness of some of E & I's contracts has been diminished by the fact that they had not dealt with major brand-name producers. Also, it was thought that the size of their staff was excessive. Saga found much sentiment in favor of the certainty of lower prices and no rebate rather than the vagaries of an uncertain and relatively small rebate.

---

[6] The Robinson-Patman Act, which prohibits discriminatory pricing by a seller under certain conditions, specifically excludes educational institutions.

The hospital market was not dominated by any one major factor. Of twenty-some existing purchasing organizations serving this market, the largest was the Hospital Bureau. Organized as an association of local New York hospitals more than 60 years earlier, by 1968, the Hospital Bureau had 750 members in roughly half of the U.S. Their staff of 27 (including one field representative) processed $9–10 million of purchasing volume in 1968. There had been a change in top management a few years earlier, and the Bureau's Board of Directors had begun to include professional businessmen as well as hospital administrators and doctors. These changes seemed to have infused a better management climate and the Hospital Bureau seemed poised for expansion. It was, however, hampered by a lack of capital, and was attempting to finance growth by giving up any form of dividend or rebate distribution and using all retained earnings for expansion.

The College Market for ISI Services. College enrollment trends provided a rough measure of the potential for ISI services (see Exhibits 3 and 4 for detailed figures). Total degree credit enrollment increased from 3.05 million students at the beginning of the 1957–58 school year to an estimated 6.35 million in Fall 1967. Recent statistical projections of the Office of Education indicated further increases to 9.7 million by 1977. A significant trend in this growth has been a shift in enrollment toward public institutions. In the 1957–58 school year, 58% of the total enrollment was found in publicly controlled schools, and 42% in private colleges and universities. By 1967 this ratio had changed to 68%–32%, and the corresponding projection for 1977 was 73%–27%. Another marked change has been the growth of the two year colleges. Enrollment in four year schools doubled during the decade 1957 to 1967, while in that period two year enrollment nearly trebled. The projections for 1967–77 show a further 73% increase in enrollment in the two-year colleges, while four-year enrollment is expected to rise by only another third. Although comparable trend and projection data were not available for categorizing enrollment by size of institution, 63.1% of total enrollment in the 1965–66 school year was in schools with more than 5,000 students. The trend away from private colleges, and the rapid growth of the two-year schools both suggest that this concentration of enrollment in the larger schools is likely to become even more pronounced.

The same type of institutional differentiation provides another measure of the potential for institutional marketing, although projections are not available and the information is neither as current nor complete (Exhibits 4 and 5). The two enrollment trends of explosive growth in two-year schools and a shift away from private colleges appear to be reflected in the number of comparable types of institutions as well. During the period 1961–67 the total number of institutions of higher education increased by 16.5%, from 2,044 to 2,382. However, the number of four-year colleges increased by only 9%, while there were 35% more two-year schools in 1967. No breakdown of public versus private control was available for 1967, but for 1961 to 1965 the rate of growth in the number of public schools (14%) was twice that of private colleges (7%), and the marked increase of two-year schools from 1965 to 1967 suggests that the public schools had accelerated their growth rate even more. The 1965 breakdown by institutional size revealed that 53.2% of all colleges had enrollments below 1,000, and the next 24.9% were in the 1,000–2,499 range. This, only 21.9% of U.S. institutions of higher education had enrollments greater than 2,500. Although statistical projections had not been made, it seemed that these figures might change, since many of the rapidly growing two-year colleges currently fell in the 1,000–2,499 range and could not be expected to remain that small, while the increasing financial difficulties of the small private colleges threatened the demise of many of the schools in the under 2,500 groups.

The attempt to estimate the potential for institutional marketing in terms of dollar volume of purchases made by the schools proved even more difficult. ISI began by dividing purchasing volume into three broad categories:

Assets: furniture and equipment for offices, laboratories, classrooms; maintenance equipment; vehicles; etc.

Supplies: stationery, forms and other office supplies; laboratory supplies; maintenance and housekeeping supplies; automotive supplies and petroleum products; etc.

Services: food service and housing for students and faculty; insurance; janitorial; medical; policy/security; etc.

These categories proved hard to track down because the typical college accounting system records expenditures by user or by source of funds used rather than by the type of goods and services purchased. For example, all expenditures for library operation are recorded together, including salaries, microfilm equipment, books, checkout forms, etc. Appendix A describes this accounting system in greater detail and presents aggregate data for the 1963–64 school year, and historical data for alternate years in the previous decade.

Using the aggregate data from Appendix A and Office of Education projections of expenditures (see Exhibits 6 and 7), a rough measure of overall potential can be made. Approximately 55% of current fund expenditures in 1963–64 were for payrolls. Applying this as an assumed constant ratio of projections of future current fund expenditures reveals that the 45% spent on goods and services would have been $7.16 billion in 1967–68, and can be expected to rise to $12.74 billion (in constant 1967–68 dollars) by 1977–78. Subtracting out the amount of current fund expenditures for plant leaves an approximation of the total purchasing volume in ISI's categories of "supplies" and "services." In order to plan specific marketing strategies these estimates should be broken down further, but they do provide a starting point. Similar analysis yields an approximation of ISI's "asset" category based on plant expenditures for "equipment." Roughly 75% of the current fund expenditures for plant and 7% of the total plant fund expenditure, in 1963–64, were specifically identified as equipment expense. Because some of the "building (including fixed equipment)" group of expenses also includes some assets ISI could provide purchasing services for, the portion of plant fund expenditures that might be considered market potential for ISI was assumed to be 10%. Combining these calculations, the total market potential for providing purchasing services for assets, supplies, and services in the college market can be approximated as follows:

(figures in billions of 1967–68 dollars)

School Year	Supplies & Services	Assets	Total
1969–70	$ 7.60	$0.67	$ 8.27
1970–71	8.05	0.66	8.71
1971–72	8.69	0.57	9.26
1972–73	9.32	0.57	9.89
1973–74	9.90	0.67	10.57
1974–75	10.48	0.67	11.15
1975–76	11.11	0.66	11.77
1976–77	11.70	0.64	12.34
1977–78	12.24	0.63	12.87

ISI'S FIRST SIX MONTHS

During this initial organization period, ISI activities were somewhat diffuse. Some effort was initiated to sign up colleges and universities as potential customers, and 28 had become ISI Associates by early June.

The process of contract negotiation had started with areas familiar to ISI personnel. While Special Assistant to the Director of Purchasing at Stanford University, Mr. Reeves had conducted a survey of the purchase and use of campus cars among 152 colleges and universities.[7] Mr. Reeves was convinced by this experience that leasing provided a valuable alternative to purchase in many circumstances and he sought to negotiate a master contract for vehicle leasing. The contract awaiting signature in early June called for the leasing company to provide a complete range of

[7] David E. Reeves, "How Colleges Manage the Purchase and Use of Official Campus Cars," *College and University Business*, Vol. 37, No. 5 (1964). The effort consisted of a letter signed by the president of Saga, which was sent to all Saga schools reporting the founding of ISI and offering membership which entitled the "buyer" the opportunity to use all master contracts negotiated by ISI. An associate paid a membership fee of $50.00 for five years. Generally, schools were enthusiastic about the new Saga venture and urged Mr. Reeves to move as quickly as possible to obtain useful master contracts. Mr. Reeves was reluctant to spend much time in the field signing up new members since this prevented him from doing the work necessary to screen potential suppliers and negotiate contracts.

services for ISI customers at a price to be kept competitive with any other leasing firm. ISI agreed to actively advertise and promote the lease contract, to add a staff member to coordinate vehicle leasing, and to provide credit screening for current Saga customers. Mr. Reeves estimated the cost of these activities at $42,000 the first year, with 10% annual increases thereafter. ISI would receive from the leasing company $3 per car per month for every vehicle leased under the contract, and Mr. Reeves was confident that 1,000 cars could be leased in 1969–70, 2,000 in 1970–71 and 3,000 by 1971–72. The question of whether Saga personnel could or should be used to market this and subsequent contracts was a matter of concern to all involved. It was decided not to attempt to use any such personnel to sell the car leasing service and instead to rely on direct mail solicitation.

One quite unforeseen development was that several opportunities had arisen for possible ISI participation that did not really fall within the charter of the company. The first such occurrence was an agreement entered into with Scope Corporation (Saga's dormitory construction and management subsidiary) to provide purchasing services for their projects. Scope agreed to pay a fixed 5% of purchasing volume for this service, and ISI hired an additional staff member, Mr. George Rawson, plus a secretary to coordinate Scope purchasing and to assist in the regular purchasing activities of ISI. It was anticipated that Scope would spend about $800,000 on furniture during the next year. This, in turn, led to another development. When Mr. Rawson began soliciting bids on beds for the Scope projects, it was revealed that there were only two institutional-bed manufacturers in the U.S., one of which dominated the market with a superior product. Thus, price negotiations were understandably stiff and one-sided. Contacts were initiated with the major institutional-bed manufacturer in Europe, and the opportunity was presented to ISI to become the exclusive U.S. market agent for that firm. The manufacturer would pay all transportation, warehousing, and distribution costs, guarantee to keep his price competitive with the leading U.S. bed, even though his product was thought to be better than the U.S.-made product. At current levels this price was expected to be $22.50, and ISI was to receive 10% of this amount for their efforts in advertising and marketing the beds. The ten-year agreement was made contingent upon ISI's meeting sales quotas of 2,000 beds in 1969, and 20% annual increases thereafter to a total of 10,000 beds in 1978.

Two other projects had come to the notice of ISI which, though outside the corporate charter, were thought to have such a substantial potential that preliminary negotiations had been conducted. The first of these was a proposal from an established foreign study and travel organization that had operated primarily in the high school market, but was now seeking an entry into the college market. It offered the opportunity for a 50% joint venture with a $40,000 initial investment from ISI. The ultimate market potential was thought to be substantial because of the expanding college population and the fact that college student travel to Europe had been growing at a 20% annual rate in recent years. In 1969, 250,000 college students were expected to go to Europe, and this figure was projected to rise to 432,000 in 1972. By forming the joint venture at this time, 1% (3,000 students) of the 1970 market was considered within reach, with added experience yielding 2% in 1971 and 3% in 1972. The anticipated pricing structure would provide $50 per student to ISI, before tax and expenses. Aside from the initial $40,000 investment the capital requirements would be minimal, because the students would pay prior to departure, thus providing the funds for flight reservations and accommodations in advance. The only expense to ISI would be marketing and overhead costs. It was planned to hire two salesmen (total costs, including travel per salesman, were estimated at $30,000 per year), and further, to have Mr. Reeves devote about one-half of his time to the new venture for at least the first year. Saga was to use its 244 resident college managers to help sell the travel service. The Foreign Study League, a subsidiary of the Transamerica Corporation, offered such courses as French language and civilization, German language and civilization, and Russian language and civilization; such courses lasted between five and six weeks and typically cost about $850 (all inclusive). High school students were solicited largely by offering a high school faculty member a "free" trip if he could attract seven or so students. Contacts with the faculty were made largely by direct mail although the League did have a sales force of about seven men who contacted various school organizations such as the Archdiocese of Chicago. They also did a certain amount of promotion work with larger schools.

There was some question as to how the Saga resident food managers would respond to this extra assignment. It was thought that they should be given an incentive to sell the program and tentatively it was planned to offer them a free trip with every ten reservations they obtained. They could take another member of their family if they sold another ten. If they did not wish to accept the trip as their reward they could accept money in the amount of $50 per student enrolled. In either case the cost would be paid by the joint venture and therefore was not charged against ISI's commission.

The foreign study proposal seemed to Mr. Reeves to represent a substantial opportunity since ISI could contract with universities and colleges to conduct their programs abroad. The school could provide faculty which would permit the granting of academic credit. It was thought that this market segment would expand substantially over time and that ISI could help the originating schools market their credit courses to students located on other campuses.

The marketing of the service to non-Saga schools could possibly be handled by the Saga District Managers. There were such managers and it was thought that they would visit non-Saga campuses for the purpose of locating a student "representative" who would then assume responsibility for selling the tours. He would be paid the same as the Saga resident food manager. It had not yet been decided how the Saga District Manager should be rewarded for his "extra" assignment.

The remaining project discussed during these first six months was comprehensive insurance service for the institutional markets ISI served. Important savings, greater convenience, and better service all seemed possible through consolidating the insurance needs of the institution into a single package or portfolio of policies in which the institutional customers might be considered as a distinct risk (and rate) class. An insurance broker was found who was sufficiently enthusiastic about the prospects for such a package that he volunteered to organize, capitalize, and devote 18 months of his time independently operating and building up a corporation designed to provide such coverage to ISI's markets. After the initial 18 months, ISI would have an option to purchase 49% of the corporation for $100,000, of a price to be determined on the basis of an independent evaluation of the worth of such an interest. After an additional seven years, the original entrepreneur would trade the remaining 51% to ISI for an equal value of public stock in Saga.

Evaluate ISI's progress to date. What recommendations should Mr. Reeves make to his board?

EXHIBIT 1

SAGA ADMINISTRATIVE CORPORATION AND WHOLLY-OWNED SUBSIDIARIES
CONSOLIDATED STATEMENT OF INCOME AND EARNINGS RETAINED FOR USE IN THE BUSINESS

	Fiscal year ended	
	June 29, 1968 (53 weeks)	June 24, 1967 (52 weeks)
Net revenues	$85,919,000	$71,732,000
Costs and expenses:		
Cost of food sold	42,203,000	36,651,000
Salaries and wages	28,187,000	23,080,000
Other operating, general and administrative expenses, including provision for depreciation and amortization of $298,000 in 1968 and $312,000 in 1967	11,887,000	9,673,000
	82,277,000	69,404,000
Income before federal income taxes	3,642,000	2,328,000
Provision for federal income taxes	1,740,000	1,045,000
Net income for the year	1,902,000	1,283,000
Earnings retained for use in the business, beginning of year . . .	5,278,000	3,995,000
Transfer to common stock in connection with 3 for 1 stock split (Note 3)	(1,107,000)	
Earnings retained for use in the business, end of year	$ 6,073,000	$ 5,278,000
Net income per share, after giving retroactive effect to 3 for 1 stock split (Note 3)	$1.18	$.78
Pro forma net income per share, assuming issuance of shares under employee stock plans (Note 4)	$1.09	

CONSOLIDATED STATEMENT OF SOURCE AND APPLICATION OF FUNDS

	Fiscal year ended	
	June 29, 1968 (53 weeks)	June 24, 1967 (52 weeks)
Funds provided:		
From operations:		
Net income for the year	$1,902,000	$1,283,000
Expenses which did not require cash outlay:		
Depreciation and amortization	298,000	312,000
Other	241,000	148,000
	2,441,000	1,743,000
Proceeds from sale of stock	60,000	
	2,501,000	1,743,000
Funds applied:		
Additions to property and equipment, net	2,920,000	203,000
Less—long-term obligation assumed in connection therewith . . .	1,938,000	
	982,000	203,000
Increases in investments and deferred charges	282,000	253,000
Reduction in long-term obligations	110,000	107,000
Purchase of treasury stock	23,000	14,000
	1,397,000	577,000
Net increase in working capital	1,104,000	1,166,000
Working capital, beginning of year	2,403,000	1,237,000
Working capital, end of year	$3,507,000	$2,403,000

EXHIBIT 2

SAGA ADMINISTRATIVE CORPORATION AND WHOLLY-OWNED SUBSIDIARIES
CONSOLIDATED BALANCE SHEET

ASSETS	June 29, 1968	June 24, 1967
Current assets:		
Cash (including time deposits of $2,500,000 in 1968 and $1,000,000 in 1967)	$ 4,963,000	$ 2,759,000
Trade accounts receivable, less allowance for doubtful accounts of $106,000 in 1968 and $23,000 in 1967	4,470,000	4,576,000
Advances to officers and employees and other miscellaneous receivables	328,000	198,000
Inventories of food and supplies, at actual cost, not in excess of market	1,210,000	1,053,000
Prepaid expenses	97,000	53,000
Total current assets	11,068,000	8,639,000
Property and equipment, at cost (Note 2):		
Land and land improvements	1,518,000	920,000
Buildings	3,503,000	1,520,000
Fixtures and equipment	1,809,000	1,625,000
	6,830,000	4,065,000
Less—Accumulated depreciation	1,095,000	952,000
	5,735,000	3,113,000
Investments:		
Cash surrender value of life insurance	339,000	260,000
Investments in affiliate and associated companies (Note 1)	179,000	292,000
Other	131,000	108,000
	649,000	660,000
Deferred charges	648,000	595,000
	$18,100,000	$13,007,000

LIABILITIES AND SHAREHOLDERS' EQUITY		
Current liabilities:		
Note payable	$ 429,000	
Current portion of long-term obligations	147,000	$ 107,000
Trade accounts payable	2,431,000	2,778,000
Accrued salaries, wages and bonuses	1,300,000	1,066,000
Other accounts payable and accrued expenses	1,416,000	1,214,000
Estimated federal income taxes	1,838,000	1,070,000
Total current liabilities	7,561,000	6,235,000
Long-term obligations (Note 2):		
7% mortgage note, payable $175,000 annually, including interest, through 1990	1,938,000	
5½% mortgage note, payable $66,000 annually, including interest, through 1980	563,000	598,000
Instalment contract, payable $75,000 annually to 1973	287,000	362,000
	2,788,000	960,000

Shareholders' equity (Notes 3 and 4):
Common stock, par value $1:

	Shares			
	1968	1967		
Authorized	5,000,000	2,000,000		
Issued	1,661,127	552,296	1,661,000	552,000
Held in treasury	45,486	6,379		
Outstanding	1,615,641	545,917		

	June 29, 1968	June 24, 1967
Capital in excess of par value	144,000	103,000
Earnings retained for use in the business	6,073,000	5,278,000
	7,878,000	5,933,000
Less—cost of treasury shares	127,000	121,000
	7,751,000	5,812,000
Contingent liabilities (Note 5)		
	$18,100,000	$13,007,000

EXHIBIT 3

U.S. Degree—Credit Enrollment in Higher Education Institution
(figures in thousands of students)

Year	Total	Type of Institution		Type of Control	
		4 Year	2 Year	Public	Private
1957.............	3,047	2,678	369	1,763	1,284
1958.............	3,236	2,851	386	1,894	1,342
1959.............	3,377	2,968	410	1,984	1,393
1960.............	3,583	3,131	451	2,116	1,467
1961.............	3,861	3,343	518	2,329	1,532
1962.............	4,175	3,585	590	2,574	1,601
1963.............	4,495	3,870	625	2,848	1,646
1964.............	4,950	4,239	711	3,179	1,771
1965.............	5,526	4,685	841	3,624	1,902
1966.............	5,885*	4,941*	945*	3,897*	1,988*
1967.............	6,348*	5,272*	1,075*	4,305*	2,043*
Projected					
1968.............	6,758	5,595	1,164	4,629	2,129
1969.............	6,906	4,698	1,207	4,775	2,131
1970.............	7,181	5,908	1,273	5,009	2,172
1971.............	7,530	6,177	1,353	5,297	2,233
1972.............	7,925	6,483	1,442	5,619	2,306
1973.............	8,322	6,789	1,533	5,944	2,377
1974.............	8,645	7,075	1,619	6,255	2,440
1975.............	9,056	7,351	1,705	6,559	2,497
1976.............	9,388	7,603	1,785	6,843	2,545
1977.............	9,684	7,825	1,859	7,102	2,581

* Estimated on basis of aggregated degree-credit and non-degree-credit data collected from *Opening Fall Enrollment* in 1966 and 1967.

Source: Compiled from U.S. Department of Health, Education and Welfare, Office of Education, Projections of Educational Statistics to 1977–78 (1968 edition); (Washington, D.C.: U.S. Government Printing Office, 1969).

EXHIBIT 4

Enrollment and Number of Institutions, by Size of Institution, 1965–66

No. of Students	Enrollment		Number of Institutions	
	Number	Percent	Number	Percent
Under 200.............	31,419	0.5	310	14.1
200–499................	132,239	2.4	377	17.2
500–999................	343,922	6.2	479	21.9
1,000–2,499.............	840,196	15.1	545	24.9
2,500–4,999.............	705,041	12.7	202	9.2
5,000–9,999.............	1,147,283	20.6	159	7.2
10,000–19,999...........	1,115,631	20.0	80	3.7
20,000 or more..........	1,254,540	22.5	40	1.8
Total.............	5,570,271	100.0	2,192	100.0

Source: U.S. Department of Health, Education and Welfare, Office of Education, *Digest of Educational Statistics, 1967* (Washington, D.C.: U.S. Government Printing Office, 1968).

EXHIBIT 5

Enrollment and Number of Institutions, by Size of Institution, 1965–66

Type and Control	Number of Institutions			
	1961–62	*1963–64*	*1965–66*	*1967–68*
Total..............................	2,044	2,140	2,238	2,382
4 Year Total....................	1,458	1,503	1,556	1,593
Public......................	376	387	403	*
Private.....................	1,082	1,116	1,153	*
University Total.............	143	146	155	157
Public......................	83	88	90	*
Private.....................	60	58	65	*
Other 4 Year Total..........	1,315	1,357	1,401	1,436
Public......................	293	299	313	*
Private.....................	1,022	1,058	1,088	*
2 Year Total..................	586	637	682	789
Public......................	348	378	422	*
Private.....................	238	259	260	*
Public Total..................	724	765	825	*
Private Total.................	1,320	1,375	1,413	*

* Date not available.

SOURCE: Compiled from U.S. Department of Health, Education and Welfare, Office of Education publications (Washington, D.C.: U.S. Government Printing Office); *Higher Education Finances* (1968); *Digest of Educational Statistics, 1967* (1968); *Opening Fall Enrollment in Higher Education, 1967–68* (1968).

EXHIBIT 6

Expenditures from Current Funds and Total Current Expenditures (1967–68 Dollars) by Institutions of Higher Education: United States, 1957–58 to 1977–78
(amounts in billions of 1967–68 dollars)

Year and control	Expenditure for educational and general purposes				Expenditure for auxiliary enterprises and student aid [3]	Total expenditures from current funds	Capital outlay from current funds only	Total current expenditures [4]
	Student education [1]	Organized research	Related activities [2]	Total				
(1)	(2)	(3)	(4)	(5)	(6)	(7)	(8)	(9)
1957–58:								
Total	$3.1	$0.9	$0.3	$4.3	$1.0	$5.3	$0.2	$5.1
Public	1.8	.5	.2	2.5	.5	3.0	.1	2.9
Nonpublic	1.3	.4	.1	1.8	.5	2.3	.1	2.2
1958–59: [5]								
Total	3.4	1.0	.3	4.7	1.2	5.9	.2	5.7
Public	2.0	.5	.2	2.7	.6	3.3	.1	3.2
Nonpublic	1.4	.5	.1	2.0	.6	2.6	.1	2.5
1959–60:								
Total	3.7	1.2	.4	5.3	1.2	6.5	.3	6.2
Public	2.2	.6	.2	3.0	.6	3.6	.2	3.4
Nonpublic	1.5	.6	.2	2.3	.6	2.9	.1	2.8
1960–61: [5]								
Total	4.1	1.4	.4	5.9	1.4	7.3	.3	7.0
Public	2.4	.7	.2	3.3	.7	4.0	.2	3.8
Nonpublic	1.7	.7	.2	2.6	.7	3.3	.1	3.2
1961–62:								
Total	4.4	1.6	.5	6.5	1.6	8.1	.3	7.8
Public	2.6	.8	.3	3.7	.8	4.5	.2	4.3
Nonpublic	1.8	.8	.2	2.8	.8	3.6	.1	3.5
1962–63: [5]								
Total	4.9	1.9	.5	7.3	1.8	9.1	.5	8.6
Public	2.9	.9	.3	4.1	.9	5.0	.3	4.7
Nonpublic	2.0	1.0	.2	3.2	.9	4.1	.2	3.9
1963–64:								
Total	5.5	2.2	.5	8.2	1.9	10.1	.5	9.6
Public	3.3	1.0	.3	4.6	1.0	5.6	.3	5.3
Nonpublic	2.2	1.2	.2	3.6	.9	4.5	.2	4.3
1964–65: [6]								
Total	6.2	2.4	.6	9.2	2.2	11.4	.6	10.8
Public	3.7	1.1	.4	5.2	1.2	6.4	.4	6.0
Nonpublic	2.5	1.3	.2	4.0	1.0	5.0	.2	4.8
1965–66: [6]								
Total	7.2	2.6	.7	10.5	2.6	13.1	.6	12.5
Public	4.4	1.2	.4	6.0	1.4	7.4	.4	7.0
Nonpublic	2.3	1.4	.3	4.5	1.2	5.7	.2	5.5
1966–67: [6]								
Total	8.0	2.8	.8	11.6	2.8	14.4	.6	13.8
Public	4.9	1.3	.5	6.7	1.5	8.2	.4	7.8
Nonpublic	3.1	1.5	.3	4.9	1.3	6.2	.2	6.0
1967–68: [6]								
Total	8.8	3.1	.8	12.7	3.2	15.9	.6	15.3
Public	5.5	1.4	.5	7.4	1.8	9.2	.4	8.8
Nonpublic	3.3	1.7	.3	5.3	1.4	6.7	.2	6.5

EXHIBIT 6 (Continued)

Year and control	Expenditure for educational and general purposes				Expenditure for auxiliary enterprises and student aid [3]	Total expenditures from current funds	Capital outlay from current funds only	Total current expenditures [4]
	Student education [1]	Organized research	Related activities [2]	Total				
(1)	(2)	(3)	(4)	(5)	(6)	(7)	(8)	(9)

PROJECTED [7]

1968–69:								
Total	$9. 6	$3. 3	$0. 9	$13. 8	$3. 4	$17. 2	$0. 6	$16. 6
Public	6. 0	1. 5	. 6	8. 1	1. 9	10. 0	. 4	9. 6
Nonpublic	3. 6	1. 8	. 3	5. 7	1. 5	7. 2	. 2	7. 0
1969–70:								
Total	9. 9	3. 5	. 9	14. 3	3. 7	18. 0	. 5	17. 5
Public	6. 2	1. 6	. 6	8. 4	2. 1	10. 5	. 4	10. 1
Nonpublic	3. 7	1. 9	. 3	5. 9	1. 6	7. 5	. 1	7. 4
1970–71:								
Total	10. 5	3. 7	1. 0	15. 2	3. 8	19. 0	. 5	18. 5
Public	6. 6	1. 7	. 6	8. 9	2. 2	11. 1	. 4	10. 7
Nonpublic	3. 9	2. 0	. 4	6. 3	1. 6	7. 9	. 1	7. 8
1971–72:								
Total	11. 1	4. 0	1. 1	16. 2	4. 0	20. 2	. 4	19. 8
Public	7. 0	1. 8	. 7	9. 5	2. 3	11. 8	. 3	11. 5
Nonpublic	4. 1	2. 2	. 4	6. 7	1. 7	8. 4	. 1	8. 3
1972–73:								
Total	11. 9	4. 2	1. 2	17. 3	4. 3	21. 6	. 4	21. 2
Public	7. 5	1. 9	. 8	10. 2	2. 5	12. 7	. 3	12. 4
Nonpublic	4. 4	2. 3	. 4	7. 1	1. 8	8. 9	. 1	8. 8
1973–74:								
Total	12. 8	4. 4	1. 2	18. 4	4. 7	23. 1	. 5	22. 6
Public	8. 1	2. 0	. 8	10. 9	2. 7	13. 6	. 4	13. 2
Nonpublic	4. 7	2. 4	. 4	7. 5	2. 0	9. 5	. 1	9. 4
1974–75:								
Total	13. 4	4. 6	1. 4	19. 4	5. 0	24. 4	. 5	23. 9
Public	8. 5	2. 1	. 9	11. 5	2. 9	14. 4	. 4	14. 0
Nonpublic	4. 9	2. 5	. 5	7. 9	2. 1	10. 0	. 1	9. 9
1975–76:								
Total	14. 3	4. 8	1. 4	20. 5	5. 3	25. 8	. 5	25. 3
Public	9. 1	2. 2	. 9	12. 2	3. 1	15. 3	. 4	14. 9
Nonpublic	5. 2	2. 6	. 5	8. 3	2. 2	10. 5	. 1	10. 4
1976–77:								
Total	15. 0	5. 0	1. 5	21. 5	5. 6	27. 1	. 5	26. 6
Public	9. 6	2. 2	1. 0	12. 8	3. 3	16. 1	. 4	15. 7
Nonpublic	5. 4	2. 8	. 5	8. 7	2. 3	11. 0	. 1	10. 9
1977–78:								
Total	15. 7	5. 2	1. 5	22. 4	5. 9	28. 3	. 5	27. 8
Public	10. 1	2. 3	1. 0	13. 4	3. 5	16. 9	. 4	16. 5
Nonpublic	5. 6	2. 9	. 5	9. 0	2. 4	11. 4	. 1	11. 3

NOTES:
1. Includes general administration, instruction and departmental research, extension and public services, libraries, and operation and maintenance of the physical plant.
2. Includes expenditures for such items as laboratory schools, medical school hospitals, dental clinics, home economics cafeterias, agricultural college creameries, college-operated industrial plants connected with instructional programs but not actually integral parts of it, etc.

EXHIBIT 6 (Continued)

3. Auxiliary enterprises include student dormitories, dining halls, cafeterias, student unions, bookstores, faculty housing, athletic programs not part of the instructional program, lectures, concerts, etc.

Student aid consists of scholarships, fellowships, and prizes and includes remission of fees.

4. Current-fund expenditures less capital outlay from current funds.

5. Interpolated.

6. Estimated.

7. The projection of expenditures from current funds is based on assumption that: (1) Expenditure per student and the percent of college-age persons attending college, on which expenditures for student education depend, will continue to increase as they did during the years 1957–58 to 1967–68; (2) expenditures for organized research will follow the 1957–58 to 1967–68 trend; (3) the relationship to student education of expenditures for related activities, for auxiliary enterprises, and for student aid will each continue the 1957–58 to 1967–68 trend; and (4) the 1967–68 to 1977–78 expenditures from current funds for capital outlay will approximate 16 percent of total capital outlay.

Data are for 50 States and the District of Columbia for all years.

Conversion to 1967–68 dollars was based on the Consumer Price Index published by the Bureau of Labor Statistics, U.S. Department of Labor and (for capital outlay) on the American Appraisal Company Construction Cost Index.

SOURCE: U.S. Department of Health, Education and Welfare, Office of Education, *Projections of Educational Statistics to 1977–78* (1968 edition; Washington, D.C.: U.S. Government Printing Office, 1969).

EXHIBIT 7

Capital Outlay of Institutions of Higher Education: United States, 1957–58 to 1977–78

Year	Total		Public		Nonpublic	
	Billions of current dollars	Billions of 1967–68 dollars	Billions of current dollars	Billions of 1967–68 dollars	Billions of current dollars	Billions of 1967–68 dollars
(1)	(2)	(3)	(4)	(5)	(6)	(7)
1957–58	$1. 161	$1. 610	$0. 732	$1. 015	$0. 429	$0. 595
1958–59 [1]	1. 304	1. 754	. 721	. 970	. 583	. 784
1959–60	1. 354	1. 768	. 807	1. 054	. 547	. 714
1960–61 [1]	1. 737	2. 216	. 932	1. 189	. 805	1. 027
1961–62	1. 714	2. 137	1. 010	1. 259	. 704	. 878
1962–63 [1]	2. 534	3. 074	1. 596	1. 936	. 938	1. 138
1958–59 to 1961–62	8. 643	10. 949	5. 066	6. 408	3. 577	4. 541
1963–64	2. 466	2. 906	1. 518	1. 789	. 948	1. 117
1964–65 [2]	3. 089	3. 549	2. 064	2. 371	1. 025	1. 178
1965–66 [2]	3. 323	3. 687	2. 233	2. 478	1. 090	1. 209
1966–67 [2]	3. 293	3. 462	2. 279	2. 396	1. 014	1. 066
1967–68 [2]	3. 462	3. 462	2. 396	2. 396	1. 066	1. 066
1963–64 to 1967–68	15. 633	17. 066	10. 490	11. 430	5. 143	5. 636

PROJECTED [3]

Year	Total		Public		Nonpublic	
1968–69	3. 409	3. 268	2. 413	2. 313	0. 996	0. 955
1969–70	3. 191	2. 935	2. 326	2. 139	. 865	. 796
1970–71		2. 838	----------	2. 106	----------	. 732
1971–72		2. 731	----------	1. 999	----------	. 732
1972–73		2. 658	----------	1. 974	----------	. 684
1968–69 to 1972–73		14. 430	----------	10. 531	----------	3. 899
1973–74		2. 879	----------	2. 115	----------	. 764
1974–75		2. 903	----------	2. 139	----------	. 764
1975–76		2. 831	----------	2. 115	----------	. 716
1976–77		2. 637	----------	2. 016	----------	. 621
1977–78		2. 490	----------	1. 933	----------	. 557
1973–74 to 1977–78		13. 740	----------	10. 318	----------	3. 422

NOTES:
1. Interpolated.
2. Estimated.
3. The projection of capital outlay is based on assumption that: (1) capital outlay per additional full-time equivalent of total opening fall enrollment will follow the 1957–58 to 1967–68 trend insofar as capital outlay resulting in increased value of trend insofar as capital outlay resulting in increased value of plant is concerned; (2) capital outlay for replacement and rehabilitation will remain constant at the level of 1% of value of plant each year through 1977–78; and (3) since capital outlay related to increased numbers of students over a number of years rather than annually, a moving average would more reasonably reflect annual capital outlay.
SOURCE: See Exhibit 6.

APPENDIX A: ACCOUNTING FOR EXPENDITURES IN INSTITUTIONS OF HIGHER EDUCATION

The financial statistics maintained by the Office of Education are both shaped by, and help to standardize, the type of accounting systems in use in higher educational institutions. This appendix describes and presents the expenditure portion of those statistics as they relate to ISI's attempts to estimate the potential dollar volume of the institutional market they serve.

An initial distinction is made in this system between funds used for the day-to-day operation of the institution (Current-Fund), and funds used for capital improvements and expansion (Plant-Fund). Each of these funds is further divided into categories by the end-use of the expenditure. The Plant-Fund broad division is between disbursements for additions to plant assets (including renewals, replacements, major repairs, and building materials as well as finished construction), and the interest expense on borrowed capital. The Current-Fund divides initially into three broad categories: (1) Educational and General Expenditures, which are the daily expenses of operating the educational activities of the institution; (2) Auxiliary Enterprise Expenditures, consisting of the administration, operation and maintenance expense of cafeterias and dining halls, student residence halls, bookstores, student unions, student health care facilities, intercollegiate athletics, concerts, university presses, etc.; and (3) Student Financial Aid Expenditures.

The Educational and General Expenditures are further divided into seven categories of expense:

1. *General Administration and General Expense.* General executive and administrative offices serving the institution as a whole, and expenditures of a general character. Includes student personnel services such as admissions, counseling and guidance, dean's office, placement, registrar, student activities, etc.

2. *Instruction and Departmental Research.* All current expenditures of instructional departments, colleges and schools, *including* expenditures for research not separately budgeted or funded. Includes office expense and equipment, laboratory expense and equipment, salaries of instructional staff, secretaries, technicians, etc.

3. *Extension and Public Service.* Includes nondegree courses, public lectures and institutes, public television and radio programs, etc.

4. *Libraries.* Includes salaries, books, operating expenses, binding, etc.

5. *Operation and Maintenance of Physical Plant.* Includes salaries, supplies, equipment and other maintenance expenses, but *not*, however, maintenance of auxiliary facilities like dormitories and dining halls, or activities related to educational departments (see item 7).

6. *Organized Research.* Separately budgeted or financed research

either from outside contracts and grants or from the institution's regular funds.

7. *Organized Activities Related to Educational Departments.* Administration, operation and maintenance of such activities as experimental agricultural farms, medical school hospitals, materials testing laboratories, etc.

Within the Plant-Fund, the broad group of expenditures for Additions to Plant Assets are further divided into: (1) Land; (2) Buildings—including fixed equipment; (3) Improvements Other Than Buildings—roads, landscaping, etc.; and (4) Equipment—laboratory and office machinery and equipment, furniture and furnishings, library books, vehicles, farm implements, nonlaboratory livestock, etc.

The tables which follow present pertinent expenditure data.

APPENDIX A—TABLE 1

Current-Fund Expenditures of U.S. Higher Educational Institutions by Category of Expense, Biennial from 1953–54 to 1963–64
(figures in millions of dollars)

	1953–54	1955–56	1957–58	1959–60	1961–62	1963–64
Total Current Fund Expenditures	2,902	3,525	4,544	5,628	7,190	9,225
Educational and General	2,288	2,789	3,634	4,536	5,789	7,466
Gen. Administration & Gen. Expense	291	358	478	587	736	964
Instruction & Dept'l Research	467	1,149	1,477	1,803	2,216	2,821
Extension & Public Services	115	141	179	208	245	298
Libraries	73	86	111	136	178	238
Plant Operation & Maintenance	280	326	409	474	566	689
Organized Research	375	506	734	1,024	1,481	1,983
Related Activities	181	222	246	303	375	473
Auxiliary Enterprises	539	640	778	918	1,161	1,455
Student Aid	75	96	131	174	231	303

SOURCE: U.S. Department of Health, Education and Welfare, Office of Education, *Higher Education Finances* (Washington D.C.: U.S. Government Printing Office, 1968).

APPENDIX A—TABLE 2

Expenditures of U.S. Higher Educational Institutions, by Type and Control of Institution, 1963–64

(figures in millions of dollars)

	Current Expenditures	Educational & General	Gen'l. Admin. & Gen. Exp.	Instruction & Departmental Research	Extension & Public Service	Libraries	Plant Operation & Maintenance	Organized Research	Related Activities	Auxiliary Enterprises	Student Aid	Plant-Fund Expenditures	Addition to Plant
Total	4,225	7,466	964	2,821	298	238	689	1,983	473	1,455	303	2,295	1,408
4 Year Total	8,739	7,063	892	2,567	293	225	634	1,982	469	1,376	300	2,119	1,760
Public	4,750	3,884	410	1,503	270	123	351	936	291	757	109	1,279	1,064
Private	3,989	3,179	482	1,064	23	102	283	1,046	178	619	191	840	696
Univ. Total	5,435	4,539	436	1,484	270	129	337	1,499	384	721	175	1,199	966
Public	3,543	2,958	263	981	257	81	219	899	258	504	81	825	660
Private	1,892	1,581	173	503	13	48	118	600	126	217	94	374	306
Other 4 Yr.	3,304	2,524	456	1,083	23	96	297	483	85	655	125	920	794
Public	1,207	926	147	522	13	42	132	37	33	253	28	454	404
Private	2,097	1,598	309	561	10	54	165	446	52	402	97	466	390
2 Yr. Total	485.5	403	71.5	253	6	13.5	55	1	3	79	3	176	147
Public	364	315	46	210	5	10.5	41	*	2	48	1	140	118
Private	121.5	88	25.5	43	1	3	14	1	1	31	2	36	31
Public Total	5,114	4,199	456	1,713	275	134	392	936	293	805	110	1,419	1,182
Private Total	4,111	3,267	508	1,107	24	105	297	1,047	179	650	193	876	727

Note: * less than $100,000.
Source: U.S. Department of Health, Education and Welfare, Office of Education, *Higher Education Finances* (Washington, D.C.: U.S. Government Printing Office, 1968).

APPENDIX A—TABLE 3

Supplemental Data on 1963–64 Expenditures of U.S. Higher Educational Institutions, by Control of Institution
(figures in millions of dollars)

	Total	Public	Private
Current-Fund Expenditures for Payroll:			
Total	5,068	3,060	2,009
Instruction & Dept'l Research			
Professional	2,023	1,250	773
Nonprofessional	230	147	83
Organized Research	985	526	458
Auxiliary Enterprises	406	242	164
All Other	1,424	893	531
Current-Fund Expenditures for Plant:			
Total	371	218	152
Equipment	278	186	92
Plant Expansion & Improvement	93	32	60
Plant-Fund Expenditures			
Total	2,295	1,419	876
Addition to Plant: Total	1,908	1,182	727
Land	88	62	26
Buildings (incl. fixed equipment)	1,588	979	609
Improvements other than building	67	51	15

SOURCE: U.S. Department of Health, Education and Welfare, Office of Education, *Higher Education Finances*, Selected Trend and Summary Data (Washington, D.C.: U.S. Government Printing Office, 1968).

Genesys Systems

It is a very small percentage of today's practicing engineers who are willing to put in two to five years of dedicated effort to obtain an advanced degree on a part-time basis, while maintaining essentially a full-time job. A larger percentage, but still too small a number, take occasional non-degree-oriented courses. What we need to do is look at the continuing education of the practicing engineer as a marketing problem. We know he needs the product; he knows he needs the product; yet only market penetration is poor. . . . The product must be easier to obtain, less expensive, newly packaged, and the customer must get a bargain, i.e., his boss must pay for it.

To implement a plan with these characteristics requires establishing an expanded community of scholars, essentially a partnership between universities and the surrounding industrial community, to the mutual benefit of both.

The above is an excerpt from a speech made by Albert J. Morris, President of Genesys Systems. An engineer himself, Mr. Morris was acutely aware of the problems of keeping the engineer's skills up-to-date after graduation.

It is felt in many circles that a four year undergraduate engineering education is insufficient training for much of the work demanded of an engineer; five years is the minimum needed. Part of the problem arises from the dichotomous treatment of theory and application in engineering programs. A theoretically oriented program leaves a man able to adapt to a variety of practical areas and easily update or modify his training. Unfortunately, having little practical training, his immediate vocational value is limited. Conversely, the practically trained engineer, while finding a ready application of his skills, is often narrowly educated and ill-suited to adapting to a changing technological environment.

Because the technological environment is changing so rapidly an engineer's skills quickly become obsolete. Estimates of the "half-life" of an engineer, i.e., the period that it takes for half his knowledge to become obsolete, range between five and nine years after the end of his formal education. Even engineers with Ph.D.'s often find themselves obsolete as the narrow area in which they specialized is superseded by advanced applications in other areas.

In the past industry has tried to cope with the problem of the outdated engineer in several ways. As an engineer's specific knowledge became less and less applicable to the work being done by the company many engineers were moved out of direct research and development work and assigned supervisory or managerial duties. The "promotion" of such men from technical to administrative work is not so much a result of the man's administrative ability, as it is of his technological obsolescence. As a consequence much of the first-line engineering work in many companies is done by the younger, more currently competent men.

Some companies regularly attempt to rejuvenate the expertise of their engineering staffs through regular periods of intensive formal education. Several universities, with the support of the Ford and Carnegie foundations, have established programs specifically for returning engineers. Typically these programs are three to nine months in length. They are intended for men who have been out of school for ten years or more. The intensive programs require a great deal of adjustment from both the company and the engineer himself. Many firms feel that they cannot give up a senior engineer for several months. For a man who has been out of school for a decade, it is difficult to readjust to the life of a student. These few intensive reeducation centers are hopelessly incapable of solving the problem.

Another remedy for the obsolescing engineer, and the one used by most, is to try to keep current by continually getting more formal education, a little at a time. This usually means taking a course a year, usually at night, from a nearby university. In 1965 one half of all M.S. degrees in engineering in the U.S. were awarded to part-time students.

It is difficult for a man to work all day and go to school at night. Not only are there problems involved in commuting to school, work and home, but going to evening classes often interferes with a man's family life. As a result fewer than half of all engineers have ever enrolled for any additional formal education. Of those who do enroll, the overwhelming majority take only one or two courses and then stop. Even in the prestigious Stanford University Honors Co-operative Program, where employer-sponsored students attend daytime classes and usually work half-time for their companies, only 30% of the students complete a master's degree.

Programs that allow an engineer to work for an advanced degree on a part-time basis are too limited in their application. The demands they place upon the student are such that only the most highly motivated men are likely to even enter them, much less persevere to get an advanced degree. The admission requirements for graduate programs screen out all but the most capable men. Yet it is often the less capable engineer who most needs the additional formal training.

Some companies sponsor regular in-house formal courses, conducted either by their own personnel or outside instructors. These are good for updating engineers in a particular field. However, since most engineers have diverse interests and needs, these programs are only efficient in a very large company.

Professional societies often offer short courses or workshops in conjunction with regular conferences. These, however, often have limited appeal and are of course, of limited duration.

A man with advanced engineering degrees and considerable experience in the electronics industry, Mr. Morris was aware that as technological advances accelerated the usable life of an engineer was becoming shorter and shorter.

A 1965 University of California School of Engineering study decided that a program of continuing education was necessary: one that could reach all engineers and cause a minimum of sacrifice on the part of the engineer. A system of limited transmission television instruction was recommended by the study.

Genesys Systems was formed in 1967 to implement such a TV system. In cooperation with the School of Engineering at Stanford University, the first system was designed and built.

THE STANFORD SYSTEM

The system Genesys designed for Stanford was the pilot upon which subsequent installations were based.

The origination point of the system is any of four television equipped studio classrooms on the campus, each of which is a conventional classroom, with a blackboard, instructor's desk, student desks, etc., to which modifications have been made. At the rear of the room is a control booth and remote operated television camera. (See Figure 1.)

The classroom has been carpeted, sound proofed and draped to facilitate the television transmission without interference from sunlight or outside noise. Two cameras are mounted in each classroom. The rear camera can be focussed on either the instructor or the blackboard. It gives a picture much like the view a student sitting in the class would have. The overhead camera focusses on the instructor's desk and can give a closeup view of either experimental apparatus or a notepad. By writing on the notepad rather than a blackboard the instructor can make his notes or calculations more quickly and without losing visual contact with his TV class. This also allows the instructor to quickly illustrate his discussion or to prepare visual aids without pre-processing them. At the instructor's request either the rear or overhead camera's image can be transmitted to remote receiving stations.

For the students actually in the classroom the lack of blackboard tech-

FIGURE 1

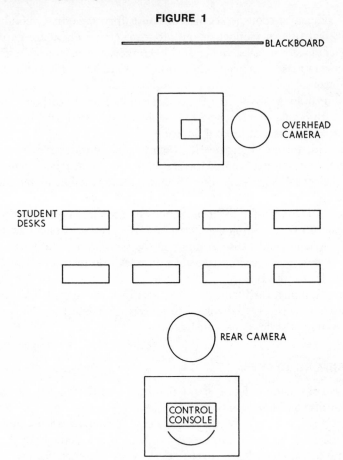

niques is no problem. Between each pair of students is a television monitor upon which is the same image as is transmitted to remote locations. The Stanford classrooms can accommodate 54 students.

At the rear of the classroom is a control booth, manned by an operator. The operator can see the classroom through a glass wall and via two monitors, one for each camera. He can switch from one camera to another or focus, pan, or zoom either camera. In addition the control console enables the operator to check on the transmission of the signal.

Adjacent to each teaching classroom are two satellite classrooms. Each of these has a large screen monitor mounted at the front of the room and speakers to broadcast the audio portion of the transmission. In addition there are about twenty student desks, like those in the "live" classroom, with smaller television monitors. In addition each desk has a microphone and signal switch, with which the student may speak to the instructor. Each satellite classroom holds about 30 students.

Atop the building housing the classroom are the transmitter and sending antenna. The audio-visual signals are transmitted on the Instructional Television Fixed Service (ITFS) band to a relay station atop Black Mountain. Stanford has four channels in the ITFS band, each of which can transmit from one classroom on campus.

At Black Mountain the signals are relayed to any of about twenty receivers located at cooperating companies throughout the Bay Area. It has a range of about 40 miles.

At each company the signal is conducted to a remote "classroom," the receiving end of the system. The classroom may be nothing more than an ordinary company conference room that is intermittently used for the TV classes. Some companies find that a mobile-home shell can be easily adapted for this purpose at little cost without the sacrifice of a meeting room. The interior of the remote classroom can be as plush or plain as the company wishes. The minimum configuration necessary is one television monitor, with speakers and a microphone and signal device for the students to contact the instructor. This "talk-back" facility gives the remote student every advantage that the student in the real classroom has. The talk-back is accomplished by an FM radio transmitter. Some companies outfit their remote classrooms like the on-campus satellite facilities, with the monitor-equipped student desks, carpeting, drapes and sound proofing. Videotape equipment is also desirable. Since there are four channels on the Stanford system a company may wish to have up to four remote classrooms, although each is not restricted to any one channel.

The costs of the Stanford system were as follows:

System design	$ 79,000
Studio classrooms & satellite classrooms	170,000
Studio transmitter link	39,000
Black Mountain transmitter	106,000
Spares & other equipment	44,000
System implementation	79,000
	$517,000

This $517,000 probably doesn't represent the true cost of the system. Both Genesys staff and Stanford liaison personnel costs were reduced because of the prototypical nature of the system. In addition purchasing and fabrication policies have resulted in some substantial savings on subsequent system hardware.

At the receiving end of the system, the cost for the hardware and installation at a company was $9,000 for the first classroom, plus $1,625 for each additional classroom. The addition of videotape equipment adds another $1,000 per classroom.

The operating expense for the Stanford four-channel system is estimated at about $96,000 annually. The operating cost of the system is borne by charging a television surcharge on top of the tuition paid by students using the system.

The $517,000 needed for construction of the Stanford system was raised by assessing those companies that wished to use the facility on a one time "fair-share" basis. Assessments, based upon size of company, varied from $3,000 to $50,000. Each company paid for the hardware used in its own remote classrooms, as well as providing for the classroom space.

The utilization of the Stanford system is rather diverse. Each of the programs will be described below:

First, regular engineering graduate courses are televised on the system. These may be taken by registered degree candidates, including those on the Honors Cooperative Program, either for credit or as auditors. They may also be taken by non-degree-candidate special graduate students, for academic credit which may be applied if they become degree candidates.

Tuition charges have been set by Stanford as follows. Since regular students' tuition covers only about half of the actual cost of teaching them, those on the Honors Cooperative Program are charged a matching fee of 100% of tuition. This is borne by the company. In addition, the television teaching surcharge, equal to 50% of tuition, is added to cover system operating costs. Auditors pay no tuition, but do pay half the matching fee plus the television surcharge. At Stanford's current rate of about $40 per credit hour, a registered TV student pays $100 per credit hour, or $300 per course. This is usually paid by his company, or reimbursed to the student upon successful completion of the course.

Typically the student goes to class during working hours, 8 A.M. to 5 P.M. Whether he must make up this time or not is a matter of individual company policy. The student usually does his homework and studying on his own time. This arrangement makes considerably fewer demands on the man than does the commuting to and from evening classes previously did.

For these graduate credit courses there is additional opportunity for student-faculty interaction, beyond the talk-back system. Instructors hold telephone office hours to discuss course materials with students. Homework assignments and tests are picked up and returned by a courier each day. In addition students often make video tapes of classes for make-up and review.

The second use of the system is for transmission of seminars and workshops. These are scheduled on a regular basis. They are available to interested employees of affiliate companies free of charge. Academic credit is not given.

The third general class of use for the system is for giving formal classes to persons other than engineers, on a nondegree-credit basis. For this purpose the Association for Continuing Education was established. ACE organizes courses that are taught over the Stanford system during its otherwise slack hours. ACE courses range from shorthand for secretaries to Advanced Engineering mathematics. ACE provides certificates for successful completion of its courses; however these are not applicable for academic degree credit. The cost for ACE courses, which are open to anybody on a first-come basis, are significantly lower than those for Stanford credit. Typical costs are $45 per course, $22.50 for auditors.

After three quarters of full scale operation, the Stanford system was serving over 750 ACE students in fifteen courses and about 250 degree candidates in 35 Stanford University graduate engineering courses.

Present utilization of the Stanford four-channel system is as follows:

8 A.M.–12 noon 1 P.M.–4 P.M.	Stanford Engineering Department
7 A.M.–8 A.M. 12 noon–1 P.M. 5 P.M.–9 P.M.	ACE
4 P.M.–5 P.M.	Seminars and workshops

Preliminary results of the Stanford system bear out other research on television teaching systems. Those students who took courses on a remote basis did as well on examinations and homework problem set assignments as those who took them in person.

THE THREE PHASE PLAN

Once the construction of the Stanford system was begun, Mr. Morris began to look for other university-industry communities that could benefit from such a system. He established a three phase program for the study, design and implementation of an educational television system. The three phase program described below is really an archetype since Genesys' policy is to modify both the program and the system to meet the needs of the community concerned.

Phase I

Initial contact is made with the university concerned, usually through the Dean of the Engineering School. If the school agrees to consider the installation of a TV system, it enters into a consulting agreement with Genesys. Under this agreement Genesys, often in conjunction with a local electronics consulting engineer, provides a feasibility study for the university. This study is really an analysis of the market, i.e., surrounding industry, for the product of the university, i.e., its faculty and curriculum. The cost of Phase I is usually about $15,000, and is the only out-of-pocket expense incurred by the university. This is for the consulting services of Genesys' principals, usually Mr. Morris, plus travel expenses.

Often before the university even consents to having Phase I undertaken there is much internal discussion in the university. Many faculty members feel that television education will undermine the regular resident graduate programs. Some feel that it will make the university a mail order degree facility by removing personal supervision of students. Others are uncertain about the teaching demands that will be made upon them. Some request reduced teaching loads or additional clerical staff because of television teaching. Others feel that the television camera will allow university administration to spy on a professor's classroom behavior. Many questions arise about the rights to these televised lectures, with respect to taping, copyrights, reproduction, royalties, etc.

The university must satisfy its faculty on these counts before it proceeds to commit itself to a complete installation of such a system.

Phase I requires one to four months to complete.

Phase II

Once Phase I is completed and the university has committed itself to a TV system, the next phase begins. First, Genesys assigns one man to be a full-time project director; he stays with the system until it is operational. The university also assigns its own liaison man to work with the director. He is usually a senior engineering professor who puts in about half his time on the TV system. Before anything else is done the university must assure itself that local industry will provide the funds for the hardware. It is the university that actually solicits these funds; however Genesys provides assistance based upon its experience.

The minimum commitment required from industry is about $375,000. This will provide a two-channel system. Additional channels (up to a total of four) will cost about $100,000 each. The initial funds are raised from industry on a "fair-share" basis, similar to the assessment method used on the pilot Stanford system. Provision is made for the fair share to be paid over a ten-year period. Thus a large company, making a maximum fair-share contribution and building four classrooms each fully equipped, is paying out less than $70,000. Spread over ten years, this is less than the salary of one junior engineer.

Genesys attempts to demonstrate to industry the value of its TV system in continuing education of engineers. The approach is basically one of cost-effectiveness. The TV system, if properly utilized, provides quality continuing education at less total cost to the company than any other system. By including the costs of lost man-hours due to travel, study and class-time in its calculations, the cost-effectiveness can easily be demonstrated.

Once the university has received fair-share pledges from industry, it usually factors these itself, paying for the system out of general funds and then collecting the industry fair-share pledges over the ten-year period. The major argument used to get industry to affiliate with the TV system is the cost-effectiveness of the education it can provide for the company's personnel.

Depending upon the response from local industry, the university will design a two- three- or four-channel system. Those companies that join after the system is build are still required to pay the fair-share assessment. These additional funds go to expand or improve the system as they are received.

Concurrently with the funds solicitation the university applies to the Federal Communications Commission for an ITFS license and is assigned up to four of the 31 channels reserved for ITFS.

At this stage specific design of the system is undertaken. The design represents the physical and logistic needs and resources of the university and industrial community.

Phase II usually costs the university about $75,000, about $30,000 of which represents Genesys' out-of-pocket costs. The time for Phase II is about three to six months, although some of the design work, particularly soliciting additional funds and making design modifications, continues throughout Phase III.

Phase III

The final phase, the only one involving actual hardware, then begins. Genesys now acts as both design engineer and equipment supplier for the system.

Genesys procures hardware from manufacturers and often modifies it to suit the system, then installs the equipment. Genesys bills the university for equipment at catalog (list) price, but purchases it as an OEM at a discount (20–40%).

Genesys also assembles many components into certain items which it then catalogs as Genesys standard products. Genesys uses a simple pricing structure for its catalog items. At the moment Genesys' catalog items include the audio-visual carrel (a two-student desk, with TV monitor, the remote controlled focus/pan/zoom camera, the control room console, and the talk-back transmitter.

During Phase III Genesys also provides and is compensated for actual physical installation of the equipment. Genesys also sells and installs the hardware at the remote industry classrooms.

Once the hardware is installed and tested Genesys now acts as a consultant in training the university employees in the operation of the system. This only takes a few weeks of the four to six months required for Phase III.

For a minimum configuration, during Phase III the university pays Genesys about $300,000. Of this about $160,000 represents actual hardware cost to Genesys. The remainder is Genesys actual labor cost, about $40,000, plus overhead, G&A and profit.

GENESYS' FUTURE

As of the end of 1969 Genesys had four systems upon which it was working. Their status is as follows:

Stanford: system operational, with a few glitches to be corrected.

U.S.C.: system in the middle of Phase II, but due to university delays is about twelve months behind schedule.

R.P.I.: (Albany–Schenectady–Troy, New York): Phase I completed.

Colorado State: middle of Phase I.

In addition about six other universities are presently exploring the possibility of building a TV system with Genesys.

In addition to its work in TV systems, Genesys is experimenting with the application of microwave technology to industrial drying operations. However this represents a very small part of Genesys' business.

The company is closely held, with fewer than 100 shareholders including employees, many of whom have acquired shares in lieu of salary. As of the end of 1969, Genesys had 22 employees. It had shown its first profitable quarter. (An income statement and balance sheet are included in the exhibits.)

Genesys would like to develop a technological monopoly in the design and implementation of TV systems based upon its experience. It tells prospective universities that Genesys brings with it over $100,000 worth of development effort spent on the Stanford system, which is available free on a new system.

Presently there is no threat of competition from the giant electronics companies such as RCA and General Electric, although both are component suppliers to Genesys.

Morris estimates that there are at least 100 university-centered industrial areas in the United States that could utilize an ETV system. As the use of such TV systems expands to cover more nontechnical employees the number of potential systems should increase.

Genesys has been well received by almost all of the 40 or so institutions it has approached. The individual professors and deans have been very receptive to such a project. The undertaking of a TV system is a large project for any university. Usually there is a long delay between initial contact with Genesys and the decision to build a TV system.

While there is no other company directly competing with Genesys, several universities are designing their own systems and assembling them, bypassing Genesys as a middleman. Many multicampus universities have systems designed not for continuing education in industry, but for campus-to-campus remote classroom instruction.

Genesys has two senior engineers doing R&D on new system hardware, such as a multichannel talk-back transmitter. It is expected that there will be little change in the basic technology that Genesys uses in its TV systems over the next few years. Specific pieces of hardware will be improved, perhaps by Genesys' suppliers, but they are expected to be compatible with existing equipment. More frequencies for ITFS transmission will be allocated by the FCC; in some areas all 31 channels are in use.

Genesys has been willing to make extraordinary concessions to universities because of special circumstances. For one university Genesys "donated" two studio classrooms and two channels because sufficient industry funds could not immediately be raised. When such funds are raised they will be paid to Genesys; additional revenue will be used to expand the system to four channels. Any fair-share revenue over and above this will be split equally between the university and Genesys.

For another proposal Genesys has agreed to build transmission facilities at its own expense, approximately $300,000. The university in question already has videotape facilities. Genesys would be repaid out of tuition fees over a five-year period. Some of these unusual situations would make Genesys a profit oriented partner with the university in the revenue it receives from the system.

Work is underway in Colorado on using a TV system with delayed feedback via telephone office hours. This no talk-back system has the advantage of being compatible with video-taped lectures, although it sacrifices the immediate student-faculty contact. Should such systems be satisfactory, the accumulation of a videotape library is being considered by Genesys.

Further delays have been experienced in negotiating with several state-supported universities. Requirements that state legislatures approve any capital expenditures, and reticence to expand state-supported higher education beyond degree programs, have made entry into public universities more difficult for Genesys.

Just as the Stanford system has been quickly expanded from just graduate engineering degree credit courses to areas as removed as shorthand, other systems are expected to expand their scopes.

Mr. Morris has expressed the hope that many people, technical and supervisory, will use remote television teaching systems on an ongoing basis. It could become quite conventional for each member of the technostructure to always be taking some formal courses, perhaps two or three a year. He would attend class during working hours and study on his own time. His employer would pay the tuition and would benefit from having better-trained employees.

Despite optimistic forecasts for the future of TV systems, Morris was uncertain about the future of Genesys systems in light of its low market penetration after two years of operation.

EXHIBIT 1

The Top Management Team

Name	Position
Albert J. Morris	President and General Manager
John E. Gerling	Vice President, Manager, Industrial Microwave Division
Gene E. Tallmadge	Chief Engineer
Stanley Corbett	Manufacturing Manager
Donald Dunn	Consultant, Industrial Microwave Division
Fred Kolleck	Financial Consultant

EXHIBIT 2

Balance Sheet
9–30–69

ASSETS

CURRENT ASSETS:

Cash on hand and in banks........................	$ 68,658.98	
Cash on loan (commercial paper)...................	100,000.00	
Accounts receivable............ $129,592.37		
Less allowance for		
bad debt.................. (660.83)	128,931.54	
Inventory.......................................	106,730.82	
Total current assets.......................................		$404,321.34

FIXED ASSETS:

Office furniture and equipment.....................	$ 4,306.67	
Manufacturing and engineering equipment...........	14,368.35	
Leasehold improvements..........................	3,223.68	
Total cost..............................	$ 21,898.70	
Accumulated depreciation.........................	(7,053.74)	
Total fixed assets..........................		14,844.96

OTHER ASSETS:

Notes receivable................................	$ 25,220.00	
Deposits and prepaid expenses.....................	4,541.97	
Organization expense—(Net of		
amortization)................................	5,933.26	
Total other assets.........................		35,695.23
TOTAL ASSETS.........................		$454,861.53

LIABILITIES AND CAPITAL

CURRENT LIABILITIES:

Accounts payable—trade.........................	$ 45,597.04	
Taxes payable..................................	9,214.89	
Accrued payroll................................	6,097.11	
Warranty reserve................................	2,349.39	
Deferred sales.................................	9,440.55	
Total current liabilities....................		$ 72,698.98

CAPITAL:

Capital stock issued and outstanding		
(90,072 shares of 200,000 authorized).............	$486,187.20	
Deficit prior to		
12–31–68.................... ($78,183.75)		
Deficit first nine		
months—1969............... (25,840.90)		
Retained earnings (deficit)		
through 9–30–69.............................	(104,024.65)	
Total capital............................		382,162.55
TOTAL LIABILITIES AND CAPITAL...		$454,861.53

EXHIBIT 3

Statement of Income and Retained Earnings (Deficit)
Nine Months Ending 9–30–69

	First Quarter	Second Quarter	Third Quarter	Nine Months 1969	Nine Months 1968
Revenue	$ 88,190	$138,791	$201,092	$ 428,073	$ 61,042
Cost of revenue	83,904	106,821	146,520	337,245	68,800
Gross profit (loss)	$ 4,286	$ 31,970	$ 54,572	$ 90,828	$ (7,758)
Operating expenses					
Research and development	$ 2,948	$ 7,597	$ 2,408	$ 12,953	$ 23,844
General and administrative	33,382	37,931	38,912	110,225	50,067
Net operating profit (loss)	$ (32,044)	$ (13,558)	$ 13,252	$ (32,350)	$ (81,669)
Other income	3,123	1,368	2,018	6,509	11,302
Net profit (loss)	$ (28,921)	$ (12,190)	$ 15,270	$ (25,841)	$ (70,367)
Retained earnings (deficit) on 12–31–68				$ (78,184)	
Retained earnings (deficit) on 9–30–69				$ (104,025)	

EXHIBIT 4

Genesys Consulting Fee Structure

Fee = 225% direct labor/salary
Travel and other costs at actual

Genesys Manufacturing Cost Structure

List Price = 1.25 (material cost + labor cost + overhead + G&A)
Overhead = 1.00 (labor)
   G&A = .15 (labor)

Concorn Kitchens

Mr. Conrad, marketing director of the Packaged Foods Division of the Concorn Kitchens expressed reservations about the planning process used in his division. Previously, brand managers had prepared a document containing a review of the performance of each product and a pro forma profit and loss statement which implicitly contained a recommended price, promotion and advertising strategy for the following year. It was viewed by most brand managers as a "commitment" for sales and profits that would be forthcoming from the product.

Mr. Conrad felt that these documents were "ploys" used by his subordinates to obtain as many marketing resources as possible. He felt that the plans often had little relation to historical performance and that generally no clear meaning could be assigned to the sales and profit numbers included in the plan. He was frequently not sure if these numbers represented goals or predictions. It was never clear how the sales figures were related to the marketing inputs nor what would be the consequences of certain resource allocations.

As an example he cited the lack of relationship between the 1969 plan and actual performance, particularly for one of the company's products—instant puddings. He noted that because sales did not develop as anticipated during the first part of the year he had been forced to cut advertising budgets for subsequent quarters. He stated, "If the original projections had been better this would not have happened and we would not be in the profit squeeze we now face."

The Operations Research Manager, Mr. Kendall, suggested that the preparation of the marketing plan could be expedited by the development of some computer models. He recommended that he be authorized to develop such models. An Operations Research project was approved and undertaken, the results of which were summarized in a report to Mr. Conrad from Mr. Kendall (see Appendix A). Based on this report, Mr. Conrad decided to try the system out on two products—instant puddings and instant breakfasts. The marketing research staff was requested to get together the necessary information to use the models. The result of this effort is reported in Appendix B. Mr. Conrad issued orders to the applicable product managers to, first, develop a planning base which would typically require modifying the straight line projections made by the computer. He requested that all changes be supported with a "logical explanation." Once a base plan had been accomplished his instructions were to get quantified goals for the period 1970–1974 with respect to the company's case sales, dollar sales, total dollar gross margin contribution, and profits before taxes.

He reminded all concerned that these goals should be consistent one with another. Once the goals were set then the individual managers were to determine how they should be obtained. This required set annual expenditures with respect to advertising and promotion and possible changes in the list price of a case. All strategy decisions were to be supported logically.

In setting forth the new strategic planning method Mr. Conrad noted that it might be that the goals which were set were unobtainable in which case the manager would explain "why" and then proceed to set up new goals. If the goals were attainable then the manager would be asked to determine whether higher goals were possible. "In this way," stated Mr. Conrad, "we hope to come reasonably close to an optimization scheme through interactions which match inputs with outputs. While I'm very interested in the numbers which emerge from this planning exercise I am more interested in how they were derived. In this connection a man's thinking will be on display—starting with the magnitude of the planning gap; i.e., the difference between his goals and the planning base. To repeat, each product manager should do the following:

1. Analyse the past data on his brand and evaluate the complete projected data for 1970–1974. (See Appendix B for data on instant puddings and instant breakfasts.)
2. Make any changes in the projected data thought necessary based only, however, on historical trends.
3. Set goals for his brand; i.e., sales in cases, market share, and profit goals for the period 1970–1974.
4. Determine the "gap" between goals and the corrected projections.
5. Strategize expenditures to accomplish these goals.
6. Change goals up or down to optimize expenditures (as best possible)."

APPENDIX A

To: Mr. Conrad
From: Mr. Kendall
Subject: Computer Planning Model (PLAN)

We believe that a planning process should include the following steps:

1. Data on past performance should be stored in an easily accessible way and these data should form the basis of a first projection of future outcomes.
2. Projections of key components of the plan should be made assuming continuation of past trends and strategies. These component projections should then be combined into a pro forma profit and loss statement for each product. (We call this a *Planning Base*.)
3. Alternate plans should then be developed which explicitly take into account the relationships between changes in spending, prices, and resulting levels of sales and profits. These alternate plans *should be* evaluated by comparison to the Planning Base.

These ideas have been incorporated into a model called PLAN. It should be possible for your staff to use the model simply by making either manual or machine changes in the sample output.

The model has made linear extrapolations of key planning components. These extrapolations are purely mechanical in nature and will not always be appropriate. Provisions for overriding the projections have been made so that when you feel market share or costs can be better projected subjectively this can be done—again manually or by the computer. In the case of costs we have projected totals, but as you can see from the printout, you can consider cost a function of sales, rather than fixed in total.

Given that these first projections are intended to show the results of *continuing historical strategies* any changes or overrides should not be used to indicate new trends that might develop *from a shift in strategy*. Such effects are considered in the next stage of analysis.

The remainder of the effort is designed to allow experimentation with alternate marketing plans in order to improve on the base projection—i.e., obtain any goals which have been set. To use this section, the individual involved must know something about the responsiveness of sales to various marketing tools. This knowledge is summarized in the form of response coefficients to be supplied by the user. These are defined as:

$$\frac{\%\ \text{change in sales}}{\%\ \text{change in inputs (e.g., price, adv., etc.)}}$$

The way in which these coefficients affect sales is illustrated in the following tables:

Change in Advertising (Percent Change from Planning Base)	Percent Change in Sales for an Advertising Response Coefficient of:	
	.2	.4
+20%	+4% .005	+8%
+10%	+2%	+4%
Same Adv. as in Planning Base	Same Sales as PB	Same Sales as PB
−10%	−2%	−4%
−20%	−4%	−8%

Change in Price (as % of Price Planning Base)	Percent Change in Sales for a Price Response Coefficient of:	
	−1	−2
+10%	−10%	−20%
No change	No change	No change
−10%	+10%	+20%

We realize that complete knowledge is not always available on response coefficients but believe that your years of marketing experience and past research efforts should allow reasonable estimates to be made. When you are unsure of the exact value you may wish to use sensitivity testing through trying the same plan with different response coefficients.

When attempting to test the sensitivity of response coefficients remember that the coefficients are defined in terms of *changes* from the Planning Base; hence a sensitivity test can only be performed on a plan that is *different* from the base plan.

The following technical notes are provided on the program:

A. *Units of Measure*
   (1) Market and sales are measured in thousands of cases (12 units to the case).
   (2) All dollar values are in thousands.
   (3) Price is the case price charged by Concorn. Retail prices are roughly 30% higher.

B. *Accounting Conventions*
   (1) Gross Contribution Margin = Price − Variable Production Cost
   (2) Overhead includes only manufacturing expense. General and administrative expenses are not included in product level profit and loss statements at Concorn (sales force expense is considered G & A).
   (3) Promotional includes expenditures on:
        (a) Trade allowances (temporary price reductions)

      (b)   Cents-off packs and coupons
      (c)   Point-of-sale material
C. A sample output is attached.

Which product do you want to consider
$ *"test product"*
HISTORICAL FILE

	1965	1966	1967	1968	1969
Market—total cases.........	1,000,000	2,000,000	3,000,000	4,000,000	5,000,000
Share.....................	.20	.20	.20	.20	.20
Price per case $...........	2.50	2.50	2.25	2.25	2.25
Gross C margin $..........	1.00	1.00	.80	.80	.80
Sales volume in cases.......	200,000	400,000	600,000	800,000	1,000,000
Sales $...................	500,000	1,000,000	1,350,000	1,800,000	2,250,000
Gross C margin $..........	200,000	400,000	480,000	640,000	800,000
Overhead $................	100,000	100,000	100,000	150,000	150,000
Gross margin $............	100,000	300,000	380,000	490,000	650,000
Advertising $..............	20,000	20,000	20,000	20,000	20,000
Promotion $...............	30,000	30,000	30,000	30,000	30,000
Net operating profit $.......	50,000	250,000	330,000	440,000	600,000

	1970	1971	1972	1973	1974
Market—total cases.........	6,000,000	7,000,000	8,000,000	9,000,000	10,000,000
Share.....................	.20	.20	.20	.20	.20
Price per case..............	2.125	2.05	1.98	1.90	1.825
Gross C margin $..........	.70	.64	.58	.52	.46
Overhead $................	165,000	180,000	195,000	210,000	225,000
Advertising $..............	20,000	20,000	20,000	20,000	20,000
Promotion $...............	30,000	30,000	30,000	30,000	30,000

Do you wish to override any projections "yes"
Which line 3
Input new values for line   2.25, 2.25, 2.25, 2.25, 2.25
Any others "yes"
Which line 4
Input new values for line   .8, .8, .8, .8, .8,
Any others "yes"
Illegal use of tabs, please retype
Any others "yes"
Which line 6
Input new values for line   150, 200, 200, 200, 250
Any others "no"

PLANNING BASE P/L

	1970	1971	1972	1973	1974
Sales volume—cases..........	1,200,000	1,400,000	1,600,000	1,800,000	2,000,000
Sales $......................	2,700,000	3,150,000	3,600,000	4,050,000	4,500,000
Gross C margin $............	960,000	1,120,000	1,280,000	1,440,000	1,600,000
Overhead $..................	150,000	200,000	200,000	200,000	250,000
Gross margin $..............	810,000	920,000	1,080,000	1,240,000	1,350,000
Advertising $................	20,000	20,000	20,000	20,000	20,000
Promotion $.................	30,000	30,000	30,000	30,000	30,000
Net operating profit $........	760,000	870,000	1,030,000	1,190,000	1,300,000

Specify response coefficient to be used for each of 5 yrs.
Price $-2,-2,-2,-2,-2$
Advertising   .2, .2, .2, .2, .2
Promotion   .4, .4, .4, .4, .4
Time dependency
0,0,0,0,0
Which marketing variable do you wish to change "advertising"
Specify new levels by year 30, 40, 50, 60, 70
Any others "no"

	1970	1971	1972	1973	1974
Sales volume................	1,301,000	1,608,000	1,922,000	2,242,000	2,569,000
Sales $......................	2,928,000	3,618,000	4,324,000	5,045,000	5,781,000
Gross C margin..............	1,041,000	1,287,000	1,537,000	1,794,000	2,056,000
Overhead...................	150,000	200,000	200,000	200,000	250,000
Gross margin................	891,000	1,087,000	1,337,000	1,594,000	1,806,000
Advertising.................	30,000	40,000	50,000	60,000	70,000
Promotion..................	30,000	30,000	30,000	30,000	30,000
Net operating profit.........	831,000	1,017,000	1,257,000	1,504,000	1,706,000

Do you wish to try another plan "yes"
Which marketing variable do you wish to change "price"
Specify new levels by year 2,2,2,2,2
Any others "no"

	1970	1971	1972	1973	1974
Sales volume	1,647,000	2,035,000	2,432,000	2,838,000	3,252,000
Sales $	3,294,000	4,071,000	4,865,000	5,676,000	6,504,000
Gross C margin	906,000	1,119,000	1,338,000	1,561,000	1,789,000
Overhead	150,000	200,000	200,000	200,000	250,000
Gross margin	756,000	919,000	1,138,000	1,361,000	1,539,000
Advertising	30,000	40,000	50,000	60,000	70,000
Promotion	30,000	30,000	30,000	30,000	30,000
Net operating profit	696,000	849,000	1,058,000	1,271,000	1,439,000

Do you wish to try another plan "no"
Do you wish to change a response coefficient "yes"
Which one "price"
New values −2.5, −2.5, −2.5, −2.5, −2.5
Any others "no"

	1970	1971	1972	1973	1974
Sales volume	1,747,000	2,159,000	2,580,000	3,010,000	3,449,000
Sales $	3,494,000	4,318,000	5,160,000	6,020,000	6,898,000
Gross C margin	961,000	1,187,000	1,419,000	1,656,000	1,897,000
Overhead	150,000	200,000	200,000	200,000	250,000
Gross margin	811,000	987,000	1,219,000	1,456,000	1,647,000
Advertising	30,000	40,000	50,000	60,000	70,000
Promotion	30,000	30,000	30,000	30,000	30,000
Net operating profit	751,000	917,000	1,139,000	1,366,000	1,547,000

Do you wish to try another plan "no"
Do you wish to change a response coefficient "no"

APPENDIX B

To: Mr. Conrad
From: Marketing Research Staff
Subject: Data for PLAN Computer Model

Per Mr. Kendall's request we have provided historical data on instant breakfasts and instant puddings for inclusion in the computer data base.[1] This information will be updated as it becomes available.

The request for response coefficient information is more difficult to satisfy. A controlled experiment was conducted on these products two years ago which provides some information on this product. The results of that test were:

---

[1] No effort was made in the initial plan to detail the sales of the product in question by subproducts. Thus, with regard to puddings, no plans were to be formulated by type or flavor of mix. Such detailing would be accomplished later.

price coefficient.................. −1.6 *for instant pudding*

advertising coefficient............ .1

Promotional coef. *not yffect*

We suspect that over time the price elasticity coefficient is rising (larger negative values) while the advertising coefficient is falling although we cannot prove this assertion.

There are no data available on instant breakfasts, but we do have some estimates on some other products which may have similar values to those of instant breakfasts in that they are also *new* package foods in our line.

They are:

	Price Coef.	Adv.	Prom.
Corn muffin mix........	−1.2	.3	.6
Soy Snacks............	−1.4	.4	.6

prom

There does not exist any hard data on the promotions question although our sales manager feels that the response to cents off promotions is rather large for all our products. He feels that doubling promotional allowance might increase sales by 50 to 70% (he is unable to say which of our products are most responsive to promotion). We feel that his estimates represent a short run view and that such promotion may not be nearly as effective in the long run.

average it to .6

INSTANT PUDDINGS

Product History

The instant pudding market started in the early 1950's as a commercialization of some processing methods that were developed as part of World War II technology. Concorn was one of the first national brands in the market, and, for a number of years was the leading brand.

As the market grew, several other major companies entered the market. These companies had the advantage of having major sources of revenue in other higher margin industries plus experience in technologies important to the instant pudding market.

By 1965, the market had slowed and Concorn was tied for second place with Julia Childs at about 20% of the market. Gambles Deluxe had become the leading brand with 27% of the market following many years during which they dominated the market in terms of spending, primarily on advertising.

During the past five years, sales promotion has become an increasingly important marketing tool. In 1969, 90% of Concorn's volume moves at a dealing rate of 50 cents per case. There are no clear data about whether as high a percentage of competitor tonnage moves under a deal. About 40 cents per case is spent on cents off promotions which are not typically supported by media advertising.

There is some indication that Concorn technology has not kept pace with the industry and that Concorn may have a marginal product disadvantage.

Ingredient costs have been rising causing a deterioration in our margin. In the past Concorn has felt that these rising costs could not be passed on to the consumer given the highly competitive nature of the market.

While ad tests show Concorn advertising to be of equal quality to competition and perhaps marginally superior, awareness studies show the leading brand to be getting credit with consumers for the principal product benefits claimed by Concorn.

The following are the 1969 share of market and media expenditure data:

	Share (Percent)	Media $ Million
Concorn	16	1.5
Gambles Deluxe	30	3.5
Julia Child	20	2.5
Private label	25	—
All others	9	—

Plan vs. Actual	Plan (000)	Actual (000)
Market	41,000	40,800
Share	.17	.157
Sales volume	6,970	6,406
Sales $	36,592	33,629
price 5.25 case (.55 per pkg. retail)		
Gross contribution margin unit	12,615	11,466
	(1.81)	(1.79)
Overhead	2,000	2,000
Gross margin	10,615	9,466
Advertising	2,000	1,500
Promotion	5,500	5,783
Net operating profit	3,115	2,183

Which product do you want to consider
$ Instant Puddings*
HISTORICAL FILE

	1965	1966	1967	1968	1969
Market (cases)..........	39,000	40,000	40,600	40,800	40,800
Share....................	.192	.1849999	.16	.165	.1569999
Price....................	5.25	5.25	5.25	5.25	5.25
Gross C margin..........	1.9	1.87	1.839999	1.809999	1.79
Sales volume (cases)......	7,488	7,400	6,496	6,732	6,406
Sales $..................	39,312	38,850	34,104	35,343	33,629
Gross C margin..........	14,227	13,838	11,953	12,185	11,466
Overhead...............	2,160	2,160	2,100	2,100	2,000
Gross margin...........	12,067	11,678	9,853	10,085	9,466
Advertising.............	2,114	2,105	1,561	1,610	1,500
Promotion..............	5,028	5,032	5,101	5,500	5,783
Net operating profit......	4,925	4,541	3,191	2,975	2,183

	1970	1971	1972	1973	1974
Market..................	41,559.98	41,999.98	42,439,98	42,879.98	43,319.98
Share....................	.145	.136	.127	.118	.109
Price....................	5.25	5.25	5.25	5.25	5.25
Gross C margin..........	1.757999	1.73	1.702	1.674	1.646
Overhead/constant.......	1,990	1,952	1,914	1,876	1.838
Advertising constant......	1,261.1	1,088.8	916.5	744.2	571.8999
Promotion constant.......	5,882.191	6,079.992	6,277.789	6,475.59	6,673.391

PLANNING BASE P/L

	1970	1971	1972	1973	1974
Sales volume... cases..........	6,018	5,704	5,381	5,051	4,713
Sales $........................	31,594	29,944	28,252	26,519	24,744
Gross C margin................	10,579	9,867	9,159	8,456	7,758
Overhead.....................	1,990	1,952	1,914	1,876	1,838
Gross margin..................	8,589	7,915	7,245	6,580	5,920
Advertising...................	1,261	1,089	917	744	572
Promotion....................	5,882	6,080	6,278	6,476	6,673
Net operating profit...........	1,446	746	51	−640	−1,325

NOTE: To all figures except those in dollars and percentages add 000.

INSTANT BREAKFASTS

Product History

Concorn entered the instant breakfast market in 1964, correctly antici-
pating the growth trend in that segment of the food market. At that time,
the major competitors in the market were the first national brands—

Paulicci's Best with 40%, Obrien with 20% and a number of local or regional brands concentrated in major metropolitan areas—New York, Miami Beach, Los Angeles, Chicago, and Philadelphia.

By 1967, the growth trend in the market and the attractive margins had led the major chains to introduce private labels (store brand) with strong local advertising and shelf space support. Paulicci's Best initiated a price cut—which the other brands followed—in an effort to reduce the price spread between the advertised and private label brands.

In addition, each brand reacted to the 1967 market situation in different ways. Paulicci's Best de-emphasized sales promotion, and increased its advertising. Obrien held to its historical pattern of promotion and advertising spending.

Concorn's response to the situation is reflected in the historical file— a strong emphasis on sales promotion and sales execution efforts to get in-store trade support.

The following are the 1969 share of market and media expenditure data:

	Share (Percent)	Media $ Million
Concorn	10.0	2.0
Paulicci's	42.5	7.5
Obrien	18.0	4.0
Private label	21.0	
All others	8.5	

Product quality and advertising claims are effectively equal for all brands.

	1969	
Plan vs. Actual	Plan (000)	Actual (000)
Market	36,500	36,500
Share	.105	.10
Sales volume	3,832	3,650
Sales $	15,711	14,945
price 4.59 case (.49 retail)		
Gross cont. margin	8,430	8,030
unit	(2.20)	(2.20)
Overhead	1,500	1,500
Gross margin	6,930	6,530
Advertising	2,000	2,000
Promotion	3,400	3,600
Net operating profit	1,530	930

Which product do you want to consider
$ Instant ~~Puddings~~ *Breakfast*
HISTORICAL FILE

	1965	1966	1967	1968	1969
Market	21,000	24,500	28,900	32,700	36,500
Share	8.999997E-02	.105	.105	9.999996E-02	9.999996E-02
Price	4.599999	4.599999	4.099999	4.099999	4.099999
Gross C margin	2.599999	2.599999	2.2	2.2	2.2
Sales volume	1,890	2,572	3,034	3,270	3,650
Sales $	8,694	11,833	12,441	13,407	14,965
Gross C margin	4,914	6,688	6,676	7,194	8,030
Overhead	1,500	1,500	1,500	1,500	1,500
Gross margin	3,414	5,188	5,176	5,694	6,530
Advertising	2,000	2,000	2,000	2,000	2,000
Promotion	1,420	1,700	3,030	3,200	3,600
Net operating profit	−5	1,488	146	494	930

INPUT PROJECTIONS FOR USE IN BASE PLAN

	Line Number	1970	1971	1972	1973	1974
Market	1	40,479.93	44,399.98	48,319.98	52,239.98	56,159.98
Share	2	.10399997	.1059999	.107	.109	.11
Price	3	3.849999	3.7	3.549999	3.4	3.25
Gross C margin	4	2	1.879999	1.759999	1.639999	1.52
Overhead/unit	5	0	0	0	0	0
Overhead/constant	6	1,500	1,500	1,500	1,500	1,500
Advertising/unit	7	0	0	0	0	0
Advertising constant	8	2,000	2,000	2,000	2,000	2,000
Promotion/unit	9	0	0	0	0	0
Promotion constant	10	4,347.992	4,933.992	5,519.992	6,105.992	6,691.988

Do you wish to override any projections "no"

PLANNING BASE P/L

	1970	1971	1972	1973	1974
Sales volume	4,230	4,706	5,194	5,694	6,206
Sales $	16,286	17,414	18,440	19,360	20,168
Gross C margin	8,460	8,848	9,142	9,338	9,433
Overhead	1,500	1,500	1,500	1,500	1,500
Gross margin	6,960	7,348	7,642	7,838	7,933
Advertising	2,000	2,000	2,000	2,000	2,000
Promotion	4,348	4,934	5,520	6,106	6,692
Net operating profit	612	414	122	−268	−759

Specify response coefficient to be used for each of 5 years.

New York State Lottery (A)

In June, 1968, at the end of its first year of operation, the New York State Lottery seemed well established. A public survey, held in fall, 1967, indicated eight out of ten state residents were in favor of continuing the lottery, and the strident criticism of opponents of the lottery that had marked its early months seemed diminished. But lottery sales had continued to fall throughout the year, and there was considerable uncertainty among responsible officials as to what steps might be taken to increase sales.

GENERAL BACKGROUND ON THE LOTTERY

The New York State Lottery was approved in referendum by New York State voters in November, 1966, by a vote of 2.46 million to 1.60 million. The State Lottery Law, required to put the lottery into operation, was passed during the 1967 session of the New York Legislature and was the result of a series of compromises between Governor Nelson A. Rockefeller and high legislative officials.

The first major compromise concerned the form the lottery was to take. Governor Rockefeller favored a simple, direct drawing to determine a winner. Anthony J. Travia, Speaker of the New York Assembly, wanted the winners to be determined by a horse race in part, because the addition of a horse race to the lottery meant New York State could avoid paying the U.S. Federal Gambling Tax of 10 percent on all gross gambling receipts, except receipts from horse racing. The form decided on was that winners would be determined in a two-stage process, the first stage separating winners from non-winners, the second deciding the dollar amount each winner would receive. Names of winners in the first stage would be drawn from a bowl. For each million tickets sold, fifteen names would be

This case was prepared by Professor David L. Rados of the Graduate School of Business, Columbia University. Reproduced by permission.

drawn and assigned numbers from one to fifteen, equivalent to fifteen post positions in a horse race already held at a specified track during the previous week. Then the horse race ticket was drawn from a second bowl. The winners' prizes would then be determined by the finish of the horse starting in the equivalent numbered post position. For example, in the first round a winner's name might be drawn and assigned post position No. 6. In the second round if the horse that ran from post position No. 6 finished first, the winner would receive the top prize. If the horse finished fifth, the fifth highest prize would be awarded. This process would be repeated for each million dollars in sales.

The total payout was to be $300,000 per million dollars of sales. The prize schedule was:

Number of Winners	Size of Prize
1	$100,000
1	75,000
1	50,000
1	20,000
11	5,000
Totals 15	$300,000

A second major compromise concerned the administration of the lottery. Governor Rockefeller wanted the lottery to be under the full control of the State Department of Taxation and Finance, while Speaker Travia wanted it controlled by an independent commission. The compromise solution resulted in a four-member, bipartisan commission within the Department of Taxation and Finance to advise the Commissioner of Taxation and Finance. Actual operation of the lottery was the responsibility of the Division of the Lottery within the Department of Taxation and Finance. The Division would be headed by a Director and three Deputy Directors of Sales and Administration, Prizes and Drawings, and Security and Accounting. A former agent for the Federal Bureau of Investigation, Ernest T. Bird, was hired as Director.

Even with these compromises, continued dispute between the Governor and Speaker Travia and various maneuvers by opponents of the lottery delayed passage of the legislation until the final day of the 1967 legislative session. The final bill specified that the lottery tickets be priced at one dollar, that drawings be held once a month, and that sales be allowed in hotels, motels, banks, Western Union offices, and some New York State offices. The ticket form was also decided on: the ticket was to be check sized, pale green, and consist of two portions separated by a piece of carbon paper. The buyer would write his name and address on the ticket and deposit half in a lottery box at the point of sale. The ticket design also included several features to help detect illegal tampering. Excerpts from the State Lottery Law are found in the Appendix.

Following passage of the State Lottery Law, State Tax Commissioner,

Joseph H. Murphy, had approximately eight weeks in which to prepare for the start of sales on June 1, 1967. After holding hearings on the size of commission to be paid sales outlets, he ruled that retail sales agents would be paid a commission of five cents on each dollar ticket. Commissioner Murphy announced that this ruling was subject to review and possible change at the end of six months' operation. Some prospective sellers had asked for commissions ranging from ten to twenty cents per ticket. Shortly after this decision Western Union announced that it would not sell lottery tickets, because 5 percent commission was insufficient to cover costs.

At this time a sales forecast of $360 million dollars was prepared for the first year's operation. Pro forma income statement for the year is found in Exhibit 1. The Lottery Law required that the payout in prizes not exceed 30 percent of sales and that 55 percent of sales be used for educational purposes in the state.

OTHER FORMS OF GAMBLING

Competing with the new lottery were several other forms of gambling. The New Hampshire Sweepstakes, like New York's lottery, was designed to raise money for education. Until passage of the New York lottery, the New Hampshire Sweepstakes had been the only legal lottery in the United States. The winner of the New Hampshire Sweepstakes was determined by an annual horse race run at Rockingham Race Track in New Hampshire, a procedure modeled on the Irish Sweepstakes. Bettors bought tickets on the race for three dollars. There were approximately two thousand prizes; six first prizes of $100,000 each, six of $50,000, six of $25,000, and the remaining prizes of lesser amounts. Results for the first four years are given in Exhibit 2. Poor results in 1965 led the Sweepstakes Commission to give prizes on two Sweepstakes races; there were twice as many prizes, each worth half the amount given above. This prize schedule was still in effect in mid-1967. A survey of New Hampshire ticket buyers showed that most were purchased by middle class, out-of-state residents, including many residents of New York State. In 1967 New Hampshire's population was approximately 690,000.

A second form of gambling, illegal in the United States, was the "numbers" or "policy" game. The most popular form of this game was the three-digit number bet, in which payments were based on a three-digit random number published in the daily newspaper, such as the last three digits of the total number of shares traded on the New York Stock Exchange or the "mutual handle" at the Aqueduct (N.Y.) Race Track. The player chose any three-digit number, say 007, and bet as little as ten cents or as much as one hundred dollars, the limits depending on local conditions. He placed his bets with a local collector who followed a daily route or at neighborhood businesses. After a compulsory tip of 10 percent on all

winnings, paid to the collector, net payoff odds were between 450:1 and
540:1. The numbers game was believed to thrive in low income neighbor-
hoods, and the net amount bet in New York City alone was estimated at
about $200 million per year.

As a form of gambling the numbers game seemed to offer residents of
New York State several advantages. Distribution was widespread, making
it easy to place a bet. There was flexibility in the amount wagered; the
minimum bet in New York City was believed to be twenty-five cents. The
bettor could play hunches and choose his own "lucky" number. Results
of wagers were known the same day or the following day. There were
frequent opportunities to play, usually six days per week. Finally while it
was a criminal offense in New York State to receive bets it was not illegal
to place them. Many numbers players were believed addicted to the game,
as the following quote from a detective in the New York City Police Department illustrates:

> We made an arrest, and we took the collectors away, and people came in—
> you know, people from the street, housewives and such—and their eyes must
> have been glazed. They'd walk up to us and try to place bets. We'd show
> them the police shield, and they'd still try. They just *had* to get their numbers
> in that day.

Bingo[1] was widely played in New York State, being legal in almost
seven hundred cities, towns and villages, and it appeared to be becoming
an increasingly popular way of raising money for non-profit organizations such as churches, temples, fraternal organizations, hospitals and
veterans posts (see Exhibit 3). In its annual report for 1966 the State
Bingo Commission cited three factors in explaining the popularity of
bingo: the large share of gross receipts returned as prizes, approximately
64 percent; the respectability of bingo as a way of raising funds; and the
rigid supervision of bingo games and operators throughout the State by
the Bingo Commission.

Tickets for the Irish Sweepstakes were also sold in the United States.
Owned and operated by Hospitals' Trust Ltd., Dublin, Ireland, a private
firm that had invested its sweepstakes profits in a number of industrial
enterprises, the Irish Sweepstakes was one of the best known and most
popular sweepstakes in the world. Estimates of United States sales varied
from $21 million to $33 million per year, with sales in New York State
estimated between 10 and 30 percent of the total. Each ticket cost three
dollars; the odds against winning exceeded 500:1; and drawings, based on
horse races, were held three times a year.

Prize money was divided into units, each containing a full set of prizes,

---

[1] Bingo, a variant of lotto, was played on boards divided into twenty-five numbered
squares. Numbers selected by lot were called out and players covered the numbers
on their boards with markers. The winner was the first player to cover the numbered
squares on his board in any of several standard configurations.

i.e., one first prize, one second prize, and so on. Thus if the total prize money to be awarded on a race amounted to $2,940,000 and each unit contained $294,000 worth of prizes, there would be ten first prizes, ten second prizes, and so on. Usually over 50 percent of net proceeds was paid out in winnings. The approximate prize structure for a typical drawing was as follows:

Approximate Prize Structure of The Irish Sweepstakes, Typical Drawing

Size of Prize	Number of Winners	Totals
$119,500	17	$2,031,500
47,800	17	812,600
23,900	17	406,300
1,280	952	1,218,560
97*	5,600†	543,160
	6,600	$5,012,120

* Average figure only.
† Approximate.
SOURCE: *New York Post.*

Sales for this particular drawing are not known.

Sales of Irish Sweepstakes tickets were illegal in most countries of the world, except Ireland, making it difficult to assess methods of distribution. In the United States tickets were apparently imported by a few "importers." These men sold to "distributors" who in turn sold to "retail" salesmen. These resold the tickets to friends and acquaintances, receiving thirty cents per ticket as commission. It was believed both the distributors and importers received gross commissions exceeding 10 percent. The buyer kept part of this ticket; the other part, the counterfoil, containing his name and address, was sent to Dublin to be placed in a drum for the drawing. The buyer was supposed to receive a receipt acknowledging that his ticket had been received in Dublin. This method of distribution offered little control over distributors, and because it was relatively easy to counterfeit both tickets and receipts, the vast majority of Sweepstakes tickets sold in the United States were believed to be forgeries.

There were also other opportunities to gamble in New York State. In 1967, for example, attendance at thoroughbred tracks was 6.7 million with $667 million bet; and harness racing attendance was 9.9 million with $745 million bet. There was believed to be substantial illegal off-track betting as well. In 1967 the U.S. Attorney Robert Morgenthau, on the basis of figures obtained from recent arrests, estimated that bookmakers in metropolitan New York handled more than $100 million per year in bets on horse races and sporting events. And it was also possible to engage in sports pools, private games of chance, and charitable gambling for prizes. Moreover it seemed likely in mid-1968 that several other states might adopt lotteries, among them New Jersey, Kentucky and Florida.

RESTRICTIONS ON LOTTERY OPERATIONS

There were several important restrictions on the alternatives available to a lottery operator such as New York State. Many states in the United States had laws making purchase or possession of any type of lottery ticket a misdemeanor. Both New Jersey and Connecticut had had such laws until 1967, when they were repealed by their legislatures.

Advertising the lottery on radio was forbidden by Section 1304 of the U.S. Criminal Code:

Whoever broadcasts by means of any radio station for which a license is required by any law of the U.S., or whoever, operating any such station, knowingly permits the broadcasting of, any advertisement of or information concerning any lottery . . . offering prizes dependent in whole or in part upon lot or chance . . . shall be fined not more than $1,000 or imprisoned not more than one year, or both. Each day's broadcasting shall constitute a separate offense. SOURCE: 18 U.S.C. 1304.

Federal Communications Commission rules had extended the reach of this section to television as well. In a declaratory ruling in September 1968 the Commission upheld the ban on use of radio and television for lottery advertising, but it indicated that reasonable, good faith news coverage was permissible:

. . . the phrase "any information" about lotteries, should not, in our view, be construed to bar ordinary news reports concerning legislation authorizing the institution of a State Lottery, or of public debate on the course State policy should take. Licensee editorials on public debate in this area are also not, in our view, proscribed by the statute, and our rules are not to be read as prohibiting them. In the category of news, any material broadcast in normal good faith coverage, which is reasonably related to the audience's right and desire to know and be informed of the day-to-day happenings within the community is permissible. SOURCE: F.C.C. Declaratory Ruling, #68-976 (Sept. 25, 1968).

In addition federal law made it a crime to publish full lists of lottery winners, but not interviews with local winners or top prize winners as matters of general interest. U.S. Post Office regulations forbade mailing lottery tickets, full lists of names of winners, and any materials pertaining to the operation of a lottery. Publications not in interstate commerce and not using the mails could carry full names of winners; for example the *Manchester Union Leader* published full lists of New Hampshire Sweepstakes winners in editions not distributed by mail. Only such publications could carry advertising for any lottery. Federal law also forbade transporting lottery tickets across state lines for sale.

A different type of restriction was the political circumstances surrounding the lottery. The Governor and several powerful members of the State Legislature had not supported the lottery referendum but had reluctantly accepted its results. Criticism of the lottery had diminished during its first year, but if results remained poor criticism was likely to mount, including efforts to resubmit the entire question to the voters via another referendum. Moreover, major changes in the lottery such as enlarging the pool of prospective sales agents required approval by the State Legislature of an amendment to the State Lottery Law.

FIRST YEAR SALES

Sales on the first day, June 1, 1967, were heavy, later estimated to be somewhat over one million tickets in New York City alone. Many distributors throughout the state had underestimated sales and doubled or tripled their first reorders. A spokesman for Manufacturers Hanover in New York City indicated that sales had been particularly heavy at branches in business districts of the city and in low-income residential areas. Sales for the month were approximately $6.5 million, far below the forecast of $30 million. Commissioner Murphy offered several explanations. The division of the Lottery was virtually unstaffed. Distribution was considered poor. By the end of June only 4,200 of the potential 10,000 sales agents had been licensed. Moreover the advertising campaign was not fully under way nor were adequate point-of-sale display and promotional materials available. For example, the official blue and yellow sign announcing "New York State Lottery Tickets For Sale Here" was unavailable in most outlets during June.

Criticism began to mount during the month, as it appeared sales would fall far short of the forecast. State Education Commissioner James D. Allen said that the Lottery was "completely inconsistent" with such objectives of education as teaching children that gambling was evil. *The New York Times* criticized the use of billboards to promote the lottery as "sad and ironic" because billboards tended to diminish scenic and esthetic values. It also said that the planned promotional budget of $1.5 million was too much, particularly as the lottery at that time, June 9, appeared to be selling itself.

In addition the lottery received poor news coverage during the month. Even on the first day not all three of New York's major television stations carried news stories. NBC carried no news of the lottery at all, neither on network or local news broadcasts. CBS gave a brief report on its local news report, as did ABC. All three were reported to be concerned about Section 1304 of the U.S. Criminal Code mentioned earlier.

The New York Times also published an interview during June with several operators of the numbers game. These anonymous operators reported that the lottery had not hurt their business, citing that the numbers game provided action six times per week, and that winners were not publicly announced, and thus not subject to "relatives moochin' around" or to taxes.

For the remainder of the year sales continued below initial forecasts. In September the forecast itself was revised. Initially the state had hoped to realize $198 million for education from the lottery. In September this was revised to $35 million for the first year. Monthly gross receipts were as follows:

Month	Gross Receipts (millions)
June 1967	$ 6.45
July	4.13
August	5.99
September	5.80
October	6.02
November	5.45
December	4.77
January 1968	4.92
February	4.93
March	5.22
April	4.23
May	4.53
	$62.44

Sixty-six percent of total sales for the year had been made in New York City, which contained 8 million of New York's 18 million residents. Surveys also indicated that about 30 percent of ticket sales were made by nonresidents of New York State.

LICENSED SALES AGENTS

In the weeks immediately preceding June 1, considerable interest was shown by potential vendors in becoming sales agents, so that by June 1 some 3,800 hotels, motels, banks, and their branches had been licensed to sell lottery tickets. In addition some of the state's 1,700 offices were to be licensed. Not all possible distributors were licensed, however, due in part to the short time the Division of the Lottery had had to prepare for the beginning of sales. It is estimated that another 3,000 banks and bank branches and 4,500 hotels and motels were potentially available, although lottery officials felt some were of dubious size and stability.

Licensees were given a seventeen-page manual with instructions for obtaining and selling tickets and for preparing weekly and end-of-month sales reports, a kit containing advertising and promotional materials, a list of free point-of-sale materials available and instructions on the legal limitations on lottery advertising and promotion. A monthly newsletter for sales agents called "Profit Margin" was also distributed. It contained news of successful promotions by agents, pictures of agents selling winning tickets, and merchandising tips. Like all such promotional material,

"Profit Margin" had to be delivered by hand. In addition a bonus plan for agents selling winning tickets was put into effect during the year:

Size of winning ticket ($)	100,000	50,000	20,000	10,000
Bonus to agent selling the winning ticket ($)	500	250	100	50

The number of licensed sales agents varied between 4,100 and 4,400 during the first ten months of lottery operations. The number rose to over 9,000 by the beginning of May, 1968 and over 9,800 by the beginning of June.

Also on June 1, 1967, Representative Wright Patman, Chairman of the House Banking Committee, announced hearings to consider a bill banning participation by national banks and federally insured banks in the sale of lottery tickets. Action on this bill proceeded rapidly and on June 13, 1967, the House passed the bill. The Director of the New Hampshire Sweepstakes stated that the bill would not affect New Hampshire because no tickets were sold through banks. A spokesman for Commissioner Murphy estimated switching the bookkeeping done by the banks to the State would raise the administrative costs of the lottery from $500,000 to $1 million. At the time banks comprised approximately 2,400 of the total lottery outlets. The bill subsequently passed the Senate and on December 15 was signed into law by President Johnson without comment. It banned sales of lottery tickets or disbursing of prize winnings by federally insured banks, effective April 1, 1968.

As a result it became clear that new outlets for lottery tickets sales would have to be found. To this end a series of sales tests were conducted in five of the state's twelve tax districts in selected supermarkets, drugstores and department stores. Since none of these outlets was licensed to sell lottery tickets, state employees were used, thus making the test outlet a temporary state office, where sales were legal. The typical test ran two or three days. One, conducted at the Daitch-Shopwell supermarket, 90th street and Broadway, New York City, was typical of the results: In two days three state employees sold 705 tickets, 305 the first day, 400 on the second. The employees sat at a table near the exit of the supermarket from 10 A.M. to 6:45 P.M. Average daily sales of tickets were obtained from two nearby banks, one a branch of Chemical Bank New York Trust, one block to the north, the other a branch of the New York Bank for Savings, four blocks to the south. The Chemical Bank branch reported sales averaging 3,000 per month. The Bank for Savings reported average sales during the first four days of the week as 200 and on Friday, when it stayed open until 6 P.M., as 500. In another sales test, state employees sold 2,000 tickets in two days in a "poor" location in the lobby of the Pan American building in New York City. Buyer reaction at both test sites was favorable, with buyers citing the convenience of the purchase and the generally long lines at banks. It appeared that a majority of purchasers in the sales tests had not bought lottery tickets before. Overall test results showed an average sale of 221 tickets per day in the test outlets, versus 98 per day in banks.

As a result Commissioner Murphy recommended to the Governor that he propose new outlets to the Legislature, which the Governor did in his annual message to the Legislature. Senate Majority Leader Brydges stated at that time that while he still opposed the lottery he would reluctantly accept the Governor's recommendations. The Lottery Law was amended so that any store or place of business could be licensed to sell lottery tickets with the exception of bars, schools, banks, and religious, charitable, or scientific organizations. In voting for the bill Senator Brydges said the lottery deserved "one final fling." The bill took effect April 1. Until this time banks had accounted for approximately 75 percent of all ticket sales.

While this major change was taking place several minor developments occurred. Sales at racetracks in the state were good. At Yonkers Raceway sales averaged more than 10 percent of daily attendance, exceeding the expectations of lottery officials. As a result application was made to the State Racing Authority for permission to sell tickets at more tracks in the state. This permission was granted and by September 1967 tickets were being sold at Roosevelt, Yonkers, and Monticello Raceways, at Batavia Downs and at Finger Lakes Track, but not at Saratoga, which did not open until summer 1968. The New York Transit Authority considered selling lottery tickets in a few high traffic locations in the subway system but because of the insufficient manpower rejected the proposal. Selling tickets at all token booths in the system was not considered, apparently because of possible difficulties in the Transit Workers' Union.

In the spring 1968 the Lottery Commission entered into negotiations with the American News Company, which operated almost 500 retail newsstands in the state, mostly in New York City. A contract was ultimately reached and signed by July 30, 1968 providing a commission of 5¾ percent per ticket if sales exceeded 500,000 tickets per month and an additional 1¾ percent if the Company performed all distribution, accounting, administrative and promotional activities which otherwise would have been performed by the state.

SALES REPRESENTATIVES

Licensed agents were to be visited by a force of eighteen sales representatives, most of whom had been hired by September, 1967. Each representative was assigned to a tax district—for example, there were eleven representatives in New York City—and was responsible for calling on sales agents within the district. Sales representatives were expected to answer questions, deliver promotional materials, assist the agent in merchandising the lottery, and enlist new sales agents. A sales meeting was held during the year at which sales techniques were discussed and future advertising plans were explained to the representatives.

Sales representatives reported to the local District Tax Supervisor for day-to-day supervision, and to the Supervising Lottery Sales Representative in Albany for policy matters. Efforts were begun during the year to establish hiring standards for sales representatives. The position of a lottery sales representative was a non-civil service job that paid about $9,000 per year. The Supervising Lottery Sales Representative received about $14,000 per year. Sales representatives received a travel allowance but no expense account.

LOTTERY ADVERTISING

As indicated above, federal law forbade use of forms of advertising media, including broadcast media and direct mail. Initial media were limited to transit and outdoor advertising. A heavy schedule of transit advertising was employed. Each of the 7,000 cars in the New York subway system was double-carded and another 1,800 posters were placed in the stations. Bus advertising was used both in New York City and upstate, principally in Rochester, Buffalo, and the trading areas of Albany, Syracuse, and Niagara Falls. In all cases interior cards were used.

Outdoor advertising began on June 15, 1967 with the purchase of approximately 2,000 30-sheet boards throughout the state. After two months this was reduced to 1,000 boards. The amount of outdoor advertising declined during the year and the funds released went into newspaper advertising. In summer 1967, Commissioner Murphy, apparently concerned about criticism of lottery outdoor advertising, announced guidelines for its use. These included using only existing boards, erecting no new signs and concentrating outdoor advertising in the state's urban areas where the opportunity to spoil natural scenery was small.

Efforts made before the start of the lottery to purchase newspaper space had been unsuccessful. The principal difficulty had been the fact that all newspapers distributed at least part of their circulation by mail. But in July, 1967, two newspapers agreed to carry lottery advertisements. Editions going through the mails were replated so as not to carry lottery ads. By the end of the first year of operation, forty of the state's approximately seventy-five dailies were carrying lottery ads. (All materials were sent to newspapers by bus carrier or railway express.) The schedule was three weekly insertions in every four-week month and four weekly insertions in every five-week month. Each month there was no advertising in the week of the drawing because it was felt the drawing itself generated considerable publicity.

There were two principal copy themes. Initial copy stressed that purchase of a lottery ticket would help education. In mid-August, 1967, copy began to emphasize prize winnings. Both appeals continued to be used through the first year. Photographs of winners were also used in some ads.

The total budget, approximately $1.5 million, is given in Exhibit 4.

Not much

PRIZE STRUCTURE AND DRAWINGS

Two changes were made in the form of the lottery during the first year. On May 24, 1967, one week before the first public ticket sale, Governor Rockefeller announced the addition of 225 prizes to the prize schedule. Prizes were now divided into two tiers: a Grand Prize Tier with an allocation of $240,000 and a Consolation Prize Tier with an allocation of $60,000. In the Grand Prize Tier the prizes were top, $100,000,000; second, $50,000; third, $25,000; fourth $10,000; the remaining eleven prizes being worth $5,000 each. In the Consolation Prize Tier there were fifteen prizes of $1,000 each; fifteen of $700 each, fifteen of $400 each, fifteen of $250 each, and one hundred and sixty-five of $150 each. As a result of these changes there were now 240 prizes for each million dollars in sales. Furthermore, the Governor announced an annual bonus drawing worth $250,000 to be held each March. Names of past winners were to be placed in a drum and one drawn. The prize would be $250,000, payable $25,000 per year for ten years, to reduce income taxes.

The second change dealt with the frequency of drawings. Legislation was passed by the New York State Legislature permitting prize drawings to be held as often as once a week. This was an apparent attempt to answer some of the lottery's critics who claimed that monthly drawings were too infrequent to stimulate interest among potential bettors. Upon passage of the bill, which became effective April 1, 1968, Commissioner Murphy announced he would start with two drawings a month, because the Department of Taxation and Finance did not have the necessary manpower to control weekly drawings. By June 1, 1968, semimonthly drawings had not yet begun.

ACTIVITY IN OTHER STATES

In September, 1967, New Hampshire made the following changes in its sweepstakes. The number of drawings per year was doubled to four. The value of the top prize in each drawing was increased from $50,000 to $100,000. At the same time other changes in the prize schedule were announced. The result of these changes was that the proportion of prize money to total gross receipts was increased from 36 to 38 percent. The Sweepstakes Commission also began efforts to persuade corporations in New Hampshire to use sweepstakes tickets in various incentive schemes, such as a reward to an individual worker for low absenteeism or as an award in a sales contest.

After some changes in announced position, Governor Hughes of New

Jersey said he would support placing a lottery referendum on the New Jersey election slate for November, 1968.

LOTTERY RESEARCH

A survey of New York State residents was conducted in September, 1967.[2] Ninety-six percent of the respondents were aware of the lottery's existence, and awareness of individual components of the lottery was generally high. For example, slightly more than one-half of the respondents came reasonably close (within $25,000) to being able to name the top monthly prize, and 86 percent knew that banks sold lottery tickets. But when classified as to awareness of three aspects of the lottery together —its purpose, prize structure, and ticket-selling locations—almost half were considered poorly informed.

Almost one-half of the sample had already bought lottery tickets by the time the interviewing was conducted, in late September, of which three-quarters were repeat buyers. Ninety-five percent of past buyers indicated they intended to purchase more in the future. (Exhibit 5 contains selected data on both buyers and nonbuyers.)

Number of tickets purchased was distributed as follows:

Largest Number of Tickets Bought at Any One Time	Percent of Ticket Buyers
1	35
2	30
3	13
4 or more	21
Did not specify	1
	100

In response to a question dealing with the degree of planning in a purchase, one-third of the respondents said they purchased on "the spur of the moment," while the remainder indicated they decided to buy ahead of time. Respondents were also asked how often they had purchased tickets.

Number of Times Purchased	Percent of Ticket Buyers	Percent of Total Sample
Once	23.1	11.3
Twice	15.8	7.8
Three times	24.1	11.8
Four times	17.4	8.6
More than four times	13.9	6.8
Other replies	5.7	2.8
	100.0	49.1

[2] A stratified, random sample was used, designed to approximate the New York State population over eighteen years old. It contained 1,202 respondents.

The survey attempted to identify interest in gambling by asking how frequently respondents engaged in various types of gambling activities. Respondents were classified as Outright Gamblers if they frequently or occasionally engaged in any form of "hard" gambling such as playing the numbers, placing off-track bets (both illegal in New York State) or betting at the horse track; as Quasi-Gamblers if they frequently or occasionally engaged in "soft" gambling such as charitable chances with interest in a prize, product purchases with a prize chance, or games with a money chance; as Low-Interest Gamblers if they seldom engaged in "soft" gambling; and as Non-Gamblers if they never engaged in any gambling except for charitable chances without interest in a prize. Exhibit 6 classifies the total sample by these categories. The distribution of buyers and non-buyers by these classifications is found in Exhibit 7.

Respondents were also asked why people bought lottery tickets and shown a card listing "Help Education, Hope of Winning, Excitement and Suspense" as possible reasons. Sixty-one percent of respondents picked "Hope of Winning" and 23 percent picked "Help Education."

A number of questions dealt with factors inhibiting sales. Forty-two percent of respondents said they would be more likely to buy if purchases could be made at supermarkets, 38 percent at drugstores, and 29 percent at department stores. Two out of three thought they would become buyers if there were more winners and smaller prizes, while 15 percent felt sales would increase with fewer winners and bigger prizes. About 40 percent said more frequent drawings would increase sales. Many also felt that smaller, tax free prizes would increase sales.

Attempts were made to develop some measure of the lottery's potential by asking non-buyers if they planned to buy tickets in the future and how many; and if they might buy under certain conditions such as wider distribution of sales outlets. Those who said they would buy under certain conditions or who gave a specific number of tickets they planned to buy in the future were classified Likely New Buyers. This group comprised 55 percent of non-buyers.[3] The highest percentages of Likely New Buyers were found among women, the young (18–29 years of age), those with family incomes under $5,000 per year, Negroes, Puerto Ricans, and Protestants.

PROPOSED CHANGES

As of June, 1968, lottery officials still did not feel they had the key to successful promotion of the lottery. Numerous options had been suggested by hostile and sympathetic critics. One legislator had introduced into the 1968 Legislature a bill that would have abolished the lottery. It had been

---

[3] The researchers estimated that 0.7 percent of the total sample could be classified as Low-Interest Gamblers *and* Likely New Buyers, and 13.2 percent of the total sample as Non-Gamblers *and* Likely New Buyers.

killed in committee. Some suggested doubling the number of prizes to
480 while keeping the total payout the same. Others suggested use of
street vendors to sell tickets, a practice common in many foreign countries. Commissioner Murphy did not feel street vendors were appropriate,
however, nor did he feel such a proposal could pass the Legislature. Many
suggestions dealt with reducing or eliminating the state income tax on
winnings, and the research on lottery buyers cited above indicated that
many respondents were concerned about taxes on winnings. There were
three arguments against such a course: it would entail considerable administrative difficulties; it would conflict with the income tax conformity
agreement between state and federal tax authorities; and it would likely
draw demands for similar treatment from parimutuel operators, a far
more important source of tax revenues. Machine vending of tickets had
also been proposed. But there was concern that machines would enable
persons under eighteen years of age to buy tickets, in violation of the
Lottery Bill. If machines were to be used, it was felt, they would require
operators.

By mid-June the first preliminary estimate of June sales became available. It was $4.05 million, the lowest since the start of the lottery.

EXHIBIT 1

**Pro Forma Income Statement, New York State Lottery
(June 1967–May 1968)**

		Millions of Dollars	Percent
Gross receipts...................		$360	100
Expenses......................			
Commissions................	$ 18		5*
Administration...............	36		10
Prizes......................	108	162	30†
Net receipts		$198	55†

* As determined by the State Tax Commissioner.
† As required by State Lottery Law.
SOURCE: *New York Times*, May 11, 1967.

EXHIBIT 2

Operating Results, New Hampshire Sweepstakes, 1963–1967*
(000 omitted)

	July 29,1963 to Sept. 30,1964		Oct.1,1964 to Sept. 30,1965		Oct.1,1965 to Sept. 30,1966		Oct.1,1966 to Sept. 30,1967	
Gross ticket revenue........	$5,729		$3,901		$3,862		$2,567	
Gross operating expenses....	1,071†		478		433		377	
Prizes:								
Sweepstakes purse......	100		200		200		200	
Prizes................	1,800	2,971	1,400	2,078	1,415	2,048	944	1,521
Net ticket revenue..........		2,758		1,823		1,814		1,046
Other income..............		10		661‡		26		9
Net income available for distribution.............		2,768		2,487		1,841		1,055

* Figures may not add, due to rounding.
† Includes Internal Revenue 10% tax and stamps ($588).
‡ Includes refund of 1964 Internal Revenue tax plus interest ($617).
SOURCE: New Hampshire Sweepstakes Commission.

EXHIBIT 3

Bingo in New York State: Gross Receipts
Net Profit and Number of Conducting Organizations, 1953–1966*

Year	Gross Receipts (millions)	Net Profit (millions)	Number of Organizations Conducting Bingo
1959.................	$21.4	$ 4.8	1,501
1960.................	41.4	9.4	1,441
1961.................	45.4	11.0	1,296
1962.................	50.6	13.6	1,232
1963.................	57.3	16.1	1,242
1964.................	64.9	18.7	1,337
1965.................	74.1	21.6	1,449
1966.................	83.3	24.6	1,543

* Bingo was legalized in 1958 on a local option basis.
SOURCE: Fifth Annual Report (N.Y.), State Bingo Control Commission (1967).

EXHIBIT 4

Advertising and Promotional Budget by Media, June 1967–March 1968*

Transit..	$ 255,000
Newspaper......................................	214,000
Matchbooks.....................................	21,000
Billboards.......................................	745,000
Other...	8,000
	$1,245,000
Production......................................	150,000
Total media and production budget...........	$1,395,000

* Figures do not add because of rounding. Total budget for the period June, 1967 to May, 1968 was $1,500,000.
Source: Fuller & Smith & Ross.

EXHIBIT 5

Selected Characteristics of Lottery Buyers and Non-Buyers, October, 1967

	Total Sample (percent)	Non-Buyers* (percent)	Repeat Buyers (percent)	Non-Repeat Buyers (percent)
Total state...........................	100	51.0	37.3	11.7
Age				
18–29...........................	19.2	65.8	25.5	8.7
30–49...........................	39.6	46.0	41.0	13.0
50 and over.....................	38.9	49.0	39.0	12.0
Income				
Under $5,000...................	26.2	64.0	26.0	10.0
$5,000–$9,999..................	46.3	44.5	44.0	11.5
Over $10,000...................	25.1	49.6	36.1	14.3
Occupation				
Business & professional...........	23.9	57.8	30.7	12.5
Clerical & sales.................	13.2	40.9	47.8	11.3
Manual.........................	42.2	46.3	42.4	11.3
Religion				
Protestant.......................	33.1	66.0	23.2	10.8
Catholic........................	50.2	41.6	45.6	12.8
Jewish..........................	11.9	47.3	42.4	10.3
Region				
New York City..................	50.9	41.4	46.3	12.3
New York suburbs..............	12.1	42.4	42.5	15.1
Upstate cities...................	21.3	64.5	24.6	10.9
Upstate towns..................	15.7	70.7	21.3	8.0
Number of respondents...........	1,202	613	448	141

* Including "not heard of."
Source: Division of the Lottery.

EXHIBIT 6

Survey Respondents Classified by Interest in Gambling

	Outright Gamblers (percent)	Quasi-Gamblers (percent)	Low-Interest Gamblers (percent)	Non-Gamblers (percent)
Total state...................	17.2	31.9	2.3	48.6
Age				
18–29.....................	17.7	28.6	4.3	49.4
30–49.....................	20.8	34.9	1.5	42.8
50 and over...............	13.7	30.2	2.4	53.7
Income				
Under $5,000.............	14.0	23.5	3.8	58.7
$5,000–$9,999.............	18.8	35.4	1.8	44.0
$10,000 and over..........	17.3	34.9	1.7	46.1
Occupation				
Business & professional.....	13.9	28.2	1.8	56.1
Clerical & sales...........	20.8	37.7	1.9	39.6
Manual...................	19.5	34.1	2.4	44.0
Religion				
Protestant................	12.6	27.4	2.5	57.5
Catholic..................	21.2	35.5	1.8	41.5
Jewish...................	14.0	30.8	3.5	51.7
Region				
New York City............	20.6	31.7	3.3	44.4
New York suburbs.........	13.0	41.1	.0	45.9
Upstate cities.............	16.8	27.3	2.0	53.9
Upstate towns............	10.1	31.4	1.6	56.9
Number of respondents..........	207	383	28	584

SOURCE: Division of the Lottery.

EXHIBIT 7

Buyers and Non-Buyers Classified by Interest in Gambling

	Total Sample (percent)	Outright Gamblers (percent)	Quasi-Gamblers (percent)	Low-Interest Gamblers (percent)	Non-Gamblers (percent)
Buyers................	49.0		72.0		63.5		35.7		32.2
Repeat.............	37.3	60.9		50.7		28.6		20.7	
Non-repeat........	11.7	11.1		12.8		7.1		11.5	
Non-buyers............	51.0*		27.5		35.2		42.9		60.8
Never heard of.........			0.5		1.3		21.4		7.0
	100.0	100.0	100.0	100.0	100.0
Number of respondents.	1,202	207	383	28	584

* Including "never heard of" category.
SOURCE: Division of the Lottery.

APPENDIX: EXCERPTS FROM THE STATE LOTTERY LAW

Section 1305. Powers and duties of the commissioner of taxation and finance

[The commissioner shall have the power:]

1. (A) To establish the time and place of regular drawings of the state lottery, but limited to not more than one regular drawing in any week.

(B) To establish the time and place of special or bonus drawings.

4. To provide for compensation in . . . manner and amounts to . . . licensed sellers of lottery tickets only where the commissioner finds that such compensation is necessary to assure adequate availability of lottery tickets . . .

5. To decide . . . the price at which tickets are sold.

(b) . . . to determine the method . . . used in selling lottery tickets and . . . to purchase or lease machines through which tickets may be sold. Such machines may not be coin operated . . .

(d) . . . to license agents to sell tickets for the state lottery. The commissioner may require a bond from any licensed agent, in an amount to be determined by the commissioner.

Section 1306. Lottery sales agents

(a) The commissioner may license as agents to sell lottery tickets such persons as in his opinion will best serve public convenience, except that no license shall be issued to any person to engage in business exclusively as a lottery sales agent, nor shall any license be issued to any person for the sale of lottery tickets within . . . premises licensed to sell beer, liquor or wine. . . .

(c) . . . before issuing a license . . . the commissioner shall consider, with respect to each person:

1. Financial responsibility and security of the business or activity.

2. Accessibility of the place of business or activity to the public.

3. Sufficiency of existing licenses to serve public convenience.

4. Whether the place of business or activity is predominately frequented by minors.

5. Volume of expected sales.

Section 1310. Lottery tickets

The price at which tickets are sold shall not be less than one dollar for each ticket. . . . [E]ach ticket shall bear the name and address of the person entitled to receive any prize. . . . No ticket shall be sold at a price greater than that fixed by the commissioner nor shall a sale be made by any person other than a licensed lottery sales agent . . .

Section 1311. Sales to certain persons prohibited

(a) No ticket shall be sold to any person actually or apparently under eighteen years, but this shall not be deemed to prohibit . . . purchase . . . for the purpose of making a gift . . . to a person less than [eighteen].

(b) No ticket shall be sold to, and no prize paid to . . . : (i) any officer or employee of the department of taxation and finance, (ii) any member of the [state lottery] commission, or (iii) any spouse, child, brother, sister or parent residing as a member of the same household in the principal place of abode of any of the foregoing persons.

Section 1314. Disposition of revenues

All moneys received by the commissioner from the sale of lottery tickets . . . shall be used for the payment of lottery prizes, but the amount so used shall in no event exceed thirty percent of the total amount for which the tickets have been sold. On or before the twentieth day of each month, the commissioner shall pay into the state treasury . . . not less than fifty-five percent of the total amount . . . sold during the preceding month . . .

SOURCE: New York State Tax Law Sections 1300–1315, April, 1967, amended March, 1968.

Standard Electronic Development, Inc.
Commercial Microwave Operation (A)

Late in 1966, Mr. James Gailer, in charge of Standard Electronic Development's (SED) Commercial Microwave Operation (CMO), was faced with a critical decision concerning future strategy. The potential market for microwave heating applications in industrial markets appeared enormous, but neither SED nor its competitors had made much tangible progress. It seemed to management that market acceptance of microwave heating was hindered by the revolutionary nature of the process, high costs, and the large development expenditures required to test the technical and economic feasibility of proposed applications. Thus, CMO management was convinced that it had to shift from a "shotgun" marketing approach to one of specific focus on early payoff opportunities.

BACKGROUND

SED was a large electronics manufacturer with sales in 1964 of $270,-000,000. Two thirds of the sales emanated from the Communications Equipment Group, which produced communications systems, primarily for the Department of Defense. These complicated systems (such as a radar network) contained a number of electronic components produced in SED's Microwave Tube and Components Group. This group also sold its products to other systems houses such as Raytheon and Westinghouse. SED's third operating group, Medical Electronics, was formed in early 1963 as a result of acquiring two small firms which specialized in medical research machines. There was almost no technical or marketing relationship between this third group and the first two.

The Commercial Microwave Operation had its origins in early 1964 when SED's top management decided to explore the possibilities of selling microwave power tubes for industrial heating equipment. Power tubes were already produced and marketed by the company for government and communications markets, but little attention had been paid to industrial applications of the microwave technology except for some limited experimentation with the blanching of fruits and vegetables and the use of combined dielectric and microwave heating for freeze-drying. SED's management was not interested in developing the consumer market, since Raytheon, Tappan, and General Electric had had microwave ovens on the market for several years. That market had never matured, apparently because of the initial expense of the equipment, the short life of the magnetron tubes, and the uncertain results of the cooking operation.

The impetus for launching the new operation came from SED's Planning Committee.[1] Early in 1964 this committee made a preliminary study of the potential for microwave energy in industrial applications and concluded that "there are many opportunities, most of which presently exist in potential form, for the beneficial introduction of electrical power into industry at frequencies above the reach of rotating machinery." The Committee foresaw a multitude of potential applications which warranted study, including laminating plywood, dehydrating or cooking food, sterilizing pharmaceuticals or surfaces of food products, and inducing precise chemical changes in material.

In order to implement this proposal, SED appointed Mr. James Gailer to spearhead a new industrial microwave unit. Mr. Gailer had an M.B.A degree as well as a B.S. in physics. His prior experience with SED had been in market research and product planning relating to the sale of certain microwave tubes to industrial markets.

One of Mr. Gailer's first acts was to commission an outside consulting firm, Jerut Research Associates, to conduct a $12,000 study of potential applications for industrial microwave. Jerut's report, completed in April 1966, evaluated a total of 45 potential applications and concluded that 20 warranted more detailed study on the basis of favorable preliminary technical, cost, or market factors (see Exhibit 1).

Of the 20 promising applications, Jerut felt that only 7 represented either an outstanding or a good opportunity for microwave processing with favorable markets and apparently favorable technical and economic characteristics. The applications and their estimated potential market size (in KW) were:

To dry adhesive in the manufacture of heavy corrugated board (7,000–10,000 KW)

To heat wet paper to improve water extraction during pressing operations (85,000 KW)

To dry adhesive in packaging operations (15,000 KW)

---

[1] This committee consisted of SED's president, the group vice-presidents, and the director of planning.

To dry and cure foundry cores (600,000 KW)
To cure adhesive in the manufacture of plywood (28,000 KW)
To heat gypsum board before normal drying operations (28,000 KW)
To heat and cure tires in retreading operations (9,900 KW)

To determine the feasibility of any one of these potential applications would require an average investment of $10,000 to $25,000 or more. Once the feasibility could be established, Jerut estimated that R & D expenditures for building a prototype unit would be anywhere from $50,000 to $250,000, depending on the application. Even if a technically sound product could be developed, Jerut felt that the major deterrent to broad acceptance of microwave processing by industry was its high cost relative to other forms of energy (steam, electricity, hot air, etc.). The cost of microwave energy, based on SED's estimated installed capital cost of equipment and tube replacement costs, was found to exceed the costs of other types of energy by at least a factor of two for most applications studied—although SED estimated that capital equipment and tube costs could be reduced by one-third by 1968.

Estimated Costs of Microwave Equipment

Unit Size	Equipment Cost ($/KW)		Tube Cost	Tube Replacement Cost (¢/Hr of Operation)		
				2,500 Hr/Life	3,750 Hr/Life 1966	11,000 Hr/Life 1968
	1966	1968				
25 KW..........	$1,000	$750	$1,850	3.3	2.0	0.7
75 KW..........	750	400	3,700	2.1	1.4	0.4
225 KW..........	600	350	7,400	1.5	0.9	0.3

Although the cost of microwave energy was higher than conventional sources of energy on a direct BTU basis, microwaves had a much higher coupling efficiency. For example, in producing 3,413 BTU's per KW/hour, microwaves could put about 2,730 of those BTU's into the product without loss to the surrounding air or equipment. Of BTU's generated in gas or electric ovens, however, only a few percent were of consequence to the product. Thus, SED felt that realistic cost comparisons should be based on the cost of BTU's at work within the product rather than their cost of generation.

Another limiting factor was the long lead time required to gain market acceptance; Jerut estimated that it would take at least one to two years for most applications and considerably longer for others. Furthermore, Jerut found that although many of the industry representatives were aware of microwave processing, most had no accurate idea of its capabilities or costs.

MICROWAVE TECHNOLOGY

Heat can be applied to matter in three basic ways: conduction, convection, and radiation (infrared). Most heating methods in general use depend upon conduction. The surface of the material to be heated is exposed to high temperatures; heat is then conducted through the mass to the center. Convection is used to heat fluids (liquid or gas) by means of a heat source which is progressively exposed to the entire fluid as a result of currents created by temperature gradients or fans. Radiation heating allows materials to be heated by thermal energy created by electromagnetic fields in a controlled atmosphere or vacuum. Microwave heating is a form of radiation heating—at microwave wavelengths.

Microwaves are rapidly alternating electrical fields with frequencies considerably higher than more commonly known sources of electromagnetic energy, such as dielectric heating and VHF or UHF television. Because microwaves are located between the UHF and infrared regions of the electromagnetic spectrum, they possess characteristics of both. Like infrared rays, microwaves can be reflected, refracted, and made to interact with matter. Like radio waves, they can be propagated through various media and can be focused and conducted through waveguides and coaxial lines. The relative position of these sources on the electromagnetic spectrum is as follows:

Frequency Millicycles/Second	Energy Source
10–100 MHz	Dielectric heating
88–108 MHz	FM radio
54–216 MHz	VHF television
470–890 MHz	UHF television
300–30,000 MHz	Microwave
Up to 5×10^8 MHz	Infrared rays
1×10^9 MHz	Visible light
Up to 10^{13} MHz	Ultraviolet and x-rays

Only four operating frequencies—915 MHz, 2,450 MHz, 5,800 MHz, and 22,000 MHz—had been approved by the Federal Communications Commission for Industrial, Scientific, and Medical use (ISM). No limitation had been placed by the FCC on radiated power levels. Microwave heating systems were being produced only at the two lower frequencies since economical sources had not been developed for the two higher frequencies.

The heating of certain materials exposed to microwave energy was probably first noted in World War II work with magnetrons used in radar. Microwaves were known to be reflected by metal objects, and were observed to pass through many materials such as air, glass, pottery, and paper without significant attenuation. Thus, none of these materials *absorbed* much heat-producing microwave energy. However, microwave energy penetrated some distance into and was completely absorbed by materials which had electrical properties similar to those of water. Such penetration enabled microwaves to generate heat in this class of materials both at the surface and in the interior of objects simultaneously. The depth to which the radiation penetrated depended on its frequency and the composition of the material.

The advantages of microwave energy arise for the most part from the fact that the fields instantly penetrate significant distances into dielectric materials, thus producing thermal energy throughout the volume of the material. Specific advantages include (1) speed through substantial reductions in process time; (2) uniformity through simultaneous penetration of the entire mass; (3) self-regulation in water removal processes, because power absorption decreases as evaporation nears completion; (4) moisture levelling through energy concentration in wettest areas; (5) efficiency (70% and higher) through relatively low heat loss to the surrounding environment; and (6) lower costs for specific applications. Typical processes utilizing microwave heating would include pasteurization, sterilization, large scale food processing, polymerization, curing, sealing, and freeze-drying.

Although the capital cost of microwave equipment was considerably higher than for conventional equipment, microwaves had been shown to compete favorably on an economic basis for some applications. Cost savings could be realized from the increased efficiency of the energy generated, the ability to conveyorize a given process thereby reducing both the labor and floor space requirements, lower expenditures to maintain satisfactory working conditions (e.g., air conditioning), and fast "warm-up" time (minutes rather than hours).

In addition to the generation of heat through the use of microwave sources, it has been suspected that specific chemical and biological reactions can be effected. The distinguishing feature of such reactions is that they occur at nearly room temperature, because the energy input is selective. This contrasts sharply with conventional or thermochemistry, where the initiating temperature for useful reaction rates might be over 1,000° F., as in the case of reducing iron ore. The difference in energy requirements might make the use of microwave power economically competitive in chemical applications. Although most research in this area has been proprietary, some industry sources felt that microwaves could ultimately restructure the chemical industry.

MICROWAVE INDUSTRY

In general, the microwave industry was made up of components and systems. Although components (including microwave tubes) were sometimes sold directly to the end user as replacement parts, most component sales were to manufacturers of systems such as radar and electronic countermeasures equipment, communications systems, and scientific and test equipment.

In the early 1960's, about 16 companies, including Litton, North American, Phillips (Amperex), Raytheon, SED, and Varian, were manufacturing microwave tubes. Most of the tube manufacturers, particularly the smaller ones, had chosen to specialize in one or a few types of tubes, rather than compete across the board in all tube types. Although a number of companies manufactured magnetrons, SED was one of the only two companies offering klystrons for microwave heating applications.

By the mid-1960's, the market for industrial microwave applications was still in its infancy. Sales of industrial microwave processing equipment for 1966 were estimated to be approximately $1.25 million, broken down as follows:

Company	Date of Entry into Microwave Equipment Market	Estimated 1966 Sales
Raytheon	1964	$200,000
Litton	1962	500,000
Cryodry	1963	350,000
Comtek	1964	50,000
Reeve Electronics	1960	50,000
RCA	1965	25,000
SED	1964	50,000
Varian	1965	60,000

Most of the large suppliers of tubes and equipment for microwave heating entered the field to diversify their activities and lessen their dependence on military procurements. However, those companies which had not separated their microwave heating activity from their tube production organization had experienced difficulty changing from military component suppliers to industrial capital equipment suppliers.

Most of the significant firms in the industry had specialized in one or a few applications. Cryodry's main interest, for example, was in food. Cryodry was the first to perfect a system for the final drying of potato chips and accounted for most of the sales to that segment of the food industry (although both Litton and Raytheon also had operating systems).

The primary interest of Litton's Atherton Division was in both food and pharmaceuticals. In addition to successfully developing systems for the industrial cooking of chicken and potato chips, Litton was conducting significant technical work investigating biological phenomena caused by microwave irradiation of foods.

Raytheon's work had been focused on large systems in chemicals, printing, and textiles designed to use its high power proprietary tubes.

Varian produced high power magnetrons and klystrons, as well as equipment based on the use of these tubes. Its application efforts had been concentrated in the food, wood, paper, and plastics industries.

Reeve Electronics had a number of small glue drying systems in operation, while RCA's studies had been focused upon freeze-drying. Comtek, originally organized to manufacture magnetrons for home cooking aplications, had also entered the industrial processing area. DuPont had perfected various heating systems for synthetic yarns utilizing microwave energy for use in its own operations.

As of mid-1966, there were 41 known installed microwave heating systems with a total estimated value of $4 million:

	No. of Systems	Application	Value (000,000)	
Food industry.............	12	Potato chip friers	$1.20	
	4	Meat	0.40	
	3	Miscellaneous food	0.20	
	1	Drug	0.05	
	1	Freeze-drying	0.05	
				$1.90
Plastics industry...........	17	Synthetic yarn	1.90	
	1	Foundry core drying	0.05	
	1	Poly foam curing	0.07	
				2.02
Forest products............	1	Finish coating	0.08	
				0.08
				$4.00

The final heating and drying of potato chips had proved to be one of the more successful applications of microwave energy. In addition to increasing process speed, microwaves improved the quality, durability, and appearance of the final product, and eased the quality requirements of the raw vegetable so that good quality potato chips could be produced from potatoes costing $2 per hundredweight rather than $6. Microwave processing also increased the shelf-life from days to weeks by altering the chemical composition of the oils in the final product.

The cooking of chicken with microwave energy had also been tested, and Ocoma Foods (a subsidiary of Consolidated Foods) had ordered a microwave system from Litton to precook chicken parts for restaurant use. The speed and flexibility of this process made possible a conveyorized production line (rather than a batch process) and resulted in less weight loss in the finished product.

The pharmaceutical industry had begun to experiment with microwave heating for the removal of solvents from various drugs. One application that had been tested, the removal of alcohol during the manufacture of penicillin, had increased the process speed. The main advantage, however, was that the penicillin need not be heated above the boiling point for alcohol because of preferential heating of the alcohol by the microwave energy. Conventional heating techniques sometimes raised the temperature of the drug to the point where damage might occur.

Freeze-drying of food, a process which completely dehydrated the material and eliminated the need for refrigeration during storage, required that the food be frozen and the water sublimated under combined conditions of vacuum and applied heat. Use of microwave heating during the sublimation phase had experimentally reduced process time to one-eighth of that required with conventional techniques.

One of the earliest industrial microwave applications to reach the production stage was a system for curing polyurethane foam for bucket seats installed at a British Motors Corporation facility. The process was expected to halve mold costs, thereby effecting considerable savings in labor, materials, and capital equipment.

Another major applications area was in the forest products industry, where several applications had already demonstrated technical and economic feasibility and others were in various stages of development. A number of companies had studied the use of microwaves in drying lumber, plywood, and paper. The ability of microwaves to penetrate material completely and to focus energy on the wettest areas made its use in such applications highly desirable. For example, lumber drying depended on evaporation of moisture at or near the surface, which could not proceed at a rate faster than water would diffuse outward. Wood was generally heated in a dry kiln to increase this diffusion rate, but too rapid removal of the surface moisture caused stresses that produced warping, cracking, case hardening, and surface checking. In microwave drying, the surface of the wood actually remained cooler than the interior due to heat losses by convection and radiation, and moisture was driven out rather than drawn out. Other advantages were a reduction in process time, the possibility of a conveyorized process, and elimination of most labor associated with stacking.

Studies of paper drying using microwave energy had also demonstrated potential advantages and cost savings. Since the cost of water removal by conventional means generally increased exponentially as the water content of the material was lowered, microwave energy became an attractive means of drying paper in the final stages of the process (from 20% water content down to 6%). Moisture levelling could be accomplished without overdrying, and the paper thus had greater strength, better printability, and higher overall quality. Furthermore, a level moisture profile allowed the product, which was sold on a weight basis, to be sold at the highest acceptable total moisture content.

CMO'S OBJECTIVES

SED's overall objective for the Commercial Microwave Group was to "enter a new commercial market area that is technically related and offers reasonable profit potential, with minimum risk, in order to expand the market for SED electron devices and expand total SED sales." The general approach was to develop, manufacture, install, and service energy conversion equipment (emphasizing high power and high frequency and using electron devices for converter elements). The stated long-range objective was thus "to supply (on a profitable basis) high-power radio frequency energy to industry to perform existing processes more quickly, more economically, or in some way better; and to develop a proprietary position (techniques and patents) in special processes utilizing microwave interaction with materials to generate or improve products."

MARKETING STRATEGY

Mr. Gailer decided to concentrate his efforts on the manufacturers who made equipment for purchase by such end users as food processors, paper mills, and pharmaceutical houses. Because these end user segments were unduly scattered and divorced from electronics technology, Mr. Gailer felt that better results could be obtained by going after the OEM's (Original Equipment Manufacturers).

First, Mr. Gailer surveyed SED's existing tube buyers in order to assess their potential interest in making industrial microwave equipment. He planned to explain microwave energy to these buyers, to convince them of the impending emergence of industrial microwave systems, and to assure them of SED's willingness to provide technological assistance in applications development.

In order to further develop a market for industrial microwave equipment, Gailer's strategy was (1) to use direct mail and periodical advertising to inform industry that SED was building such equipment; (2) to build a selected mailing list and periodically send out articles, design information, and other related technical data; and (3) to work diligently toward getting laboratory microwave sources and microwave test chambers into a large number of the industrial laboratories in order to stimulate interest and experimentation.

The sales strategy was multi-faceted, and made use of SED's tube sales force as well as manufacturers' representatives. Although the tube field sales force gave CMO broad market coverage, the technical requirements of specific applications and the more pressing demands of the tube division lessened the salesmen's effectiveness. The CMO intended to set up its own field sales network as soon as sales volume warranted. CMO was also negotiating joint venture arrangements with customers, including pilot experiments with end users or with engineering firms and OEM's.

PRODUCT AND MARKET DEVELOPMENT

In 1965, a year after the launching of CMO, Mr. Gailer proposed four major projects based on a year-long study of potential applications:

(1) Drying paper and paper coatings
(2) Drying wallboard, plywood products, and latex (tennis shoes)
(3) Liquid and solid particle heating (carbon and PVC)
(4) Solid material heating (asbestos, galena, rubber)

The company laboratory was experimenting with the hardware needed to process these various materials and with the use of 915 and 2,450 MHz tubes. In addition to providing design and application assistance to potential equipment users and OEM's, Mr. Gailer encouraged the Tube Division to develop specialized tubes for the Commercial Microwave Operation.

Specifically, CMO intended to develop and market: (1) 2.5 KW radio frequency (r.f.) sources, applicators, and accessories (i.e., test equipment) for research laboratories to use for their own microwave studies and for quality control use where rapid drying was important; (2) 25 KW r.f. sources, applicators, and accessories for research laboratories requiring higher power for their own studies and for pilot line experiments to prove out a production process; (3) high power r.f. systems (100 KW, 250 KW, and 1 megawatt modules) for on-stream production processes. By early 1966, CMO had completed development work on a 2.5 KW 2,450 MHz Power Pack, a 25 KW 915 MHz Power Pack, and waveguide components for use at both frequencies. Work had also been started on a 25 KW 2,450 MHz Power Pack, which was scheduled for completion late in the year.

CUSTOMER PROJECTS

By early 1966, Mr. Gailer had research projects underway with five different companies involved in paper products, paperboard and wallboard, plywood glue curing, veneer redrying, and fluid bed carbon extraction. Two of the most promising applications at that time appeared to be plywood glue curing and veneer redrying. For example, Mr. Gailer estimated that a plywood plant with annual production of 50 million square feet (average size plant), requiring an investment of $300,000 in microwave processing equipment, could produce a higher grade plywood which would result in a net return on the investment of 31% after taxes. For the veneer redrying process, CMO estimated that a plant producing 450 million square feet would require an investment of $120,000 for microwave processing equipment and would yield an ROI of 47% after taxes due to the increased efficiency of the process and higher yields of saleable product.

In the fall of 1966, the CMO had a number of additional in-house R & D projects.

One project for Johnson Rubber was to test the feasibility of drying latex on canvas shoes mounted on a metal last. CMO had built a rotary turntable with a microwave exposure position, but the results had been inconclusive. Further action was awaiting Johnson Rubber's evaluation of the results.

In August, SED signed an agreement for a joint project with Wood-Dry, Inc., a manufacturer of forest products drying and heating equipment. Wood-Dry had annual sales of $10 million and provided 80% of the wood veneer drying equipment in the United States and Canada. The project was in three phases—economic investigations, prototype installation, and production installations—and was to cover the drying process for gypsum wallboard, lumber, particle board, wood veneer, hard board, soft board, logs, raw lumber, and finish coatings. The economic and technical investigations were to be conducted during a one-year period, with the total expense to either company not to exceed $50,000. A prototype installation was to be made on the basis of guaranteed performance; otherwise, the equipment would be removed at no cost to the customer. In the production phase, the sales responsibility was to rest with Wood-Dry, and all system elements were to be purchased from SED for five years.

SED had also had preliminary discussions with a major forest products company (sales $200 million) on the use of microwave energy in a newly developed continuous press for manufacture of glued wood products.

From October 1965 through August 1966, CMO made 132 quotations to 111 different companies for a total of $3.5 million, and received 17 orders totaling $103,000 (see Exhibit 2). In assessing the status of those quotes, SED found that two companies (total bid of $175,000) had been sold by a competitor, that active negotiations were still underway with 18 companies (for orders amounting to $1.37 million), that 10 companies had a mild continuing interest, and that the rest probably had no further interest. The quotations were based on a markup of 25% over estimated cost of sales.

FINANCIAL DATA

By the end of 1965, SED had invested over $400,000 in pursuit of the industrial microwave market:

Capital investment—Actual	$ 49,800
Capital investment—Committed	26,700
Company sponsored R & D	254,200
Value of inventory	61,000
Overhead variable	24,700
	$416,400

Another $300,00 in expenditures would be incurred by the end of fiscal 1966 (year ending September 30).

Total sales in 1966 would be approximately $50,000 with a back-log of an additional $50,000.

SED projected that annual sales to the industrial microwave equipment market would grow from virtually nothing in 1965 to over $25 million in 1970. SED expected to be a major factor in that market—along with Litton, Raytheon, Varian, Cryodry, and Phillips—and projected in early 1966 that it would have a 25% share of that market by 1970, and that it would reach breakeven in 1968 (see January, 1966 Fiscal Plan, Exhibit 3).

By late 1966, SED revised its sales projections downward to reflect the longer-than-anticipated lead times for product development and market acceptance. However, SED still estimated that CMO could reach the breakeven level in fiscal 1968 (see Exhibit 4, Cash Flow Projections).

PERSONNEL

By mid-1966, Gailer's team had grown to 12, as shown in Figure 1.

Mr. Gailer had to prepare a Five Year Plan and submit a budget for 1967 to the SED Corporate Management Committee by November 1st. That plan had to include a detailed outline and justification of a specific strategy for bringing SED's expertise in microwave technology to bear profitably upon the industrial processing market.

FIGURE 1

Organization Chart,
July 1, 1966

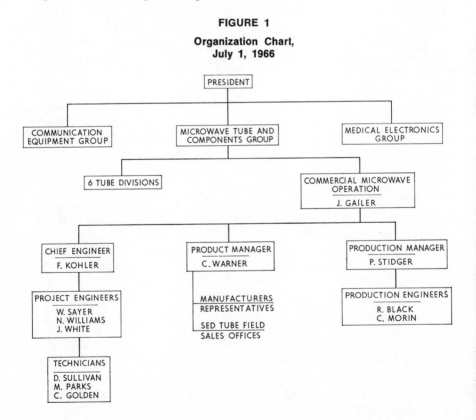

EXHIBIT 1

Market Opportunities
Based on the Study of Some Likely Industrial Applications*

	Number of Applications Investigated	Number of Applications That Appear to Be Economically Doubtful for Microwave	Number of Applications That Appear to Be Economically Promising for Microwave	Estimate† of Potential Microwave Market Millions of $
Mineral industries.................	4	3	1	15
Chemicals and allied products........	15	13	2	10
Primary metals industry............	3	3	0	
Food and kindred products..........	8	4	4	20
Paper and allied products‡..........	5	0	5	550
Lumber and wood products‡........	6	1	5	70
Textile mill products..............	3	1	2	10
Rubber and plastics products........	1	0	1	5
			Total	680

* Preliminary view from Jerut survey.
† Estimate of Potential Microwave Market figures are based on installed kilowatts. Only those applications that appear to be economically promising (column 3) are considered.
‡ Current marketing effort is concentrated mainly in these areas.
SOURCE: Standard Electronic Development, Inc.

EXHIBIT 2

Quotations and Orders by Application, Oct. 1965 through Aug. 1966
($000)

	Quotes		Orders	
	$	No.	$	No.
Chemical, plastic rubber, coatings....................	1,750	52	50	5
			Johnson Rubber	
			DuPont	
			Goldsworthy	
			Martin-Orlando	
Mineral, glass, ceramics..........	140	5	20	3
			Int'l Converters	
			State of California	
Thin film.....................	15	3	10	3
			Fairchild	
			Stanford Res. Inst.	
			Dyna Metric	
Forest products, paper............	710	26	6	5
			Weyerhaeuser	
Intracompany...................	15	7	5	4
			Microlink	
Other equipment manufac- turers......................	390	8	4	5
			Cryodry	
			Reeve	
			Comtek	
Food.........................	360	22	8	2
			U.S. Dept. Agriculture	
			Pet Milk	
Leather.......................	60	4	—	—
Undisclosed...................	60	7	—	—
Total..................	3,500		103	

EXHIBIT 3

Fiscal Plan
($000)

	Actual 1965	Projected 1966	1967	1968	1969	1970	Total through 1970
OPERATIONS:							
Sales......................	$ 0	$ 200	$ 600	$1,500	$3,000	$6,000	
R & D...................	150	300	200	200	200	300	
Other cost................	0	300	500	1,100	2,300	4,500	
Total................	$ 150	$ 600	$ 700	$1,300	$2,500	$4,800	
Net profit.................	$(150)	$(400)	$(100)	$ 200	$ 500	$1,200	
Net profit (after taxes).......	$(75)	$(200)	$(50)	$ 100	$ 250	$ 600	
ASSETS EMPLOYED (annual additions):							
Bldg. × Equip..............	$ 0	$ 160	$ 340	$ 440	$ 540	$ 600	
Working capital:							
Inventory...............	0	50	100	220	350	700	
Other...................	0	35	70	155	260	530	
Total....................	$ 0	$ 245	$ 510	$ 815	$1,150	$1,830	$4,550
CASH FLOW:							
(+) Assets acquired........	$ 0	$ 245	$ 510	$ 815	$1,150	$1,830	
(−) Operating P & L......	(75)	(200)	(50)	100	250	600	
(−) Depreciation (50%)....	0	10	30	60	90	130	
Cash required annually......	$ 75	$ 435	$ 530	$ 655	$ 810	$1,100	$3,605

RETURN ON INVESTMENT
Calculated using the discounted
cash flow method 16%

EXHIBIT 4

Cash Flow Projections
($000)

	Years 1 1965	2 1966	3 1967	4 1968	5 1969	10 1974
Sales......................	0	55	425	1,000	2,000	9,500
Incremental cost of sales excluding depreciation.....		73	335	665	1,220	5,984
Depreciation...............	8	17	26	35	40	96
Research & development.....	150	260	100	150	200	475
Other costs General administration.....	0	7	64	150	300	1,425
Profit before taxes...........	(150)	(302)	(100)	0	240	1,520
Net profit after taxes........	(75)	(151)	(50)	0	120	760
Add back depreciation.......	8	17	26	35	40	96
Net cash inflow (outflow)....	(67)	(134)	(24)	35	160	856

ROI—16% (A.T.)

Standard Electronic Development, Inc. Commercial Microwave Operation (B)

INTRODUCTION

In late 1968, SED's Commercial Microwave Operation was finally beginning to tap the large potential market for industrial microwave processing equipment. During the past two years a number of major developments had taken place: the market strategy had been shifted toward the end user and focused on a limited number of applications; the technical and economic feasibility of certain applications had been demonstrated; a new manager had been installed; the total CMO staff had grown to 45 people; a reorganization had shifted the CMO to the Equipment Group; and CMO was operating at or close to breakeven for the first time. Nevertheless, sales and profits had not expanded at the rate first envisioned by CMO—largely due to the slower-than-anticipated rate of market adoption and to an underestimation of initial engineering and manufacturing costs. Thus, the role of the new manager was to devise a strategy for more effectively translating CMO's efforts and resources into profitable sales.

ORGANIZATION

In 1968, CMO was removed from the Microwave Tube and Components Group and given project status in a newly created division of the Equipment Group, Industrial Systems Activity. In October 1968, Dr. George Emmanual was hired to head ISA and the expanding Commerical Microwave Operation. Dr. Emmanual had a Ph.D. degree in electrical engineering and had worked extensively in the research and development of the klystron tube and other high power microwave tubes. He had previously managed a highly successful klystron engineering and manufacturing profit center. It was felt that his recognized technical and managerial competence would be a significant asset to CMO. At the same time, Mr. Gailer was relieved of all administrative details so that he could concentrate upon applications for the forest products industry, an area in which he had much experience and competence.

The total CMO staff by the end of 1968 was 45 people: 4 in sales and marketing; 13 in the development and model shop; 18 in production; 9 in services; and the General Manager. The organization chart is shown in Figure 1.

FIGURE 1

Organization Chart,
Fall, 1968

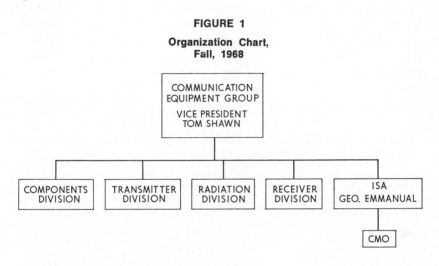

INDUSTRIAL SYSTEMS ACTIVITY (ISA)

The Industrial Systems Activity was established in 1968 to concentrate on systems having a significant content of equipment produced by divisions or operations making up the Equipment Group—where the division management considered the scope of the opportunity to be beyond the capability or interest of the division.

Tom Shawn, Vice President of the Group, described ISA this way:

There have been opportunities in the past, and we expect more in the future, to give customers a more complete system than lies within the competence of any one division. The attempt in ISA is to take a broader view of industrial systems opportunities. In this way we can enlarge SED's role in industrial equipment and develop new opportunities based upon an appropriate combination of our technologies.

ISA was established to achieve greater sales and exposure for CMO and the Equipment Group as a whole, and it was ultimately expected to reach a sales volume comparable to that of the other divisions in the Equipment Group.

COMPETITION

SED had developed numerous applications for industrial microwave processing and was expected to account for over one third of 1968 industry sales. Competitors had elected to limit their applications to specific fields. Varian was SED's strongest competitor due to its long time corporate interest in industrial microwave and its dominant position in microwave electron tubes. Raytheon had only recently entered the potato chip processing field. Litton was no longer a factor as it had shifted its interest from industrial to institutional and home applications. RCA had demonstrated an interest in freeze-drying and had the capability to make a strong entry. Smaller companies, such as Reeve and Comtek, were expected to make minor penetrations in specific fields. Except for Varian and perhaps RCA, SED did not anticipate any significant, across the board competition within the next four years.

Sales and areas of concentration in the industry are summarized below:

Competitor	1968 Sales (millions)	End Markets				
		Plastics	Paper	Wood	Food	Chemicals
SED	$1.3	X	X	X	X	X
Varian	1.1	X	X		X	
Cryodry	1.0	X		X	X	
Reeve	0.2	X				
RCA	0.1				X	
Genesys	0.05				X	
American Microwave	0.05				X	
Raytheon	0.4	X			X	
Comtek	—	X				

MARKETING STRATEGY

Although CMO's initial marketing thrust had been component sales to OEM's, the emphasis had shifted recently to sales of complete systems and services to end users. In order to create a market for microwave equipment, CMO found that it had to work closely with each customer and custom design each system to meet the unique requirements of a given process. While most of SED's competitors had adopted the approach of designing a single piece of equipment which they hoped to place in many applications, SED felt that its custom job-shop type of operation would ultimately pay off. Once the technical and economic feasibility of given applications could be established in an on-stream production line, competitive pressure within that industry was expected to force other industry factors to adopt microwave equipment.

Besides developing, manufacturing, and marketing industrial microwave systems and components, CMO made laboratory and pilot scale equipment and engineering services available either internally or externally to customers who wanted to test the feasibility of a process. CMO was willing to work with a customer on a number of bases: providing laboratory facilities and staff on a daily fee basis; arranging a joint venture to study and exploit a given process; or selling and leasing equipment for experimental use in the customer's own facilities.

Although CMO had explicitly stated its willingness to accept all commercially viable challenges, George Emmanual's initial thought was to "stop proliferating" and to limit efforts to the six applications which not only showed greatest promise of economic feasibility but also had some favorable operations history. These included poultry processing, plastic pipe production, pharmaceutical solvent extraction, polyurethane foam curing, doughnut proofing and baking, and crumb polymer drying.

The major challenge, as Dr. Emmanual saw it, was to convert these demonstrated applications into broad markets. Since SED had had little experience in this kind of selling, he thought that CMO would ultimately have to guarantee performance of process and equipment in order to penetrate beyond the relatively small pioneering sector of any given industry.

Dr. Emmanual felt that CMO should concentrate upon proving the cost and product advantages inherent in microwave processing. He argued that microwave equipment should not be developed unless its unique advantages made it capable of performing where conventional heating methods were inefficient, time consuming, or impractical. He did not regard microwave equipment as a general replacement for fossil-fuel energy sources, but rather as a supplemental heating system.

Sales were no longer handled by the tube field sales force since the reorganization which moved CMO out of the Tube and Components Group. However, that sales force had not proven to be effective for CMO and recent sales efforts had been handled entirely by CMO's staff. Dr. Emmanual had suggested that each manager within CMO be responsible for two or three major accounts.

PRODUCT AND MARKET DEVELOPMENT

In late 1967, CMO received a $511,000 order from Auto Seats, Inc. for a 210 KW on-stream installation for curing polyurethane foam car seats. The system was delivered and successfully producing 360 parts/hour by early 1968. Auto Seats, Inc. cited several advantages over the old hot air ovens, including two-thirds reduction in manufacturing space, improved product uniformity, two-thirds reduction in mold inventory, and two-thirds or more reduction in manufacturing labor. In the sales contract, CMO was responsible for thermodynamic and mechanical parameters, but was not responsible for the process. CMO expected follow-on orders from Auto Seats, Inc., for three more units and additional sales of $1–2 million from other automobile manufacturers in the next 1–2 year period.

CMO had also developed, built, and sold a system for curing epoxy-impregnated filament-wound pipe on a continuous basis to a European concern at a cost of $42,000. The system was curing pipe at four times the specification rate and greater production was limited by mechanical winding speed rather than curing capacity. Since the market for plastic pipe was growing rapidly and manufacturing methods were becoming highly competitive, CMO expected to sell at least ten units in 1969 at $40,000 each.

Another application in the plastics field was crumb polymer drying. CMO had sold a 90 KW, $150,000 pilot line to Interstate Oil in 1968, and anticipated additional sales of $600,000 in 1969.

CMO had also spent much time and money developing forest products applications, some on a joint venture basis. The most successful application to date had been drying tanoak wood (which was impractical by conventional methods) for baseball bat manufacture. A 30 KW installation was operating successfully, and CMO expected an order for a 120 KW installation (about $150,000) in 1969. All other forest products applications were still in the R & D stage and no major sales were anticipated within the near future.

The food processing industry also represented a large potential market. CMO's major effort here was poultry processing. Although no sales had yet been made, the company anticipated 1969 sales of $60,000. Other development work had been in grain drying, potato chip drying, and the cooking of bacon and shrimp. A pilot system for baking doughnuts had been installed at SSD Foods in 1967. Orders for production equipment totalling $150,000 were expected in 1969.

Another potential market appeared to be chemicals and ores, where microwave excited plasma techniques promised to drastically simplify processing sequences and thereby produce important economic advantages. Through its microwave chemistry development work, partially funded by SED's central research funds, CMO had sold $95,000 worth of laboratory equipment for use in a wide variety of possible applications, including pharmaceutical drying, ore processing, and plasma chemistry. Order prospects for these applications for 1969 were $400,000–$600,000.

JOINT VENTURES

CMO had placed increasing emphasis upon joint venture arrangements. Proprietary relationships were established with some of the principal manufacturers and users of process equipment. CMO's objective was to become the exclusive supplier of radio frequency modules (power supply, tube, and applicator) rather than to assume overall systems responsibility. This arrangement allowed SED to couple its microwave know-how with the partner's knowledge of customers and technical processes.

A jointly-funded program with Bechtel was currently underway for a pilot paper drying installation at Reginald Paper to determine design data for a full-scale production system. The first test program had been completed and preliminary results indicated satisfactory performance. Orders for such a system were expected to start in 1969. Costs for the microwave power and closely associated equipment for a 100 ton/day paper mill were projected at $500,000 to $1 million, with an industry potential for more than 100 units.

CMO also had undertaken a joint project with Moore-Oregon of Portland to study veneer and wood drying. CMO had invested $35,000 and Moore-Oregon $20,000 to complete a pilot installation. The advantages for veneer drying were unclear at this point; however, it was thought that specialty wood drying results might lead to 1969 sales.

Haida Industries and CMO were also jointly engineering the development of a system for continuous manufacture of plywood. Initial studies indicated no serious technical problems, and sales of production equipment were expected in 1969.

(See Exhibit 1 for a "Rate of Adoption" summary.)

FINANCIAL DATA

During CMO's first few years, most of its sales were to laboratory-type markets, i.e. for performing experiments to determine new processes or develop new products. Although this was a growing market, the sale of production equipment, characterized by large individual orders, was beginning to develop even more rapidly:

	Sales		Cost/Sales		Gross Profit	
	$000	%	$000	%	$000	%
FY 1968 Actual						
Production	782	60	588	61	194	58
Laboratory	515	40	375	39	140	42
Total	1,297	100	963	100	334	100
FY 1969 Budget						
Production	1,333	74	885	76	448	71
Laboratory	467	26	280	24	187	29
Total	1,800	100	1,165	100	635	100

CMO's long range goal was to generate orders in excess of $10 million in 1974 with an after tax return on assets in excess of 15%. (See Exhibits 2 and 3 for Statement of Income and Expenses, 1966–1973, and Sales Summary by Product, 1966–1973.)

*   *   *   *   *

George Emmanual's job, as the new General Manager of ISA and the CMO project, was to devise a total market strategy and a Three Year Plan that would increase the rate of adoption of microwave process equipment and effect a sales volume comparable to that of the other divisions in the Equipment Group.

EXHIBIT 1

Rate of Adoption

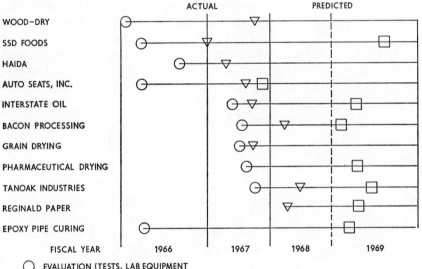

    ○ EVALUATION (TESTS, LAB EQUIPMENT
    ▽ ORDER PILOT EQUIPMENT
    ☐ ORDER PRODUCTION EQUIPMENT

EXHIBIT 2

Statement of Income and Expenses (FY ending 9/30)
($000)

	1966 Act.	1967 Act.	1968 Bud.	1968 Est.	1969	1970 Proj.	1971	1972	1973
Orders Entered............	$ 110	860	1,200	1,200	2,600	4,225	6,690	8,365	10,725
Sales (net)...............	55	315	900	1,200	2,050	3,475	5,250	7,280	9,450
Costs of Sales............	79	315	550	780	1,262	2,140	3,260	4,494	5,880
Gross Margin............	(24)	–0–	350	420	788	1,335	1,990	2,786	3,570
% of Sales...............	(44)	–0–	39	35	39	39	38	38	38
Mktg. Expense............	26	57	120	120	150	200	270	410	550
Proj. G & A.............	22	21	68	68	90	135	165	195	230
Grp. Corp G & A........	11	35	77	77	120	230	350	485	630
R & D Expense...........	280	134	130	130	180	250	335	480	610
Total Expense............	$ 339	247	395	395	540	815	1,120	1,570	2,020
Operating Profit..........	$(363)	(247)	(45)	25	248	520	870	1,216	1,550
Domestic Taxes..........	(181)	(124)	(23)	13	124	260	435	608	775
Net Income..............	(182)	(123)	(22)	12	139	260	435	608	775
% of Sales...............	(330)	(39)	(2)	1	6	7	8	8	8
Backlog.................	55	600	900	600	1,150	1,900	3,340	4,425	5,700
Assets Employed..........	208	485	791	820	1,127	1,728	2,543	3,405	4,360
Asset Turnover...........	0.5	0.7	1.1	1.5	1.8	2.0	2.1	2.1	2.2
After Tax Return on Assets Emp. %.......	(88)	(25)	(2)	1	11	15	17	18	18
R & D Expense % of Sales.............	510	43	14	11	9	7	6	6	6
Mktg. Expense % Ord. Entered........	24	7	13	10	5	4	4	4	5

EXHIBIT 3

Sales Summary by Product (FY year ending Sept. 30)
($000)

	1966 Act.	1967 Act.	1968 Est.	1969	1970	1971 Proj.	1972	1973
1. Low Power Catalog.........	55	175	200	280	360	440	500	600
2. 25 KW, 915 MHz...........	—	20	100	200	300	400	530	600
3. 30 KW, 2,450 MHz.........	—	60	550	840	1,240	1,760	2,370	3,100
4. 100 KW, 2,450 MHz........	—	—	—	—	300	600	800	900
5. 20 KW, 8 GHz.............	—	—	50	150	200	300	400	400
6. 25 KW, 5.8 GHz...........	—	—	—	40	100	200	400	600
7. Non-Microwave............	—	60	300	540	975	1,550	2,280	3,250
Total..................	55	315	1,200	2,050	3,475	5,250	7,280	9,450

NOTES:
a) Group 1 consists of laboratory scale equipment and waveguide items.
b) Groups 1 through 6 consist of power sources as indicated together with simple microwave applicators without conveying means.
c) Group 7 includes conveying means, and other system elements which include hot air, steam, gas and other energy handling means used in conjunction with microwaves. Also included is process instrumentation, systems design, installation and service.

Standard Electronic Development, Inc. Commercial Microwave Operation (C)

INTRODUCTION

Early in 1970 SED management was again reviewing its Commercial Microwave Operation in the hope of establishing a more effective marketing strategy for developing and penetrating the large potential market for industrial microwave processing equipment. More than ever SED management was convinced that such equipment was a technically and economically sound investment. The question remained, however, of how to communicate these facts to the end user.

DEVELOPMENTS IN 1969

When 1969 sales did not materialize as anticipated, SED began drastically reducing the R & D and overhead costs of CMO. In the first half of fiscal 1969, sales were $277,000 and after tax loss was $150,000. Second quarter sales were down 50% from the first quarter and inventories reached a high of $461,000.

Despite this deteriorating trend, Dr. Emmanual recommended that CMO be retained, at least temporarily, for two reasons: (1) the inventory would have little value without a marketing organization; and (2) the recent program of concentration on a few chosen applications, as well as the newly appointed Marketing Manager, George Vixen, should be given a chance to reverse the trend. Inventories were to be reduced to no more than $200,000 by year end and all non-sales costs eliminated. In mid-1969, with a total staff of 16, costs (labor, allocations, and expenses) were running approximately $55,000 per month. All of the marketing and engineering efforts were focused upon three applications, chicken processing, wood drying, and flexible packaging.

The forecast for second half orders was $600,000, including one system in each of the target areas. Unless at least two of the three orders materialized, a major retrenchment would have to be undertaken at the end of the fiscal year.

Total sales at year end (i.e., September) amounted to $500,000, but on October 1, 1969, CMO received an order for a $300,000 microwave chicken-cooking system. The system was scheduled for delivery in early 1970. At the same time George Vixen was promoted to General Manager of CMO.

Not only were CMO sales disappointing, the entire market for microwave processing equipment also declined. SED estimated that total industry sales were less than $1.9 million and that CMO had 40% of that market.

CURRENT POSITION

In March, 1970, CMO consisted of five men and one secretary. George Vixen was an electrical engineer who had worked for SED for 18 years on numerous projects concerned with high power electron tube technology. Dr. Carl Hansen, CMO Manager of Applications, held a Ph.D. in plant pathology and was considered an expert on the effects of microwave radiation on biological systems. He was largely responsible for the development and promotion of the poultry processing system. CMO also had two applications engineers and one technician. All of the men were spending half their time on promotional efforts.

Organizationally, CMO now reported to the Radiation Division of the Equipment Group. The Industrial Systems Activity did not develop successfully, largely due to the severe problems of CMO. Thus, ISA was eliminated when CMO was transferred to the Radiation Division. (See Figure 1 for the latest organization chart.)

The entire staff was devoting its efforts to sales in two proven applications, chicken processing and flexible packaging. Once the economic advantages were proven in a large scale field operation, George Vixen hoped that CMO could saturate these industries. He felt that a realistic potential for the chicken cooker was 20 units during the next four years, or $6 million. He also estimated the potential for power packs sold to food OEM's at 200 per year by 1973, or $600,000 per year. Although CMO was anxious to develop these markets, it was not willing to sell below cost.

CMO's research and development budget had been reduced to virtually zero. CMO's only R & D expenditures were for a joint venture with Guardian Packaging Corporation for the developing of a plastic film dryer for the flexible packaging industry. CMO's costs to continue the de-

FIGURE 1

**Organization Chart,
Spring, 1970**

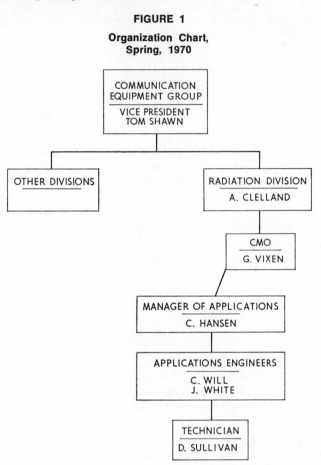

velopment were expected to total $30,000, but preliminary results looked promising and the potential market was practically unlimited.

Research on any other applications had to be financed by the customer on a per diem basis. SED made its facilities and engineers available to any serious customer who was willing to pay $360 per day for their use.

OBJECTIVES

The stated goals and strategies for fiscal 1970 were as follows:

1. To get orders totaling $500,000 by closing contracts on the chicken cooker.
2. To make shipments totaling $400,000 by completing the chicken cooker order and others.
3. To realize a gross profit of $140,000 (35% or sales) by careful cost control, particularly on salaries and services.
4. To have a clear outlook to fiscal 1971 orders of $1 million by con-

centrating on poultry, flexible packaging, and one other target industry.

5. To work out a low cost joint venture in the fast food industry by completing discussions with New York Canning.
6. To complete development of a plastic film dryer with Guardian Packaging by devoting all R & D to it.
7. To maintain a high level of customer contact, sufficient to support the budget for miscellaneous orders and shipments by continuing to meet customers on a broad front.

(See Exhibit 1 for FY 1970 Budget.)

In early March, 1970, Mr. Vixen was optimistic about CMO's performance and thought that the turnaround point might have been reached. In January, an order for $220,000 worth of equipment was received from Auto Seats, Inc., and the order outlook for the next six months exceeded that budgeted for the entire year. Furthermore, the chicken processing equipment had been delivered for installation and was expected to be in operation in April. CMO was anxious to have it operating successfully not only because the sales contract had called for graduated payments based on meeting performance requirements but also because many other potential customers for poultry processing equipment had been awaiting the results before making any commitments.

* * * * *

A Three-Year Outlook for the Commercial Microwave Operation was due by April 1st. Although CMO appeared to be near the turning point, George Vixen was not certain that the present marketing strategy was the best for profitable development of the industrial microwave processing market. (See Exhibit 2 for financial status as of the end of February, 1970.)

EXHIBIT 1
Budget, FY 1970
($000)

	Orders	Shipments	Gross Profit
October	8	124	31
November	8	4	1
December	9	4	1
January	8	4	1
February	8	4	1
March	59	129	31
April	308	4	1
May	8	4	1
June	9	34	31
July	8	54	9
August	8	4	1
September	59	35	31
Total	500	404	140

EXHIBIT 2

Income Statement and Performance Report, February, 1970
($000)

	Year-to-Date	
	Budget	*Actual*
Sales		
Chicken cooker.................	120.0	128.0
Other........................	20.0	67.0
Total....................	140.0	195.0
Cost of Sales		
Chicken cooker.................	90.0	113.0
Other........................	15.0	52.0
Total....................	105.0	165.0
Gross Profit		
Chicken cooker.................	30.0	15.0
Other........................	5.0	15.0
Total....................	35.0	30.0
Other Costs		
Marketing.....................	51.0	66.0
Admin. alloc...................	—	5.0
Controller alloc................	—	2.5
Corporate alloc................	10.0	10.0
Safety and purch. alloc...........	—	2.5
Total M. G. and A...........	61.0	86.0
Pretax profit on operations..........	(26.0)	(59.0)
Other income...................	—	6.0
Total pretax profit................	(26.0)	(53.0)
Tax...........................	(13.0)	(27.0)
Net profit.......................	(13.0)	(26.0)

Beneficiadora de Cafe S.A.

Mr. Enrique Lopez, vice-president of marketing for Beneficiadora de Cafe S.A., a firm in Monterrey, Mexico, was asked by the president of the company, Mr. Manual Garcia, to develop a marketing program for 1964. It was to be submitted to the board of directors at their meeting on August 23, 1963, only six weeks away. Mr. Lopez realized the company's very survival could well depend upon the program adopted.

Beneficiadora de Cafe's only product, BECA brand instant coffee, had first been placed on the Monterrey market three and one-half years earlier in January 1960. The unprofitability of these three and one-half years was largely due to the intense requirements of promotional competition. For 1964, the company had only MP$800,000 available for promotional purposes. Additional expenditures for promotion would have to be supported either by bank loans, at 15% per year on the unpaid balance, or a bond issue at an annual rate of interest of 8 to 10%.

Mr. Garcia had suggested that funds be borrowed in order to finance promotional expenditures of MP$300,000 per month.[1] He estimated that this level of expenditure was required if the company was to maintain national distribution and its market share of 8%. Mr. Garcia, who owned majority interest in Beneficiadora de Cafe, argued that this was the only course of action open to the company if it was to prevent foreign competition from gaining complete control of the Mexican coffee market. "We gained our present market share by hard work and much financial sacrifice," he maintained, "and I want to continue the fight until that investment pays off."

Mr. Lopez was of a different opinion. He favored a more conservative approach, based on consolidating the company's market position in Monterrey. He visualized a program which would incorporate three major features. First, the company would curtail distribution beyond the metro-

[1] In this case, MP$ means Mexican pesos. One peso is equivalent to 8 U.S. cents. One U.S. dollar equals 12.5 pesos.

185

politan area of Monterrey City. Second, the company would add to its regular line a new package size, containing enough coffee for 15 cups (28 grams). This package, to be made of either aluminum or polyethylene plastic, would retail for one peso. The company had previously featured this package in a one-time "15 cups for one peso" promotion, but it was not a permanent part of the product line in 1963. The third feature of the program which Mr. Lopez advocated was an MP$50,000 per month promotional budget, which would have as its sole purpose the promotion of the new "one peso" package to the lower and lower-middle socioeconomic groups in Monterrey.

Mr. Lopez stated that this strategy would be short-lived and that its primary purpose was to put the company in a better position to compete successfully in the national market over the long run. In response to the president's plan for a frontal attack on the major competitors, Mr. Lopez replied: "It would look like a fight between a heavyweight and a featherweight. We are better advised to stay out of the ring for the time being and come in when they are tired."

BACKGROUND INFORMATION ON BENEFICIADORA DE CAFE S.A.

At the beginning of 1958, the principal stockholders of Cafes del Norte S.A., a firm established in 1940, in Monterrey, Mexico, voted to establish a new firm to be known as Beneficiadora de Cafe S.A. This new company would produce and market a new brand of instant coffee, BECA. Cafes del Norte S.A. had been very successful with three brands of "substitute" coffee.

Substitute coffee is a mixture of coffee and other materials, such as chick-peas and beans. The proportion of non-coffee is always less than 40% of the total weight, and the formula used must be approved by the government. A complete listing of the contents of the product, and the proportions of each additive, must be specified on the package label. Substitute coffee had achieved good consumer acceptance, especially among the lower and lower-middle socioeconomic classes. The reasons for the widespread acceptance of substitute coffee included: (1) its lower price (about 50% of regular coffee prices); (2) the belief of many heavy coffee drinkers that it did not produce the ill effects attributed to regular coffee; and (3) the custom of adding coffee to milk in order to combine milk's health benefits with coffee's pleasant taste.

In 1959, Cafes del Norte's three brands of substitute coffee had an estimated 28% of total coffee sales in Monterrey. (This was the equivalent of 35% of ground coffee sales, which were 80% of total coffee sales.) Instant coffee sales accounted for about 20% of the Monterrey market. (All instant coffee was 100% coffee.) In small rural Mexican towns, it was estimated that substitute coffee accounted for 70 to 80% of all coffee consumed. In Monterrey, it was estimated that substitute coffee accounted for between 50 and 60% of *all* coffee sales.

Sales of Cafes del Norte's three brands of substitute coffee were concentrated in the lower and lower-middle socioeconomic classes who represented about 60% of the total families in urban regions and about 80% in rural sections. Monthly incomes for these families were less than MP$1,500.00. Table 1 presents estimates of the distribution of the population of the Monterrey market by income group.

The success of Cafes del Nortes' three brands of substitute coffee was attributed by the company's executives to promotional efforts consisting primarily of in-package coupons which offered a prize depicted on the coupon. Because not all packages contained coupons offering prizes, the consumers did not know if the purchased package contained a prize cou-

TABLE 1

The Monterrey Market

Income Class	Monthly Income (in '000 pesos)	% of Total Population	Number of People
a) Upper.....................	5.0 and above	4.9	35,550
b) Upper-middle...............	3.0 to 5.0	10.1	73,275
c) Middle....................	1.5 to 3.0	25.0	181,375
d) Lower-middle...............	0.5 to 1.5	45.0	326,475
e) Lower....................	Below 0.5	15.0	108,825
Total........................			725,500

SOURCE: Estimated by BECA S.A. management from various sources. The management believed that the characteristics of the population in the Monterrey market were similar to the ones of urban Mexican markets which were comprised of about 40% of the total population of Mexico.

pon until the package was opened. This promotional device was therefore somewhat like a contest or lottery. The prizes offered were of medium value and included movie tickets, home furnishings such as tables and chairs, household items such as kitchen pots and pans, bed linens, and so on. Consumers exchanged the coupons found inside the packages for the indicated prizes at a redemption center, maintained by Cafes del Norte in Monterrey.

COMPETITION IN THE MONTERREY MARKET BEFORE BECA'S INTRODUCTION

The new product of Beneficiadora de Cafe, BECA, was directed to the higher-income market which included the upper, upper-middle, and middle socioeconomic groups. When the company introduced BECA into this higher-income segment of the Monterrey market, executives of Beneficiadora de Cafe knew that they would be facing two competitors.

IMESA brand instant coffee had been introduced into the Mexican market shortly after the Second World War by Internacional Mexicana S.A. This company, which did business all over the world, also sold several complementary lines of food products, including canned milk and cream, powdered milk and cream, powdered chocolate, and chocolate bars. Although IMESA's main offices were in Europe, its Mexican offices were in Mexico City. The company held a strong financial position and a healthy share of the market. In 1959, IMESA's share of the instant coffee market in Monterrey and throughout Mexico was estimated to be 92%.

Cafeteros Asociados S.A., the other competitor, held an estimated 8% of the instant coffee market in 1959. This firm, established in 1956 by some members of the National Association of Coffee Growers, produced and marketed only one product, CASA brand instant coffee. Executives of BECA believed that CASA had neither the financial strength nor the marketing power of IMESA.

In 1959, the BECA management estimated the total Mexican market at about 80,000 cases per month, of which probably 5,000 were distributed in Monterrey. This information was based on estimated production and discussions with various retailers and wholesalers. Instant coffee was sold in two sizes, 170 grams (6 oz.) and 56 grams (2 oz.). A case contained 12 bottles of 170 grams or 30 bottles of 56 grams and was sold to retailers for MP\$160.20. It was estimated that 75% of total instant coffee sales were made in the large (170 grams) size and 25% in the smaller size.

Both CASA and IMESA had traditionally sold at the same prices and with the same margins. Retail sales prices established by both IMESA and CASA were MP\$13.50 for the 170 gram bottle, and MP\$5.40 for the smaller size.[2] Although the price to the consumer and the list price to the retailer were almost equal, in actual practice the retailers paid only MP\$157 per case because they were always given a 2% cash discount, even though some sales were made on credit. (Most sales to retailers were on a strictly cash basis.) This allowed the retailer a margin of only MP\$5 per case.

IMESA sold only on a cash basis (except to a few very large buyers), whereas CASA offered the 2% cash discount for payment within 30 days. Both producers granted wholesalers a functional discount of 5%. Additional quantity discounts were obtainable from both sellers for the 170-gram-bottle cases, according to the following schedule, in which all prices quoted were *f.o.b. city of destination.*

Over the years, IMESA had been supported by a continuous advertising effort. Executives of BECA estimated that, before they entered the market, IMESA advertising expenditures in the Mexican market averaged one million pesos per month during the months of August through March,

---

[2] Regular ground coffee sold at MP\$12–MP\$20 per kilo and substitute ground coffee at MP\$6–MP\$8 per kilo. A kilo of ground coffee would make 110 cups of coffee at average strength.

Size of Order (Cases)	Discount on Cases Ordered (%)	Per Case Price after Discounts (including 2% Cash Discount)
5	2	MP$153.80
50	5	MP$149.00
100	7	MP$145.80
500	10	MP$141.00
2,500	14	MP$134.60

and 850,000 pesos from April through July, the latter being months of relatively low coffee sales. The main appeals used in the IMESA advertising were prestige, quality, and adaptability to Mexican tastes, achieved during more than 20 years of experience. Because virtually no *national* advertising media were available in Mexico, IMESA used local media, and advertising budgets were allocated to different metropolitan markets according to past sales and local market potentials. In the larger cities, such as Mexico City, Guadalajara, and Monterrey, advertising expenditures were allocated among the various local media as follows:

	Percent
Radio	40
Newspapers	30
Television	20
Other (movies, outdoor, etc.)	10

Cafeteros Asociados, on the other hand, had not pursued an aggressive or continuous advertising effort to promote the CASA brand. CASA's promotional dealings, either at the consumer or retailer level, were almost insignificant. A small public relations effort was directed mainly to large buyers. CASA's promotions and deals were not conducted on a national scale, as were IMESA's, but were confined to isolated markets. CASA's promotional activities were believed to be largely a matter of bargaining between buyers and CASA's salesmen. Although CASA did not have the strong *brand image* of IMESA, the CASA salesmen had been very successful in gaining acceptance with small retail accounts. For this reason, CASA was much stronger in the smaller retail outlets than in the larger accounts. BECA executives estimated, however, that IMESA outsold CASA in the typical small retail store five-to-one.

Beneficiadora de Cafe S.A. originally planned to enter the instant coffee market on a market-by-market basis. The first market to receive attention was the metropolitan area of Monterrey, where the parent company enjoyed a favorable reputation among consumers, retailers, wholesalers, and advertising media. BECA's ultimate goal was to obtain a sales level of 2,000 cases per month, 40% of the total Monterrey instant coffee market.

BECA's initial marketing strategies were to:

1. Produce and market a product of superior quality. Company officials believed that they had the best instant coffee, at least with respect to its formula and production process.
2. Sell this superior product at the same retail price as competing brands.
3. Use the same marketing channels as competitors but place more emphasis on personal selling (at least in the introductory stages) to retailers, who were favorably oriented toward the parent company and its salesmen.
4. Invest in intensive introductory advertising and sales promotion directed to both consumers and retailers.

MONTERREY MARKET ACTIVITY AFTER BECA INTRODUCTION: 1960 TO 1963

In the third week of January 1960, the BECA brand instant coffee was introduced into the Monterrey market. BECA was introduced in both the large size (170 grams) and the small size (56 grams). Additionally, smaller packages containing enough instant coffee for one cup were introduced for use in coffee shops and restaurants. They were also used for promotional purposes, especially consumer sampling.

The strategy followed by BECA was approximately the same as that followed by its principal competitors, IMESA and CASA. BECA, however, relied more heavily upon advertising and introductory personal selling directly to the retailer, than had characterized competitors' previous marketing activities. Selling prices to the consumer, retailer, and wholesaler were set at the level established by competition. As part of its introductory offer, BECA offered retailers a 2% cash discount if they paid for their initial orders within 30 days.

Under an agreement which had been reached with the sales manager of Cafes del Norte, the sales force for Beneficiadora de Cafe was recruited from the Cafes del Norte sales force. This sales force was to be assigned first to the Monterrey area. When BECA moved into other market areas, one or more salesmen would be relocated. Replacements for the men moved out of Monterrey would be recruited from outside of the company. BECA obtained eight salesmen and two sales supervisors from the Cafes del Norte sales force. These men were regarded by Mr. Lopez as "the best coffee salemen available in the country," in part because they had important contacts with retail and wholesale buyers in the Monterrey market. The sales supervisors, who also did some selling, reported directly to Mr. Lopez. Salesmen were paid MP$1,500 per month plus a 5% commission on sales.

During the first year of BECA's introduction, the company spent an average of MP$100,000 per month on advertising and sales promotion. The media used were radio, newspapers, television, movies, and point-of-

SOURCE: J. Walter Thompson de Mexico, S.A., *The Mexican Market*, 1963, p. 121.

purchase displays. Expenditures were allocated among these various media in substantially the same proportion as IMESA's expenditures, with radio receiving 40%, newspapers 30%, etc.[3] The main themes of BECA's introductory advertising campaign were quality, nationality, and novelty. During the first three months of the new product introduction, BECA used full-page advertisements on alternate days in the two major newspapers of Monterrey. *Saturation spot* advertising was used in both radio and television. The sales force attempted to set up point-of-purchase displays in every retail outlet. Finally, BECA had a 12-minute motion picture presentation, which appeared in every movie theater in Monterrey and surrounding towns.

All of the management and purchasing representatives of the wholesale grocery trade and the larger retail accounts were invited to dine at the BECA factory and to tour the plant to see its complete operations. Every small grocery in Monterrey was visited by salesmen, supervisors, and even top-management executives. Some grocers were invited to visit the plant, and special luncheons for this purpose were held every day, in the factory dining room, during the introductory three-month period.

As competitors observed the introductory promotion of BECA, they reacted differently. CASA did not take any retaliatory steps, and their sales efforts remained unchanged. IMESA adopted a more aggressive approach and fought BECA almost from the very beginning of its entry into the Monterrey market. Neither the approach taken by IMESA nor the strength of the IMESA efforts had been properly anticipated by the executives of BECA and their consultants.

As soon as IMESA learned that BECA had started to contact retailers and to place advertising messages in the various media, a complete IMESA marketing *task force* left the central offices in Mexico City for Monterrey. Knowing that BECA would be entering the market, IMESA had carefully planned this move and had developed a comprehensive counter-strategy. The Mexican general manager for IMESA, the marketing manager, the sales supervisors, and at least 10 specially trained salesmen formed the IMESA task force.

The first step in the counter-strategy of IMESA was to attack the stronghold of BECA's marketing, the retailers. This they did with sales promotions and deals which were financially very attractive to the trade as well as to the consumer. Up to that time, IMESA had sold only on a *cash in advance* or *cash on delivery* basis. IMESA's wholesalers were responsible for extending credit to retailers. During the retaliatory period, almost every retailer was visited by the IMESA staff, no matter what the size of its account, and was offered, either directly by IMESA or indirectly through the wholesaler serving that account, 30 days to pay the net invoice value of purchases, irrespective of quantity. Whenever retailers

[3] In Monterrey City, 87% of all families had radios, and 33% had television sets in their homes.

were late in paying, IMESA took no action, and the *net* was extended to 60 and even 90 days in some cases. This change in policy was designed to encourage retailers to stock and display IMESA, regardless of their financial ability to pay for the merchandise.

Every small and medium-sized retailer was given a *free* case of IMESA instant coffee for every five cases displayed. Larger retailers and wholesalers were offered new prices ranging from 10 to 15% lower than formerly, from the initial date of the retaliation campaign to an indefinite terminal date. A special task force was employed to *demonstrate* and offer free cups of coffee in supermarkets, department stores, groceries, and at all types of conventions and meetings.

IMESA advertising budgets were also increased by at least 100% in the Monterrey area, with emphasis on such appeals as *proven quality by Mexican taste*, prestige, etc. Sales promotions directed to ultimate consumers by IMESA in 1960 were numerous. Among them were the following:

1. *A Two for One* deal. For the regular price of MP$13.50 for one 170-gram jar, a smaller 56-gram jar was given free of charge.
2. A *Coffee and Cream* deal. For every purchase of a 170-gram bottle, a can of IMESA condensed milk was given free.

BECA, with its smaller resources, had not expected this strong competition, but did its best to compete by using similar practices. Their promotional and selling visits to retailers were increased both in number and in the amount of time spent on each sales call. Some retailers, who at the beginning of the period were overstocked with IMESA, refused to handle BECA. BECA sales personnel, however, used all means of persuasion available, and, in Mr. Lopez's opinion, an *acceptable* degree of distribution was achieved. The strong reputation of the products of the parent company, Cafes del Norte, facilitated this difficult task.

Advertising efforts by BECA were increased above the planned levels, but were still considerably lower than IMESA expenditures. BECA's main promotional theme was *Our Best Deal to You: Quality*. After several months of concentrating on the ultimate consumer, BECA shifted its promotional efforts to the retailer, although a strong consumer effort was still maintained. During 1960 and the first part of 1961, several consumer promotional campaigns were conducted, including the following:

1. A *Two for One* deal. This was similar to the IMESA *Two for One* promotion but was initiated prior to the IMESA deal. In other words, IMESA had copied the BECA *Two for One* promotion.
2. An *Introductory Price* deal. This promotion was started in the spring of 1960, three months after BECA had entered the market.
3. A *Cups for Your Coffee* promotion. Included with the standard 170-gram jar of BECA instant coffee were a cup and small saucer.
4. A *Coffee and Sugar* promotion. Every bottle of 170 grams was ac-

companied by a polyethylene bag which contained 1 kilo (2.2 lbs.) of first-quality refined sugar.

In June 1961, the marketing manager of BECA, Mr. Lopez, received the results of a market survey, conducted for the company among 150 families in the city of Monterrey (see Exhibit 1). The study found that 25% of the respondents purchased instant coffee as a *favored brand* and that five respondents favored IMESA, to every one respondent who favored BECA. Of those people who had purchased BECA, 25% gave *taste* as their major buying reason, and 22% gave *curiosity.* Of all respondents, 38% purchased coffee most frequently in a supermarket,[4] 32% in a grocery store, and 25% through a *despensa.*[5]

From the summer of 1961 to the summer of 1962, several changes occurred in the competitive situation including the following:

1. Sales of BECA improved slightly, mainly at the expense of CASA. The location of BECA's production facilities in the Monterrey area and the familiarity of the residents of Monterrey with the company were believed to be major reasons for this slight improvement.
2. By the summer of 1962, BECA had been introduced nationally. Expansion to national distribution was achieved by adding 12 salesmen and 3 sales supervisors to the sales force. Each of these men was given some experience in the Monterrey market before being transferred to another area. Media advertising expenditures in areas other than Monterrey were very low. BECA management hoped that the promotional battle in Monterrey could be financed, in part, by earnings on sales made in outlying areas without advertising. BECA was also being sold to foreign markets. The major export markets were those of Northern Europe. Some export sales carried the BECA label; others were unbranded.
3. Several new brands of instant coffee entered the Mexican market.

---

[4] In Monterrey, the three large supermarket chains, which consisted of over four units each, were supplemented by a number of smaller chains and independents. Supermarkets were common in the large Mexican cities (found in all 45 Mexican cities of over 50,000 inhabitants). Generally, these supermarkets appealed to the middle, upper-middle, and upper classes (see Table 1). The largest chain in the country (30 units) was located in Mexico City.

[5] *Despensa Familiar* is a system by which a marketing intermediary, frequently an established wholesaler, signs a contract with a business firm to assume the responsibility for providing an assortment of grocery products to the employees of that firm on a weekly, biweekly, or monthly basis, as stipulated in the contract, at a *wholesale* price, with the understanding and agreement of the recipient that the amount of purchase will be deducted from his next pay check. The wholesaler is reimbursed by the business firm in a single transaction. A list is given to the employees by the marketer, which includes a group of products, one or more brands of each, from which the employee can select the grocery products which he wants to receive. There is no minimum, but a maximum according to a family size and salary. It is estimated that about 30,000 families in the Monterrey area have this service through their place of employment.

Virtually all of them carried a relatively lower consumer price. None of these new products were supported by extensive promotional efforts, although most of them did have somewhat larger retail and wholesale margins. The market did not appear to be receptive to these brands. Two of these brands were produced by IMESA and one by CASA. Two others were introduced by marginal producers.

4. Promotional efforts of both IMESA and BECA were reduced, but in the summer of 1962 these efforts were still of major size. BECA's expenditures in 1962 averaged MP$75,000 per month; IMESA's were estimated at twice that by BECA management. Retailers were the target of most of these promotions.

In the fall of 1962, Compania Mundial S.A. began selling a new brand of instant coffee to the Mexican market. This brand, KAFE, which already enjoyed a large share of the U.S. market, was now produced in Mexico. At the time of its introduction, KAFE was expected to constitute a major competitive threat to IMESA, because of its reputation as an international-firm, high-quality product. It was estimated that IMESA enjoyed an 80% share of the instant coffee market at the time of the introduction of KAFE.

In October 1962, IMESA started a new consumer promotion in the form of a lottery to be held in 1963. Advertisements publicizing the lottery announced: *Two million pesos in prizes!! 50 new automobiles to be given away including 10 Mercedes-Benz!! 2,500 additional prizes!!* The Mexican people's favorable attitude toward lotteries had been repeatedly demonstrated by the success of the Loteria Nacional, a lottery sponsored by the Federal Government of Mexico to raise funds for public welfare purposes. In the IMESA lottery, tickets would not be purchased, but would be given in exchange for labels from jars of IMESA instant coffee. One label from a 170-gram jar of IMESA instant coffee could be exchanged for one lottery ticket; labels from the smaller-sized jars could be exchanged at proportionately higher rates.

A very large advertising budget supported the IMESA lottery promotion. The executives of BECA estimated that IMESA spent ten million pesos from October 1962 to March 1963 on this campaign, five times the value of the prizes offered. By March 31, 1963, the end of the winter season, when coffee sales were at their highest, virtually every citizen of Monterrey knew about the IMESA lottery.

In order to achieve a greater promotional effect in Monterrey, IMESA sponsored a special one-hour televised program on two local channels in April 1963, during which regional prizes were distributed to the holders of the lucky lottery tickets. Seven automobiles were given away on this television show.

While the IMESA lottery promotion was in progress, IMESA's competitors did very little except to sit back and watch, for none could afford the expenditures required to match such a promotional effort. Mr. Lopez thought that if any product other than IMESA had been sold off the retail shelf during this period, it was BECA. In the course of this six-month period, a two-months shortage of first-quality sugar had occurred, and BECA still had its *Coffee and Sugar* promotion in operation.

In April 1963, after the conclusion of the IMESA lottery promotion, BECA launched a new promotion called the *Summer Deal*, which offered the consumer a price reduction on the 170-gram jar of BECA, from MP$13.50 to MP$9.95. BECA's monthly peso sales increased slightly as a result. In the same month, IMESA marketed a new product, *IMESA Express*, which was not successful. In May 1963, BECA introduced a small aluminum bag package and featured the promotional message: *15 cups of the best coffee for only MP$1.00.* This packaging innovation in the Mexican instant coffee market increased BECA sales among middle and lower-middle income groups.

Also in May 1963, Compania Mundial S.A., marketers of KAFE, merged with Cafeteros Asociados S.A., marketers of CASA, but this action had no noticeable effect on the marketing programs of either brand. No special promotions of CASA or KAFE were made during this period. BECA executives believed that the merged companies would produce primarily for the export market.

In June 1963, BECA started another promotion. This was an in-package coupon campaign. The consumer who purchased a jar with a lucky coupon inside would receive a prize. The prize to be given was described on the coupon. Prizes ranged from a free 170-gram jar of BECA instant coffee to such large appliances as refrigerators and stoves.

In early July 1963, IMESA announced its *Second Grand Lottery*, which now included prizes worth more than three million pesos. Another manufacturer, Chavela Products, cooperated in this promotion. The Chavela line of products included instant soups, canned jams and jellies, chilis, and other canned foods. Labels from specified Chavela Products packages as well as IMESA labels could be exchanged for lottery tickets. Altogether, more than 15 combinations of labels could be exchanged for a lottery ticket, for example, three instant soups, or one large IMESA, or one small IMESA and two instant soups, etc.

Mr. Lopez received the results of another market study in July 1963, based on interviews among 100 families, using a quota sample, in Monterrey (see Exhibit 2). Forty respondents indicated that they purchased instant coffee more frequently than ground coffee; six of these respondents said that BECA was their favorite brand, compared to 32 for IMESA.

Early in July 1963, Mr. Lopez reviewed the events of the past three years in preparation for developing the BECA marketing strategy for the coming year. He hoped to be able to develop a marketing program that would effectively compete with IMESA's, as well as provide a sound basis for competing with the KAFE-CASA combination, should the latter develop a new and aggressive marketing approach. The program's sales goals were to sell 2,500 cases per month in the Monterrey market. He expected that sales in July 1963, would not exceed 1,200 cases and estimated that the total instant coffee market in Monterrey had increased from 5,000 cases in early 1960, to between 7,500 to 8,000 cases per month in 1963.

Mr. Lopez knew that any marketing program which he submitted would have to convince Mr. Garcia that the company could not reasonably borrow funds to continue fighting IMESA on a national scale. At the same time, Mr. Lopez recognized that his own strategy involved a high risk, since an increased share of the Monterrey market would also have to come at the expense of IMESA. He hoped, however, that the smaller package, aimed primarily at the lower-income groups, would reach a market segment where retaliation by IMESA would be less certain.

Mr. Lopez was also considering making two other recommendations to Mr. Garcia. The first involved the possibility of selling through the *despensa familiar* system. The second would be the recommendation that the company offer private labels to major customers throughout Mexico. If the latter course of action was followed, he argued, the company could maintain its level of national distribution, while virtually eliminating promotional expenditure.

Mr. Lopez was still not certain of the final course of action to recommend. He did know, however, that the plant was capable of producing up to five times as much instant coffee as his organization had been selling.

Questions for Discussion

1. Evaluate the marketing strategy of BECA over the past three years. What was the company's underlying strategy?
2. Develop a marketing program for 1964 for BECA.

EXHIBIT 1

Results of June 1961 Market Survey

A. *Questions asked of all respondents*

    1. Does anyone in your family consume coffee?
        (a) Yes 97.4%
        (b) No 2.6*

    2. What is your favorite brand of coffee?
        Instant:
        (a) IMESA 20.0%
        (b) BECA 4.0
        (c) CASA 1.3
        Regular:
        (a) Cafes del Norte (3 brands) 24.7%
        (b) Other 50.0

    3. Who drinks more coffee at home?
        (a) husband 45.3%
        (b) wife 26.7
        (c) no difference 28.0

    4. When is coffee consumed at home?
        (a) breakfast 96.0%
        (b) lunch 37.3
        (c) dinner 86.6
        (d) other times 60.0

    5. How is coffee consumed?
        (a) black 31.3%
        (b) in milk 46.0
        (c) both black and in milk 20.0
        (d) no response 2.7

    6. Where do you most frequently purchase coffee?
        (a) supermarket 38.0%
        (b) grocery 32.0
        (c) despensa 24.7
        (d) other 5.3

B. *Questions asked of all instant coffee purchasers.*

    1. Why do you purchase instant coffee?
        (a) ease of use 56.0%
        (b) other reasons 44.0

    2. Which size do you purchase most frequently?
        (a) 170 grams 84.2%
        (b)   56 grams 15.8

    3. How long does a jar of instant coffee last?
        (a) less than one week 5.3%
        (b) one week 47.4
        (c) two weeks 28.9
        (d) three weeks 13.1
        (e) one month or more 5.3

* If the respondent answered *No* to this question, the interview was terminated at this point. Out of 154 families interviewed, four respondents answered *No*. The remaining 150 interviews provided the basis for the other questions.

C. *Questions asked of respondents who indicated that they had purchased either BECA or IMESA at least once.*

   1. What was your major reason for buying IMESA?
       (a) taste................................. 28.3%
       (b) habit................................. 20.0
       (c) easy to use........................... 18.3
       (d) other................................. 33.4

   2. What was your major reason for buying BECA?
       (a) taste................................. 25.0%
       (b) curiosity............................. 22.0
       (c) other................................. 53.0

D. The sample consisted of 154 families (150 of which included at least one coffee user). This sample was selected through the use of area probability sampling techniques. Families in the sample were distributed among five socioeconomic groups as follows:

	Number	Percentage
Upper	2	1.3
Upper-middle	9	5.8
Middle	68	44.2
Lower-middle	60	38.9
Lower	15	9.7

E. It was noted by the research team that some people referred to *all* instant coffee as "IMESA," and the new BECA product was frequently called "BECA IMESA."

EXHIBIT 2

Results of July 1963 Market Survey

A. *Questions asked of all respondents.*

1. Which brand of coffee do you purchase most frequently?
    Instant:
    (a) IMESA............................ 32%
    (b) BECA............................. 6
    (c) KAFE............................. 1
    (d) CASA............................. 1
    Regular:
    (a) Cafes del Norte (3 brands).............. 28%
    (b) other................................. 32

2. Where do you most frequently purchase coffee?
    (a) supermarket......................... 30%
    (b) despensa............................ 31
    (c) other.............................. 39

3a. How many people in your household?
    Average: 6.00

3b. How many of them drink coffee?
    Average: 5.13

B. Each of the families interviewed was classified in one of four socioeconomic groups. Analysis of responses according to socioeconomic group is presented below.

	Upper and Upper-Middle (N = 12)	Middle (N = 29)	Lower-Middle (N = 37)	Lower (N = 22)
Average monthly expenditure on coffee (MP$)..............................	50.24	36.80	27.88	21.71
Purchase IMESA.......................	67%	55%	11%	18%
Purchase BECA.......................	8%	3%	5%	9%
Purchase CASA.......................	0%	3%	0%	0%
Purchase at least one Cafes del Norte brand............................	0%	0%	41%	50%

This chart is interpreted as follows: The average monthly expenditures for coffee of a family in the middle socioeconomic group was MP$36.80; of respondents in the lower-middle socioeconomic group, 11% reported that they purchased IMESA, 5% reported that they purchased BECA, and so on.

C. *Instant coffee users were asked the following question.*

1. Which size do you purchase most frequently?
    (a) 170 grams............................ 80%
    (b)   56 grams............................ 20%

SECTION III

PRODUCT AND PRODUCT LINE

Hardy Toilet Soap

Handle-Soap was the latest and most promising of the projects in which Guy Hardy, a free lance engineer-designer, had been involved. A mechanical engineer by training, Hardy had always been interested in creative activities. In fact, he hoped that he might someday start his own engineering company with the specific objective of inventing and developing new products. The several products that Hardy had worked on before his development of Handle-Soap had never been entirely successful. On one occasion he developed a product improvement that seemed to have substantial potential but he could not convince manufacturers to change their production to this design. The improvement apparently was not a significant one as far as the consumers' subjective reaction to its use was concerned.

For over five years Hardy had been interested in improving the conventional cake of toilet soap. He had several ideas for accomplishing this and made up a few samples. Primarily he wanted to eliminate soap waste. Of secondary interest was providing a better grip on the soap cake. After considering several new ideas Hardy finally decided to make up a few samples based on an earlier but untried idea. The idea represented quite a radical departure from the conventional concept of a toilet soap bar; it was a round soap cake with an attached handle of new and unusual concept. The product proved rather difficult to make, but the finally completed samples were tried out by several of Hardy's friends. Despite the crudeness of the design, the idea appeared to have real merit. It took several months to improve the design further, to build semi-production molds, and to produce more samples; then to reappraise the past design, to evolve a new theory of design, and to test numerous new designs before achieving a near-optimum product-form.

The final test model could be clasped comfortably and securely between two adjacent fingers with little effort. An important feature of this design was that the single using surface of the cake remained approximately constant in area regardless of how much of the cake was worn away in use. There was almost no wasted leftover soap. When not in use, the cake could be stood upside down on its handle around the tub or basin, or be hung up from a simple wire hanger affixed to the wall with a suction cup. Every cake of Handle-Soap would float, with the handle protruding above the water's surface. This was achieved by providing an air-chamber with the handle base. Each soap cake had a shallow plastic cup imbedded in its top surface into which the handle could be easily fastened by the consumer. At most, the consumer needed only one handle and one hanger for any single location of use.

CONSUMER TEST

Hardy was satisfied that the product really worked and noted that it seemed especially desirable for shower use. However, he realized he could not approach a prospective manufacturer on the strength that he and his friends liked Handle-Soap. He decided to obtain the results of an objective, consumer test of the product in order to really have something to talk about. He hoped that at least 20% or 25% of all households would want Handle-Soap for one or more uses in their home. He anticipated that product acceptance might run as high as 40%, but tended to discount this as probably reflecting an unduly favorable personal bias. With annual toilet soap sales approximating 3 billion cakes, Hardy concluded that even if Handle-Soap captured but 10% of the market, it would be exceedingly profitable.

Hardy then approached a marketing research group in the San Francisco Bay Area. They seemed intrigued by the product and undertook to run a small consumer test of the Handle-Soap in a medium-sized city in that area. The minimum-sized sample believed necessary to determine if there were a real market for the product was 100 households. Soap samples were provided and the test run. Four interviewers left a cake of Handle-Soap with its soap-hanger at each of 106 households randomly selected, asked a few preliminary questions, then called back in about 5 weeks to learn what was the reaction to use of the product. Product acceptance ran 72% of the sample. After trial use over an average 5 week period, 70% bought a second cake of Handle-Soap at a premium above the usual retail price—the interviewer made no sales "pitch" at this time. About 63% of the sample agreed to pay a premium of 5¢ per cake to obtain the product. A very high percentage indicated they would change to other than their favorite brand of toilet soap to obtain Handle-Soap. These findings did not appear improbable since some survey questions plus research carried out by a well-known national marketing research agency indicated that many if not most consumers were not of unchanging brand loyalty and that these consumers were not very conscious of the price they paid for such a low-cost necessity as toilet soap. About 25% of the sample was enthusiastic over the product. On careful examination, the test sample appeared to be highly representative of toilet soap users nationwide.

The survey uncovered a number of possible uses or specific markets for Handle-Soap, which were mentioned in the report. Some of these related to the soap cake content, others to the circumstances of use or the individuals who used it. The uses and markets are listed below:

1. Volume Toilet Soap Market. This was believed to represent roughly about 85% to 90% of the total market and was handled mostly by the grocery stores. The average retail margin for toilet soap sold in grocery stores was about 17%.

2. Specialty Soaps. These were highly perfumed and expensively packaged. They sold at prices usually ranging from 50¢ to $5.00 per cake —with the bulk probably selling for between $1.00 to $2.50 for packages of 2 or 3 cakes. They were sold mostly by drugs, department, and specialty stores. Drugstore margins were believed to run about 33% while department and specialty stores got about 40% on their toilet soaps with usually a 10% advertising allowance on top of this.

3. Medicinal Soaps. These sold at prices ranging from 20¢ to $1.20 with the bulk of sales apparently lying within a range of about 29¢ to 49¢ each. There is a large market for special skin soaps of numerous types. (Acne, allergies, etc.) Their sales were handled chiefly by drugstores.

4. Shampoo Cake. There was some indication that a Handle-Soap shampoo cake might find a good market. It should be more economical than liquid and cream shampoos. Both drug and grocery store sales were indicated.

5. Shaving Soap. Two people who tested Handle-Soap reported it convenient for use as a shaving soap. If successful, this would represent quite a departure from the trend to aerosols. Drug and grocery stores would handle retail sales.

6. Use in Hospitals. Handle-Soap should prove especially handy for bathing patients. It should be made available in small sizes for this purpose. When a nurse has one hand busy manipulating a patient, Handle-Soap should be easy to hold onto and sanitary to stand up or hang up when not in use. Economy is an important factor here as hospitals use large quantities of soap.

7. Pet Soap. Handle-Soap should prove very handy for this use. It lends itself to rubbing and scrubbing. Also the soap would float in the tub with the handle up. Drug and pet stores would carry it.

8. For Babies and Small Children. Handle-Soap was found exceedingly handy for this use by several mothers. Drug and grocery store sales were indicated.

9. Physically Handicapped. People who tend to drop soap or who have difficulty in picking up a dropped cake because of any physical impairment should represent an excellent market potential. Several arthritics in the survey were enthusiastic over Handle-Soap. According to published data, the sizes of some of these handicapped groups are estimated as follows: Diagnosed arthritics—7,500,000; heart disease impairment—9,200,000; hemiplegics—1,000,000; major amputees—400,000; blind—330,000; cerebral palsy—300,000 (rough est.); multiple sclerosis—200,000; muscular dystrophy—100,000; and paraplegics—82,000. (Total about 20,000,000 persons).

  10. *Aboard Naval and Commercial Ships.* Soap won't fall from soaphangers even in rough seas.

  11. *Hotels and Motels.* Small-sized Handle-Soap might be useful and economical here—especially in showers. It may offer some institutional advertising possibilities.

HANDLE-SOAP "MILEAGE" TEST

  While the market test was underway, Hardy arranged for an industrial engineer to run a "mileage" test comparing the life of Handle-Soap to a standard bar of bath soap under conditions of ordinary shower use. After several weeks this engineer made a report showing that pound for pound, Handle-Soap lasted about twice as long as the standard bar of soap. Apparently this was due to the thorough and quick drying of the Handle-Soap suspended where air could circulate freely around it. Hardy felt that ideally Handle-Soap should last enough longer for its economy to impress the user but not so long as to markedly reduce potential sales. What this optimum life should be Hardy did not know. But he guessed it should be between 67% to 75% longer than the standard bar on a pound for pound basis. On inquiry he learned that bar "mileage" could be controlled to some extent by varying the composition and drying time during manufacture. Therefore, it would be possible to reduce Handle-Soap "mileage" somewhat if it lasted too long.

COST OF SOAP

  During the market test, Hardy was able to collect some detailed information about costs. He found that toilet soap of top quality could be purchased in bars under contract manufacture at a cost of between 15¢ to 16¢ per pound depending on the quantities involved. Perfume had to be supplied to the manufacturer. Since the two most common bar sizes were nominally 3 and 5 ounces, these being used by the consumer in about equal amount, an average 4 ounce bar would calculate in cost (without perfume) to about 4¢ each. Therefore, a 4 ounce toilet soap bar would ordinarily cost the manufacturer between 3¢ to 3½¢ for the soap content. The optimum weight for Handle-Soap as determined from actual usage appeared to be about 4 ounces.

Perfume costing from \$2.00 to \$4.00 per pound would, in a 1% concentration, cost about ½ ¢ to 1¢ per cake of Handle-Soap. A bacteriostat such as Hexachlorophene would cost about 0.6¢ per cake if used in the 1% concentration recommended for deodorant use. Monsanto's "Actimer," which was about equally effective, would only cost about ⅓ ¢ per cake.

COST OF PLASTIC PARTS

An estimate was obtained from a production plastic injection molding company for the plastic parts. If impact polystyrene or linear polyethylene were used in production quantities the plastic insert would probably cost about 0.2¢ to 0.3¢ each. The handle was estimated at slightly over 1¢ and the plastic hanger at about 2¢. If nylon was used the costs would be about 3 times as high. Apparently the cost of plastic parts would be no obstacle to marketing Handle-Soap—especially with the buyer willing to pay at least a 5¢ premium for it, i.e., for the soap cake with an insert.

SOAP MANUFACTURE INCLUDING EQUIPMENT COSTS

Hardy visited two different soap manufacturing plants as an "observer" to learn what he could about the process of manufacturing bar soap. He discovered that most toilet soaps were made up in the proportion of about 80% bleached white tallow from the meat packing houses and 20% imported coconut oil. Some olive and cottonseed oils were used in some bars. The detergent toilet soaps (Dove, Zest, Praise, Vel, etc.) were produced by organic synthesis, mostly from petroleum but also from animal and vegetable fats and oils. These so-called "detergent" bars were not affected by water hardness and dissolved readily in both hot and cold water. They contained almost no water whereas regular toilet soaps carried about 12% moisture.

Soap making is an easily acquired art. One can buy a soap plant practically "off the shelf." Apparently almost any company with the funds could enter the soap industry and soon be turning out large quantities of soap—provided they could sell it. Selling appeared to be the one real problem. One eastern manufacturing firm would supply a line of equipment, from the initial kettles down to the final soap wrapper machines, capable of producing 250,000 lb. of toilet soap per week—for approximately \$200,000. The plant could produce over 12,000,000 lbs. of toilet soap per year, which is equivalent to between 1% and 2% of reported total industry shipments of toilet soap.

Some small toilet soap manufacturers buy their white soap chips already produced, from anyone of several manufacturers. They then mill in their coloring and perfume, and extrude this soap in a continuous long bar which is cut to the desired length to produce "blanks" for feeding automatically (or manually) into the dies of the soap press. This not only reduces their investment in equipment but also in building, since the initial processing equipment is bulky.

Since Handle-Soap represented such a radical change in product-form, Hardy made a visit to a prominent eastern manufacturer of soap presses and packaging equipment. Convinced that he should gain all the information he could about the manufacture of Handle-Soap before he tried to promote the production of this product, Hardy spent an entire day with the engineering staff of this company discussing the problems involved and their solutions. Production apparently presented no real problem. Hardy learned that most toilet soaps were produced in a Box Type press. These usually operated at a rate of about 110 to 120 cakes per minute. Such a press with a double set of dies could produce from 180 to 220 cakes per minute. A cake of soap of the Handle-Soap design, however, would have to be produced on what was called a Pin Die press. This latter press usually operated at speeds of about 80 to 100 cakes per minute. However, an automatic feed mechanism would have to place the plastic insert into the die for each cake of Handle-Soap, and was expected to reduce the production rate to between 45 to 60 cakes per minute. The press manufacturer indicated that later on a double set of dies (Duplex) or even 2 presses could be installed in the same production line to double the production rate of the line.

The cost of the modified simplex (single die) press was estimated at $17,000. A pre-trimmer costing $8,000 would also be needed for each press, if 2 were used. The Handle-Soap cake would not lend itself to paper wrapping and would probably have to be cartoned. Automatic cartoning machines that could easily handle the production from 2 soap presses (if not more), would cost $35,000. An extra $10,000 was estimated for tying the cartoner into a production line that included 2 Pin Die presses.

The estimated costs for a manufacturer to change his present toilet soap production line over to Handle-Soap are summarized as follows:

a)   A single press-line capable of processing roughly 25 million cakes or 6,000,000 lbs. of Handle-Soap per year. (4 ounce cake)—$60,000

b)   A double press-line for processing roughly 50 million cakes or 12,000,000 lbs. of Handle-Soap per year. (Only 1 cartoner needed.) —$95,000

The *initial* single press line was estimated at $68,000 to allow for some special development costs. Subsequent lines were estimated as shown above. A duplex press should be less expensive than the double line, although no estimate was obtained for this. The mechanism to place the plastic insert within the dies would be designed according to known, proved techniques developed for use in the plastic industry.

The soap dies themselves were inexpensive. Those of the best manufacture cost about $350 per set. These would be far cheaper than the estimated cost of dies for making the previously discussed plastic parts. For large quantity manufacture, a 32-cavity hot-runner die for the plastic inserts could cost as much as $8,500; a 16-cavity die for the handle might cost $7,500; and a 16-cavity die for a plastic hanger could cost $6,500. But these costs if amortized over reasonably large production quantities would not be significant.

COST-PRICE ANALYSIS

Handle-Soap appeared to Hardy to offer an unusual profit opportunity. For example, a 4 ounce bar of bath soap, at the "usual" margins and markups, would sell for about 12¢ retail. The manufacturer's pretax profit would ordinarily amount to about 1¢ per bar. According to the consumer test this same amount of soap made up into Handle-Soap could be sold readily for about 19½¢ each. Due to its new and unusual shape, the consumer could not tell very well just how much soap Handle-Soap contained. Its longer "mileage" also would serve to confuse him in this regard.

At the 19½¢ retail price, everything above the "usual" 12¢ price excepting ½¢ maximum allowance for the insert would be "extra." Of the 7½¢ retail price increment, the retailer would take his usual gross margin of about 17% or 1.3¢—thus leaving 5.7¢ (6.2¢–.5¢) extra profit to the manufacturer. Added to the 1¢ profit included within the 12¢ basic price structure the manufacturer could increase his profit to about 6.7¢ per cake of Handle-Soap. Obviously, if Handle-Soap lasted twice as long, pound for pound, the manufacturers would sell roughly half as many bars. This would reduce his net pretax profit to 3.3¢ per normal unit of purchase; still well above his previous 1¢ per cake. A further offset to the profit would be the necessity of utilizing part of the 3.3¢ to maintain the same advertising budget as formerly—providing only a given share of this manufacturer's existing market switched over to Handle-Soap. This is at least in part an unreal assumption because some proportion of his competitors' market shares should also change to Handle-Soap. Further, for such a highly differentiated product represented by this basic innovation, the effectiveness of each advertising dollar should fall on a new higher level than formerly.

Mr. Hardy reasoned that if he knew the demand curve even approximately, it would help him in determining the "best" price. He reasoned that it might be better to overprice Handle-Soap at the outset, then come down in price later if it should seem desirable. But he recognized that this might create the impression in the consumers' mind that Handle-Soap was a high-priced luxury item. However, in a field such as toilet soap, a manufacturer might later introduce a new lower-priced brand to overcome this objection. One thing that seemed clear after studying the toilet soap industry was the necessity of multiple branding to maximize profits. Some people want deodorant soaps. Some want beauty soaps. Some want detergent soaps. The consumer must be offered a choice. Also, price-lining had proved successful in the toilet soap industry.

One good argument for under-pricing Handle-Soap at the outset was to gain maximum usage at an early date. Hardy reasoned that the consumer test showed that the best way to convert people to Handle-Soap was to get them to use it. Seemingly, once they changed their using and buying habits to Handle-Soap, they would become loyal customers. Many, if not most of them according to Hardy, indicated they would continue to buy the product even if the price was increased by small increments from time to time. If later on the Handle-Soap content were altered so as to last only 75% longer than standard bar soap, (wear factor = 1.75) profits would naturally be expected to increase substantially.

Hardy was not positive in his own mind what would be the best price for introduction of Handle-Soap. He noted that retail prices had recently risen on most toilet soaps in his area of the country. Standard bath bars selling 2 for 31¢ had jumped to 2 for 33¢. And premium bath bars that sold 2 for 39¢ had increased to 2 for 41¢ and in some stores to 2 for 43¢. Because of this trend, Hardy was more inclined toward a higher introductory price for Handle-Soap than formerly.

In making a cost-price breakdown for the volume market Hardy decided to consider (for purpose of his analysis) a retail price of 25¢ per unit of purchase. He assumed that a 25% retail gross margin would help to obtain the cooperation of retailers over the first year or two. He analyzed the cost-price structure both with and without included low-cost promotion-type Handles and Hangers. The results showed that a manufacturer could probably obtain a gross margin ranging from about 47% to 61% under the stated assumptions and with various costs. Later on the manufacturer might attain as high as a 67% gross margin, if he were able to reduce retail margins down to 22%—still considerably above the 17% average retail margin for toilet soap enjoyed by U.S. grocery stores. All in all, the profit picture was very encouraging for the volume toilet soap market.

Hardy decided he should make a somewhat similar analysis for Handle-Soap sold in the specialty market. Here the sales would be smaller and the amortization costs of dies would be significant. He assumed that the soap would be purchased under contract and packaged 3 units per box. The box would be of high quality, but the soap cakes would not be individually wrapped in cellophane or polyethylene film since this would cost nearly 4¢ per cake. Utilizing information acquired from various sources including contract soap manufacturers, Hardy came up with a practically attainable retail price range of from $1.15 to $1.58 depending on the assumed gross margin and number of years over which the dies were to be amortized. He assumed annual sales of 1 million units of purchase, which he thought was conservative. Hardy believed this was a good practical price range for attaining the maximum possible volume in the specialty toilet soap market. Hardy was satisfied at this time that the cost-price analyses for Handle-Soap both in the volume and specialty markets indicated that an attractive profit margin should be attainable in each market.

PATENT

When Hardy first conceived his idea for Handle-Soap, he arranged for a preliminary patent search to determine the uniqueness of his invention. After gaining a "Green Light," he proceeded with the development of this product.

Hardy had been careful to protect his patent position over the years of the Handle-Soap development. He had kept a bound engineering notebook with consecutively numbered pages. In this he entered chronologically every idea contained in his invention as it was conceived. Periodically he had this witnessed by competent engineers. When his first working model of Handle-Soap was made up, he had two engineers try it out under conditions of actual use, and he had them attest to this use in writing. This, in patent terminology, was the "reduction to practice" of the invention and was an important date should any future litigation arise between two inventors who conceived the same product. Providing the development of the invention was carried on with due diligence from this date to the filing of the actual patent application, the inventor with the earlier date of reduction to practice usually is considered the first inventor. (This date is also of importance tax-wise to an investor in connection with the development of a new product. Under the then existing internal revenue code, all income received from a new product by an investor who invested his money in and gained an equity in an invention prior to this date of reduction to practice would be treated as a capital gain.) Hardy then had his entire engineering notebook microfilmed, sealed the film in a self-addressed registered package, and upon receipt through the mail placed it unopened in a bank safety deposit box. At this time he enlisted the services of a reputable patent attorney. Several weeks later his patent application was filed with the U.S. Patent Office in Washington.

SOAP INDUSTRY

Hardy decided that next he would be wise to look up some information on the soap industry so that he could approach prospective licensees with at least some knowledge of the field. The history of the industry was not only interesting but informative.

In 18th century America the housewife saved all the refuse grease from cooking and the wood ashes from the fireplace, and by a long and arduous process she prepared and blended these into a rank, jelly-like mass which served as a practical cleansing agent about the home.

In the early 19th century commercial production of soap got underway, and soap was sold in the cities and larger towns as a "body cleansing agent and beautifier." Prior to 1830 soap was sold to retailers in long bars, and storekeepers sliced off the quantity desired by the customer. Then B. T. Babbitt, a peddler turned soapmaker, began to sell soap in cakes cut to uniform size and wrapped separately in paper carrying his name. To promote his soap, Mr. Babbitt offered premiums for returned wrappers. His was the first soap bar imprinted with a brand name.

In 1837 Procter & Gamble was formed. All of the company's early output was sold in bulk. In 1879, Procter & Gamble introduced its first branded soap, IVORY. This floating soap resulted from a mistake by a workman who forgot to shut his mixing paddles off at lunchtime.

Another early giant in the soap field was Lever Brothers. This company produced Lifebuoy as early as 1900 and introduced LUX flakes in 1906, after having first pioneered the revolutionary use of soap chips in England. LUX bar soap was not introduced until 1925, one year before Procter & Gamble introduced its CAMAY toilet soap. Lever brought out RINSO in 1918, a soap for heavy duty laundry and cleaning. In 1919 Procter & Gamble began selling IVORY Flakes as a competitor to Lever's LUX Flakes.

The Colgate Company, founded in 1806, and the Palmolive Company, which, as the B. J. Johnson Soap Company, had its beginning in the 1860's, merged with the Peet Company in 1927 and 1928. This new company consistently promoted its PALMOLIVE and CASHMERE BOUQUET toilet soaps, which had been nationally advertised for many years.

These companies, Procter & Gamble, Lever Brothers, and Colgate, were the 3 giants who have consistently dominated the U.S. soap industry. Their sales have ranged from an estimated 65% to perhaps 80% of the annual U.S. output over the past several decades.

The pioneer brand of synthetic detergent was introduced in 1933 by Procter & Gamble under German patents. But the major shift in emphasis from soaps to synthetic detergents occurred after World War II, led off by the introduction of Procter & Gamble's TIDE.

The first floating soap in competition with IVORY was Lever's SWAN, introduced in 1940. Procter & Gamble had learned back in 1937 about Lever Brothers having produced a superior product to IVORY, that lathered better, had a finer texture and contained less moisture. Apparently Procter & Gamble gained advance knowledge of this soap, for it was able to beat Lever to the market with a similar new product by 9 months. In the ensuing litigation three Procter & Gamble employees were fined $6,500 for using the mails to defraud, and Procter & Gamble had to pay Lever Bros. an estimated $10 million.

Other litigation of similar nature had occurred in this industry. In the late 1920's Colgate sued Procter & Gamble over use of a spray drying process that infringed Colgate's patent for SUPER-SUDS. The suit was settled with Procter & Gamble purchasing half interest in the process. The two companies then sued Lever Brothers over manufacturing methods being used for RINSO. They won the suit, although it had little practical effect since Procter & Gamble had by then obtained volume standing with its OXYDOL.

In 1948 Armour & Company introduced a good-smelling deodorant soap containing hexachlorophene, a germ-killing agent. The surprising success of DIAL soap led to its capturing as much as 18% of the dollar toilet soap market by 1956.

The newest developments in the toilet soap field were:

a)   The introduction of vari-colored soaps by Lever Brothers with LUX; other manufacturers following suit, and

b)   The introduction of synthetic detergent soaps such as ZEST and DOVE, which in their first 3 years had between them captured about 13% of total U.S. toilet soap sales. Other detergent bars were soon introduced to the market. Because none of the synthetic detergent soap was used up to overcome water hardness, these soaps tended to slow any increase in per capita consumption. So far, detergent bars had all been sold at premium prices.

Hardy noted particularly that ever since Mr. Babbitt introduced the first cake of packaged toilet soap in 1830, practically all efforts at improvement had gone into improving the content of a cake of soap. Little effort had been spent in improving the scent and color. Also, the shape of the bar had undergone some refinement, as with DOVE. But it appeared that little or no effort had been expended to improve the basic concept of a cake of toilet soap per se.

The total market for toilet soap at factory price was estimated at between $225 and $300 million. Over the period of 1909 to 1940 per capita annual consumption had risen from 1.2 to 3.0 pounds. Disregarding variations of consumption during war years, per capita consumption during the 1950's and 1960's leveled at about 3.2 pounds per year. For a theoretical average size soap-cake weighing 4 ounces, this would calculate to 13 cakes per person per year or on the average about 1 bar per person per month.

MAJOR SOAP COMPANIES

Hardy decided that he would eventually want to approach the major soap companies for licensing Handle-Soap and set about gathering what little information he could find about them. From financial reports and articles in business publications he learned that over 60% of all U.S. soaps and synthetic detergents were sold by the Big Three—Procter & Gamble selling more than Lever Brothers and Colgate combined. The foreign market was dominated by the Unilever Group. In Europe alone they sold well over twice the total volume of sales made by the Big Three in the

United States. Much of this was in edible fats. Unilever's operations in the United States were all handled by Lever Brothers, a wholly owned subsidiary.

In recent years Procter & Gamble's operating income before depreciation had ranged from about 13½% to 14%. Income on Colgate's 1957 domestic sales was about 8% and foreign and domestic sales combined was 10%. In recent years the same ratio for Unilever had dropped from 7% to 6%.

For 1958, *Printers' Ink* revealed that advertising expenditures for 7 reported media were as follows: Procter & Gamble—$99 million, Lever Brothers—$51 million, and Colgate-Palmolive—$46 million. Armour's expenditure was reported at $10½ million, but the proportion of this spent on toilet soap was not known. The total promotion-advertising expenditures for these companies were not available.

During the late 1950's and early 1960's the toilet soap industry entered into a highly competitive period. According to published information, the major companies were eagerly watching all the fast-breaking developments that might open up new opportunities. A big market expansion was believed to lie ahead, both in the United States and abroad. Reportedly, the Big Three were well-equipped with new soaps in new packages and had available large amounts of advertising and promotion dollars. They were out to regain ground lost to Armour's DIAL, Purex's SWEETHEART, and to Andrew Jurgen's WOODBURY toilet soaps. The explanation for this activity in toilet soap was found largely in the DIAL success story. In only a little more than a decade Armour's DIAL rose from nothing to nearly 20% of the dollar toilet soap market.

Procter & Gamble was first in soaps and detergents. Toilet soaps were reported to make up less than 10% of their gross sales. For them every new product must have some distinctive characteristic that can be dramatized. To help achieve this they employed a number of advertising agencies. For promotion deals they were reported to spend between $30 to $50 million annually. When launching a new product, Procter & Gamble usually gave out samples by the tens of millions. Trade sources estimated they spent about $20 million on advertising and promotion of GLEEM toothpaste. Within 2 years this product became number 2 in sales, grossing $25 million annually.

Past experience is reportedly a constant reminder to Procter & Gamble executives of THE IMPORTANCE OF BEING 1ST IN THE FIELD WITH A NEW PRODUCT. Crisco was introduced in 1911 and Lever's Spry in 1936. Crisco outsells Spry by about 3 to 1. A management theory within Procter & Gamble was "don't be afraid to spend money to make money."

Procter & Gamble's principal toilet soaps were Personal IVORY, CAMAY, and ZEST. The American Institute of Management had singled this company out as being the best managed company in the United

States. The success of their sales program was illustrated by the fact that one or more of their products was used in 95% of U.S. homes, a penetration unequalled by any other manufacturer of anything.

Colgate-Palmolive Company was a substantial factor in toothpaste, second in detergents, and 4th in toilet soap sales. Sales of PALMOLIVE and CASHMERE BOUQUET toilet soaps had fallen off in recent years. During the 1930's, sales of PALMOLIVE toilet soap were reported by trade magazines at more than one-third of the entire market. During the period following World War II the company spent nearly $100 million on new plants and equipment. They built plants in a dozen European cities and substantially had increased new foreign sales.

In the early 1960's Colgate-Palmolive management was reported to be spending substantially over $5 million on research and development as contrasted to about $400,000 per year prewar. It was about this time that the company's board chairman stated that it now required over $6 million to introduce a new product whereas it used to take only $1,000,000. In an effort to keep pace with DOVE and ZEST, they had tried to introduce two different detergent bars but without success. Their position in toilet soap sales was considerably behind both Procter & Gamble and Lever Brothers.

The American Institute of Management rated Colgate-Palmolive as having excellent management.

Unilever Group. Lever Brothers was the wholly owned American subsidiary of the parent companies, Unilever N.V. (Dutch) and Unilever Ltd. (English). Their U.S. sales represented only a small portion of their total world sales. Unilever's capital investment in Europe was many times their investment in the United States. Their return on capital (before interest but after taxes) was considerably less than that of Procter & Gamble's. In Canada, the United States, Argentina, and Brazil a substantial majority of their business was in soap.

In the late 1950's Lever Brothers acquired the "ALL" detergent line from Monsanto. They became especially active in this period, introducing several new products to the U.S. market. By introducing LUX toilet soap in 4 new colors they pushed it back up to the number one position in volume toilet bar sales. Their DOVE detergent toilet soap grew rapidly in sales, and they introduced GAYLA, a green translucent toilet soap, into some parts of the United States. In promoting DOVE they distributed tens of millions of samples to consumers throughout the nation. Their latest addition to the detergent bar parade was PRAISE.

Purex Corporation was the fastest growing soap company in the United States although much of this was achieved through acquisitions. They acquired the Manhattan Soap Company in the mid-1950's, which produces SWEETHEART soap. And more recently they acquired the Allen Wrisley Soap Company in Chicago. Purex gave SWEETHEART soap a new look in a new wrapper, but did not change the soap.

Armour & Company achieved enviable success with DIAL soap, introduced in 1948. DIAL rose to 18½ of the dollar toilet soap market in 8 years, despite obtaining only about 12% in tonnage sales. Armour added ½ ¢ extra cost per bar in Hexachlorophene and sold the product for 4¢ to 5¢ higher on the retail level than did their competitors. DIAL was the first deodorant soap that actually smelled good. With it Mr. Wilson of Armour proved that the Big Three did not have an unbreakable grip on the market.

Swift had introduced soap brands of its own at different times over the past years, none of which succeeded on a national scale. In view of this experience the company's management concentrated on manufacturing soap for private brand labels.

After studying the soap industry and its individual companies Hardy decided to direct his efforts specifically toward the toilet soap market. Some general information was available about retail sales from magazine articles, but little detailed information could be found in publications about different brands and company activities.

During the period of the Handle-Soap market test and after, Hardy often discussed the Handle-Soap prospect with some of his business associates. He welcomed any new ideas that appeared to have merit. One of his associates suggested he might approach a local group who had backed a number of new ventures. He thought they might put up several hundred thousand dollars to launch this product.

Hardy still believed that his best opportunity probably lay with an existing company with good management which was already selling soap through nationwide grocery outlets. But he felt he should consider the private venture capital group as a possible alternative.

In the course of one such discussion the possibility was brought up of getting a major grocery chain to produce and to market Handle-Soap. Some chains were known to be marketing their own private brands and very successfully, and at least one of them owned and operated its own soap factory. This appeared to offer interesting possibilities, and Hardy thought he should give this careful consideration.

In anticipation of a possible meeting with the officials of one such grocery chain, Hardy decided he would talk to one of the nation's leading industrial designers. Before Handle-Soap should be marketed, he believed that the optimum design of the production prototype should be determined by an outstanding design firm. Hardy wanted a cost estimate for this service so he could inform the grocery executives of what to expect.

He made an appointment with the senior member of this design firm and called to see him on the following day. As soon as Hardy showed pictures and a sample of Handle-Soap this designer called in two of his top staff to show them the product. Hardy was pleased at their excitement over Handle-Soap although he was not sure exactly what it was that occasioned this reaction. This half-hour meeting lengthened into one of four hours that included a most pleasant luncheon. The complete design work through packaging would cost probably between $20,000 to $30,000 and take about 90 days. Of special interest was an offer by the head of this design firm to handle all this work with the only compensation being a small participation in the product's future. Hardy was grateful for the offer but explained that he had been advised at least for the present to keep the situation free of all attachments or possible encumbrances. He thanked the designer and said he would keep the proposal in mind should the Handle-Soap program develop in such a way as to make this feasible and desirable.

In further discussions the possibility was considered of approaching some company who might be persuaded to enter the toilet soap field. Hardy did not think this prospect would be nearly as promising as going directly to the major soapers. But he agreed that perhaps some thought should be given to this. Lists of prominent and financially able companies could be found in *Fortune's* annual report on the "500 Largest Industrial Corporations" and also in *Printers' Ink* annual advertising expenditures edition which showed the "100 Top Advertisers in 7 Media." *Standard & Poor's* "industrial surveys" also gave the names of the more prominent corporations broken down by industry.

Hardy knew his period of patent coverage would last for 17 years plus the time it took for his patent to be granted. Usually it was desirable to extend this patent pending period prior to the actual issuance of the patent as long as possible so as to gain the maximum period of coverage. When the patent finally expired, all royalties would cease. Hardy thought that perhaps he would be wise to reserve certain Handle-Soap applications outside the volume toilet soap market for his own exploitation. If he were able to establish a substantial sales volume for perhaps a pet soap, shampoo, or for medicated soaps over the patent protection period, he might have a nice little business that would continue to bring in a profit long after his patents had expired. So Hardy tentatively accepted this in his long-range planning. Of course, Hardy stated that his primary long-range objective was still to establish his own engineering company for the development of new products.

He believed that from time to time such a company might find itself in such a highly favorable patent position that, if possible financially, it could reap a far greater reward by direct exploitation than through a licensing program. And even if the chief objective were to license others, he probably could get better terms after the product had been successfully marketed, even if only in a preliminary way. Hardy believed he already had enough good ideas in mind to keep a couple dozen people busy full-time. Handle-Soap he believed would be the springboard for gaining the money needed to launch this enterprise.

On looking into the tax situation he discovered that for him to be given capital gain treatment on his Handle-Soap income, he would have to sell all substantial rights in the invention in a single transaction. He could not license more than one company directly. But this transaction could be with a corporation that he controlled with his two brothers, since under the internal revenue code blood brothers and sisters were considered not to be relatives but "outsiders." This corporation in turn could make all the licenses it could arrange. Hardy could then "license-back" to himself any particular application of Handle-Soap he desired. But, aside from any royalties he fed back through the licensing company, all income under the "license-back" provision would be ordinary income.

Hardy believed the way was clear to approach prospective licensees for Handle-Soap. Before doing so he felt he should develop in some detail a marketing plan for his product complete with a profit and loss statement so as to indicate what potential existed for the item.

Lex Computer Systems, Inc.

On April 14, 1969, the *Palo Alto Times* reported that five Mid-peninsulans had formed a computer-programming company named LEX. A similar story appeared in the issue of *Electronic News* for April 21, 1969. These two articles were part of LEX's initial attempt to inform the community of its existence. (See Exhibits 1 and 2 for the text of these two articles.)

LEX was incorporated in November 1967 as the result of discussions between Dr. Kenneth Knight, an assistant professor at the Stanford Business School, and Kent Mitchell, a local practicing attorney. They felt that a computer oriented service company could be of great benefit to the legal profession and the long run returns to a pioneer in the field appeared to be attractive. Although there had been similar attempts by several other groups that had failed, Knight and Mitchell thought that LEX would be profitable if the goals set for it were relatively modest. Accordingly, their plan was to develop a central computer program that would do routine accounting and record keeping, and yet satisfy the unique information needs of a law firm. Nevertheless, many of their colleagues remained skeptical. The costs of developing the central program could run into the hundreds of thousands of dollars and the variable costs of servicing a law firm might also be very high. Their potential market, although extremely well defined and accessible, was small, and almost completely unfamiliar with the computer. Sales and profits would come slowly. Although Knight and Mitchell remained enthusiastic, it was apparent that they could not attract sufficient capital unless outside investors could be given the assurance of a broader and more readily profitable sales base.

This was done in August 1968 by merging with a small programming company which was not connected with the law in any way. It had been started recently by Dr. Bud McClelland, manager of the Operations Research Group at Varian Associates, and Lou Pennington, an operations research analyst also from Varian. The third man in this group was Mr. Stuart Lamont, who was the Regional Sales Manager for Xerox at the time. After the merger, the company retained the original directions of its various founders by "splitting" into two virtually autonomous divisions—the Decision Assistance Division (DAD), co-directed by McClelland and Pennington, and the Legal Services Division (LSD), directed by Mitchell. Dr. Knight became LEX's President. He and Harry Turner, the Corporate Treasurer were the only company executives who were not exclusively devoted to one division or the other. (Biographical sketches of Messrs. Knight, Mitchell, and Turner are included as Exhibit 3.)

Mr. Lamont was particularly important in the search for outside financing inasmuch as he was the only one in the company with substantial sales experience. Although he did not plan to actively participate in the company until its products were marketable, he could be presented to potential investors as the link between product development and revenue. Lack of such a link was widely regarded as being a serious deficiency in a software house. As a result, his wishes carried substantial political weight within the company.

The merger itself was not accomplished smoothly. Mr. Lamont wanted to have a separate Sales Division which would service both the DAD and LSD, thereby making him directly accountable only to the President and not to the chiefs of either operating division. He planned to build from a base of five or six salesmen to a large national marketing organization. Mr. Mitchell was strongly opposed to this plan. He felt that with regard to the LSD, he was the only one in the firm competent to supervise the sales effort by virtue of his legal training. Under Mr. Lamont's plan, he would have little control over the hiring, training, developing or firing of the salesmen assigned to his product. Furthermore, he felt that the likely expansion of his division could accommodate the cost of one salesman at the most and that not even one should be hired until he could conclude the first few contracts himself. Mitchell was overruled and Mr. Lamont was established as Marketing Vice President, reporting directly to the President, although salesmen and their costs would be assigned to the operating divisions.

The disagreement remained, however. Dr. Knight had accepted a teaching position at the University of Texas and unfortunately would remain in Austin until the end of the 1968–69 school academic year, leaving Marketing and the LSD to work out their own problems.

The combination of the two groups under the LEX name subsequently succeeded in attracting $1.5 million of outside capital. Of this, $750,000 was to be available to LEX on April 1, 1969. The remainder would be delivered in two equal installments on April 1 and October 1, 1970, contingent upon the attainment of certain goals set by the outside investors. The benchmarks for the April 1970 delivery were $125,000 in billings in either of the preceding two quarters and losses to that time not to exceed $460,-000; that is, in the first year of operation with the new financing. Projections in late 1968 placed the time of first overall profitability in late winter 1971.

THE PRODUCT

The LSD's objectives were the development and sale of a software package designed to facilitate office management, accounting, and billing for law firms. It was to be a proprietary service system: data would be collected from law firms on forms provided by LEX and processed through a central program to final computer printed reports. The first marketable version of the Law Office Package (LOP), scheduled for substantial completion in June 1969, would provide the following:

1. A full ACCOUNTING service for recording hours worked, disbursements, billings and receipts. These would be organized according to a particular subject area or case for a client (Client Ledger), client (Summary Client Ledger) or attorney (Attorney Activity Report). Examples of the accounting reports (and a general explanation of them) which were distributed to attorneys as part of the marketing effort appear in Exhibit 4.

2. A DOCKET and JOURNAL service. This was a computer kept calendar of coming (DOCKET) and past (JOURNAL) events in the legal history of a case. There were two general benefits of doing this by computer. First, some positive response was necessary to erase an entry from the computer file. If a deadline were missed it would reappear on the calendar, marked as overdue, until action was taken. Second, the data on the file could be easily searched or organized in a variety of different ways, a useful aid to a large law firm. (See Exhibit 5 for a more detailed description.)

3. A LEGAL MEMORANDUM INDEX of the work product of the office. This was designed to reduce duplication of past effort by allowing a quick, comprehensive search of all research done in a law office. (See Exhibit 6.)

Until the volume of information to be processed justified the expense of a computer terminal in a law office, all processing would be done on a batch basis. This involved setting up a regular, fixed schedule for picking up the input data from the law firm and delivering the final reports to it. The input data would be checked for errors, key-punched and verified, and then fed to a computer at an outside installation. The printout would be returned to LEX for bursting, further quality control, and delivery to the firm. Although the basic procedures were simple, it was suspected that the actual operating costs would be significant. Firm projections could not be made without some operating experience. This was particularly true with respect to quality control. Although the LOP program was designed with numerous, sophisticated error checks, it could not guarantee complete accuracy. Certain types of undetectable errors could result in data misplacement, reruns and the expense of considerable personnel time.

Kent Mitchell had done most of the preliminary system design and development work on the LOP himself. He felt that other systems had failed because "a standard accounting package tends to slight the needs of lawyers by ignoring the complex relationship between record keeping, deadline control, and monitoring the progress of cases." Therefore, he had specifically tailored the LOP to the needs of a law firm as he knew them. For example, a law firm's output is generally measured in terms of "billable hours." The dollar value of an attorney's work is calculated from a set fee per hour and the number of hours he works. Typically, however, the value of the hours worked is posted directly to "Receivables," yet actual billing is done infrequently and at irregular intervals and no "inventory" of hours worked is kept. As a result, "Receivables" begin to age only from the date of billing, although in fact the work may be months old at that point. It had been Mitchell's experience that if actual hours were accumulated until billing time, a greater percentage of the older work than the newer was "written off." In response to these problems, he had designed the accounting portion of the LOP to keep and age the inventory of hours worked and to compare these figures with what had been billed and remained unpaid. This would not replace the law firm's accounting system, but would be a supplement to it. He felt that use of the LOP would enable a law firm to significantly increase its revenues through better control of its "inventory" and billing process and by relieving attorneys of clerical tasks which consumed productive time. In addition, part of the computer printout could be included with the bill. He thought that it would be reasonable to expect that a prompt, itemized billing would improve payments.

In reality, the three parts of the LOP were distinct products, with different inputs and uses and subject to different operating constraints. For example, batch processing of the DOCKET system was a potentially severe problem. The maximum economically feasible frequency of data pick-up was weekly. An attorney's schedule for the week could be given to him on Monday if the data was available to LEX the Friday before, but this would not allow the posting of short term deadlines within the week. A duplicate system would be required to handle the inadequacy. There was a similar problem with the work product INDEX. When attorneys wanted to know what research had been done in the past, they would want immediate response. A rigid access schedule would present retrieval difficulties on the output side which attorneys would find inconvenient and therefore undesirable. LEX executives believed that full realization of the Docket and Index benefits could be achieved only with the installation of remote access terminals. For these reasons, their primary concern was initially with the marketing of the accounting services portion of the LOP.

THE LEGAL INDUSTRY

Of the several hundred thousand attorneys in the United States today, only about 35,000 work in firms of ten or more. A little more than 1,000 attorneys belong to firms of this size in the San Francisco Bay Area, LEX's chosen territory of initial penetration.

The typical law firm is a self-contained unit of highly trained professional counselors. It processes no raw material and has no final output in the industrial sense. Instead, its basic inputs are its own time and expertise; its outputs are advice and the structural ordering of other people's affairs. While the drive for immediate profit is seldom overlooked entirely, the typical firm assiduously seeks to establish and maintain a reputation for professional legal competence and service. These circumstances have naturally affected procedures of production control and internal accounting employed by attorneys and their billing practices as well.

Allocation of the work load in a law firm is generally done on an *ad hoc* basis, particularly among the newer attorneys in a firm. Whoever is available does the work. A large number of attorneys still do not keep time records, and the systems utilized by those who do keep records vary widely.

Typically, time is recorded on chits or estimated at the end of the day or week and reported to a central secretary, who adds them to a client's file. A similar system is used to keep track of expenses advanced on the client's behalf and billable to him. Retrieving the information in a different form is usually avoided. For example, often a firm will not have any idea of the burden assumed by each attorney or the receivables position of the firm as a whole. No law firm could put together reports of the LOP type with the same ease and speed as LEX could.

Docketing (scheduling) of future events is generally done by a central secretary, based on memos received from attorneys in the office. Firms of 10–25 attorneys often post a calendar for the entire office, but individual calendars and reminders of past due events are frequently omitted.

The legal profession as a whole has only recently become concerned with the economics of office management. The first national conference on the subject was sponsored by the American Bar Association in 1965. By 1968, when a third conference was convened, the general level of efficiency in law offices had still not significantly changed. Nevertheless, the opening address of the conference highlighted its growing importance:

> The overall conclusion to be drawn is that the demand for legal services is mushrooming and will continue to do so. In addition, as private practitioners, we are running into competition with broad areas of government competing for the manpower. In a very real sense, the phenomenon parallels the experience of the medical profession following the introduction of the Medicare programs. Although we might be merely on the threshold of it, the trend of more consciousness of the lawyer and of increased use of the lawyer's services is a continuing one.

In this regard, it is instructive to take a look at the lawyer manpower and how it is divided. Based on past figures, our 1968 lawyer population is approximately 300,000. Of this number, there are approximately 110,000 who are solo practitioners, 75,000 who are in small firms and associations, 35,000 in large firms with five or more partners. This represents the spectrum of private practice. The rest of the population is made up generally of House Counsel (which includes lawyers working in educational institutions in all capacities), and governmental lawyers. The former employs 35,000 persons, and lawyer personnel in all governmental levels, including Judicial, Executive and Legislative, amounts to another 45,000. Interestingly enough, the employment of the latter two groups is constantly growing. Thus these groups, as well as the military are competing for lawyer manpower.

With this competition, we must look to either new lawyers or more efficient practice to take up the slack. The estimates of new lawyers per year is approximately 16,000. Any estimate of a new increase in lawyers would appear to be hardly adequate to handle the growing demand.

The law of supply and demand, as complicated by the draft, tends to confirm all of this. It was a national sensation when the Wall Street firms announced that they would begin young lawyers at salaries of $15,000 per year right out of law school. Already in Pennsylvania in certain non-metropolitan areas, beginning salaries are as high as $11,000 for the well-qualified young graduate. This emphasizes the importance of the cost factor. It's a national phenomenon, not just a metropolitan problem.

The conclusion to be drawn is that we, as lawyers, are facing unusual demands; and that in attempting to provide service, we cannot necessarily think solely in terms of hiring young lawyers. Those days are gone. We must concentrate on efficiency and the productivity of our operation.

We must consider the ever increasing demand for lawyer services and explore means of providing those services most effectively. If we are to survive as a profession, we must operate efficiently and promptly, and with the greatest quality possible. We must assume that our lawyers are capable, qualified, intelligent and progressive in keeping up with developments in the law.

We must also assure that lawyers practice law. This is basically our work. It's the application and interpretation of the law, whether in the courtroom or in the wills or contracts we draw, that is our principal function. We must, in every way, strive to reduce our non-legal or mechanical functions.

In summary, let me say that the law explosion is real—it's current—it is with us. Whether we choose to admit it or not, the demand for legal services is exceeding the supply. A key indication of this is the salary inducements being offered to new lawyers upon completion of their law school courses. This demand is going to continue to grow. In view of the fact that the demand is exceeding the supply, it is incumbent upon us to improve the quality and the efficiency of our legal services. We seek those management and professional skills which are prerequisite to handle the changes which are being thrust upon us.[1]

---

[1] Andrew Hourigan, "Today's Lawyer in a Changing Society," in *Proceedings of the Third National Conference on Law Office Economics and Management* (1969), pp. 1–8.

The basic charge for legal services can be determined in four ways: (1) from the number of hours spent on a project and a set charge per hour; (2) on a contingency basis—for example, 30% to 50% of the proceeds won in a personal injury suit; (3) by law, as in probate matters, where the maximum fee is set by statute as a percentage of the estate; and (4) on a retainer basis, either for a single matter, such as an uncontested divorce, or for a period of time, such as a year. Generally, attorneys use the hours expended as a guide in billing their clients. Almost every local bar association publishes a schedule of minimum fees, and each attorney has a "rough" idea of what he will charge per hour, but the ultimate bill is most often an exercise in subjective evaluation and not a simple calculation of hours multiplied by the rate. Often no precise record of the time spent is available. In one notable case, a $90,000 fee was justified on the basis of an ex post facto estimation of the hours spent during several years. Furthermore, if an attorney can achieve excellent results with little effort, the bill will not reflect any relationship to the time actually expended. Much of the time spent on a matter by younger attorneys will be absorbed by the firm on the theory that it is part of their training. In any event, the estimation process is rarely indicated to the client. Characteristically, this adjustment is assumed to be of no concern to the client. For example, following is a bill which LEX received from *its* counsel in December 1968:

Services rendered during the months of October and November, 1968, with respect to miscellaneous corporate problems, adjusted as per agreement of December 5, 1968 . . . . . . $2,100.00

Xerox charges 20.00

$2,120.00

In fact, a recent survey among lawyers had turned up the following replies to the question, "With reference to the client's views on billing, what factors do you believe the client considers to be the most important?"

Factors	Number of Replies
Results	76
Service	34
Time	26
Amount of money involved	15
Difficulty of problem	13
Price of service rendered fee	12
Effort expended	8
Personality	6
Importance of matter	5
Prestige of lawyer	4
Ability to pay	3

SOURCE: J. E. Roehl, "Modern Billing Techniques—1968 Survey" in *Proceedings of the Third National Conference on Law Office Economics and Management* (1969), pp. 171–95, 182.

To Kent Mitchell, these characteristics of a law firm and attorney attitudes presented important and subtle marketing problems. Attorneys were 20 years behind the times in their accounting procedures alone, seemed very resistant to change, and did not perceive the benefits that could be obtained by a subtle change in the treatment of clients. In January 1969, he again found himself arguing that salesmen without a legal background would be unable to effectively present the aspects of the LOP which had been tailored particularly for attorneys. For example, it would be difficult for a layman to explain to an attorney who charged on a contingent fee basis why he should reassess his fees or the timing of his billing based on his inventory of hours worked.

On the other hand, attorneys were well aware of the problems which could arise in other areas. For example, missed deadlines could be very serious. The law provides stringent penalties for an attorney's negligence, including complete forfeiture of the client's cause and consequent impairment of the attorney's professional stature. The following memo hints at the extent of the problem and a potential benefit on which LEX executives thought they might capitalize with their Docket Service:

May 6, 1969
MEMORANDUM TO FILE
Subject: Impact of the Lex Docket Service on Attorneys' Errors and Omissions Insurance

Interview with Mr. Roland C. Williams, a Commercial Casualty Manager of Fireman's Fund American

I interviewed Mr. Williams on the 2nd of May. We discussed the condition of errors and omissions insurance for attorneys as seen by Fireman's Fund. Mr. Williams feels that the field is in trouble. Fireman's Fund does not see themselves in the business because of the high loss ratios that they experienced. They really only sell it to accommodate existing clients. Mr. Williams feels that over 50% of his claims come from failure to file, and that the majority of these failures are the very first filing and that, furthermore, a prevalent problem is failure to file against public agencies with short deadlines. He gave me a list of 15 or so recent claims, providing me with good specific information about the ways attorneys can get into trouble.

Mr. Williams gave me the following factual information with respect to rates and claims. He used the term loss ratio; that is, the ratio of premiums to claims. Generally, he said, rates have gone up 50% in various states in the last two years. A plan with a $2,500 deductible and $25,000/$75,000 coverage would cost $185.00 per attorney per year. Hawaiian rates went up 100% last November from $35.00 to $70 for low limit policies. In northern California, the five-year loss ratio has been 85%. In addition to this, Fireman's Fund has about $.50 of expense on each dollar, so that they are losing money on this type of insurance. In southern California, the five-year loss ratio is 117%.

How is an application reviewed for insurability? These general principles are followed. They avoid abstract work, patent attorneys (litigation is very prevalent here), attorneys new in practice, elderly attorneys operating by themselves. Normally, they have their claims manager underwrite the application. Mr. Williams volunteered that his company would not be ready yet to give a rate credit for the Docket System, but that was a possibility after some field experience was obtained.

The State Bar Association is trying to work up a group insurance program. Apparently, attorneys are finding difficulty in obtaining insurance. . . .

I went over the Docket System with Mr. Williams and left him copies of the input and output forms. Due to its simplicity, he understood it promptly and observed that it only had value if attorneys really used it; that is, if they remembered to put their self-imposed deadlines into the Docket.

Harry A. Turner

* * * * *

Given its initial operational problems and costs affecting marketing, the Docket part of the LOP depended on the isolation of subgroups of attorneys who were particularly hard hit by deadline problems, for example, patent attorneys. Mitchell felt that the Docket should be presented to attorneys along with the Accounting portion of the LOP, but that emphasis of it should depend on an assessment of the particular problems of a given firm.

At least one point was clear to everyone: the LOP could not be presented primarily as a means of cutting clerical costs. The Accounting portion alone would cost each attorney in a firm approximately $50 per month. While the system was expected to make secretaries capable of handling more work over the long run, it would impose new and rigid demands on existing personnel for quality work on the data inputs. On the other hand, potential revenue gains were nebulous. The system was designed to reduce the clerical work done by an attorney, allowing him more time for legal work, and to provide him with the information necessary in order to "turn over" his inventory more efficiently. The benefits to an attorney did not depend on doing something better than he had been doing, but on doing something new.

These product characteristics—immediate, definite cash outflow and nebulous revenue return—presented a difficult marketing problem in an area where existing procedures were entrenched by habit and tradition.

THE MARKETING PLAN

At the start of 1969, Mr. Lamont was still with Xerox. He did not plan to actively participate in LEX affairs or recruit the salesmen he wanted until June, when the LOP would be ready for marketing. His plans called for team canvassing of San Francisco, Los Angeles, and New York in rapid succession, leaving one or two salesmen behind in each of the first two areas to "mind the store" and hiring others as he went along. The target date for initial entry into the New York market was September 1969.

In his absence, Mr. Turner, the Treasurer, was given the role of Director of Marketing. He was to be in charge of preliminary market research and development, including advertising. In June, his role would change somewhat. He would then be responsible for coordinating supportive services and LOP development with the sales force. This timetable had barely been set up before it had to be abandoned. Mr. Lamont's conflicting positions at Xerox and LEX forced him to assume an active role at LEX in late January. By March 16, he had brought six of his former Xerox salesmen to LEX. All of these men were in their late twenties or early thirties, the average age being 28. All were college graduates, and most had done some postgraduate work. Two of the younger men had M.B.A.'s. They had all been with Xerox for 1½ to 2½ years, and several had marketing experience prior to joining Xerox.

Kent Mitchell objected to the new salesmen. He argued that they were costly and unnecessary. The cash drain per salesman was about $2,000 a month and the LOP could not even be demonstrated until June. Mr. Lamont argued that the Xerox training in paper flow analysis made the salesmen uniquely suited to sell the LOP and that his own ability to recruit them would have decayed if he had waited until June. In addition, he asserted that a broad assault on the market was the best way to insure that the LSD could meet its share of the April 1970 billings benchmark. In rebuttal Mitchell noted that the five "extra" salesmen represented a $120,-000 cash drain over the next year. He was more concerned with the "losses" benchmark and felt that the outside investors would give LEX the second installment even if the billings benchmark were not met, so long as the company had good prospects and had managed its resources well.

A compromise resulted. Mr. Lamont and three of the new arrivals concentrated their efforts on finding potential buyers for a DAD package which was being developed. This left Mitchell and Turner in effective control of all LSD sales force training for the time being. Together with the three new salesmen they spent two weeks, until the first of April, concentrating on the development of a sales presentation and supporting material for the LOP. Although this involved intensive instruction by Mr. Mitchell about the benefits of the system and the problems of attorneys as well as exposure to a videotape of a "typical" sales call prepared by Messrs. Mitchell and Turner, the focus of the period was on a cooperative pooling of ideas. The salesmen were eager to contribute their impressions of the proper way to present the system to law firms and these impressions were warmly received since neither Mitchell nor Turner had any marketing or sales experience.

At the same time, Mr. Turner was coordinating the efforts of LEX's advertising agency with those of the salesmen to produce the necessary supporting sales aids. These included stationery; looseleaf binders; calling cards, brochures in explanation of the benefits of the system in general terms; and portable presentation easels with flip-over pages which set forth the problems of attorneys, their solutions, and other benefits offered by the Law Office Package.[1] Mock-ups were made of the forms on which LEX would ask attorneys to record the basic inputs to the system, but no examples of the output reports were provided since the LOP was still in the final stages of formation and no one knew exactly what the format of the output reports would be.

The real development of the sales presentation began in April, when the three salesmen began calling on law firms in San Francisco. Together with questions and answers, the presentations took about three hours and typically a salesman could make two presentations a day. Although most firms required two or three such presentations, because it was usually not possible to have all the partners in a firm present at any one time, canvassing the area seemed to move quickly.

By the middle of May it became apparent that the DAD project would be a failure. The DAD executives discovered that because of their experience and contacts in the industry, they could market the product better than the former Xerox salesmen. Accordingly the three salesmen were transferred back to the LSD and Mr. Lamont redirected his efforts to the supervision of a six man team. Harry Turner remained the liaison between the salesmen and the LOP development personnel under Kent Mitchell. With the "old" salesmen training the new, several LEX executives began to express concern about the professionalism of the sales force and the possible negative reaction to LEX that might be generated by calling on firms without a product which could be demonstrated. There appeared to be no immediate solution, however.

With regard to the advertising program, Mr. Turner planned several news releases, Exhibits 1 and 2 among them, and a three-month ad campaign in the *Journal of the American Bar Association* starting in June. The first ad would take two full pages, while the next two would use similar art work and copy on a single page. (Correspondence between Mr. Turner and the advertising agency concerning the objectives and execution of the ads is included in Exhibit 7.) Projected total cost for the series, including the development of mats and [insertion] charges, was approximately $5,000. At the time, there was some disagreement over the choice of a slogan for the LSD. Dr. McClelland wanted to use "LEX is on your side" to emphasize that LEX would not simply dump a system on a user but would service the client continually. On the other hand, Mr. Mitchell argued that law firms had almost no experience with computer systems and that a defensive slogan might have the negative effect of making an issue of the bad experience of others. He advocated his own slogan, "LEX brings a practice back to law."

On the other hand, it was generally agreed that the purpose of the ads was to establish an image. The issue was: "What image?"

---

[1] A decision was made that the appearance of all supporting material would be of the highest quality, although the projected cost of this effort was about $4,000.

On April 24, Mr. Turner sent Dr. Knight the following report on the development of the marketing strategy. The contents of this memo were not discussed with Kent Mitchell nor did he receive a copy. This reflected again the earlier decision that the sales and marketing organization would report directly to the President, who in turn directed the overall management of the two operating divisions.

TO: Ken Knight   SUBJECT: Marketing Plan
                                                     for LSD
FROM: Harry A. Turner   DATE: April 24, 1969

The dominant but not total marketing effort in the Legal Services Division is devoted to the Law Office Package. Other product interests of LSD include the development and assessment of the market potential for a publishers package. This is a package whose services would be sold to the principal law book publishers in the field and would combine in a system three packages, all of which are already partially developed—the Shepardizing Package, the Alphabetizing Package, and the Index Office Files.

Because of the generality of application of the concept of the Accounting Package, the Publishers Package, and some of the components of the Accounting Package, particularly the Lex Docket or Diary, market research can readily be undertaken to determine the demand and the payout function for tailoring of our means of accessing and drawing from our files various output reports. A field-oriented market research effort into the application of the Law Office Package files to the problems of architects is now being conducted. Soon, market research into the applications of the Docket or Diary Package will also be conducted. Lex, being basically entrepreneurial, will also examine the market potential for tailored applications of the Law Office Package or any of its products when the customer is willing to pay for the development. Such a proposal of the San Francisco Neighborhood Legal Assistance Foundation is now being considered.

Now, to deal with the Law Office Package. The basic posture of LSD with the Law Office Package is to effectively penetrate the national market potential as soon as possible. Present timetable indicates that this can be done within about three years. The segment under most active consideration by us now is the private law firm. In the United States, there are approximately 250,000 attorneys in private practice. Approximately half of these are in partnership practice. The attorneys tend to concentrate in large firms, and it developes that approximately 30,000 attorneys reside in about 1,000 law firms. Accordingly, the sales call effort with respect to law offices is to start from the top and work down, although the economics of the Package are such that any firm larger than a few attorneys should find it effective in their practice. In addition to the law office concentration of attorneys, they also tend to concentrate in large cities. Seventy-five percent of the national potential of this market can be reached by marketing efforts in 13 cities in the United States. These cities are, in descending order of importance, (1) New York—25% of the national market; (2) Chicago—9%; (3) Los Angeles—6½%; (4) Washington, D.C.—5%; (5) Philadelphia—5%; (6) Boston—4½%; (7) San Francisco—4½; (8) Cleveland—3%; (9) Detroit—2½%; (10) Houston—

2½%; (11) Minneapolis–St. Paul—2%; (12) Dallas–Ft. Worth—2%; (13) Atlanta—2%. Lex is currently test marketing its Law Office Package in San Francisco. Its next expansion for sales force activities will be Los Angeles, followed by an expansion in the fall to New York. The timetable for marketing activities in Chicago is under active consideration at this time. The approximately 30,000 attorneys in this segment can be expected to generate revenues under the current price list and estimates of volume per attorney of about $50 per month. Fifty dollars per month times 30,000 attorneys is $1,500,000 per month, or $18,000,000 per year. There are other segments. These segments include attorneys in service of the federal government. The Department of Justice, for example, employs approximately 1,000 attorneys. A preliminary contact between Lex and the Justice Department has already been made. Another area of interest is the attorneys in public employ in the counties of the states; that is, the District Attorneys and their staffs. Lex has had preliminary communication with members of this segment also. An additional segment is the corporate staff. The attorneys work on the staffs of corporations in the United States.

The Legal Services Division is active in a test marketing program in the City of San Francisco. It has deployed in the field, working out of the San Francisco branch office, a force of three salesmen plus an actively participating Marketing Vice President. These salesmen started on the 1st of April, targeted themselves for approximately 60 prospects and will have completed their initial contacts with every one of them by the middle of May. We are currently estimating that a decision time from initial contact, if it is properly made, to a decision to receive service from Lex to the law firm is approximately 60 days. As of yesterday, April 23, two law firms have contracted for our services and several others are about to decide to receive them. The strategy of the sales call is something I do not want to discuss in detail here, but it is undergoing a continuous change and evaluation by the salesmen, the Marketing Vice President, the LSD Product Manager[2] and the LSD Vice President.

Simultaneously, as the salesmen contact their prospects, the information which they receive with respect to the product is being evaluated by the product development people in Redwood City and the product is being upgraded in direct response to the needs and the active realities of the marketplace. I emphasize that this is a basic strategy of our marketing effort. The salesmen and the product development people all are working to become educated and appreciative of the needs of the users for the Law Office Package. This is no small point because it implies a willingness to aggressively make contact with every potential prospect and to respond organizationally at the field level and at the headquarters level to our changing appreciation of his needs. We are doing this and we find that each day the product is slightly different from what it was before, although, of course, the basic strategy of the service that we are providing has not changed.

Now, with respect to competition, we find that there is a good deal of it. Competitors are numerous and active in the field. Service Bureau Corporation has been very active in the San Francisco marketplace. Every law firm in San

---

[2] Mr. Turner. He had dropped his title as Director of Marketing when Mr. Lamont began active employment in January.

Francisco that is now or has recently considered a computerized system, has been approached by SBC, although SBC has made no sales. Legal Management Services, a franchising company, has not been as active as SBC in San Francisco, but most law offices like the formats of LMS's reports. There is an NCR bookkeeping system which some firms are using. California Office Systems has a small office computer console and keyboard system which has been sold to one law office. There are many independent service bureaus and bookkeeping machines offering services to the law office. The marketing strategy of the Legal Services Division is to establish itself as a professional organization, serving the needs of its clients, the attorneys. As an informal opinion of the Ethics Committee of the ABA stated, the data processor for the attorney must ethically stand in the shoes of an attorney's employee. We are attempting to discriminate ourself from all other law office service organizations in this way. Lex is committed to an active advertising program in national and regional publications read by attorneys. To date, no competitor has advertised in any of these media. The basic strategy of initial advertising in this media is to create an awareness of Lex Computer Systems, to appeal to the law office need to reduce paperwork and to free its attorneys to become better professionals, and, finally, why Lex is to be preferred as a computerized service to its competitors. Lex is also committed to provide creative and professional literature support to its salesmen in terms of providing service brochures, analysis of competitors, brochures describing the capability of the company and materials for the customers through service representatives and it will implement strict quality control procedures on order processing procedures and on computer processing of the data that it handles for the law offices. Lex is actively committed to promotion and public relations activity. A public relations consultant has already placed articles in Bay Area newspapers and one national trade journal. LSD plans to participate in every significant ABA convention and trade show that occurs during the year, will use direct mail solicitation, and it is personally seeking to exercise contacts which it has and which it can develop in the ABA on its behalf. Lex will no doubt, for example, put together an educational program for the Continuing Education of the Bar in California and thereby effectively reach and create an awareness, some understanding and convictions about the benefits of the LSD Law Office Package in the some 28,000 attorneys residing in California.

The sales forecasts which appear in the budget for the Legal Services Division were derived in the following fashion. First, it was targeted that the Legal Services Division would produce by itself the revenues required by the first Blyth milestone and it would do them three months sooner than required. Second, it was assumed that Lex would actively market in San Francisco, Los Angeles and New York during this year. The sales estimates for the year contemplate a successful sale by the end of the year of approximately 40 law firms containing, on the average, 30 attorneys each; that is, about 1,200 attorneys. Starting from the first of April, this would amount to the successful sale of about one law firm per week between that date and the end of the year. The sales force and the Marketing Vice President feel that this is a good estimate for the most likely sales. This, of course, assumes the present pricing schedule. Deviations from this plan could occur because of the low sales rate, or reduction in the price of the service, and are quite difficult to forecast at this time.

However, I would say that a minimum likely change in the price schedule would be to reduce the monthly per attorney revenue to about $30. As far as the number of sales between now and the end of the year goes, it is extremely difficult to forecast, but I would estimate that a minimum likely sales would be 500; the most likely sales would be 1,200 attorneys, and that the maximum likely sales would be 2,000 attorneys.

HAT:bb

[Ed. Note: The two contracts referred to were for the batch Docket, the first part of the LOP completed. They were concluded by Mr. Mitchell before deployment of the sales force.]

After reading and re-reading this memorandum, Dr. Knight had a number of questions concerning the assumptions being made about the anticipated response to the selling effort. First, and foremost, he wondered whether a law firm in which partners had an equal voice would come to any quick decision about buying the LOP service. Where management was dispersed, he thought that decisions would come slowly. Secondly, he wondered whether attorneys would see the cost-benefit trade-off clearly enough in view of the immediate out-of-pocket costs of the system. If these market conditions were adverse, they would slow the adaption process and cause a lag in cash flow to LEX as well as increased selling costs.

By the end of May, the sales force had made presentations to the 60 largest law firms in San Francisco, most of which had offices within several blocks of each other. All of them employed 10 or more attorneys. No sales were made as the result of these presentations, but the sales force continued to follow up with about 20 large firms which had registered interest in the system. The results of the presentations seemed to be that attorneys were interested, but skeptical of how the service would benefit them. A number of firms indicated that they would like to talk more when LEX had succeeded in selling and servicing several other accounts. Others pointed out that LEX really wanted to charge them for being guinea pigs. Product benefits did not come across clearly and several firms noted that they felt their billing and pricing practices were satisfactory as they were.

All the salesmen had experienced a high degree of frustration since they felt that they were often at a disadvantage in answering questions which required considerable knowledge of the workings of a law office. To a man they argued for a simpler system; at the least they wanted the Docket and Index omitted from their presentations. They had also run into some price competition. Another computer oriented service claimed a price of $35 per attorney per month with a minimal installation fee. The salesmen could not match Mr. Mitchell's persuasiveness in demonstrating that LEX's $50 per attorney, $2,000 + installation charges were justified by the LOP's clear superiority to its competition. Since the pricing policy had not been set *definitely*, the salesmen responded in some instances by quoting their own prices, which subsequently generated a good deal of antagonism both within the organization and from prospective buyers. This particularly irked Dr. Knight, who returned from Austin in early June. After noting that some of the salesmen's demands on the development people were justified, he rebuked them for not "teaching" law firms more about better management techniques which the LOP would allow them to use.

It also seemed clear that the time required to close a sale might be closer to 90 days than the 60 days originally projected and that once a sale had been made, an additional 90 days would be required in order to get the system up and running.

In the middle of June, LEX's Board of Directors met to discuss the status of the company and future strategy. The results of the sales canvass generated a great deal of concern for obvious reasons, not the least of which was the cash drain it produced. The total annual costs per salesman were about $24,000. One major San Francisco firm appeared ready to sign, but the final decision would have to wait until the middle of July, when a senior partner returned from vacation. There was some question as to whether the Los Angeles area should be entered at that time and if so, what marketing approach to use. With regard to the nationwide effort, it seemed clear that the LSD could not expand its service capabilities as fast as the salesmen could move. Although it would be possible to do even the New York processing in Redwood City via cross country computer tie-ups, preliminary soundings indicated that attorneys would object to keeping their records in a distant city. On the other hand, a national effort was necessary. Cost revenue analysis showed that the break-even point might be as high as 1,800 attorneys, considerably more than San Francisco's large firms could supply even with 100% penetration.

In line with previous plans, Mr. Lamont was preparing to move four of the salesmen to Los Angeles and had already sent out an introductory letter to all law firms in the Los Angeles area over scattered protests that this was an unprofessional way to make initial contact. (See Exhibit 8 for this letter.)

EXHIBIT 1

**Midpeninsulans Form Computer
Programming Company***

Five Midpeninsula men have joined in the formation of Lex Computer Systems Inc., a new software firm set up to develop and market computer programs for general business and for law offices.

The company is based at 617 Veterans Blvd. in Redwood City.

Officers include Kenneth E. Knight of Los Altos Hills, former Stanford University assistant professor in business, who is president; Charles W. McClelland of Palo Alto, former Varian operations research manager, senior

---

* by Marge Scandling, *Palo Alto Times*, Palo Alto, Calif., Monday, April 14, 1969, p. 11

EXHIBIT 1 (Continued)

vice president; Kent Mitchell of Los Altos, attorney, vice president of legal services, and Lou Pennington of Sunnyvale, former Varian engineering specialist, vice president.

Cedric Sheerer of Los Altos, independent consultant in electronic data processing for business and industry, will be director of information systems. He will supervise and control all the software packages designed and developed at Lex.

Alfred S. Julien, a New York City attorney, is board chairman.

According to McClelland, who described the concepts underlying the company's formation in an interview, the founders believe that computer systems often produce a superfluous amount of information unusable to the person or company who originally contracted for it.

"Enormous amounts of computer printout materials are tossed out without being used," he declared. "This is partly because it is based on information the user needed, or thought he needed, at an earlier date.

"We believe that there's a limit to the volume of information an individual is prepared to handle. Instead of preparing large projects, we will specialize in smaller systems designed for a specific, immediate application," he continued.

As an example of general business programs, he cited one that encourages salesmen to report their daily results, not because the employer wants him to, but because by doing so he obtains desirable information, such as fresh lists of prospects.

Lex's second area of operations is legal services. McClelland explained that the firm considers previous attempts to provide computer services for law offices inadequate. These, he said, have included routine accounting functions and an attempt to computerize precedent, or search, activities.

The company's program for law offices includes output of an auditable index of past, present and future legal status on each active matter and memoranda on accounting information and routine billings.

"There's a real need for having legal office work done more efficiently," McClelland said.

He charged that previously announced moves to computerize precedents to aid attorneys in research have bogged down in technical difficulties.

"Basically we want to approach it from what we know we can do—handle office paperwork," he said.

"There's a solid economic reason for what we're doing," McClelland continued, "We're aiming at systems in the price bracket of between $10,000 to $20,000."

He described Lex as "a computer firm without a computer."

The founders, he said, have made a management decision to lever the company toward an intensive marketing effort and away from hardware for the time being. "We are taking a calculated risk that there will be plenty of computation power around for us to use."

Many local companies with computer installations rent the excess time out to other users, he indicated.

"The way we now see it is the most hardware we'll ever have is terminals," he said, although the company may acquire a small computer to be linked to larger ones elsewhere.

EXHIBIT 1 (Concluded)

Lex is being financed by $1.5 million supplied by Blyth Co., New York investment bankers, and by about $200,000 from its founders.

The company is privately held and will remain so for at least two to three years, according to McClelland. There are 30 employees at present.

EXHIBIT 2

Electronic News—April 21, 1969

REDWOOD CITY, Calif.—A little company with big ideas has entered the software fray here, determined to become a giant.

Dr. Kenneth E. Knight, president of the new Lex Computer Systems, Inc., at 617 Veterans Boulevard, here, said: "Our objective is to be a $1 billion corporation in 10 years." Dr. Knight is completing the academic year as associate professor of management at the University of Texas, Austin.

Chairman is Alfred S. Julien, senior partner in Julien, Glazer & Blitz, New York law firm.

Dr. Charles W. McClelland, senior vice-president and chief operations officer, was manager of the Operations Research group at Varian Associates, Palo Alto. Dr. McClelland said the Varian Aerograph and Analytical Instrument divisions are among Lex's first customers.

Stuart J. Lamont, former sales manager in the San Francisco area for Xerox Corp., is marketing vice-president.

Kent Mitchell, Redwood City attorney, is vice-president, Legal Services division.

Lou Pennington, former operatons research analyst at Varian Associates, Palo Alto, is vice-president, Decision Assistance division.

Cedric Sheerer, recently a consultant in data processing, is director of information systems.

Initial financing is by the founders and Blyth & Co., New York and San Francisco, with a money package exceeding $1 million.

Targets Attorneys

"We are organized around the markets we serve, not the computer," said Dr. Knight. "The computer must be brought back under the control of the people it serves." He said the first two market areas for Lex will be law offices, and marketing, financial and manufacturing executives.

The law office package will provide computer readout of an auditable index of present and future legal status on each active matter, with byproducts including accounting information and routine billing memoranda.

The other side of the house already has developed a system of quotation updating and sales forecasting; another for optimizing bidding, and still other packages for analysis of cash flow and risk, market research and production scheduling.

Lex has sales offices in San Francisco, New York and Los Angeles, with others to come in Chicago, Boston, Washington, Cleveland, Atlanta, Pittsburgh, Dallas, Miami and Detroit.

The company employs 30; expects a rise to 80 by year's end.

EXHIBIT 2 (Continued)

"We are entering the market with small, stand-alone products, self-justifying investments in the $10,000–$20,000 range," Dr. McClelland said. "A large system is merely a combination of a lot of small systems that really work, integrated from the user point of view, not that of the equipment."

EXHIBIT 3

KENNETH E. KNIGHT, age 32, is President and Chief Executive of Lex.

As Chief Executive he is concerned primarily with corporate development and expansion into new areas of interest; in the Lex organization, all major operations areas are the responsibility of the Senior and Divisional Vice Presidents.

Until the end of the 1968–69 academic year, Dr. Knight will be Associate Professor of Management at the University of Texas, where he has been teaching during the period while Lex was being formed. Before going to the University of Texas, he was Assistant Professor of Business Administration at Stanford Business School for five years. While on the Stanford faculty, he specialized in the area of computerized management information systems and was widely published in the fields of management and computer technology.

Dr. Knight is a nationally known consultant, and his consulting assignments both before and after receiving his Ph.D. from Carnegie-Mellon University in 1963 in Industrial Administration have included RAND Corporation, IBM, McKinsey and Co., Stanford Research Institute, G.E. TEMPO, Barnes-Hind Pharmaceuticals and Texas Instruments. Dr. Knight's Master's degree from Carnegie-Mellon and B.S. from Yale were also in Industrial Administration.

KENT MITCHELL, age 30, Vice President, Legal Services Division, is an attorney at law and mathematician. He directs all activities of Lex in the legal field, based on pioneering systems development work performed by him in the utilization of computers for the law.

Before co-founding Lex, Mr. Mitchell practiced law independently in Redwood City, California, and was associated with the San Francisco law firm of Brobeck, Phleger and Harrison. He was admitted to the California Bar in January 1965. Mr. Mitchell gained his computer experience at the University of California in Berkeley, where he was employed as a systems programmer while studying for his law degree. He also worked as a systems programmer for Lockheed Missiles and Space Company immediately after receiving his B.S.

Mr. Mitchell's academic training started in the field of mathematics, in which he received the B.S. degree from Stanford University in 1961. He went on to the University of California from which he received the J.D. in law in 1964 prior to admission to the Bar.

Mr. Mitchell is an Olympic medalist—co-winner of the Gold Medal at the Tokyo Olympic Games in 1964 and of the Bronze at Rome in 1960, on both occasions as cox in the coxed-pairs rowing event.

HARRY TURNER, age 32, is Corporate Treasurer of Lex.

In addition to his duties as Treasurer, he is responsible for directing market support and client services for the LSD.

EXHIBIT 3 (Continued)

Before joining Lex, he was a research engineer and project leader at the Stanford Research Institute. While there, he specialized in directing empirical and theoretical research in radio communications. He received an M.S. in electrical engineering in 1960 and an M.B.A. in finance in 1968 from Stanford University.

EXHIBIT 4

Law Office Accounting Program

CLIENT-MATTER DIRECTORY

DISTRIBUTION: To all attorneys and clerical-accounting staff

FREQUENCY: Monthly

A monthly updated list of all clients (in alphabetical order) and their matters. This is a housekeeping report from which client and matter numbers for input data are obtained.

```
              LIST OF ACTIVE CLIENTS AND ACTIVE MATTERS        01 OCTOBER, 1969

     CHOLIS, MAY & LEVY
     39 WEST WASHINGTON STREET
     CHICAGO, ILLINOIS
     60604
```

CLIENT NAME	CLIENT CODE	MATTER DESCRIPTION	MATTER I.D.	RESP. ATTORNEY
BANK OF CHICAGO	BKCHI	FORTUNE MAG. LOAN	F51	GEORGE N. ROBERTS
BANK OF CHICAGO	BKCHI	TOOK PLAZA LOAN	F49	GEORGE N. ROBERTS
BANK OF CHICAGO	BKCHI	VESPER PRAIRIE LOAN	F59	GEORGE N. ROBERTS
GERBAR, INC.	GERB	APPLIC FOR TRDMARK	TR880	RUDOLF H. LEVY
GERBAR, INC.	GERB	SECURITIES ISSUE	S10	RUDOLF H. LEVY
GERBAR, INC.	GERB	WRIT V. GERBAR, INC.	W41	RUDOLF H. LEVY
LOEW'S, INC.	LOEW	FERRIS V LOEW S, INC	L101	GEORGE R. CHOLIS
LOEW'S, INC.	LOEW	GEN'L CORP REORG	01	GEORGE R. CHOLIS
LOEW'S, INC.	LOEW	PETERSON V. LOEW'S	L102	GEORGE R. CHOLIS
LONDON GUARANTEE AND ACC. CO.	LOND	HOPPER V. TABBOT	P1400	S. J. CRUMBACKER
LONDON GUARANTEE AND ACC. CO.	LOND	MACHIN V LOCKS	P1410	S. J. CRUMBACKER
LONDON GUARANTEE AND ACC. CO.	LOND	ROLFS V HAWKINS, ETC	P1419	S. J. CRUMBACKER

CLIENT LEDGER

DISTRIBUTION: Billing Attorney

FREQUENCY: Monthly, although selective ledgers may be inhibited for a period of time to be defined by the using law office

Page 1—SUMMARY BILLING DATA
Provides a complete financial summary of each Case or Client (law office determines which file this represents) for the current reporting period, and cumulative financial data, year-to-date or case opening to date. Unbilled fees and disbursements and accounts receivable (billed) fees and disbursements, are

EXHIBIT 4 (Continued)

aged to provide cash flow control. Client/Case identification information is provided on each ledger. This ledger is perforated to the right of center. The right hand side is separated from the ledger by the attorney, when he enters his billing values, to initiate client billing. It is then forwarded to Lex to adjust Client/Case files. On the Billing Memo he may allocate billing credit to any number of attorneys.

Page 2—CURRENT ITEMIZED ATTORNEY ACTIVITY

A chronological detail of activity by working attorney. The first line of activity is initiated by a three (3) digit activity code on the attorney's time sheet. Following lines of descriptive text is provided by the attorney on his time sheet. Total hours and extended value (times each attorney's hourly rate) is provided on the left side of this page. Activity, in chronological order, is provided on the right side tear-off sheet to be optionally attached to the client's bill to document attorney's fees. It may also be sent separately as a status report to the client.

Page 3—CURRENT ITEMIZED DISBURSEMENTS

A chronological listing of client disbursements showing authorizing attorney if appropriate. The right hand tear-off constitutes the client's disbursement bill.

Page 4—ITEMIZED CURRENT RECEIPTS AND BILLINGS

A chronological listing of client receipts and billings. If billings or receipts are allocated to more attorneys than the billing attorney, the distribution will be reflected here. Adjustments, if any, will also be reflected on this page.

```
OFC  CLNT     CLIENT LEDGER              CURRENT DATE             OFC  CLNT       / /
056  WFB      EST OF GR HUMG,DECD        NOVEMBER 15,1969         056  WFB      EST OF GR HUMG,DECD

CLIENT NAME                              LAST LEDGER              CLIENT NAME
WELLS FARGO BANK                         OCTOBER 15,1969          WELLS FARGO BANK
100 FOURTH AVE.                                                   100 FOURTH AVE.
SAN MATEO, CALIF.            94401                                SAN MATEO, CALIF.            94401

MATTER NO          TYPE    BILL ATTY     SOURCE ATTY ASST ATTYS   MATTER NO        BILL ATTY
WEB-354-001        354     001-0                                  WFB-354-001      001-0

DESCRIPTION                              DATE OPENED                               ATTY       FEES        DISB
EST OF GR HUMG,DECD                      APRIL 23,1969

SUMMARY OF ACTIVITY SINCE LAST LEDGER                            BILL NOW
             HOURS      VALUE     DISB.    BILLINGS   PAYMENTS
FEES          2.90     101.50                 0.00       0.00
DISB                             26.60        0.00       0.00

CUMULATIVE STATUS THROUGH CURRENT PERIOD
             HOURS      VALUE     DISB.    BILLINGS   PAYMENTS
FEES         21.15     740.25                 0.00       0.00
DISB                             73.68        0.00       0.00

BILLED SERVICES AND DISBURSEMENTS THROUGH CURRENT PERIOD          WRITE UP
           OVER 90    OVER 60   OVER 30      CURR    BALANCE
FEES          0.00       0.00      0.00      0.00       0.00
DISB          0.00       0.00      0.00      0.00       0.00

UNBILLED SERVICES AND DISBURSEMENTS THROUGH CURRENT PERIOD        WRITE OFF
           OVER 90    OVER 60   OVER 30      CURR    BALANCE
FEES          0.00     540.75     98.00    101.50     740.25
DISB          0.00      47.08      0.00     26.60      73.68
```

EXHIBIT 4 (Continued)

OFC CLNT 056 WFB	CLIENT LEDGER–CONTINUED– EST OF GR HUMG,DECD		CURRENT DATE NOVEMBER 15,1969			OFC CLNT 056 WFB	/ / EST OF GR HUMG,DECD	
ATTY ACT	DATE	DESCRIPTION	HOURS	VALUE	ATTY	DATE	DESCRIPTION	
001-0 011	10-20-69	LETTER RE NON PROB PROP FOR IT-22-TO MR. FICK	1.00	35.00	K M	10 20 69	LETTER RE NON PROB PROP FOR IT-22-TO MR. FICK	
001-0 011	10 21 69	LETTER TO MR FICK RE 1968 GIFTS	.10	3.50	K M	10 21 69	LETTER TO MR FICK PE 1968 GIFTS	
001-0 014	10 22 69	PREP. PLEADINGS, OT. PAPERS PET FOR AUTH OT SELL & STOCK	1.00	35.00	K M	10 22 69	PREP. PLEADINGS, CT. PAPERS PET FOR AUTH OT SELL & STOCK	
001-0 017	11 03 69	TELEPHONE TIME W/FICK RE SUPP IVV/APP	.10	3.50	K M	11 03 69	TELEPHONE TIME W/FICK RE SUPP IVV/APP	
001-0 017	11 04 69	TELEPHONE TIME 2 CALLS-ACK&MRS.HUMPHRIES CALL FICK RE STOCK SALE ORDER	.50	17.50	K M	11 04 69	TELEPHONE TIME 2 CALLS-ACK&MRS.HUMPHRIES CALL FICK RE STOCK SALE ORDER	
001-0 011	11 06 69	LETTER TO FICK W/'COAT ON A STICK' ROYALTY ASSIGNMENT	.20	7.00	K M	11 06 69	LETTER TO FICK W/'COAT ON A STICK' ROYALTY ASSIGNMENT	

"Copyright 1969 Lex Computer Systems, Inc."

Page 2

OFC CLNT 056 WFB	CLIENT LEDGER–CONTINUED– EST OF GR HUMG,DECD		CURRENT DATE NOVEMBER 15,1969			OFC CLNT 056 WFB	/ / EST OF GR HUMG,DECD	
ATTY ACT	DATE	DESCRIPTION	HOURS	VALUE	ATTY	DATE	DESCRIPTION	
CURRENT EXPENSES ADVANCED						CURRENT EXPENSES ADVANCED		
001-0 010	10 23 69	PUBLICATION EXPENSE PETIT. FOR PROB,LTRS TEST NOTICE OF HEARING		25.00	K M	10 23 69	PUBLICATION EXPENSE PETIT. FOR PROB,LTRS TEST NOTICE OF HEARING	$25.00
001-0 005	10 31 69	CLERK'S FILING, OTHER FEE CERT COPY ORDER SELL STK		1.60	K M	10 31 69	CLERK'S FILING, OTHER FEE CERT COPY ORDER SELL STK	$1.60

"Copyright 1969 Lex Computer Systems, Inc."

Page 3

OFC CLNT 056 ARIF	CLIENT LEDGER–CONTINUED– INCORPORATION		CURRENT DATE NOVEMBER 15,1969			OFC CLNT 056 ARIF	INCORPORATION	
ATTY ACT	DATE	DESCRIPTION	HOURS	VALUE	ATTY	DATE	DESCRIPTION	
CURRENT RECEIPTS ITEMIZED								
	11-12-69	COST BILL PAID		127.150R				
	11-12-69	COST BILL PAID		127.150R				
CURRENT BILLINGS ITEMIZED								
	10-21-69			667.500R				
	10-21-69			127.15				
	10-21-69			1,000.00				

"Copyright 1969 Lex Computer Systems, Inc."

Page 4

SUMMARY CLIENT LEDGER

DISTRIBUTION: Managing Partner

FREQUENCY: Monthly

DESCRIPTION

A complete financial summary by client. This report shows: (1) the number of cases for each client, active or closed; (2) year-to-date total hours and extended dollar valce; (3) total disbursements, billings, receipts and write-offs (this is total adjustments minus or plus). For law firm cash flow analysis, billed

EXHIBIT 4 (Continued)

(accounts/receivable) fees and disbursements and unbilled fees and disbursements are displayed in an aged format. The final entry is a summary of the law office client billing position.

USE

This report is intended for monthly analysis by managing partners to identify cash flow position or problems of the firm, with a client breakdown, so that statistics can be traced back to responsible clients and billing attorneys.

```
                                              SUMMARY LEDGER
OFC                                           CURRENT DATE
056                                             11/15/69
CLNT      CLIENT NAME
CODE

ARIE   ARIES ADVERTISING ASSOCIATES   SUMMARY OF ACTIVITY & EXPENSES THRU CURRENT PERIOD              WRITE OFF
          TOT MTRS=  1 ACTV=  1 INACT=  0    HOURS     VALUE     EXPENSES   BILLINGS   PAYMENTS     HRS     VALUE
                                     FEES   10.70    414.50                1,075.00    110.00    0.00
                                     DISB                        254.30     127.15     254.30    0.00
                                       AGE OF UNBILLED ACTIVITY & EXPENSES THRU CURRENT PERIOD
                                        OVER 90   OVER 60   OVER 30     CURR     BALANCE
                                     FEES    .00       .00       .00      7.00      7.00       0.00
                                     DISB    .00       .00       .00       .00       .00       0.00
                                       AGE OF BILLED ACTIVITY & EXPENSES THRU CURRENT PERIOD
                                        OVER 90   OVER 60   OVER 30     CURR     BALANCE
                                     FEES    .00       .00       .00    965.00    965.00       0.00
                                     DISB    .00       .00       .00    127.15-   127.15-      0.00


OFC                                           CURRENT DATE
056                                             11/15/69
CLNT      CLIENT NAME
CODE

WFB    WELLS FARGO BANK               SUMMARY OF ACTIVITY & EXPENSES THRU CURRENT PERIOD              WRITE OFF
          TOT MTRS=  1 ACTV=  1 INACT=  0    HOURS     VALUE     EXPENSES   BILLINGS   PAYMENTS     HRS     VALUE
                                     FEES   21.15    740.25                   .00                 0.00
                                     DISB                         73.68     127.15                0.00
                                       AGE OF UNBILLED ACTIVITY & EXPENSES THRU CURRENT PERIOD
                                        OVER 90   OVER 60   OVER 30     CURR     BALANCE
                                     FEES    .00    540.75     98.00    101.50    740.25       0.00
                                     DISB    .00     47.08       .00     26.60     73.68       0.00
                                       AGE OF BILLED ACTIVITY & EXPENSES THRU CURRENT PERIOD
                                        OVER 90   OVER 60   OVER 30     CURR     BALANCE
                                     FEES    .00       .00       .00      .00       .00        0.00
                                     DISB    .00       .00       .00      .00       .00        0.00

"Copyright 1969 Lex Computer Systems, Inc."



OFC                                           CURRENT DATE
056                                             11/15/69
CLNT      CLIENT NAME
CODE

MSCP   MCCRILLIS, REVEREND PHILLIP   SUMMARY OF ACTIVITY & EXPENSES THRU CURRENT PERIOD               WRITE OFF
          TOT MTRS=  1 ACTV=  1 INACT=  0    HOURS     VALUE     EXPENSES   BILLINGS   PAYMENTS     HRS     VALUE
                                     FEES    3.20    112.00                 150.00                0.00
                                     DISB                        166.20     127.15                0.00
                                       AGE OF UNBILLED ACTIVITY & EXPENSES THRU CURRENT PERIOD
                                        OVER 90   OVER 60   OVER 30     CURR     BALANCE
                                     FEES    .00       .00       .00     38.00     38.00-      0.00
                                     DISB    .00       .00       .00      .00       .00        0.00
                                       AGE OF BILLED ACTIVITY & EXPENSES THRU CURRENT PERIOD
                                        OVER 90   OVER 60   OVER 30     CURR     BALANCE
                                     FEES    .00       .00    150.00      .00     150.00       0.00
                                     DISB    .00       .00     83.10      .00      83.10       0.00

OFC                                           CURRENT DATE
056                                             11/15/69
       OFC TOTALS -CURRENT           SUMMARY OF ACTIVITY & EXPENSES THRU CURRENT PERIOD               WRITE OFF
          TOT MTRS=  3 ACTV=  3 INACT=  0    HOURS     VALUE     EXPENSES   BILLINGS   PAYMENTS     HRS     VALUE
                                     FEES   35.05  1,266.75                1,225.00    110.00    0.00
                                     DISB                        494.18     635.75               0.00
                                       AGE OF UNBILLED ACTIVITY & EXPENSES THRU CURRENT PERIOD
                                        OVER 90   OVER 60   OVER 30     CURR     BALANCE
                                     FEES    .00    540.75     98.00     70.50    709.25       0.00
                                     DISB    .00     47.08       .00     26.60     73.68       0.00
                                       AGE OF BILLED ACTIVITY & EXPENSES THRU CURRENT PERIOD
                                        OVER 90   OVER 60   OVER 30     CURR     BALANCE
                                     FEES    .00       .00    150.00    965.00  1,115.00       0.00
                                     DISB    .00       .00     83.10    127.15-   44.05-       0.00

"Copyright 1969 Lex Computer Systems, Inc."
```

EXHIBIT 4 (Continued)

ATTORNEY ACTIVITY REPORT

DISTRIBUTION: To be determined by law office

FREQUENCY: Monthly

A listing by working attorney of the cases on which he worked, and the current time he spent on each case with the extended dollar value of his time. Data are presented for the current period and for year-to-date. If billings, receipts and adjustments are allocated by the billing attorney to the working attorney, these figures will be displayed both for the current period and year-to-date. The final entry is a total for all working attorneys, both current and year-to-date. At the beginning of each report, a standard of billable hours and their extended dollar value (an average of all working attorneys) is provided for comparative analysis.

```
                                      ATTORNEY SUMMARY

OFC CURRENT DATE
056    OCTOBER 13,1969
                                      HOURS                    VALUE
   SJR OFC AVERAGES                    1.55                     112.00-
   YTD OFC AVERAGES                    17.52                    354.62
   001-0 KENT MITCHELL

   CLIENT MATTER I-D    MATTER DESCRIPTION       CUR HRS   VALUE    BILLINGS   PAYMENTS   WRITE OFF
   ARIE  ARIE-026-001                              .20     7.00     1,000.00
   WFB   WFB-354-001    EST OF GR HUMG,DECD       2.90    101.50

              CURR TOTAL                          3.10    108.50    1,000.00

              YTD TOTALS                         35.55  1,284.25    1,225.00     110.00


   002-1 SECRETARIAL

   CLIENT MATTER I-D    MATTER DESCRIPTION       CUR HRS   VALUE  ' BILLINGS   PAYMENTS   WRITE OFF
                        NO CURRENT ACTIVITY

              CURR TOTAL

              YTD TOTALS


         OFFICE TOTALS

              CURR TOTAL                          3.10    108.50    1,000.00

              YTD TOTALS               2         35.55  1,284.25    1,225.00     110.00
```

OTHER AVAILABLE REPORTS

The preceding reports are standard monthly output from the Law Office Accounting Program intended to provide law firms with data for monthly activity and monthly law firm management. Input data for these reports are similar to those produced for a manual billing system, i.e., a form to open a case or client file, time sheets, disbursement memos, billing memos and client receipts. One of the benefits of filing this information on the Lex computerized accounting program is that the same data can be sorted, computed and printed in a number of meaningful reports so that quarterly, semi-yearly or yearly the firm can call for special analyses of their data. An example of this procedure is the monthly "Client Summary Ledger" and "Attorney Activity

EXHIBIT 4 (Concluded)

Summary" wherein data to construct the billing ledgers is re-constructed and computed to provide management information. Other less frequent special reports that are anticipated without further law firm input are:

Source Attorney Billing Report: Billings by source attorney are presented to analyze his contribution to the firm's business.

Case Type Financial Report: Time expended and value received are analyzed by case type, i.e., corporate, personal injury, estate, etc., to provide the using law firm with information to plan what kinds of business to encourage or what expertise to look for in new attorneys.

Inactive Case Listing: One quarterly report, not shown, which is available as regular output from the Law Office Accounting Program is a listing of all cases which have received no activity for 90 days. This report is intended to alert responsible attorneys to cases on which some work should be proceeding but has not.

EXHIBIT 5

LEX DOCKET

The Lex Docket organizes docket activity and retrieves weekly calendars for each attorney. A pad of input forms will be supplied for each attorney's secretary, or for a central register clerk, depending on who dockets activity in your office.

If secretaries docket memos, input forms will be pre-printed with attorney names and code numbers. All memos on her form would be for one attorney.

If a centrally located register clerk enters docket memos, she will fill in attorney numbers on each memo. Her memos could be for several different attorneys.

In addition to weekly calendars, you will receive a weekly transaction sheet. This sheet displays every memo that was added to your files in the previous week. This means that you can verify the accuracy of posted memos within a few days after you present them for posting.

Calendars are available five ways. They can be produced for an attorney for any specified period, or for a particular date. This feature is useful for vacation memos and when attorneys leave the office, because reassignments of duties can be effected quickly.

Calendars of all activity on a particular matter are printed. These are useful in constructing status reports on cases. All the system needs is your file number to select the proper memos.

Finally, regular reports for specified periods for all attorneys are printed. Weekly calendars for each attorney are commonly produced with this feature. You may also limit the report so that the memos for the entire office are printed for a particular date. These flexibilities let you tailor the Docket to satisfy whatever needs you have.

LEX JOURNAL

The Journal records activity in cases as it occurs. It relates to past activity and the Docket relates to future activity. These two, together, provide com-

EXHIBIT 5 (Continued)

plete case status reports. The Journal document provides a table of contents for each matter file. The pad of input forms and the format of output documents are identical to those of the Docket.

EXHIBIT 6

LEGAL MEMORANDUM INDEX

This service provides a memorandum file indexed by statutes, regulations and cases that have been cited in the work product of your office.

When a secretary finishes typing a legal memorandum, she lists the statutes, regulations and cases cited in it. A copy of the memorandum goes to your library and is assigned a book and a page number. The memorandum is then indexed by Lex under every citation listed.

This means that you can eliminate costly duplication of legal research in your office. It gives you access to every brief and memorandum which is pertinent to your current legal problems. It lists the name of every attorney in your office who has done the type of research you are about to undertake. An important feature is that the preparation of this index requires none of your attorneys' time.

EXHIBIT 7

March 12, 1969

Mr. Jim LeBoeuf
Fleig & LeBoeuf Advertising, Inc.
2300 Mason Street
San Francisco, California 94133

Re: Our Advertisement for the Journal of the ABA
Dear Jim:

Before we discuss this ad any further, we should establish the several objectives that the ad should try to accomplish. Furthermore, we should regard the ad as the first in a series of ads working towards the same set of objectives. I have given some thought to this problem and I feel that the following set of objectives is what the ad should be working toward:

1. It should create a favorable awareness of the company, Lex.
2. It should establish a general understanding of the overall benefit of Lex's principal service, the Law Office Package.
3. A strong imperative to all law offices—don't accept an automated management system before you talk to Lex.
4. The ad should generate inquiries that our sales force can use as leads. I feel that a coupon or possibly a rip-out card would serve this purpose.

With respect to the slogan, "Lex is on your side," I feel that it will not create as favorable a response as we desire. There seem to be two main problems:

EXHIBIT 7 (Continued)

Mr. Jim LeBoeuf   March 12, 1969

1. The personal reaction of most people I have talked to, including myself, is that the initial impression is one of little or no impact, but after a day or two, the response has grown to be favorable. I would like to see something making a stronger initial impression.

2. Many people react negatively in the following way. They feel that the statement is a hypocritical misstatement of the Company's real purposes. For example, Lex may be dedicated to the legal community alright, and it may be a user oriented company, but it really is in business to serve its own self-interest of creating profits. The person who makes this kind of response says, "You are trying to pull the wool over my eyes with this kind of statement because I really know that you are self-interested." These same people give a similar response to the telephone company's slogan, "We're here to help." They would say, "Well, it is true that the equipment you offer and the operators that are in your system do help, but that is not why you are here."

I do like the idea of trying to create a strong, credible statement that Lex is dedicated to the law office market.

Now, with respect to the art work, I feel that the art work is imaginative and hard hitting and it will achieve the desired purpose of getting the reader to linger over the ad. The first page is rich with possibilities, containing as it does an egg shell and the text, "In an emerging world of new ideas and fresh concepts." The art work on the second page, however, is sometimes ambiguous. Most people do not recognize that it is a hard boiled egg that is emerging from the broken shell. Perhaps this message will be much stronger when actual photographs are used. In any case, the emergence of the hard boiled egg will *have* to be clear if we are to use this ad.

I also like the association of emerging and an egg because there are so many things that can come out of that shell. For example, a chicken, a hard boiled egg, ideas, money, and several other things associated with the concept of hatching.

I don't think that we should use the word profits as the key on the second page. Many attorneys will argue that they are not in business to increase profits and may be offended at the suggestion that they are. For our first ad, I would like to use something less loaded. An obvious suggestion is "What should your attitude be toward office management." If we use this, the answer "hard boiled" should be very clearly suggested by the art work.

Here are some ideas about how we can develop Lex as an ally to the law office. Let's consider first the attitudes that an ally should have toward the law office. He should be consistent, sympathetic, understanding, dedicated and loyal. Now, let's consider the attitudes an ally should have toward the law offices' problems. He should be hard boiled toward inefficiency, waste and risk of default. He should be ruthless, uncompromising, aggressive and rigorous in his treatment of these problems. We should be very careful in keeping these features separated. That is, Lex is consistent, sympathetic and so on toward

EXHIBIT 7 (Continued)

Mr. Jim LeBoeuf   March 12, 1969

the law office and it is hard boiled, uncompromising and rigorous toward law office problems.

Now, here are some miscellaneous ideas with respect to the advertising for LSD. First of all, the state of mind of most law offices is a general innocence about automated services. The majority of them have not had bad experiences; in fact, they have had no experience at all. Many of them have read in the literature pie in the sky promises about what automation can do. I feel that these people will be best persuaded by language that is precise and rational in the style that attorneys are accustomed to in their briefs.

With respect to a slogan, we might wish to convey that Lex is a company created and run by attorneys for attorneys, or that Lex is dedicated to the legal profession. There are three features of the Law Office Package that I feel are too loaded with connotations to be used in our advertising at this time. The first of these is that we increase profits. The second of these is the itemized billing feature of the Client Ledger, and the third is the suggestion that Lex's charges to the law office can be passed on to the client because it is itemized on the Client Ledger. I feel that we could advertise the following benefits without taking a significant risk of creating unfavorable reactions.

1. Lex assists law office management.
2. Efficiency in the office resulting from our service will increase professional legal service to clients.
3. The Lex service will save the busy attorney valuable time in the following areas of activity: billing, research, docket keeping.

Finally, I am very much impressed with your creative and flexible attitude toward our advertising problems. I have put my ideas down on paper primarily as a means of assisting your understanding of my thinking and the thinking of LSD about its advertising problems.

Very truly yours,
HARRY A. TURNER
Director of Marketing

HAT:bb

EXHIBIT 7 (Concluded)

EXHIBIT 8

May 26, 1969

Leonard S. Lyon, Jr., Esq.
Lyon & Lyon
Suite 800, Havenstrite Building
811 West Seventh Street
Los Angeles, California 90017

Dear Mr. Lyon:

How much law do you really get to practice?
An attorney's administrative paper work often demands too much time—time that could be more profitably devoted to clients.
Lex has a solution for the practicing attorney who wants relief from the burden of tedious administrative detail. The secret is in adapting computer processing techniques to law office requirements without changing existing law office procedures. Lex provides a complete law office service that is attorney-oriented, using your own file numbers, time codes, and activity and matter type codes.

> The computer does all the clerical work, and gives you back simple, concise, reports on normal-size paper—You select only those reports needed for billing and review, there is no sorting through reams of print-outs—The Lex service minimizes your file-searching time, time notes posting, and duplication of original research—Docket preparation and memorandum indexing and retrieval are greatly simplified—The integrity of your files is assured through a special cross-checking code system —Your files are permanently maintained; closed matters are not erased.

These are just a few of the benefits of the Lex service. There are many more, and we will be happy to send you more information if you complete the enclosed self-mailing business reply card.
Behind the Law Office Service is Lex's team of attorneys, accountants, and computer experts, with years of experience in putting the computer to practical use. They will be happy to review *your* administrative workload and show you how to turn it into an asset. Lex *can* help you get your practice back to law.

Sincerely,
Stuart J. Lamont
Vice President, Marketing
Lex Computer Systems, Inc.

SJL:mw

. . . *The Company behind the Service*
LEX COMPUTER SYSTEMS, INC.

WHO IS LEX?

Lex Computer Systems, Inc., provides law office management services with the assistance of computer processing. Lex was organized by attorneys, accountants and computer specialists to serve the legal profession exclusively.

EXHIBIT 8 (Continued)

The company does business nationwide, primarily in San Francisco, New York, Chicago and Los Angeles.

WHAT IS LEX?

Lex, the Latin term for law, symbolizes our dedication to serving the legal profession. Lex provides a complete law office service by:

1. relieving the practicing attorney and his staff of the burden of tedious administrative detail.
2. adapting computer processing techniques to law office requirements. Reports are received only when they are needed for billing or review. Attorneys choose from a menu of services.
3. retaining each attorney's data permanently for use at any future time.
4. expanding the service as the attorney's requirements grow or change.

Lex financing has been provided by its employees, Blyth & Co., Bank of America, Hale Bros. Associates, Inc., and others.

CLIENT ORIENTED APPROACH

Lex, from its very beginning, has maintained a close, working contact with its law firm clients, responding to the detailed requirements that are unique to the profession. The Lex service does not upset traditional law office procedures. It uses the firm's own file numbers, time codes, activity codes and matter type codes. Reports are simple and concise on normal size paper for ease of reading and filing. Lex assumes the responsibility for all administrative and data preparation by processing directly from user source documents. Lex is dedicated to maintaining the absolute integrity of the privileged information that it processes according to the guidelines set forth by the ABA Committee on Professional Ethics. Lex maintains all client information in its files permanently for future use.

THE LAW OFFICE PACKAGE—ITS BENEFITS TO YOU

An attorney's devotion to his clients' needs should not be burdened by the distraction of his office's administration.

You can reduce the time spent searching through files to prepare bills. You can avoid supervising time notes posting. You can simplify docketing and control of important deadlines. You can eliminate duplication of original research.

I bring this up because Lex Computer Systems offers the only complete package of services for law office management. Lex was organized by attorneys, accountants and computer specialists to serve the legal profession exclusively. A main feature of the service is its adaptability to your office without upsetting established procedures.

1. Time sheet categories and entries are specified by you. This means no time lost with unfamiliar time sheets or complicated instructions.
2. After the *original* entry, on the time sheet or elsewhere, we do all the processing. This means that you need not transfer the information to other forms—your bookkeeper and secretaries can do other work.

EXHIBIT 8 (Continued)

Another main feature of the service is its flexibility.

1. Rather than use the rigid and stylized input and procedures required of a computer system, we use your file numbers and your time codes.
2. You receive only the reports you want from our menu of services. These reports come only when you need them for billing or review. You will not receive a pile of computer printout, only part of which is useful. Reports are simple and concise and on normal size paper for ease of filing and reading.

Another main feature of the service is its comprehensiveness.

1. It provides a full accounting service for recording time and disbursements by matter or case, client and attorney. This means that you have complete, up-to-date status reports on all of your matters, clients and attorneys.
2. It provides all the traditional docket functions and it provides additional protection.
   This means that, unlike current systems, calendared items reappear until the attorneys certify that they are completed.
   This means that a calendar is provided for each attorney in your office and that a calendar can be produced for each *matter* in your office.
3. It provides an indexed memorandum file by statutes, regulations and cases that have been cited in the work product of your office.
   This means that you can eliminate costly duplication of legal research in your office. It gives you access to every brief and memorandum which is pertinent to your current legal problems. It lists the name of every attorney in your office who has done the type of research you are about to undertake.

Another main feature of the service is its permanence.

1. Our service department stays with you. We do not become ill, take vacations or resign. We assist your secretaries and assume responsibility for all data preparation by processing directly from your source documents.
2. Your data stay in our files permanently. Unlike other services, we do not erase closed matters. This means that you can receive year-end business summaries or other special reports that you require.

There is a lot to the service. At no obligation, we can show you more about the service and the results it would produce. Please fill out the self-addressed card enclosed or telephone me at (415) 365–5691.

[Ed. note: The package also included the descriptions of the LOP in Exhibits 4, 5, and 6.]

California Canners and Growers, Inc.

Robert Gibson, the newly elected President of California Canners and Growers, Inc. (CCG), was happy as he was driving home this Friday night. It had been a difficult week, but he had managed to sort out all problems, and for the first time in months, his briefcase was empty. It would be nice to spend the weekend with Helen and the children. As soon as he walked in the front door, his wife told him that Dick Moulton[1] had called a few minutes earlier and wanted Bob to call him back as soon as possible. Bob Gibson's face fell as he said, "I think I know what that'll be about."

Dick Moulton's voice sounded tired. "Bob, I had a call from Harry Thomas of Great Western Stores in L.A. a couple of hours ago. He wants our answer on the supply contract for all their private label canned fruit and vegetable requirements by 9:00 A.M. Tuesday morning. This is two weeks earlier than we had expected to have to make this decision, but apparently the dry weather and the supply position have them worried. As you know, this contract involves about 10% of our production, and it will mean that we won't be able to consider marketing a larger proportion of our production under our own brand label."

Bob Gibson sighed. "Dick, let me spend some time over the weekend going over some of the figures we have started to prepare. Then let's meet at 9:00 A.M. sharp on Monday and decide whether we should sign the contract or not. Thanks for the call."

"It's no pleasure, but that's the way it goes in this game. See you on Monday morning then." Dick Moulton hung up.

"So much for my weekend," thought Bob Gibson as he sat down at the table for dinner.

HISTORY OF THE CCG

By the mid-1950's, it was becoming increasingly apparent to a great many California growers that the production of fruits and vegetables was

[1] Richard H. Moulton, Executive Vice President and Marketing Director of CCG.

on the increase and that this trend would continue and perhaps accelerate. After intensive study, a tight-knit group of these growers became convinced that in the food industry the "big would get bigger" and the "small would get smaller." They foresaw, as did a number of independent canning companies, that the chances were great that before too long the big buyers—the so-called majors—would have market control and, with it, increasing control of crops and of canned goods prices.

With growing production and a cost-price squeeze, this group of California growers concluded that, for their own protection, it was vital that they move toward establishing greater control over the processing and marketing of their own products.

Further research confirmed the group's opinion that they should move immediately toward the formation of a new California fruit and vegetable co-operative. They were encouraged and backed in this by the state's leading grower associations: the California Canning Peach Association, the California Tomato Growers Association, the California Canning Pear Association, the California Freestone Peach Association, and the California Asparagus Growers Association.

Most of these associations were responsible, among other things, for representing their grower members in bargaining on prices with the canners who bought their crops. They believed that the formation of a strong grower "marketing" co-operative would represent a healthy step forward for California agriculture.

Early in 1957, an aggressive membership drive was launched with prospective members asked to commit all or part of their crops and to make a contribution to capital. The original sign-up for this co-operative organization consisted of 473 growers of various California fruits and vegetables. This group put up just under $1,000,000 in capital with two banks providing considerable additional funds.

In the early talks about the formation of a co-operative with a variety of crops, the growers recognized that this kind of diversification offered them a sort of "insurance" they would never have with a single crop. For example: if it were an off-year for tomatoes but peaches were good, the tomato grower, as a co-op member, would realize some of the profits from peaches even though he didn't grow them. The next year might be the reverse and in the following year another crop might carry the load. Thus, diversification became one of the most attractive elements which the formation of a co-op offered California growers, many of whom were "single crop" operators.

At that time, the growers were faced with a critical decision: whether to build new, modern plants or whether to buy existing canning operations with marketing patterns already esablished. They made the decision to buy existing companies, and, with that, CCG became immediately embroiled in the total marketing spectrum.

Just as the growers who formed Cal Canners had seen the dangers which lay ahead, so did a number of solid but somewhat worried processors of the divergent crops which the growers raised. In the middle and late fifties, canners and marketers of California agricultural products were growing fewer but larger. The independent canners, like the growers, faced the somewhat inevitable cost-price squeeze and more intense competition.

So there was, indeed, a mutuality of interests between the growers and certain processors in the state. It seemed only logical that, with similar motivations, California Canners and Growers, Inc. would do well to buy certain processing and distributing companies as a part of a strong agricultural co-operative. In 1958, the purchase of the first two processing companies was made and they became part of the now correctly named California Canners and Growers, Inc. Three additional processing and marketing organizations were purchased in the succeeding four years and a smaller grower co-op became part of the CCG family in 1966. (See Exhibit 1 for details of product categories and acquisitions made by CCG.) CCG operated the five canning companies as subsidiaries until 1964. By that time it had become obvious that this structure was not in the best interest of the company, and the first steps toward centralization of management and operations were taken. A headquarters office was opened in San Francisco, but a number of managers and executives were unable to adjust to this new way of life, and left CCG to pursue other activities.

By the end of 1964, CCG had become a major factor in California's canning industry with sales of over $90,000,000. With this dollar volume, Cal Canners ranked well up with other large, dominant canned goods companies in the United States.

In terms of case sales of California fruits and vegetables, the figures were as follows:

Pack of total industry in California in 1964*...................... 133,200,000
Pack of California Canners and Growers in 1964*............... 19,700,000

* Excluding tomato juice.

Thus, CCG's pack represented approximately 15% of the total California fruit and vegetable pack in 1964.

The equity of members in CCG had grown from $1.0 million in 1958 to $15 million in 1964–65. At the time of formation in 1958, it had been hoped that the return to growers would be at least 15% above the market value of their crops. This objective had been accomplished, despite two bad years in 1962 and 1963. (See Exhibit 2.)

By the end of the fiscal year 1966–67 the company had been in existence for ten years, and the record looked very impressive. On May 31, 1967, CCG:

Had 1,100 member-growers and a waiting list of growers who wanted to join the group.
Had record sales of $111,000,000 and assets of over $66 million.

Owned and operated nine processing plants, was a partner in two can manufacturing plants, operated a fleet of trucks and maintained distribution warehouses across the U.S.

Had, on the average, over the ten-year span of its existence, returned 15.5% above the market value of their crops to its growers.

Was the largest grower-owned, canner-marketing co-operative in the United States.

Had completely revamped its organization, emerging as a marketing company to be reckoned with in the canned goods industry; a company with operating and marketing expertise.

The company took another step forward in early 1967 when it hired Mr. Robert L. Gibson to be the new President of CCG. Mr. Gibson had many years of top management experience and for the past five years had been president of Libby, McNeill and Libby, headquartered in Chicago. Gibson and Richard Moulton, Executive Vice President for Marketing, had joined together to head a formidable management team. (See Exhibit 3 for background of Gibson and Moulton.) The appointment of Bob Gibson as President of CCG was a bold move, for it served notice on the competition that Cal Canners was fast emerging as an aggressive, ambitious, growth-minded company, now that it had closed out its first decade with a record of success.

Mr. Henry Schacht, CCG's Vice President, Corporate Relations, summed up the company's current attitude about its future direction in an article written for the *Farmer Cooperative Service Journal* published by the U.S. Department of Agriculture:

Of our general philosophies and operating policies, the key one is our determination to be market-oriented. We attempt to govern our *pack* according to marketing plans. All of our *plans* and *programs* must reflect the needs and demands of the marketplace.

In marketing we have been developing greater brand sales, particularly through wider distribution of our low-calorie canned fruits. At present some two-thirds of our sales fall into what we call trade sales that include our private label, institutional, industrial, and export sales—and the other one-third, approximately, is brand.

We feel that stronger brands will give us a better balance in our marketing program. But the private label business will, of course, continue to be of great importance.

We expect the future will bring further refinements in distribution methods. In pursuit of lower costs and improved customer service, we have established a number of regional distribution centers in the East and Midwest.

We are also anxious to strengthen new product development. Hand-in-hand with new product research and development goes market research. Launching a full scale campaign for a new product would be foolhardy without preliminarty testing of consumer response.

Whatever we do must be done in the best interests of our 1,100 grower-members. In the first 10 years of our growth we feel that we have performed well in their behalf. We look ahead to the next 10 years as a period of opportunity. We feel that our co-operative must be able to compete with the best in the industry, and we do not intend to settle for anything less.

A great deal had been accomplished during Gibson's and Moulton's first year as the top management team of CCG. One of the first things which Bob Gibson and Dick Moulton began looking at in 1967 was the possibility of CCG expansion. Both men knew that to offer a full line to their important private label buyers in the East and Midwest areas, they would have to add peas, corn, and green beans to their product line. This meant expansion into the Midwest, where these products were grown.

Wisconsin seemed to be the best area to investigate and by mid-1967, a feasibility study was set in motion. In February of 1968, the findings of the study were exposed to the grower-owners of CCG, and a recommendation was made by management and accepted by the Board of Directors. It was decided that California Canners and Growers would begin processing corn and peas in the state of Wisconsin for the 1969 packing season and green beans in 1970. Sales and earnings for the first six years of this new venture were projected as follows:

	Sales (000's Omitted)	Increase (Decrease) in Earnings of Present CCG Growers
1968–69	$2,518	$ (414)
1969–70	5,893	(391)
1970–71	7,075	259
1971–72	7,781	567
1972–73	8,560	793
1973–74		1,056
		$1,870

This represented a return on investment on a discounted cash flow basis of 25.8%—the highest return of the alternatives considered during the course of this study.

Other highlights of the fiscal year ending May 31, 1968, included the following:

Highest profit year in Cal Canners' history—approximately $7 million.

Greatest grower equity in CCG history—$28 million.

Second largest sales volume in CCG history—$109 million.

Bob Gibson accomplished a number of other things during his first year in office. He greatly improved the morale of the company by selecting his management team and then giving them clear-cut lines of authority and the whole-hearted backing of management. He decided that his key people were substantially underpaid and he quickly corrected this. Bob Gibson's management philosophy was very simple:

> The greatest resource of any company is its people . . . preferably fewer people working harder and being given greater responsibility and higher pay. We must have highly motivated management and have a deep concern for those who are subordinate to them. CCG must create a working environment wherein people can freely express themselves and work up to their full capabilities.

Bob Gibson made this philosophy work in terms of highly motivated management and in terms of dollars and cents. In his first full year of operation, he had cut expenses by $1,200,000, almost 10% of the co-op's total cost of doing business.

The granting of greater responsibility and authority to key people accomplished one other vital thing for CCG. The company suddenly emerged as a leader rather than a follower in such important matters as pricing, which represented a complete switch from the co-op's position of a year or two before. As Gibson put it succinctly:

> Our people on the marketing and negotiating ends of the business can hold their heads high and they do! Let me tell you this: Everybody these days is wondering what Cal Can is going to do, not the other way around. These days, I get the feeling that Del Monte and CCG are *the* important leaders in the area of California fruits and vegetables.

Shortly after the Directors of California Canners and Growers had approved the co-op's expansion into the Midwest, Bob Gibson and Dick Moulton began to examine and to talk about other routes which might offer new growth and profit opportunities. There were a number of ways to go but one in particular interested them.

At lunch one day in January 1968 at the World Trade Club, Bob Gibson said to his marketing associate: "Dick, we've just completed our first year or so together, which was the best profit period in CCG's history. But, as we said in April, '67, we've got a great opportunity to make Cal Canners an increasingly important marketer of canned fruits and vegetables. Soon, we'll have the complete line that it takes to really compete with the likes of Del Monte and Libby. I think we should start talking seriously very soon about the economics of shifting our marketing away from private labels and into our own promoted brand products. We know that there are greater profits to be made if we succeed in this, but the risk of bigger losses is equally great. We know, for instance, that on a rule of thumb basis, branded merchandise will give us 10 to 15% more profit than we can provide our growers through private label sales. Let's say, for instance, that we up our volume to $115,000,000 in 1969 and switch from 60/40 in our mix to 50/50. The difference in operating profits would be in the area of a million dollars."

"What we are discussing right now," Moulton said, "is whether this might be the time to aggressively develop our 'brand franchise' business, what with a broader line and more production. But, as you say, Bob, there are pros and cons, and we'd better take a hard look at the whole picture before we start changing our marketing strategy and our 60/40 mix of private label and brand."

Bob Gibson concluded, "Let's get all the facts out on the table as soon as we can. It could be, Dick, that before too long you and I will be making a basic marketing decision that will set the course of Cal Canners for some years to come."

THE MARKETING OPERATION

Sales were made under either private or brand label to a variety of buyers, chain and wholesale organizations for retail sales, as well as institutional, industrial, and export sales. A typical year's output by CCG would be sold as follows:

40% of the pack was sold under the private labels of most of the country's leading chain and wholesale organizations. It was highly desirable and profitable business. This part of the pack was in the standard shelf sizes with which all grocery shoppers are familiar.

25% of the pack was sold under CCG's own brands, which were promoted and advertised by CCG and which competed with such other brand franchises as Del Monte, Libby, Hunt, and Stokely. (For a list of CCG brands, see Exhibit 4.)

15% of the pack was sold, under private label, to the large institutional wholesalers in the country. These were the large size containers (gallons and up) which were purchased by restaurants, hotels, hospitals, government commissaries, etc.

The remaining 20% of the pack was sold either to industrial buyers or for export. About a quarter of this amount was sold under private label while the remaining three-quarters was sold under CCG's own brands.

CCG sales were made through large broker organizations, which were supervised by company district managers. For brand sales the brokers employed retail men who worked both at chain and wholesale headquarters, as well as at the brochures and P.O.S. material. At the retail level they worked with stores to improve shelf position, get more shelf space for brands, and secure end-aisle displays. At chain and wholesale headquarters, the broker salesmen covered deals and sought chain ads and specials.

For private label sales a straight sales story was told by the brokers, with no merchandising or sales help. It simply covered the price of the goods and the labels under which the merchandise would be packed—straight selling without any attempt at merchandising.

For many years, there had been a strong private label (P/L) position with wholesalers and chains on canned goods. Movement figures on P/L's in the nine San Francisco Bay Area counties, for example, showed that they had about a 25% market share of six leading fruits and vegetables—peaches, apricots, pears, peas, corn, and beans. As far as brand products were concerned, Del Monte would probably average out around 35–40% of this, with the balance spread among such brands as Libby, Hunt, and Stokely.

Private labels in such other major categories as coffee, mayonnaise, and bleach, for example, were somewhat less than canned goods. Again using Bay Area figures, P/L coffees and mayonnaise ran in the area of 10–15% and liquid bleach around 20%.

The situation, substantiated by the attached article (Appendix A), is simply that P/L is a sizable factor today, has been a substantial factor in the past, and will doubtless continue to be in the future. But it is unlikely that it will grow or regress; it is highly probable, instead, that P/L will continue to be a large factor but not the dominant one.

Promotion of a brand nationally takes a lot of money and is a risky venture. The risk is greatly increased when an attempt is made to introduce a new brand against established competition. For example,

Del Monte spends around $9 million a year in advertising alone, plus an additional $2 or $3 million on promotions, point-of-sale, and contests. Of that $11 to $12 million, about $8 million are spent on canned fruits, vegetables, and juices.

Libby spends about $5 million annually in advertising and promoting its canned fruits, vegetables, and juices.

Hunt spends $3 to $4 million a year promoting its tomato sauces, catsup, and peaches.

Dole spends approximately $3 million annually on pineapple of various types and pineapple and mixed juices.

A dollar does not go very far in national advertising. A line such as Diet Delight spent about $1,250,000 for all media advertising. This bought six 4-color pages in six major women's magazines. On television, this amount bought three early evening one-minute spots per week for 26 weeks in the 50 major markets of the country.

The product mix of the so-called brand franchisers was much more heavily weighted toward advertised brands than it was toward private labels. Certainly that was the case with the brand operators such as Del Monte, Libby, Hunt, and Green Giant. Del Monte, for example, sold very little private label merchandise. What little it did place on the market would be surplus "inventory" that they simply wanted to dispose of. Hunt Foods sold no private label and Libby sold only surplus commodities under private label.

This situation might alter at short notice, however. The decline in export markets would place increasing pressure on private label business in the future. There was the danger that, due to the potential loss of export tonnage, companies would "dump" merchandise on the domestic market, resulting in a weakening of prices. There was a possibility, therefore, that CCG's strong position in the private label field might in the future be strongly challenged by companies such as Del Monte and Libby.

BRAND VERSUS PRIVATE LABEL SALES

Since January 1968, Dick Moulton had studied the question of whether CCG should increase its effort in the brand sales field or remain at the 60/40 split between private label and brand sales which the company currently enjoyed. As a first step, Moulton had looked at the four advertised brands currently marketed by CCG.

Diet Delight. This was CCG's line of low calorie fruits, low sodium vegetables, plus a number of low calorie specialties. It was sold nationally, and despite a few geographic areas of weakness, it was the leading national brand in canned diet foods and specialties, and its weaker markets were being gradually strengthened.

The diet fruits market had grown steadily during the last five years. For example, in 1963, 8% of households in the U.S. used some diet fruits and in 1968, the usage figure was 18%. In New York, considered a mature market for diet fruits, 18 to 19% of all canned fruits purchased were in the diet category. Diet fruits cost about 10% more than normal canned fruits.

Diet Delight was by far the dominant brand in its category, holding about 65% share of market in such a major area as New York. The brand had withstood competitive activity very well in the past.

In 1966 and 1967, three major brands came into the New York market with diet fruits: Dole in 1966 with fruit cocktail—heavily promoted and advertised; Del Monte also in 1966 and Libby a year later. Dole did well in the beginning; Del Monte, with heavy advertising and promotion, gained a 25% share in fruit cocktail and a 33⅓% share in diet peaches. However, total sales in this *category* increased about 30%. After a year, Del Monte's share settled down to about 10%. While Diet Delight was down slightly in 1966, the brand's share and sales had returned to normal at the end of 1967.

This was an encouraging trend but the questions management had to ask itself were: How close is Diet Delight to a peak in sales? Can Diet Delight continue to withstand competitive inroads, particularly if a major brand decides to *stay* with promotion and advertising, instead of backing off after a year, as Del Monte did? Can Diet Delight hold its profitable 10% price differential in a growing category which might attract more P/L or brands? Should management of Cal Canners hold firm in its determination to maintain its leadership in the low calorie category through sustained and perhaps increased advertising spending? Or could the company afford to slack off somewhat in hopes that competitive advertising spending would lift sales sharply in the whole category? Or should CCG turn a larger share of its advertising attention to another group of products, in an effort to expand its over-all brand franchise?

Red Pack. This was a line of tomatoes and tomato products, including whole peeled tomatoes, quartered tomatoes, juice, puree, paste, catsup, and tomato sauces. It was a line of premium-priced products; it had a long advertising history and had been profitable for many years.

Red Pack was a regional brand, with most of its sales being made in New York, New Jersey, and Pennsylvania. Gradually, sales had begun to expand geographically, and as they did so, Red Pack's advertising budget grew—to $600,000 in the year ending May 31, 1968.

In 1967–68, three new markets were opened for Red Pack tomatoes—Boston, Cleveland/Akron, and Minneapolis/St. Paul, all supported by advertising and promotion. Sales in established markets had been held at high levels; sales and distribution in the new markets had been quite good, somewhat beyond projections. To the marketing team at CCG, it seemed that Red Pack, principally because of the quality of the products, could be a real breadwinner. Although sales had expanded at the rate of 15% per year since 1965, there were some problems ahead. One of these came from low-priced imports from Italy and Portugal, which were expected to make inroads into Red Pack's sales. Fifty percent of Red Pack sales were institutional, and thus were especially vulnerable to price competition. About 90% of the retail sales of Red Pack were made in the New York area, and if this expected low priced competition materialized, $600,000 for advertising would be difficult to justify. Perhaps substantial additional geographic expansion of the market area and of advertising expenditure should be made, especially since the new sales areas opened up in 1967–68 were doing well.

Heart's Delight. This was a full line of California fruits and vegetables, including fruit nectars. The nectar had been advertised for a number of years, and it seemed that the name "Heart's Delight" had become synonymous with a line of fruit nectars. In the year ending in May, 1968, about $300,000 had been spent to advertise Heart's Delight Apricot Nectar on television in 34 markets, accounting for approximately one-half of the television homes in the U.S., and for promotion at the retail level.

The effort was a joint advertising and promotional plan and the combination did the job. Promotional allowances plus hard work on the part of the brokers resulted in excellent displays and substantial price features for Heart's Delight nectars. The advertising, eight 30-second spots a week in the Midwest, East, Florida, and Texas for sixteen weeks, increased consumer awareness of the product and created the required consumer demand for the line of nectars.

The Heart's Delight line of fruits and vegetables had never been advertised or promoted to any degree. It would be difficult to make a brand line out of it; since Heart's Delight was known as a line of apricot, peach, and pear nectar. However, Heart's Delight and Diet Delight did have a kinship of names, and possibly Diet Delight could pull its companion brand along with it.

Thus the questions to be answered about the Heart's Delight line were difficult ones. Should the brand be confined to nectar only and a new brand name established for fruits and vegetables? Was the association between Diet Delight and Heart's Delight something which should be cultivated, or would it just cause confusion in the consumer's mind? What total sum of advertising dollars would be needed to establish the line as a true national brand, if in fact this is what CCG should do?

Aunt Penny's. This was a line of sauces—White, Cheese, and Hollandaise—which enjoyed distribution and sales in the Western states only. While the three sauces had to be considered strictly as specialties, they enjoyed solid distribution, had a good reputation for quality, and had a good, solid brand name.

Sales were steady at about 100,000 cases annually, and the brand, without advertising, showed a good profit. Over the years, only limited advertising dollars had been expended on Aunt Penny's sauces with no measurable increase in sales. In spite of little advertising or promotion in recent years, the product continued to enjoy 100% distribution in the marketplace with two and three shelf facings. The major question with this brand was, if sales held steady with little or no advertising, would not some expenditure on advertising increase sales considerably? The other question was the expansion of the line into areas where CCG already had marketing experience and distribution outlets.

As a second step, Dick Moulton had arranged a meeting at Pebble Beach Lodge in early May of 1968, for the 14 top executives of CCG to discuss many of the marketing problems which faced the company.

Inevitably, the discussion returned to the problem of whether to change the current mix of 60% private and 40% branded products or not. By and large the major advantages and disadvantages of such a move were agreed upon. The major advantages were: (1) There was a much greater gross profit to be made from branded products than from private labels. A figure of 10–15% was thought to be possible, depending upon the nature of the products for which brands were to be established. (2) Greater marketing control could be exercised through having a well-known brand product line. The major disadvantages were the costs of advertising and promotion which would be required to establish the brand in the marketplace. There was sufficient indication that these costs would be very large, because competing brands were well entrenched.

As far as its own present branded products were concerned the company felt it had done reasonably well, at least as far as the Diet Delight and Red Pack lines were concerned. Advertising and promotional costs had been held to a reasonable level, and the lines were profitable. On the other hand, and this was true especially of Diet Delight, the product lines had yet to face sustained competition. Other companies had made several attempts at gaining market share, but had backed off after a year at the longest, for reasons which were not really known to CCG; but the high costs of advertising and promoting three products would no doubt be one of the major ones.

The second major disadvantage was that many of CCG's loyal private label customers would suffer. These buyers had long been a mainstay to CCG. If they thought that CCG was moving toward further brand development, they would begin to look elsewhere for their supplies of California fruits and vegetables. It was also a case of no second chance, because once a private label customer had tied up with another supplier there was no chance of CCG obtaining his business again in the event that the venture into branded products proved to be unsuccessful. There was a limit on how much CCG could physically produce during a season, and if the change to additional branded products was to be made, CCG would have to forego a number of private label supply contracts long before it knew whether its advertised brands were a success or not.

On this issue the group at the Pebble Beach meeting had certain questions that needed answering. There were those who asked why there was any need to change a successful operation for one where the monetary risks were very great indeed. This group argued that even if CCG succeeded in successfully establishing its own line of brand products, this would only invite retaliation from those competitors whose market share was being hurt by inroads from CCG brands. Another group argued that "standing still means retrogression." "Furthermore," members of this group asked, "what guarantee do we have that Del Monte and others will not move in on our private label business, especially in view of the export situation? We could then end up with no additional brand volume and our private label business under considerable pressure."

There were some other subsidiary matters discussed at the Pebble Beach meeting. The first of these was the question of a common brand name for all CCG branded products. Those who favored this proposal argued that such a move to a single brand name would indicate a common look to all "branded" packaging, as was the case with Del Monte. A common name or mark would make possible more efficient use of advertising dollars, greater impact at the retail level, and an easier sales operation for the brokers and their retail man. If such a brand name for all CCG products was decided upon, should the Diet Delight brand be included in this brand family or should it continue to be promoted separately, since it was the leader in its specialized category?

Finally, the company had to consider just where to expand its line of branded products, if this was the course of action decided upon. Should it concentrate on dietary products, and if so, on presently developed products only or should it consider adding new products? Alternatively, should it concentrate on non-dietary products, and if so, on presently marketed products or on new products? If the latter, then specifically what products should be added?

These were just some of the many matters discussed at CCG's first "forward planning" seminar. Returning from Pebble Beach after three days of business and golf, Dick Moulton said to Bob Gibson as they headed home,

You know, Bob, that was a very good meeting and I'm certain that a lot of good will come out of it. We covered many things and we talked about profit opportunities that may be just around the corner or well down the road. But CCG's marketing future looks mighty bright to me.

"I couldn't agree with you more," Gibson added. "But you know as well as I that profit growth doesn't come easy. Alternatives are clearly in front of us; all we've got to do now is to make the right decisions."

After the Pebble Beach meeting, Dick Moulton hoped that during the next few weeks he would have an opportunity to come to a decision on the brand products vs. private label contracts question before the contract with Great Western Stores in Los Angeles came up for signature. However, the phone call from Harry Thomas changed all that. A decision had to be made now.

* * * * *

As Dick Moulton walked into Bob Gibson's office at 9:00 A.M. on Monday, he said, "Bob, I think I have decided what we ought to do about this contract with Great Western Stores. I wonder if you will agree with me?"

EXHIBIT 1

California Canners and Growers

The Product Categories: 11 major crops.

Cling peaches, tomatoes and tomato products, apricots, pears, freestone peaches, grapes, figs, cherries, fruit salad, asparagus, and spinach.

The Acquisitions:

Filice & Perrelli Canning Company in 1958

Specialized in top quality canned fruits and vegetables since 1914, grew to be one of the largest canning companies in California. At time of purchase by CCG had 3 modern plants, and sales of $20,212,000, 30% in advertised F & P brands, 70% in private label.

Richmond-Chase Company in 1958

One of the largest independently owned canneries in the state, which sold $31,937,000 of fruit, vegetables, and nectars in 1958. Had two large plants and two important advertised lines, Heart's Delight whole fruit nectars and other fruit and vegetable products, and Diet Delight, the leader in low-calorie, low-sodium foods. Sixty percent of the pack was sold under private label, 40% as advertised brands.

EXHIBIT 1 (Continued)

Thornton Canning Company in 1959

Although this company packed some private label fruits and vegetables, the company sales of $9,451,000 were largely in fruit concentrates and in dehydrated fruits and vegetables in crystal form, both used for remanufacture. Virtually all production in its one large plant in the Sacramento Valley was classified as "Industrial."

San Jose Canning Company in 1960

At the time of acquisition, this 40-year-old company had an outstanding reputation as a packer of high quality, premium priced tomatoes and tomato products. Most of the highly efficient plant's production was sold under the well-established, advertised brand, "Red Pack," in Eastern markets. Sales in 1960 totaled $4,704,000.

Schuckl and Co., Inc., in 1963

Considered one of the finest fruit packers in the country, Schuckl processed and sold 4,000,000 cases in 1963, much of it overseas. Total sales in 1963 were $15,544,000. It had two plants, with headquarters in Sunnyvale where it packed and marketed Aunt Penny's White Sauce, Cheese and Hollandaise sauces. These specialities were advertised and distributed in the Western states only. Ninety percent of sales were in private labels.

In 1966 CCG acquired Wyandotte Olive Growers, an excellent, small cooperative with quality products and a valuable brand franchise in the field.

EXHIBIT 2

California Canners and Growers

	1959	1960	1961	1962	1963
Sales ($ millions)	53.9	68.2	77.0	79.2	88.8
Members' equity ($ millions)	2.3	4.1	6.1	9.2	11.3
Return to growers	22.2%	15.4%	19.8%	5.1%	0.5%

	1964	1965	1966	1967	1968
Sales ($ millions)	92.0	97.4	104.1	111.4	109.0
Members equity ($ millions)	14.0	16.8	20.9	24.3	28.0
Return to growers	26.6%	17.4%	21.6%	17.0%	N.A.

EXHIBIT 3

California Canners and Growers

Robert L. Gibson, Jr.

Education. B.S. in Food Technology from the University of California at

EXHIBIT 3 (Continued)

Berkeley in 1940. Following service as an officer in the Counterintelligence Corps during World War II, Gibson earned a master's degree in industrial management, as a Sloan Fellow, from the Massachusetts Institute of Technology in 1946.

Business Career. Out of graduate school into Libby, McNeill & Libby, rose rapidly in the company's most important and profitable geographic region, the West, becoming VP and General Manager of the Western Division in 1958. On the basis of an outstanding record in sales and profits, elected to the Presidency of Libby in 1962, headquartered in Chicago. After 5 years, resigned to accept the post of President and Chief Executive Officer of California Canners and Growers, Inc., in March of 1967.

Richard H. Moulton

Education. Graduated from George Washington University in Washington, D.C., where he took his L.L.B. degree in 1929 and was admitted to the bar.

Business Career. Joined General Foods Corporation following graduation and, during a highly successful 22 years with General Foods, held a number of key executive posts; he was, among other things, General Foods' first Director of Marketing Research. In 1951, Dick Moulton formed an advertising agency and marketing consultant firm in New England. Later he joined the New York business consulting firm of Lillard Syndications, where he worked closely with a number of the country's leading chains.

First served CCG in a marketing consultant capacity and, in early 1967, was named Executive VP and Director of Marketing.

EXHIBIT 4

California Canners and Growers

The following is a list of products marketed under various CCG brands:

Diet Delight, a line of low calorie fruits and fruit cocktail, vegetables, and speciality items which had long been a brand of Richmond-Chase. This line had wide distribution and was heavily advertised. It had made good sales gains in earlier years but by 1965 its sales curve had flattened.

Heart's Delight, a line of whole fruit nectars as well as various fruits and vegetables, had also been a Richmond-Chase advertised brand. It had rather wide distribution but, like Diet Delight, its sales had plateaued.

F & P Brand was Filice & Perrelli's line of California fruits and vegetables. Throughout the years it had received advertising support but it had never achieved a position of brand dominance. It was becoming, in fact, a semi-price brand with an increasingly limited distribution. Advertising of this brand was discontinued in 1966.

Red Pack Tomatoes and Tomato Products, packed by San Jose Canning Company, was a top-selling brand, mainly distributed in such Eastern states as

EXHIBIT 4 (Continued)

New York, Connecticut, New Jersey and Pennsylvania. It was a strongly advertised brand in its marketing area. The line included whole peeled tomatoes, juice, puree, paste, catsup, and tomato sauces. Red Pack was a top quality line, sold at a premium price, and was recognized as a brand leader.

Aunt Penny's Sauces, pioneered by Schuckl and Co., consisted of a line of White, Hollandaise, and Cheese sauces which were distributed in the West only. They had been advertised to some extent over the years, and they enjoyed good distribution in their limited marketing area.

General Foods Corporation—Maxim

In 1963 the Maxwell House Division of General Foods was the leading company in both the regular and soluble coffee markets. This dominant position was traceable to the company's historic strength in the regular coffee market, and the early development and introduction of high quality soluble (instant) coffees in the early 1950's. As a result of this flavor improvement in soluble coffee, category sales grew dramatically during the middle and late 1950's and were the leading growth factor in the total coffee market of that period.

Not content with this success, General Foods was aggressively developing another new coffee, produced by a process called freeze drying. This coffee was markedly different (in appearance and flavor) from either regular or "traditional" soluble coffees. The overriding problem during the initial development period was the high per unit production cost. By late 1962 the research group assigned to the problem expressed confidence that a freeze-dried coffee could be produced at a "reasonable" cost. Their recommendation to proceed was followed shortly by the assignment of a new product marketing group to the task of compiling appropriate consumer research and developing the most effective marketing positioning and strategy for the new brand. During 1963 this new product group, headed by Mr. Ken Carter,[1] who served as the product manager, worked towards the goal of preparing a fully defined national marketing plan by February of 1964. This national plan was designed to satisfy three needs:

1. Define the new product's positioning and potential share of market impact, as well as its ability to meet the company's financial guidelines for new entries.
2. Serve as the basis for a decision to either: proceed immediately to the national introduction stage, test market, or stop the development process.

[1] A disguised name used here to represent the several product executives who eventually worked on the project.

267

3. Assuming a favorable decision to proceed with test and/or national market introduction, guide the implementation of these stages. (The marketing plan for a test market or regional introduction would be a scaled down version of the national plan.)

As the deadline for the completion of the marketing plan drew near, the problem of selecting the best "mix" from many alternatives of: *market positioning, pricing strategy, promotion and advertising budgets*, became acute.

In defining the optimum market positioning for the new product, three broad potential market positions became apparent:

1. A totally new kind of coffee
2. The best of the soluble category
3. As good as ground coffee with the convenience of soluble

Another vital consideration in properly positioning the new entry was the selection of a name for the brand. Should it be:

1. Maxwell House Freeze-Dried Coffee?
2. Freeze-Dried Instant Maxwell House?
3. A name with no Maxwell House connotations?

The basic issue involved was the desire to capitalize on the strength of the Maxwell House name and consumer acceptance at minimum cannibalization risk to other Maxwell House brands.

Each of the possible positions would require a different marketing approach. Each would also have its own impact on the final share of market goal identified in the marketing plan. Each would have to be evaluated in estimating the long run financial benefits to be gained by the introduction of the new freeze-dried entry. The determination of the most effective market positioning would also have direct effects on the selection of pricing strategy, promotion and advertising strategies and budgets used to promote the brand.

The critical task of evaluating all viable alternatives involved and developing the best possible combination—to be detailed in the national marketing plan—was the assignment which Mr. Carter and the men of his Product Group faced in the closing months of 1963.

THE GENERAL FOODS CORPORATION

General Foods grew to its 1964 level of $1,338,000,000 in sales (see Exhibit 1)[2] through a series of mergers and consolidations that had begun in 1926 and that had gradually built up a corporate structure containing over sixty plants divided into six major domestic divisions: Maxwell House, Post, Jell-O, Birds-Eye, Kool-Aid and Institutional Food Service. Each division functioned as a highly autonomous unit. These divisions turned out a wide array of food products, including Maxwell House,

---

[2] Unless otherwise noted all exhibits are from company records or reports.

Yuban and Sanka Coffees; Kool-Aid; Birds-Eye Frozen Foods; Post Cereals; Jell-O Desserts; Gaines Dog Foods; Minute Rice and many more.

Maxwell House Division. The organizational structure of the Maxwell House Division reflected its marketing orientation (see Exhibit 2). The Division believed that the size, complexity and competitive nature of the coffee business created the need for the "Business within a business" arrangement of product management. Key to the success of this system was having a small group of managers—such as Ken Carter—literally "run their own business" under general philosophy and strategy guidelines administered by Division's top management. In short, subject to the approval of management, Maxwell House Division Product Managers exercised the functional responsibility and authority of a "General Manager" of a given brand. This "General Manager" responsibility required that the Product Manager initiate the development of an integrated overall plan for marketing his brand, *secure* management's concurrence with this plan and *follow through* to ensure that each element of the plan was successfully and efficiently executed.

To discharge this "General Manager" responsibility to his brand, the Product Manager had to secure management concurrence on these primary objectives: (1) The competitive position the brand expects to occupy in the marketplace, (2) The brand's profit and volume objectives, (3) The advertising, promotion and pricing strategy and execution, (4) All auxiliary plans and operations necessary to realize these profit and sales objectives—including appropriate marketing research plans, product development plans, marketing tests, etc.

New Projects Evaluation Policy. An important consideration in the development of the new freeze-dried product's marketing position, objectives and strategies, was the financial requirement specified in General Foods' corporate policy for new entries. General Foods required each division to submit rate-of-return estimates for any project involving incremental outlays of more than $50,000, specifying its expected payback period (from the date the project became operational to the repayment of the original investment) and projecting the anticipated return-on-funds employed (using average flows from the first 3, 5 and 10 years of the project's life). The policy ruled explicitly that any new venture's report must include deductions for anticipated incremental losses to *other* General Foods products occasioned by the new project. Top management generally required a *specified* projected 10 year average profit before taxes on invested funds, but it allowed the payback period to extend the full 10 years to cover losses accumulated during the market development period.

After reviewing the Product Group's profit projections and accompanying budget proposals, top management also bore the responsibility for weighing several factors: (1) duration of the period until break-even, (2) risks, (3) probable competition, (4) quality of forecasts, (5) period of greatest investment.

THE COFFEE MARKET

Coffee was, without question, the American national drink (see Exhibits 3 and 4). Coffee's position as the largest single beverage category was achieved by a broad demographic appeal and an ability to meet many needs and serve many functions. Thus coffee was seen by many consumers as being appropriate for most social occasions and at almost every time of day (see Exhibits 3 and 4).

A series of inquiries into the general motivational structure that indicated salient consumer needs and desires for the best cup of coffee were of considerable value in the development of freeze-dried coffee. Coffee was perceived as having a wide latitude of functions beyond satisfying thirst or providing warmth and comfort. The functions varied as to time of day, mood of the individual and particular needs at any given time. Some of these functions were: (1) a force to provide energy or stimulation, (2) a tension reliever with an implicit reward and consequently an aid to mental health, (3) a convenience food and a "snack," (4) an appetite-depressant, (5) a medication (with apparent emetic qualities) and (6) a "friend" in and of itself. Also coffee served as a visible symbol of adulthood.

Drinking coffee was universally associated with the sociability of a friendly gathering. Other perceptions of the coffee drinking situation were (1) an opportunity to relax, (2) a thought lubricator to help achieve concentrated thought, and (3) an excuse for sociability. The coffee break had an almost unique status as a reward for work well done, or as a legitimate escape from routinized drudgery.

Although consumers perceived coffee in a variety of ways, most agreed on what constituted the important attributes in a cup of coffee. These attributes, ranked according to the number of times they were mentioned, are shown below for two different ways of viewing the attributes:

	Attributes Desired in Everyday Cup of Coffee (Percent)	Attributes Needing Improvement for the Perfect Cup of Coffee (Percent)
Flavor/taste	62	37
Freshness	46	24
Good aroma	44	21
Gives you a lift	37	18
Relaxing	35	16
Strength without bitterness	30	22

Most consumers described their optimum cup of coffee as slightly sweet, rich yet smooth, with a minimum of calories.

Because coffee played so many roles so often, a major concern with regard to ground coffee was the bother of preparation—that is, the time consumed in preparation and the bother of cleaning the pot and disposing of the grounds. Also cited by consumers was their inability to achieve a consistently good cup of coffee, whether ground or soluble.

Size and Growth of Coffee Market

During the late fifties and early sixties, the combined instant and ground coffee market saw a period of consecutive increases well in excess of the 1.5 percent growth rate of the coffee drinking population (e.g., 14 years old and over). This growth can be traced to the introduction of a high quality soluble coffee in the early 1950's—Instant Maxwell House, and subsequently, to a general improvement in product quality for other soluble coffees, plus a limited amount of price elasticity.

Soluble coffees provided ease of preparation and made it convenient for people to serve coffee more frequently during the day. From 1950 to 1963, between meal coffee drinking doubled while meal-time coffee drinking showed small change (see Exhibit 5). Even though the between-meal convenience of soluble coffee came at some expense of flavor and aroma, its ease of preparation apparently weighed heavily enough to lead to its rapid adoption.

By 1962 instant coffee had added 0.67 cups per day to the average coffee intake while regular coffee had gained 0.14 cups per day (see Exhibits 5–7). Figures also show that the rapid growth of soluble consumption abetted the growth of the total industry until the soluble ratio[3] stood at 30.0 percent in 1964 (see Exhibit 8). This soluble ratio represented a slight decrease from the high of 31.6 percent in 1964.

Market Segmentation

Associated with the complexity of coffee buying and consumption were significant variations from the population norm in the behavior patterns of coffee drinking consumers. Maxwell House marketing executives divided the coffee market as follows:

By user type.....................	Predominantly ground
	predominantly soluble
	dual users
By geographic area.................	East
	West
By size of urban area..............	Over 1,000,000 TV homes
	250,000 to 1,000,000 TV homes
	75,000 to 250,000 TV homes
	under 75,000 TV homes

---

[3] The *soluble ratio* was the percent of total coffee volume (in units) accounted for by soluble coffee. This ratio is broken down by areas in Exhibit 16.

The usefulness of this analysis came from the very different patterns of coffee drinking displayed in the East and West. Traditionally, Westerners drank more cups per day than Easterners. Consequently, since light coffee users had converted to instant coffee most readily, the Eastern soluble ratio (i.e., soluble/regular units purchased) greatly exceeded that in the West. The East, more populous by half, accounted for half again as many unit sales of soluble. Correspondingly, it contained more densely settled urban areas; cities with over 250,000 TV homes made up 75 percent of its population, while, in the more thinly settled West, they composed 64 percent of the populace. This was important for the introduction of new General Foods' products since high-quality food innovations seemed to be adopted more readily in the larger urban areas. Exhibits 9 through 13 present the data which Maxwell House had collected to illuminate this market segmentation.

COMPETITIVE POSITION OF THE MAXWELL HOUSE DIVISION AND THE POSITIONING OF ITS BRANDS

In 1964, General Foods had a substantial share of the coffee market. Maxwell House Division marketed Sanka, Yuban and Maxwell Coffees nationally in both instant and regular form, consciously aiming each brand at a distinct consumer need to avoid "cannibalizing" sales to the extent possible.

Exhibits 14 through 16 indicate the strength of the Division's competitive position. Its soluble offerings commanded approximately 50 percent market share in both the East and the West and Instant Maxwell House sold more than three times as well as its nearest competitor. General Foods regular coffees enjoyed a 36 percent share of the Eastern market and a 13.5 percent share of the "low soluble" West, where they encountered strong competition from well-established regional brands.

Sanka was marketed to consumers who sought a coffee that could claim to let them sleep by virtue of its low caffeine content—a selling point that sharply distinguished Sanka from Yuban and Maxwell House. Since Sanka's share of the total coffee market was about 4 percent, and research indicated that about one coffee drinker in three was "concerned" about his caffein intake, there remained a considerable potential market for the Sanka brand. The major barrier to increased usage was the belief by most prospects that it was not real coffee and did not taste as good as "real" coffee. Thus Sanka tended to be used as a supplement to the usual coffee consumed, rather than as the primary coffee.

Yuban Coffee had been developed and introduced as a premium coffee differing from other brands in flavor and price. Ground Yuban had a flavor judged by consumers to be richer and more full-bodied than other ground coffees; Instant Yuban's flavor was judged to be "bitter/burnt" and more like that of ground coffee than competitive soluble brands. Ground Yuban sold at about a 10 percent premium at retail over most manufacturers' brands and Instant Yuban sold at about a 20 percent premium over most other soluble brands. Ground Yuban had been on the market for some years and in 1964 held 1.2 percent of the total coffee market, or about 1.8 percent of the ground coffee market. Instant Yuban had been introduced in 1959 in selected areas and expansion of its geographical coverage had been continuing since then. By 1964, Instant Yuban had achieved a 1.5 percent share of the total coffee market or 4.2 percent of the soluble coffee market.

In 1964, attempts were underway to reposition Yuban to replace its exotic and sophisticated, but apparently unsociable and strange, image with a warm and personable approach designed to establish it as a friendly coffee. The new plan aimed Yuban at the market segment that desired a coffee to please discriminating tastes and could (or would) afford to pay premium prices. Its product planners expected Yuban to attract older (30–50 years), better educated people in the higher income groups (upper 50 percent). Instant Yuban achieved its greatest franchise in the West and Northeast by claiming to be more ground-like than other instants (see Exhibit 16).

Regular Maxwell House, designed to appeal to the majority of ground coffee users, was sold at popular prices. A promotional goal was to achieve maximum loyalty through intensely competitive promotional programs, including strong consumer advertising. For this brand, the Division wished to develop a stronger franchise in the low soluble West where it faced stiff competition from regional brands like Hills and Folger's that had captured strong loyalty. It also sought a way to attract more young users (aged 18–25) to insure its long range market position.

Instant Maxwell House paralleled Regular Maxwell House by offering quality at a popular price and by claiming greater value than any other soluble coffee. As a foil to the potentially devastating effects of price dealing, Instant Maxwell House continually sought an improved blend which would increase consumer loyalty. The Division had also introduced a new 14-ounce jar in an effort to maintain consumer interest and to increase time between purchases so that the consumer might be less responsive to competitive promotion. To increase the number of Instant Maxwell House users in the West, the Division used heavy sampling and represented Instant Maxwell House as offering the "optimum coffee experience."

Price deals were used by Maxwell House management primarily as a defensive measure to prevent competitive retail prices from getting so far below Instant Maxwell House that previously loyal users would be lost. They were used less frequently to provide extra value inducements to encourage switching to Instant Maxwell House.

In general, soluble coffee marketers were putting more emphasis on promotions and less emphasis on media advertising (see Exhibit 17). The majority of the promotional dollars were going to off-label deals.[4] By 1964, sales on off-label promotions accounted for an estimated 50 percent of Folger's soluble sales, 80 percent of Nescafé's soluble sales and 30 percent of Maxwell House soluble sales.

DEVELOPMENT OF FREEZE-DRIED COFFEE

Through the middle and late 1950's, the Maxwell House Division had experimented with the use of a special freeze-drying process to produce a new type of soluble coffee. The Division's product planners began to focus increased attention on the still embryonic project in 1960, assigning it a top priority spot.

The freeze-drying process, the heart of the new development, closely resembled a technology long used by pharmaceutical firms. It produced a soluble coffee with a unique set of product characteristics. More concentrated than conventional instant coffee, crystalline in appearance, and soluble even in cold water, it offered flavor which rivalled that of regular ground coffee in consumer appeal.

The freeze-drying process began much like other techniques for manufacturing coffee: The manufacturer roasted and ground a carefully selected blend of green coffee beans. Then, as in the preparation of other soluble coffee, he brewed a strong coffee solution at a pressure and temperature somewhat higher than those found in normal home preparation. The next step differed radically from all other coffee-making techniques. At this point, the manufacturer flash-froze the solution. He subjected the resulting solid to a vacuum, and into this vacuum he suddenly introduced just enough local warmth to cause "sublimation" of the frozen solution's liquid content. "Sublimation," a kind of super-evaporation, resulted in a solid (ice) becoming a gas (water vapor) without passing through the liquid state. After this dehydration of the frozen coffee solution, the remaining sponge-like solids were ground up to ready them for packaging as soluble coffee.

This process departed entirely from the two more traditional techniques. The home-brewed method, used to prepare regular ground coffee, required only the first stages of the manufacturing process (blending, roasting and grinding) after which the user brewed the coffee himself in a percolator or dripolator at standard atmospheric pressure, with water heated to the boiling point (212° F.). Consumers have long regarded coffee prepared in this manner as the standard for good taste and aroma.

The spray-dried method, formerly used to manufacture all instant coffees, required similar initial preparation. But the sealed brewing system

---

[4] The term "off-label" referred to special tags or over-printing on labels, offering a special price reduction. In promotions of this type the manufacturers absorbed the drop in price and retailers received their regular dollar profit margin.

worked at super-normal pressure and temperature to make the solution dense enough to afford a profitable yield. When this liquid was sprayed into a column of hot air in a drying tower, its coffee content fell to the bottom in a fine soluble powder ready for packaging. The spray-drying process reduced the coffee's flavor and aroma somewhat.

Freeze-dried coffee suffered from the first of these disadvantages less than did spray-dried, since its brewing did not require such intense heat. And there its flavor loss ended. The freeze-drying process saved the coffee from further flavor loss that occurred when spray-dried coffee entered the drying tower. Freeze-dried coffee, therefore, closely resembled ground coffee in flavor and aroma. The following chart summarizes these and other differences that resulted from the freeze-drying process:

	Spray-Dried Coffee	Freeze-Dried Coffee
Flavor	Less quality than regular, no astringency or "mouth feel"	Comparable to regular, some astringency, but less than regular
Aroma	Very little in cup aroma	Resembles regular in cup
Appearance	Powder	Irregular crystals
Solubility	Fair in cold water, foam in cup (due to air trapped in drying)	Good even in cold water little foam in cup
Concentration (weight per unit volume)	Index = 100	Index = 125
Cost per ounce	Index = 100	Index = 135

Freeze-dried coffee performed well when subjected to blind cup taste tests. The following figures show disguised, but representative figures from two blind taste tests:[5]

Percent Preferring Maxim Versus . . .

Instant Maxwell House (Sample of 400 Soluble Users) (Percent)	Ground Maxwell House (Sample of 340 Ground Users) (Percent)
47	44

DEVELOPMENT OF A MARKETING STRATEGY

To make the planning task more manageable the new products group assigned to freeze-dry coffee first identified the following basic operating assumptions:

1. That the finished product would possess the flavor of regular coffee and the convenience of instant,

---

[5] In both these tests about 14 percent of the sample expressed no preference.

2. That its advertising could make this claim credible,
3. That it would receive backing from advertising expenditures comparable to those invested in other new General Foods products and that these would insure its domination of coffee advertising media,
4. That the product would succeed in maintaining the margin set for it.

These assumptions were necessary to provide a starting point for the setting of goals, put some constraints on the development of feasible price, advertising, promotion and position alternatives, and guide the consumer research program.

Secondly, Mr. Carter arranged a series of meetings with senior division and corporate executives to review these operating assumptions and to clarify what was expected of the new product. For the most part these performance expectations were based on requirements for a recognizable success. But success in this context was not merely achieving designated financial goals for the product itself; it also required that the new product should not prosper at the expense of other company brands.

The operating assumptions and the following performance expectations guided the thinking of the new product group during most of 1963. However, as the time came to solidify the marketing plan, some of these guides looked to be in conflict with others, or obsolete in terms of new evidence collected during 1963. Any changes made would have to be justified since the modified form would serve as the operating goal and performance criteria for the new product. Mr. Carter also suspected that it would be quite hard to have the expectations scaled down if subsequent research, planning and market experience showed them to be unreasonable.

Performance Expectations

The following are the expectations that guided the initial planning of the freeze-dry coffee strategy:

A. The franchise would be built outside that currently held by other Division products.
B. The gross margin would be at least equal to that on comparable products and better than that on cannibalized business. This was necessary to help pay for the enormous investment in new plant and equipment.
C. The product should endeavor to increase the soluble ratio, particularly in the West.
D. The benefits of the freeze-dried process would be exploited before competition broadly marketed a comparable product.

Underlying these explicit expectations was a basic requirement that the new coffee achieve a going year franchise (expressed in terms of share of the soluble coffee market plus people converted from ground to freeze-dried) that would generate enough volume to meet corporate return on funds employed criteria for new products—and still support a campaign that would dominate coffee advertising media.

The product manager's estimate of the going year franchise, and ultimately its acceptance as a reasonable performance objective, required some very difficult judgments with respect to:

1. The probable rate at which regular and instant users would convert to the new product. A major question concerned the degree to which the "soluble stigma" would make ground users more difficult to convert.
2. The variation in the franchise by market size. The range of the variation would depend somewhat on the extent to which the product was perceived as a premium coffee. Experience with premium priced coffees such as Yuban showed that the larger urban markets would be more receptive to such an innovation. The question was: how much more receptive? The answer to this question would also weigh heavily in deciding media allocations by market size and type.
3. The effect of the various performance expectations, which are discussed in more detail below:

Build a Franchise Outside That Currently Held by Other Division Products. Because the Division already commanded about half of the instant coffee market in both East and West, a sizeable share of the Eastern business would inevitably come from *other* Maxwell House Brands. Nevertheless, the greatest profits obviously lay in attracting those who had not previously used a General Foods coffee, since this new franchise would directly expand the company's volume and market share. Conversion of customers from other brands was, therefore, of primary importance.

In projecting profit figures for various marketing plans, Mr. Carter needed a device to predict the comparative likelihood of gains in company franchise as opposed to mere cannibalization. The simplest model considered was one which assumed that the new coffee's usage would come from all other brands in exact proportion to their previously existing market share (in units). Thus if Brand X currently held a 12 percent share of the Eastern soluble market, the new coffee would gain 12 percent of its Eastern soluble target from this brand. Other more complex "cannibalization" models were also considered. Their usefulness was limited because of the lack of evidence that they were any improvement over the simple model.

Maintain a Gross Margin Higher Than That on Cannibalized Business. The logic of the simple model determined that if Instant Maxwell House commanded 38 percent of the Eastern soluble market, the new product would steal 38 percent of its Eastern soluble target from Instant Maxwell House. So, in order to insure the Division an incremental profit to help pay for the tremendous investment required to produce freeze-dried coffee, Mr. Carter suggested establishing a requirement that the gross margin on the new coffee must exceed that on Instant Maxwell House ($2.50 per unit) which in turn already exceeded that on Instant Maxwell House ($2.00 per unit). The higher margin on IMH over RMH reflected the greater cost for plant and equipment required to produce this form of coffee and the need to develop a reasonable return on this investment. This meant that, within reasonable limits which did not distort the scale of production on the Division's other offering, incremental profits would result even from stealing Maxwell House customers.

Increase the Soluble Ratio, Particularly in the West. The conversion of regular coffee buyers to use of the new soluble coffee was a more profitable prospect than the conversion of instant users for two reasons:

1. The Division commanded a lower market share among regular users, particularly in the West, so that conversion of regular users produced cannibalization with fewer drawbacks than did the conversion of instant users (see Exhibit 14).
2. Even where the Division's new product cannibalized its own brands, the margin on instant coffee ($2.50 per unit) exceeded that on regular ($2.00 per unit), making conversion of the latter the more profitable prospect (by $0.50 per unit).

Exploit the Freeze-drying Process before the Competition Broadly Markets a Comparable Product. Since the Division had spent years developing its new coffee product at a time when the question of its eventual practicability remained uncertain, it had necessarily borne the expense of such exploratory research which competitors would not need to repeat. Naturally, the Division wished to reap the rewards of its advantage by establishing a strongly loyal franchise before competitors could enter the market.

Mr. Carter estimated that it would take at least two years for any company to develop an offering of comparable quality and make it operational. Following that, it would be at least another year before the competitor had acquired enough production capacity to be able to go national. He reported that while anyone could produce limited quantities of freeze-dried coffee in the laboratory, transferring the technique to a mass production scale posed difficult problems that required at least two years to solve. He added that, even then, only a major coffee producer could handle such an operation.

Nevertheless, the manufacturing process, having served pharmaceutical firms for years, remained unpatentable. The situation, therefore, presented the danger that, after cannibalizing some of the Division's share, the new brand might then lose share to some especially successful and aggressive freeze-dried competitor with the net result that the Maxwell House Division's total share could actually decline.

Rumors in the trade indicated that one major international competitor

Competition

(Nestlé) and a very few small, North American firms were experimenting with—and were about ready to test, on a limited scale—freeze-dried, concentrated coffees. The quantity and quality of these possible competitive coffees were unknown. Of the firms in question it seemed highly probable that only the Nestlé company had the technical skill and financial resources necessary to market successfully a freeze-dried concentrated coffee. An interesting aspect of the rumors was the purported Nestlé strategy—to direct its freeze-dried coffee entirely against the soluble market. It would then cannibalize from Nescafé as well as attempt to take a share from all other solubles.

On a national level, the competitive position of General Foods' innovation depended on the company's ability to achieve enough capacity to serve a national market. Mr. Carter estimated that new plants could achieve additional volume at the rate of 2 million annual units per $10 million investment at an operating cost of $5.72 per 48-ounce unit[6] (this cost does not include depreciation). Each plant would take at least a year to build, plus several months to reach capacity volume. While the minimum plant size was two million units, plants could be built to any capacity up to a maximum of four million units. The operating cost per unit was expected to be the same regardless of the capacity.

ACHIEVING THE GOALS

Mr. Carter recognized that the stringent performance expectations could only be met if the Division's marketing efforts found an effective set of appeals to give Maxim a favorable market "position." This meant that he had to decide first what image to seek for the new product, then he had to select a name, a label, a package, and other product features that would successfully conjure up this image in the public eye, and finally he had to decide how to allocate advertising and promotional funds for efficient attainment of these positioning goals.

Positioning

The initial expectations of the new product suggested that it meet the following positioning requirements:

1. That it be assigned to a unique position, clearly different from the positions of the Division's existing brands, so as to minimize cannibalization.

---

[6] A unit is a fractional composite made up of:

6 — four-ounce jars
4.8 — two-ounce jars
1.8 — eight-ounce jars

which equals 48 ounces of Maxim. This is the basic unit of analysis.

2. That it be differentiated from both other types of coffee so as to establish it as a new *form* of coffee; a third type which offers ground users their customary flavor with new convenience and which allows instant users to retain ease of preparation while improving the taste of their brew.

3. That it be an extension to the Maxwell House line rather than a completely new brand name.

Mr. Carter recognized, however, that the threefold objectives of assigning the coffee a unique position, differentiating it from all others, and registering its association with Maxwell House, while difficult enough to achieve in themselves, complicated the situation still further by conflicting with each other at several points. For example, the more the package emphasized the connection between the new coffee and Maxwell House (a fulfillment of the third goal), the more it encouraged the probability of substitution between the two (a violation of the first). And so, Mr. Carter had to handle several dilemmas to achieve the best possible balance among these three goals.

Name

To balance these positioning requirements Mr. Carter sought a name which would provide an optimum association with Maxwell House without producing so close an identity that substitution would occur to an undesirable degree. Before making his recommendation, he considered two concepts:[7]

1. Using the Maxwell House name directly with some modifier attached,
2. Using a separate brand name that implied its parentage with only minor emphasis.

For the second concept he considered several alternatives, finally narrowing the choice to three—Prima, Nova, and Maxim. A study, asking 463 women respondents to report their association with these names and rate them on various scales, produced the results given in Exhibit 19.

Alternatives based on the first concept included Maxwell House Coffee Concentrate, Maxwell House Concentrated Soluble Coffee, and Maxwell House Concentrated Instant Coffee. Of these, Mr. Carter preferred the first or second for their distinctiveness since research had shown them to be relatively unfamiliar to the consumer (see Exhibit 20). Mr. Carter rejected the first concept altogether because he felt that use of the Maxwell House name under these circumstances would merely attract current Division patrons rather than new users. He disliked the second concept because of

---

[7] These two basic concepts were subject to some further modifications according to the kind of descriptive designation associated with the chosen brand name (see Exhibits 18–21).

consumer unfamiliarity with the term soluble. Moreover, reassuring evidence came from a study which indicated that a separate brand name could generate almost as much consumer interest as the familiar "Maxwell House." Subjects who were offered a choice between three gifts—(1) Instant Maxwell House, (2) Regular Maxwell House, or (3) one of four competing alternative names—chose Maxim or Prima over 50% of the time, an acceptable frequency in Mr. Carter's judgment (see Exhibit 20).

Mr. Carter tentatively chose "Maxim" because of its easy association with coffee (22%) and favorable connotations,[8] pointing out that "Maxim": (1) Implies concentration and strength (index = 132), (2) connotates quality and superiority (37% and index = 135), (3) relates to Maxwell House (33%), and (4) is short, memorable and euphonious. However, not everyone was equally convinced that Maxim was the best choice, particularly because of the association with Maxwell House.

Jar Size and Design

Mr. Carter recommended packing Maxim in 2-ounce, 4-ounce and 8-ounce sizes. He expected the 2-ounce size to encourage purchase on a trial basis, to expand Maxim's shelf facings, and to return a higher margin than other sizes. He selected the 4-ounce size to enable Maxim to offer the consumer a middle-sized jar with price and cup yield comparable to a pound of ground coffee (about 50 cups at under a dollar). He counted on the 8-ounce size to offer convenience and economy to heavy users and to attain a price comparable to other brands' large sizes.

As a further aid in distinguishing Maxim from all other brands, the packaging department designed a jar that differed markedly from everything else on the market. Oval instead of round, it faced the buyer with a shouldered, rectangular shape, topped by a special lug-screw cap with separate label panels instead of the customary wrap-around labeling. Tests showed that this shape was superior to either a square or a round alternative in generating product interest (see Exhibit 22).

Copy Strategy

Mr. Carter proposed a copy strategy which grew out of his conviction that Maxim did indeed present an inherently superior product, combining the best features of traditional regular and instant coffees and eliminating many of the defects of both. He and his subordinates believed that Maxim's advertising must be directed to (1) convince ground users that they could continue to enjoy fine coffee flavor with new convenience, and (2) to persuade instant users that they could now make a soluble brew that tasted like regular ground coffee.

---

[8] See Exhibit 19.

To assign Maxim a position as a new type of coffee with the taste of regular and the convenience of instant, he planned to present the new entry as *being* real percolated coffee, the result of a scientific breakthrough which enabled freeze-dried coffee literally to *become* fresh perked coffee in the buyer's cup.

To overcome the slightly incredible aura of this claim, the copy strategy called for several reinforcing features. It counted on the freeze-dried process story as its "reason-why." Tangibly, the coffee's granular form would help establish it as a new type of coffee; and hopefully, the newness suggested by this crystalline shape would help reduce the "soluble stigma" that might otherwise contradict the claim to superior flavor. At the same time, the messages would offer the buyer reassurance through emphasis on the coffee's high quality and by alluding to its connection with Maxwell House—an association which would strengthen the suggestion of quality and lend an atmosphere of authority. Finally, the copy strategy proposed to reinforce Maxim's singular position by pointing to its concentration, i.e., the greater weight per unit volume. The buyer needed to use less, a characteristic which should connote both quality and economy (moreover, the consumer must recognize this fact when preparing his cupful to avoid excessively strong taste).

Assuming this was the best copy strategy to follow Mr. Carter then faced the problem of selecting the best means of translating it into complete advertisements. Two executions of the copy strategy submitted by the advertising agency for consideration by Mr. Carter are shown in Appendix I along with associated testing.

Advertising Budget

Mr. Carter felt that the adoption of the operating assumption that Maxim should dominate coffee advertising logically implied the following media objectives:

1. *To direct weight against all coffee users 18 and over, especially housewives in households with incomes above $3,500.*

Experience with other products had suggested that those with incomes below $3,500 would hesitate to accept a premium-priced, high quality food product like Maxim. In a test conducted to determine the chief source of coffee buying decisions, the housewife proved to have made the choice entirely on her own in at least 65 percent of the instant-using homes and in at least 61 percent of the ground-using homes (see Exhibit 23).

2. *To provide weight sufficient to stimulate maximum trial and repeat usage.*
3. *To achieve media dominance within the soluble coffee category.*

In this respect, the plan "aimed to insure the consumer's attention and awareness of Maxim's introduction by saturating coffee-promoting media in each area in an effort to make Maxim the most salient new food product in the public consciousness."

New product advertising was typically divided into three periods—a two-week *stocking* period (to stimulate consumer—and trade—interest so as to insure adequate distribution), a 26-week *introductory* period (to create awareness, encourage trial, and provide reinforcement to secure repurchase), a 20-week *sustaining* period to retain initial triers and extend brand awareness over introductory goals).

The final advertising budget, for the first year, had to be built from these general considerations in a step-by-step process:

1. Since it was assumed that no product trial would come without consumer awareness of the new brand, an awareness objective had to be set for each advertising period. Experience with other comparable new products showed that an overall awareness of at least 60 percent had to be achieved, by the end of the introductory period, if the product was to be successful.
2. The awareness goals needed to be scaled by market size and by shares expected in those areas. Since bigger shares were expected to come from larger urban markets, the awareness objectives should be correspondingly higher. A reasonable range of awareness objectives is shown below.[9]
3. A critical step would be the conversion of awareness goals into estimates of reach and frequency (that is, the cumulative audience, and the number of repeated messages being delivered to the cumulative audience). Sufficient impact during the introductory period could probably be generated in the largest markets with a reach of 80–90 percent and a frequency of once per week. During the sustaining period the frequency usually was cut by half or more. Also a budget at this sustaining level could probably suffice for the second year. Some adjustments might have to be made during the campaign to combat competitive advertising efforts. Usually this meant out-spending the competition by shifting funds into the period of heaviest competitive advertising.

---

[9] Reasonable share and awareness objectives during introductory period:

Market Size (TV Homes)	Estimated Maximum and Minimum Feasible Awareness (Percent of TV Homes)
Over 1,000,000	65–75%
250,000 to 1,000,000	60–70
75,000 to 250,000	50–60
0–75,000	40–60

4. There was little question that spot television would be the basic medium to be used. It was already the common media practice in the coffee industry; absorbing an estimated 59 percent of the industry's 1963 budget. Another 20 percent of the industry budget went to network television expenditures.
5. A final problem, resulting from the desire to increase the soluble ratio, was the relative allotment to the high and low soluble areas. The expenditure of the same number of dollars per capita in both areas would certainly result in regional disproportions in terms of dollars per units sold. The question was how far out of line was the extra expenditure per unit sold in the low soluble area?

Adherence to the initial assumptions of awareness, reach, frequency and media for the purpose of an "order of magnitude" estimate of the advertising investment produced an expenditure range of $9,500,000 to $12,500,000 in the first year and $6,000,000 to $7,000,000 in the second year. This clearly ensured media dominance (see Exhibit 24) but did not answer questions of adequacy or inadequacy.

Promotions

As a general policy for Maxim, Mr. Carter urged the principle that wherever possible the brand should direct promotion at the consumer rather than the dealer. He believed that the industry had subscribed to too many trade incentives, many of which proved ineffective, and preferred promotional offers such as free containers, free jars for two innerseals, free enclosed premiums, and so on—offers which exerted "pull-through" by establishing direct contact with the consumer. This, of course, ruled out off-label dealing, which often lost its impact before reaching the consumer. However, some sort of introductory trade allowance and display offer would be necessary in order to ensure rapid distribution. Based on past experience, a trade promotion budget of at least $3,500,000 would be needed to ensure 80 to 85 percent distribution by the end of the 26 week introductory period.

A great deal of emphasis was placed on a promotional plan that would secure broad product trial. There was a strong belief that a buyer's experience with Maxim would result in a high level of satisfaction and that this was the best way to overcome inhibitions resulting from Maxim's premium price, or the "soluble stigma."

To obtain cost estimates Mr. Carter asked several large promotion houses to quote on the following promotional alternatives:

1. Two-ounce samples with 25 cent repurchase coupon delivered door-to-door
2. Mailed coupons redeemable for free jar

3. Mailed packets of six individually measured servings with a 25 cent repurchase coupon.

The restriction placed on the quotes was that only urban homes with incomes over $3,500[10] be considered, in accord with the basic media objectives. One quotation, based on sending just a coupon to the smaller urban areas (which had an eligible population of 9,000,000 households), is shown in Exhibit 25. This left Mr. Carter with the problem of deciding what combination of samples, coupons and populations should be adopted. For example, if a coupon (redeemable for a free jar) were sent to all 34,000,000 households the cost would be $12,400,000, but a 2-ounce jar and 25 cent coupon would cost $16,050,000 if sent to all households. Other combinations of samples and coupons were also possible.

Pricing

Pricing presented particularly sticky problems. In the first place, Mr. Carter could not hope to set a definite or permanent price for Maxim before actually entering the market, simply because the price of coffee imports had long showed a confirmed tendency to fluctuate violently—by as much as 10 to 20 percent a year—and retail prices for the entire coffee market reflected these fluctuations. Consequently, Mr. Carter tended to view the Maxim pricing decision in terms of (*a*) Maxim's premium over Instant Maxwell House and other Division brands and (*b*) the margin generated after accounting for the retailer's mark-up.

Several other difficulties already mentioned above made the decision for pricing Maxim particularly tough. First, freeze-dried coffee cost about 35 percent more to make than the equivalent weight of spray-dried. Secondly, pricing had to reflect a result of business it took away from the Division's other brands. Thirdly, Maxim's concentrated form made the per cup premium apply to a smaller total volume per ounce. This meant that a smaller jar could be used for 2-ounce, 4-ounce and 8-ounce sizes, a confusion which might affect the consumer's perception—either favorably or unfavorably.

Indeed, Mr. Carter faced what he felt to be a sharply-pronged dilemma, for he realized that with the coffee market's high price elasticity Maxim might not realize its market share goals (especially for ground user conversion) if it were priced at a differential high enough to bring an incremental profit on cannibalized business.

To aid in clarifying the problem, several alternative price structures were drawn up—each with a different margin and a different premium

---

[10] This was a total of 34 million homes, of which 25 million were in major urban areas. This excluded 23 million homes that were either in rural areas or had incomes less than $3,500.

relationship to Instant Maxwell House and other Division brands. Discussion was not limited to the price structure shown in Exhibits 26 and 27; nor was everyone willing to consider these two prices to be the extremes that were possible. Those who were more concerned with the market's price elasticity generally favored the price structure shown in Exhibit 26. This structure would establish a premium relationship to Instant Maxwell House of 12.2 percent/28.8 percent/43.0 percent for the 2-, 4-, and 8-ounce sizes respectively, and would yield a higher margin to reflect high investment in plant and equipment. The per cup cost to the consumer would be close to that of Regular Maxwell House.[11]

A second alternative with a great deal of support was based on the feeling that a higher premium such as 16.3 percent/40 percent/51.9 percent (see Exhibit 27) would not injure consumer acceptance of Maxim. This prediction came from the view that Maxim, as an inherently superior product, might show less price sensitivity than other coffees. On the other hand, the Yuban experience showed that it was harder to gain trade support for premium priced coffees. This was in spite of the fact that retailers would require a margin of 13 percent of the retail price, regardless of the price level chosen.

A further alternative, with some potential legal drawbacks, was to price Maxim lower in the West. The desired result was to lure a larger number of ground users, since the Division had less to fear from cannibalization.

Choice of Alternatives

The final decision on the price level was bound up with the concurrent decisions on positioning, advertising and promotion. The approach used to consider the logical combinations of these elements was to create a "pro forma" share, budget and profit projection for each combination.

However, before these projections could be made, a number of problem areas had to be resolved:

1. The gross margin and cost projections could be tentatively established from the requirement that Maxim demand a margin greater than that of other Maxwell House coffees.
2. A more difficult problem concerned the state of the market to be expected in the three years following the introduction. Three years was a typical planning horizon for the financial evaluation of a new food product. But even this period was long when it came to estimating future sales trends and competitive responses.
3. A broader policy question concerned the effect of the reduced sales volume of other Division brands (because of Maxim cannibalization) on the advertising and promotion budgets of these brands. If these

---

[11] Per cup costs were computed on the assumption that both spray-dried and freeze-dried coffee would yield the same number of cups per ounce. However, since Maxim was more concentrated the volume per cup would be smaller.

budgets were fixed at 1963 levels the rest of the Division would lose its entire margin on each unit cannibalized. This loss would have to be charged to Maxim profits. On the other hand, if these advertising and promotion budgets were reduced in proportion to the decrease in sales, the incremental loss to the rest of the Division would be limited to the customary net profit per unit.

APPENDIX I: ALTERNATIVE EXECUTIONS
OF THE COPY STRATEGY

Ogilvy, Benson & Mather prepared two television commercials embodying the general copy points outlined above, each with a somewhat different emphasis. The "Freeze-dried Announcement" stressed the effectiveness of the innovative manufacturing discovery; the "Perfect Percolator Cup" concentrated on the claim that Maxim tastes even better than ground coffee because it has no bitter aftertaste. The agency tested each ad with forced in-home trials. O. B & M also submitted two newspaper advertisements (one of which included a 10 cent coupon) stressing the theme that freeze-drying produces a crystalline coffee with the power to turn every cup into a percolator. The agency further suggested outdoor and transit displays proclaiming first "Maxim Is Coming" and then "Maxim Is Here."

(A)   Freeze-dried Announcement

ANNOUNCER: You are looking at an entirely new form of coffee. You are looking at freeze-dried coffee. Tiny, concentrated crystals that have the power to turn every cup in your house into a percolator! This is Maxim, the entirely new form of coffee from Maxwell House. After years of research, it was discovered that freshly brewed coffee could be frozen. The ice could be drawn off in a vacuum, and you would have freeze-dried coffee, concentrated crystals of real percolated coffee. That's Maxim. Rich, full bodied, exactly like the finest coffee you ever brewed. Let Maxim turn every cup in your house into a percolator! Get Maxim, the entirely new form of coffee from Maxwell House.

(Accompanied by appropriate *sound effects:* crystals dropping into cup, water pouring, coffee perking, vacuum being applied, more water pouring and perking; and by appropriate *visual effects:* close-up of crystals on spoon, cup changing into percolator, close-up of jar, perked coffee being frozen and vacuumized, man savoring taste, close-up of label.)

(B)   Perfect Percolator Coffee

PRETTY YOUNG HOUSEWIFE: I make better coffee than you do. That's right. I make better coffee than you do. Without a coffee pot. Without a powdery instant coffee. (Slams cupboard door.) But *with* an entirely new kind of coffee! It's Maxim. (Close-up of jar.) And it's fantastic! Maxim turns every cup in your house into a percolator. (Cups turning into percolators.) Yes. Maxim makes better coffee right in the cup than you can brew in a coffee pot. Perfect percolator coffee with none of that harsh, bitter taste you sometimes get with ground.

ANNOUNCER: Maxim's secret? A totally new process from Maxwell House turns real percolated coffee into crystals. Tiny concentrated crystals with the power to turn every cup in your house into a percolator. (Repeat visual sequence of cups turning into percolators.)

PRETTY YOUNG HOUSEWIFE: That's why I make better coffee than you do. Unless you've discovered Maxim too.

ANNOUNCER: Maxim, the entirely new form of coffee from Maxwell House.

Test of "Freeze-dried Announcement" vs. "Perfect Percolator Cup"

	Freeze-dried Announcement		Perfect Percolator Cup	
	Immediate (Percent)	24-Hour (Percent)	Immediate (Percent)	24-Hour (Percent)
Recall:				
It's Frozen............................	63	72	—	—
It's Dehydrated, Dried..............	36	42	—	—
It's Perked, Brewed.................	26	22	4	4
It's Crystallized.....................	18	14	40	40
8 Pots in One Jar...................	36	15	—	—
It's Concentrated...................	15	10	10	10
Tastes Like Real Perked............	20	14	16	14.
Can Make Better Coffee Than You.......................	—	—	20	12
Turns Every Cup Into a Percolator....................	16	7	24	18
An Instant Coffee..................	18	8	24	26
Connotation:				
Maxim Different...................		84%		74%
Reference to Process............		46		23
Reference to Flavor.............		20		41
Reference to New, Different......		35		19
About the Same................		14		22

EXHIBIT 1

General Foods Financial Statistics, Fiscal Years*

(all dollar amounts in millions, except assets per employee and figures on a share basis)

	1964 (Est.)	1963	1962	1961	1960	1959	1958
INCOME							
Sales to customers (net)	$1,338	$1,216	$1,189	$1,160	$1,087	$1,053	$1,009
Cost of sales	838	774	769	764	725	734	724
Marketing, administrative and general expenses	322	274	267	261	236	205	181
Earnings before income taxes	179	170	156	138	130	115	105
Taxes on income	95	91	84	71	69	61	57
Net earnings	84	79	72	67	61	54	48
Net earnings per common share	3.33	3.14	2.90	2.69	2.48	2.21	1.99
Dividends on common shares	50	45	40	35	32	28	24
Dividends per common share	2.00	1.80	1.60	1.40	1.30	1.15	1.00
Earnings retained in business each year	34	34	32	32	29	26	24
ASSETS, LIABILITIES, AND STOCKHOLDERS' EQUITY							
Current assets	$ 436	$ 411	$ 387	$ 360	$ 357	$ 329	$ 313
Current liabilities	202	162	142	123	126	107	107
Working capital	234	249	245	237	230	222	206
Land, buildings, equipment, gross	436	375	328	289	247	221	203
Land, buildings, equipment, net	264	223	193	173	148	132	125
Long-term debt	23	34	35	37	40	44	49
Stockholders' equity	490	454	419	384	347	315	287
Book value per common share	19.53	18.17	16.80	15.46	14.07	12.87	11.78
OPERATING STATISTICS							
Inventories	$ 256	$ 205	$ 183	$ 189	$ 157	$ 149	$ 169
Capital additions	70	57	42	40	35	24	28
Depreciation	26	24	21	18	15	14	11
Wages, salaries, and benefits	195	180	171	162	147	138	128
Number of employees (in thousands)	30	28	28	25	22	22	21
Assets per employee (in thousands)	24	23	22	22	23	22	21

* Fiscal 1964 ended April 2, 1964. Other fiscal years ended March 31.

EXHIBIT 2

Organizational Chart for Maxwell House Division

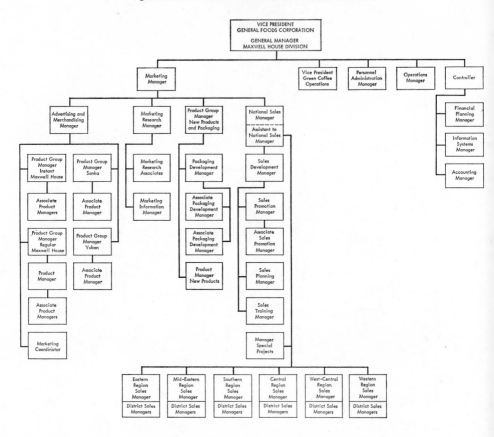

EXHIBIT 3

Consumption of Coffee and Other Beverages
(percentage of persons 10 years of age and over)

	1950	1962	1963
Coffee	74.7	74.7	73.2
Milk and milk drinks	51.0	52.6	52.3
Fruit and vegetable juices	32.8	41.4	38.3
Soft drinks	29.1	32.6	34.0
Tea	24.0	24.7	24.7
Cocoa, hot chocolate	5.4	4.5	4.0

EXHIBIT 4
Coffee's Share of Beverage Market
(Index 1961 = 100)

	Consumer $ Bases	Liquid Consumption Basis
1961	100	100
1962	95	98
1963	90	97

SOURCE: Maxwell House Market Research Department.

EXHIBIT 5

Trends in Coffee Drinking
(cups per person per day)

	Fiscal Year						
	1950	1953	1960	1961	1962	1963	1964 (Est.)
Regular:							
At home	N.A.	N.A.	1.78	1.90	1.95	1.93	1.86
At eating places	N.A.	N.A.	0.25	0.26	0.28	0.22	0.24
At work	N.A.	N.A.	0.18	0.17	0.22	0.21	0.19
Total Regular		2.31	2.21	2.33	2.45	2.36	2.29
Instant:							
At home	N.A.	N.A.	0.52	0.59	0.62	0.60	0.56
At eating places	N.A.	N.A.	0.00	0.01	0.01	0.00	0.00
At work	N.A.	N.A.	0.04	0.04	0.04	0.05	0.05
Total Instant		0.56	0.56	0.64	0.67	0.65	0.61
Breakfast	1.03	N.A.	1.11	1.18	1.17	1.18	1.14
Other meals	0.91	N.A.	0.89	0.92	0.98	0.90	0.85
Between meals	0.44	N.A.	0.77	0.87	0.97	0.93	0.91
Total for day	2.38	2.57	2.77	2.97	3.12	3.01	2.90

EXHIBIT 6

Coffee Drinking by Age Groups
(cups per person per day; percentage of age group drinking coffee)

| | Fiscal Year | | | | | | | | | |
| | 1950 | | 1962 | | 1963 | | 1964 (Est.) | | % Change 1950–64 | |
Age	Cups	Percent	Cups	Percent	Cups	Percent	Cups	Percent	Cups	Percent
10–14..........	0.21	(16.0)	0.18	(13.4)	0.18	(13.1)	0.18	(12.2)	− 14.3	− 3.8
15–19..........	1.13	(53.8)	1.09	(40.2)	0.89	(37.1)	0.71	(31.7)	− 37.2	− 22.1
20–24..........	2.34	(75.2)	2.99	(76.6)	2.70	(69.1)	2.30	(68.4)	− 1.7	− 6.8
25–29..........	2.78	(83.3)	3.88	(85.2)	3.76	(81.4)	3.64	(84.3)	+ 30.9	+ 1.0
30–39..........	3.02	(87.4)	4.50	(88.8)	4.38	(89.7)	4.14	(85.8)	+ 37.1	− 1.6
40–49..........	2.98	(88.0)	4.44	(91.4)	4.27	(90.7)	4.33	(89.6)	+ 45.3	+ 1.6
50–59..........	2.85	(91.2)	3.83	(92.9)	3.75	(89.3)	3.68	(88.2)	+ 29.1	− 3.0
60–69..........	*2.22	(86.0)	3.01	(89.8)	3.17	(89.8)	3.06	(90.6)	—	—
70 and over.....			2.39	(85.8)	2.40	(86.8)	2.47	(88.7)	—	—

* Figures include all persons 60 years of age and older.

SOURCE: Pan-American Coffee Bureau, based on a national probability sample survey of 6,000 civilians over 10 years of age, taken at midwinter.

EXHIBIT 7

U.S. Per Capita Coffee Consumption, 1946–1964
(pounds per capita)

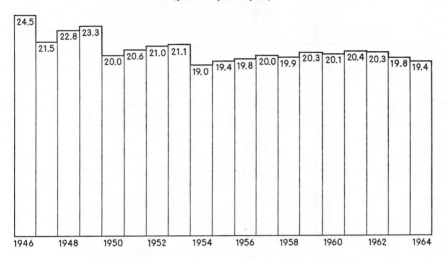

EXHIBIT 8

Coffee Consumption Trends, Fiscal 1955–1964

Fiscal Years	Total Coffee (000,000 lbs.)	Total Coffee Equivalent Units (000,000)	Soluble Ratio	Growth of Soluble Sales vs. Year Ago (Percent)	High Sol. East (000,000) Reg. Units	High Sol. East (000,000) Sol. Units	Low Sol. West (000,000) Reg. Units	Low Sol. West (000,000) Sol. Units
1964 (est.)	2,102	174.5	30.0	–2.1	63.0	38.2	59.1	14.2
1963	2,171	170.9	31.3	0.2	59.9	38.8	57.5	14.7
1962	2,163	168.8	31.6	5.6	58.4	38.9	57.0	14.5
1961	2,080	163.2	30.9	7.4	57.7	36.6	55.0	13.9
1960	1,984	155.9	30.1	5.3	55.4	33.6	53.5	13.4
1959	1,955	154.1	29.0	9.3	55.7	32.0	53.7	12.7
1958	1,863	147.5	27.7	19.4	54.3	29.3	52.3	11.6
1957	1,738	138.6	24.7	20.8	54.1	25.4	50.2	8.9
1956	1,654	131.5	21.6	21.5	54.8	21.2	48.3	7.2
1955	1,500	120.4	19.4	—	52.0	17.4	45.1	5.9

EXHIBIT 9

**Coffee Drinking by Region
(cups per person per day)**

	1950	1962	1963	(Est.) 1964	Percentage Change 1950–64
East..................	2.27	2.91	2.76	2.54	+11.9
Midwest.............	2.72	3.34	3.30	3.20	+17.6
South...............	1.91	2.78	2.54	2.61	+36.6
West...............	2.79	3.52	3.56	3.38	+21.1
U.S.A...............	2.38	3.12	3.01	2.90	+21.8

SOURCE: Pan-American Coffee Bureau Annual Study.

EXHIBIT 10

Sales and Soluble Ratio by Area—Fiscal 1964 (Est.)

	East	West	Total U.S.
Population over 14 (000,000).......	81.0	53.0	134.0
Total coffee market *(000,000 units)................	101.2	73.3	174.5
Soluble ratio (Soluble/Total units).........................	42.9	22.9	30.0

* (Unit = 48-ounce soluble or 12-pounds ground)

EXHIBIT 11

Geographical Distribution of Coffee User Types

Type of Coffee	Total U.S. (Per-cent)	North-east (Per-cent)	South (Per-cent)	Mid-west (Per-cent)	West Central (Per-cent)	Pacific (Per-cent)
Ground only users...............	37	24	40	34	49	51
Users of both....................	48	57	35	52	42	32
Instant only users................	15	19	25	14	9	7

EXHIBIT 12

Composition of the Coffee Market by User Type

	Percentage of Families (Percent)	Percentage of Coffee Volume (Percent)	Percentage of Regular Coffee Volume (Percent)	Percentage of Instant Coffee Volume (Percent)
Exclusively Regular..................	48	54	76	2
Predominantly Regular (60–89 percent)..................	14	15	17	12
Instant and Regular (40–59 percent)..................	5	5	4	8
Predominantly Instant (60–89 percent)..................	10	8	3	20
Exclusively Instant..................	23	18	—	58

SOURCE: Maxwell House Market Research Department.

EXHIBIT 13

Population by Size of Urban Area
(in 000s)

Number of TV Homes	East	West
Over 1 million.............	42,896	20,454
250,000–1,000,000..........	41,348	27,071
75,000–250,000.............	22,520	18,116
0–75,000.................	5,481	8,483
Total	112,245	74,124

EXHIBIT 14

Competitive Position—Fiscal 1964 (Est.)

	Percentage		
	East	West	Total U.S.
Division Share:			
Regular...............................	36.0	13.5	24.9
Instant................................	50.7	47.1	50.3
Volume.................................	76	24	100
Gross Profit............................	77	23	100
Advertising and Promotion.................	62	38	100
Merchandising Profit.....................	84	16	100

EXHIBIT 15

Competitive Position—Fiscal 1964 (Est.)
(brand share)

Soluble Market	Percent	Ground Market	Percent
Instant Maxwell House	36.8	Regular Maxwell House	21.4
Nescafé	12.2	Folger's	15.1
Sanka	9.3	Hills	9.7
Chase and Sanborn	6.6	Chase and Sanborn	6.5
Folger's	5.9		
Yuban	4.2		

EXHIBIT 16

Soluble Ratio and Market Share by Region

	East	Mid-East	South	Central	West Central	West
Fiscal 1963						
Maxwell House:						
Instant	39.2	40.2	43.1	37.4	39.4	28.1
Regular	32.1	35.9	32.7	16.1	7.6	8.9
Yuban:						
Instant	7.6	3.3	2.6	2.4	0.8	7.9
Regular	2.2	1.2	0.8	0.5	0.1	4.8
Soluble Ratio	39.3	40.2	38.4	27.8	18.9	20.4
Fiscal 964 (Est.)						
Maxwell House:						
Instant	37.9	38.4	41.1	36.9	36.4	24.4
Regular	33.1	36.9	31.4	16.1	8.8	8.9
Yuban:						
Instant	6.7	3.3	2.3	2.5	0.9	8.2
Regular	2.1	1.1	0.7	0.5	0.1	5.1
Soluble Ratio	39.5	39.2	37.0	21.1	18.2	19.7

EXHIBIT 17

A Comparison of the Trend for Estimated Advertising Expenditures

Year	Total Coffee	20 Leading Grocery Product Manufacturers	$ Coffee Expenditures
1958 = index	100	100	$43 million
1959	88	109	37
1960	117	109	50
1961	119	117	51
1962	106	120	45
1963	104	130	44

EXHIBIT 18

Research on Eight Product Descriptions for Freeze-Dried Coffee
(February 27, 1963)

	Percentage Rating As "One of Best" on Attributes					Would Buy
Description	Flavor	Aroma	Strength	Quality	Freshness	(Percent)
Extract of coffee...............	14	16	37	20	29	43
Freeze-dried coffee.............	17	16	17	19	49	48
Dry frozen coffee..............	10	7	25	17	46	52
Crystal coffee.................	14	14	6	21	40	45
Groundless coffee..............	12	13	21	21	38	45
Coffee concentrate.............	11	8	39	18	30	51
Whole coffee without grounds....................	26	27	30	26	42	52
Concentrated Crystals of Real Coffee.....................	22	23	25	23	44	55

	Spontaneous Associations	
	Instant Coffee (Percent)	(Other)
Extract of coffee..............	22	(Flavoring agent, 19 percent)
Freeze-dried coffee............	18	(Frozen, 32 percent)
Dry frozen coffee.............	17	(Frozen, 34 percent)
Crystal coffee.................	19	(Crystal clear, 47 percent)
Groundless coffee.............	29	(No sediment left in cup, 16 percent)
Coffee concentrate............	42	(Stronger—won't need as much, 25 percent)
Whole coffee without grounds....................	41	(Whole coffee beans, 26 percent)
Concentrated Crystals of Real Coffee.....................	44	(Grains/beads of coffee, 10 percent; Concentrated, 10 percent)

EXHIBIT 19

**A Study of Four Candidate Names
(May, 1963)**

Base: 463 respondents (women "heads of households")

	MAXIM (Percent)	PRIMA (Percent)	NOVA (Percent)	KAABA (Control) (Percent)
Spontaneous Association				
With coffee....................	22	5	4	14
With Maxwell House...........	7	—	—	—
Spontaneous Association When Identified as Coffee				
Major association...............	Best/Maximum (37) Maxwell House (33)	High Quality (43)	New (24)	Foreign (45)
Not a suitable name............	5	6	12	15
Anticipated Likes				
Will like nothing about it........	12	13	25	32
Will dislike nothing about it......	37	31	24	18
Expected Type				
Instant coffee...................	34	39	44	26
Regular coffee..................	51	35	22	34
New third type coffee...........	15	21	38	40
Rating Index by Characteristics (7 point scale: 4 = 100 index)				
Fresh..........................	148	148	132	130
Fine aroma.....................	135	132	112	118
Highest quality.................	135	135	110	112
Strong.........................	132	115	100	130
Dark...........................	125	110	102	132
Expensive......................	118	120	100	112
Modern........................	112	122	122	112
For men.......................	106	90	90	112

EXHIBIT 20

Name Test—Choice of Gift Product from Three Alternatives*
(June, 1963)

Chose	Total	Regular Ground	Instant	Both	Maxwell House	Regular Maxwell House	Instant Maxwell House	Both Maxwell House	Not Maxwell House
					Percent of Users of				
MAXIM..........	53	41	63	56	52	47	56	53	55
Nova..........	57	45	67	57	53	42	64	55	60
Maxwell House concentrated soluble......	62	52	71	62	60	53	69	60	63
Maxwell House concentrated instant......	62	48	73	64	59	47	73	55	64
Regular Maxwell House (average four tests)......	28	50	4	29	28	50	5	29	28
Instant Maxwell House (average four tests)......	14	3	27	8	16	3	24	15	12
Base: (average)......	(300)	(100)	(100)	(100)	(150)	(56)	(56)	(38)	(150)

* In four matched tests the respondent was offered one of three products as a gift; namely, Regular Maxwell House, Instant Maxwell House, or one of the four descriptions for freeze-dried coffee. The table should be read as follows: Among all coffee drinkers (i.e., the total sample), who were given a choice of a description MAXIM versus IMH or RMH, 53 percent chose MAXIM, about 28 percent chose RMH and 14 percent chose IMH. Similarly if Nova was the description it was chosen 57 percent of the time over either IMH or RMH.

EXHIBIT 21

Telephone Study on the
Awareness, Association, and Connotations of "Soluble"
(April 6–7, 1963)

Association	*Instant* *Coffee*	*Other*	*None* *Don't Know*
Soluble coffee..................	36%	24%	40%
Concentrated soluble coffee........	50	19	31
Soluble coffee concentrate.........	52	18	30

Awareness	*Heard of Before*		*NOT Heard of Before*
Soluble coffee..................	14%		86%
Concentrated soluble coffee........	7		93
Soluble coffee concentrate.........	8		92

Definition (unaided)	*Heard of* *Synonym*	*(Instant)*	*(Other)*	*Not* *Heard*	*Don't* *Know*
Soluble coffee..................	16%	(14%)	(2%)	44%	(40%)
Concentrated soluble coffee........	19	(18)	(1)	38	(43)
Soluble coffee concentrate.........	15	(15)	—	43	(42)

Definition *(aided)*	*Regular Ground*	*Instant*	*Neither—* *3rd Type*
Soluble coffee..................	34%	37%	29%
Concentrated soluble coffee........	20	53	27
Soluble coffee concentrate.........	2	61	37

Connotation	*Better Than* *Instant*	*Same as* *Instant*	*Not as Good* *as Instant*
Soluble coffee..................	7%	12%	10%
Concentrated soluble coffee........	10	8	10
Soluble coffee concentrate........	18	14	14

EXHIBIT 22

Test of Consumer Reaction to Maxim Square, Round, and Rectangular Jars
(January, 1964)

	Shown Square and Round		Shown Square and Rectangular	
	Square (Percent)	Round (Percent)	Square (Percent)	Rectangular (Percent)
Interest in Buying........................	59	58	55	64
Use instant only....................	62	70	62	78
Use only ground..................	40	38	40	40
Use both.........................	72	66	64	74
Consider Different from Other Coffees........	77	57	85	79
Favorable Product Evaluations				
Flavor...........................	71	81	80	80
Aroma...........................	69	79	82	84
Color............................	83	87	86	89
Strength.........................	75	80	83	85
Overall quality...................	77	78	83	84
Improvement over other products........................	80	81	88	88
Favorable Packaging Evaluation				
Ease of handling..................	77	88	87	91
Ease of removing coffee.............	80	88	86	91
Ease of storage...................	82	86	92	94
Attractiveness....................	72	75	72	81
Cap style........................	87	90	88	88
Base: Female Heads of Households........	(150)		(150)	

EXHIBIT 23

Male Influence in Coffee Brand Buying Decision Study (1962)

	Instant			Ground		
Household Coffee Usage	Total (Percent)	Use Instant Only (Percent)	Use Instant and Ground (Percent)	Total (Percent)	Use Ground Only (Percent)	Use Ground and Instant (Percent)
Husband asked directly for a brand, and wife bought it	18	18	18	16	15	17
(Wife did not buy it)	(1)	(—)*	(1)	(—)	(—)	(1)
Husband mentioned a brand, and wife bought it	8	5	8	9	7	10
Husband indicated dissatisfaction, and wife bought another brand	15	14	16	20	17	22
Husband bought a different brand	7	8	7	7	6	8
Husband shopped with wife and suggested a different brand, and wife bought it	8	10	8	9	8	10
(Wife did not buy it)	(—)	(—)	(—)	(1)	(2)	(—)
Husband did none of the above	65%	66%	65%	61%	61%	61%
Base: Total housewives in each group (no male interviews)	(753)	(96)	(657)	(200)	(88)	(112)

* Less than 0.05 percent.

EXHIBIT 24

Soluble Coffee Brand Expenditures on Media Advertising (Estimated 1963)

Total Dollars*—By Region	Total	East	Mid-East	Central	West	South	West Central
IMH	$6,490	$1,710	$1,153	$1,048	$821	$1,053	$705
Nescafé	4,673	1,286	829	748	673	669	468
Sanka	2,981	675	448	462	520	464	412
Chase & Sanborn	3,243	946	582	574	267	611	263
Folger's	1,627	—	143	192	732	194	366
Yuban	2,440	1,221	433	255	352	162	17

Dollars per Thousand Population—By Region

	Total	East	Mid-East	Central	West	South	West Central
IMH	$34.33	$40.83	$43.09	$34.01	$25.63	$32.26	$28.29
Nescafé	24.72	30.71	30.98	24.28	21.01	20.49	18.78
Sanka	15.77	16.12	16.74	14.99	16.24	14.21	16.53
Chase & Sanborn	17.16	22.59	21.75	18.63	8.34	18.72	10.55
Folger's	8.61	—	5.34	6.23	22.85	5.94	14.69
Yuban	12.91	29.16	16.18	8.28	10.99	4.96	0.68
1/1/64 Population (000)	189,039.3	41,878.6	26,755.1	30,813.4	32,028.3	32,645.2	24,918.7

EXHIBIT 25

Comparative Projected National Costs of Alternative Promotional Techniques

	Cost Per Thousand	Extension
2-Ounce Jar and 25-Cent Coupon		
(Base: 25,000,000 homes)		
Product and package..................	$241.00	$ 6,025,000
Distribution.........................	120.00	3,000,000
Carrier.............................	13.00	325,000
Freeze-dry leaflets...................	6.00	150,000
25-cent coupon......................	5.00	125,000
Coupon redemption (25 percent)........	67.50	1,687,500
Scoop..............................	10.00	250,000
Transportation......................	6.00	150,000
Warehousing........................	5.00	125,000
	$473.50	$11,837,500
Free Coupon		
(Base: 9,000,000 homes)		
Coupon............................	$ 6.00	$ 54,000
Freeze-dry leaflets...................	6.00	54,000
Distribution.........................	10.50	94,500
Postage............................	27.50	247,500
Coupon redemption (50 percent)........	315.00	2,835,000
	$365.00	$ 3,285,000
6 Single Serving Packets and a 25-Cent Coupon		
(Base: 34,000,000 homes)		
Product............................	$130.50	$ 4,437,000
Container and top....................	4.50	153,000
Package............................	26.50	901,000
Handling...........................	25.00	850,000
Postage............................	39.00	1,326,000
Leaflets............................	6.00	204,000
25-cent coupon......................	5.00	170,000
Redemption (25 percent)..............	67.50	2,295,000
Mailing carton......................	10.00	340,000
	$314.00	$10,676,000

EXHIBIT 26

Pricing Alternatives—Maxim

Brand	Size	Retail Price	Retail Price per Ounce	Retail Economy vs. Next Smaller Size	Cost* per Cup	Maxim per Ounce Premium
Maxim	2-oz.	$0.55	$0.2750	—%	2.12¢	—%
	4-oz.	0.85	0.2125	29.4	1.63	—
	8-oz.	1.59	0.1988	6.9	1.53	—
IMH	2-oz.	0.49	0.2450	—	1.88	12.2
	6-oz.	0.99	0.1650	48.5	1.27	28.8
	10-oz.	1.39†	0.1390	18.7	1.07	43.0
	14-oz.	1.89†	0.1350	3.0	1.04	47.3
IY	2-oz.	0.53	0.2650	—	2.04	3.8
	5-oz.	0.99	0.1980	33.8	1.52	7.3
	9-oz.	1.39†	0.1544	28.2	1.19	28.8
IS	2-oz.	0.53	0.2650	—	2.04	3.8
	5-oz.	1.09	0.2180	21.6	1.68	(7.5)
	8-oz.	1.49†	0.1862	17.1	1.43	6.8
RMH	1-lb.	0.87	—	—	1.74	(2.3) A
	2-lb.	1.71	—	—	1.71	(7.0) B

* Soluble—13 cups per ounce.   (A) versus 4-ounce.
Ground—50 cups per pound.   (B) versus 8-ounce.
† Reflects retail shelf price when label packs of the following values are in distribution:

IMH	10-ounce	20 cents
IMH	14-ounce	30 cents
IY	9-ounce	20 cents
IS	8-ounce	10 cents

EXHIBIT 27

Pricing Alternatives—Maxim

Brand	Size	Retail Price	Retail Price per Ounce	Retail Economy vs. Next Smaller Size	Cost* per Cup	Maxim per Ounce Premium
Maxim	2-oz.	$0.57	$0.2850	—%	2.19¢	—%
	4-oz.	0.99	0.2475	15.1	1.90	—
	8-oz.	1.69	0.2112	17.2	1.63	—
IMH	2-oz.	0.49	0.2450	—	1.88	16.3
	6-oz.	0.99	0.1650	48.5	1.27	50.0
	10-oz.	1.39†	0.1390	18.7	1.07	51.9
	14-oz.	1.89†	0.1350	3.0	1.04	56.4
IY	2-oz.	0.53	0.2650	—	2.04	7.5
	5-oz.	0.99	0.1980	33.8	1.52	25.0
	9-oz.	1.39†	0.1544	12.8	1.19	36.8
IS	2-oz.	0.53	0.2650	—	2.04	7.5
	5-oz.	1.09	0.2180	21.6	1.68	13.5
	8-oz.	1.49†	0.1862	17.1	1.43	13.4
RMH	1-lb.	0.87	—	—	1.74	13.8 A
	2-lb.	1.71	—	—	1.71	4.7 B

* Soluble—13 cups per ounce   (A) versus 4-ounce
  Ground—50 cups per pound   (B) versus 8-ounce
† Reflects retail shelf price when label packs of the following values are in distribution:

IMH	10-ounce	20 cents
IMH	14-ounce	30 cents
IY	9-ounce	20 cents
IS	8-ounce	10 cents

Metal Products, Inc.

NEW PRODUCT POLICY

The five year objectives of Metal Products, Inc., as stated in early 1966, were listed as:

1. Growth—20% per year minimum increase in sales.
2. Profit—20% return on the yearly beginning net worth.
3. Continued work in the building field, strengthening our position and increasing our volume with door, window and window wall products.
4. Develop real strength and depth in our management team by having each member of the first-line management backed up by strong potential management men.

One method under consideration by the company's New Product Development Committee for providing the increased sales volume required by these objectives was the addition of a commodity or low-price door to the company's existing line of high-quality sliding glass doors. While commodity doors held tremendous sales potential, Metal Products' president was not convinced that the company should compete for this market.

Background

Metal Products, Inc. manufactured and sold a quality line of sliding glass doors and windows. Incorporating under the laws of the state of California on July 30, 1948, three engineers and an architect started the company in Southern California on a total investment of $13,000. Plant facilities included a house trailer and a quonset hut.

Metal Products' early success was attributed to the timely exploitation of a new market. Following World War II, a number of young and unrestrained architects identified themselves with the tremendous housing boom in Southern California and introduced the concept of "California" or "outdoor" living. The idea became an immediate local success and the close tie-in with sliding fenestration[1] devices was obvious. The company's founders, seizing upon this opportunity, became one of the first manufacturers of sliding glass doors.

A steel door made only to customer order was the original product. Contractors and builders were the primary customers. Sales of $120,000 in 1949 increased to over $4 million by 1965. Comparative financial statements for 1960 to 1965 are included as Exhibits 1 and 2.

THE INDUSTRY

Background

Evidence of a sliding fenestration industry did not exist until late 1948. The only limitation to the industry's potential was the number of yearly housing starts and the market acceptance of the "outdoor living" concept. Recent estimates indicated that one out of every two new houses used some form of sliding glass doors and windows.

For the first five or six years, steel was the basic raw material used by the sliding door manufacturers. A few companies dominated the industry during this period because a door manufacturer could only guarantee a volume supply of steel door frames by purchasing and placing with the steel supplier $70,000 worth of rolling and shaping equipment. Metal Products was one of the few companies in the industry owning the required equipment.

The situation changed in the mid-1950's when the aluminum companies, searching for new product uses, introduced aluminum to sliding door manufacturers. Investment in expensive equipment was not required. Consequently, for as little as $10,000, a sizable operation could be started.

With this shift to aluminum, the small operators, producing stock sizes only, became significant marketing factors. By the late 1950's an estimated three hundred builders of sliding doors blanketed every major marketing center in the country. The small companies flourished because patent protection was difficult to obtain and it was easy to copy the designs of the leading firms. These copies resembled quality doors and apparently met the needs of the majority of the market. Distribution by small operators was usually direct and concentrated in a local area. Overhead was low, with little emphasis on research and engineering. Consequently, the product reached the buyer at a price some 40% below the cheapest Metal Products door. Turnover was high among these small operators, but the Metal Products company sales manager stated, "For every two that go under, three more seem to start."

---

[1] A term used commonly in the trade which refers to the decorating of an architectural composition by the window and door openings, their ornaments and proportions.

Industry Channels

Firms striving for national sales coverage originally distributed through specialty dealers. The dealers, under this system, did not stock glass or have the facilities for glazing.[2] Consequently, the door companies had either to glaze all products prior to shipment or the dealer had to sub-contract the work at the job-site. As the cost of this arrangement became prohibitive, manufacturers shifted to selling through large glass distributors who had facilities for glazing. Glass distributors found the carrying of sliding doors and windows a must if they expected to protect their sales of the glass panels going into these products.

Market

The sliding door market was classified by price and ultimate user. Assuming a total market of $60 million, the following relationship was found:

Price		*Ultimate User*	
Commodity	$42,000,000	Tract and low cost housing	$33,000,000
Intermediate	15,000,000	Southeastern multislide*	10,500,000
Custom deluxe (architectural)	3,000,000	Better-class housing	15,000,000
		Pre-fabs	1,500,000

* All panels of the door compact into the width of a single panel or disappear into wall pockets. Popular mainly in the Southeastern states.

Almost all sliding door sales were made to contractors. A few do-it-yourselfers bought doors from distributors, but their number was insignificant. The contractor made the choice of which type and make of door to buy about 95% of the time. The other 5% of the sales were purchased by contractors, but the type of door was specified by an architect.

There was general disagreement as to how many builders engaged in residential construction, but it was believed that there were about 100,000, of which about 5% accounted for 70% of the homes.

Builders specializing in low cost, high volume tract developments purchased by far the largest number of sliding glass doors. With price as the major consideration, the builder usually decided which door to buy after requesting bids from door distributors and manufacturers. Brand name or company reputation rarely received attention in such transactions. The home buyer, quite obviously, had no choice of the type of door used in the tract houses.

Contractors who built higher priced tract houses and those who built

[2] Glazing means installing the glass into the door or window frame.

a limited number of custom houses each year were the next largest sliding glass door buyers. This group looked beyond price to design, quality, service, and company reputation. Quite often, they established strong product preferences, thus making it important for manufacturers to have sales people in the field calling on builders and selling the features of their products. The home buyer played an insignificant part in the choice of the sliding door.

The remaining sliding door sales were to contractors building houses to architectural specifications. Special products and innovation were used extensively in such houses, and, consequently, most sliding doors were custom made. The sale resulted from close liaison between the architectural representatives of door manufacturers and the architects designing the houses. An architectural representative objective was to have the specifications so written that the contractor had no choice in his purchase of the door.

Metal Products' sliding doors appealed mainly to contractors building better class housing, to some higher priced tract developers, and to architects. Metal Products' prices ranged from upper intermediate to custom deluxe.

Since there was no trade association, there was little pooling of industry information by sliding door manufacturers. Estimates of future sales were tied to residential building starts, but obviously were influenced by other factors.

Product Policy

The Metal Products basic product line was well established with all items except sliding windows meeting sales expectations. (See Exhibit 3.) On the average, 65% of the company's production was to stock sizes, which differed from earlier experience. Custom products, however, showed signs of increasing. Stock sizes, which could be inventoried, were important in helping to level the production schedule and stabilize the work force. Sliding doors (including screens) announced for 90% of total sales. Roughly 65% were credited to residential building. Sliding window sales were to be curtailed until an improved model could be placed in production. A window wall line, introduced a few years earlier, was to be pushed actively.

The window wall, designed primarily for commercial structures, was a pre-fabricated wall section that could be delivered to a job as an assembled unit. Having unlimited flexibility in size and color, the product competed with the popular but sometimes troublesome curtain wall. Window wall was installed in sections with the exterior surface of the building broken by the framework of the walls and floors. Leakage and other maintenance problems were confined to the individual sections. By contrast, curtain wall hung from the upper story of a building, providing a continuous exterior wall covering. Water entering the wall at the tenth floor might not seep through until several floors below. Window wall sales in 1965 were 6.6% of sales and were expected to increase to $1,000,000 or 20% of sales in 1966. Eventually window wall sales were expected to equal those of the other products combined.

Sales

The Metal Products, Inc. Sales Division organization is shown in Figure 1. The sales office was located at the company plant in Southern California.

FIGURE 1

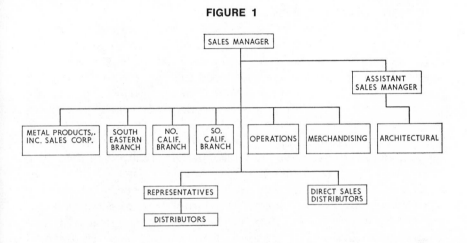

Channels

Metal Products' products were sold directly and through distributors with the latter accounting for 85% of sales. Sales efforts were primarily directed at contractors and builders. Missionary work by sales personnel brought these customers to the distributors or branch outlets. Because of the influence of specifications drawn into building plans, however, sales contacts with architects were also important. Metal Products found this particularly true in selling quality products where often the architect was the only one to recognize the added features.

Regular salesmen and architectural promotion men performed the field sales work. Salesmen called on contractors and architects with the intent of filling specific product needs. Architectural promotion men, on the other hand, worked with architects to sell ideas that later could be translated into products.

Large distributors, employing sizable sales forces and architectural staffs, assumed their own sales responsibility and worked directly with the

Metal Products' main office. Distributors without adequate staffs were provided sales and technical support by Metal Products' personnel. Either company salesmen or commissioned sales representatives were assigned to territories with full responsibility for the performance of the distributors within the territory. Architectural assistance was obtained from the home office or nearby branches.

To exploit the direct selling opportunities offered in concentrated areas, branch operations were set up in Los Angeles, San Francisco, and Miami. Where distributors were located within a territory served by a branch, conflict was avoided by having the branch handle directly only those jobs beyond the capabilities of the distributors. Company salesmen working out of the branch provided the same support to the distributors as in an area where there was no branch office.

The company had one hundred and sixteen franchised outlets throughout the country. Exhibit 4 shows their approximate locations. The United States, as can be seen, was divided into twelve territories. Unshaded areas represent those covered by salaried personnel. Two company men were assigned to Southern California and one each to the remaining company supervised territories. With but three exceptions, Southern California differed from other territories in that distributors were not used. Instead, thirty dealers sold Metal Products' products in this area with all field sales support coming from the company salesmen and architectural promotion men who worked out of the Los Angeles branch.

The shaded areas on the map were served by six sales representatives whose functions were the same as the company's salaried salesmen. Territory 12 was served by the Metal Products Sales Corporation. This subsidiary was established for tax reasons. Two company men were responsible for promoting sales and managing distributors in the territory. A company plane was provided to insure coverage of this extended area. Approximate sales volume for each of the territories was as follows (see map for areas covered):

Territory No. 1	$873,000.00
No. 2	715,800.00
No. 3	115,300.00
No. 4	111,000.00
No. 5	92,600.00
No. 6 and 7	83,000.00
No. 8	524,500.00
No. 10	29,000.00
No. 11	148,000.00
No. 12	597,000.00
House Accounts (including Area No. 9)	930,600.00

Compensation

Compensation of field sales personnel was based on the performance of distributors rather than orders taken. When the occasion arose to write up a sale, it was credited to the local franchised distributor. Company salesmen were paid a salary and a 1% override on sales in their territories exceeding $22,000. The average salary was $880 per month with car and expenses paid by the company. The lowest yearly salary was $9,500 and the typical earnings were between $12,000 and $17,500. Sales representatives were paid a 5% commission on the sales of distributors under their supervision. The average earned by the representatives on company products was $5,500.

The nature of the sales work made an engineering or technical background desirable. Moreover, salesmen and agents were hired for management ability since they were directly responsible for the performance of the distributors assigned to their territories. It had been found in the past that when the company added a salaried salesman, he had to be carried for a year. Within two years, however, sales for the assigned area could be expected to double. The development of a new distributor was also figured at two years.

Methods of Selling

The basic sales appeal used by company sales personnel emphasized the quality features of the product. Samples and demonstration kits were used extensively. Company willingness to stand behind its products, the thoroughly engineered features of the products, and the company's financial stability and tenure in the field were all strong selling points. If for any reason a salesman felt a product would not perform under given conditions he was encouraged to turn the job down.

Sales literature, incorporating the company's attitude toward design and quality, was widely used. A substantial portion of the $80,000 advertising and promotion expenditure went into the preparation of such material.

New sales personnel were given two weeks of in-factory training followed by a short field service-call assignment. Similar programs were conducted for distributors and their sales personnel.

Approach for Selling the Low-Price Door and Window Wall

Should the company enter the low-price door market, it was expected that the use of supporting literature for this line would be restricted greatly. Selling costs would have to be drastically cut if the line were to be competitive. The unit would have to be designed to require little service, thus minimizing the cost of post-installation repairs. In addition to existing outlets, the company anticipated taking on a number of volume distributors who engaged in limited field sales work, but were known to the building trade as low-price operators.

The sales manager saw some difficulty in achieving national coverage for the window wall line. He knew that one order from each of the distributors would provide sufficient business but the low volume and widely fluctuating demand would not justify the distributors' full time efforts. Being a highly specialized item, no two jobs were alike and considerable architectural liaison would be required. The size of the individual jobs ran quite high; four recent jobs in Texas totaled sales of $210,000.

Architectural promotion men would bear the brunt of this sales effort. While the existing distributors in major marketing areas had their own staffs, the smaller distributors were not qualified to sell window wall either from a personnel or a financial standpoint. Initial steps to introduce window wall involved promotional meetings with architects in such key areas as Miami, Houston, and Denver.

Architectural Department

The architectural department was important to Metal Products because of the need to work closely with architects, meeting their specifications, selling them ideas or new uses of company products, and convincing them to draw up specifications that only company products could meet. The home office staff was responsible for receiving and bidding on architectural jobs submitted by distributors. Preliminary plans were drawn and the bid price determined.

The department also prepared scaled detail packets for use by architects and builders. Preparation of such material was expensive, but management was convinced that this type of service had been responsible for building the company's name as the leader in quality sliding doors.

Merchandising Department

The head of the merchandising department acted as the coordinator of advertising, promotions, conventions, and training activities required by the sales division. The company's main advertising emphasis was upon a number of regional architectural books and Sweet's catalogue (an architectural service published by F. W. Dodge, considered to be the architectural Bible). No program using nationwide mass media advertising had been used since the late 1950's. While the company had advertised in *Sunset* and other leading publications, these were dropped in favor of increasing the emphasis on improved sales tools (such as detail packets, product catalogues, distributor aids, etc.) and distributor training programs. The need to sell the quality advantages and long run savings of the company products required the distributors to be well versed and themselves sold on the products' virtues. Training programs consisted of bringing the distributor to the plant for extended tours, study of the Metal Products facilities, and instruction in the use of the sales tools. A similar program involved ten or twelve yearly meetings with leading architects throughout the country.

Local advertising programs were carried on by the distributors themselves, and for the most part, were quite effective. Ad mats were prepared by Metal Products and sold to distributors for local use. A four page quarterly house organ, *News 'n Views,* was sent to all persons associated with the company.

Product and brand acceptance had been developed to a point where the term "a Metal Products door" had become generic for sliding doors. This sometimes worked to the disadvantage of the company. People asking for a Metal Products door were often satisfied with any sliding glass door. Model houses in many large tract developments displayed Metal Products doors, while the actual houses included a cheaper door.

Selling Expense

A breakdown of major selling expenses for 1964 and 1965 is presented below:

Selling Expense
Major Items, 1964–65

	1964	1965
Fixed (rent, dep'n, ins., etc.)	$20,656	$25,210
Variable		
Advertising	80,898	80,941
Agent commissions	37,849	92,158*
Office supplies	9,726	10,748
Freight out	13,219	16,410
Telephone and telegraph	23,290	29,941
Travel and entertainment	46,230	48,397
Labor		
Executive and supervisory salaries	62,875	82,840
Clerical wages	31,313	32,370
Salesmen's salaries	47,424	37,350†
Salesmen's commissions	6,138	7,159
Delivery, salaries-wages	13,974	8,665
Service and installation, salaries-wages	45,973	71,902

* Includes commissions to representatives in areas that have since come under coverage of company salesmen.

† Actual number of company salesmen (salaried) has increased. However, 1964 salary figures include the two men who now work for Metal Products Sales Corporation (Texas, Oklahoma, Louisiana).

Based on the year's master schedule, the sales manager was responsible for submitting his own division budget. In 1965, the variance was $75,000 over budget, but the original figure was based on projected sales of $3.6 million as opposed to actual sales of $4.2 million. More important, selling expenses as a percent of sales dropped from 14.39% in 1964 to 12.90% in 1965.

Pricing

The sales division set prices subject to revision by the president and the controller. Sales and accounting people worked closely in tieing in cost figures with the final selling price.

A standard six-foot door of the Series 102 is best used for comparison of company prices with those of the industry. Priced to sell to the distributor (with glass and screen) at $106, this door was competing in the intermediate range against doors selling for from $70 to $80. However, in the quality markets, the special features of the door and the follow-up service offered by the company tended to overcome the price differential. The commodity door, which commanded 70% of the market, reached the distributor at a price of $60. With this type of door going almost entirely into tract housing, and with price being the important factor, the $70 to $80 door of the intermediate range offered little competition. There were no listed prices for the custom deluxe doors. Most jobs were on a bid basis and the architectural specifications were often the determining factor in who made the sale. One job of this nature that went to Metal Products involved a steel sliding door that was 19 feet high and 75 feet long.

Terms of sale were 1–10 prox-net 30. Quantity discounts were given for orders exceeding 100 units. The sales department was against discounts at a lower level because it felt they did not reward the small distributor who really worked to sell fifteen doors as opposed to the large distributor who might sell fifty doors with half the effort.

Manufacturing

The manufacturing function was broken down into three divisions: engineering, manufacturing control, and production. With all facilities under one roof, this group was able to work closely together in manufacturing the company's product lines.

Quality standards both in terms of raw materials and finished products were extremely high and the management would tolerate no compromise in this respect. The printing on the shipping crates, "Metal Products Glass Door—Handle with Pride," was emphasized at every work station.

Raw materials consisted of variable lengths of aluminum and cold rolled steel and such smaller component items as screws, rollers, neoprene glazing channels, handles, latches, etc. Dyes for extruding the metals were owned by the Metal Products company but installed in the plants of the metal suppliers. The annual purchase of aluminum was $2\frac{1}{2}$ million pounds. Inspection of the extrusions was carried out at the supplier's plant and for aluminum materials had resulted in as high as 75% rejection.

The major components of a sliding door or window included a sill and other metal sections making up the window or door frame. This frame was installed as part of the building just as for any door or window. A combination of fixed and sliding panels was placed into the frame. When drawn closed, the panels offered an airtight and watertight glass wall.

The production process started when lengths of steel or aluminum extrusions were drawn from the raw material storage area located outside and to the rear of the plant. At the first work station the pieces were cut to the size specified on the work order. They were next passed along a production line where the necessary holes were drilled and the ends of the pieces milled. For aluminum products, the doors were either shipped as knocked-down units or, on occasion, were assembled and packed in regular shipping crates. For knocked-down packaging, the framing members, or as defined before, the parts making up the door frame, were packaged in polyethylene sleeves and placed in a cardboard carton approximately 4 feet x 6 feet x 8 feet in size. The polyethylene sleeve was designed to be left on during installation and until the building was completed. This eliminated the costly clean-up of paint, plaster, and grime. All fixed and sliding panel members and components were placed in a second carton of the same size, and the two, consisting of a complete door, were bound together for shipping. Aluminum doors to be glazed at the plant were fully assembled on racks and sent to the glazing department to have the glass installed. The finished product was packaged in a cardboard carton which enclosed the entire door.

Steel products, after all members were cut and prepared for assembly, were clamped in an assembled state on large revolving racks and then arc welded. The doors were then sprayed with a semi-gloss enamel and carried through a drying oven on overhead conveyors. Steel doors were normally shipped without crating, although special two by four wooden crates were available to the customer on request.

Most of the company's tooling and machinery had been designed and built by Metal Products people. Engineered to meet the company's specific manufacturing needs, this machinery offered greater flexibility than standard purchased equipment. The production control division indicated that under present volume, the plant was at more than full one-shift capacity. Two shifts were run to meet peaks in demand for specific products such as the standard 102 or heavy-duty 201 sliding doors. Each week the emphasis might change, but there was nearly always a second shift at work. It was felt that labor costs of a third shift would be prohibitive should sales volume require any significant increase in the present level of production. The shop was unionized, but good working relations had prevailed with the union.

CONSIDERATION OF ENTERING LOW-PRICE DOOR MARKET

The question of entering the low-price door market arose again in late 1965 during a meeting of the New Products Development Committee. The discussion on this subject follows:

SALES MANAGER: "I have been collecting information and putting together next year's sliding door sales forecast and am impressed with the share of the market going to low-price or commodity doors. They currently account for 80% of the total. We should seriously consider the position we want to take with respect to this segment of the market. This chart (see data below) projects our door sales to 1969, assuming no change in our product policy. The second chart reflects the added sales we could expect to receive by adding a low-price door to our line.

Projected Door Sales If Basic 1965 Product Line Is Unchanged
(millions of $'s)

	1966		1967		1969	
	Industry	Company	Industry	Company	Industry	Company
Commodity*........	$42	$0.25	$54	$1.5	$73	$1.70
Residential..........	15	3.00	15	2.7	14	2.70
Architectural........	3	0.50	3	0.5	3	0.55
	$60	$3.75	$72	$4.7	$90	$4.95

* Sales in this category based on the theory that a small number of tract developers would come to appreciate the long-run advantages of installing quality sliding doors.

Projected Door Sales If Low-Price Door Is Added to Product Line
(millions of $'s)

	1966		1967		1969	
	Industry	Company	Industry	Company	Industry	Company
Commodity.........	$42	$0.25	$54	$3.5	$73	$5.00
Residential..........	15	3.00	15	2.0	14	2.00
Architectural........	3	0.50	3	0.5	3	0.75
	$60	$3.75	$72	$6.0	$90	$7.75

Most of our distributors now carry a low-price door. Very few, however, have stayed long with one manufacturer. This seems to present a real opportunity for us to establish ourselves in a growing market.

PRESIDENT: What reasons have you heard given for this shifting from one low-price manufacturer to another?

SALES MANAGER: Well, first of all, we know that a number of the little companies are going out of business. Also, it's pretty hard for the small operator to face the large promotional and sales push programs used by new firms. Distribution policies, in general, are weak for the small firms, with many now reverting to direct sales in local areas.

VICE-PRESIDENT, ENGINEERING AND MANUFACTURING: If this is true, what are our chances in competing for this business?

SALES MANAGER: Our biggest asset in entering the low-price door market is an established distribution system. We have a ready market in our franchised outlets and the know-how we've gained in distribution gives us a real jump. Financial stability would be another factor in our favor. As I see it, we now command 25% of the market available to us; to gain a larger share of this market (residential and architectural) will become increasingly difficult. We can increase the overall company sales with other products —window wall and windows—however, this does not increase our position in the sliding door field. We are missing out on a very large market which could enable us to become the dominant company in sliding doors.

At this point in the meeting, the president felt that prior to further discussion, some basic information still needed to be collected. Calling the meeting to a close, he asked the vice-president of manufacturing to estimate the cost of starting a facility for the manufacture of this type of product and also to look into possible purchase of existing companies. The sales manager was to conduct further study about the market.

At the next committee meeting some preliminary cost estimates were presented as follows:

VICE-PRESIDENT OF MANUFACTURING: Assuming we build a new structure, our costs should run between $50,000 and $60,000 for the building. By doubling this figure, we could provide the capacity needed for expansion in our other lines. Tooling and equipment for the project will run about $50,000 and inventory requirements about the same. As of now, I have found no companies that look right for buying.

MANAGER OF ENGINEERING: I have talked somewhat with the sales department about the criteria for the low-price door and have concluded that the mass buyer is interested in a plain door of good design that needs to meet only the minimum standards.[3] The door should be designed for shop glazing using standard glass sizes. The neoprene channels we use for field glazing would price us out of the market.

The price of the door to the builder including glass, screen, installation and distributor mark-up will have to be between $85 and $95. The price to the distributor with screen will have to be between $44 and $60.

Assuming the criteria I have outlined, and applying labor, burden, and selling costs at our established rates, this chart (see below) gives a cost comparison between our 102 door and the proposed low-price door.[4]

PRESIDENT: What would you say is the competitive price that we would have to meet with this line?

SALES MANAGER: There are products on the market that sell for $35.00. However, during my recent inquiries, the distributors indicated that they would accept our product as long as the delivered price, less glass and screen, was close to $45.00.

PRESIDENT: Did anything else come up during your market survey?

SALES MANAGER: In general, the work I have done confirmed our original idea that the mass buyer is interested mainly in price. Several of the distributors

---

[3] It was felt by some that the Metal Products door was over-built for the California market considering the moderate climate conditions. However, standards set for nationwide distribution and pride in the product led to these quality features.

[4] The $57 and $39 price do not include glass and screen. These items would each add about $12 to the price if supplied by Metal Products, Inc.

Cost Comparison

	102 Door	*Low-Cost Door*
Aluminum	$20.38	$15.60
Aluminating	1.95	1.80
Misc. (hardware, etc.)	10.00	6.25
Packaging	(included)	(none)
	$32.33	$23.65
Labor	$ 3.42	$ 2.35
Burden	6.49	4.50
Selling	11.83	8.55
	$54.07	$39.05

stated that one reason for this is the lending agencies are not giving credit for quality products in large tract developments. Typical replies of "reasonably good and cheap," "cheap, simple design," "low cost," etc., were given when distributors were asked the type of door needed to reach the mass market.

To show a profit in this line, I have estimated that we will need monthly sales of 3,000 units at $45 each. If we start the project in the near future, we can easily reach this figure in a couple of years.

PRESIDENT: So far I am impressed with the potential of this market. Particularly since it offers us a chance to continue or exceed our current rate of growth. However, there are certain aspects that still bother me. We are at a point now where our brand name implies quality, and I am opposed to any action that might reflect poorly on the company's name. Entering a market characterized by price competition makes me wonder if we could actually produce a satisfactory door—one upon which we would want to attach our name.

MANAGER OF ENGINEERING: I'm not so sure that the only way we can expand door sales is through entering the low-price market. A stripped-down version of the 102, priced to sell to distributors between $80 and $90 could well be the answer. With this type of door, we can still offer the basic quality features of our existing products and at the same time provide our distributors with a wider line.

SALES MANAGER: I can't agree. I think that this is the time to make a move. Our relationship with our dealers, in particular, worries me. With our products appealing to a limited segment of the market, each distributor has to go elsewhere to secure a full line. Right now, with no one else strong in the production of quality doors, this may not be significant. However, we don't know when some of the existing commodity door manufacturers might get on their feet and add an acceptable quality product. With the leverage provided by the large sales volume in commodity doors, these manufacturers might well be able to force the distributors to drop our line in favor of their own. Right now, we have the advantage and if we could offer a full line of doors, we can go a long way in protecting our position.

PRESIDENT: I think the low-price door offers a real challenge. With the econo-

EXHIBIT 1

Comparative Balance Sheets, 1960–1965

	1965	1964	1963	1962	1961	1960
Current assets						
Cash	$ 60,552	$ 16,108	$ 16,150	$ 11,489	$ 38,366	$ 56,101
Trade accounts rec'vble (Net)	825,695	419,455	306,492	296,679	166,870	81,748
Inventories						
Finished	230,331	99,354	84,526	57,886	41,101	27,306
Work-in-process	62,213	72,893	88,528	53,154	31,780	8,755
Raw material	374,359	259,166	228,522	395,664	187,447	105,285
Pre-paids	20,055	22,080	19,010	14,608	11,191	5,702
Total current	$1,573,205	$ 889,056	$743,228	$ 829,480	$476,755	$284,897
New plant under construction	—	—	—	304,561	35,239	—
Other assets	26,135	29,998	31,688	17,530	—	1,118
Plant and equipment	389,527	420,282	374,634	261,731	198,366	126,376
Less allowance for depreciation	177,457	222,817	158,546	102,399	110,566	64,252
	$ 212,070	$ 197,465	$216,088	$ 159,332	$ 87,800	$ 62,124
Total assets	$1,811,410	$1,116,519	$991,004	$1,310,903	$599,794	$348,139
Current liabilities						
Notes payable						
Bank	$ 450,000	$ 50,000	$ 90,000	$ 249,293	$ —	$ 8,585
Officers	10,150	16,879	13,544	11,573	—	—
Other	4,105	4,105	4,105	—	—	—
Accounts payable	192,902	105,016	75,343	111,491	81,487	25,541
Salaries, wages, etc.	57,264	36,823	35,249	102,556	31,029	10,083
Taxes	207,339	128,224	104,646	229,570	138,633	64,981
Dividends payable	—	13,890	13,890	13,890	—	—
Miscellaneous	5,367	14,022	5,466	19,941	12,684	—
Total current	$ 927,127	$ 368,959	$342,243	$ 738,314	$263,833	$109,190
Capital stock and surplus						
Capital stock	$ 277,800	$ 277,800	$277,800	$ 277,800	$150,000	$150,000
Paid-in surplus	58,176	58,176	58,176	58,176	—	—
Earned surplus	548,307	411,583	312,784	236,613	185,961	88,949
Total capital stock and surplus	$ 884,283	$ 747,559	$648,760	$ 572,589	$335,961	$238,949
Total liabilities	$1,811,410	$1,116,518	$991,003	$1,310,903	$599,794	$348,139

EXHIBIT 2

Statement of Income and Expenses, 1960–1965

	1965 ($)	1965 (%)	1964 ($)	1964 (%)	1963 ($)	1963 (%)	1962 ($)	1962 (%)	1961 ($)	1961 (%)	1960 ($)	1960 (%)
Net sales	4,234,111	100.0	3,127,632	100.0	2,823,258	100.0	2,882,419	100.0	1,982,070	100.0	1,329,323	100.0
Cost of goods sold	3,071,433	72.5	2,236,224	71.5	2,008,215	71.1	1,884,495	65.1	1,321,645	66.7	948,570	71.4
	1,162,668	27.5	891,408	28.5	815,043	28.9	997,924	34.9	660,425	33.3	380,753	28.6
Expenses												
Selling	546,185	12.9	449,946	14.4	475,808	16.9	399,760	13.9	239,434	12.1	113,194	8.5
Administrative	191,478	4.5	171,149	5.5	145,160	5.1	202,499	7.0	181,440	9.1	156,861	11.8
	737,663	17.4	621,095	19.9	620,968	22.0	602,259	20.9	420,874	21.2	270,055	20.3
	425,005	10.0	270,313	8.6	194,075	6.9	395,665	14.0	239,551	12.1	110,698	8.3
Other income	29,464	.7	32,869	1.0	0		0		0		0	
	454,469	10.7	303,182	9.7	194,075	6.9	395,665	14.0	239,551	12.1	110,698	8.3
Other expenses	122,870	2.9	96,386	3.1	32,014	1.1	48,410	2.0	28,626	1.4	30,015	2.3
Income before income taxes	331,599	7.8	206,796	6.6	162,061	5.8	347,255	12.0	210,925	10.7	80,683	6.0
Income taxes	167,094	4.0	94,106	3.0	72,000	2.6	188,458	6.5	112,837	5.7	45,466	3.4
Net income	164,505	3.8	112,690	3.6	90,061	3.2	158,797	5.5	98,088	5.0	35,217	2.6

mies of volume production, I'm sure we can lower the price of the door
to a more competitive level. From an engineering standpoint, the door
won't measure up to existing standards, but I'm confident that the product will perform satisfactorily and be as good or better than the low-price
doors now on the market.

EXHIBIT 3

Metal Products, Inc. Product Line

Product	*Percent of Sales*			
	1965	*1964*	*1963*	*1962*
Aluminum Sliding Doors				
Series 102—First announced in 1964, this product became the work horse of the company line. Offered in both stock and custom sizes, this door was largely responsible for the jump in 1965 sales........	31.6	—	—	—
Series 104—Duplicating the 102 door, the 104 series accommodated ⅝ feet insulating glass. Offered in both stock and custom sizes..............	1.4	—	—	—
Series 201—Designed for uses requiring added strength and rigidity, this series was particularly suitable for commercial and institutional type buildings. Available in stock and custom sizes.......	13.1	—	—	—
Series 221—This was the multislide door in which all panels compact upon themselves into the width of a single panel, offering ideal flexibility. Particularly popular in the Southeastern market. All doors of this series were custom-made.............	1.9	—	—	—
TOTAL (including custom and miscellaneous sales).......................................	54.5	43	27	2
Steel Sliding Doors				
Series 301—To meet architectural requirements for steel sliding doors, this series met the same exacting standards as the aluminum units. Available in stock and custom sizes....................	18.3	36	54	79
Aluminum Windows				
Series 501—Designed as a look-alike to the sliding door, this product had met with vigorous competition on the market where sliding windows had not been accepted as readily as the sliding door. Offered in both stock and custom sizes..............	4.1	5	2	3
Window Wall				
A prefabricated wall section delivered to a job as an assembled unit, this product was first included in the regular product line in 1965. All work was custom in nature with units available in either aluminum or steel.............................	6.6	—	—	—

NOTE: Sales not represented in the percentages were in screens and items relating to the listed products.

EXHIBIT 4

Sales Territories

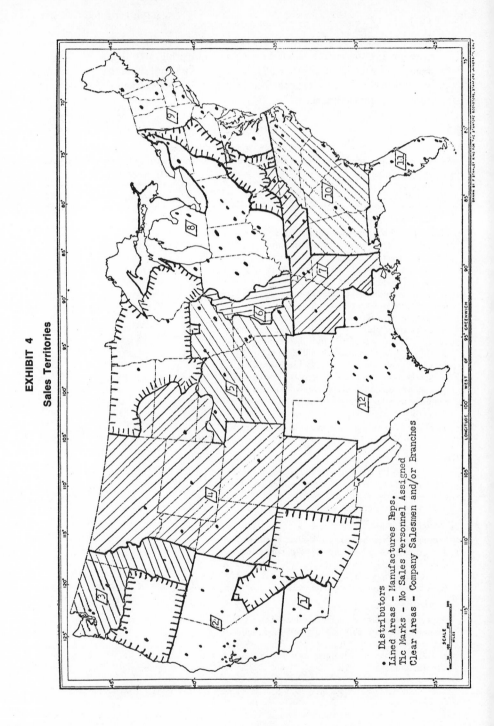

• Distributors
Lined Areas – Manufactures Reps.
Tic Marks – No Sales Personnel Assigned
Clear Areas – Company Salesmen and/or Branches

Honchan Company

Honchan was a large producer of cooking oil in Malaya and Singapore, with extensive interests in the soap business. Its soap sales in 1962 totaled M$2.8 million.[1] The company, which was owned by a Chinese family, sold soap to lower- and middle-income consumers in Malaya, from 1949 through 1960. During 1961 and 1962, Honchan introduced two new soap products to compete in the upper- and middle-income markets, which were dominated by foreign companies. In May 1965 Mr. Hock Wong, who was responsible for Honchan's domestic sales, wondered what changes he should make in his marketing strategy in order to compete more effectively in the toilet and household soap markets in Malaya.

COMPANY BACKGROUND

Honchan Company was formed in Singapore in 1945 by Mr. Lee Wong, Sr. to can meat, vegetables, and sauces for the local Chinese market. Over the next 18 years, the company gradually changed from a small backyard operation to an integrated cooking oil and soap producer with plants in Singapore and Malaya. The second phase of Honchan's growth started in 1947, when the company began crushing coconuts in Singapore, to produce cooking oil for sale in Singapore, Malaya, and overseas. The third phase commenced in 1949, when Honchan entered the soap business. Mr. Wong, Sr. decided to refine the cooking oil to produce two brands of low-quality laundry soap for sale in Singapore and Malaya. The company expanded until 1955, by concentrating on the distribution of cooking oil and laundry soaps manufactured at its Singapore plant. While Honchan's cooking oil products were sold mainly in the high-quality, high-priced market, its laundry soaps were produced for the low- and middle-income buyer.

---

[1] Malayan $3.00 = U.S. $1.00.

The company's market strategy was adversely affected by the decision of the Malayan government in 1955, to impose a duty on laundry soap imported into Malaya. The new tariff forced Honchan to set up its own plant in Kuala Lumpur in 1956, so that the company could remain competitive in the Malayan market. It was decided to build a large-scale plant with capacity to produce coconut oil, refined oil, blended oil, laundry soap, toilet soap, margarine, and scouring powder. The relation of soap production to the oil business is shown in a brief technical note in Appendix A.

Mr. Wong, Sr.'s two sons had joined the company in 1953. Shortly thereafter they assumed direct responsibility for company operations, because of their father's illness and subsequent retirement. The elder son, Mr. Chuk Wong, who joined Honchan at the age of 28, had previously

FIGURE 1

Company Organization Chart

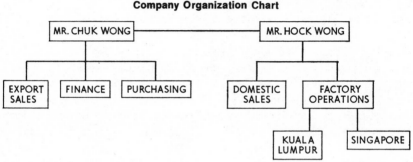

SOURCE: Described by Mr. Hock Wong, May 1963.

acquired accounting and financial experience in Singapore and Malaya. The younger brother, Mr. Hock Wong, had studied chemistry in the United States. After 1956, the brothers shared the management of Honchan (as shown on the organization chart in Figure 1). Mr. Hock was responsible for domestic sales in Singapore and Malaya and for factory operations in Singapore and Kuala Lumpur. Export sales, purchasing, and the finance function were administered by Mr. Chuk.

Between 1956 and 1959, Mr. Hock gradually expanded the distribution system in Malaya for Honchan products. Sales branches had been established earlier in Malacca and Kuala Lumpur. Four more branches were set up in Penang, Klang, Ipoh, and Kota Bharu to serve the growing Malayan market. Figure 2 is a map of Malaya, showing the location of Honchan branches in 1961. The domestic sales organization administered by Mr. Hock in Malaya is shown in Figure 3. By 1963, Honchan employed about 35 salesmen in Malaya and 15 in Singapore. Each branch sales force called directly on wholesalers, retailers, and industrial consumers in its territory, and maintained its own delivery fleet.

FIGURE 2

**Federation of Malaya
Honchan Branch Offices, 1961***

Thailand

Kota Bharu

China Sea

Penang

FEDERATION OF MALAYA

• Ipoh

• Kuala Lumpur

• Klang

• Malacca

Sumatra

Singapore

• Honchan branch office

SOURCE: Described by Mr. Hock Wong in 1963.
* No significant changes had been made in the distribution system by May 1963.

Mr. Hock encouraged each sales group to implement a marketing strategy which was tailored to the needs of its territory. Consequently, different sales campaigns and price structures were sometimes employed by Honchan in various parts of Malaya. The domestic marketing operation was supervised by Mr. Hock through monthly sales reports and frequent telephone calls to the field on special problems. Explaining Honchan's marketing policy, Mr. Hock said that the company tried to sell in every part of Malaya, no matter how small the local demand. "We may lose by this policy for a while," he said, "but it will pay off in the long run." No targets were fixed for the sales force, but Mr. Hock was satis-

FIGURE 3

Domestic Marketing Organzation Chart

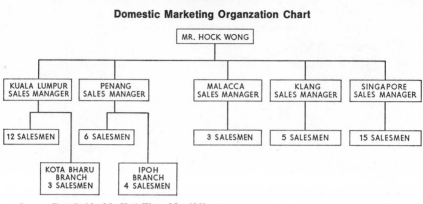

Source: Described by Mr. Hock Wong, May 1963.

fied so long as Honchan's total sales grew faster than the country's rate of population growth.

SOAP MARKET IN MALAYA

The soap market in Malaya was dominated by Weaver Brothers (Malaya) Ltd., an English company which had sold soap in the country since before the Second World War. Weaver Brothers had a plant in Kuala Lumpur which produced three different types of soap for all income levels in the Malayan market. Its toilet soap (*Fresh*) and the household-laundry soap (*Clean*) had over 50% of the urban soap market. Weaver Brothers also produced a low-quality soap called Village, which had a high market share in the rural areas. All three products had good acceptance in Malaya, which Mr. Hock attributed partly to the market preference in Malaya for goods produced by a foreign manufacturer.[2]

Mr. Hock thought Weaver Brothers had other competitive advantages over Honchan. The higher production volume of the English company meant lower manufacturing and advertising costs per unit sold. Also, Weaver Brothers had larger financial resources, more experienced management, and better information about the market. The company had its own plantation in Malaya which gave it direct access to raw materials, possibly at lower costs. Mr. Hock believed Weaver Brothers had the resources to cut soap prices long enough to squeeze Honchan out of the market if it so desired. He thought, however, that this would not happen, because Honchan would then be bought cheaply by a new owner, who could reopen with low production costs.

Weaver Brothers concentrated on the manufacture of soap products.

---

[2] Table 1 shows available published information on soap production, imports and exports in Malaya, between 1953 and 1961.

It did not produce coconut oil and had gained only limited penetration of the blended cooking-oil market, which was dominated by Honchan. Mr. Hock described Honchan as primarily a cooking-oil manufacturer, with an interest in the soap market as a second line of defense. In 1961, Honchan's two soap brands were sold through the direct sales force in Malaya, which was principally concerned with distributing the company's well-established oil products. This practice made it easier for Honchan to persuade retailers to carry its *Pick* and *Tiger* brands of soap. Mr. Hock thought that his company had further competitive advantages in its better knowledge of local market conditions, lower overhead expenses, more flexible management, and its more efficient modern plant.

TABLE 1

Federation of Malaya
Total Market Supplies of Soap ('000 cwt.)*

Year	Production	Imports	Exports	Total Market Supplies
1953	215	153	37	331
1954	264	135	50	349
1955	287	141	87	341
1956	298	121	87	332
1957	307	112	99	320
1958	313	114	103	324
1959	320	88	81	327
1960	356	65	85	336
1961	378	42	45	375

* Total market supplies refer to production plus imports less exports. Soap refers to all types of soap, including toilet, household, and laundry soap.
SOURCE: Department of Statistics, Federation of Malaya, Kuala Lumpur, *Monthly Statistical Bulletin of the Federation of Malaya*, June 1962, p. 60. Reproduced by permission.

Honchan produced two brands of low-priced laundry soap for the middle- and low-income soap market in Malaya. Pick brand, distributed at M$11.25 per 44-lb. case, was sold mainly to Chinese and Malays in the rural areas. Tiger brand, wholesaled at M$14.10 per 44-lb. case, was bought mainly by middle-income Chinese in the town areas. Mr. Hock thought that both of these products were competitive with the Village brand produced by Weaver Brothers. Up to 1961, Honchan had concentrated its efforts in establishing the laundry soaps firmly in the Malayan market. "We were preoccupied with our oil products," said Mr. Hock, "and we did not have the technical people or sophisticated equipment necessary to expand into higher-quality soap production." After it was decided to build a modern plant in Kuala Lumpur, Mr. Hock planned to enter the toilet and household soap market to compete with the Weaver Brothers' Fresh and Clean brands. The volume and value of Honchan's soap sales by type of product between 1960 and 1962 is shown in Table 2.

The Malayan market was supplied with Honchan products from the

TABLE 2

Honchan Company
Annual Soap Sales by Product between 1960 and 1962 in Malaya

	1960		1961		1962	
Product	Quantity ('000 lbs)	Value (M$'000)	Quantity ('000 lbs)	Value (M$'000)	Quantity ('000 lbs)	Value (M$'000)
Tiger Soap........	3,076	982	2,513	801	2,812	897
Pick Soap.........	2,076	497	3,656	843	6,586	1,495
Jasmine Soap......	*	*	113	113	178	178
Honchan Soap.....	—	—	—	—	343	215

* Not available.
SOURCE: Honchan Company Records.

Singapore plant until the Kuala Lumpur factory was completed in 1958. In 1960, the technical equipment to produce the higher-quality soap was installed and tested.

NEW PRODUCT PLANNING

Commenting on Honchan's decision to enter the higher-quality soap business, Mr. Hock said that "consumer products trends in advanced countries, such as the U.S.A. and Europe, indicate what will happen eventually in Malaya." His assumption that the Malayan market for higher-quality soaps was growing was confirmed by reports from Honchan's sales force that Weaver Brothers' sales of Fresh and Clean were increasing. Mr. Hock also noticed that Weaver Brothers' recent advertising campaigns were directed at persuading Village buyers to upgrade their soap purchases to Clean. In time, Mr. Hock believed, the market for lower-quality soaps, like Pick and Tiger, would decline. Although no clear-cut signs pointed that way in 1960–61, he thought Honchan should take action as soon as possible to expand its line of toilet and household soaps.

To penetrate the Clean market, Honchan decided to produce a soap which could be sold either as an expensive laundry soap, a competitive household soap, or a cheap toilet soap. Mr. Hock said that, although Honchan did no formal market research, his impression was that the Malay and Indian population used Clean as a toilet soap, whereas the Chinese used it as a household soap.[3] Honchan tried to copy the Clean soap tablet in color, size, and perfume.[4] The yellow color was somewhat modified so that the consumer could identify it with Fresh yellow-colored

[3] Ethnic data concerning the population of Malaya are shown in Table 3.

[4] Tablet and cake are used interchangeably in Malaya to describe the size of a piece of soap which is approximately 4" x 2¼". Bar soap refers to a larger size of soap, which measures 9" x 3".

toilet soap, as well as the yellow Clean soap. Mr. Hock wanted the new soap to look suitable for both household and toilet uses.

The brand name chosen for the soap was Honchan. Mr. Hock thought that by using the name of the company for the name of the new product, the consumer goodwill associated with Honchan in the oil business would help to interest customers in Honchan soap. The only information featured on the package were the two English words, Honchan Soap, because Mr. Hock believed that quality products in Malaya were associated with labels in English. The type of wrapping used for the package was an essential part of the company's marketing strategy.

Clean soap was packaged in a wax-paper wrapper. Mr. Hock decided to use an aluminum foil wrapper for Honchan soap, because he thought

TABLE 3

Federation of Malaya
Population Analysis
(000)

Period (12–31)	Malaysians	Chinese	Indians and Pakistanis	Others	All groups
1950	2,599	2,002	566	80	5,247
1955	2,991	2,229	681	104	6,005
1956	3,078	2,297	704	111	6,190
1957	3,188	2,378	723	116	6,405
1958	3,293	2,445	740	118	6,596
1959	3,406	2,520	767	122	6,815
1960	3,510	2,595	786	126	7,017

SOURCE: *Monthly Statistical Bulletin of the Federation of Malaya*, June 1962, p. 3. Reproduced by permission.

that the market identified aluminum foil wrapping with high-class soaps. In 1960–61, all toilet soaps in Malaya were wrapped in aluminum foil, and all household-laundry soaps were wax-paper wrappers. The Honchan package was selected to tell the consumer that this household-laundry soap was a very high-class product. Mr. Hock made this decision in full awareness that consumers might assume Honchan to be only a toilet soap and thereby eliminate it from the household-laundry soap market.

Mr. Hock believed that the toilet-soap market in Malaya offered outstanding prospects for growth. He thought that population growth and rising living standards would enlarge the Malayan toilet-soap market by 7 to 8% per year, and his goal was a market share of 40% of the toilet-soap market in Malaya. His best information was that Fresh had about 60% of this market in 1960–61; imports accounted for the remainder.

Honchan's decision to market a high-class toilet soap required selection of a suitable name. Mr. Hock thought that the name of a flower was appropriate for the soap, particularly if the flower was well known, expensive, and considered to be high-class. He selected the brand name Jasmine Soap because the Jasmine flower was highly regarded and widely known in Malaya.

The size and shape of Jasmine soap was made the same as Weaver Brothers' toilet soap, because Fresh was the most popular brand on the market. "If we made it bigger than Fresh, it would increase our costs," said Mr. Hock. "If we made it smaller, who would buy from us?" Weaver Brothers sold Fresh in five colors: white, pink, green, yellow, and blue. According to earlier practice, each toilet-soap company sold only one color (for example, Fresh was white, Coldgate was green), but the recent trend had been toward a wider selection of colors for each brand. In 1961, about 60% of the Malayan market bought white toilet soap, about 35% pink and green toilet soap, and the remaining 5%, an assortment of colors.

Mr. Hock thought that the Chinese tended to prefer white soap, whereas most Malays and Indians favored colored soaps. If Honchan produced only one color, Mr. Hock believed that Jasmine soap would be able to capture only a limited segment of the market. Consequently, he decided that Honchan would produce toilet soap in three colors: white, pink and blue. He selected white and pink because of their market popularity. Although he considered marketing a green soap, it was decided to produce blue instead because Honchan was negotiating to manufacture the green Coldgate soap for the Coldgate Company in Malaya.

The aluminum foil wrapper selected for Jasmine soap had a beautifully printed jasmine flower on the front, and the rest of the package was the same color as the soap inside. On the front and sides were printed the English words *Jasmine Soap*. A brief statement on the back of the wrapper described the benefits of the product for the user's complexion, as well as words identifying the soap as a Honchan product. Mr. Hock tried to match the colors of the soaps with attractive fragrances. He thought that the Chinese liked a mild odor, while the Malays and Indians preferred something more pungent. No other soap manufacturer linked color differentiation with differences in fragrance.

PRICING AND PROMOTION PLANS

Mr. Hock decided to introduce pink Jasmine soap onto the Malayan market first, because it was the company's only new soap product with a satisfactory aluminum foil wrapper available. Months of work in 1960 and 1961 went into package planning, designing, and printing. Delays were experienced because the work and printing had to be done by an overseas company. By September 1961, only the wrapper for pink Jasmine soap met the quality standards set by Mr. Hock. The wrappers for the other colored toilet soaps and Honchan were not yet satisfactory.

The basic strategy adopted by Honchan was to market Jasmine as a high-quality, high-priced toilet soap backed by extensive sales promotion. It was planned to sell Jasmine soap at the same retail price as Fresh, 30¢ per cake or M$43.20 per case of 144 cakes. Both companies sold toilet soap to retailers at M$36.00 per case. Honchan offered dealers a 3% cash discount. Until the full color line of toilet soap was available, Honchan did not intend to match Weaver Brothers' dealer discounts, which could total 8%.

Mr. Hock planned to use Honchan's existing distribution system to reach wholesalers and retailers throughout Malaya. Company branches would act as local warehouses, and the sales force would sell at prices fixed by the head office, with only minor modifications authorized by the branch manager if local conditions required it. Mr. Hock estimated that the company's products reached about 12,000 retail outlets throughout Malaya.

Honchan introduced Jasmine soap to the Malayan market by combining a sampling campaign with extensive radio, newspaper, and magazine advertising over the last three months of 1961. Every customer who bought a tin of Honchan oil was given a small sample size of Jasmine soap. Mr. Hock estimated that about 80,000 samples of toilet soap were distributed in this way. During the same period in 1961, about M$30,000 was spent by the company on its advertising program.

Mr. Hock had a movie advertisement prepared for showing at cinemas throughout Malaya. Twenty copies of the film were produced in Europe at a cost of M$10,000. He also arranged to have Jasmine soap exhibited at trade fairs around the country, and he planned to use the sales force for house-to-house calls, to introduce Jasmine soap into as many homes as possible. Except for small signs in public transportation, Mr. Hock did not use outdoor advertising signs.[5] He thought that it was too difficult for an artist to draw a large attractive picture of the flower trademark.

Mr. Hock believed that the sale of Jasmine soap would depend on Honchan's ability to generate "consumer pull" for the product. Until this demand built up, retailers would carry the new toilet soap because of their goodwill for Honchan, based on the company's oil products.

Delays in the production of a satisfactory aluminum foil wrapper prevented the distribution of Honchan soap until April 1962. Departing from the market strategy he used for Jasmine soap, Mr. Hock decided not to use advertising to introduce Honchan into the Malayan market. Instead he relied on a lower wholesale price than Clean soap, backed up by good product quality and an aluminum foil wrapper.

The retail selling prices recommended for Honchan and Clean soaps were identical at M$14.40 per case of 72 cakes. Weaver Brothers sold Clean to stores at M$12.55 per case, although it was possible for the re-

---

[5] Trade fairs were held twice a year in Kuala Lumpur and three other towns in Malaya, to promote consumer products and entertain the public. Honchan planned to invest about 25% of its advertising expenditure for all of its products, on trade fairs.

tailers to earn up to an 8% discount for cash payments and volume purchases. Mr. Hock planned to sell Honchan to stores at M$11.50 per case; this gave the retailers a margin of M$3.90 per case, which would be increased if they took advantage of the 3% cash discount. Mr. Hock thought that retailers would be interested in the Honchan brand because they could earn M$1.00 more per case, excluding discounts, than they could from selling Clean.

EXPERIENCE IN THE MARKET

Because Jasmine soap was given away free with purchases of Honchan oil until December 1961, cash sales of the company's pink toilet soap were slow during this period. Sales started increasing in January 1962 when the introductory deal was stopped. Mr. Hock thought that the Jasmine soap movie was particularly effective for contacting consumers in both urban and rural areas in Malaya. Inasmuch as Malaya had no television, the cinema was considered a cheap and popular form of entertainment. Both English and Cantonese narratives were used, because most of the servants in Malaya were Cantonese Chinese. Mr. Hock hoped that the movie reached the illiterate market with an attractive visual message.

Radio, newspaper, and magazine advertising were maintained at about half the 1961 monthly rate until June 1962. Altogether, Honchan spent M$39,000 on Jasmine soap advertising for the year ending December 1962, but most of this was spent in the first six months. Mr. Hock decided to reduce expenditures in the second half of 1962 because he had arranged a special promotion campaign with the company selling Slick hairdressing preparation.

In May 1962, the Slick company informed Honchan that it would be interested in buying 700,000 cakes of Jasmine soap to distribute as "free" gifts with Slick hair lotion. Mr. Hock was surprised and pleased. He knew that Slick was sold more heavily than any other hair preparation in Malaya and he believed that this offer would enable Jasmine soap to be tried by almost half the Malayan market. Assuming that a family would purchase one jar of Slick at M$2.00 with a free cake of Jasmine soap attached, and assuming that each family had five members, Mr. Hock estimated that the pink toilet soap would be used by about 3.6 million people in 1962. Honchan negotiated a price of 18¢ per cake on the 700,000 standard cakes of Jasmine soap sold to Slick in June 1962.

After the "free" distribution, Jasmine was unable to maintain its previous monthly sales volume. Mr. Hock concluded that the market had been flooded. Despite the introduction of blue Jasmine soap in February 1963, total monthly sales of Jasmine soap in 1963 were below those of the previous year. (Table 4 shows the monthly sales of Jasmine and Honchan soap, from their introduction until May 1963.)

It was difficult for Mr. Hock to evaluate the market penetration of

Jasmine soap, but he estimated in May 1963 that it had probably captured about 5% of the total toilet soap market. Reports from his sales force suggested that pink Jasmine soap was the best selling pink toilet soap in Malaya. Mr. Hock guessed that Jasmine had gained sales by collecting a little volume from each of the other companies which were supplying the market. So far, Honchan's market strategy had not produced any significant retaliatory action from its competitors. Mr. Hock believed, however,

TABLE 4

Honchan Company
Monthly Sales of Jasmine and Honchan Soaps
January 1962–May 1963*

Period	Jasmine Soap		Honchan Soap	
	(*'000 lbs.*)	(*M$ '000*)	(*'000 lbs.*)	(*M$ '000*)
1962				
January...............	11.8	11.8		
February..............	16.7	16.7		
March................	21 1	21.1		
April................	15.1	15.1	50.7	31.8
May..................	19.3	19.3	33.1	20.8
June.................	11.9	11.9	50.3	31.6
July.................	13.2	13.2	46.9	29.4
August...............	13.3	13.3	45.9	28.8
September............	10.1	10.1	31.8	20.0
October..............	10.8	10.8	31.6	19.8
November.............	12.6	12.6	25.1	15.7
December.............	14.7	14.7	28.6	17.9
1963				
January...............	7.7	7.7	20.3	12.8
February..............	15.8	15.8	27.6	17.3
March................	11.6	11.6	29.9	18.8
April................	9.1	9.1	21.3	13.4
May..................	17.8	17.8	27.1	17.0

* Sales data do not include sales of Jasmine soap during September to December 1960, nor Jasmine soap distributed during the Slick campaign. May 1963 is estimated.
Source: Honchan Company Records.

that his competition might retaliate when Honchan introduced its white Jasmine soap in June 1963.

The major reason for Honchan's delay in the introduction of its blue and white toilet soaps was continued trouble with the aluminum foil wrapper. In early 1961, the first overseas supplier approached by Mr. Hock produced a wrapper on which the color would not hold fast. After repeated attempts, the wrapper manufacturer came up with a color which did not smudge, but was dull in appearance. Because all other toilet soaps in Malaya had shiny packages, Mr. Hock decided to switch to another European manufacturer, who produced a satisfactory pink aluminum foil wrapper by September 1961. While this supplier was developing other Honchan wrappers, the pink Jasmine soap wrappers on the market showed signs of fading after a few months. Furthermore, during 1962 the wrappers were becoming increasingly uneven in quality. By May 1963, the supplier had worked out these wrapper problems for the pink package and had produced satisfactory wrappers for the blue and white toilet soaps. In order to ensure the continuous availability of quality wrappers, Mr. Hock had selected a second European producer as a backup supplier in 1962.

The introduction of Honchan soap onto the Malayan market was also delayed by wrapper production difficulties. When it finally came out in April 1962, Weaver Brothers responded by increasing their already extensive advertising campaign for Clean. About the same time, a bar-size Clean was added to the tablet size copied by Mr. Hock. Dealer acceptance of the Honchan tablet was good, and the immediate sales results pleased Mr. Hock. Two problems adversely affecting sales and dealer reaction appeared after the first few months. Frequent complaints were received that the wrapper's appearance deteriorated and that the Honchan soap was too soft.

APPENDIX A: HONCHAN COMPANY COOKING-OIL AND SOAP PRODUCTION

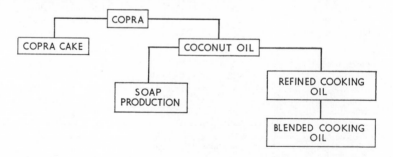

Copra was brought from northern Malaya to the Honchan plant in Kuala Lumpur. This basic raw material from coconut plantations was processed to produce copra cake and coconut oil. The copra cake was sold as animal feed, and a small part of the coconut oil was sold as cooking oil to the Malays.

The bulk of the coconut oil was processed further to produce refined cooking oil. Most of the refined cooking oil had other oils mixed with it, such as ground nut oil, to produce blended cooking oil which was mainly sold to the Chinese in Malaya.

The coconut oil used for cooking-oil production was sold to approximately the following market segments:

10% as coconut oil almost exclusively to the Malays.

25% as refined oil to all groups in Malaya.

65% as blended oil almost exclusively to the Chinese, mainly in the middle- and higher-income groups.

About 93% of the coconut oil was used for cooking-oil production, 1% was lost through waste or impurities, and 6% was used to supply part of Honchan's raw material needs for soap production.

The fatty acid is an excess acid in coconut oil which can be neutralized by the addition of an alkali. This process "wastes" 6% of the coconut oil, but the "waste" by-product is the raw material for soap production.

If the "waste" by-product is not used for soap production, it has a very low market price. Honchan's expanding soap output used all of the by-products produced by its oil refining process and went outside for a large proportion of its additional requirements.

Coconut oil was sold at a relatively stable commodity price; copra cake prices tended to fluctuate; but soap and blended oil were branded products which could be sold at differentiated prices.

"Looking back over its first year on the market," said Mr. Hock, "our Honchan soap had a very unfortunate beginning." After changing from the first supplier of aluminum foil wrappers in 1961, Mr. Hock had thought that the Honchan wrapper problem had been overcome by the second overseas supplier. In the middle of 1962, he had learned that Honchan soap wrappers soon faded on the dealers' shelves, and the color on the package tended to come off on the consumer's hands. Occasionally, the wrapper also became spotty in appearance. Mr. Hock believed that these problems were caused by the action of sunlight on the package and the effect of alkali chemicals in the soap. By May 1963, the company's two wrapper suppliers had been able to improve the quality of the Honchan package considerably, so that its appearance was no longer an adverse marketing factor.

The fragrance and color of Honchan soap had won favorable market acceptance, but consumers soon complained about its softness. Mr. Hock had known that the soap should be seasoned, to develop the appropriate hardness before being used by the consumer, but because he was anxious to place Honchan on the market, he had not waited long enough before distributing the soap to dealers. The hardness of the soap gradually improved as Honchan's production increased and the inventory built up at the plant. By the end of 1962, Mr. Hock was able to market a well-seasoned Honchan soap.

Weaver Brothers continued advertising its Clean soap by radio, movie, and newspapers in 1962–63, while Mr. Hock continued to depend on dealer interest and favorable consumer acceptance to market Honchan. "I hope that once consumers use it," said Mr. Hock, "they will stick with us. Both the Clean and Honchan soap tablets sell for 20¢ each, but ours is better. Not only is Honchan's fragrance, color, and texture superior, but its percentage of pure soap is higher." Since March 1962, Mr. Hock had run four dealer specials, so that when the retailers purchased other Honchan products, they were given free cakes of Honchan soap. For example, one special deal offered retailers five free cakes of Honchan soap for each case of Tiger brand soap purchased.

"We thought that Honchan soap was going to displace Clean soap," said Mr. Hock in May 1963. "I didn't set a specific market target, but so far, I don't think it has done too well." He estimated that Honchan sales had probably reached about 10% of Clean's monthly sales. This result was so disappointing to Mr. Hock that he wondered whether or not the Honchan brand should be considered a failure.

FUTURE MARKET STRATEGY

Reviewing the market performance of Jasmine and Honchan soap in May 1963, Mr. Hock wondered what changes, if any, he should make in his plans to compete with Fresh and Clean. Higher profit margins in the middle- and upper-income soap market continued to promise better long-run profits for Honchan than the lower-income market covered by its Pick and Tiger brands. Mr. Hock had refrained from altering his market strategy for Jasmine soap after June 1962 because he saw no point in making any changes until his company's white toilet soap was available. Inasmuch as blue Jasmine soap was first sold in February and white Jasmine soap would be distributed to dealers in June 1963, Mr. Hock was concerned about what action he should take to ensure the success of the Jasmine product line. "I personally think our current standing in the toilet soap market is weak," he said. "My target is to follow Fresh. I want 40% of the market; otherwise Jasmine soap will be in danger. I have a small share now, and that is very bad. This month my toilet soap sales improved, but, compared with last year, the recent results have not been satisfactory."

To increase his toilet soap sales significantly, Mr. Hock planned to give his dealers, for an indefinite period, an additional 10% discount on their purchases of Jasmine soap. At the same time, he planned to resume a full-scale sales promotion campaign for Jasmine soap, utilizing radio, newspapers, and magazines as well as trade fair exhibitions and movie advertisements. He did not contemplate any change in the recommended retail price for the toilet soap, because he thought it should remain at the same price as Fresh. Reports from his sales force indicated that Weaver Brothers intended to supplement their existing cash and turnover discounts, totaling 8%, with a special 5% discount to dealers on Fresh purchases.

Mr. Hock was less sure about what action he should take with Honchan soap. He said that the main elements in his market strategy up to

May 1963 had been: (1) product quality; (2) a fair-to-good dealer margin; and (3) gifts to retailers.

"From the company point of view," said Mr. Hock, "Honchan soap has been used on about four occasions to promote other Honchan products to retailers." The product problems which faced Honchan soap in its first year had been overcome. "Judging the current market situation," he said, "I think there is nothing much we can do immediately. I'll wait for the market to forget Honchan's introductory problems, and then I'll do something later."

Most of the sales of Honchan soap had been in the rural areas. The Clean bar, introduced in 1962, had captured the Chinese market in the towns. Mr. Hock acknowledged that if Honchan were to be sold to Chinese in urban areas, it would have to be produced in bar form. The Chinese purchased soap in bar form because of their experience in buying the less expensive Tiger, Pick, and Village bars. The rural areas bought cakes of soap because they couldn't afford to buy soap bars. Mr. Hock was undecided as to what brand of bar soap he should promote to compete with Clean.

One possibility was to upgrade the existing quality of his company's Tiger soap. This brand could be produced as a translucent bar with English and Chinese labeling on the wrapper. Everything would be changed except the name Tiger. At present, Honchan Company had a small advertising expenditure for Tiger soap and none for Pick. Under this alternative, the new Tiger bar would compete with the Clean bar, and Honchan cake-soap would sell against the Clean cake. Another possibility was to produce a Honchan bar to compete directly with the Clean bar. The same soap qualities would be retained by simply enlarging the Honchan cake, and marketing the two sizes against the Clean bar and cake.

"When we are well established in the upper- and middle-income soap markets," said Mr. Hock, "Honchan will probably enter the growing detergent business. Eventually detergents may displace laundry soaps in Malaya. If Honchan goes in for selling detergents, I estimate we shall have to spend M$0.5 million to M$1 million in introductory sales promotion. For the time being, I'm going to concentrate on finding ways to improve soap sales in competition with Fresh and Clean."

SECTION IV

PRICE

Grey Electronics, Inc.

Grey Electronics, Inc., a multi-divisional producer of electronics equipment headquartered in Iowa, was founded in 1936 by John Forman, a graduate engineer with an interest in electronics. During its early years the company survived by assembling various types of radio equipment for Midwestern manufacturers. Operations expanded substantially during World War II as the company obtained large amounts of subcontracting work, mainly of an assembly nature. During and immediately following the war, Forman changed the character of his firm in an attempt to develop a proprietary product. His first effort was an improved version of a high frequency radio receiver which one of his associates had designed. The "new" product was immediately successful and the profits generated enabled Forman to invest heavily in research and development. During the late 1940's and early 1950's the company successfully introduced a series of new products and by 1960 sales had grown to almost $40 million a year. By 1965 the company consisted of three major producing divisions (consumer products, radio equipment and solid state) as well as several staff departments (see Exhibit 1).

The solid state division's products were high quality, technically sophisticated electronic subassembles and integrated circuits designed for limited, specialized uses, with about 75 percent of division sales going to the U.S. government. The products were constantly changing and the division regularly worked near the "state of the art" in either its product development work or its production methods.

The division was organized with four major departments—all of which reported to a decision manager. In 1964 a solid state oscillator department was added to the division.[1] (See Exhibit 2.) This department was respon-

---

[1] An oscillator is a source of power used in technically advanced laboratory and field test sets. A test set might contain a series of oscillators, each capable of producing a signal over a given frequency range, making the set useful for checking the accuracy and receiving power of a piece of electronic equipment.

sible for its own research and development, engineering, manufacturing, and marketing activities. Grey's market share for this product was estimated to be about 35 percent versus 40 percent for the industry's largest producer, Standard Parts.

Because such a large portion of its sales were to the government, the manager of the oscillator department, Ned Seymoure, was constantly troubled by the problem of bid pricing. Competition was severe and he was often forced to bid on a variable cost basis—or even below—to secure some business. In 1965, Seymoure asked Tom Moore, Director of Corporate Operations Research, to investigate the feasibility of preparing a model which would help in determining the price to bid on contracts.

In his preliminary work, Moore found that the oscillator subassembly group's cost on a job was often a function of the price bid. Thus, if a low bid was submitted and accepted the manufacturing group worked hard to keep its costs down. Conversely if a "profitable" bid had been accepted, the manufacturing group did not strive as hard to hold down its costs. He also determined that substantial variations existed between contracts and bids in the gathering and utilizing of marketing information concerning the customer's needs and competitor's strengths, weaknesses, and probably bids.

At the end of three months, Moore and other members of the Operations Research Group had completed the job of constructing and programming the model. The actual construction consisted of two steps:

1. *Determining the Objectives of the Model.* After careful deliberation it was decided that, since the manager of the oscillator department was the person who would ultimately accept or reject the model, it would be useless to try to sell him a model which did not meet his objectives. "Therefore," stated Moore, "I asked Seymoure what his own goals were relative to the operations of the division. It would have been possible for us to construct a model which best served the interests of the corporation, the product managers working for Seymoure, and/or of Seymoure himself. We knew, in advance, that the objectives of these three parties were not necessarily compatible. For example, the corporation tends to set year to year objectives on return on investment while product managers often become excessively concerned about winning or losing a particular contract. Seymoure, on the other hand, tends to look at the long run—the next five years. He worries about getting enough volume to hold his research group together, to hold his manufacturing schedule fairly constant throughout the year, and about getting a big share of the market. We finally decided we'd try to construct a model which would be predicated on the long run, but which would show what would happen in the short run also."

2. *Determining the Bidding Process.* The Bidding Procedure in the oscillator department involved the representatives of several functional areas. Chronologically, the steps appeared as follows:

1. A request to submit a bid was received by the department's Marketing Manager.
2. He referred the bid request to a Product Marketing Specialist whose specialty was within the product line concerned.
3. The Product Marketing Specialist requested a cost estimate from the Accounting Department.
4. A cost estimator from the Accounting Department obtained from the Product Line Manager estimates of the cost of manufacturing the product; i.e., the cost data, both historical and estimated, that he could use to produce a bid. This bid was always based on full-cost-recovery pricing.
5. This analysis was returned to the Product Marketing Specialist who prepared an analysis of the market to supplement the financial analysis.
6. These analyses were presented to the Product Line Manager. The Product Marketing Specialist and the Product Line Manager jointly prepared a bid which was submitted to the Marketing Manager for approval.
7. If the Product Line Manager and the Product Marketing Specialist could not agree on a bid, the Marketing Manager would resolve their differences.
8. If the contract to be bid was large or particularly significant for other reasons, the Division Manager approved the final bid. He also resolved any remaining disagreements or even changed the suggested bid to one which he felt was more appropriate.

FULL-COST-RECOVERY PRICING

A full-cost-recovery price, as prepared by the cost estimator, was designed to recover *all* variable costs plus all allocated costs of a contract. The procedure for preparing such a bid was:

1. Direct labor for the contract was estimated. Direct labor included a 25 percent charge for employee fringe benefits.
2. An overhead charge was allocated based on 70 percent of direct labor. Overhead included depreciation on the division's equipment, the costs of the machine shop and service departments of the division (e.g., divisional R & D, etc.), and all fixed charges not included in the General and Administrative allocation.
3. Material costs were estimated.
4. (1), (2), and (3) were totaled to get manufacturing cost.
5. General and Administrative burden was computed as a percentage of manufacturing cost. G & A included: an allocation for the expenses of the corporate staff; corporate building; corporate service; the division manager's salary and his staff salaries; and costs of moving and

rearranging equipment. G & A normally ranged from 35 to 65 percent of manufacturing cost.

6. An allocation for profit was computed as a percent of the total of (4) and (5). The percentage used depended on the type of contract being negotiated and also varied according to the Federal Government's pricing guidelines.

Description of the Model

The basic model represented an attempt to simulate the process by which an experienced manager prepared a bid. The probability of getting the contract if a given price was bid was of critical importance. By multiplying this probability with the expected payoff, the model showed the probable value of submitting a particular bid. Mr. Moore explained: "We repeat their process for many different bids until we find the optimal price, that is, the bid which was the highest expected value of those bids we are willing to submit. Naturally, we don't blindly accept what the model puts out. We know we can't describe all bidding situations in this one model and even if we could, the cost would be exorbitant. We submit the model's output to the department manager for further action. If his intuition agrees with the model, we'll have done a pretty good job. If not, either some factor has been left out of the model or the manager is biased by some personal consideration. Once we determine what the problem is, the model's suggested bids can be accepted or rejected."

Inputs to the Model

In its completed form, the model made use of four inputs. The first input was an estimate of the most critical competitor's probable bids. Factors considered in preparing this estimate included the opposing firm's financial condition, the capacity at which the firm was estimated to be operating, its bidding history, and the bidding history of the person preparing that firm's bid, the firm's estimated cost structure, its capacity to develop or produce the product involved, the firm's policies relating to long-run versus short-run gains, any unique rivalry existing between Grey and that firm, the firm's position in (or out of) the market involved, the price structure of the market (e.g., firm or deteriorating), and any other information relevant to the opposing firm's probable bid.

One or several people might prepare this assessment. Usually those persons most familiar with the market would be the manager of the manufacturing group for that product and his counterpart in the marketing department. Their estimates were quantified in the model using a probability distribution. A normal-type distribution was assumed with the competitor's most likely bid equalling the mode.

(As an example, if a competitor's most probable bid was expected to be $50,000 and there was felt to be 1 chance out of 40 that he would bid below $35,000, a normal-type distribution was created with $50,000 equalling the mode while $35,000 and $65,000 equalled the plus and minus two standard deviation points.)

The second input involved an estimate of the amount of bias which the customer held for or against Grey or its products. To prepare this estimate it was necessary to determine the basis on which the contract would be let. A customer might be concerned about a number of factors including price, the ability of the supplier to meet delivery schedules, unusual technical characteristics of a product, the back-up service which a firm offered—or any of a number of other factors peculiar to a customer and a contract.

This estimate was quantified in terms of the probability of Grey being awarded the contract if its bid was a certain percent above or below the competitor's bid. Such an estimate might appear as follows, for example:

Percent Grey's Bid Above (+) or Below (−) Competitor's Bid	Probability Grey Will Get Contract
+20%	.025
+ 5%	.5
−10%	.975

Once again, a normal-type distribution was assumed with the mean equalling the point at which there was a 50–50 chance Grey would get the bid. This estimate was prepared by the product sales manager and the manufacturing group manager.

The third input consisted of the production costs of the contract. An estimate of the labor and material costs was prepared by the manager of the manufacturing group. He considered historical performance, learning curve effects, start-up costs, equipment required and all other factors which influenced his production costs. Overhead rates were allocated by the Division Controller.

The fourth input was the long-run effects of the contract. Effects of the contract on catalogue prices and prices which would have to be submitted on succeeding bids such as follow-on contracts, reduced overhead allowances on renegotiable contracts, gains and losses in market position and prestige, and any other factors not included in the costs of production were computed to determine the rewards and penalties of losing the contract. These payoffs or losses were present-valued at an annual rate of 10 percent to determine the "extra" benefits and costs of the contract. The manufacturing group manager and the marketing manager prepared this estimate.

Output of the Model

The model's output was a payoff table showing the expected value of a given bid. This table might appear as follows, for example:

Bid	Probability of Winning	Profits (Losses)	Probable Profits (Losses)
$70,000	.05	$40,000	$ 2,000
60,000	.3	30,000	9,000
50,000	.55	20,000	11,000
40,000	.70	10,000	7,000
30,000	1.0	–0–	–0–

Other Factors

Several additional factors were built into the model. The model could produce two suggested bids, one based on full-cost and the other on variable cost. The model could also be used to compare the effect of several different estimates of cost and market inputs.

The SSI Job

An opportunity for the oscillator department to reach its goal of becoming the leader in the solid state oscillator field arose in April, 1966 when Systems Suppliers Incorporated (SSI) solicited bids for a large number of oscillators to be used in laboratory test sets designed for the military. SSI received the contract from Redstone Arsenal at a time when SSI was reportedly in financial trouble due to low sales volume.

The contract was for 57 sets. Each set contained two separate oscillator units each of which required one oscillator subassembly for each of eight frequency bands, A, B, C, D, E, F, G, and H. Bids were therefore being solicited on 912 subassemblies in total or 114 in each frequency band. In addition, bids were requested for a possible follow-on order should Systems Suppliers wish to raise the total procurement to either 1,200 or 1,600 units.

SSI did not restrict itself to one supplier for the entire contract. Bids were requested on several options so that SSI could split the contract if it wished. The options were:

Option Number	Frequency Bands to Be Covered
1	A, B, C, D, E, F, G, & H
2	A, B, C, D, E, F, & G
3	H
4	A, B, & C
5	D, E, F, & G

Grey asked for and received permission to bid on one other option:

Option Number	Frequency Bands to Be Covered
6	A, B, C, D, & E

Grey requested this option because it closely matched Grey's present capabilities and its market expansion plans. Option number 6, therefore, was the option the company was most interested in winning.

Grey believed it held a technical advantage in three frequency bands (A, B, and C) amounting to a virtual monopoly. Standard Parts, Grey's only significant competitor, was known to have started working on these oscillator subassemblies, but had not yet displayed any capacity to produce or deliver in quantity any oscillators in these frequency ranges. In the past year, Grey had successfully marketed an oscillator at H band, one which was expected to be extremely competitive in terms of the SSI contract. Grey did not have, or plan to develop, an oscillator at G band, but at F band, an oscillator was in the final stages of development. At E band, the company was preparing a pilot production run, while both Grey and Standard Parts had successfully marketed D band subassemblies.

Grey believed it held a technical advantage on all oscillators from A through E band, and in H band, because its products were magnetically shielded. Magnetic shielding was important to SSI as Redstone's specifications required close physical storage of the oscillators, a layout which might cause equipment failure if their magnetic fields interacted. It was known that Standard Parts proposed to overcome this weakness by lining the storage containers with magnetic shielding material. It was not known with certainty if this technique would work.

The Customer

Determining the basis on which SSI would award the contract was relatively easy. SSI had the reputation of making decisions which maximized short-term profits. In other words, they were thought to be willing to take a high risk of a long-term loss in return for a high assurance of a short-term gain. Price, therefore, was thought to be the key to obtaining the contract.

This situation operated to Grey's disadvantage because, in issuing the contract, Redstone Arsenal had specified Standard Parts oscillators rather than "Standard Parts or equivalent." This oversight on Redstone's part had probably occurred because Redstone copied SSI's specifications when the contract was written. Grey was not successful in attempting to get Redstone to change this specification. Although Grey might legally have forced Redstone to change the specifications, this would have created ill-will which the company was reluctant to incur.

Redstone's oversight worked to both SSI and Standard Part's advantage. SSI told Grey it would be willing to purchase Standard's oscillators in all frequency bands despite the risk of technical difficulties and failure to meet delivery schedules, knowing they could escape any repercussions by maintaining they had exactly followed the contract's specifications.

On the other hand, Grey was reasonably sure that SSI did not really wish to do this. Grey felt that SSI probably wanted to split the order, with Standard Parts getting options 3 and 5, and Grey getting option 4. It was also felt that Standard Parts would be determined to get as much of the contract as possible since their market share had dropped substantially over the past two years. This contract was quite large and the firm which got the contract would probably gain or hold a leadership position in the market for some time to come. The combination of these circumstances meant that the SSI job was a prize well worth seeking but one that would be difficult to attain.

Estimates of Competitive Bids

Assuming the contract would be let on price alone, Grey prepared estimates of Standard Part's probable bids.[2]

Option	Frequency Band	Bid Range Estimate A	Estimate B
1	A	$1,990–1,390	$1,530–1,630
	B	1,170–1,420	1,020–1,120
	C	765– 865	765– 720
	D	690– 740	665– 765
	E	665– 740	640– 690
	F	665– 740	640– 690
	G	690– 765	690– 740
	H	2,500–2,750	2,100–2,500
2	Same as 1 above except eliminate H Band		
3	H	$2,500–2,750	$2,100–2,500
4	A	$2,040–3,040	$1,840–1,940
	B	1,220–1,720	1,220–1,320
	C	820– 920	870– 970
5	D	$ 720– 770	$ 720– 770
	E	690– 765	665– 720
	F	690– 740	665– 720
	G	720– 820	720– 770
6	A	$1,990–2,390	$1,530–1,630
	B	1,170–1,420	1,020–1,120
	C	765– 865	765– 715
	D	690– 740	665– 765
	E	665– 740	640– 690
7 Standard Parts Reaction to Option 6	F	$ 690– 665	$ 714– 765
	G	700– 800	790– 840
	H	2,325–2,550	2,375–2,495

Estimates A and B were made by knowledgeable people who were intimately familiar with the market, historical bids made by Standard Parts, their general financial position, and other intangibles which might

---

[2] While Grey was preparing bids on all seven options, only option number 3 will be costed in this case; the cost per oscillator is given in Exhibit 3.

influence Standard's bid. They were made independently, and there was no attempt to "correct" the estimates once each estimator knew what the other had estimated. They were therefore a reliable indicator of Grey's knowledge of Standard Part's intentions.

Historical Costs

The company possessed a substantial amount of cost data on oscillator subassemblies in bands A, B, C, and D; several successful bids had been made for contracts involving these subassemblies, and the company was confident that this information could provide the basis for a successful bid on this occasion. The company had only been marketing band H subassemblies, on the other hand, for some four months. The technical breakthrough which had enabled Grey to manufacture band H oscillator subassemblies at relatively short notice had led to wide customer acceptance of the product. Nevertheless, Grey was a little uncertain of the value of the five months' cost data on band H components, in view of the relative experience of its competitors. In spite of this, Grey was very anxious that the company's bid on Option 3 should be competitive, in view of the boost to development that would be provided by winning the band H contract. The first five months' labor and material costs (Exhibit 3), are those actually incurred during the first production runs of band H components. The last seven months' costs (of the full year's contract) were estimated by the Product Line Manager.[3]

Although lacking marketing experience in bands E, F, and G, the company prepared bids using the following criteria:

1. Costs for the band E oscillator should equal band D. Equivalent effort should be the same.
2. Costs for band F should be the same as those for band D except that the costs for labor category 2 should be doubled. Equivalent effort should be the same.
3. Costs for the G band oscillator should be the same as for D band for labor category 1, the same as the F band for labor category 2, 1.25 times the cost of D band for labor category 3, and the same as D band for material cost. Equivalent effort should be the same as the D band.

All labor costs included an overhead charge of 70 percent.

Additional Labor Costs

If Grey obtained the order, it was felt that additional people would be required. Estimates of these needs were as follows:

---

[3] The company felt it had a good chance of being awarded the contract for option 4. At all events, Grey anticipated spreading the production of the subassemblies over a year's operations.

Labor	Salary (Not Including 25% Fringe Benefits)	Order Size*
Jr. Tech................................	$115/wk	Three or more bands
Assembler A........................	$2.75/hr	Three or more bands
Assembler A........................	$2.75/hr	Six or more bands
Assembler B........................	$2.41/hr	Three or more bands
Experimental Assembler.............	$2.75/hr	Any order
Assembler B........................	$2.41/hr	Four or more bands
Technician.........................	$136/wk	Six or more bands
Prod. Eng. B.......................	$180/wk	Four or more bands
Clerk (half time)..................	$88/wk	Four or more bands

* The necessity for these labor force additions varied with the number of types for which an order was received. If Grey received an order for any three oscillators, for example, it would have to hire four people: a senior technician; an Assembler A; an Assembler B; and an Experimental Assembler. If it obtained an order for all eight oscillators, it would have to hire all of the people listed.

Equipment Required

In addition to labor force additions, an order from SSI would force Grey to purchase equipment. The following table summarizes these requirements:

Equipment	Approximate Cost*	Order
Assembly Station.................	$ 5,000	Three or more bands
Assembly Station.................	5,000	Four or more bands
Processor........................	1,200/pair	Any order
Console..........................	10,000	Any order
Console..........................	10,000	Four or more bands
Microscope.......................	600	Each added assembler
Spotwelder.......................	1,000	Any order
Spotwelder.......................	1,000	Three or more bands
Two Spotwelders..................	1,000 ea.	Six or more bands
Test Bench.......................	500	Each added assembler
Furnace..........................	7,500	Seven or more bands

* Installation costs included.

Other Costs

Several miscellaneous costs had to be considered. Training costs historically equalled about six weeks' salary per person. There were also warranty provisions; about 5 percent of the oscillators in each of the top five bands would have to be replaced, while in the lower three bands, about 15 percent would have to be replaced. Royalties were also a factor; a royalty consisting of one-half of 1 percent of the selling price would have to be paid on the top six oscillators. Finally, there was the problem of deciding which, if any, of the bids would bear the departmental overhead of $480,000 a year. The management assumed that the contract, if awarded, would run for one year, and that the overhead rate on all of the oscillator business was effectively the same. This did not mean, however, that a marginal cost bid could not be made.

In addition to these costs, increases would be necessary in some liquid assets. In general, a contract would increase cash requirements by about two or three weeks' total cost, receivables by between three and four weeks total cost, and inventories by about seven to eight weeks' total cost.

Intangibles

No matter what the factory costs, Grey did not want to lose all of the SSI business. Recent technical developments in test sets indicated the feasibility of substituting integrated equipment for low frequency oscillators. If Standard Parts got a contract for high frequency units, they could develop a shielded oscillator subassembly and compete more favorably with Grey elsewhere. Grey, therefore, did not want Standard Parts to get the order for high frequency oscillator subassemblies.

Output

The final output of the program, based on the information given in the case for band H subassemblies, is presented in Exhibit 5.

EXHIBIT 1

Organizational Chart of the Grey Electronics Company in 1965

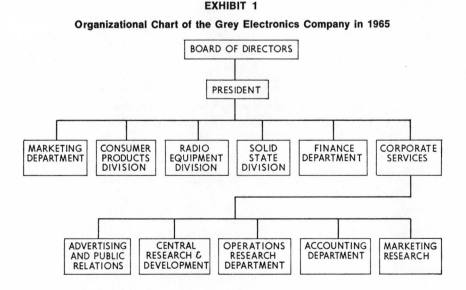

EXHIBIT 2

Organization Chart of the Solid State Division of the Grey Electronics Company in 1965

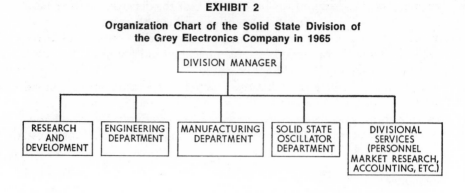

EXHIBIT 3

Grey Cost Data for Frequency Band H

Month	No. of Weeks	Labor Category			Total Labor	Material	Equivalent Effort*
		1	2	3			
1.....	4	$ 4,290	$ 5,110	$ 2,450	$ 11,850	$ 4,700	11.70
2.....	4	3,330	4,330	3,860	11,520	2,420	8.65
3.....	4	2,865	3,870	2,370	9,105	3,440	8.50
4.....	5	3,905	2,480	2,125	8,510	2,820	1.15
5.....	5	3,120	3,860	4,050	11,030	1,775	12.25
6.....	4	3,770	2,825	3,115	9,710	1,570	13.35
7.....	4	3,535	3,165	2,655	9,355	1,570	12.65
8.....	4	2,170	3,350	2,830	8,350	1,175	8.25
9.....	5	2,285	2,110	3,160	7,555	590	8.15
10.....	4	3,410	2,735	2,660	8,805	785	9.35
11.....	4	3,265	3,150	2,210	8,625	980	'9.55
12.....	5	2,985	2,845	3,615	9,445	590	10.45
		$38,930	$39,830	$35,100	$113,860	$22,415	114.00

* "Equivalent effort" referred to the number of oscillator subassemblies produced during the period. With respect to the above, for example, output at the end of the first month might consist of the following:

No. of Oscillators	Percent Completed	Equivalent Effort
1......................	100	1
20......................	50	10
2......................	25	0.5
1......................	20	0.2
Equivalent effort at end of 1st month		11.70

EXHIBIT 4

Evaluation of Cost of H Band Oscillator
Subassembly: Options 1 & 3

Direct labor	$113,860	
Material	22,415	
Additional labor	11,690	
Training costs	660	
Additional equipment	1,590	
Manufacturing cost	$150,215	$150,215
Warranty provisions	$ 22,530	
Royalties	—	
Other costs	485	
Miscellaneous costs	$ 23,015	23,015
Allocation of department overhead	$ 42,860	42,860
Cash	10,660	
Receivables cost	15,275	
Inventory cost	30,545	
Total increase in liquid assets	$ 56,480	56,480
Total cost:		$272,570
Units produced:		114
Full cost per unit:		$ 2,391
Marginal cost per unit:		$ 2,015

NOTE: Costs are calculated on the basis of information given on pages 345–346 and in Exhibit 3 of this case. General & Administrative overhead of $42,860 (29% of manufacturing cost) was a result of (1) allocating the total factory overhead "reasonably" between not only the expected SSI contracts, but also over the other work on which the department was engaged; (2) an assessment of the major long term benefits to which success with the Option 3 bid was expected to lead.

EXHIBIT 5

Grey Electronics, Inc.

GREY ELECT FULL COST

Q =	0.95
A =	2100.00
M =	2500.00
B =	2750.00

ALPHA = 0.0 Percent (competitive advantage)

FIRST TRIAL PRICE = 2000.00

TRIAL PRICE INTERVAL = 10.00

NUMBER OF TRIAL PRICES = 80.00

PRODUCT COST = 2391.00

NUMBER OF UNITS = 114.00

EXTRA PROFIT = 0.0

EXTRA PENALTY = 0.0

PSTAR INTERPOLATION PERMISSIBLE ERROR = 0.10 Cents

EXHIBIT 5 (Continued)

GREY ELECT FULL COST

BID PRICE	PROBABILITY OF WINNING	EXPECTED PROFIT
2CCC.CO	0.991	-44182.81
2010.CO	0.990	-42997.70
2C20.00	C.989	-41808.76
2C3C.CC	0.987	-40615.91
2C40.00	0.985	-39419.04
205C.CC	0.983	-38218.12
2C6C.00	0.981	-37013.14
2C70.00	0.978	-35804.15
2080.0U	0.976	-34591.25
2C90.00	C.973	-33374.60
2100.00	0.969	-32154.44
211C.00	0.966	-30931.10
2120.0C	0.962	-29704.97
2130.00	C.957	-28476.56
2140.CO	C.952	-27246.46
2150.0C	0.947	-26015.39
2160.C0	0.941	-24784.16
2170.0C	0.935	-23553.72
218C.00	C.928	-22325.13
2190.0C	0.921	-21099.59
22C0.0C	C.913	-19878.41
2210.00	0.904	-18663.04
2220.00	0.895	-17455.07
223C.C0	0.886	-16256.20
2240.00	C.875	-15068.27
225C.CC	0.864	-13893.22
2260.00	C.853	-12733.11
227C.C0	0.840	-11590.11
2280.0C	0.827	-10466.46
229C.0C	C.813	-9364.50
23C0.CC	0.799	-8286.62
2310.00	0.784	-7235.26
2320.0C	C.768	-6212.89
2330.00	C.751	-5221.99
2340.00	C.734	-4265.04
2350.00	C.716	-3344.48
2360.C0	C.697	-2462.69
2370.00	Q.678	-1621.99
2380.0C	0.658	-824.60
2390.0C	0.637	-72.62

EXHIBIT 5 (Continued)

GREY ELECT FULL COST

BID PRICE	PROBABILITY OF WINNING	EXPECTED PROFIT
2400.00	0.616	631.98
2410.00	0.594	1287.42
2420.00	0.572	1892.06
2430.00	0.550	2444.51
2440.00	0.527	2943.54
2450.00	0.504	3388.19
2460.00	0.480	3777.74
2470.00	0.457	4111.70
2480.00	0.433	4389.86
2490.00	0.409	4612.25
2500.00	0.385	4779.23
2510.00	0.361	4891.56
2520.00	0.337	4951.25
2530.00	0.313	4961.09
2540.00	0.290	4924.44
2550.00	0.267	4845.16
2560.00	0.245	4727.52
2570.00	0.224	4576.08
2580.00	0.204	4395.64
2590.00	0.185	4191.08
2600.00	0.167	3967.30
2610.00	0.149	3729.09
2620.00	0.133	3481.05
2630.00	0.118	3227.52
2640.00	0.105	2972.51
2650.00	0.092	2719.61
2660.00	0.081	2472.02
2670.00	0.070	2232.47
2680.00	0.061	2003.22
2690.00	0.052	1786.08
2700.00	0.045	1582.41
2710.00	0.038	1393.14
2720.00	0.032	1218.82
2730.00	0.027	1059.66
2740.00	0.023	915.55
2750.00	0.019	786.13
2760.00	0.016	670.82
2770.00	0.013	568.89
2780.00	0.011	479.47
2790.00	0.009	401.62

MAXIMUM PROFIT =   4963.18   PRICE =   2527.10

EXHIBIT 5 (Continued)

GREY ELECT. MARGINAL

$Q =$ 0.95

$A =$ 2100.00

$M =$ 2500.00

$B =$ 2750.00

ALPHA =   0.0 Percent (competitive advantage)

FIRST TRIAL PRICE =   2000.00

TRIAL PRICE INTERVAL =   10.00

NUMBER OF TRIAL PRICES =   80.00

PRODUCT COST =   2015.00

NUMBER OF UNITS =   114.00

EXTRA PROFIT =   0.0

EXTRA PENALTY =   0.0

PSTAR INTERPOLATION PERMISSIBLE ERROR =   0.10 Cents

EXHIBIT 5 (Continued)

GREY ELECT. MARGINAL

BID PRICE	PROBABILITY OF WINNING	EXPECTED PROFIT
2000.00	0.991	-1694.99
2010.00	0.990	-564.27
2020.00	0.989	563.46
2030.00	0.987	1687.64
2040.00	0.985	2807.62
2050.00	0.983	3922.68
2060.00	0.981	5032.00
2070.00	0.978	6134.66
2080.00	0.976	7229.68
2090.00	0.973	8315.93
2100.00	0.969	9392.19
2110.00	0.966	10457.13
2120.00	0.962	11509.30
2130.00	0.957	12547.14
2140.00	0.952	13568.95
2150.00	0.947	14572.93
2160.00	0.941	15557.16
2170.00	0.935	16519.58
2180.00	0.928	17458.04
2190.00	0.921	18370.29
2200.00	0.913	19253.95
2210.00	0.904	20106.59
2220.00	0.895	20925.67
2230.00	0.886	21708.59
2240.00	0.875	22452.72
2250.00	0.864	23155.37
2260.00	0.853	23813.83
2270.00	0.840	24425.44
2280.00	0.827	24987.50
2290.00	0.813	25497.41
2300.00	0.799	25952.61
2310.00	0.784	26350.65
2320.00	0.768	26689.19
2330.00	0.751	26966.04
2340.00	0.734	27179.20
2350.00	0.716	27326.81
2360.00	0.697	27407.32
2370.00	0.678	27419.31
2380.00	0.658	27361.74
2390.00	0.637	27233.72

EXHIBIT 5 (Concluded)

GREY ELECT. MARGINAL

BID PRICE	PROBABILITY OF WINNING	EXPECTED PROFIT
2400.00	0.616	27034.78
2410.00	0.594	26764.75
2420.00	0.572	26423.66
2430.00	0.550	26012.09
2440.00	0.527	25530.72
2450.00	0.504	24980.73
2460.00	0.480	24363.70
2470.00	0.457	23681.29
2480.00	0.433	22935.79
2490.00	0.409	22129.52
2500.00	0.385	21265.38
2510.00	0.361	20347.27
2520.00	0.337	19382.81
2530.00	0.313	18381.02
2540.00	0.290	17351.23
2550.00	0.267	16302.91
2560.00	0.245	15245.55
2570.00	0.224	14188.41
2580.00	0.204	13140.41
2590.00	0.185	12109.92
2600.00	0.167	11104.65
2610.00	0.149	10131.54
2620.00	0.133	9196.65
2630.00	0.118	8305.12
2640.00	0.105	7461.11
2650.00	0.092	6667.77
2660.00	0.081	5927.34
2670.00	0.070	5241.11
2680.00	0.061	4609.49
2690.00	0.052	4032.13
2700.00	0.045	3507.93
2710.00	0.038	3035.21
2720.00	0.032	2611.76
2730.00	0.027	2234.97
2740.00	0.023	1901.93
2750.00	0.019	1609.48
2760.00	0.016	1354.37
2770.00	0.013	1133.28
2780.00	0.011	942.92
2790.00	0.009	780.09

MAXIMUM PROFIT = 27422.98   PRICE = 2366.70

NOTES to Output, Exhibit 5

1. "Q" relates to the degree of certainty which Grey had for the estimates of its competitors' most probable bids; figure A refers to the minus 2 standard deviation point; figure B to the plus 2 SD point, and M to the mode. See pages 346–347, this case.

2. "Alpha" is an input measure of any (non-price) competitive advantage which Grey was thought to have over the competitor. Alpha = 0.5, for example, would mean that Grey could bid 5 percent more than the competitor and still win the contract. If the contract was being let on price alone, then there could be no competitive advantage, and Alpha would equal zero. See page 347.

3. Extra Profit, Extra Penalty: These dollar inputs quantify the extra (particularly longer term) benefits (or penalties) which the company might expect as a result of winning (or losing) the contract. For example, success in this contract might lead to a reduction of costs in the production of another assembly. See page 347.

4. P* is the allowed error in the estimate of the price (to produce the expected maximum profit).

APPENDIX A

Government Contracts

Among the problems faced by firms supplying sophisticated parts and equipment to the government or its suppliers is the contracts which the government negotiates.

As a first-order generalization, government contracts are very precise in terms of specifications, both technical and other. The custom of phoning or writing a customer to submit an order, common in some business and industries, is not common when doing business with the government. Technical specifications in government contracts are very specific and inclusive in describing the desired product. Other specific provisions of these contracts might include delivery dates, profits which the supplying firm is allowed to make, sharing of research and development costs, and privileges which the government reserves for itself with respect to the product, its development, and the knowledge which a firm gains from developing that product.

With respect to systems, the government reserves the right to accept or authorize the manufacture of a system until the pilot models have been demonstrated to be fully workable and the supplying firms have proved their capacity to supply the system and its components. Thus, if five firms are supplying components to a systems manufacturer and one of the components fails, neither the systems manufacturer nor the components manufacturers will receive authorization to commence production until the problem is solved. This can create many scheduling problems as a firm might receive a contract for a component but not get authorization for production until some time later, with that time depending on another supplier.

Contracts which the government might negotiate with respect to profits can also create problems. In general, there are three types of contracts: a "fixed-price" contract; a "cost-plus-fixed-fee" contract (CPFF); and a "target-incentive" contract.

A fixed-price contract means that a company agrees to supply a given quantity of a given product for a fixed amount of money. If the company loses money on the contract, it suffers the entire loss. If the company makes money on the contract, it enjoys the entire gain.

A cost-plus-fixed-fee contract might cover a research and development project with the government agreeing to pay for the cost of the project plus some amount or percent of profit. Such contracts are renegotiable as differences of opinion may arise concerning exactly what the costs are or were. Disagreements can arise over whether machinery investments should be allocated fully to a given contract or should be partially supported by other aspects of a firm's operations. Overhead and administrative expenses are also common areas of disagreement, not only because of the difficulties involved in allocating these costs, but also because of the difficulties created by the fluctuating volume of business which a company might do. For example, an overhead allocation rate based on the level of business a firm is doing now might be unacceptable to the government six months from now if the firm's business increased significantly in the interim. The opposite would be true if the firm's business declined.

A target-incentive contract involves several negotiated figures—a target price, a target cost, a ceiling price, and a profit formula. Target cost represents the expected cost of the job. Target price is the price the government expects to pay and represents target cost plus an allowance for profit. Ceiling price is the highest amount which the government will pay for the job. The profit formula represents the division which will be made of the costs or profits if they differ from the targets. If target cost is less than actual cost, the government shares part of the cost and the company takes the rest. If actual cost is less than target cost, the government shares part of the savings and the company gets the remainder.

The government handles problems over CPFF and target-incentive contracts by reserving the right to audit a company's books whenever it chooses. For example, if a company is working on a CPFF contract and the company receives another large contract from the government or a significant amount of business from elsewhere, the government might audit the company's books to renegotiate the overhead and administrative allowances on the CPFF contract. As a consequence, when a company is bidding on contracts, it must consider the effect of those contracts on any government business it currently has if that government business is renegotiable or requires cost breakdowns.

The government also audits a firm's books before it negotiates a fixed-price contract if there is insufficient competition for the contract.

Another aspect of government contracts deals with the ownership of products developed through government sponsored research. If the government has financed the development of a product, it can require the firm which performed the work to supply blueprints to competing firms to allow the government to develop alternative sources of supply. It should be noted, however, that supplying blueprints does not imply that production know-how must also be supplied. In practice, the difficulties involved in manufacturing many technical items reduces substantially the usefulness of blueprints.

APPENDIX B

Some Competitive Characteristics of the SSO Market

SSO's are utilized as subassemblies of systems designed mainly for military use. It has been estimated that as much as 90 percent of the SSO's produced are ultimately delivered to the government. In this field, Grey is an "independent" producer. That is, Grey is not a systems designer but, instead, supplies SSO's to other firms which are systems designers and which often have their own SSO departments. Independent producers sometimes find that a systems designer will ask for bids from the independents, then offer the contract to their own division if it can produce the SSO's at a lower cost.

About 25 percent of Grey's SSO sales are the result of contracts for which bids are required. However, these bid contracts serve as the price leaders in the field. As the price structure of this and other electronics markets is historically deteriorating, it is necessary for a manager to consider not only the effect of a bid price on a given contract, but also the effect of that bid on his "catalogue" prices and the profits resulting from these sales.

Producers compete in several ways in this market but not all firms elect to follow the same paths. As the products are often "state-of-the-art" in terms of their advanced technical design, the capacity to develop and produce high-quality, technically advanced and often highly-specialized equipment is one area of competition.

In general too, allegedly competitive items produced by different manufacturers are not directly interchangeable. For example, if a system is designed to use Company A's SSO's, it might be very difficult or expensive to alter that system in order to use Company B's SSO's. This situation places a premium on being either the first producer of an item or getting a firm to design their system specifically to use your products.

Firms may compete by having an intelligence system which informs them of the probable need for a given new product or an adaptation of an existing product in order that they can develop the item. They may also compete through the use of highly-skilled, technical field men whose job it is to sell the systems designer on the merits of their company's products and to suggest to the systems designer ways in which new uses or adaptations can be made of existing products. It is sometimes said that the field men must "live in the customer's pocket."

The importance of price in this market is very great. Systems designers must submit bids to the government which force the designer to seek the lowest-cost suppliers he can. In addition, contracts with suppliers are usually negotiated by the business managers of a system design firm rather than by the technical men. Thus, even though the technical designers may be convinced of the merits of Company A's products, it may be very difficult to convince the business managers of this fact. This problem is compounded by the fact that technical specifications of competing products are often the same while their performance characteristics may not be.

Several other factors also compound the price problem. The effect of volume on the costs of production is substantial. Learning curves play an important role in this industry so that the variable costs of producing SSO's is significantly reduced with increased volume. In addition, the high costs of research and development represent a substantial fixed investment in a given product which often requires a large volume of production to recover. As government contracts are often followed by additional "follow-on" contracts for the same products, the necessity for volume production places another premium on securing the initial contract. Finally, as initial contracts sometimes include an allowance for R & D, yet another premium is placed on securing the first contract.

The characteristics described so far also apply to the systems manufacturers so that price pressures are extremely strong throughout the industry. Systems designers and components manufacturers will sometimes deliberately take a loss on an initial contract in order to gain a competitive advantage. When a systems designer has done this, he will exert pressure on the components manufacturers for lower prices in order to recover part of the expected loss. Similarly, a components manufacturer may do the same thing to its suppliers or to its own manufacturing groups in order to reduce costs.

One of the more interesting ways in which suppliers may be pressured is by means of a practice referred to as a "Chinese Auction." A systems manufacturer might solicit bids from components manufacturers with the understanding that the contract will be awarded to the low bidder. After bids have been submitted, the customer might call components manufacturer company X and hint that he would prefer X's products but that company Y submitted a lower bid. If X responds by submitting a lower bid, the process is then repeated with Y. Since X and Y do not know what the competing firm has bid or whether or not the customer is in fact telling the truth, the amount of uncertainty faced by a supplier is very great. X and Y cannot reveal their respective bids for competitive reasons nor will they do so for fear the Justice Department might regard this as collusion. They cannot mutually agree to stop bidding since that would definitely be collusion. The only alternative is to unilaterally elect to stop bidding, inform the customer of this decision, and run the risk of losing the contract. Needless to say, the customer may not believe a company when it has made this decision and may find itself placed in an untenable position as a consequence. The Chinese Auction is a practice followed by only part of the industry, so a supplier must know who might engage in this practice and be prepared to act accordingly.

Another practice consists of varying the technical specifications of a contract. A customer might specify loose or misleading technical specifications in a contract to be bid on. After the contract has been awarded, the customer will tighten and reinterpret the specifications, so that he gets an expensive part or component for the price of a cheap one.

It would be misleading to say that these practices prevail in the electronics industry. However, they are practiced enough, particularly on large contracts, that they must be taken into account by suppliers through strategic bidding. Some of the ways in which a supplier might combat these practices would include submitting an initially higher bid than the contract is expected to go for in order to be able to reduce the bid later. Alternatively, a supplier might demand technical concessions in exchange for a lower bid or even demand that his technical specifications be written into the customer's contract.

Another way in which a supplier might combat the Chinese Auction problem or escape price pressures consists of reject-bidding. If a components manufacturer is producing an SSO which must produce a certain amount of power, he may find that he is getting a significant number of rejects which do not meet the power requirements for the item he is selling. If he can find a customer for these rejects, he has the opportunity to make very large profits since, in effect, the cost of these items is virtually minimal to him.

Reject bidding, however, is also quite hazardous. It is based on the assumption that rejects will be available to be sold. If a production improvement eliminates the rejects or the market for higher-power products runs out, the supplier may find himself trapped with an unrealistic price. Alternatively, if the lower-power products are not acceptable, renegotiating the contract would be both difficult and embarrassing, if not impossible. The problem of renegotiation is further hampered by the responsibility a manufacturer assumes when he accepts a contract. If a system fails, even though it is the fault of the designer, the manufacturers whose components are involved suffer a very real loss of reputation and feel called upon to do what they can to correct the problem. If this involves supplying primary rather than reject products, they may be forced into this position to avoid the stigma attached to the failure of the system.

Cryovac Division,
W. R. Grace & Company

Cryovac introduced a new process for packaging and preserving such foods as fresh meats, poultry, cheese, and fish in 1947. Although there were some 20 other firms manufacturing fresh food packaging materials, none had the patented features of the Cryovac process, which management considered to be the only truly satisfactory method of packer packaging for self-service retail sale. From its inception, therefore, Cryovac sold its process at a considerably higher price, generally 50–100 per cent higher, than other packaging materials. The firm's sales climbed rapidly from $1.5 million in 1947 to about $40 million. Sales in recent years had not been up to expectations. Cryovac executives believed that this failure to achieve the planned sales volume was the result of prices higher than competitive prices and that this was especially true during a period when economic and competitive factors were unfavorable.

Cryovac is the name of a vacuum-sealing process designed to protect products from damage and deterioration during handling, storing, and shipping. The process involves four steps:

1. The item to be packaged is placed in a loose-fitting bag made from special plastic.
2. Air is withdrawn from the bag by a vacuum pump.
3. The neck of the bag is twisted tightly and sealed with a metal clip.
4. The package is then dipped in hot water at about 200° F., which causes the plastic to shrink and to cling tightly to the contours of the product like a second skin.

Cryovac bags are made from an airtight film that is a modified type of Saran, a plastic resin produced by Dow Chemical Corporation. When a food is sealed in a Cryovac bag and the air withdrawn, the food is protected against spoilage and shrinkage (loss of weight from loss of moisture) and the flavor does not deteriorate. The food can be seen clearly through the plastic. Many foods wrapped by Cryovac can be kept under refrigeration for many weeks without spoiling, whereas with other wrappers spoiling sets in within a week. Cryovac-wrapped meats can be frozen without the discoloration that usually occurs. A number of foods, such as ready-prepared corned beef, which had practically disappeared from meat counters, are now being sold again in Cryovac wrappings.

Cryovac's strongest selling points to food packers were that the Cryovac package would (1) stop shrinkage of the product completely, (2) control the color of the product, and (3) prevent spoilage and thus permit retail shelf life of from three to seven weeks versus a shelf life of only a few days to a week with other types of packages. Competitors in food-packaging materials had processes for packaging foods in plastic bags, but none had the airtight vacuum or the durability features of Cryovac.

Cryovac licensed their entire process to packers. This included sale of three items: the bags, the clips, and the equipment. Manual, semiautomatic or automatic equipment was available, depending on the needs and desires of the packer. The equipment included (1) a vacuumizing unit that drew out the air in the bags, (2) a clipping machine that fastened clips on the bags, and (3) a bath unit that shrank the bag tightly around the product. One person could operate one complete unit. Working with small-unit products, one man in an eight-hour day could package 1,000–1,200 units; with the automatic or semiautomatic equipment, he could do 2,000–3,000 units. On products packaged in larger units, one man could handle 800–1,000 units in a day with the manual equipment and 1,500–1,750 units with the automatic equipment.

Manual equipment generally costs $500–$700 for each set, and the automatic equipment $5,000–$7,000 a set. The equipment wore out very slowly, so that replacement sales were negligible. Small packers might buy one set; large national packers might buy 75 to 100 sets. The bags were sold at prices that varied with the quantity bought, the size of the bag, the type, and the printing desired. About 60 per cent of all bags sold were printed. The price schedule for a typical bag size was as follows:

Nonprinted Bags		Printed Bags*	
Quantity Purchased	Price per Thousand	Quantity Purchased	Price per Thousand
1,000	$40.00	2,500 (Min.	$83.00
5,000	38.00	5,000 order)	63.00
10,000	36.00	10,000	53.00
20,000	34.00	20,000	48.00
50,000	32.00	50,000	45.00
100,000	30.00	100,000	44.00
250,000	29.00	250,000	43.50
500,000	28.50	500,000	43.00

* The prices shown are for three-color printing.

It was possible for a packer to purchase bags on a split-shipment basis. He could place an order for a number of bags and have portions of the order shipped at different times within a six-month period; however, a minimum of 20,000 bags had to be shipped at any one time. The clips were sold in three sizes in cases of 10,000; medium size clips sold at about $25 per case.

A small meat packer who did about 25 per cent of his dollar volume in package meats would use the following Cryovac equipment: one semi-automatic vacuum and fastening machine set, one manual vacuum and fastening machine set, and one automatic shrink tunnel. This equipment would cost about $6,000 and would enable him to package up to 2,000 units a day. This packer would use $10,000 to $15,000 worth of bags and clips in a year.

Initially, the packers of poultry, especially turkeys, were the biggest customers for the Cryovac process. It was estimated that some 86,000 farms produced 82 million turkeys, but that about 2,000 of these accounted for 56 million. Many of the larger farms were owned by large meat packers, grocery manufacturers, and animal feed processors. Locker plants were important customers, but after they reached a total number of about 15,000, they began to decline in importance and currently represented a negligible market. Early in its career Cryovac began an all-out campaign to convince meat and poultry packers of the desirability of prepackaged goods for consumers, a somewhat new concept at the time. To accomplish this task, Cryovac made extensive appeal to retailers, in the hope that retailers would encourage food packers to prepackage more products. Direct-mail pieces, articles in trade publications, demonstrations at trade shows and conventions, and calls by Cryovac salesmen were used. Cryovac salesmen also called on food packers with a presentation that included (1) a list of items to prepackage, (2) a description of how to prepackage them, (3) a statement of how to prepare the food for prepackaging, and (4) a blueprint of how to install a production line using the Cryovac process.

Cheese packers, especially those in Wisconsin, were next in using the Cryovac process because they could age the cheese in the package. Fish and meat packers were also beginning to be important sales sources, but poultry packers were still the largest customers.

The firm split into three regional divisions, each having its own plant and personnel. The western division included the territory west of Michigan to the Texan line, with headquarters in Cedar Rapids, Iowa; the eastern division was centered in Greenville, South Carolina; and the third division was in Canada. The general administrative office, where all research, promotion, and general policies were developed, was located in Cambridge, Massachusetts. In addition, a Chicago office was maintained to handle a group of large national accounts, which included Armour, Swift, Kraft, Wilson, A & P, and National Food Stores. These large accounts generally produced sales of between $100,000 and $1 million each per year. One salesman was required to handle two to four accounts. National accounts represented approximately 25 per cent of Cryovac's volume.

Originally Cryovac had five salesmen, who called on some 25 to 30 distributors who sold the product to packers. The distributors were selected on the basis of experience in the food industry, ability to merchandise, and willingness to crusade for a new process that was costlier than competitive processes. The distributors realized an average 18 per cent discount from list price. After several years the company reappraised this policy in the light of the growing frozen-food market and the general consumer acceptance of prepackaged fresh foods. The executives believed that an all-out sales campaign was needed if Cryovac were to receive its share of the packaging market and that distributors could not do as effective a job as could Cryovac's own sales force. Prospects had to be sold aggressively because of the high cost of the Cryovac process, and accounts had to be serviced. Cryovac salesmen were more skilled in handling the service problems than were distributor salesmen. In addition, the Cryovac management believed that Cryovac salesmen were actually doing most of the selling for the distributors. Therefore, all distributors were dropped, and 60 salesmen were added to Cryovac's existing force, which had grown to 20.

Only two years later the management decided on another major expansion of the sales force and about 80 salesmen were added, bringing the total to more than 160. Each salesman had an assigned territory and was expected to call on each account at least once every 30 days. A sizable and growing volume of business had been developed with smoked meats, and the company then campaigned to get the packers and wholesalers of red meats to use the Cryovac process. The advantages of aging such meats in the Cryovac package rather than unwrapped was emphasized. Normal practice was to age meats in a refrigerated warehouse and then to package them, using a process of one of Cryovac's competitors that would permit shelf life of only a few days. The Cryovac salesmen could cite the following problems in aging by this method: (1) weight loss due to shrinkage; (2) color loss from bacteria activity; and (3) the trimming required to take off the edges that had spoiled. Shrinkage ran to as much as 8 per cent of the weight of some meats but averaged about 4 per cent. Generally, only the finest meats were aged—those sold to high-class restaurants and similar customers. Aging was believed to make meat more tender and to improve its flavor. Despite aggressive selling, Cryovac salesmen found considerable resistance to dropping the traditional method of aging red meat. This market segment, however, represented a large potential.

Cryovac faced competition from a few large firms and some twenty smaller firms. The larger ones were Visking, Tee-Pak, Milprint, Dobeckmun, Continental Can, and Goodyear. These firms had many other packaging lines that did not compete with Cryovac's line, but it was estimated that they had combined sales of $40 to 50 million that could have been replaced by Cryovac.

All competitive firms sold packaging materials, but few sold a packaging process, and none had all the features of Cryovac's vacuum-sealing method. Cryovac, therefore, offered the best method for preventing shrinkage and assuring longer shelf life. It was generally accepted in the field that the Cryovac bag was of a quality superior to that of competitors. How much the added quality was worth was not clear. A typical comparison was a bag used for pork butts. Cryovac's bag sold for $44 per thousand and would preserve a butt for three weeks or more, compared to $30 per thousand for a competitor's bag that would be adequate protection for only 10 to 14 days.

Although the company sold flat film, pouches, and equipment, bags were the key item in the line. They represented the major part of the sales volume and produced the greatest margin. Therefore, it was the price competition in bags that was crucial; equipment sales and prices were relatively unimportant. Cryovac bags were priced from 50 to 80 per cent above competing bags.

During a recession there was a rather pronounced effort by most food packagers to reduce expenses because of a profit squeeze. Many firms reported to Cryovac that they were well satisfied with the line but that the advantages gained from Cryovac over other packaging lines in terms of what was needed did not justify the additional costs of the Cryovac line. Cryovac's competitors generally used the argument that meat packers should package to sell, not to keep, and that the most effective way to maximize profits was to package as cheaply as possible while maintaining minimum package requirements. Cryovac salesmen also ran into other objections, as follows:

1. The labor costs of operating the Cryovac process was generally 10–15 per cent higher than others because somewhat more skilled

workers were needed. The manual and semiautomatic machines, especially, required a great deal of dexterity on the part of the operator.

2. The initial cost of the packaging line averaged 50 per cent more than competitive lines.

3. Cryovac offered no cash discount or free freight, as was the general practice in the field. All Cryovac prices were F.O.B. factory, and terms were net 30 days.

4. Cryovac-wrapped fresh red meats changed color because of the absence of air. When the package was opened, however, the original color returned.

In considering the problem, the Cryovac general manager listed the things that Cryovac salesmen had to offer:

1. A process that would stop shrinkage of the product completely, which would mean that a packer would incur virtually no weight loss during aging or handling.

2. A process that would retard color fade in smoked meat, making it more inviting to purchase, with resultant higher turnover.

3. A process that permitted the package to have a retail shelf life of three to seven weeks, depending on the product, which meant fewer returns and less dissatisfaction from consumers and retailers.

4. A bag that was stronger and clearer than any other plastic bag on the market.

5. The only process that permitted aging of product, when desirable, right in the package.

As an example of the savings possible through prevention of shrinkage loss, one Cryovac customer, a hotel and restaurant meat purveyor, reported the following savings from using the Cryovac process: A choice boneless sirloin strip steak might weigh 17 pounds and, at $1.50 per pound, be worth $25.50. The cost to package it with Cryovac, including the bag, clip, and labor, was 26.5 cents. Shrinkage during aging of such steaks usually ran 4 per cent or more. Such shrinkage in this case cost the purveyor over $1.00 in loss of weight, an amount far more than the cost of packaging. Meats aged outside of Cryovac developed mold, which had to be trimmed off, causing further loss of weight.

Figures from the various industries showed that average shrinkages were as follows: Cheese, 3 per cent; smoked meats, 4 per cent; red meats, 6 per cent; and poultry, 3 per cent.

Meat wholesalers also gave a saving in the use of Cryovac in that the longer shelf life it gave meat permitted them to build up inventory during slack periods. This resulted in labor savings and also permitted the wholesalers to buy larger quantities when they had opportunities to get lower prices.

Cryovac's management was disturbed by the apparent resistance in the market to its prices. This was particularly noticeable among smoked meat packers, whose preservation requirements were not as critical as in some other lines. Cryovac's margins were such that it could cut prices to some degree, but it could not meet the prices of lower-quality bags. If it cut prices, however, it would lose margin on all sales. There was a possibility that an intensified sales and promotion program could offset a price cut.

What pricing action, if any, should the Cryovac management take?

McBride Printing Company

In the late 1950's and early 1960's competition in the printing industry increased steadily and profits of many firms declined accordingly. The McBride Printing Company was no exception. As they studied the problem, however, the McBride executives became convinced that small orders were a substantial part of the problem. In commenting on this the marketing vice-president, Kenneth Olds, said: "We have always gone out of our way to compete aggressively for any account—regardless of size—for fear of losing volume. We have an expensive set of machinery housed in an expensive plant. If we don't keep these resources fully utilized we lose money. It's really that simple."

McBride Printing was founded in 1936 and after several mergers in the late 1940's emerged as one of the largest commercial printing houses on the East Coast with plants in Philadelphia, New York, and Baltimore. Its equipment consisted of a variety of large scale letterpress and offset presses as well as binding and engraving capabilities. Total sales in 1966 were in excess of $28 million with an after tax loss of over $800,000. The company employed a total of 36 salesmen who not only operated in the markets where the company had plants, but also ranged the nearby areas to generate sufficient business to keep the plants busy. Salesmen were compensated on a salary plus commission basis, with commissions accounting for about 60 percent of the total. Salesmen were fully compensated for all expenses. In 1966 the company estimated that its plants operated at 94.7 percent of capacity. "We can't very well get more production out of our plants," said Ken Olds, "but we can strive for a more profitable mix of orders."

The company sold a variety of products including package inserts, company phone directories, retail mail order catalogs, wholesaler catalogs, annual reports, airline and railroad timetables, school catalogs, newsprint flyers, forms, instruction manuals, small circulation business magazines, programs, and workbooks. Some were sold on a contract basis (e.g., where the account required repetitive and scheduled printing such as would be the case with magazines). A majority of the company's sales was "bid" business. Such accounts required at least two calls. On the first call the salesman would obtain the job specifications. These would be turned over to the estimating department which, on the basis of standard costs obtained from the comptroller's office would cost out the job and add a profit margin to obtain the "full" price. The salesman and the sales manager then consulted and on the basis of the competitive situation in that particular account, the prevailing price in the market, and the return on investment expected by management, a final or "bid" price was set. Actually this latter price was meant to be the lower limit; i.e., the point below which the salesman was not to quote. The salesman was supposed to try and obtain as high a price as possible. In actuality the bid price typically ended up as the final and accepted price. In some cases the sales-man was authorized to bargain with the customer if he met considerable resistance and to go no lower than bid price less 10 percent. "We fre-quently do this with business we really want and where we know we haven't time for a second round of discussions between the sales manager and the salesman," said Ken Olds.

Once a job was secured the production specifications were prepared by the customer service department. This group of specialists ordered the necessary paper stock, indicated the quality standards, specified who would approve the work at each critical stage in its production, the delivery schedule, and the quantities required. A customer service man was assigned to the order and he was responsible for seeing to it that the production department performed in accordance with the job specifica-tions. This individual was often referred to as "the customer's representa-tive" in the McBride organization.

In 1964 a new comptroller was hired and in 1966 the entire accounting procedure was computerized. One of the cost breaks requested by the marketing department was that having to do with size of order. Initially, the cost data were run off for accounts of $10,000 and under, $10,001–$50,000, and over $50,000. The cost report on these categories is shown as Exhibit 1. In explaining the cost report to the marketing group the comp-troller stated:

First, we analysed all 1966 jobs to get direct labor hours for each dollar vol-ume group. This information was used to distribute plant overhead expense. Inevitably some cost items are grouped together and distributed as a total. A good example is building expense which includes janitor and maintenance la-bor, supplies, fringe benefits, repair parts, taxes, pension, and even deprecia-tion. In this case I actually pulled out the pension and depreciation for a separate distribution.

Selling expenses were distributed first as commissions to the various groups then the office expense was allocated. General administrative such as customer service, purchasing, traffic, and estimating were distributed on the basis of estimates made by the department head. I, personally, distributed such expenses as switch board, mail girl, officers' salaries, etc. For the most part I was guided here by dollar sales and the number of orders.

Other expenses, such as the retirement plan, were distributed on the basis of direct labor charges and selling commissions. Waste sales were allocated largely on the basis of sales. Discounts and any special paper price reductions were distributed on the basis of material costs. Some income such as surplus machinery sold and insurance refunds are shown under "other expenses" as a credit. Bad debts and donations are deducted from this "other" category. Allocations here were pretty much based on direct labor. Depreciation was distributed on the same basis.

There were a total of 1,730 jobs in the $10,000 and under category. To obtain these jobs it was necessary to "cut" a total of $662,450; i.e., this was the difference between the "full" or initial price and the "final" price. Nearly 500 of the 1,730 jobs were from accounts with larger billing and another 260 repeated two or more times in this same dollar volume category. In the over $10,000 through $50,000 category there were 540 jobs and it was necessary to "cut" the initial prices by $782,000 to obtain these. In the over $50,000 volume category there were 105 jobs and the extent of the "cuts" was $981,000.

The marketing manager was naturally disturbed by the results of the cost breakdown and the company's inability to make money on both the "small" and "medium" size jobs. He did not see any way to reduce expenses and he knew that the severe price competition, especially from the small local printer, would continue indefinitely.

EXHIBIT 1

Case Report on Commercial Jobs with Gross Sales of 0–$10,000, $10,001–$50,000, and over $50,000, for the Fiscal Year 1966

	$0–10,000	*$10–50,000*	*Over $50,000*
Gross sales	$7,210,000	$10,420,000	$10,345,000
Less: Materials at cost	3,140,000	4,675,000	5,930,000
Net sales	$4,070,000	$ 5,745,000	$ 4,415,000
MANUFACTURING COST			
Direct labor	1,500,000	2,275,000	1,360,000
Overhead	1,870,000	2,685,000	1,730,000
Total	$3,370,000	$ 4,960,000	$ 3,090,000
Manufacturing profit	$ 700,000	$ 785,000	$ 1,325,000
OPERATING EXPENSES			
Division selling (commissions)	465,000	685,000	460,000
Corporate G. & A.	. . .	25,000	75,000
Division G. & A.	595,000	475,000	260,000
Total	$1,060,000	$ 1,185,000	$ 795,000
Operating profit (loss)	(360,000)	(400,000)	530,000
OTHER EXPENSE			
Retirement plan	130,000	150,000	100,000
OTHER INCOME			
Waste paper sales	50,000	50,000	50,000
Discounts earned on paper and supplies	60,000	90,000	100,000
Other income	40,000	60,000	70,000
Total	$ 150,000	$ 200,000	$ 220,000
Net operating profit (loss)	(340,000)	(350,000)	650,000
CONVERSION TO NET PROFIT			
Depreciation	165,000	325,000	230,000
Rent	10,000	10,000	10,000
Long term interest	15,000	20,000	15,000
Total	$ 190,000	$ 355,000	$ 255,000
Profit before tax	(530,000)	(705,000)	395,000

Container Corporation of America

Increased competition and its resultant pressures on salesmen and profits led the Container Corporation of America, the largest manufacturer of corrugated and solid fiber shipping containers in the United States, to reappraise its market objectives. Part of the pressure on profits, in the opinion of management, was the result of salesmen's taking any orders they could get without regard to plant operating efficiency or profit. It was proposed that this tendency be controlled by changing the pricing procedure to make all types of orders approximately equal in profitability, even though this might result in lost sales. Since prices were established from cost estimates for each job, a program was outlined to revise the estimating system so that it would more accurately reflect the marketing objectives of the company.

The Container Corporation was a completely integrated company, with sales exceeding $250 million. Its own forests and wastepaper processing plants supplied its fifteen paper mills with raw materials. The paper mills supplied paperboard to the company's twenty-five shipping container factories and twenty folding carton and fiber can factories. Each of the forty-five container and carton plants operated independently and was responsible for meeting competition in its area and for making a profit. Paperboard was sold by the mills to the plants at market prices.

The shipping container market extended to all manufacturers who needed to package their products. Potential order sizes ranged from orders of one hundred or less units from a small manufacturer of specialized products to orders for five or more carloads at a time from large canners and brewers. Variations in types of materials ordered ranged from display materials, which required complicated manufacturing procedures, to plain regular "slotted containers," the industry term for ordinary boxes, which were run routinely at the rate of 10,000 per hour.

Container's shipping container factories were primarily designed for large-volume operation. For example, the Chicago plant had two corrugators for producing corrugated paperboard with a capacity in excess of 2.5 million square feet of corrugated board per day, which represented thirteen to fifteen carloads of finished boxes per day. The company did not manufacture any stock items or maintain an inventory of finished material. Everything was made to order.

The manufacture of an ordinary box, one for canned foods or beer, normally involved three operations. First, the order went to the corrugator, where the corrugated sheets were made, cut to size, and scored[1] to make the flaps of the box. The sheets then went to a printer-slotter machine, where they were printed, scored to form the sides, and slotted to separate the flaps of the boxes. In the final operation, the ends of the sheets were folded and joined either by taping, stitching (stapling), or gluing to form the finished box. The finished boxes were tied in bundles or palletized and moved almost immediately into trucks or freight cars for shipment. Orders were timed to be finished at the scheduled time for shipment, since the volume of materials produced each day made storage impractical.

To get maximum production out of a box plant such as Container's Chicago plant, it was necessary to have a major proportion of large orders. This reduced the down time of machines for changing "setups" for each new order. But the large-volume business was generally low-profit business because of competition. Therefore, to maximize profits, it was necessary to have a mixture of large-volume orders and small or more specialized but more profitable orders.

Management believed that the cost-estimating methods led to prices that did not indicate the real profitability of an order. The estimating methods were thought to overstate profits on small-volume business and understate profits on large-volume business. This had led to a situation in which the plants were getting too many small orders to operate efficiently, because these orders looked more profitable than they were. Furthermore, some large-volume business was being lost because it did not look profitable when actually it was. A study of sales records revealed less than 10 per cent of the company's customers accounted for 90 per cent of the volume.

Further thought on this problem led management to the conclusion that a box factory was not primarily selling paper, but was selling the skills and process of converting paper into boxes. It was on these conversion costs that profits should be based. Under the existing system, sales and administrative expenses and profits were estimated as percentages of full cost, including materials. Also, under the existing estimating system,

---

[1] "Score" is the industry term for creases put in the corrugated board so that it will fold at the proper points.

costs of certain groups of similar operations were averaged. It was thought that a new method should be found that would be based on the specific cost of each operation. This would make it possible to determine much more accurately the profitability of an individual order.

Exhibit 1 shows the prices arrived at from costs estimated by the existing average cost method and by the proposed specific cost system, with overhead and profits based on conversion costs. Four examples are shown. The first illustrates the case of an ordinary box, for which material costs were large in proportion to factory conversion costs, and the fourth example illustrates the case of a more complicated item, for which factory costs greatly exceeded material costs. The second and third examples are in between. Factory conversion costs consisted of two parts, the setup cost, or cost of preparing the machines for a particular operation, and the base cost, which was the cost of the machine time and labor used to run 1,000 units. All material and factory costs were for 1,000 units.

The profit percentage, 10.9 per cent of total conversion cost, including materials for the average cost method and 24 per cent of total conversion costs for the specific cost method, was calculated to bring a return of 20 per cent on invested capital after taxes. Factory costs that were included in factory conversion costs were allocated to units on the basis of an assumed minimum volume. The sales and administration cost percentage and the profit percentage were also based on this assumed minimum volume. In the case of the Chicago plant the assumed minimum volume was 63 million square feet of corrugated board per month.

Base and setup costs were not ordinarily quoted to customers. Prices were quoted for a specific quantity or quantities and were always quoted on a per thousand basis. These prices were arrived at by dividing the setup cost by the quantity in thousands and adding the base cost. For example, given a setup cost of $10 and a base cost of $100, the price quoted for 1,000 units would be $110 per thousand; for 500 units, $120 per thousand; and for 5,000 units, $102 per thousand.

Exhibit 2 shows the prices that would be quoted for orders of different quantities when the prices were determined by both the old and the new methods. Prices are shown for the same four hypothetical products shown in Examples 1, 2, 3, and 4 of Exhibit 1. The specific cost method resulted in generally higher prices, especially for small quantities. Where factory conversion costs were less than material costs, as in Examples 1 and 2, however, the specific cost method of computing prices resulted in lower prices than the average cost method. For products in which the conversion costs exceeded material costs, prices were consistently higher under the specific cost method than under the average cost method. Since most of the company's business, particularly the large-volume business, resulted from items similar to Examples 1 and 2, the specific cost system would improve Container's competitive position.

The responsibility for establishing the actual prices quoted to cus-

EXHIBIT 1

Two Methods of Cost Estimating for Four Hypothetical Jobs

	Example 1		2		3		4	
	Setup	Base	Setup	Base	Setup	Base	Setup	Base
Average Cost Method with Profit Calculated on Full Cost								
Material................		$ 70		$ 60		$ 40		$ 30
Factory conversion costs......	$10	20	$10	30	$10	50	$10	60
Total factory conversion costs, including materials......	$10	$ 90	$10	$ 90	$10	$ 90	$10	$ 90
Sales and administration costs, 10 per cent of total factory conversion costs...	1	9	1	9	1	9	1	9
Total conversion-cost, including materials......	$11	$ 99	$11	$ 99	$11	$ 99	$11	$ 99
Profit, 10.9 per cent of full cost...	1.20	10.80	1.20	10.80	1.20	10.80	1.20	10.80
Price............	$12.20	$109.80	$12.20	$109.80	$12.20	$109.80	$12.20	$109.80
Specific Cost Method with Profit Calculated on Total Conversion Costs								
Factory conversion costs......	$10	$ 20	$10	$ 30	$10	$ 50	$10	$ 60
Sales and administration costs, 25 per cent of factory conversion costs......	2.50	5	2.50	7.50	2.50	12.50	2.50	14
Total conversion costs......	$12.50	$ 25	$12.50	$ 37.50	$12.50	$ 62.50	$12.50	$ 74
Profit, 24 per cent of total conversion costs......	3	6	3	9	3	15	3	18
Materials............		70		60		40		30
Price............	$15.50	$101.00	$15.50	$106.50	$15.50	$117.50	$15.50	$122.00

EXHIBIT 2

Prices Calculated from Exhibit 1

		Price per Thousand	
Quantity	Example	Average Cost	Specific Cost
100	1	$231.80	$256.00
	2	"	261.50
	3	"	272.50
	4	"	277.50
500	1	134.20	132.00
	2	"	137.50
	3	"	148.50
	4	"	153.00
1,000	1	122.00	116.50
	2	"	122.00
	3	"	133.00
	4	"	137.50
10,000	1	111.02	102.55
	2	"	108.05
	3	"	119.05
	4	"	123.05

tomers rested with the sales managers at a step beyond the cost-estimating process described above. The estimated price was the price needed to give the standard profit. The price actually quoted to a customer might vary up or down from the level, depending on information sales manager had on market conditions and competition for the specific account involved. There were no "standard prices" in the industry. It was not unusual for two companies buying boxes identical in size and material from the same box manufacturer to pay different prices. Some box companies tried using a "price list" that would permit the customer to calculate what the price would be on a given box by using the number of square feet of corrugated board in the box, multiplying this by a price per square foot, and then adding special charges for printing or other special features. In all cases, these "price lists" had been short-lived.

Examples of two typical pricing situations are shown in Exhibit 3. In both situations the estimating department figured estimated prices based on the minimum return desired by management. The sales manager established the market prices, i.e., competitive prices, on the basis of his knowledge of the market and information from salesmen as to competitors and the prices they usually quoted these accounts. In the first situation the market price was lower than the estimated prices. It offered no profit under the average cost method of estimating costs, but it showed a profit of 12.4 per cent on conversion costs if the specific cost estimating method was used. In the second situation, which represents a small order that required more conversion, the market price was above the average

EXHIBIT 3

Two Typical Pricing Situations

	Average Cost Method	Specific Cost Method
Price per Thousand for 20,000 Ordinary Boxes Similar to Example 1, Exhibit 1		
Estimated price.........................	$110.41	$101.78
Full cost..............................	99.55	95.63
Market price..........................	99.55	99.55
Profit................................	...	3.92
Per cent profit		
On total conversion cost..............	N.A.	12.4%
On full cost........................	0	3.9%
Price per Thousand for 500 Complicated Boxes Similar to Example 4, Exhibit 1		
Estimated price.........................	$134.20	$153.00
Full cost..............................	121.00	129.00
Market price..........................	146.20	146.20
Profit................................	25.20	17.20
Per cent profit		
On total conversion cost..............	N.A.	17.4%
On full cost........................	20.8%	13.3%

cost price and below the specific cost price, but showed a profit in both cases. The average cost method showed more profit on market price than did the specific cost method.

With this information at hand, the sales manager could decide how badly he wanted these particular orders. Container's policy was to develop long-standing accounts that were profitable. Once a profitable price level was established in these accounts, it was generally maintained to the best of the company's ability. Constant attention was necessary, however, because of possible price cutting by competitors.

Constant attrition of accounts because of product changes, moves, and losses to competitors required the regular addition of new accounts if the company was to maintain its position. Container's main emphasis in acquiring a new account was on quality and design rather than on price. Price competition was avoided whenever possible, but it was sometimes necessary, particularly in large accounts using relatively standard types of boxes. Generally, when a company designed a new package for an account, it got the first order before the other box companies quoted on the item. Competitors could be expected to bid on later orders.

Salesmen were given some latitude for bargaining with an account. If the price the sales manager quoted was high, the salesmen could, if the customer was willing to bargain, meet the competitive price to get the order. Experienced salesmen were even given the authority to go below competitors' prices for some accounts.

Management did not expect that a change to the specific cost method of estimating prices would result in radical price changes and immediate improvement in profits. The estimating system approximated prices, actual prices were established by the sales manager in light of market conditions. Since the latter would not change, no great changes could be made in Container's prices. Management believed, however, that the new pricing system would cause sales managers to re-evaluate the importance of various accounts and hence to make some price adjustments.

1. Would the new pricing system lead to higher profits for Container Corporation?
2. What other actions, if any, could have been taken in lieu of or in addition to the new pricing system to accomplish the same objectives?

SECTION **V**

CHANNELS OF
DISTRIBUTION

Oak Creek Furniture Company

Each December was budget time at the Oak Creek Furniture Company and Sales Manager, Jack Renfro, like other division heads, turned his full attention to this task. Renfro considered for some time, but with little satisfaction, the approaches he might take in preparing what he hoped would be an ideal sales budget. Last year's budget, in his opinion, was unsatisfactory because it had lacked the flexibility necessary to combat an unfavorable sales trend which caused Oak Creek's net profit to drop to its lowest level since 1960. When it became obvious in the previous May that Oak Creek sales would fall short of the forecasted $3,300,-000 by $300,000, Renfro could take little action because the money set aside for advertising and sales promotion was already either spent or committed and there was no other ready source of funds. Unfortunately a big portion of the sales budget was committed to such fixed expenses as salaries, showroom rental, freight, catalog printing costs, and so forth. The largest of costs was the amount earmarked each year for agents' commissions—5.9 percent of sales and approximately 50 percent of the entire sales budget.

As Renfro faced the problem, he knew that to meet the company's objective of a 20 percent sales increase next year, he would have to base his budget on a $3,600,000 volume. This meant that assuming the same percentage of expenses as in the current year, about $215,000 of an expected $540,000 sales budget had to be earmarked for agents' commissions. The remainder, which represented only a slight increase over the funds available in the current year, had to support the projected increase in sales. (The distribution of the sales division's expenses for the past three years are presented in Exhibit 1.)

Renfro thought that one answer to the budget problem might be to have the agents agree to take a smaller commission on sales up to 80 percent of their budgeted volume. Then, if it became obvious that the forecast would not be reached, Renfro would have some reserve funds for stepped-up advertising and promotion. If forecasted sales were achieved without added stimulus, the reserve would then be distributed to the agents to bring their commissions up to 7 percent.

Over the long run, Renfro felt that it could not be possible for sales commissions to remain as large a percentage of total sales and the sales budget. In fact, commissions to some agents were already becoming so large that Renfro questioned the reasonableness of the company's existing distribution system. Obviously, when Oak Creek Furniture Company was in its infancy and its product line unknown, the agents were the key to its success. In the meantime, however, the Oak Creek name had become well enough known that Renfro believed continued sales gains were no longer entirely related to the agents' efforts.

The recurring temptation was to replace sales agents with company salesmen on a salary plus commission basis. Sales in some areas, however, had not yet reached a volume sufficient to sustain the salary and travel expenses of a company man. To make the change in areas with higher volume would be to lose the best of the sales agents and would certainly be demoralizing to sales agents in those areas where they are retained. Assuming a change to direct salesmen Renfro also anticipated disproportionate initial costs and the possibility of a serious public relations problem with Oak Creek Furniture's customers who, in many cases, had a strong personal loyalty to the sales agent with whom they had been working for so many years.

THE COMPANY AND THE INDUSTRY

The Oak Creek Furniture Company was founded in 1952 in Oak Creek, Wisconsin, by Aaron Forester. Until that time, Forester had been the chief furniture designer for the Logan Furniture Company of North Carolina. He broke from this firm over a disagreement with the president concerning the style trend that the Logan Company should follow. Forester advocated a shift to the clean straight lines characterizing the modern furniture that had become so popular since World War II, but the president of the Logan Company insisted on staying with traditional carved and curved surfaces.

Early in 1952, Forester found financial backing to start his own company, and the end of the year witnessed the first piece of furniture emerge from the Oak Creek plant. Forester had earlier designed a full line of home furniture of contemporary style. The line included seating units for both living and dining rooms, dining room tables and cabinets, and bedroom furniture. Forester chose to manufacture a high quality line which maximized the use of carefully selected hard woods. Consequently, the price of Oak Creek furniture was in the more expensive range for manufactured furniture. Only antiques and other unique pieces sold for more.

A number of people apparently agreed with Forester's designing, because Oak Creek furniture was well received from the start and sales grew rapidly. The price of the furniture dictated that it reach the consumer through fine furniture stores and interior decorators. Several of the country's better department stores eventually accepted the line, but since the individual pieces were manufactured to order, Oak Creek furniture was not the rapid turnover type of merchandise desired by the average department store.

The company competed in an industry that had been long established as an important segment of the U.S. economy. Of the twenty major industrial groups used in the Census of Manufacturers, the furniture industry ranked 16th in the number of employees and 17th in value added by manufacture. Manufacturers' shipments of wood (and upholstered) furniture were estimated to be over $2.5 billion.

The furniture industry was highly competitive, nonintegrated and characterized by a number of relatively small, closely held companies. No one, or even few companies, dominated the industry. There were about 700 metal furniture plants, 1,700 upholstered furniture plants, and 2,500 wood furniture plants. Few employed as many as 500 workers. In fact, 50% of the establishments employed less than 21 and the industry average was about 50. Only 1,200 plants in the industry topped $400,000 a year in sales and these plants accounted for better than 80 percent of industry sales.

Two-thirds of all furniture plants were located in the Middle Atlantic Southeast and Great Lakes States. North Carolina, with 12 percent of the plants, led all the states. The trend in industry location, however, was to the Middle West following the population shift. An excellent supply of hardwood in Michigan and other midwestern states further encouraged this move.

Most furniture companies produced a wide range of style patterns and suites in particular lines. Consumer tastes varied widely and retailers felt the need to keep a broad selection on the floor in order to meet these diverse needs. Moreover, retailers preferred new styles to feature in their sales talks and in their advertising programs. Consequently, most furniture manufacturers used designers, some with original and creative talent and others who adapted from successful items. This preoccupation with design was matched by the larger furniture department stores, most of which employed full time decorators.

Distribution in the furniture industry centered around a number of furniture markets located throughout the United States. At these markets, manufacturers periodically displayed their products to the trade. Retailers representing 29,000 furniture outlets from all parts of the country visited the markets to select stock to see what was being offered for the coming year. Manufacturers maintaining booths went all out to induce visiting retailers to make purchase commitments. Needless to say, salesmen had to follow-up such voluntary commitments, but the difficult part of selling the line—actually showing the pieces—had already been accomplished. Most retail buyers would not consider taking on a line unless they had seen it at one of the markets. These markets, which were closed to the public, lasted from one to two weeks and were held twice a year. In order of importance, the furniture markets were located in Chicago, Highpoint, N.C., Los Angeles, New York, San Francisco, Grand Rapids, Dallas, Jamestown (N.Y.), and Boston.

Chicago set the pace of industry activity. The other cities waited until Chicago established its semiannual market dates—usually in January and June—and then scheduled their dates accordingly. Between 500 and 1,000 manufacturers participated in the Chicago market.

Widespread distribution of its products was the typical pattern for the furniture manufacturer. Because each manufacturer concentrated on particular groups of furniture he needed a wide market to secure volume. The demand for furniture, moreover, was sensitive to business conditions and a regional economic down-turn could easily destroy a market. No manufacturer, nonetheless, had ever achieved intensive national distribution. The largest firms were able to place their products in about one-third of the furniture outlets.

Manufacturers typically used sales representatives who carried the products of noncompeting manufacturers and who were paid a commission of 5 to 10 percent of the sales that they made. Few manufacturers had been able to establish sales forces to handle their products exclusively.

Attempts by manufacturers to create brand preference were relatively unheard of until 1949. Since then, the number of firms spending over $25,000 a year for advertising had increased substantially. With many firms in the industry grossing less than $500,000, however, few had much of a chance to launch costly advertising programs.

Retailers, in many cases, tended to discourage the development of manufacturers' brands. Some even went so far as to conceal the identity of a manufacturer on floor samples. Retailers taking this position did so for several reasons. They believed that no manufacturer advertised enough to make his brand mean more to a community than the name of a reputable local store. Furthermore, retailers were concerned that advertised names would be disparaged by unscrupulous salesmen in other stores. The average consumer's inability to ascertain the quality of furniture by visual inspection made him particularly vulnerable to such tactics. Finally, the retailers did not want to promote manufacturers' brands because they feared they would become the "showrooms" for many of the small decorators and dealers not maintaining such a facility. Decorators could easily place an order for a customer once they knew who manufactured the pieces the customer wanted.

To stock a furniture store, retailers found it necessary to buy from several different manufacturers in order to obtain the styles, types and quality grades required. While a typical store might buy from six to eight different manufacturers, they did try to limit the number as much as possible in order to minimize inward freight costs.

Most of the dealings between furniture stores and manufacturers were carried on by sales representatives and store buyers. The number of buyers in a store depended largely on the store size. A large store would probably have a buyer in each department, i.e., lamps, upholstered furniture, modern furniture, etc. A buyer had complete responsibility for the purchase and sale of the items in his department. He supervised the sales force and was responsible for its training and performance.

Buyers selected new lines of merchandise and dropped other lines generally with the approval of the store merchandise manager. When a buyer selected a new line, he asked the following questions:

Is it an accepted name and style?
Will the quality of the line fit in with the other items in the store?
Will it add prestige to the store and the department?
Does the price fit into the pattern in the store?
Does the price represent the true value of the item?
Is there an adequate markup?
Is similar merchandise sold in the area?
Is the price protected?
Is there adequate selectivity in the fabrics, finishes, frames, etc.?
Can I get rapid delivery?
Is the line advertised?

Of equal importance were another set of questions regarding the agent selling the furniture:

Do I already know the agent? (Possibly he is already selling me a line.)
Does he have a good personal reputation?
Is he experienced in selling this type of merchandise?
Will he visit me often enough to give me the selling support required?
Will he immediately take care of my complaints about damaged pieces and delivery errors?
Will he spend time with the floor salesmen to support the training that I give them?

OAK CREEK DISTRIBUTION POLICY

Oak Creek, in 1965, employed nine selling agents and one company salesman. Eight of the agents were independent and carried other, non-competing lines. The ninth sold Oak Creek furniture exclusively. The company salesman, holding the title of Eastern Sales Manager, was located in New York City. There he sold to furniture stores and contract dealers,[1] and also directed the operation of Oak Creek's New York showroom. The showroom was one of five that Oak Creek maintained in major U.S. cities. (These showrooms were used to exhibit the Oak Creek line to visiting retailers. The remainder of the year, the showrooms were open usually one day a week for conducting business with local decorators, architects, non-stocking dealers, and in some cases, retailers.)

Future plans called for the ten Oak Creek territories to be organized under three field sales managers. In 1965 the eastern sales manager who sold in territory #2 supervised the agents in territories 1, 3 and 4. Jack Renfro supervised the remaining agents. Renfro's responsibilities as sales manager included selecting and supervising agents, managing the company's advertising and promotional activities, preparing the sales budget, and providing company representation at the various furniture markets.

SALES AGENTS

Renfro believed that he had assembled a highly competent group of agents. Most had joined Oak Creek during the company's first two or three years and worked hard to establish the line. Renfro exercised great care whenever it was necessary to select a new agent. He did not use personality or sales ability tests, but thoroughly screened each applicant by interview and carefully investigated their backgrounds. Renfro relied much upon recommendations from other manufacturers who had used or were using the agent. He looked particularly at the following elements when considering prospective agents:

1. Sales experience with furniture.
2. Amount of uncommitted sales time which could be given to the Oak Creek line.
3. Types of other merchandise sold by the agent.
4. Types of outlets covered by the agent.
5. Appearance and carriage of the applicant. Does he have the "Oak Creek look?"[2]

Probably the most important determinant for selecting a new sales agent was the candidate's present territory. The most effective agents sold Oak Creek furniture through channels which they had already set up; thus it was important that these channels did not overlap those of other sales agents.

Oak Creek agents generally represented several manufacturers of

---

[1] Contract dealers were individuals who sold only to commercial accounts.

[2] Renfro explained that the agent's appearance was extremely important since the company tried to maintain the quality image in its salesmen that it maintained in its furniture.

furniture or home furnishings. A typical mix might include the Oak Creek line and lines of traditional furniture, lamps, garden furniture and accessories. In larger stores, the agent often sold each line to a different buyer, although this was not considered the optimum use of the agent's time.

Because Oak Creek furniture was not intensively distributed there were only a few franchise dealers in a given area. The agents called about every two weeks on stores which sold large volumes of Oak Creek furniture, but only two or three times a year on remote stores that did not show particularly active sales.

On a typical visit to a furniture store, the agent first made an appointment to see the buyer. During the interview, the agent presented new pieces and fabrics which had been added to the Oak Creek line. He talked over the items which were moving most easily in the area and told of new promotions sponsored by the company. The buyer then ordered the items that he believed he would need in the interval between the agent's visits. Sometimes the agent had to suggest tactfully to the buyer that the order was either too large or too small. Most buyers respected the agent's opinion on such suggestions.

After visiting the buyer, the agent usually inspected the floor samples. He looked for soiled or damaged pieces which would reflect poorly on the quality of the line. (The majority of the stores selling Oak Creek furniture were on a basic stock plan which meant they displayed representative items of the line. The amount of basic stock was generally decided upon by the agent and the buyer in terms of the store's size and volume.) If the agent found that any of the basic stock had been sold from the floor, he noted this along with data on soiled pieces. While on the floor, the agent talked with the furniture salesmen explaining many of the same details about the line that he had with the buyer earlier. One of the agent's prime objectives was to develop the floor salesmen's enthusiasm for the Oak Creek line.

After inspecting floor samples and talking to the floor salesmen, the agent returned to the buyer and wrote up the order. He suggested that soiled pieces be marked down and sold, and he made arrangements to have damaged pieces repaired at one of the company's warehouses.

AGENT SUPERVISION

Renfro exercised little direct selling supervision over the eight independent agents. He did not attempt to tell the agents to whom they could sell, except that it was understood that the agents would not sell to discount houses or other cut-rate merchandisers. The agents recommended the discount to be allowed to various retail dealers. The established discount schedule was:

50 percent of retail—to furniture and department stores stocking and displaying Oak Creek furniture.

40 percent of retail—to furniture and department stores not stocking and displaying Oak Creek furniture, and to interior decorators having a legitimate office and showroom.

33 percent of retail—to interior decorators not having an office or showroom.

Agents were watched carefully to see that they were selling up to their area's potential. If they were considerably low, Renfro could threaten to withdraw the agency. Renfro determined area potential, which he called a "style quota," through a city-by-city analysis of the national market. An index published by *Sales Management* gave the relative buyer power of each metropolitan area. This index was based upon population, retail sales and family income. The index gave Renfro a tool with which to compare the efforts of each agent against the others and against the country as a whole. Sales data were collected weekly and graphs were drawn monthly for each agent comparing territorial sales and total sales for the country.

In the fall of 1965, Renfro sent a questionnaire to each agent requesting information about the other lines carried and the percent of the agents' income each represented. Some agents responded with complete details while others provided only fragmentary information. Because of the great quantity of data, Renfro grouped the style quotas and corresponding sales figures by state rather than by city. A sampling of the reports is included in Appendix A.

SELLING AIDS

Renfro attempted to provide his agents as much help in making a sale as possible. He regularly placed Oak Creek ads in *Holiday*, *Town & Country*, and *Bride*. (Exhibit 2 outlines the 1965 advertising schedule.) Renfro also supplied the agents with various descriptive materials about new items or lines of furniture, gave the agents samples of new fabrics, and offered special merchandise for sales and promotions. Agents received monthly a letter from Renfro informing them of how they were doing with respect to the total sales picture and how the merchandise was moving in the various territories. Moreover, each sales agent was given a "Manual of Standard Procedures" which contained descriptive material about all the Oak Creek products and prices as well as reprints of current magazine ads and samples of the advertising mats which were available to the retailers.

THE 1966 BUDGET

If he could find a way to cut back the dollars going out as agents' commissions, Renfro planned to redistribute the budget to place emphasis on the following:

1. A total reduction in the overall sales budget to assist in delaying possible price increases owing to: (*a*) Increased costs of design and product research; (*b*) Increased costs of labor and materials.
2. Funds to support hiring two more field sales managers.
3. A larger investment in advertising space and production, dealer aids and printing (catalogs, consumer brochures, etc.).

EXHIBIT 1

Sales Division Expenses
(1963–1965)

	1965*	1964	1963
TOTAL SALES	3,300,000	2,858,710	2,308,500
Commissions	185,900†	200,400	161,500
Salaries	45,400	29,800	29,500
(Agency fee)	2,900‡	7,600	4,200
Travel	6,400	4,500	13,800§
Entertainment	2,200	1,200	9,340§
Sales promotion	6,850	5,900	9,250§
Advertising space	38,400	19,650	27,900
Advertising production	7,740	2,460	3,500
Photography	5,800	4,900	3,000
Dealer aids	7,600	5,750	4,560
Printing	24,300	10,800	14,850
Sample expense	13,600	6,150	9,500
Freight	3,500	4,090	. . .
Postage	6,800	6,100	. . .
Repairs & maintenance	1,450	715	1,060
Showroom rent	28,500‖	8,700	1,020
Miscellaneous	3,870	3,700	3,600
	391,210	322,415	296,580

* 1965 figures are as budgeted.

† During 1964, a 22 percent commission was paid to the separately owned New York showroom. The drop in commission in 1965 reflects the beginning of a company owned showroom there, but overall expenses were increased to cover the cost of the company's showroom in salaries, showroom rent, etc.

‡ Agency fee was substantially reduced when the company hired its own full time Advertising Public Relations Manager.

§ In 1963 and before the travel and entertainment expenses of all executives in the company as well as all company gifts and gratuities normally charged to sales promotion were charged against the sales budget.

‖ 1965 was the first full calendar year reflecting cost of rent of showrooms in New York and San Francisco.

EXHIBIT 2

Advertising Schedule, 1965

Book	Space	Color	1	2	3	4	5	6	7	8	9	10	11	12	Total
									Months						
Holiday	1/4	2				1	1				1	1	1		5
Town & Country	1/4	2	1	1	1	1	1				1	3	1		10
Bride	1/4	2	1	1		1									3
			2⁄3	2⁄4	1⁄2	3⁄4	2⁄4				2⁄5	4⁄6	2⁄4		18
Furniture Forum		B/W		1			1				1		1		4
Int. Dec. Hand-book	1	2									1	1			2
Interiors	1	B/W	1		1	1	1			1	1				6
Interior Design	1	B/W		1				1				1	1		4
			1⁄3	2⁄4	1⁄2	1⁄4	2⁄4	1⁄1		1⁄1	3⁄5	2⁄6	2⁄4		16⁄34

APPENDIX A

Oak Creek Furniture

| AGENT: | Dick Newton | | TERRITORY: | 1 |
| HOME: | Massachusetts | | JOINED OAK CREEK: | 1956 |

OTHER LINES:

NATURE OF LINE	APPROX. % OF INCOME
Rattan furniture	NA
Fabrics	NA
Accessories	NA

YEARLY SALES VOLUME:	1965	1964	1963
	(11 mo. total)		
	$228,300	$228,400	$158,000

QUOTA PERFORMANCE: STYLE QUOTA   ACTUAL SALES
(1st 6 mos.)

	STYLE QUOTA	ACTUAL SALES	
Connecticut............................	$ 25,193	$ 12,965	
Maine.................................	3,619	548	
Massachusetts..........................	44,957	49,379	
New Hampshire........................	2,227	100	
NY (excluding NY City).................	49,343	48,673	
Rhode Island..........................	6,263	6,962	
Vermont..............................	5,217	1,450	% of U.S.

TERRITORY COMPARISON (1965 Data)	% of Co. Sales	% of U.S. Population	% of U.S. Metropolitan Population
	8.0	10.3	12.3

| AGENT: | Allan Connell | | TERRITORY: | 2 |
| HOME: | New York | | JOINED OAK CREEK: | 1957 |

OTHER LINES: None—
Employed by company as Eastern sales manager and also responsible for the New York City territory and showroom. Paid a $16,000 salary in 1965.

YEARLY SALES VOLUME:	1965	1964	1963
	(11 mo. total)		
	$242,600[1]	$271,200	$169,500

QUOTA PERFORMANCE: STYLE QUOTA   ACTUAL SALES
(1st 6 mos.)

	STYLE QUOTA	ACTUAL SALES
New York City........................	$214,972	$126,067

TERRITORY COMPARISON:	% of Co. Sales	% of U.S. Population	% of U.S. Cosmopolitan Population
	9.5	4.9	18.2

[1] Include sales through N.Y. showroom which became company owned and operated in 1965. Showroom sales for first 11 months of 1965 were $151,800. Connell's sales outside the showroom for the same period were $90,800.

AGENT:	Paul Kearns		TERRITORY:	1
HOME:	New Jersey		JOINED OAK CREEK:	1952
OTHER LINES:	Would not list			

YEARLY SALES VOLUME:	1965	1964	1963
	(11 mo. total)		
	$285,100	$323,900	$258,700

QUOTA PERFORMANCE: STYLE QUOTA   ACTUAL SALES
(1st 6 mos.)

	STYLE QUOTA	ACTUAL SALES
Delaware..............................	$ 3,201	$ 11,236
District of Columbia....................	33,900	25,155
Maryland..............................	21,991	27,643
New Jersey............................	62,912	32,872
Pennsylvania..........................	84,208	52,071

% of Co. Sales	% of U.S. Population	% of U.S. Cosmopolitan Population
11.3	12.6	18.1

AGENT:	Carl Gilman		TERRITORY:	4
HOME:	Florida		JOINED OAK CREEK:	1955
OTHER LINES:				

NATURE OF LINE	APPROX. % OF INCOME
Traditional	NA
Woven Woods	NA
Lamps	NA
Accessories	NA

YEARLY SALES VOLUME:	1965	1964	1963
	(11 mo. total)		
	$116,000	$110,000	$116,600

QUOTA PERFORMANCE: STYLE QUOTA   ACTUAL SALES
(1st 6 mos.)

	STYLE QUOTA	ACTUAL SALES
Alabama...............................	$ 8,073	$ 2,424
Florida................................	30,064	21,246
Georgia...............................	13,222	8,207
Mississippi............................	3,480	1,182
N. Carolina...........................	12,109	4,431
S. Carolina...........................	5,567	475
Tennessee.............................	11,692	6,560
Virginia..............................	12,031	2,540
W. Virginia...........................	7,658	2,303

TERRITORY COMPARISON:	% of Co. Sales	% of U.S. Population	% of U.S. Cosmopolitan Population
	3.9	17.2	6.1

AGENT: Dean Metcalf   TERRITORY: 9
HOME: Southern California   JOINED OAK CREEK: 1958
OTHER LINES:

NATURE OF LINE	*APPROX. % OF INCOME*
Garden Furniture	15%
Custom Designs	5%
Accessories	5%

YEARLY SALES VOLUME:	1965	1964	1963
	(11 mo. total)		
	$371,100	$294,700	$245,600

QUOTA PERFORMANCE: *STYLE QUOTA   ACTUAL SALES*
(1st 6 mos. 1959)

	STYLE QUOTA	ACTUAL SALES
Southern California......................	$120,084	$173,017

TERRITORY COMPARISON:	% of Co. Sales	% of U.S. Population	% of U.S. Cosmopolitan Population
	10.3	4.1	3.7

AGENT: Harry Preston   TERRITORY: 10
HOME: California   JOINED OAK CREEK: 1954
OTHER LINES: Exclusive Oak Creek
                 Preston received a 5% commission on all sales. Oak Creek
                 provided Preston a completely financed showroom in lieu of
                 the normal 7% commission.

YEARLY SALES VOLUME:	1965	1964	1963
	(11 mo. total)		
	$360,600	$375,500	$350,400

QUOTA PERFORMANCE: *STYLE QUOTA   ACTUAL SALES*
(1st 6 mo.)

	STYLE QUOTA	ACTUAL SALES
California (Northern).....................	$ 60,399	$ 80,601
Oregon...............................	12,388	25,968
Washington...........................	21,574	65,968
Nevada...............................	1,854	299
Idaho................................	2,784	2,285
Montana..............................	3,201	2,834
Alaska...............................	...	5,220

TERRITORY COMPARISON	% of Co. Sales	% of U.S. Population	% of U.S. Cosmopolitan Population
	13.1	7.8	13.5

Barton Company

The Barton Company, with headquarters in New York City, imported a line of European china and glassware for resale to major department stores and leading gift stores located in the larger cities of the United States. The line included such items as china vases, bowls, and ashtrays; Venetian and cut crystal glass animals, birds, candle holders, ashtrays, salt and pepper holders, butter dishes, candy dishes, and centerpiece bowls; and barware from France and Portugal. Retail prices of these items varied from less than a dollar to over $100 for a dozen cut crystal goblets. The average retail price per item, excluding drinkware was $8–$10. Company sales were $5,250,000 annually with a gross margin of 39.6 percent. The company was considering whether to sell to discount department stores.

The company had always sold exclusively to department stores and large gift stores through its own sales force. Only stores located in metropolitan areas were contacted. Until recently such stores, despite the fact that they were typically large stores, did not send buyers to Europe to procure the items. Barton salesmen had always stressed the advantages of buying from their company. These advantages were specialized buying skills, a wide assortment of goods warehoused in New York ready for immediate delivery, an ability to forecast the market a year in advance, and a willingness to take back merchandise which did not sell. They also pointed out that importing required a substantial amount of knowledge about tariffs, customs, foreign exchange, and handling adjustments. The company served as the exclusive representative in the United States for a number of small glass factories and, in one case, served as the exclusive representative for the glassware produced by one of the Iron Curtain countries. About 30 percent of the company's sales in the 1953–1956 period were of products for which it had exclusive representation.

An increasing number of the large department stores were sending buyers to Europe. At about the same time the sales of the company's line of cut crystal—a major part of the company's sales—started to decline. Even so the company's sales increased owing to the addition of new glassware items.

It was the belief of the company that many of the stores which had started the practice of sending a buyer abroad to buy glass and china items would later resume buying from Barton. This belief was based on not only the company's experience, but on the knowledge that many stores viewed their china and glass departments as a necessary evil. Such departments had a small stock turn—often under three times a year. Despite the high markups of about 50 percent, the breakage, markdowns, and gift wrappings prevented satisfactory profits.

The Barton Company labelled all of their products using Barton's name plus the country of origin. The latter was required by law. Barton did no advertising, but it did pay for certain cooperative advertising which was typically negotiated by one of its salesmen. Nor did the company grant any exclusives, although upon occasion a salesman in return for a large order of a single item would agree not to sell any other store located in the same city the identical item.

Recently the company had received an increasing number of inquiries from discount department stores about the purchase of certain items. Because of its close relations with its customers the Barton Company turned down such inquiries although it knew that such stores would have no difficulty in obtaining the desired items from a variety of other sources. The china and glass importing industry was highly competitive. Barton, one of the largest importers, faced strong competition from three other importers of approximately equal size and from many smaller importers.

By the mid-1960's discount department stores had grown substantially in numbers. Increasingly, they were known to be buying items similar to or even identical with those sold by Barton. Department store buyers constantly complained to company salesmen about the fact that discount department stores were selling these items at lower prices than those charged by the "regular" department and gift stores. An investigation by Barton revealed that the discounters were indeed stocking such items, but that the extent of the lines carried and the prices charged varied a great deal from discounter to discounter. Some of these stores appeared to be selling these items for about the same price as did the more traditional stores while others were apparently applying only a 25 percent markup. Some stores had a china and glass department while others would make a "buy" and after disposing of it would not restock the items again for several months. In only a very few cases did these stores advertise such items.

The company received an order from the buying headquarters of one of the largest discounter chains, with store units located in the East and as far west as Ohio, for the purchase of about $50,000 worth of merchandise at regular company prices. The company had such merchandise in stock and could replenish it without difficulty. This chain was thought to have a potential to the company of nearly $100,000 a year. The Barton Company president was reluctant to refuse such a large order although he recognized that to accept it would mean a significant change in company policy. He estimated that the discount segment of the market might be worth between $750,000 and $1 million annually to his company, assuming that the company was not forced to lower its price. He knew that his salesmen would argue strongly against taking the order.

Should the Barton Company accept the $50,000 order from the buying head-quarters of a large discount department store chain?

Skyline Petroleum Company

"Congratulations, Joe," said Phil Keller, a regional credit manager for the Skyline Petroleum Company, "your new assignment to the Watertown Sales District is a good promotion." Joe Smith was the district sales manager of Skyline's small River Bend Sales District, and had recently received word of his transfer to Watertown. "Just think," Phil continued, "old Dick Owen has finally reached retirement age. Forty-two years is a lot of service."

The Skyline Petroleum Company, a large and well-established oil distributor, operated in Texas, Oklahoma and Louisiana. The company's marketing division was divided into Wholesale and Retail Departments. Both the River Bend and Watertown Districts were part of the Wholesale Marketing Department.

Wholesale distribution involved all customers not buying through service stations of the Retail Marketing Department. Customers included farmers, contractors, truckers, and manufacturing and commercial establishments. The three-state marketing area was divided into regions which in turn were organized into sales districts. As shown in Figure 1, a sales district was a purely line organization; staff support was centralized at the regional headquarters.

District organizations varied depending on the business density and volume of the area served. Typically, however, districts consisted of some ten bulk plants or depots, a majority of which were operated on a commission basis. Facilities included storage tanks for gasoline and diesel products and a warehouse for lubricating oils, greases, and other packaged materials. Tank trucks distributed Skyline products from the local bulk plant to the customer, although certain customers with large requirements and adequate storage were served direct from the refinery or major distribution terminal. The company owned bulk plant facilities and leased them to Commission Agents.

A sales manager headed each district, but staffing below that level again depended on the size and nature of the area. Assistant sales managers were assigned to larger districts. An average-sized district employed two to three Wholesale Salesmen, a Fuel and Lubricant Engineer, and the necessary operating personnel to receive, store, and deliver the products. All operating personnel engaged in some way in direct contact with customers. Office personnel sold to walk-in customers, while truck

FIGURE 1

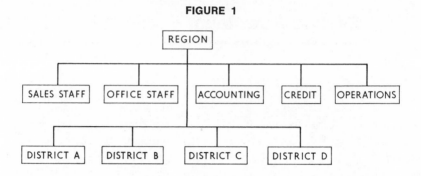

drivers delivered and sold products from tank trucks. Job titles and brief job descriptions of all district positions follow:

District Sales Manager—manages the activities of the sales district and administers established policies and procedures relating to sales, delivery, accounting, credit, operations and personnel to secure a representative portion of the available business at maximum realization and minimum operating cost.

Assistant District Sales Manager—assists the district sales manager in managing the activities of the sales district and administering established policies and procedures relating to sales, delivery, accounting, credit, plant-operations and personnel to secure a representative proportion of the available business and maximum realization at minimum operating cost.

Fuel & Lubricant—provides technical and specialized solicitation and service to accounts which require full engineering help, technical service and experienced assistance beyond the ability of general sales organization through one or a combination of the following activities: (1) solicitation of all product requirements and servicing of accounts which requires constant fuel and lubricant engineering effort beyond the ability of other sales positions; (2) furnishing regularly assigned support to other sales positions on accounts requiring a high degree of fuel and lubricant engineering effort; or (3) providing on-call technical specialized service to accounts requiring fuel and lubricant engineering effort at intermittant or infrequent intervals.

Wholesale Salesman—responsible for sale of the full line of products and related services to an assigned group of accounts (both Skyline and competitive) within a designated area. Keeps constantly alert to the entrance of new accounts into the field, and programs solicitation efforts to best serve such accounts. As appropriate, and when so directed, performs designated administrative and clerical functions closely related to sales and operations.

Office Salesman—directs and performs plant sales and clerical work for the district sales manager. In the absence of the district sales manager, acts as a company representative at the station and coordinates station activities. Responsible for meeting standards in the preparation of reports, records and correspondence; for accurate advice to customers on products, prices and sales policies; for securing maximum orders from each customer contacting the plant; and for direction of warehouse and delivery functions as required to coordinate station activities.

Assistant Office Salesman—as a primary function, i.e., at least 25% of the time, performs one or a combination of the following duties: (1) taking orders and soliciting business at the counter and on the phone, advising customers on product characteristics, applications, prices and sales, operating or credit policies; (2) performs negotiation-type credit control duties such as soliciting payments on accounts from customers on the phone or in person; (3) dispatches delivery trucks. Responsible for giving accurate information to customers and for completing assigned clerical and operating duties accurately and expeditiously.

Head Route Salesman—operates a small sales office and bulk plant at a location remote from the district sales office to provide service and facilities for the receipt, storage, sale and delivery of bulk and packaged petroleum products in the area. Performs all functions involved in the receipt, storage and delivery of packaged and bulk petroleum products. Responsible for plant and operations, safety practices, solicits business of regular and new accounts, collects and arranges for banking of funds, performs accounting functions, prepares sales, stock, credit, personnel and accounting forms, and reports, and necessary correspondence.

Route Salesman—delivers company products by tank, combination or package truck to accounts within an assigned area or an assigned route. Loads or assists in loading trucks, drives truck, delivers product from truck, collects for product at the time of delivery or in accordance with established line of credit. Accounts for all products and funds handled. Reports any pertinent competitive activities observed. Services the truck.

THE JOB OF THE DISTRICT SALES MANAGER

One of Skyline's top wholesale marketing executives explained that the job of the district sales manager consisted of three basic functions—

He has to make day-to-day operating decisions to keep the business running smoothly.

He has to plan ahead, setting worthy objectives for each component of the organization; and follows through to assure that progress actually made is in keeping with goals established.

And finally, he has to train, counsel and motivate the people comprising the organization.

Administering these functions required a number of skills on the part of the district sales manager. He maintained a good deal of the physical plant; he sought out and reported price actions by competitors; he assigned sales territories; was the company representative in the community; recommended manpower changes; and so forth. The regional office reserved final approval on price changes, hiring, wage and salary matters, etc., but the district sales manager initiated such recommendations.

Forms for recording district activity were important to the manager in the effective discharge of his basic responsibilities. Several served as the basis for recommendations to regions. For example, Exhibit 1 is the form used for determining the delivery work load for the route salesmen. The district sales manager used this information periodically to reapportion the work load within the district or to recommend additional personnel to the region.

Sales personnel were expected to record available business information on the customer data sheet, D102 (Exhibit 2). This form provided up-to-date data on the pertinent circumstances surrounding each account, including responsibility for solicitation. Form D105 (Exhibit 3), the account change card, kept the manager informed on sales gains and losses. District managers varied in their insistence on current maintenance of these forms. Some felt that this attention to detail was burdensome and not overly productive, while others insisted that the reported information was their only way of keeping aware of district activity.

The Commission Agents submitted monthly operating and financial statements which the sales managers were to evaluate and use in consultation with the agents. Agents had no formal business training and relied greatly on the supervision of the district sales manager.

The Regional Office provided the district with information compiled by three staff services. Form R30, for instance, reported cumulative monthly sales results by product for the district and its components. Form R31 showed the number of accounts to which credit has been extended. Form R35 provided expenses per gallon delivered.

THE WATERTOWN DISTRICT

Following several trips to the Watertown district, Joe wondered just what his course of action would be on assuming his new duties. Dick Owen had been at Watertown for 29 years and appeared to be an established part of the community. Joe noted during visits at several service clubs that Dick knew nearly all the town's business people. In fact, at one time or other Dick had served as president of several of the organizations.

Also going through Joe's mind was the material he had encountered at a recent administrative functions course for district sales managers held at Skyline's home office in Dallas. Joe had not been back at River Bend long enough to really apply the material but he recalled how they had covered the basic management responsibilities of planning, organizing, directing, coordinating and controlling.

The Watertown District spread over a large area, with a concentration of business activity and population as shown on the map in Exhibit 4. Petroleum and related needs were diversified to the extent that the portion south of the Blue River was highly industrialized while to the north the mainstay was agriculture. District population figures recorded at 321,000 in 1964 had reached 400,000 in 1968 and were projected to 675,000 in 1980. This growth was based primarily on expected manpower requirements for new business establishments moving into the area. The following figures show new plant construction since 1964:

Number of New Plants and Expansions (and of Capitalization—Millions)

1964		1965		1966		1967		1968	
55	($10.5)	82	($12.0)	99	($15.0)	153	($24.6)	176	($35.1)

Fabricated metal products manufacturers ranked first in number of firms followed by electrical machinery, chemicals, and food and kindred products. Active promotion of five major industrial parks promised a continuation of this trend.

Navigable waters along the Blue River, adequate rail and trucking facilities, and moderate year-round weather were considered basic attractions to new plant growth.

With the increase in population and industrialization, the area within the district devoted to agriculture had been declining over the past five years. However, mechanical efficiencies in farming and an improved price structure in 1968 helped achieve a record value for agricultural production of $16,500,000. Flowers, vegetables and livestock accounted for the major share of the total.

Watertown, the heart of the area's heavy industrial growth, was the home of the district office and the main salaried sales office. Encouraged by liberal zoning laws, "smoke-stack" type operations had increased 40% over the last five years. A new industrial park consisting of 300 acres was soon to open near the city.

There were four rather sizable airports in the Sales District—located at Watertown, Alpine, Poplar Bluff and Garden City. The Watertown Airport, five miles outside the city limits, was the largest, providing facilities for commercial and private aircraft. The District had been successful in establishing dealerships at each of these airports. Bulk storage facilities at the Watertown Airport were under supervision of the District Sales Manager and required the services of four warehousemen.

A smaller salaried sales office was located 20 miles from Watertown, in the city of *Poplar Bluff.* This was primarily a residential center, but a recently developed light industrial tract brought 20 new manufacturing firms to the city within the past two years. Commercial establishments, warehousing facilities, and some farming rounded out the activities of the area. Several large accounts were important in maintaining the gallonage position at this station. The light industrial plants, in general, were not large users of petroleum products.

The city of *Alpine,* served by a Commission Agent, was involved in an overnight transition from an agricultural-commercial economy to one centered around light industry. Electronics asd precision-type manufacturing firms were predominant in the area. Industrial sites covering 250 acres were at the time being sold along the Blue River with reports that actual sales and inquiries had already exceeded expectations. Keeping pace with industrial growth, the city's population now at 50,000, had doubled in the past five years. Joe was visiting the Watertown office when it was learned that Mac McMurtry, a commissioned distributor for Skyline's largest Alpine competitor, was going to retire in several months. McMurtry had always been a leader in Alpine (mayor, city council, etc.) and was held in high esteem by many accounts in the area. A salaried plant was scheduled to replace the old operation.

Garden City and *Mansfield* were both unincorporated farming centers served by Commission Agents. The total number of agricultural accounts had been declining over the last three years due to the failure of the marginal operators to keep up with new farm innovations. However, those still in business were producing larger quantities through use of more and more mechanized equipment. The Garden City area showed the most promise in terms of agricultural growth, while the future of Mansfield was uncertain. Recent plans for improving Highway 7 and the low cost of land had attracted the interest of several real estate promoters to the Mansfield area. One manufacturing firm had already constructed plant facilities near Mansfield, and from all reports its management was quite happy with the results.

An organization chart for the Watertown sales district would have been as shown in Figure 2.

Exhibit 5 shows the district's 1968 market position in terms of number of accounts and percent of gallonage for both motor gasoline and diesel sales. These figures were developed from existing customer data sheets, Form D102, which admittedly had received very little attention from the district sales manager. Comparable figures for prior years had never been developed. Some picture of district growth, however, can be gained from

FIGURE 2

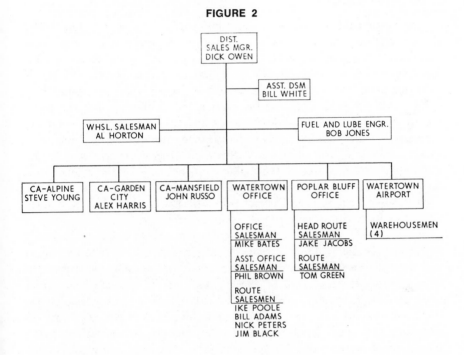

a composite of the R31 Credit statements. Quarterly and yearly averages of accounts to which credit had been extended are shown in Exhibit 6 for the last four years.

Sales results for the district and its components are shown in Exhibit 7 for the period covering 1966–1968. Dick set the district goals for 1968 at a general increase over the 1967 results. Several large losses, as noted in the exhibit, resulted from situations over which the district had no control. Expenses, as listed in Exhibit 8, showed some improvement for the year. The large decrease per gallon at the Poplar Bluff Plant related to the elimination of a Route Salesman following a regular workload study.

Credit collections for the district ran below the Company objectives of 75% current. Figures ($ & Accounts Current) for September, 1967, and September, 1968 are indicative of the yearly results.

	Sept. '67*		Sept. '68*	
	$	Accts.	$	Accts.
District	71	62	66	63
Watertown	77	68	71	70
Poplar Bluff	78	63	68	60
Alpine	75	54	63	60
Mansfield	52	48	53	50
Garden City	54	61	71	59

* SOURCE: CD-35.

Commission Agent operations are outlined in Exhibit 9 which shows the number of employees, major expense items, gross commissions, total expenses, net commissions, commission rates, and equipment. Several monthly statements (Exhibit 10) are included for the operation at Mansfield. Realizing that such earnings would not support the distributorship, John Russo was paid, as a common carrier, for picking up and transporting the product needs for both his own and the Garden City operation. As a part of the trucking business Russo often hauled farm products for other members of the community. Such trips might cover a distance of 200 miles, with fertilizers often making up the load for the return haul. Russo's 22 year old son tended the CA operations during these absences.

Dick Owen, the retiring District Sales Manager, had, during his tenure, advanced with the organizational changes of the company. His duties over the past 29 years had changed from Agency Manager to Resident Manager and finally District Sales Manager. He was alert, enthusiastic and a good personnel salesman. As a result of his long association in Watertown, he knew most of the accounts in the immediate' area and often supplemented the solicitation efforts of other district employees. To make sure operations continued smoothly, Dick was quite active in checking on clerical details, handling many himself. He insisted on opening all the company mail as a precaution against missing any important correspondence.

The following people were relied upon to carry out district operations:

White Collar Personnel

Bill White—Assistant District Sales Manager. Age 36, had been with the company 11 years and in his present position 3 years. Held a B.S. degree in engineering and started with Skyline as a route salesman. His ability was obvious as he moved rapidly through the positions of head route salesman, Fuel and Lubricant Engineer, and regional specialist. As Asst. D.S.M., he handled a number of accounts, which greatly relieved the load on the wholesale salesman. He also took the responsibility for planning the activities of the Fuel & Lubricant engineer. Joe had formed the impression that Bill was not being used to his full capabilities and was not functioning within the proposed scope of the A.D.S.M. position.

Bob Walters—Fuel & Lubricant.   Age 62, had been with the company 35 years and in his present position 16 years. A graduate engineer, he had held a previous position as a home office specialist. He was very conscientious but needed to be told exactly what to do, where to be at a given time, etc. The A.D.S.M. had set up certain days when the Engineer was to be at stations in the district. He reported to the District Office twice a week for instructions.

Al Horton—Wholesale Salesman.   Age 60, with the company 35 years and in his present position 12 years. A high school graduate, previously a bottled gas salesman, he was considered to be a good salesman; was energetic and enthusiastic. While not particularly effective in organizing his own time, once told to do something he required little follow-up. He reported each day to the District Office, left (about 9:30 A.M.) to make his calls, returned in the afternoon to set up appointments on the telephone and then out again about 3:00 P.M. Al seemed to be left pretty much on his own in terms of planning his sales approach and setting up his calls for the day. Very little of his time was actually spent in the area north of the Blue River. Occasionally, when a problem was heard of through one of the Commission Agents, Dick would instruct him to take a run out and see what was taking place. According to both Dick and Al, the nature of these accounts did not warrant a more intensive solicitation effort.

Operating Personnel: Watertown Sales Office

Mike Bates—Office Salesman.   Age 32, with the company 10 years and in present assignment for the last 4 years. Had completed two years of college and seemed to possess the necessary qualifications for the job although it was noted that he was not particularly exacting in his work. There was evidence that he needed training in the clerical aspects of his job but this seemed to stem from the fact that he had not been delegated the full responsibility called for in this position. Normally Mike should have been the spokesman for the rest of the operating personnel, but very seldom was he included in problem solving or planning conferences held by Dick Owen.

Phil Brown—Asst. Office Salesman.   59 years old, had been with the company 35 years and in his present assignment for the past six months. Previous positions included time as a field salesman and head field salesman. There were indications that he didn't work well under pressure and lacked knowledge of many company policies.

Ike Poole—Route Salesman.   57 years old and had been with the company for 30 years in his present position. Performed his work well.

Bill Adams—Route Salesman.   59 years old and had been with the company for 40 years as a field salesman. Performed work well and required a minimum of supervision.

Nick Peters—Route Salesman.   Age 45, with the company as a field salesman for 20 years. An energetic and enthusiastic worker with real concern for company welfare. Well acquainted with company policy and required little supervision.

Jim Black—Route Salesman.   Age 38, had been a field salesman for 11 years. Had potential for position of head field salesman or head office salesman. Followed directions well.

It was noted that the work done by the above men consisted principally of delivering to accounts, taking orders, truck maintenance, etc. However, in terms of solicitation of new and existing small accounts, all needed development of sales desire and techniques. Few tangible results were being recognized from their efforts to gain new accounts or increase sales from present customers.

Personnel: Poplar Bluff Sales Office

Jake Jacobs—Head Route Salesman.   Age 58, had been with the company 38 years. Very energetic and conscientious. Required a minimum of supervision but did require occasional counseling from the district management. Noted as a good salesman.

Tom Green—Route Salesman.   58 years old and with the company 35 of these. Had no formal sales training but was very alert to duties involving filling orders, maintenance, etc.

Commission Agents

Steve Young—Alpine.   50 years old with eight years as agent. Was at one time a bottled gas salesman for the company. Steve was sized up as a rather retiring individual and, while effective in selling agricultural accounts, was not particularly suited to the growing industrial trend of his area. It was felt that he was making little effort to keep the district office posted on potential business that entered the area.

John Russo—Mansfield.   Age 59, had been agent for 15 years. Previously worked 15 years for the company. In addition to the low area potential his operation was somewhat sloppily run. John did not seem to be particularly concerned with company welfare. Much of the area was of the same nationality and was extremely clannish. Consequently, there was danger that business could well follow the distributor rather than the company, should he become alienated. The present CA agreement was soon due to expire and regional reports that always preceded renewal of such contracts showed considerable weakness, particularly in the areas of plant maintenance and credit collections.

Alex Harris—Garden City.   58 years old, with 16 years as agent. Was head field salesman at the same station before it was converted to an agency. Similar to John Russo, he had greatly tied up the area business in an extremely clannish community. Although he needed considerable supervision the operation had always been independently profitable. Alex had always been very cooperative and receptive to suggestions.

* * * * *

As implied earlier, supervision of district functions was closely held by Dick Owens. Having grown with most of the local accounts, he seemed to feel that he owed personal attention to them. During one of the visits Dick said to Joe, "I know everything that happens in this district. If I walk into the front office of any of our accounts here in Watertown they know who I am. Knowing as much as I do about the accounts saves a lot of time in working with my sales personnel. Unless a special problem arises, it's very seldom that we have to sit down and plan an approach to a particular customer."

"One thing I've really limited," continued Dick, "is the use of sales meetings for district personnel. If you ask me, they are a pure waste of time; most people form a negative attitude when they are asked to attend these meetings. I see all of my white collar people every day, and believe me, the grapevine takes care of passing on information of interest to the operating personnel."

Apparently Dick was satisfied with the job being done by his sales force, as he spent relatively little time with them observing sales techniques. "If I play nursemaid to these people," he said, "they would never learn to go out on their own. Hell, I'll know anyway when one of them goofs-up."

District sales coverage logically broke down into geographical areas with the Wholesale Salesman and Fuel and Lubricant Engineer providing white-collar support to the entire district. Alpine, Poplar Bluff, Garden City and Mansfield, with their relatively limited number of accounts, posed no real problem of area breakdown. Within the Watertown area, the responsibility of the four route salesmen was originally organized by geographical boundaries. However, local revisions over a period of time had finally resulted in each route salesman serving a certain list of accounts. This occurred as account status changed and Dick found it necessary to add or subtract gallonage as a means of maintaining an equal workload for each salesman. Finally, Jim Black was pulled off regular business and given the responsibility to service contractor accounts only. The net result of the shifting had been a composite of accounts for each salesman which no longer followed the original geographical breakdown. A two-year record by route salesmen of miles run, gallons delivered, number of deliveries, and average gallons delivered is offered in Exhibit 11.

EXHIBIT 1
Tank Truck Performance Analysis

1	2	3	4	5	6
Truck No.	Capa- city	Gals. Delv'd	# of Loads	# of Del'ys	Miles Run

7	8	9	10	11	12
Loads @ 25/min	Del'ys @ 20/min	Drive @ 20 mph	Total #7, #8 & #9	Office Plant Solic. Etc.	Total Hours Required

The following indicates the source of data entered in Columns 1–2–3–4–5–6 and the basis as well as method of computation of figures entered in Columns 4–7–8–9–10–11:

Column 1 —*Truck Number*
        From Statement of Miles Run by Motor Equipment, D-123.

Column 2 —*Capacity*
        If the exact truck capacity in gallons is not known, average ca- pacities can be used, i.e., 750 for T1, 950 for T2, 1,250 for T3 and 1,650 for T4.

Column 3 —*Gallons Delivered*
        From Statement of Miles Run—D-123.

Column 4 —*Number of Loads*
        Divide gallons delivered (Col. 3) by truck capacity (Col. 2).

Column 5 —*Number of Deliveries*
        From Statement of Miles Run—D-123.

Column 6 —*Miles Run*
        From Statement of Miles Run—D-123.

Column 7 —*Loading*

Multiply Col. 4 by .42 (the fractional hour equivalent of 25 minutes per load). For package trucks, full loads, multiply Col. 4 by 1 hour.

Column 8 —*Delivering*

Divide Col. 5 by 3 (hourly equivalent of 20 minutes per delivery —a liberal average for all types of deliveries).

Column 9 —*Driving*

Divide Col. 6 by 20 (average truck speed under normal operating conditions).

Column 10—*Total of Loading, Delivery and Driving Time.*

Column 11—*Office, Plant, Solicitation, Collection and Miscellaneous*

Multiply Col. 10 by .28 which is the standard percentage of tank truck workload time allowed for these functions. (The office and plant standard allowance to handle daily turn-ins, checking orders, servicing and garaging equipment, etc., is 40 minutes a day. Allowance for solicitation, collection and miscellaneous is 60 minutes per day. This total, plus 20 minutes for personal time, reduces the average available time for delivery operations to 360 minutes. 100 minutes is 28% of 360 minutes.)

EXHIBIT 2

Customer Data Sheet—D102

ASSIGNED TO:	CALLS ASSIGNED	NAME					
		LOCATION					
SUPPORTED BY:		HEADQUARTERS					
		TYPE OF BUSINESS					
		EQUIP. OPERATED: PASS. CARS _____ TRUCKS _____ TRACTORS _____ NO. CREDIT CARDS _____					
		OTHER EQUIP.:					

KEY PERSONNEL—SPECIAL DATA—CONTRACT INFO.—ETC.	ANNUAL AVAILABLE BUSINESS					
	PRODUCT	STGE. TANKS	TOTAL	SKYLINE	COMPETITIVE	CO.
	GASOLINE (Gals.)					
	DIESEL (Gals.)					
	FURNACE (Gals.)					
	STOVE/KERO. (Gals.)					
	AUTO OILS (Gals.)					
	AUTO LUBS./GRS. (Lbs.)					
	INDUSTRIAL OILS (Gals.)					
	INDUSTRIAL GRS. (Lbs.)					
	THNRS./SOLVS. (Gals.)					
	WAXES (Lbs.)					
	OTHER SPECIAL PRODUCTS (Gals.)					
	TOTAL LIGHT PRODUCTS					

CALLS MADE	YEAR	JAN.	FEB.	MAR.	APR.	MAY	JUNE	JULY	AUG.	SEPT.	OCT.	NOV.	DEC.

EXHIBIT 3

Skyline Petroleum Company
Account Change Card—D105

Account Change					
District_____ Office_____ Date_____					
Name of Account_____					
Type of Business_____					
Product	Annual Require-ments	Volume Gained Lost	Distribution of Requirements after Change		Compet. Gained from or Lost to
			Skyline	Compet.	
Gasoline-gals Motor Aviation					
Diesel fuel-gals					
Furnace oil-gals					
Stove oil-gals					
Kerosene-gals					
Fuel oil-gals					
Auto oils-gals					
Auto grease-lbs					
Ind. oils-gals					
Ind. greases-lbs					
Thinners and Solvents-gals					
Liquified pet. gases-gals					
Other gal or lbs					

Reason for Gain or Loss_____

Sales Rep_____ Office Manager_____
District Manager_____
(over)   D-105

Contracts in Effect (if Gained, What Type Signed: If Lost, What Paper in Effect):_____
_____
_____

If Account Lost, What Action Taken to Regain:_____
_____
_____
_____
_____
_____
_____

Should Appreciation Letter Be Sent to Account

Yes ☐   No ☐

Changes in Key Personnel, Subsidiaries, Etc.:_____
_____
_____
_____
_____
_____
_____
_____

EXHIBIT 4

Geography of Watertown Sales District

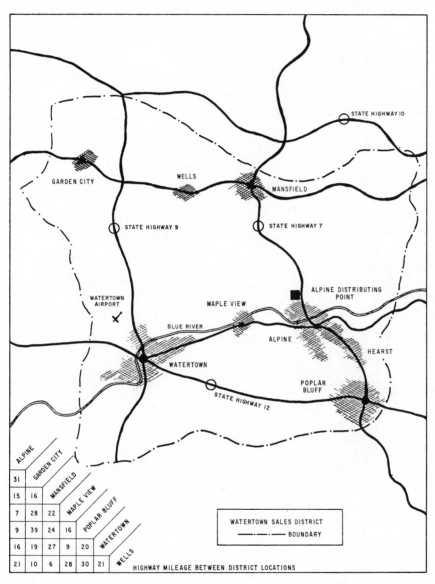

EXHIBIT 5
Market Position* 1968
(by number of accounts and per cent of gallonage)

Watertown District—(5,000 gal. per year and over)

Company	Motor Gasoline				Diesel Fuels			
	C.A & I		Other		C.A & I		Other	
	# Accts.	% of Gallonage	# Accts.	% of Gallonage	# Accts.	% of Gallonage	# Accts.	% of Gallonage
Skyline	244	38.3	8	34.1	69	30.6	2	12.3
Company A	61	14.7	2	11.7	18	15.3	1	5.5
Company B	95	25.7	—	—	20	19.8	—	—
Company C	86	11.3	6	19.0	16	5.6	—	—
Company D	6	1.1	11	25.5	5	20.1	1	54.3
Company E	10	2.4	2	2.3	1	.5	1	27.9
Other	55	6.5	2	7.4	11	8.1		
Accounts Available	557		31		140		5	
Total Gallonage	8,918,800		1,118,400		2,776,700		107,200	

Watertown Office—(5,000 gal. per year and over)

Skyline	81	46.1	3	24.3	27	25.7	—	—
Company A	14	15.8	1	16.0	1	7.9	—	—
Company B	56	25.3	—	—	7	20.9	—	—
Company E	5	2.5	—	—	1	1.	1	34.1
Company C	19	6.4	3	26.4	3	4.1	—	—
Company D	1	.9	6	22.6	3	36.4	1	65.9
Other	16	3.0	1	10.7	2	4.0	—	—
Accounts Available	192		14		44		2	
Total Gallonage	5,009,000		409,000		1,515,000		88,000	

* SOURCE D-102. Excludes some company's activities where minor sales involved.

EXHIBIT 5 (Continued)

Poplar Bluff Office—(5,000 gal. per year and over)

Company	Motor Gasoline				Diesel Fuels			
	CA & I		Other		CA & I		Other	
	# Accts.	% of Gallonage	# Accts.	% of Gallonage	# Accts.	% of Gallonage	# Accts.	% of Gallonage
Skyline	27	25.6	1	70.8	3	17.0	1	100
Company A	13	14.1	1	26.4	5	49.3	—	—
Company B	3	8.2	—	—	—	—	—	—
Company F	4	5.4	—	—	1	19.7	—	—
Company G	3	10.8	—	—	1	9.8	—	—
Company C	23	28.5	—	—	3	4.2	—	—
Other	2	7.4	1	2.8	—	—	—	—
Accounts Available	75		3		13		1	
Total Gallonage	1,980,000		212,000		507,000		12,000	

Alpine—(1,200 gal. per year and over)

Skyline	34	23.0	2	24.0	6	48.5	1	100
Company A	16	13.9	—	—	3	5.3		
Company B	35	38.9	—	—	13	41.3		
Company C	31	12.9	2	20.4	2	3.2		
Company D	5	2.3	5	48.5	2	1.7		
Other	18	9.0	2	92.9	—	—	—	—
Accounts Available	139		11		26		1	
Total Gallonage	2,391,000		416,000		562,000		13,000	

EXHIBIT 5 (Concluded)

Mansfield—(1,200 gal. per year and over)

| Company | Gasoline | | | | Diesel Fuels | | | |
| | CA & I | | Other | | CA & I | | Other | |
	# Accts.	% of Gallonage	# Accts.	% of Gallonage	# Accts.	% of Gallonage	# Accts.	% of Gallonage
Skyline	49	52.8	—	—	10	62.1	—	—
Company A	5	7.5	—	—	5	12.2	—	—
Company F	6	10.1	—	—	3	6.2	—	—
Company C	10	29.6	1	100	7	19.5	—	—
Accounts Available	70		1		25			
Total Gallonage	199,000		4,000		98,000		—	

Garden City—(1,200 gal. per year and over)

Skyline	53	76.6	2	100	23	43.3	1	100
Company A	13	8.1			4	12.8		
Company F	11	8.3			4	6.9		
Company C	3	7.0			1	37.0		
Accounts Available	81		2		32		1	
Total Gallonage	239,800		17,400		94,700		1,200	

EXHIBIT 6

Number of Accounts to Which Credit Has Been Extended

	1968	1967	1966	1965
District				
1st Qtr.	701	648	730	677
2nd Qtr.	706	651	705	685
3rd Qtr.	721	659	680	685
4th Qtr.	713	676	689	650
Year Avg.	710	659	701	674
Watertown				
1st Qtr.	223	177	188	167
2nd Qtr.	224	172	184	183
3rd Qtr.	238	173	174	177
4th Qtr.	234	220	184	163
Year	230	186	182	172
Poplar Bluff				
1st Qtr.	91	78	88	85
2nd Qtr.	88	83	81	86
3rd Qtr.	96	93	89	85
4th Qtr.	93	81	87	79
Year	92	84	86	84
Alpine				
1st Qtr.	123	119	148	121
2nd Qtr.	131	118	142	129
3rd Qtr.	132	130	135	129
4th Qtr.	133	121	123	129
Year	130	122	137	127
Mansfield				
1st Qtr.	93	84	112	104
2nd Qtr.	96	95	109	104
3rd Qtr.	94	96	111	104
4th Qtr.	86	89	108	102
Year	92	91	110	103
Garden City				
1st Qtr.	171	190	194	200
2nd Qtr.	167	182	189	183
3rd Qtr.	161	167	171	190
4th Qtr.	167	165	187	178
Year	166	176	185	188

Source: R 31 (compiled through averaging to obtain data by quarters).

EXHIBIT 7

Sales Results by Product, 1966–1969
(gallons)

	1968	1967	1966
DISTRICT			
Motor gasoline			
Agriculture.................	413,211	410,733	423,592
Const. & contr..............	675,031	518,116	634,570
Comm. & ind..............	2,316,641	2,187,287	1,973,751
Jobbers...................	30,264	137,998	25,861
Government...............	429,345	146,052	179,462
Total...................	3,864,492	3,400,186	3,237,236
Auto diesel..................	126,705	114,517	114,100
Truck diesel.................	695,846*	1,083,705	877,275
Aviation gasoline.............	18,699,930	18,961,370	16,483,800
Auto oils....................	113,000	118,899	112,000
Thinners & solvents..........	2,350,074	2,334,249	2,561,540
Refined wax.................	476,344	660,778	191,297
Total light products...........	26,326,391	26,673,704	23,577,248
WATERTOWN PLANT			
Motor gasoline			
Agriculture.................	141,119	137,365	144,307
Const. & contr..............	304,499	287,146	292,250
Comm. & ind..............	1,876,132	1,832,996	1,559,580
Jobbers...................	11,014†	125,015†	12,500
Government...............	209,300	100,105	50,674
Total...................	2,542,064	2,482,627	2,059,311
Auto diesel..................	76,443	78,388	82,647
Truck diesel.................	346,360	454,469	406,284
Auto oils...................	52,543	54,997	50,674
Thinners & solvents..........	2,046,644	2,149,941	2,180,938
Refined wax.................	367,334	264,037	287,653
Total light products...........	5,431,388	5,484,459	5,067,497
POPLAR BLUFF PLANT			
Motor gasoline			
Agriculture.................	8,934	12,699	8,710
Const. & contr..............	136,126	94,674	96,852
Comm. & ind..............	173,003	168,020	164,412
Government...............	115,884	34,169	36,358
Total...................	433,947	309,562	306,332
Truck diesel.................	77,975‡	182,892	92,783
Aviation gasoline.............	137,859	117,468	100,848
Auto oils....................	9,245	10,327	9,503
Thinners....................	48,493	62,564	81,098
Total light products...........	707,519	682,813	590,564
ALPINE			
Motor Gasoline			
Agriculture.................	29,842	25,315	22,358
Constr. & contr.............	232,033	121,384	218,095
Comm. & ind..............	202,618	258,345	282,590
Jobbers...................	19,250	0	0
Total...................	483,743	405,044	523,043

EXHIBIT 7 (Continued)

	1968	1967	1966
Auto diesel...................	5,740	7,644	7,534
Truck diesel..................	191,378	351,600	269,199
Aviation gasoline..............	136,937	127,613	105,006
Auto oils.....................	20,856	22,447	18,142
Thinners & solvents...........	253,776	145,277	230,305
Refined wax..................	10,010	49,737	20,013
Total light products...........	1,102,440	1,109,362	1,173,242

MANSFIELD

Motor gasoline

Agriculture.................	82,455	77,448	87,824
Constr. & contr.............	311	5,432	15,131
Comm. & ind...............	28,507	29,228	32,977
Total....................	111,273	112,108	135,932
Auto diesel...................	14,961	16,450	10,741
Truck diesel..................	40,879	49,092	81,668
Auto oils.....................	3,122	3,220	4,720
Bottled gas...................	58,968	61,969	64,831
Total light products...........	229,203	242,839	297,892

GARDEN CITY

Motor Gasoline

Agriculture.................	150,861	142,304	148,142
Constr. & contr.............	1,062	0	0
Comm. & ind...............	33,650	37,673	44,042
Government...............	13,800	2,400	2,111
Total....................	199,373	182,377	194,295
Auto diesel...................	21,766	3,871	3,377
Truck diesel..................	39,245	45,644	51,080
Aviation gasoline..............	28,640	25,844	25,413
Auto oils.....................	4,043	4,274	4,067
Refined wax..................	99,000	61,600	64,000
Total light products.........	392,067	323,710	342,232

WATERTOWN AIRPORT

Aviation gasoline..............	18,396,500	18,690,445	16,252,433

* Lost (completed) highway contract—nonrecurring business.
† Gained and lost jobber—not under District or Region control.
‡ Loss of large account—moved to other District.
SOURCE: R 30 (Based on 10-month period).

EXHIBIT 8

Expenses Per Gallon Delivered*

(1967–1968)

		1967 (cents)	1968 (cents)
Total Sales District.	1st Qtr.	3.34	3.06
	2nd Qtr.	3.00	2.93
	3rd Qtr.	3.20	2.75
	4th Qtr.	3.30	2.94
	YEAR	3.21	2.92
Supervision/Solicitation.	1st Qtr.	0.64	0.69
	2nd Qtr.	0.57	0.58
	3rd Qtr.	0.49	0.48
	4th Qtr.	0.56	0.57
	YEAR	0.56	0.57
Plant Cost—Watertown.	1st Qtr.	1.05	0.71
Sales Office.	2nd Qtr.	0.50	0.75
	3rd Qtr.	0.82	0.86
	4th Qtr.	0.80	0.83
	YEAR	0.79	0.79
Marketing Delivery Cost—.	1st Qtr.	2.07	1.90
Watertown Sales Office.	2nd Qtr.	1.78	1.72
	3rd Qtr.	2.04	1.47
	4th Qtr.	1.95	1.70
	YEAR	1.96	1.70
Total Cost—Watertown.	1st Qtr.	3.12	2.61
Sales Office.	2nd Qtr.	2.28	2.47
	3rd Qtr.	2.86	2.33
	4th Qtr.	2.75	2.53
	YEAR	2.75	2.49
Plant Cost—Poplar Bluff.	1st Qtr.	0.78	0.51
Sales Office.	2nd Qtr.	0.76	0.27
	3rd Qtr.	0.72	0.42
	4th Qtr.	0.77	0.40
	YEAR	0.76	0.40
Marketing Delivery Costs—.	1st Qtr.	2.12	2.24
Poplar Bluff Sales Office.	2nd Qtr.	2.15	2.04
	3rd Qtr.	2.27	1.75
	4th Qtr.	2.17	2.01
	YEAR	2.18	2.00
Total Cost—Poplar Bluff.	1st Qtr.	2.90	2.75
Sales Office.	2nd Qtr.	2.91	2.31
	3rd Qtr.	2.99	2.17
	4th Qtr.	2.94	2.41
	YEAR	2.94	2.40
Total Cost—Commission Agents.	1st Qtr.	1.99	1.89
	2nd Qtr.	2.35	2.02
	3rd Qtr.	2.35	1.89
	4th Qtr.	2.36	1.91
	YEAR	2.26	1.93

* Excludes airport gallonage.
SOURCE: R 35.

EXHIBIT 9

Commission Agent Operations

	1966	1967	1968
	ALPINE		
Gross Commissions....	$24,240	$23,395	$25,193
Expenses			
Salaries.............	$7,621	$7,986	$8,274
Gas & oil...........	1,225	1,091	1,294
Tires & batteries.....	195	178	329
Repairs.............	923	711	383
Rental..............	—	—	—
Dep................	2,136	637	323
Lic. & tax..........	191	145	195
Ins.................	723	769	774
Bus. lic.............	56	130	126
Work. comp........	103	190	138
U. C. tax..........	—	—	—
F.O.A.B............	201	147	173
Utilities............	137	111	137
Postage.............	268	301	307
Tel. & tel..........	572	390	409
Tool & sup.........	243	164	228
Dues & dons........	212	231	194
Adv................	196	—	—
Dep. P & T........	—	—	—
Stor. ded...........	—	—	—
W/D allow.........	739	13	—
Spec. allow.........	—	—	—
Enter..............	381	548	680
Other.............	64	161	110
Total Expenses.......	$16,186	$13,903	$14,074
Net Commissions.....	8,054	9,492	11,119

	Commission Rates	Equipment	Full-Time Employees
Airport & Airline................	1.10¢	1962 Dodge—710 Gal.	1 @ $500 per month
All Other Resale.................	1.10¢	1961 Ford—12 BBL	
Government.....................	.80¢	1966 Dodge—Pickup	
Other Consumer—gasoline and kerosene.....................	1.70¢		
Diesel/Furnace & Auto...........	1.35¢ + .2¢ = 1.55¢ Gas Oil		
Stove Oil.......................	1.45¢ + .2¢ = 1.65¢		

EXHIBIT 9 (Continued)
Commission Agent Operations

	1966	1967	1968
	GARDEN CITY		
Gross Commissions....	$15,457	$14,464	$18,222
Expenses			
Salaries.............	$3,900	$3,900	$5,608
Gas & oil..........	650	574	721
Tires & batteries.....	394	465	356
Repairs............	1,009	720	550
Rental.............	—	—	—
Dep................	1,320	1,320	1,416
Lic. & tax..........	217	175	342
Ins................	712	1,011	759
Bus. lic.............	—	—	—
Work. comp........	—	—	—
U. C. tax..........	—	—	—
F.O.A.B...........	—	—	—
Utilities...........	144	144	145
Postage...........	122	121	144
Tel. & tel.........	562	561	516
Tool & sup........	—	—	—
Dues & dons........	300	275	300
Adv...............	—	—	—
Dep. P & T........	—	—	12
Stor. ded...........	87	115	54
W/D allow.........	—	—	—
Spec. allow.........	—	—	47
Enter.............	—	—	—
Other.............	—	—	—
Total Expenses........	$ 9,417	$ 9,381	$10,970
Net Commissions.....	6,040	5,083	7,252

	Commission Rates	Equipment	Full-Time Employees
Airport and airline*..............	1.60¢	1967 Chev—970 Gal.	1 @ $457 per month
Gov't—All bulk products.........	1.60¢	1956 Chev—930 Gal.	
All other resale*.................	1.60¢	1959 Ford—Pickup	
Other consumer—gasoline and kerosene*.....................	2.10¢		
Diesel/furnace & auto*...........	1.95¢		
Stove oil*......................	2.05¢		

EXHIBIT 9 (Concluded)
Commission Agent Operations

	1966	*1967*	*1968*
	MANSFIELD		
Gross commissions........	$7,971	$6,812	$6,986
Expenses			
Salaries................	$1,597	$1,812	$1,956
Gas & oil..............	690	724	678
Tires & batteries........	506	161	408
Repairs................	1,830	280	270
Rental.................	—	—	—
Dep...................	564	564	654
Lic. & tax..............	132	150	138
Ins....................	337	458	162
Bus. lic................	10	—	—
Work. comp...........	—	—	—
U. C. tax..............	—	—	—
F.O.A.B..............	—	—	—
Utilities...............	54	54	52
Postage...............	50	38	43
Tel. & tel.............	118	108	131
Tool & sup............	73	53	29
Dues & dons...........	47	42	36
Adv...................	27	—	—
Dep. P & T...........	—	—	—
Stor. ded..............	22	12	19
W/D allow............	—	—	—
Spec. allow............	—	—	—
Enter.................	343	327	387
Other.................	114	178	9
Total Expenses..........	$6,514	$4,961	$4,972
Net Commissions........	1,457	1,851	2,014

	Commission Rates†	*Equipment*	*Full-Time Employees*
All other resale...................	1.40¢	1959 Chev—760 Gal.	1 @ $163 per month
Consumer—all gasoline and kerosene.....................	2.10¢	1958 Ford—Stake	
Diesel/furnace & auto.............	1.95¢	1962 De Soto—Sedan	
Stove oil........................	2.05¢	# Pd. to Pete Russo, John's son	

* Plus .50¢ TSC (Temporary Supplemental Commission)
† Workload shows that TSC's not warranted.

EXHIBIT 10

Monthly Statements for Mansfield

JUNE—68

Gross Commissions......................			607.35
Expenses...............................			
Wages.............................		163.13	
General			
Gas and oil........................	57.03		
Tire and battery...................	53.48		
Repairs...........................	11.53		
Depreciation......................	57.00		
Licenses..	2.40		
Insurance	15.64		
Utilities..........................	13.85		
Miscellaneous.....................	7.89		
Club dues........................	2.50		
Advertising and entertainment.........	22.20		
Total Expenses.................		243.52	406.65
Total Net Commissions..................			200.70

JULY—68

Gross Commissions......................			591.49
Expenses			
Wages.............................		163.13	
General			
Gas and oil........................	45.47		
Tire and battery...................	156.06		
Repairs...........................	7.94		
Depreciation......................	57.00		
Licenses..........................	2.36		
Insurance.........................	15.64		
Utilities..........................	24.98		
Club dues........................	2.50		
Advertising and entertainment.........	19.90		
Total Expenses.................		331.85	494.98
Total Net Commissions..................			96.51

EXHIBIT 10 (Continued)

AUGUST—68		
Gross Commissions......................		608.06
Expenses		
Wages..............................	163.13	
General		
Gas and oil.........................	75.71	
Repairs............................	52.95	
Depreciation........................	57.00	
Licenses...........................	2.61	
Insurance..........................	15.64	
Utilities...........................	18.82	
Club dues..........................	2.50	
Advertising and entertainment.........	32.70	
Total Expenses..................	257.93	421.06
Total Net Commissions..................		187.00

SEPTEMBER—68		
Gross Commissions.....................		533.65
Expenses		
Wages..............................	163.13	
General		
Gas and oil.........................	61.76	
Repairs............................	34.06	
Depreciation........................	57.00	
Licenses...........................	2.22	
Insurance..........................	15.64	
Utilities...........................	25.27	
Club dues..........................	2.50	
Advertising and entertainment.........	20.95	
Total Expenses..................	219.40	382.53
Total Net Commissions..................		151.12

EXHIBIT 11

Route Salesman Performance
(1967–1968)

Route Salesman	Miles Run		Light Products Delivered (Gal.)		Number of Deliveries		Average Gal./Del.	
	1967	1968	1967	1968	1967	1968	1967	1968
Jim Black—T2—Capacity 850								
1st Qtr.	3,146	2,547	78,697	99,554	217	318	312	313
2nd Qtr.	3,473	5,044	89,256	124,525	258	440	344	287
3rd Qtr.	2,899	3,404	58,282	119,132	167	330	304	358
4th Qtr.	3,133	3,191	62,878	118,005	209	410	292	282
Year.	12,651	14,186	289,113	461,216	851	1,498	313	310
Bill Adams—T2—Capacity 977								
1st Qtr.	2,719	1,963	114,693	141,621	406	431	281	328
2nd Qtr.	2,664	2,113	127,813	157,392	457	484	280	325
3rd Qtr.	2,687	2,182	127,633	176,900	451	629	283	283
4th Qtr.	2,369	2,023	120,889	177,000	452	590	252	300
Year.	10,439	8,281	491,028	652,913	1,766	2,134	274	313
Ike Poole—T2—Capacity 814								
1st Qtr.	3,225	3,293	168,433	128,564	487	435	342	296
2nd Qtr.	2,813	3,585	162,500	157,624	503	509	329	310
3rd Qtr.	3,317	3,490	156,824	178,958	487	522	322	348
4th Qtr.	3,050	3,030	133,122	134,368	383	442	366	299
Year.	12,405	13,398	620,879	599,514	1,860	1,908	340	313
Nick Peters—T3—Capacity 1130								
1st Qtr.	2,360	3,457	157,020	126,627	449	408	351	288
2nd Qtr.	1,970	3,938	166,070	158,651	435	430	375	369
3rd Qtr.	2,178	3,688	162,693	170,154	452	520	339	329
4th Qtr.	3,033	4,462	152,109	157,885	474	468	299	358
Year.	9,541	15,545	637,892	613,317	1,810	1,826	341	336
Composite.	45,036	51,410	2,038,912	2,326,960	6,287	7,366	317	318

SOURCE: D-123.

Suprema Dairies

By June, the early part of winter in Chile, plans for constructing the new Suprema Dairies plant in Santiago had been completed, and the general manager turned to the problem of establishing a distribution system for the company's products. Direct distribution through the company's own force of driver-salesmen was not feasible because the capital required to buy the necessary trucks and other equipment was lacking. Inasmuch as the plant was scheduled to begin production early in the following year, arrangements for distribution had to be made soon. Initial plant capacity was to be 100,000 liters[1] of milk daily. Other dairy products such as butter, cheese, cream, and chocolate milk were to be added later. After the second year of operation, daily plant capacity was to be expanded to 200,000 liters of milk. Suprema's sales manager recommended that the company sell only through retail stores. The general manager, on the other hand, favored selling at street-corner stops and through home delivery.

ORIGIN OF SUPREMA DAIRIES

The Suprema Dairies plant was located in Santiago, the capital of Chile, because of that city's particular need for improved dairy services. Owing to Chile's marked seasonal milk production and the great distance of most dairy farms from Santiago, the supply of fresh milk varied sharply from relative abundance during the summer to scarcity during the winter. In response to this inadequacy, a group of independent businessmen decided to organize Suprema Dairies to supply Santiago with "recombined" milk.

Modern processing techniques and facilities make it relatively easy to convert fluid milk to powdered milk by separating the cream (butter fat)

---

[1] One liter = 1.057 U.S. fluid quarts.

and then eliminating the water content from the milk. The resulting powdered skimmed milk can be stored without refrigeration and can be transported cheaply and safely. It is a simple operation to reconvert the powdered skimmed milk to fluid whole milk by adding water and cream. The quantity of recombined milk necessary to supply a particular market area can be produced and distributed on a day-to-day basis. The Suprema plant in Santiago was equipped to combine powdered skimmed milk with water and cream, to bottle the fluid milk, and to store it under refrigeration. Suprema's executives believed that they could eliminate the milk shortages of the winter months and provide whole milk to the Santiago market throughout the year, by obtaining powdered milk from plants in the southern part of Chile.

Suprema executives were convinced that recombined milk tasted like fresh whole milk and was no more perishable. A product test conducted among Santiago housewives by Ingenieros Consultores Asociados (ICA), a large local consulting firm specializing in engineering and management services, confirmed these beliefs. The ICA study found that consumers could perceive no differences in taste, color, or appearance between Suprema recombined milk and fresh whole milk when comparing unidentified glasses of milk. In the ICA study, consumers reported a preference for the deeper "cream line" on the top of a bottle of Suprema milk, compared with the two brands of fresh milk sold in Santiago. Finally, the ICA product test found no differences in perishability between recombined milk and fresh milk. Because the Suprema plant was not in operation at the time of the study, samples of recombined milk were prepared for the product test. Until the plant was completed, possible variations in the product resulting from variations in the production process could not be tested.

The company's general manager had acquired several years of experience as an executive of a major Santiago dairy company. He had an intimate knowledge of the marketing methods used by the existing dairies in Santiago, and of the characteristics of this market.

THE SANTIAGO MILK MARKET

The Marketing Research Branch of ICA had recently conducted a survey for Suprema, to determine the present milk consumption habits of the Santiago market. The Santiago market area covered ten counties. The Chilean National Statistics Service published estimates of the total population for each county, the number of households, and the average number of inhabitants per household. By working with these estimates, together with the results of previous market studies, ICA was able to estimate the population of each county by socioeconomic groups. (These estimates are presented in Table 1.)

To determine the milk consumption and purchasing habits of each of

TABLE 1

Distribution of Population in Each County in the Santiago Market Area, by Socioeconomic Classification
(percentage of total population)

	Total Population	Upper Class	Middle Class	Lower Class
Santiago...........	638,741	15	55	30
Couchali..........	150,642	0	10	90
Providencia.......	83,551	20	70	10
Nunoa............	193,904	5	70	25
Quinta Normal.....	150,560	0	20	80
San Miguel........	274,185	2	45	53
Renca.............	51,164	0	40	60
La Cisterna........	149,205	0	30	70
Los Condes........	70,597	40	50	10
La Granja.........	60,735	0	10	90
Total.............	1,823,284	155,939 (8.6%)	820,684 (45.0%)	846,661 (46.4%)

TECHNICAL NOTE: Because it was socially unacceptable in Chile to ask people about their income (due partly to taxation policies), the following criteria had been developed by ICA to classify families by socioeconomic groups:

1. Upper-Class Profile:
   a. large house with garden;
   b. two or more automobiles;
   c. five or more servants, including chauffeur;
   d. children being educated in one of the most expensive private primary or secondary schools.
2. Middle-Class Profile:
   a. occupation of head of household either self-employed small businessman, employed by corporate enterprise, or employed by government;
   b. house must include at least one bedroom for every two children (plus one bedroom for the parents) and either one or "one and a half" bathrooms; house must provide necessities but not luxury;
   c. only one or two servants;
   d. children being educated in low-cost private schools or public schools;
   e. housewife may be employed.
3. Lower-Class Profile:
   a. head of household in employment requiring manual and physical skills, not mental skills or abilities based on formal education;
   b. small house with all members of family in one or two bedrooms;
   c. toilet and bathing facilities may or may not be in the house.

In practice, it was fairly easy for the interviewers employed by ICA to determine the socioeconomic status of a family. Interviewers were trained by viewing film slides showing the exterior and interior of houses, classifying the houses, and then learning the correct classification. Interviewers were also trained by accompanying experienced interviewers in the field for several days.

the three major socioeconomic divisions, ICA conducted interviews with 446 respondents, of whom 156 were in the upper-class group; 162 in the middle-class group; and 128 in the low-class group. In this survey, which was made in April, people were asked about their milk consumption during the previous thirty-day period. The survey's results are presented in Table 2.

The results of the ICA market survey confirmed many of the general manager's assumptions about milk consumption in Santiago. Because the average housewife did not have a home freezer or refrigerator, she bought such food items as bread, milk, eggs, and meat at a neighborhood store every day. Many housewives purchased milk from milkmen who stopped daily at certain street corners. Daily home delivery was also available but was used mainly by upper-class families.

846,661 / 6 ...42 × 2/3 = >100,000/Day — mkt is there

TABLE 2

Results of April Market Survey Conducted by ICA on Milk Consumption and Purchasing Habits

	Upper Class	Middle Class	Lower Class
A. Milk Consumption			
Percentage of families reporting that milk was consumed in the past 30-day period	90.6%	84.4%	67.0%
Percentage of families reporting no milk consumed in the past 30-day period	9.4%	15.6%	33.0%
B. Types of milk consumed*			
Fresh	86%	81%	47%
Condensed	11%	8%	18%
Powdered	13%	10%	32%
Evaporated and baby formulas	8%	2%	1%
C. Quantity of milk consumed by family last month, in liters†			
None	15	25	43
1–8	0	3	4
9–22	17	25	22
23–44	36	47	45
45–72	38	42	8
73–96	44	20	6
97–165	6	0	0
Total number of families	156	162	128
Average number of liters per consuming household	70.26	55.37	42.92
D. Where purchased			
Percentage of families who purchased in a store	16%	38%	66%
Percentage of families who purchased from a milkman, either house delivery or street-corner purchase	84%	62%	34%

* Figures are stated as a percentage of families reporting milk consumption; many families reported consumption of more than one type of milk.

† Powdered, condensed, and evaporated milk consumption was converted to fluid milk equivalent in liters for the purpose of this analysis.

MARKETING OF DAIRY PRODUCTS IN SANTIAGO

Two large dairy firms supplied fresh milk to the Santiago market. The larger of the two, Soprole Dairy Company, had a plant capacity of 160,000 liters per day, and the other, Delicias Milk Company, had an estimated daily capacity of 70,000 liters. The general manager of Suprema Dairies estimated that Suprema would have to obtain a 30 percent share of the market when it began production, as follows:

Company	Capacity	Market Share (Percent)
Soprole.................	160,000	49
Suprema.................	100,000	30
Delicias.................	70,000	21

Both Soprole and Delicias employed their own driver-salesmen, who were paid a straight salary, without commission or any other incentive payment. These driver-salesmen were assigned routes throughout the Santiago market area, which they covered daily. These consisted of fixed routings which included home delivery, store delivery, and several street-corner stops. Driver-salesmen attempted to arrive at each stop at approximately the same time every day. Both companies virtually blanketed the Santiago market with their distribution networks.

Retail prices for all products declared to be of prime necessity or habitual use were fixed by the Chilean government. The retail price of milk was fixed by the government at $82.50 per liter.[2] Recombined milk would sell at the same price as fresh milk. Soprole and Delicias allowed a margin of $2.00 to retailers. Milk left in the retail store from the previous day was returned to the plant (most retail stores did not have refrigeration facilities). The retailer was given full credit for all returned milk.

Because milk was scarce in Santiago during much of the year, especially in the five months from May through September, the two dairy companies did not find it necessary to promote the sale of their products. The driver-salesman did not have to "sell," in the sense of "pushing" the product. In fact, driver-salesmen often requested a small tip (gratuity) before selling to a consumer, especially when milk was scarce. Sometimes they required the consumers to buy other products such as butter and cheese[3] before they would sell them milk. It was also reported that some driver-salesmen would dilute the milk with water in order to increase the quantity of milk which they could offer for sale.

PROPOSED DISTRIBUTION PLAN FOR SUPREMA

When Suprema's general manager asked the sales manager to recommend a distribution plan, he pointed out that it would be financially impossible for the company to support its own sales force of driver-salesmen. He suggested that the company rely upon a system of independent distributors to provide market coverage, in which each area-distributor would be assigned an exclusive sales territory. He believed that the com-

[2] In this case, the symbol "$" signifies Chilean pesos, of which 2,000 = U.S. $1.00.
[3] Although salesmen were not paid a commission incentive, they were assigned daily quotas for by-products such as butter and cheese.

pany should find distributors with previous experience in distributing and selling bottled beverages, such as Coca-Cola and Pepsi-Cola, as well as beer companies which had experimented successfully with similar distribution systems.

The general manager thought that Suprema's distribution system should follow substantially those of Soprole and Delicias. He wished to establish extensive in-store distribution and also to provide home delivery at no additional charge for all who desired it. Finally, he wanted distributors' routes to include street-corner stops.

According to the general manager's plan, distributors would be required to buy one or more new trucks (the number depended upon the market potential of the assigned area), to cover the trucks with a roof or hood, and to paint them in the style and colors prescribed by Suprema. Distributors would buy the bottled milk from Suprema at a price of $75.50 per liter and sell it at their own risk. Every milk bottle carried the Suprema brand name and trademark. Distributors would be required to take back day-old milk from retailers and to give them credit for it, but Suprema would take back milk from area distributors only up to 5 percent of the daily order. The general manager believed that this system would furnish the area distributors with an incentive, while providing a solution to Suprema's distribution and selling problem. He estimated Suprema's cost to be about $71 per liter with the plant operating at 75 percent or more of capacity. Selling to area distributors at a price of $75.50 would allow Suprema a margin of $4.50 per liter. If the distributor allowed retailers a margin of $2.00 per liter, the distributor's margin on store sales would be $5.00. At a retail price of $82.50, the distributor would realize a margin of $7.00 on street-corner sales and on home deliveries. The general manager's estimates of the expenses incurred by the distributors are presented in Table 3.

TABLE 3

Daily Cost of Operation in Pesos for an Average Truck Route by Type of Truck

	Trucks				Wheel Tractors	
Items	2.5 Tons	4 Tons	6 Tons	8 Tons	4 Tons	6 Ton
Salaries*	8,200	8,200	8,200	8,200	8,200	8,200
Depreciation	1,805	2,361	3,612	4,433	2,500	2,638
Insurance	1,100	1,280	1,350	1,528	1,065	1,065
Gasoline	1,900	1,950	2,210	3,200	1,900	1,900
Adaptation†	474	474	474	474	474	474
Registration	164	164	164	164	164	164
Uniforms	200	200	200	200	200	200
Tires	1,252	1,252	1,252	1,252	1,252	1,252
Maintenance	4,150	4,150	4,150	4,150	4,150	4,150
Unexpected	575	575	575	575	575	575
Total	19,820	20,606	22,187	24,176	20,480	20,618

* Salaries were estimated at approximately 156,000 pesos per month for a driver salesman and 90,000 pesos per month for his helper.

† Only for the first two years. Includes cost of painting and roofing the truck.

Two types of vehicles were considered feasible for use by the area-distributors. Trucks were available in four capacities and price ranges: 2.5 tons at $6.6 millions each; 4 tons at $8.6 millions; 6 tons at $13.2 millions; and 8 tons at $16.0 millions. Wheel tractors for use with a coupled-car or trailer were available in two capacities and prices: 4 tons at $9.2 millions and 6 tons at $9.6 millions. Other types of trucks or pickups were not considered because they were subject to very high customs duties.

ALTERNATIVE PROGRAM SUGGESTED BY SALES MANAGER

Suprema's sales manager was a thirty-two-year-old man whose previous business experience had been in the sales department of a firm selling imported machinery. He had no special education or training and no previous dairy or other food products experience. His major assets were his pleasant outgoing personality, friendliness, and facility in dealing with people.

The sales manager accepted the general manager's suggestion of using independent distributors with assigned and exclusive territories but argued that they should sell only to retail stores. He pointed out that inasmuch as ICA's market survey had found that the lower-class population constituted the largest market segment with the lowest rate of consumption, it represented the largest potential market for milk. He further argued that the lower-class consumer purchased most frequently in a retail store, partly because retailers sold on credit, whereas driver-salesmen did not.

If Suprema were to reach its sales objectives, the sales manager contended, it would have to concentrate on the market segment with the greatest unfulfilled demand. "Why try to sell house-to-house," he asked, "when the upper-class market is already being served adequately? Only upper-class families can afford to pay the milkman the tips which he demands. Further, without additional service charges for home delivery, the retail price remains the same, even though the cost is higher. We must not forget that consumers who can afford it will still prefer fresh milk to recombined milk. Our market will be among the lower-class consumers who cannot afford the additional costs of tipping a milkman to encourage him to sell fresh milk to them. We should also consider allowing a higher retail margin to encourage store cooperation. Distributors would make less per unit but would benefit from greater volume."

The general manager disagreed with the sales manager and asserted that the upper-class and middle-class groups represented the largest market potential for Suprema Dairies. He pointed out that 91 percent of upper-class families and 84 percent of middle-class families consumed milk, compared with only 67 percent of lower-class families. Furthermore, among consuming families, the average upper-class family used more than 70 liters of milk per month, compared with 43 liters for lower-class families. He estimated that the lower-class market segment accounted for less than one-third of the potential market for milk. In order to reach the other two-thirds of the potential market, Suprema would have to sell house-to-house and at street-corner stops.

The general manager supported his argument in favor of all three distribution methods with three additional observations. First, because the area distributors would realize a margin of $7.00 on direct sales to consumers compared to $5.00 on sales to retail stores, distributors would prefer to make direct sales. Second, as the company added additional product lines such as butter and cream, a more extensive distribution system would be required. Third, because of the nature of the relationship with distributors, having additional distributors involved no additional costs.

The sales manager was not satisfied with the general manager's analysis of the problem. A decision had to be reached in the near future, and he had to consider the time required to select distributors, to order trucks and have them painted, and to develop methods of supervising, controlling, and administering the distributor system.

SECTION VI

PERSONAL SELLING
AND ADVERTISING

Gloss Wax Company

The general manager of Gloss Wax Company, Mr. Peter Tantoco, had asked his newly appointed sales manager, Mr. Manuel Garcia, to review the performance of the company's sales force with him in early September 1965. Gloss Wax used 76 salesmen to sell floor wax house-to-house, to lower- and middle-income families in Manila. After three years of operations, Mr. Tantoco estimated that the company had captured about 85% of the city's lower- and middle-income floor-wax market. Since 1961, monthly sales in the city had expanded rapidly, and had reached a peak of 24,409 gallons in August 1964. By September 1965, however, Mr. Tantoco thought that a leveling out of monthly sales below 20,000 gallons seemed to be indicated.

At this stage, Mr. Tantoco wondered if the Gloss sales force was being used to best advantage. He believed that Gloss salesmen were spending more time than was necessary, in traveling between the company's main office and their territories each morning and evening. By setting up branch offices in other parts of Manila, Mr. Tantoco believed that the actual selling time of the sales force would be increased.

Mr. Garcia, who had been the part-time attorney for Gloss Wax until his appointment as sales manager in July 1965, proposed another idea. His brief experience in managing the sales force influenced him to point to the possibility that the large number of salesmen was an unnecessarily heavy drag on profits. By changing the call patterns of the salesmen, Mr. Garcia thought that the number of salesmen might be cut down, without reducing company sales.

Mr. Tantoco told Mr. Garcia that he was reluctant to make significant changes in the operations of the Gloss sales force until the matter had been given more detailed consideration. He requested that, at their next meeting, Mr. Garcia submit recommendations on a plan of action which would improve the operating efficiency of the sales force.

COMPANY BACKGROUND

Company Founders

Gloss Wax Company was a partnership organized by Mr. Tantoco and his sister, both naturalized Filipino citizens of Chinese descent. Both partners initially contributed P1,000 each, to purchase the basic equipment necessary for the manufacture of floor wax.[1] At the age of 24, Mr. Tantoco had developed his own formula for floor wax, which he thought could be sold profitably in competition with other brands on the Filipino market.

The Product

Gloss Wax was manufactured from a synthetic paraffin base, with a very small amount of natural wax, turpentine, and insecticide. More expensive floor waxes used a higher proportion of natural wax.

Mr. Tantoco believed that Gloss Wax would have a stronger appeal to the Filipino housewife than other waxes on the market. It produced a brilliant shine and the surface to which it was applied did not become sticky when subjected to moisture. Other brands on the market contained larger amounts of detergent, for easy removal of the wax before application of a new coat. When water was spilled on the floor, the surface tended to become somewhat dull and sticky. This was an important consideration, particularly during the rainy season. Also, Mr. Tantoco thought it was unrealistic to assume that the old wax coating would be removed before the new one was applied. He believed that the practice in most Filipino homes was to apply new applications of floor wax again and again, without attempting to remove the remains of earlier waxings.[2]

Another characteristic which distinguished Gloss Wax from most other brands was the short duration of its shine. Other waxes on the Filipino market usually kept their luster for about a month, whereas a single application of Gloss stayed shiny for only 10 to 14 days. Mr. Tantoco did not think this characteristic affected his product's market acceptance. In his opinion, most Filipino homes had their floors waxed at least once,

---

[1] The free rate of exchange of the peso against the U.S. dollar in 1950 was approximately P3.00 = U.S. $1.00. In 1962, the free exchange rate changed so that P3.90 = U.S. $1.00, *Source: International Financial Statistics* (International Monetary Fund, Washington, D.C.), XVII, Number 1, January 1964, pp. 222–223.

[2] In Mr. Tantoco's opinion, almost all houses in the Philippines were potential customers for floor wax. Floors were usually made of concrete or wood. A survey by the Philippines Bureau of Census and Statistics in Manila proper during 1960 indicated that 60% of dwelling units were constructed of durable materials (i.e., concrete, brick, wood, with galvanized iron roofing or aluminum sheets, asbestos, etc.). About 14% of dwelling units in Manila were made of nondurable materials like bamboo, nipa, sawali, etc.; and the remaining 26% were a combination of durable and nondurable materials.

and frequently twice a week, often with the help of servants. He thought that it was unnecessary to produce a floor wax which retained its shine for long periods. "The Gloss formula," he said, "is adapted to the system of house cleaning in the Philippines." The company made no attempt to promote other uses of Gloss, outside of its use as a wax for polishing floors.

Gloss Wax was manufactured in natural and red colors, but red contributed the greater part of sales. The product was first packaged in one-gallon cans for the home market; and, in February 1965, five-gallon cans were introduced especially for institutional users. One-pound cans were tried for a while, but were dropped after a brief trial, so that the company could concentrate its selling efforts on the one- and five-gallon cans, where profits were larger per unit of sales. All containers were bright red with the brand name *Gloss* printed in black.

Market Strategy

Before Gloss Wax entered the Filipino market, floor wax was generally purchased from hardware stores, *sarisari* (general merchandise) stores, supermarkets, and grocery stores. Institutional buyers usually ordered direct from manufacturers. Government purchases were either made by procurement officers or by competitive public bidding, if the quantity and peso value were substantial. Prior to Gloss's market entry, Mr. Tantoco estimated that S. C. Johnson and Son, Philippines (a subsidiary of a large United States company), accounted for over 80% of floor-wax sales in the Philippines. The bulk of Johnson's sales came from institutional users, and households belonging to higher- and middle-income groups in Manila and suburbs, as well as from provincial cities.

A lack of capital at first prevented Mr. Tantoco from distributing Gloss through retailers, or from spending funds on consumer advertising. "My limited financial capacity forced me to sell direct to the housewife, which I thought was the best approach anyway," he said. "I don't believe much in advertising. Besides we didn't want our competitors to know we were in the market. If they knew, they would have put us out of business before we got started. We used the back-door system, and introduced Gloss by house-to-house selling on limited credit terms."

Mr. Tantoco initially rented space in the Manila district, and hired a laborer to help him produce the wax. Production required only such simple equipment as drums and burners. The plant had a capacity of 200 gallons a day, on one shift. To start, however, the company produced 60 gallons per day, which Mr. Tantoco himself sold to housewives in Manila. Buyers were given one week's credit, but accounts were collected promptly, to provide much needed working capital. Collections held up well, and sales improved steadily. Within a month, Mr. Tantoco had hired four salesmen.

TABLE 1

Philippines

Population and Households by Region: 1962

Regions	Population		Households		Average Size
TOTAL PHILIPPINES	29,698,000	100.00	5,042,105	100.00	5.89
Urban.................	10,810,072	36.4	1,714,316	34.0	6.31
Rural.................	18,887,928	63.6	3,327,789	66.0	5.68
Region 1 (Metropolitan Manila).................	2,304,100	100.00	349,106	100.00	6.60
Manila Proper..........	1,239,606	53.8	200,387	57.4	6.63
Suburbs..............	1,064,494	46.2	148,719	42.6	6.56
Region 2 (Ilocos Region).....	1,593,600	100.00	316,819	100.00	5.03
Urban.................	471,706	29.6	91,561	28.9	5.15
Rural.................	1,121,894	70.4	225,258	71.1	4.98
Region 3 (Cagayan Valley).................	1,121,600	100.00	183,268	100.00	6.12
Urban.................	296,102	26.4	43,985	24.0	6.73
Rural.................	825,498	73.6	139,283	76.0	5.93
Region 4 (Central Luzon).....	3,995,600	100.00	633,217	100.00	6.31
Urban.................	1,346,517	33.7	206,429	32.6	6.52
Rural.................	2,649,083	66.3	426,788	67.4	6.21
Region 5 (Southern Tagalog Provinces and Islands)..............	3,527,100	100.00	598,829	100.00	5.89
Urban.................	1,407,313	39.9	216,776	36.2	6.49
Rural.................	2,119,787	60.1	382,053	63.8	5.55
Region 6 (Bicol Region)......	2,567,200	100.00	414,733	100.00	6.19
Urban.................	716,249	27.9	106,586	25.7	6.72
Rural.................	1,850,951	72.1	308,147	74.3	6.01
Region 7 (Western Visayas).................	4,119,894	100.00	699,474	100.00	5.89
Urban.................	1,050,574	25.5	168,573	24.1	6.23
Rural.................	3,069,320	74.5	530,901	75.9	5.78
Region 8 (Eastern Visayas).................	4,316,400	100.00	774,937	100.00	5.57
Urban.................	1,113,631	25.8	191,409	24.7	5.82
Rural.................	3,202,769	74.2	583,528	75.3	5.49
Region 9 (South and Western Mindanao)..............	3,687,500	100.00	640,191	100.00	5.76
Urban.................	1,076,750	29.2	177,973	27.8	6.05
Rural.................	2,610,750	70.8	462,218	72.2	5.65
Region 10 (North and Eastern Mindanao)........	2,465,000	100.00	451,465	100.00	5.46
Urban.................	744,430	30.2	123,250	27.3	6.04
Rural.................	1,720,570	69.8	328,215	72.7	5.24

SOURCE: The urban-rural percentage breakdown of the population and households is based on the Statistical Survey of Households, October 1961, Bureau of Census and Statistics, Philippines.

The company planned to sell Gloss to the lower- and middle-income market, first in Manila and later throughout the Philippines. (See Tables 1 and 2 which indicate the Filipino population by regions, and the regional distribution of annual income groups in the Philippines.) It was not planned to sell Gloss to upper-income families. To encourage the market to try Gloss, Mr. Tantoco thought that it was necessary to have the housewife think that it was superior to S. C. Johnson's product. Consequently, he used a special introductory pricing policy, which allowed the housewife to try Gloss on a trial basis without obligation to purchase.

Mr. Tantoco decided that a satisfactory profit could be obtained by selling Gloss at a price equivalent to P3.80 per gallon. S. C. Johnson was

TABLE 2

Philippines

Distribution of Total Annual Income of Filipino Families by Three Income Groups within Regions, 1961

Region	Total	Under P2,500	P2,500 to 4,999	P5,000 and over
TOTAL PHILIPPINES	100%	87.1	9.1	3.9
Region 1	100	46.7	28.9	24.4
Region 2	100	90.6	6.6	2.6
Region 3	100	90.3	7.7	2.1
Region 4	100	75.1	12.0	2.8
Region 5	100	86.4	10.3	3.2
Region 6	100	94.1	3.9	2.0
Region 7	100	88.6	9.5	2.0
Region 8	100	95.4	3.4	1.4
Region 9	100	91.8	6.4	5.9
Region 10	100	92.1	5.7	2.2

NOTE: Percentages have been rounded.
SOURCE: Bureau of Census and Statistics, Philippines.

selling their floor wax at P7.50 per gallon. To suggest that Gloss was a superior product, Mr. Tantoco used an invoice price of P7.60 per gallon; as an introductory offer, however, an additional gallon was given free with each gallon purchased. Also, the superior luster of Gloss's shine was compared with the S. C. Johnson finish, and the product's water-resistance was emphasized through demonstration. These inducements, together with the credit and free home trial, successfully introduced Gloss to the market.

The company was faced with the problem of expanding the sales force to meet its growing market opportunities. From four salesmen the sales force was increased to 41 in October 1963 and to a peak of 99 in August, 1964. By 1965, the size of the sales force had stabilized at about 75. (See Table 3, which shows data on the number of Gloss salesmen and the vol-

TABLE 3

Gloss Wax Company

Sales Volume by Months and Number of Salesmen in Manila (Region 1)
for the Period September 1963–August 1965

Period		Volume of Sales (Gallons)	Salesmen* (Number)	Average Monthly Sales per (Gallons)
1963	September	14,289	37	386
	October	15,577	41	380
	November	12,428	31	401
	December	12,350	31	398
1964	January	16,503	44	375
	February	13,266	36	369
	March	14,675	36	408
	April	19,017	61	312
	May	13,365	72	186
	June	20,295	67	303
	July	21,377	80	267
	August	24,409	99	247
	September	21,168	81	261
	October	24,347	80	304
	November	22,929	78	294
	December	20,187	84	240
1965	January	23,577	78	302
	February	21,459	78	275
	March	23,940	78	307
	April	20,450	78	262
	May	20,202	69	293
	June	18,173	76	239
	July	19,394	76	255
	August	18,289	76	241

* *Salesmen* includes salesmen whose primary function is credit collection; all salesmen, however, do some credit collection work.

Source: Company records.

ume of monthly sales.) The office staff was composed of two female clerk/typists and three dispatcher/checkers.

FORMATION OF SALES FORCE

Recruitment and Selection

Mr. Tantoco personally selected all Gloss salesmen from applicants who were usually recruited from newspaper advertisements in Manila papers. An advertisement which ran for three days would produce about 50 applicants, from whom 5 to 7 men would be selected. Most of the men accepted by Mr. Tantoco were between 21 and 28 years old. Ideally, he preferred to choose his salesmen from high school and college graduates who had no practical selling experience, because he thought that older experienced salesmen were wise to many "loopholes" which might lead them to take advantage of the company. Men with some education were desired, because of the need to keep sales records and to handle money. In addition, Mr. Tantoco thought that greater employment of graduates was a positive contribution to the social and economic progress of the Philippines. Younger men were preferred for their greater enthusiasm and higher capacity for physical work. Sales managers and supervisors were selected by Mr. Tantoco on the basis of their honesty, seniority, and demonstrated capacity for hard work. With one or two exceptions, all sales managers and supervisors were promoted from within the Gloss sales organization.

All new salesmen were appointed for a probationary period of two weeks. During the first week they underwent formal training, which included lectures about the Gloss product, competitors' products, competitors' prices, *do's and dont's* in selling, and methods to use in closing a sale. Demonstrations and sales talks in the morning were followed by closely supervised field selling experience in the afternoons. Since all salesmen were engaged in credit collections at some time during a month, instructions were given on this responsibility.

Salesmen acted as order-takers for Gloss, and the product was delivered one or two days later by one of the company's drivers. In 1965, the company owned 18 panel vans, 2 trucks, and 6 jeeps. The drivers' responsibilities were confined to driving and delivery. All delivery-drivers employed by Gloss were trained by the company, to assure the high standards of courtesy and service to customers which Mr. Tantoco demanded.

"Today Gloss is on top," said Mr. Tantoco, "because our salesmen-collectors and drivers help each other. I don't consider myself boss. We work as a team. The average age of all employees is only 25 years. We encourage bachelor salesmen to marry, feeling that marriage increases their sense of responsibility. I am working on a plan now to provide furnished apartments for my managers and supervisors. This will give them a strong incentive to work hard, and to stay on with Gloss. The primary motivation for the sales force, however, is salary increases."

Sales Organization

The Gloss sales force in Manila made house-to-house calls seven days a week. Individual salesmen worked only six days each week, but Mr. Tantoco usually worked the full seven days. The company had no formal marketing organization until November 1963, when the sales force was split into five selling groups. When more salesmen were hired in April and May 1964, the number of selling groups was increased to ten. Each group consisted of about seven salesmen, an assistant supervisor and a supervisor. The supervisor was responsible for determining the routing and scheduling of customer calls. Eight of the groups were engaged in house-to-house selling, but two teams were established to canvass schools, hospitals, and business firms. Two unit managers were appointed by Mr. Tantoco, each to supervise five of the selling groups, and these two managers in turn reported to a branch manager responsible for all of Manila.

The same sales organization was used by Mr. Tantoco in 1965, when approximately 65% of Gloss sales were made in the Manila area. Three branch offices established in Northern, Central, and Southern Luzon dur-

FIGURE 1

Organization Chart, September 1965

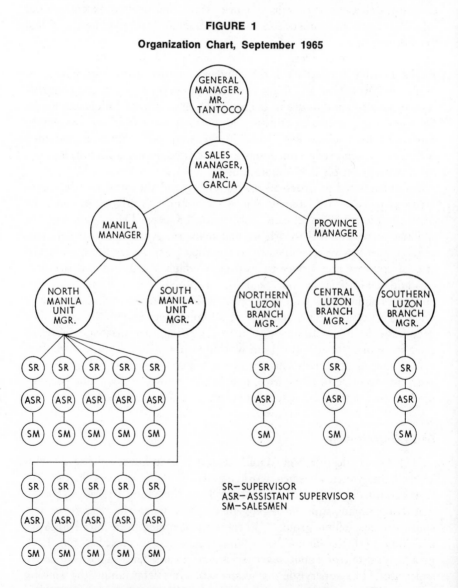

SR—SUPERVISOR
ASR—ASSISTANT SUPERVISOR
SM—SALESMEN

Source: From a description by Mr. Tantoco in September.

ing 1964, accounted for the remaining company sales. Each Luzon branch was staffed by one selling group, an assistant supervisor, a supervisor, and a manager. The three branch managers were responsible to a manager for the provinces, and along with the Manila manager, he reported to the company sales manager. Mr. Tantoco kept in close touch with the Gloss marketing organization through frequent consultations with Mr. Garcia, the new company sales manager. The former sales manager had recently resigned from the company for personal reasons. (The Gloss sales organization chart is shown in Figure 1. The specific responsibilities and duties of the marketing organization are shown in Appendix A.)

Compensation

It was useless, in Mr. Tantoco's opinion, to offer salesmen commissions based directly on the volume sold, when the market for a product of low unit value was good. He thought that it was better to provide each salesman with the opportunity to earn a salary increase every three months, based on their individual sales during the period against a daily sales quota. Company policy authorized a salary increase of P15 to P20 every three months. Starting salaries for salesmen were usually P120 per month. Mr. Tantoco was prepared to let salesmen's salaries increase to P300. The highest monthly pay for a Gloss salesman in September was P165. Company drivers were paid P120 per month.

Sales supervisors were paid between P180 and P240 monthly, but Mr. Tantoco thought that their salaries could increase to P350–P400. Branch and unit managers were paid in a range between P300 and P700 monthly, and the company sales manager received P800 per month. All members of the staff were paid an annual bonus in December, usually equivalent to one-month's salary, depending on profits. Cash bonuses were awarded occasionally for exceptional sales performances.

SALES FORCE OPERATIONS

Manila Sales Territories

In 1962, Mr. Tantoco first started selling in the middle- and lower-class suburban areas around Manila. Having no idea what the market reaction would be, he systematically moved his growing sales force throughout the Manila metropolitan area. Wherever a concentration of buying interest took place, salesmen were instructed to work the area thoroughly before moving on. Within six months, the company had covered the Manila market about three times. By 1965, Mr. Tantoco estimated that one call in seven produced an average sale of one gallon. Each salesman kept a daily record of sales, and of the brand of floor wax used, other than Gloss.

It was not until November 1963, that Mr. Tantoco set up sales territories in Manila and organized his salesmen into five groups. After one year of operations, the company had a good idea of those middle- and lower-income suburban areas where Gloss sales were strongest. Territories were divided by Mr. Tantoco according to the productivity of each area, as measured by the level of income and the number of homes. The objective was to develop territories with equal sales potential.

The slow growth of sales in early 1964, together with more competitive conditions, made Mr. Tantoco increase the number of sales territories and the size of the sales force in April and May 1964. The number of salesmen was nearly doubled and the sales territories were increased from five to eight. This action became necessary, in Mr. Tantoco's judgment, to meet S. C. Johnson's recent move into C.O.D. (collect on delivery) house-to-house selling, the main impact of which was felt in the middle-income market areas in Manila. Price competition also had become more severe. In 1963, S. C. Johnson had reduced its price of a gallon of floor wax from P7.50 to P6.30. A major price reduction was introduced by the company again in early 1964, when the price of Johnson's floor wax was lowered to P3.95 per gallon. About the same time, another competitor had moved into the house-to-house market, with credit terms similar to Gloss.

During this period of increased competition, the company made certain that the Manila home market was saturated by Gloss. This was accomplished by increasing the call frequency of the sales force, so that each territory was covered at least once every three to four weeks. Mr. Tantoco planned to serve all fast-consuming customers so that they were never without Gloss. Although no special analysis had ever been made, he estimated the following usage rates of Gloss in 1965:

Percent of Customers	Time Period Required to Use 1 Gallon of Gloss
5	less than 2 weeks
10	2 weeks–1 month
80	1 month–6 months
5	6 months–12 months
100	

In May 1964, two more selling groups were established to concentrate on the floor wax market in schools, hospitals, and business. One institutional group worked in Manila north of the Pasig river, while the other worked the southern part of the city. The company frequently submitted bids for government contracts, but Gloss had not made significant sales to this market. Mr. Tantoco said that it was difficult to meet competitive price levels on sealed government bids. In 1965, he estimated that 80% of Gloss' sales were made by house-to-house selling, and 20% of sales were to institutional users.

Every day, each company sales group made about 700 calls. Around 100 of these calls produced sales with an average of one gallon of Gloss per call. Most salesmen were able to make 90 to 100 calls per day. Each salesman was given a daily quota of 20 gallons, which he was not expected to achieve on any given day, but he was expected to average over a three-month period. Performance against this quota was used by Mr. Tantoco to decide salary increases every three months. Each salesman spent about six to eight days of each month doing credit collection work.

Relations with the Consumer

Every morning, company salesmen in Manila met at the Gloss head office for 15 to 30 minutes. The sales managers used these daily briefings for administrative purposes, sales pep talks, and checks on the salesmen's appearance. Sales supervisors and their groups reviewed selling techniques and whatever problems arose. The supervisors issued instructions on customer call patterns for the day.

Mr. Tantoco encouraged his salesmen to be friendly and courteous to the housewife. *The Mrs.*, as Mr. Tantoco called her, made the buying decision on household purchases almost all the time. In very few families were household servants given authority to buy from door-to-door salesmen. Each Gloss representative wore a white shirt and carried a company identification card. On days when salesmen made collections in the field, they returned to the head office in the afternoon to bank their receipts with the company.

During Gloss's introductory period in the Manila market, the salesmen used the "free sample" approach, product demonstrations, and credit extension, to induce the housewife to try the new floor wax. Over the next three years, Gloss gradually gained outstanding acceptance in lower- and middle-income homes. The need for product demonstration fell off as salesmen did more repeat business, but pricing strategy and credit policy continued to play an important part in maintaining sales.

In early 1964, when housewives complained about having to take two gallons of Gloss to obtain a price of P3.80 per gallon, Mr. Tantoco changed his sales appeal by offering one-half a gallon of Gloss for P3.95 and giving every buyer an additional half a gallon free. Later in 1964, when S. C. Johnson suddenly reduced the price of a gallon of its wax to P3.95, Mr. Tantoco did not reduce the price of his wax. Instead, he retaliated by raising his price to P4.00 per gallon. Included in his price were two boxes of cleaning powder. Next time around, the customer was offered only one box of cleaning powder with the wax, and on the third call Gloss was sold by itself at P4.00 per gallon. In 1965, the price was raised to P4.50.

Each selling group included three or four men whose primary responsibility was collection of accounts due. Ordinarily, Gloss was sold on credit terms of 7–15 days. For several days after the bimonthly Filipino paydays on the 15th and 30th of every month, the Gloss sales force returned to the homes where recent purchases had been made. Each month, it was necessary to call on about 3,000 customers for collection purposes.

Mr. Tantoco considered the excellent collection record maintained by Gloss salesmen to be a major factor in his company's success. He estimated that only 1% of accounts receivable became bad debts. The first call for payment usually recovered 60%, the second call 20% and the remainder was collected by the fifth house call. The timing of the collection was an important reason for the low credit losses. The relatively small amount owed by the customer, and the regular personal follow-up by the company, kept bad debts to a minimum. The main cause of bad debts was the unexpected change-of-address of families. In 1964–65, 5 to 10 customers moved away without warning every month.

Controlling the Sales Force

One of the principal purposes of the daily briefing sessions was to motivate the sales force. This regular meeting was important to Mr. Tantoco, since he believed that the behavior of Gloss salesmen reflected the personality of the company. In his view, the company should do what it could to help the development of individual salesmen.

After three years of operations, Mr. Tantoco believed that he was familiar with the major problems of his sales force. These problems fell into three categories. First there was the salesman who joined the company simply to learn about Gloss's plans and strategies. This type later left the company and sold his services to a competitor at a higher price. Because of this, Mr. Tantoco was careful to prevent the salesmen from knowing very much about the overall operations of the company. A second problem was that some Gloss salesmen tended to lose their selling enthusiasm after a period which ranged from four months to two years. Mr. Tantoco said that he or his managers personally encouraged individual salesmen whose productivity showed signs of falling seriously.

The third problem was the behavior of dishonest salesmen. Mr. Tantoco said that experience had taught the company what "tricks" to expect. One of the major responsibilities of Gloss managers was to follow up any evidence of dishonest actions by salesmen. For example, a salesman would make a credit sale to a customer, for which he would collect during a later collection period. Instead of passing on the payment to the company, the salesman would pocket the money himself. To cover his action, he would mark on the credit invoice that the customer had left his residence without a forwarding address. Between 1962 and 1964, Mr. Tantoco was very lenient with offenders. He tried to help such employees by talking to them and giving them a chance to reform. Only five sales-men were actually dismissed for dishonest behavior during the company's first 2½ years. The increasing incidence of offenses during 1964, forced him to change company policy on this problem.

Early in 1965, he selected about 15 of the worst offenders, dismissed them from the company, and laid formal charges against them with the local police station. After several days in jail the men were released, and the charges were withdrawn. Mr. Tantoco intended this action to pro-vide a lesson for the rest of the sales force. Over the next several months, about 20 more salesmen resigned, but new acts of dishonesty were effec-tively discouraged. In the first six months of 1965, the Gloss sales force underwent about a 50% turnover.

Mr. Tantoco measured the efficiency of each salesman by the follow-ing three criteria: (1) Did he meet his quota? (2) Did his customers pay on schedule? (3) What amount was outstanding on his customers' ac-counts after collection day?

A system was introduced so that for every three gallons for which a salesman could not collect from his customers, the salesman was docked one gallon by the company. This was designed to teach the salesman a lesson and to keep down the rate of bad debts. Despite his many other activities in the company, Mr. Tantoco kept a close watch on the opera-tions of the Gloss sales force. "As a Chinese," he said, "I cannot let other people handle my business completely."

Other Selling Methods.   As noted earlier, an important part of Mr. Tantoco's strategy was to keep the Manila floor wax market saturated with Gloss at all times. He was, therefore, concerned about the supply problem for customers who unexpectedly ran out of Gloss, between calls by company salesmen. For the convenience of such customers, he attempted to appoint selected retailers in those suburbs where Gloss was in strong demand, but he found it difficult to find retailers who were willing to cooperate. Many protested that Gloss would not offer a fast stock turnover, because of the company's home distribution policy. A limited number of retailers in Manila agreed to carry stocks of Gloss on a consignment basis, for a 10% markup on cost. Mr. Tantoco estimated that Gloss sales through retail outlets accounted for only 10% of total sales in 1965.

The company did not undertake any consumer advertising. From 1962 to 1964, the company's marketing strategy relied completely on personal selling. During this period, Mr. Tantoco resisted frequent ap-proaches from advertising agencies. Finally, in January 1965, he agreed to try sporadic radio spot announcements and medium-sized billboards in heavy traffic areas in Manila and its suburbs. This small-scale advertising campaign was discontinued after a few months because Mr. Tantoco thought it was not adding significantly to the company's sales.

COMPETITION

In 1965, the 14 floor-wax manufacturing companies in the Philippines were distributed as follows: Manila and suburbs—7; Cebu City—3; other areas in Visayas—2; and Mindanao—2. The dominant brands in the market were Johnson Wax, YCO Wax, Gloss Wax, and Sanitone. S. C. Johnson and Son was estimated by Mr. Tantoco to have less than one-half of the total national market in 1965.[3] The other leading manufacturers, including Gloss, were primarily owned and operated by permanent residents of the Philippines.

Like Johnson Wax, the sales volume of YCO came primarily from institutional sales, government sales, and high- and middle-income group households. Other brands derived sales primarily from middle- and low-income group households and medium-sized commercial establishments in Manila and the suburbs.

Floor-wax companies typically relied on their own salesmen to distribute their products directly to the approximately 90,000 retailers throughout the Philippines. Following Gloss's success with house-to-house sales, the other leading producers attempted to duplicate the personal selling system introduced by Mr. Tantoco. Competitors attracted Gloss salesmen away by higher salary offers, and later tried to copy Gloss's higher-price strategy. The policy of market saturation implemented by Gloss Wax made it difficult, however, for competitors to make serious inroads into the Gloss markets.

S. C. Johnson engaged in heavy advertising expenditures. Johnson's natural and red paste wax were advertised along with its family products (i.e., insecticides, air freshener, furniture wax, and car-washing cream) in colored advertisements in the *Sunday Times Magazine*, the *Weekly Women's Magazine*, and other nationwide publications. Johnson's also sponsored "People Are Funny," a highly rated television program which came on at eight o'clock on Sunday evenings.

The manufacturer of YCO floor wax advertised exclusively through the use of national magazines and radio and TV spots. Both Johnson and YCO wax products used such slogans as: *Shines are longer lasting. For easy application. Protects as it beautifies. One waxing lasts for months. Never sticky or smeary. Made of quality hard wax.*

FUTURE SALES FORCE PLANS

Mr. Tantoco had invited his sales manager to discuss ways in which the operations of the Gloss sales force in Manila could be improved. Recent signs that the level of Gloss sales was stabilizing had pleased Mr. Tantoco. He believed that the company should not try to eliminate competition, but aim to hold its market share among lower- and middle-income families

---

[3] No official published data were available on total floor-wax sales in the Philippines.

at between 70 and 85%. Under the present distribution system, Mr. Tantoco estimated that selling expenses for Gloss were about 33% of sales; thus, for every gallon of Gloss sold at P4.50, about P1.50 was used to cover selling costs.

Present trends in the industry suggested that Gloss could expect increasing competition from other manufacturers. Several companies had copied Gloss's system of house-to-house selling in selected districts of Manila, and some had increased their advertising expenditures. Mr. Tantoco believed that he could keep his company one step ahead of its competitors. In October 1965, for example, he planned to introduce an innovation in Gloss's Floor Wax container. Instead of the usual tin, he intended to pack Gloss in a plastic jug, which the consumer could use in the home after the wax was used.

Mr. Tantoco found justification for his company's large sales force chiefly in the following four reasons: (1) It enabled the company to give prompt service to fast consumers of Gloss; (2) It kept the market saturated with Gloss and helped to prevent the entry of competitive products; (3) The company did no advertising; (4) It promoted the socio-economic program of the government. He thought, however, that increasing their available selling time might improve the use of the existing sales force. Mr. Tantoco considered that the time now used by salesmen in traveling to and from the head office for briefings, and to deposit cash collections with the company, could be reduced. He wondered whether the company should set up branch offices in each territory in Manila to handle such administrative functions.

Mr. Garcia thought that the time saved might not be worth the loss of control now exercised by top management. He was more in favor of reducing the size of the existing sales force. He considered that the present requirement of making a monthly call on all lower- and middle-class homes in Manila was an unnecessary waste of sales effort. He proposed that a selective call pattern policy be adopted, so that fast consumers of Gloss might be given the service which they required, while the bulk of the market could be approached on a less frequent basis, say, every two to three months.

This discussion made Mr. Tantoco uncertain about what changes should be made in the operations of the company sales force. He believed that he and Mr. Garcia needed time to review the matter more carefully. For their next meeting, Mr. Tantoco asked Mr. Garcia to prepare a list of whatever changes the sales manager felt were necessary to improve the operating efficiency of the Gloss sales force, together with a valid argument for the adoption of these changes.

APPENDIX A: RESPONSIBILITIES AND DUTIES OF THE GLOSS MARKETING ORGANIZATION, SEPTEMBER 1965[1]

A Sales Supervisor

1. Acts as the leader of the group in the field. Before leaving for the field assignment, he checks the number of stocks actually assigned for sale. He checks the invoices that are assigned to each and every salesman. He furnishes himself with all the necessary forms, which he fills out with information for the guidance of the office. He receives instructions for the day from the unit managers before actually leaving for the field.
2. While in the field, he gives a five-minute briefing and lecture on the strategy of sales for the salesmen to assimilate and follow in a given assigned territory.
3. While the salesmen are actually selling the product to the house-to-house customers, the sales supervisor observes their manner of presenting the product and convincing the prospective customer.
4. He back-checks all invoices issued by the salesmen for all sales on account, and thereafter countersigns the invoices, to certify that the sale is really on account, that the name of the customer is correctly specified, and that the house number and street are correct and specific.
5. He fills out all the office forms furnished to him with the required information.
6. While back in the office during the afternoon, he checks the number of stocks left unsold and returns them to the stock clerk. Finally, he submits his reports for the day to the unit manager.
7. He performs any other duties and functions that the exigencies of the service may demand.

Unit Managers

1. Are responsible for the preparation of daily territorial assignments for each group or team of salesmen.
2. Give daily instructions and briefings to the sales supervisors before leaving for the field assignments.
3. Check the daily reports being prepared and submitted by the sales supervisors, and make proper observation and comments.
4. Prepare weekly reports about the achievements of all salesmen, and submit said reports to the sales manager.
5. Conduct monthly meetings with the sales supervisors and salesmen, with the aim of assisting them in the solution of whatever problems are encountered in the field.
6. Conduct field investigations to find out the prevailing conditions of

---

[1] *Source:* Company records.

competition and other material matters which may affect the flow of sales of Gloss wax.

7. Pay courtesy visits to good customers of Gloss. They also try to discover why certain customers find it hard to pay their bills within the allowed time. They receive comments from Gloss customers and submit them to the sales manager.

8. Perform whatever other functions may be required by the exigencies of the service.

A Manager for Manila and Suburbs

1. Is directly responsible to the sales manager for the conduct of the sales force and the success or failure of the sales for each and every period of time.

2. Is responsible for the preparation of the plans, systems, and procedures to be undertaken which may tend to combat and weaken competition in any given area or territory.

3. Conducts monthly meetings with the senior members of the sales force and periodically briefs the salesmen whenever it becomes necessary.

4. Prepares and submits monthly reports to the sales manager about the actual status and condition of the sales for the month.

5. Assists the unit managers in field investigations whenever necessity so requires.

6. Performs such functions that may be assigned to him by the sales manager and assumes responsibilities as required by the nature of his office.

A Manager for the Provincial Branches

1. Is directly responsible to the sales manager for the conduct of the personnel and sales condition of the different branch offices.

2. Prepares monthly report on the sales condition of the different provincial branch offices.

3. Conducts investigations at the different branch offices to observe the operation and projects being undertaken.

4. Checks the stocks and invoices sent to the branch offices.

5. Conducts seasonal inventory of the stocks, money, properties, and other assets of the company in the branch offices.

6. Receives remittances from the branch offices, to be accounted for in the central office.

7. Requires the branch managers to make the requisite reports and to provide information for the guidance of the central office.

8. Performs such other functions as may be assigned from time to time and assumes such other responsibilities that the assignment may require.

A Company Sales Manager

1. Is responsible for the success or failure of the marketing function.
2. Approves recommendations by the subordinate members of the staff which may ultimately serve the interests of the concern.
3. Conducts monthly staff meetings.
4. Represents the management in all affairs and activities with public and government personnel.
5. Reports to the management about the state of affairs of the concern.
6. Performs such other duties and functions which may be required by the assignment.

Sierra Chocolate Company

Starting in 1961 management of the Sierra Chocolate Company had initiated a program to upgrade the competence of the company's field sales organization. Special steps were taken to recruit college and MBA graduates with high management potential. These men were given initial job assignments in the sales force to better prepare them for product management and other positions. At the same time training practices, manpower evaluation programs and compensation plans were altered to encourage a higher level of sales performance.

In 1965 the National Sales Manager commissioned a consultant to "give us an outside view of how things are going." It was decided that the study should focus upon Sierra's compensation plan because it was argued that performance and incentives should be closely related. But the consultant was asked to consider compensation in its broadest aspects, namely to consider not only the mechanics of the plan but its administration.

After reading the report the Sales Manager was convinced that its findings required significant alterations in Sierra sales management practices. He debated what action to take.

The Company and Industry

The 1965 sales for Sierra were close to $100,000,000, placing the company among the giants of the food industry. Its product lines included eating chocolate, cooking chocolate, pre-packaged desserts, frozen specialties and cookies. Exhibit 1 shows in summary the Company's organization.

The 245 general line salesmen called on wholesalers and direct retail accounts. There were 3,000 direct retail accounts which contributed 60% of Sierra's sales volume. There was a trend toward direct selling because of the manufacturer's need to obtain prime retail shelf position and because of recent consolidation trends within the retail trades. As a rule wholesalers were used in sparsely populated areas or in the solicitation of smaller retail accounts.

Sierra salesmen had two responsibilities: to obtain trade cooperation (in the form of shelf position, floor displays, advertisements, etc.) and to write orders. Some salesmen spent 90% of their time "servicing" individual chain outlets even though a direct salesman had already received an order from the chain buying office. Direct salesmen, usually the senior and most experienced men, concentrated on the chain buying offices and large independents. All salesmen were paid within a range of $85 to $140 per week and participated as well in a district bonus pool based upon reaching quota.

It was the function of the supervisor to lead a team of between 4–10 salesmen and to sell personally a few of the most important direct accounts in the territory. The supervisors averaged three days each week traveling with the salesmen and reviewing their progress.

District managers spent most of their time on administrative matters, being responsible for local inventory, the flow of reports and local strategic recommendations, personnel matters, the supervision and development of supervisors and the handling of one or two major direct accounts.

Competition was fierce in the industry but Sierra's overall share of market was 22%. It ranged from 40% in sweet chocolate to as low as 8% in frozen specialties and cookies. Districts, in turn, had various levels of acceptance with the share of market varying between "less than 1%" (in the midwest) and 48% (in New England).

The regional managers were primarily "large scale" district managers and operated out of the firm's Chicago headquarters. These men averaged 40% of their time in the districts and 60% at the home office. An important part of their function was to help the product managers develop promotions pertinent to the separate regions. They also approved district recommendations for salary increases, the hiring, firing and promotion of local personnel, and changes in account coverage tactics.

In addition to its field sales organization, Sierra placed heavy emphasis upon advertising and product management. In 1965, for example, the Company spent $15 million dollars for national advertising and local promotional programs. Whereas national advertising expenditures (TV primarily) exceeded promotional expenditures 2 to 1 in 1957, the pendulum had swung by 1965 so that local deals and promotions represented 55% of the total budget. Local deals included such examples as buying allowances (to the retailers), feature payments (for retailer-placed advertisements), and off-label packs (such as "10¢ off").

For each product line there was a product manager whose job it was to decide the advertising and promotional budget, to introduce package and price variations, to suggest research and test market projects and to help set yearly quotas. Most men in these positions, and their assistants, were hired from MBA programs and given a six-month field selling assignment before being returned to the home office. The starting pay for such trainees was considerably higher than for new salesmen (about $150 higher per month) and a product manager earned about the same as a regional manager (between $18,000 and $26,000). The product managers in 1965 were respectively 31, 32, 32, 35 and 36 years old. In contrast, the average regional manager was 44 years old and the average district manager 36.

The Consultant's Report

The compensation audit was based upon in-depth interviews with all personnel in 5 of the 20 districts. It was the National Sales Manager's belief that the five districts selected for analysis represented a fair cross section of the field sales organization. In addition, the consultant made use of certain national sales data maintained at headquarters.

The consultant's report is summarized below and organized as follows:

1. A summary of local salary practices (in five districts)
2. National averages
3. Implications of current compensation practices
4. Factors that determine local salary practices

A SUMMARY OF SALARY MATTERS

Knowledge of Salary Matters

Among the five districts there are wide differences in knowledge of compensation matters. Some salesmen know the range for their job; others do not. Some understand how budgets are set for the bonus plan; others do not. It follows that some local managers tolerate, and even encourage, discussions of salary while others refuse to let their men raise such issues. As a result, the intensity and extent of compensation complaints among the salesmen varies widely throughout the districts.

Use of the Range

It is somewhat surprising that few field sales managers make use of the full salary range of $85–$140 per week. Most managers avoid the extremes and defend their action by voicing strong opinions about the purpose of the low and high limits of the salary range.

For example, the starting pay is ordinarily set above the minimum, but by varying amounts. Some supervisors stretch the initial offer in order to attract the unusual man. But not all. Other supervisors are violently opposed to such tactics. One, for example, regularly pays his new men $5 or $10 below the "going rate" so that he can give an early raise. There is, in short, no real agreement among the managers about the proper starting salary.

There are, similarly, disagreements about the top of the range. In general most field sales managers operate within the confines of self-imposed limitations concerning maximum earnings. Thus, one district manager leaves a cushion at the top of the scale to be used only for the outstanding salesman "about to retire." Another remarked: "You never put a salesman at the top unless he is perfect or going on to new opportunities." And a third maintains; "Men should be paid their worth." This same manager, on the other hand, went on to describe how he had limited to $6 the final increase for his best salesman due to retire in five months: "You never give a bigger raise than $4, $5, or $6." Despite his qualifications, the senior man was deprived of the $140 maximum.

Although the evidence to support their position is not convincing, some managers argue that the top of the scale in Sierra is reserved to senior career men because "able young men will be promoted before they reach that level."

Size and Frequency of Raises

Although most managers argue that they grant wage increases "as earned," the fact is that increases are better explained as being *automatic*, *emotional* or *opportunistic*. Merit may play a part but it is mentioned as the cause by the managers only because they know the "approved vocabulary" of the home office.

Several managers had a *balance concept*—they tried to maintain an "acceptable" distribution among the salaries of their men. An acceptable distribution presumably resembles the traditional "bell-shaped" curve; that is, a concentration of payments at the mid-point of the range and a gradual decline toward the extremes. Although balance in this sense is not generally discussed, it does exist, and tempers the salary practices of the managers. There was no evidence, however, that supervisors were influenced similarly, possibly because each supervisor handles too few salesmen to permit an even distribution of compensation.

Another criterion for granting a wage increase is *time since the last raise*. It outranks merit most of the time. Before he recommends an increase a typical manager will ask: "Is the timing correct?" There is no absolute formula for the answer, though the acceptable company standard seems to be a time between increases of 12 months.

In two of the districts, to be specific, it was evident that most salesmen received raises about once each year. The pattern, it is important to note, was not entirely regular. During a salesman's early days with the company, the raises came faster; they slowed down when earnings hit "the average." In each of these districts, the neophyte's first increase was granted between the 4th and 6th month of employment. The next raises were at longer intervals until finally the 12 month average was attained. Some managers took the position that whereas time was the major criterion for an increase during the early days of a man's employment, merit was the eventual factor. Actually this is not always true—time is always the dominant consideration but because field managers informally recognize $120 to $130 as a "normal wage" they are forced to lengthen the span between increases when salaries reach this norm. Time, as a criterion, was well described by two of the managers:

I would sure like to award increases whenever I felt they were due, but for now I am going along with the boss.

If I put a man in for a raise every 3 or 4 months, the raises would never be granted—so I don't bother anymore unless 10 or 20 months have passed.

A third supervisor said that he recently found himself considering a man for an increase because "it had been so long since the last one." Upon closer examination the supervisor realized that the man was incompetent. So he fired him instead.

Seniority is another basis for giving wage increases and is related

FIGURE 1

Wage Level in Relation to Seniority, District "A"

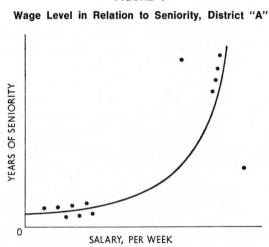

closely to this question of timing. Wage practices throughout the Company, as a result, reflect considerably the seniority of the men. In one district, for example, the wage/years-of-service relationship can be plotted as shown in Figure 1.

Each dot represents a salesman in the district. With but two exceptions, it can be seen that high income is reserved for senior salesmen.

Evaluation of Performance

Evaluation and compensation are intimately related. Whether the compensation is financial or nonfinancial, it should reward a salesman for a measurable level of performance. Measurement justifies the payment. Measurement, because it is so critical, warrants further discussion.

What to measure is a provoking consideration. Should a salesman, to be exact, be held accountable for his volume, his selling techniques and practices, his habits, his personal traits, or his potential for advancement? Managers can be found who support one or more of these alternatives. Some, therefore, want their men to reach quota (results), to use their selling aids in making each presentation (techniques), to be aggressive and imaginative (personal traits), or to have the breadth of vision to move ahead into management.

These measurement differences mean that the evaluation aspects of compensation are as varied among districts as the pay practices already cited. Such variations mean also that local managers typically introduce into their ratings a number of personal biases.

Whatever the bias, however, it appears further that wage increases are usually granted in the spirit of "well done," instead of "here's how you can improve to get even more."

NATIONAL AVERAGES

Are these illustrations from the 5 districts typical of the national organization? An analysis of headquarters' data shows that the problem is national and permits a number of generalizations:

1. Salesmen's Salaries Do Not Correlate with Selling Ability. Perhaps the easiest way to illustrate this disturbing observation is by a simple table. Thus below, salary averages are shown by years of service (from "less than 1 year" to "over 10") and by performance rating ("Satisfactory," "Good," "Superior"). We would hope to find higher salaries for the Good and Superior salesmen, but do not:

Salary Averages by Performance Rating and Seniority

Performance Rating*	Years of Service					
	−1	1	2	3	4	5
Satisfactory	$103	$105	$110	$127	$125	$132
Good	109	108	114	114	118	110
Superior	106	110	112	114	—	115
No. of men	27	58	22	7	5	3

Performance Rating*	6	7	8	9	10	10+
Satisfactory	—	$120	$123	$119	$120	$126
Good	122	122	128	125	128	125
Superior	127	124	126	119	130	130
No. of men	12	19	34	13	15	70

* The assumption is made that the performance ratings for salesmen made during the Sales Selection Procedure Study in 1958 and in subsequent follow-up studies, represent reasonable indicators of actual performance.

It is clear that the salary averages do not distinguish Superior (and Good) from Satisfactory salesmen. Seniority is the important explanation of salary level.

This fact can be deducted by another comparison, this time between "level of education," "seniority," and "average pay." We would hope to find education rewarded:

All Sierra Salesmen

	Years of Service				
Educational Level	0–1	2–3	4–6	7–10	11+
High school..................	$110	$115	$121	$126	$125
1–3 yrs. college...............	106	116	125	125	125
College graduate..............	110	113	123	125	123

We can only conclude from this table that either education and selling ability have no relationship (which is certainly possible) or seniority overpowers other considerations when increases are granted.

2. *Salary Increases Are Awarded Every 12 Months.* To prove the accuracy of this statement is easy. We can calculate the average time between the last two raises for salesmen throughout the United States. These averages are 11.8 months and 11.6 months respectively.

3. *Managers Themselves Impose Informal Limits on Wages.* It was stated earlier that in the districts studied, it seemed that salesmen received regular and frequent pay increases until their earnings reached some norm or midpoint. From that time on, raises were less frequent and in smaller increments. The national averages prove that this observation is the rule, not the exception:

All Sierra Salesmen

	Service (in Years)				
	0–1	2–3	4–6	7–10	11+
No. of salesmen........	134	36	22	88	79
Average salary.........	$109	$114	$123	$125	$125
Range...............	$90–140	$100–134	$110–134	$105–148	$105–145

It should be noted that the average salary rises nicely from $109 for men with less than 1 year of experience to $123 for men between 4 and 6 years. At that point the typical increase diminishes and the average wage for the two senior categories is the same.

4. *Men with Management Potential Are Paid the Same as Men Without.* Once again we are faced with the overpowering impact of seniority

upon wages. The next table summarizes average salary by years of senior-ity, but sub-classified between those men who are considered promotable within one year and those who are not:

Promotability/Salary/Years of Service

Promotability Rating	Years of Service				
	0–1	2	3	4	5
Within 1 year-Salary.............	$109	$114	$117	—	$111
No. of Men.....................	20	13	3	—	1
Not within 1 year-Salary..........	$108	$111	$121	$122	$124
No. of Men.....................	66	12	5	4	2

Promotability Rating	6	7	8	9	10+
Within 1 year-Salary.............	$125	$137	$125	$125	$126
No. of Men.....................	5	6	13	6	29
Not within 1 year-Salary.........	$123	$124	$127	$121	$126
No. of Men.....................	7	12	18	5	57

These data dramatize the fact that those recommended for immediate promotion earn no higher salaries than their colleagues. The able men, to be sure, seem to have a slight edge during their first two years of employ-ment (indicating perhaps a higher starting wage) and after the 6th year. Any conclusions, however, must be tempered by the inadequate number of cases in some of the seniority categories.

If we examine wage data in a slightly different way, we can find some evidence that young men with management ability receive a slight salary advantage. Let us assume, for this purpose, that "$131 or over" represents top pay. Our query is: "What percentage of the salesmen in various se-niority categories receive top money?" The results are interesting:

Sierra Salesmen

Years of Seniority	Ratio of Men Making $131+ to Total Men in Category	Percentage of Men in Category
2–3......................	1/36	3
4–6.....................	5/22	23
7–10....................	10/88	11
11+....................	16/79	20

What does this mean?

Intriguing though this evidence is, it is embarrassingly sketchy. The numbers are small (only 32 men in all) and the age brackets have been arbitrarily selected. We must assume, also, that men with over 7 years of service have no management potential (otherwise they would have been promoted).

In terms of these limitations, we can observe the data. The top pay percentages are at 4–6 years and over 11. In the younger group we would expect to find the promotable men. They move into management before the next seniority bracket. By this reasoning, the 7–10 year men are the career salesmen. Their peak wages are not attained until they arrive at the most senior category.

IMPLICATIONS OF CURRENT COMPENSATION PRACTICES

Sierra salary policy is not consistent. Local field sales managers impose their own criteria, yet there seem to be some generally held field beliefs about a salesman's "worth" or "value."

There is quite evidently an overriding bias toward seniority, at least after the salesman's salary has reached $125 per week. This phenomenon may be understandable, but it creates a situation of potential conflict as top management tries to apply new value or performance standards, namely merit.

Field managers, when caught in this predicament, are prone to say one thing (i.e., "raises are based on merit") while practicing another (i.e., granting increases for seniority). By this subterfuge, the managers preserve their traditions while demonstrating (verbally) to the outside world their conformity with the new standards.

That many field sales managers can be so described is not due solely to their perversity. Home office requirements do not always conform with local definitions of "fairness." For example, top management argues that raises should be given when earned, and not on an annual basis. There is, however, no cost of living allowance built into the salary structure. Many local managers, whether justifiably or not, consider minimum annual increases as necessary, if the salesmen are to keep abreast of increased living costs.

But these managers must "disguise" the real purpose of the increases by describing them as "earned" and by insuring that they are spaced just short of, or just beyond, 12 months.

The local argument is telling. If a salesman does not receive a boost he has taken, ipso facto, a cut in pay. Managers, it can be added, are more aware of this reality than the salesmen, and not only talk about it openly but include it in their salary philosophy.

This same philosophy has one unexpected twist which explains why some top salesmen earn less than the maximum salary. Unless the top producer can be given an increase, he cannot keep up with inflation. The weakness to this position, of course, is the implied assumption that the company will not raise the salary limits—an argument without foundation.

A second sales management conflict centers about the cost of hiring college graduates. Headquarters is willing to pay the market price for men with presumed potential. Field sales managers, in contrast, are less willing. They are under pressure to produce immediate volume; their world is today's problems. They are less inclined, as a consequence, to pay a premium for potential results.

One aspect of this concentration upon current volume is the occasional temptation for local managers to retain, by hiding, their best salesmen. Unless the home office is alert to this possibility, it is no trick for the hard-pressed field supervisor to raise a few well-timed doubts about the readiness of his key men for advancement.

To some extent, field practices are the result of honest confusion about the company's real intention. It is the official policy, for example, to grant wage increases on the basis of merit. Such a policy implies that selling jobs have definable values. Compensation is the reward for producing these values. Nonetheless, the home office promotes some men without paying the minimum of the new job. This inconsistency happens, presumably, because the candidate has recently received a raise, or, if he were to receive the full amount, would be paid "too large a single increase." Through the eyes of the field men this practice supports their assumptions that "time since the last raise," "size of the last raise," and "seniority" are preferred criteria. Field personnel, in effect, interpret home office practice as evidence that selling positions do not have absolute values and that salary range is partly fiction.

A further area of disagreement centers about field and home office viewpoints about the bonus plan. A number of local personnel have concluded that the "original" plan worked well (and the present one doesn't) because the first plan was accompanied by the successful introduction of new products. With this as the hypothesis, these people have been led to ask whether headquarters really wants to pay a bonus on existing products or only when there is need to get new products "off the ground."

In a number of respects, then, there is misunderstanding between field and home office managers. What, if anything, is the effect of these differences upon the salesmen themselves?

Potentially the most "explosive" problem is that of the lost generation. As top management introduces new performance standards, there is created in the field a "lost generation." This is the group of 35 to 40 year old salesmen who joined the company when seniority and experience were prerequisites for advancement. Suddenly these men find that promotion goes to the young man with analytic ability. Old timers are not only unqualified, but "over age."

There are times when salesmen evidence concern about local salary practices. Occasionally they are given "a glimpse" of reality when one of their colleagues quits the company and, before going, talks about his pay experiences. Such insights can be disturbing if they fail to match the listener's own monetary experiences and assumptions about compensation.

The fact that MBA's are often granted unusual salaries is learned, at times, by the local salesmen. Such information usually invalidates personal beliefs and concepts and reveals a double standard of pay. Fortunately, this kind of knowledge is restricted typically to local managers, whose resentment about this inequity is no less genuine.

One can speculate that much of the salesman's disillusionment (when it happens) occurs because his standards and beliefs have been a projection of his own salary experience. His assumptions about Sierra pay practices, the realizable range, and the value of a given performance are personal. Indeed, he usually exaggerates the speed and limit of raises because of his early experience in these regards.

It is not surprising, therefore, that there are some bitter complainers in the field. The trouble spots seem to concentrate (1) on the bonus system in districts where the men had realized high earnings before the changeover and where they have had subsequent difficulty in making budget, (2) where the local manager is incompetent, (3) where there are weak salesmen. It is typically true that the poorest salesmen complain the most about money. The reasons seem apparent. Not only do these men fail to receive regular increases but their selling deficiencies are masked behind a smoke screen of belligerent verbalizations about "inadequate pay." Although the company has only a few such malcontents, their presence is a reminder that any worsening of general field conditions will fan the dissent and cut into productivity.

Management should be concerned about another aspect of the compensation problem. Today's practices, as well as field attitudes toward compensation, contain elements of inflexibility. To hire competent new men in most markets the company must "break the scale." But we have observed that many local managers resist such wage "erosion." They fail to understand the reasons and reject them even when they are told.

The final problem, and perhaps the greatest, is the fact that weaknesses in the compensation plan restrict the impact of financial and nonfinancial incentives upon the behavior of the salesmen. For these several reasons, it is imperative that we examine the factors that determine local salary practices. Corrective action presupposes understanding.

FACTORS THAT DETERMINE LOCAL SALARY PRACTICES

There are four explanations for local salary practices: (1) the field sales manager; (2) the characteristics of the district; (3) the Sierra organization; and (4) the nature of the salesmen and their jobs.

The Field Sales Manager

A number of managers, as we have seen, encourage a climate of "no knowledge" regarding monetary matters. Thus, in these geographic areas, ignorance of the facts is the rule rather than the exception. This ignorance accounts for some of the local peculiarities. Despite such secrecy, it should surprise no one that local managers in general consider themselves fair when it comes to salary administration. After all, it is natural that managers should describe a weak manager as "weak also in salary matters." Salary administration is viewed as an essential of good management. It follows that requests by salesmen for increases in pay are regarded as criticisms of the manager. Incompetent managers, moreover, regard money as their fundamental "hold" over the men. An open discussion of money could threaten this root of authority. Salary discussions thus are considered taboo. It frequently happens, as well, that a supervisor who is under constant harassment for a raise from a particular salesman will keep a "file" of negative points about the man to use "in defense." Such a reaction obviously is of little value to either party.

The compensation attitudes of local managers reflect, moreover, their own backgrounds. Because managers are given few official rules they are guided in their operations by tradition. They behave as they do because they "know no better."

This fact tempts one to conclude that a manager's treatment of his men will mirror the treatment he receives—that a poorly paid manager, with infrequent and small raises, will subject his men to a similar treatment. The evidence does not support this conclusion. Managers, apparently, can divorce their salesmen pay action from their personal compensation experience.

Yet, it seems reasonable (but impossible to prove) that managers who feel insecure are less willing to fight for salary increases—indeed, may perpetuate their "God-like" self-image by a penurious attitude toward money. After all, it is easier not to recommend for a full raise a "doubtful" candidate than to have to defend an increase later when the man fails.

We must conclude that in a number of ways local sales managers can impose personal salary rules. Although local patterns of behavior are hard to isolate, it seems possible to draw these two generalizations:

1. *Managers who advance rapidly are more liberal in their pay practices than managers who have many years of service in a single location.*

The evidence to warrant this assumption is summarized below. Two groups of districts have been identified, those with high management turnover and those with low. For each group a comparison is made of the "average salesmen $ wage increase in %" and the "average salesman maximum $ wage increase." The reader can see that the high turnover districts lead on both counts:

Raise Policies

	Districts with High Management Turnover (Percent)	Districts with Low Management Turnover (Percent)
Average $ increase in %.	7.25	4.7
Average maximum $ increase.	13.5	6.7

2. *Weak managers frequently try to "buy the support" of their men with small, frequent increases, rosy promises, and soft evaluation.*

On the surface, this proposition seems to contradict the first one. How can managers be generous and penurious simultaneously? Only if, in fact, small, frequent raises are less generous in total than the normal increases of competent managers. Incidentally, the manager who is lenient is seldom regarded as competent by his men.

Categories of Managers. The importance of the local manager is not to be denied. At this point it may be useful to summarize the important differences in attitudes among these managers, differences which relate to various aspects of the compensation problem. Thus, managers can be grouped as favoring either *merit* or *seniority* as the reason for giving wage increases. We have already discussed this distinction. Among the managers interviewed, the supervisors were more apt to support a seniority criterion than their district managers. In a classic example, the district manager defended merit and analytic know-how but constantly had to urge his supervisors to submit recommendations for pay increases. Why? The supervisors were conservative, their seniority criteria demanded less frequent increases than the *performance* criteria of the district manager. Such divergence, however, is limited by the normal reaction of supervisors to analyze their men in terms of the district manager's standards.

Seniority is so basic a consideration in most territories that local managers constantly modify their interpretation of the regular salesman rating forms to allow for it. Even though these forms purport to measure "absolute merit," the practical modifications permit the manager to factor in his seniority prejudices.

Managers can also be categorized as those who evaluate salesmen on the basis of *personal traits* and those who evaluate on the basis of *skills*. The former rely upon any number of personality or physical characteristics, often of their own choosing. These criteria may be explicit or implicit. The second group of managers, on the other hand, look for such attributes as persuasive ability, selling prowess and administrative competence. These criteria may be personal and may or may not be explicitly stated.

A third category of manager evaluates on the basis of the *selling methods* employed. Such raters can be spotted by their interest in the man's work habits, attention to paper work, and selling techniques.

There is a final group of managers whose salary practices reflect their fear that "too much money will ruin a good man." Several of the interviewed managers volunteered such sentiments. These managers have established their own definitions of worth which are smaller in monetary equivalent than the "normal" definition. In a similar category are those managers who fear that if a young man gets to the top of the scale too early, an indispensable motivating and control tool is lost. In the case of the young man with management potential this salary limitation causes little difficulty. But what of the young career salesman? The only way he can get a raise is to leave the company or wait until he has gained seniority.

The Characteristics of the District

The second factor to which we can turn for an understanding of local salary practices is the essential nature of the district itself.

For example, "time since the last raise" is a critical consideration because every district manager has a salary budget. In order to receive maximum mileage each year from his salary budget, the manager must space the increases over the full 12 months. His natural tendency, therefore, is to appraise each recommendation for a raise against a time standard such as "time since the last increase." However, by the same token, the average manager would prefer to give each man a 3% raise rather than assume the cost of one additional salesman.

There are other district differences. Newly created districts seem to give smaller increases, but at more frequent intervals. The next table is illustrative:

All Districts

Age of District	Average Time between Increases	Average Increase	Average Minimum Increase	Aver. Maximum Increase
Before 1960	12.8 mos.	5.8%	4.3%	9.6%
After 1960	11.3	4.9%	4.1%	6.5%

There are two possible explanations for these differences: (1) new districts are poorer and tend to hold down their expenses, including salaries; (2) new districts have younger salesmen who earn, as we saw earlier, frequent but small raises.

Districts with primarily senior salesmen are in a special salary quandary. Their average salary is high. To the people involved this average, being related to seniority, is equitable and fully earned. Home office managers, in contrast, who rely upon a merit standard may conclude that the fat earnings are not fully deserved. This conflict poses a dilemma for the local manager. He is caught between contrasting philosophies and is "damned if he does and damned if he doesn't."

The salesmen in a senior district, for their part, are apt to draw erroneous conclusions about salary matters. We noted earlier that during a man's career his raises taper off at about $125 per week. In a senior district, the men interpret this general slowdown as evidence that "headquarters" is tightening up on expenses.

The nature of the district, therefore, explains in part local salary practices.

The Sierra Organization

The third major influence on salary is not peculiar to Sierra; it is the consequence of any sales organization having a home office and scattered field personnel. Such separation, by encouraging contrasting definitions about common phenomena, explains many compensation differences.

Home office and field sales management jobs are quite dissimilar, not only in obvious activities but in fundamental objectives and responsibilities. It is useful to summarize these differences:

Lower (i.e., Field) Management	*Top (i.e., Home Office) Management*
1. Manages "doers"	Manages "delegators"
2. Deals in the immediate	Deals in the long run
3. Treats specifics	Considers over-all issues
4. Has professional or technical status (i.e., sales manager)	Is a general manager or administrator

Managers at each level, by these definitions, naturally have particular and contrasting attitudes, approaches to problems, and basic definitions of what is important and what is not. Inevitably, such managers reach different conclusions about identical problems, one of which concerns salesmen and their compensation.

Such logic supports our earlier contention that field managers will pay salesmen for current performance while home office managers will pay for potential. Because the latter candidate commands a higher wage on the open market, there is a natural internal conflict between the field and home office about pay, ranges, and starting salaries.

This growing preference for men with college and higher degrees portends a future moral problem. Today's "lost" group is the 35 year old; tomorrow's will be the college graduate without management ability. Until selection know-how becomes more refined, such a result is inevitable.

The dichotomy of management is augmented by the narrowness of the salary range for salesmen. The $50 spread, in other words, magnifies the philosophic differences between the two levels of management. We know that a salesman's earnings are a function of seniority and, to a lesser degree, ability. Because the dollar spread is fine, the influence of seniority and ability upon a given wage is hard to distinguish. To make matters worse, the narrow range is squeezed even more as the company raises the starting pay.

What does this mean in the field? We know that seniority is important —field men feel that old timers deserve some pay recognition. But a differential is hard to establish within a $50 range.

Moreover, seniority advantages are eaten away continually as the hiring pay increases. The injured party in this progression is the old timer. Higher starting wages reflect demand and cost of living increases; the old timer loses on two counts—in status (as measured by absolute pay differences) and in real income.

As a result, field people, to some extent, subconsciously consider small differences in dollar pay of more importance than would be suggested by the actual dollars themselves.

The Selling Job and the Salesmen

The final explanation for district salary practices rests with the salesmen and the nature of the selling job. Because salesmen usually work alone and have little opportunity to communicate with each other, they form many ill-supported opinions.

In recent years, to compound this difficulty, the selling job has changed and the change accounts for some of the current compensation problems. Until recently salesmen were hired, trained, judged and rewarded in terms of "boxes sold" as well as numbers of accounts and calls made. Such measures reflect the traditional picture of the retail salesman which is perpetuated, to some extent, in the basic philosophy of the bonus plan. Two developments have altered drastically this old concept of selling:

1. A job evolution—The emphasis has been taken from case sales and placed on merchandising, effective calls, selling owner benefits, service, and follow-through. This array signifies a new approach to selling in which advertising, sales promotion and point of purchase inducements assume dominant importance.
2. A manpower evolution—As we noted earlier, the division has started to feed into the sales organization young men with advanced educational training. The price tag on these men is high.

Both of these changes have created internal pressures to redefine traditional concepts of selling and its worth. But such changes take time to effect and the transition period, as we know, can be painful. Field managers are not the only ones to drag their feet about new concepts of compensation and performance—their attitudes are supported generally by the salesmen. The men, for example, almost instinctively accept "time since the last raise" as proper. A normal self-query is to ask: "Aren't I about due for an increase?" The philosophy of many salesmen is contained in the following quote by one of the better men: "Senior men built this business—they deserve the promotions and rewards." Such salesmen would agree that the skills of the supervisor take years to develop. These skills, the argument continues, resemble the interpersonal relationship skills possessed by the competent salesmen. Men of this philosophy invariably accept experience as worthy of special recognition.

Logic of this type lives on, in part, because it is hard to define the essential requirements of the selling job. The intangibles make it so. No one is really sure what the ideal behavior of a salesman should be. This uncertainty shows up in local compensation and evaluation variations. In short, different measurements for performance support different compensation practices. Until there is a standard procedure for measuring performance there can be no consistent compensation policy.

EXHIBIT 1

Organization Chart of Sierra Chocolate Company (1965)

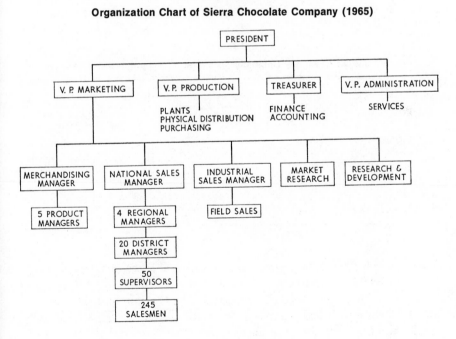

Servel Office Supply Company

The Servel Office Company manufactured a wide line of office cements, pastes, artists' supplies, stamp pads, ink, ink eradicators, crayons, tempera paints, marketing pencils, and ink solvents. During the past four years sales had increased from $1,504,881 to $2,359,337. In December, the president received the final income statement for the company's fiscal year ending November 30. He was extremely disappointed in the net income figure of $23,595. Exhibit 1 shows this income

EXHIBIT 1

Servel Office Supply Company Abbreviated Income Statement

Net sales........................	$2,359,337	100.0%
Cost of sales....................	1,403,805	59.5
Gross margin....................	$ 955,532	40.5
COMMERCIAL EXPENSES		
Shipping and delivery............	$ 224,137	9.5
Selling expense.................	408,165	17.3
Administrative..................	198,184	8.4
Advertising & promotion.........	101,451	4.3
Total Expenses...........	$ 931,937	39.5
Net operating income............	$ 23,595	1.0

statement. The president immediately began an analysis of the company's plans for the following year.

Servel, which had originally specialized in the ink business, was an old and well-established company. With the decline in the sale of conventional writing ink as the result of the popularity of the ball-point pen, it had expanded into other lines of expendable office supplies. The policy of adding new products was successful, and the fastest-growing items in

Servel's line were tempera opaque water-color paints, rubber cement, stamp pads and stamp-pad inks.

The Servel sales force consisted of twenty salesmen, five manufacturers' representatives, and a promotion man. Sales were made directly to large retail stationers and to wholesale office supply companies. Many customers were both wholesalers and retailers. Institutional and industrial customers were not typically sold direct; they generally bought from retail stationers. One salesman handled sales to all the major chains regardless of the location of the chain buying office. The balance of the sales force worked in specifically defined territories. The entire continental United States was covered by the sales force, with some salesmen having territories as large as five or six states. The same salesman who handled the chain-store business was also responsible for export sales, which were a growing factor accounting for about 6 percent of the company's current sales.

One manufacturer's representative covered the state of Washington, another Oregon, and a third northern California. These were supervised by the salesman in that territory. Another representative covered Colorado, New Mexico, and Arizona, but he was dropped recently because his volume was too small to be worthwhile. The fifth manufacturer's representative covered almost all the rest of the United States. Salesmen from these representatives competed with Servel's own salesmen, who were often perturbed when the representatives got orders from their customers. The management felt, however, that this competition was good because it forced Servel's salesmen to be more aggressive and because it was one way to raise the firm's sales volume quickly.

The president believed that the recent policy followed by the company in selling more aggressively in all territories had resulted in sales growth over the past five years but that, in turn, it had been responsible for higher selling costs, thus reducing net income to a smaller percentage of sales. Salesmen had been placed in new territories where there was no established volume. The firm had to support these men until they developed the market to a profitable level. The president considered this "an investment in market development." Such investments could not be capitalized, however, and had to be carried as expenses, thus making a poor showing on the operating statement. He had the controller prepare a study of the sales potential for the company's products by areas. This study (Table 1) substantiated his belief that more effort had to be expended to develop areas in which Servel's present sales were relatively low, even if this meant a reduction in current profits.

Servel sales had always been relatively low in New York City, for example. This city had previously been part of two larger territories, but in the previous year two men, Clark and Woodbury, were assigned to New York City alone. One of these men, Woodbury, was to concentrate on industrial accounts to be sold directly—a new procedure for Servel.

Strand and Stevenson were also new salesmen who were given new territories in which to build up Servel's volume.

In checking selling costs in established territories with costs in some of the new areas, the president found that selling costs ran as high as 24

TABLE 1

Office Supply Potential and Servel Sales

Salesman	Territory	Share of U.S. Potential	Annual Servel Sales	Share of Servel Sales
Payne	New England & part of New York..........................	5.4%	$ 130,943	7.1%
Clark	Part of New York City...........	4.1	45,641	2.5
Woodbury	Part of New York City...........	4.1	63,793	3.4
Dillion	Parts of New York, Pennsylvania, W. Virginia and Maryland........	6.4	52,681	2.8
Strand	Delaware, New Jersey, and parts of Pennsylvania and New York.....	6.7	70,344	3.8
Adams	Virginia, District of Columbia, Tennessee, Kentucky, and parts of W. Virginia, Maryland and Indiana......................	6.5	125,915	6.8
Pospisil	N. Carolina, S. Carolina, Georgia and Florida....................	6.9	125,840	6.8
Berwick	Ohio..........................	5.7	80,631	4.4
Stevenson	Alabama, Mississippi, Louisiana, and Arkansas..................	4.7	50,037	2.7
Thomas	Southern Michigan and parts of Indiana......................	4.3	64,655	3.5
MacRae	N. Dakota, S. Dakota, and parts of Minnesota, Wisconsin and Michigan......................	3.7	104,547	5.6
Herbert	Parts of Minnesota, Wisconsin, and parts of Chicago............	4.4	81,751	4.4
Finan	Northern Illinois and northwest Indiana......................	4.7	167,043	9.1
Ragsdale	Part of Chicago................	4.0	251,761	13.6
Henderson	Missouri and Iowa..............	4.8	110,079	5.9
Lewis	Kansas, Nebraska, Oklahoma, Wyoming, Colorado, New Mexico......................	4.8	69,937	3.7
Miller	Texas....:....................	5.6	97,604	5.3
Hinit	Washington, Oregon, Northern California, Montana, Idaho & Northern Nevada..............	7.4	74,852	4.0
Dashiell	Southern Nevada, Arizona, and Southern California.............	5.8	84,948	4.6
	Total Territories...............	100.0%	$1,853.002	100.0%
Strother	Chain stores and export.......................		420,550	
Naismith	Promotion man.............................		3,964	
5 manufacturers' representatives.........................			78,126	
House sales*...			3,695	
	Total Sales..................................		$2,359,337	

* Sales made by major officers of the company.

percent of net sales in the latter. In the more established territories covered by experienced salesmen, the costs of selling averaged approximately 13 percent (see Table 2). The company did not have a uniform sales compensation plan, as shown in Table 2, but believed that the ideal plan for controlling sales costs would be straight commission and hoped that ultimately all salesmen could be compensated on a straight commission basis.

In spite of the president's belief that the high cost of selling in the underdeveloped territories was justified on a long-term basis, he decided that in planning for the next year a reappraisal of this policy should be made. He believed that in view of the fact that the net operating profit was small, this budget must be highly accurate. The precision of such a budget would naturally be dependent upon a correct estimate of sales for the coming year. With this situation in mind, the company had started to work on the new budget early in December.

Sales forecasts were prepared in three independent procedures. First, each salesman was instructed to submit a realistic estimate of his next year's sales, broken down by fifteen major product groups. This estimate was to reflect current trends in the salesman's territory. It was hoped that the newer territories would show encouraging expectations.

The second sales projection was made on a product basis—a separate estimate for each of the 150 items handled by the company. The president, controller, and sales manager worked on this forecast. A product-record card showing production by months for each item for the past three years was analyzed. A projection was then made for each month of the entire coming year. In making this projection the historical record was first considered and then modified by knowledge of industry conditions with respect to the specific item. Long-term trends in demand and competitive conditions were considered. For example, heavy sales promotions in the previous year or price cutting that resulted in the dumping of unusually large supplies on the market were factors which would affect sales in the following year. Upon completion of this analysis, all product forecasts were converted from units to sales dollars.

The third sales projection was made at a round-table discussion among the president, sales manager, controller, and several of the older, more experienced salesmen who represented widely separated geographical areas. At this conference, sales were forecast for each of the fifteen product groups: (1) writing ink, (2) stamp pads, (3) stamping ink, (4) paste, (5) gums and thinners, (6) cements, (7) tempera paints, (8) solvent, (9) ink eradicator, (10) artists' supplies, (11) indelible inks, (12) shipping supplies, (13) laundry-marking pens, (14) crayons and pens, and (15) specials. All Servel products were classified in one of these categories. Each group was considered as a unit, and dollar volume was estimated for the coming year from data on past sales, current trends, economic conditions, and any other information possessed by the sales-

TABLE 2

Servel Sales and Selling Expenses by Territory

Salesman	Sales	Salary and/or Commission	Expenses*	Total Selling Cost as of Sales (Percent)	Method of Compensation
Payne	$ 130,943	$ 13,094	$ 3,000	12.3	$250 monthly expense allowance plus 10% of net sales
Clark	45,641	8,645	1,000	21.1	Reimbursed expenses and salary
Woodbury	63,793	15,000	1,500	24.3	Car, reimbursed expenses and salary
Dillion	52,681	6,720†	2,400	17.3	$200 monthly expense allowance plus 12% of net sales†
Strand	70,344	8,400	5,500	18.3	Car, reimbursed expenses and salary
Adams	125,915	12,592	3,000	12.4	$250 monthly expense allowance plus 10% of net sales
Pospisil	125,840	12,584	3,000	12.4	$250 monthly expense allowance plus 10% of net sales
Berwick	80,631	8,063	2,400	13.0	$200 monthly expense allowance plus 10% of net sales
Stevenson	50,037	6,000	5,000	22.0	Car, reimbursed expenses and salary
Thomas	64,655	9,600	5,000	22.6	Car, reimbursed expenses and salary
MacRae	104,547	10,454	2,400	12.3	$200 monthly expense allowance plus 10% of net sales
Herbert	81,751	8,200	4,100	15.0	Reimbursed expenses and salary
Finan	167,043	12,000	2,800	8.8	Car, reimbursed expenses and salary
Ragsdale	251,761	15,500	3,200	7.4	Car, reimbursed expenses and salary
Henderson	110,079	11,008	3,000	12.7	$250 monthly expense allowance plus 10% of net sales
Lewis	69,937	8,392	3,000	16.3	$250 monthly expense allowance plus 12% of net sales
Miller	97,604	8,088	5,000	13.4	Car, reimbursed expenses and salary
Hinit	74,852	9,600	5,600	20.3	Car, reimbursed expenses and salary
Dashiell	84,948	11,000	4,300	18.0	Car, reimbursed expenses and salary
Strother	420,550	28,000	5,800	8.0	Reimbursed expenses and salary
Naismith	3,964	10,000‡	4,300†	360.7‡	Car, reimbursed expenses and salary
5 mfr.'s reps	78,126	8,472		10.8	See footnote§
House sales	3,695	#	18,000‖	487.0‖	
Totals	$2,359,337	$241,412‖	$93,300¶	14.1	

* Rounded to nearest $100 because final expense reports were not in.

† Commission rate was 13 percent part of year.

‡ Naismith was the company promotion man. While his salary and expenses were properly chargeable to selling expenses in the broadest sense, they could not be compared directly with his own sales, since he spent only a small part of his time in face-to-face selling.

§ Three representatives were paid commissions of 10 percent; one got 15 percent; and one had a sliding scale of 5 percent on all sales over $10,000.

‖ House sales were made by company officers, whose salaries and expenses were not directly chargeable as selling expense. Travel expenses of $18,000 were not all properly allocated to selling.

¶ The difference between total selling expenses shown here and the total in the operating statement is made up of the sales manager's salary and expenses and office sales expenses.

men. The estimated dollar sales of each group were then added to give a total company sales estimate.

The three independently achieved sales forecasts for each of the fifteen products groups were then considered and a "best" forecast selected. The three forecasts for writing ink, for example, were $240,000, $245,000, and $250,000. Since sales of writing ink had been declining, the conservative lower estimate was taken. On the other hand, the forecasts for tempera paints were $290,000, $300,000, and $327,000. Since this was a growing product line with Servel, the highest estimate was chosen. The total of the product group forecasts was $2,500,000. Since this represented an increase in sales over the previous year, but still seemed to be readily attainable, it was set as the company's sales forecast for next year. This total was then broken down by salesmen on the basis of their forecasts and past performances (see Exhibit 2).

EXHIBIT 2
Forecast of Sales and Selling Costs by Salesman

Salesman	Forecast Sales	Forecast Selling Costs	
		Salary and/or	Commission Expenses
Payne	$ 130,000	$ 13,000	$ 3,000
Clark	75,000	11,000	2,500
Woodbury	70,000	16,000	2,500
Dillion	*	*	*
Strand	74,000	8,000	5,500
Adams	135,000	13,000	3,000
Pospisil	135,000	13,500	3,000
Berwick†	130,000	9,000	2,400
Stevenson	65,000	6,000	4,200
Thomas	80,000	9,600	4,000
MacRae	108,000	10,800	2,400
Herbert	80,000	8,700	4,000
Finan	182,500	13,000	3,000
Ragsdale	263,000	16,500	3,800
Henderson	125,000	12,500	3,000
Lewis‡	90,000	9,900	2,400
Miller	90,000	9,000	5,000
Hinit	85,000	10,000	5,600
Dashiell	95,000	11,500	4,000
Strother	450,000	36,000	6,600
Naismith	§	10,000	4,500
4 mfr.'s reps.‖	75,000	7,500	......
House sales¶	5,000	†	12,000
Total	$2,542,500	$254,500	$86,400
Less cash discounts	42,500		
Net Sales	$2,500,000		

* Dillion resigned. His territory was divided between Clark and Berwick.
† Berwick's compensation plan was changed, when he got part of Dillion's old territory, to a monthly expense allowance of $200 and a $9,000 salary.
‡ Compensation rate changed to $200 monthly expense allowance and 11 percent commission on net sales.
§ It was planned that Naismith would devote all his time to promotion.
‖ One manufacturer's representative who had covered Colorado, New Mexico, and Arizona was dropped.
¶ House sales would be made by company officers whose salaries could not be charged directly to sales.

Next the controller was instructed to prepare the expense budget for the year based upon this level of sales. The most important selling expenses—those involving salesmen's salaries and/or commissions and travelling expenses—were projected, based upon the tentative sales volume expected from each salesman (see Exhibit 2). All other items of expense were also estimated and a forecast income and expense statement prepared (Exhibit 3).

EXHIBIT 3

Projected Annual Operating Statements at Three Sales Levels

Net sales..................	$2,359,000	100.0%	$2,500,000	100.0%	$2,600,000	100.0%
Cost of sales...............	1,389,000	58.9	1,473,300	58.9	1,531,400	58.9
Gross margin.............	970,000	41.1	1,026,700	41.1	1,068,600	41.1
Shipping and delivery—variable.	188,700	8.0	199,800	8.0	208,000	8.0
Shipping and delivery—fixed...	39,600	1.7	39,600	1.6	39,600	1.5
Total shipping and delivery..	228,300	9.7	239,400	9.6	247,600	9.5
Selling expense—variable*.....	99,100	4.2	104,700	4.2	109,200	4.2
Selling expense—fixed†........	316,300	13.4	316,300	12.7	316,300	12.2
Total selling expense........	415,400	17.6	421,000	16.9	425,500	16.4
Administrative expense........	209,000	8.9	209,000	8.4	209,000	8.0
Advertising and promotion.....	96,000	4.1	96,000	3.8	96,000	3.7
Total expenses............	948,700	40.2	965,400	38.7	978,100	37.6
Projected net profit..........	21,300	0.9	61,300	2.4	90,500	3.5

* Variable selling expenses included commissions only.
† Fixed selling expenses included salesmen's salaries, the salaries of five sales clerical people, sales meeting expenses, and miscellaneous other selling expenses.

The president directed that this statement be prepared based upon three different sales levels. In addition to a statement based on the projected sales of $2,500,000, he asked for a projected statement showing the results that would accrue if sales continued at the present annual volume level of about $2,359,000, and for a third projection showing the results if sales should exceed the estimate of $2,500,000 by $100,000.

In order to make projected income statements for three levels of sales, the controller made extensive studies of which expenses would be variable and which would remain fixed. Exhibit 3 shows the resulting changes in net income based upon the three projected levels of sales. The president considered these budgets adequate to reappraise the problem of whether to continue to develop some territories at a high sales cost in order to continue increasing the company's sales volume.

Another use for the budgets developed when the president and the sales manager had to decide whether or not to take part in a $38,000 promotional program that had been presented to the company. This program had not been included in the present budget. In general, the program involved a special dealer promotion on paste and the awarding of many prizes, including a number of English bicycles to leading salesmen and dealers. The president believed that this program had a great deal of merit. He planned to present it at a sales meeting in order to get the re-action of the entire sales force. The reaction he received would have some bearing on his final decision as to whether the expenditure of $38,000 for additional promotion would produce enough added sales to justify itself and whether it would be wise to take such a step at this time, when selling expenses were running well above the desired level because of heavy expenses in new territories.

Appraise the Servel sales budget as a planning and control device.

Imperial Belting Company

For over fifty years Imperial Belting Company had been the sales leader of stitched canvas belting, which was used primarily with conveyors and elevators. Each of the nine men on the sales force was a highly trained industrial salesman with considerable knowledge of engineering problems, who earned between $12,000 and $15,000 annually. The general sales manager was concerned with salesman turnover; at least one salesman had left the company each year for the past several years. The sales that were lost while these men were being replaced plus the cost of training a new man, which was estimated at $15,000, made this turnover expensive.

The belting industry consisted of two major segments, manufacturers of rubber belts and manufacturers of canvas belts. There were approximately fifty companies making belts, of which some forty manufactured the rubber type and ten the canvas and cotton woven type. Imperial accounted for about 40 per cent of the total quality canvas belting business, or more than the next three largest canvas belting manufacturers combined. Canvas belts were considered to have a major advantage over the rubber variety—they resisted oils and acids and cost less to maintain. Imperial produced quality belts that sold for 5–15 per cent more than most competitive belts. The company executives believed that their belts lasted two to five times longer than most ordinary rubber or canvas belts.

Each Imperial salesman was expected to make about one hundred calls a month, of which 20 per cent should produce sales; the typical order was for about $1,200. The sales manager expected that about 40 per cent of all calls would be made on new prospects and the remaining 60 per cent on established accounts. All established accounts were to be called on at least once a year. Larger-volume accounts were expected to receive from four to eight calls a year, depending on their size.

A new salesman normally needed nearly a year to acquire the technical information needed to be fully versed on the entire line. An ability to read blueprints was essential. Each salesman was on his own, once he was out in the field, except for monthly visits by the general sales manager. A two-day sales meeting was held once a year. All other contact with the home office was by mail or telephone. The nine sales territories are shown in Exhibit 1. Each salesman had to adapt his sales personality to a number

EXHIBIT 1

Geographic Territory Assignments

Salesman 1: Connecticut, Massachusetts, Vermont, New Hampshire, Maine, 50 per cent of New York, and 50 per cent of New Jersey.

Salesman 2: Maryland, Delaware, Virginia, 50 per cent of West Virginia, 50 per cent of North Carolina, 50 per cent of Pennsylvania, and 50 per cent of New Jersey.

Salesman 3: Canada (basically Montreal and Toronto), 50 per cent of New York, 50 per cent of Pennsylvania, and 25 per cent of Ohio.

Salesman 4: Kentucky, 50 per cent of West Virginia, 75 per cent of Ohio, and 75 per cent of Indiana.

Salesman 5: Alabama, Georgia, S. Carolina, Tennessee, and 50 per cent of North Carolina.

Salesman 6: Michigan exclusively.

Salesman 7: Wisconsin, Minnesota, 50 per cent of Iowa, and 50 per cent of Illinois.

Salesman 8: 50 per cent of Illinois, 25 per cent of Indiana, and 50 per cent of Iowa.

Salesman 9: Arkansas, Colorado, Kansas, Mississippi, Nebraska, and Oklahoma.

of varied situations. On one occasion he might deal with the plant superintendent or with the maintenance foreman, who often had worked his way up from the ranks; at other times his contact would be with the chief engineer, who perhaps had one or more college degrees. The job description for an Imperial sales engineer is shown in Exhibit 2.

All salesmen received the same base salary—$8,000 a year—and expenses which averaged about $6,000. In addition, each salesman received a bonus of 10 per cent on all sales that exceeded the quota established for his territory.

The general sales manager recruited new salesmen primarily through newspaper advertising, employment agencies, and referral of noncompetitive salesmen by Imperial's customers. Management believed that the sales force was not large enough to justify a sales training man; therefore, all training was done by the general sales manager. Since he had many other responsibilities, he was willing to pay a premium to obtain the services of an experienced industrial salesman.

Imperial executives had developed the following list of characteristics, which they believed a salesman would need to have in order to be successful with their firm:

1. Be married.
2. Have two or more children.
3. Be 28–35 years old.
4. Have had some engineering courses.

5. Be a college graduate.
6. Not be an only child in his family.
7. Enjoy traveling and being on his own.
8. Have a wife who would be a social asset.

A candidate for a selling position usually went through the following procedure:

1. Filled out an application blank.
2. Had preliminary interview with general sales manager (generally 15–20 minutes).

EXHIBIT 2
Job Description of an Imperial Sales Engineer

A job description is a written record of the duties, responsibilities, skills, and requirements of a particular job. It is concerned with the job itself and not with the individual. The individual is selected and trained to perform the duties it outlines.

An Imperial representative is the sales manager of his territory and must perform the following essential functions for best performance. (1) sales, (2) service, (3) territory management, (4) sales promotion, (5) executive duties, and (6) goodwill.

1. Sales:
   Make regular, productive calls.
   Sell the line, demonstrate.
   Handle questions and objections.
   Estimate customer's potential needs.
   Emphasize quality.
   Explain company policies on price, delivery, credit.
   Explain benefits of product to customer.
   Get the order.
2. Service:
   Report product adaptability, complaints.
   Handle adjustments, returns, and allowances.
   Show customer how to get the most from the product.
   Advise and assist customer on his belt problems.
3. Territory Management:
   Arrange route for best coverage.
   Balance effort with customer against potential.
   Maintain sales portfolio, samples, kits.
4. Sales Promotion:
   Develop new prospects and new accounts.
   Call on conveyor manufacturers' headquarters.
   Present suggestions, layouts, and proposals.
5. Executive:
   Each night make a daily work plan for the next day.
   Prepare and submit daily reports to home office.
   Organize field activity for minimum travel and maximum calls.
   Prepare and submit special reports on trends and competition.
   Collect and submit data requested by home office.
   Investigate lost sales and the reasons for loss.
   Prepare reports on developments, trends, new objections met, and new ideas on meeting objections.
   Attend sales meetings.
   Build a prospect list.
6. Goodwill:
   Counsel customers on their problems.
   Maintain loyalty and respect for firm represented.

3. Awaited word relative to (1) checking on references given on application blank and (2) evaluation of interview.

4. If step 3 was favorable, he was asked to return with his wife for a final interview.

The general sales manager believed that the yearly turnover of at least one salesman was primarily the result of faulty selection, since he was not able to determine whether or not a candidate possessed the psychological attitudes that would fit him for the job. He could only guess at answers to such questions as: How well can he take being on his own? How well can he take company direction? Does he resist help? Should he be in selling at all?

To help him select salesmen, the sales manager decided to use the services of a psychological testing company, which would test prospective salesmen for $50 per candidate. The testing company suggested that each candidate be given a battery of six tests:

1. Mental ability (Otis Employment Test).
2. Personality portrait (Washburne S-A Inventory).
3. Social intelligence (George Washington University Series).
4. Personality adjustment (Bernreuter Personality Inventory).
5. Interests other than selling (Strong Vocational Interest Test for Men).
6. Sales aptitude (sales sense).

To verify the validity of these tests, the battery was given to each salesman in the company. From analysis of each salesman's test and the correlation of test scores, criteria were established to evaluate the test scores of potential salesmen as shown in Exhibit 3. Upon seeing the results of these tests the sales manager was convinced that they could be a useful tool to help separate the undesirable from the potentially good salesmen. Shortly after completion of this validity work, he was faced with the problem of hiring a salesman. After several months of recruiting, a number of candidates were obtained. Of the group, two men, Mr. Harold R. Overstreet and Mr. George Paddock, appeared to be the best prospects. The selection problem was a difficult one for the general sales manager because both candidates appeared to have equal abilities:

1. Both were married and had children.
2. Both had wives who would be social assets to their work.
3. Both had their own homes.
4. Both had about equal previous industrial selling experience.
5. Both were college graduates with over a year of study in engineering.
6. Both had been in the service as officers.
7. Both were in their early thirties.

Paddock and Overstreet took the aptitude tests, after which the testing firm submitted the reports shown as Exhibits 4 and 5. Each report consisted of a "graphic analysis" and a commentary by an analyst.

EXHIBIT 3

Graphic Test Analysis

	Score to Be Not Less than	Score to Be Not More than
1. Mental ability		
Speed in arriving at conclusions on new problems	35	90
Accuracy in finding the right answers under time pressure	35	100
Capacity—mental adaptability and trainability	35	100
2. Personality portrait		
Stability—ability to take adversities or turndowns	65	90
Self-sufficiency—capacity to stand on one's own two feet	30	75
Objective-mindedness—treating situations unaffected by own feelings	75	95
Dominance—ability to control interviews and situations	60	90
Self-confidence—confidence in one's own ability to achieve	65	90
Social mixing qualities—need for group sociability	70	90
Aggressiveness and driving power	50	90
3. Social intelligence		
Tact and diplomacy—knowledge of diplomatic things to say and do	50	100
Sizing up—sizing up people in face-to-face social situations	75	100
Judging behavior—judging human behavior correctly	75	90
Sense of humor—ability to take kidding at one's own expense	75	95
4. Personal adjustment		
Sincerity in taking these tests	30	100
Happiness—tendency toward personal and domestic happiness	90	100
How others take to him—feeling of being accepted	50	95
How he takes to others—sympathetic interest in others	15	75
Purposiveness—goals and objectives in business	75	95
First things first—in business situations	90	100
Self-control—capacity for control in business situations	80	100
5. Sales aptitude		
Interest in selling as expressed by sales managers	A	. . .
Interest in selling tangibles	A	. . .
Interest in selling intangibles	A	. . .
Sales sense	85	100
6. Interests other than selling		
Engineer	C	. . .
Chemist	A	. . .
Production	B	. . .
Personnel	B	. . .
Accountant	No rating	. . .
Office worker	No rating	. . .
Purchasing agent	No rating	. . .
Advertising	No rating	. . .

not close enough to actual job

EXHIBIT 4
Graphic Test Analysis
George R. Paddock

	Danger	Desirable	Caution
1. Mental ability			
Speed in arriving at conclusions on new problems.........		40 *5*	
Accuracy in finding the right answers under time pressure...		35 *0*	
Capacity—mental adaptability and trainability............		35 *0*	
2. Personality portrait			
Stability—ability to take adversities or turndowns.........		84 *19*	
Self-sufficiency—capacity to stand on one's own two feet..		35 *5*	
Objective-mindedness—treating situations unaffected by own feelings..		93 *18*	
Dominance—ability to control interviews and situations....		58 *2*	
Self-confidence—confidence in one's own ability to achieve..		65 *0*	
Social mixing qualities—need for group sociability.........		88 *18*	
Aggressiveness and driving power.....................		34 *16*	
3. Social intelligence			
Tact and diplomacy—knowledge of diplomatic things to say and do......................................	34 *16*		
Sizing up—sizing up people in face-to-face social situations...	99 *24*		
Judging behavior—judging human behavior correctly......	29 *46*		
Sense of humor—ability to take kidding at one's own expense..			99
4. Personal adjustment			
Sincerity in taking these tests.....................		30 *45*	
Happiness—tendency toward personal and domestic happiness..		99 *9*	20
How others take to him—feeling of being accepted.......			20
How he takes to others—sympathetic interest in others.....		35 *0*	
Purposiveness—goals and objectives in business...........		75 *65*	
First things first—in business situations..................		99 *2*	
Self-control—capacity for control in business situations.....		74 *16*	
5. Sales aptitude			
Interest in selling as expressed by sales managers..........		A	
Interest in selling tangibles............................		A	
Interest in selling intangibles...........................		B *A*	
Sales sense..			15
6. Interests other than selling			
Engineer..		○	
Chemist...		○	
Production..		B-plus	
Personnel...		○	
Accountant..		A	
Office worker..		A	
Purchasing agent.....................................		A	
Advertising..		○	
7. Other factors			
Analytical tendency..................................			X

EXHIBIT 5

Graphic Test Analysis
Harold R. Overstreet

	Danger	*Desirable*	*Caution*
1. Mental ability			
Speed in arriving at conclusions on new problems.........		55 2ˢ	
Accuracy in finding the right answers under time pressure...		80 45	
Capacity—mental adaptability and trainability..........		45 / ὀ	
2. Personality portrait			
Stability—ability to take adversities or turndowns........		65 ı	
Self-sufficiency—capacity to stand on one's own two feet...	30 → 21		
Objective-mindedness—treating situations unaffected by own feelings......................................		86 //	
Dominance—ability to control interviews and situations....		78 / 8	
Self-confidence—confidence in one's own ability to achieve..		75 / ὀ	
Social mixing qualities—need for group sociability.........		75 ʂ	
Aggressiveness and driving power.....................		84 ʂ⁴	
3. Social intelligence			
Tact and diplomacy—knowledge of diplomatic things to say and do......................................		99 4ⁿ	
Sizing up—sizing up people in face-to-face social situations..		89 /ⁿ	
Judging behavior—judging human behavior correctly......		54 ²¹	
Sense of humor—ability to take kidding at one's own expense..		94 /ⁿ	
4. Personal adjustment			
Sincerity in taking these tests.......................		35 ʂ	
Happiness—tendency toward personal and domestic happiness.......................................		99 ⁹	
How others take to him—feeling of being accepted........		94 ⁴⁴	
How he takes to others—sympathetic interest in others.....		15 ὀ	
Purposiveness—goals and objectives in business..........		95 ²ⁿ	
First things first—in business situations.................		99 ⁹	
Self-control—capacity for control in business situations.....		99 /ⁿ	
5. Sales aptitude			
Interest in selling as expressed by sales managers.........		A ὀ	
Interest in selling tangibles.........................		A ὀ	
Interest in selling intangibles........................		A ὀ	
Sales sense..................................		90 ʂ	
6. Interests other than selling			
Engineer....................................			
Chemist....................................			
Production..................................			
Personnel...................................		A +ⁿ	
Accountant..................................			
Office worker................................			
Purchasing agent.............................			
Advertising.................................		B-plus	
7. Other factors			

DETAILED ANALYSIS: PADDOCK

Objective of This Report.   To evaluate Paddock for the position of industrial salesman.

1. *Mental Ability.*   The ratings are in line for the job. Paddock has the capacity for absorbing the essentials of new duties and responsibilities.

2. *Personality Portrait.*   Paddock has a strong personality portrait. He reveals capacities for taking it when it comes to the impact of disappointments, defeats, and obstacles and resistances. He has aggressiveness, inner energy, dominance, and driving power, as well as confidence in himself and his abilities and high objective-mindedness.

The following factors should be explored: Paddock was analytical in his approach to the test. Many technical men tend to be analytical, are accustomed to weighing carefully the pros and cons of situations before reaching decisions or making commitments. We have placed this tendency in the caution zone on the color chart because it is important to determine whether or not Paddock may still be in the state of "analysis" relative to the job opportunity being offered him with Imperial Belting. In other words, does Paddock have any uncertainties or doubts or mental reservations concerning the job or his ability to handle the job or the future. If so, these should be completely resolved before he is put on the payroll.

3. *Social Intelligence.*   Paddock has capacities for tact and for sizing up people in face-to-face social situations. He earned a fairly good rating for judging behavior.

Paddock earned a top rating for sense of humor. We have placed this in the caution zone on the color chart because it is important for him to recognize the fact that many of the people with whom he will be working out in the field cannot begin to match his own high sense of humor. He must be alerted against impressing such individuals as taking too lightly or airily situations that they would rather have him consider seriously.

4. *Personal Adjustment.*   Paddock seems to feel that others may not take to him too readily. Why? Is there any aspect of his appearance, speech, personal mannerisms, or background about which he is sensitive and which he believes others do not like in him?

Ratings for the other adjustment factors are in line for the job.

5. *Sales Aptitude.*   Paddock has live interest in selling, but his rating for sales sense is that of the individualist, and usually the individualist sells the hard way and only the rugged survives.

Paddock is not bringing what might be termed an inherent or intrinsic sales sense to the new job with Imperial Belting. Thus he is a risk for employment unless he has had very thorough and specific experience in exactly the same field of work in which he will be operating if employed as an Imperial Belting industrial salesman. If he has this experience, then he is a fair or calculated risk for employment by Imperial Belting; perhaps he will carry over in the new job some specific sales experiences he has had in the same or related field.

It is important in working with Paddock to make certain that at all times he follow through on specific Imperial Belting methods and techniques of selling rather than depend on his own individualist's approach to sales situations.

6. *Interests Other Than Sales.* Paddock's other interests are in line for industrial selling, particularly his interests in manufacturing processes and in purchasing.

Conclusion and Recommendation. Paddock is recommended for employment as an industrial salesman with Imperial Belting Company.

DETAILED ANALYSIS: OVERSTREET

Objective of This Report. To evaluate Overstreet's potentials for a sales position with the Imperial Belting Company. In this capacity he would be covering New England and New York City, being away from home for several days to a week at a time but never for week ends.

1. *Mental Ability.* Overstreet's performance on the mental ability test is quite good. It indicates that he should be able to absorb training, new information, and new ideas without any particular difficulty.

2. *Personality Portrait.* Overstreet appears to be a generally sociable individual who is quite amiable and amenable to guidance. He should be a good company man in terms of being willing to follow through on established policies and procedures without making sudden and unexpected changes on his own.

From that standpoint, he should be a good company man. He shows good over-all self-confidence, can take most emotional pressures without becoming easily discouraged, and is sufficiently objective-minded to be able to keep most personal worries or troubles apart from his work. He shows good dominance, drive, and aggressiveness.

The marginal rating for self-sufficiency has positive as well as negative implications. From the positive standpoint, it reflects the type of individual who fits well into a large, smoothly running organization, where he is expected to operate as a member of a closely knit and well co-ordinated team.

By the same token, such a man typically needs to feel that he has the support of his organization and of his manager behind him if he is to function at his best. It is also important, from the standpoint of the traveling aspects of his job, that he have the full support of his family and those who are nearest and dearest to him, since otherwise it may be difficult for him to "take" traveling which keeps him away from home for days and nights at a time. Not only his attitude but the attitude of his wife and family should be checked carefully to be sure that all are in full accord with the desirability of his entering into a position of this type.

It should also be noted that Overstreet apparently has high hopes and great expectations for the future. He seems to expect big things to happen and great events to occur. The question is: Are his "great expectations" realistic and in accordance with the plans and expectations that management has for him? If not, they could lead to ultimate disappointment and a letdown in his efforts.

3. *Social Intelligence.* Overstreet has a fine understanding of what it takes to get along well with other people. He can be so highly tactful and diplomatic as to be almost suave, and he has fine capacity for sizing up other people face to face. He has a good understanding of human nature generally and a fine sense of humor.

4. *Personal Adjustment.* The indications are that Overstreet has made a good adjustment to his home, personal, and business environments.

5. *Sales Aptitude.* Overstreet has a strong interest in the selling field, or the type commonly associated with men who regard that general field of work as a career. Furthermore, he has an excellent understanding of and insight into the "sales-wise" approach to situations.

6. *Interests Other than Sales.* Overstreet also has a strong interest in working with and handling personnel and a secondary interest along advertising, merchandising and sales promotional lines.

Conclusion and Recommendation. On the basis of the over-all test pattern, Overstreet is recommended for employment as a salesman with the Imperial Belting Company.

Which candidate, if any, should Imperial hire?

Evaluate the use of this psychological testing program in recruiting salesmen.

The Benson Chemical Company

"A substantial growth in sales and a shift in market strength from the Northeast to the South and Southwest have knocked our sales territories completely out of line," said Bill King, sales manager of the Benson Chemical Company. "The morale of the sales force is low," he continued, "because some of the men feel that the present territories don't afford an equal opportunity to earn commissions."

THE COMPANY

Benson Chemical was a wholesale chemical house supplying specialized chemicals to paper processors throughout the country. The several thousand potential users of the company's products ranged in size 'from small operators to giants such as International Paper and Crown Zellerbach. Competition was intense with sales going to the firms offering the best combination of quality, service, and price.

The company's sales increased significantly between the years 1966 and 1969. A continuation of this trend was expected in 1970. Although the company started in the East, it extended operations westward after World War II. Twenty-four states were serviced in 1969.

THE SALE

The typical Benson customer purchased $8,500 in chemicals yearly, although the range was from $25 to over $60,000. Some sales were contracted but most were solicited directly by the company's ten man sales force. About 70% of the Benson line consisted of standard items for which purchasing agents made the final buying decision. The remaining items were specialized "brand" products and required the approval of production personnel. The chemical companies, in 1969, faced a buyers' market; thus the demands for service were heavy. A purchasing agent from one of the larger paper firms recently said to a Benson salesman, "We might as well get one thing straight. You know as well as I do that your competitors can meet you in price and quality so if you want our business we had better see some real service."

Salesmen, during their calls, checked the performance of products sold previously, followed up delivery promises and sought to introduce the customer to new uses for existing products as well as to new products. Benson salesmen were expected to have a chemical engineering background because of the technical orientation of their customers.

Salesmen averaged five calls daily in metropolitan centers and four in non-metropolitan areas. Typically the men spent four days of each week on metropolitan calls. Accounts were classified by purchases as A, B, or C—the limits for A accounts being "over $25,000," for B accounts "between $5,000 and $25,000," and for C accounts "below $5,000." A accounts were called on weekly, B accounts monthly and C accounts quarterly. About 10% of a man's time was devoted to "service callbacks."

THE SALESMEN

The Benson Company employed ten salesmen ranging in experience from 6 months to 25 years. Mr. King was generally satisfied with his sales force and thought them technically qualified to sell the full line.

Each salesman had a monthly drawing account of between $500 and $600. "This," said Mr. King, "is justification for the missionary work that they are required to do." Above the draw, compensation was by straight commission. Commission rates varied with the profitability of products and according to the sales manager there was no apparent tendency for salesmen to overlook the full-line in favor of higher-margin items. "The nature of our selling is such," said Mr. King, "that the salesman first has to establish himself with the account. Once this is done full-line selling is no problem."

Mr. King was convinced that differences in compensation (see Exhibit 1) arose from the distribution of territories rather than the individual abilities of the salesmen. Of this he said, "I would expect some variations in commissions earned, but not to the extent we've experienced. I don't see that much difference among our salesmen."

Mr. King gave the following appraisal of his ten salesmen:

Phil Haney is our "old timer," having been with us since 1945. He is one year from our mandatory retirement age of 65 and he likes to remind people of his 20-odd years of seniority. He hasn't been particularly easy for me to work with. Phil has strong personal ideas about selling, many of which are "academically" outdated but are apparently accepted by his customers. He has what you might call an old-time personality and has been tremendously successful over the years. I often wonder what kind of volume could be generated by combining Phil's personality with some of our new merchandising techniques. Phil has always worked Manhattan, although initially he sold to all of New York City.

Gary Whalen is in his sixth year with the company and sells to accounts in the New Jersey–Pennsylvania area. Whalen is an excellent salesman who is obviously aware of the "smoothness" of his sales approach. He carries this self-assurance to the extent that he often becomes very indifferent whenever I offer a few suggestions for improvement in his sales techniques.

Norman Ives is probably the most ambitious, aggressive, and argumentative salesman we have. He has been with the company since 1956 following his discharge from the Army. He reached the rank of Lt. Colonel at the age of 30 but had no interest in a military career. Norman really stormed into his present territory in 1959 and in the first year doubled its volume. He's extremely independent but will work hard to implement any sales program that he agrees with. If he doesn't agree, though, I get absolutely no cooperation. In 1966, Norman's territory began to slip; I think primarily because of a shift in market strength. Moreover, his compensation fell from $15,000 in 1966 to $12,600 in 1969.

Bob Ericson has been with the company three years now and I still get the feeling that he is unsure of himself. He seems somewhat confused and overworked, probably because he's trying to serve too many accounts in too large an area. Surprisingly enough, though, the general growth in the territory has given Bob a significant increase in sales for 1969.

Dick Richards is the "mystery man" of the sales force. Neither the other salesmen nor myself know very much about Dick's personal life. He's quiet and unassuming and knows the Benson line amazingly well. I've often wondered why Dick chose sales over research work. Sales in his territory have continued to grow which is unusual considering an opposite trend in neighboring territories.

Warren Sharp is the guy on the sales force who keeps the rest of us going. Warren is slightly rotund and always good natured. His accounts seem genuinely happy to see him when he makes a call. He worked the New York State territory for his first two years and then moved into the West Coast when we took on Joe Gordon. At first I worried about Warren's ability to get serious long enough to make a sale. However, this has not proved to be a problem.

Gus Billings joined the company in 1963 after four years with a competitor. Gus is easygoing, even tempered, and very popular with his customers. Despite his even temperament Gus was somewhat upset the last time I saw him. We plan to activate five more states in his territory during 1970 which would make Gus responsible for a geographic area covering roughly one fourth of the United States. He is already calling on 81 accounts in six states and this keeps him away from home much of the time.

Ben Owens joined us in 1964 after receiving an M.S. degree in Chemistry from the University of Pennsylvania. After the normal three-month training program during which time Ben travelled with Gary Whalen, he stepped into his territory and was immediately successful. Ben is earnest and conscientious and has increased his sales volume each year. He's not what you would call the "salesman type" but he is always exceedingly successful in using the merchandising techniques that I try to implement.

Joe Gordon is the youngster of our sales force at 23. Joe went into New York State in the spring of 1969. The territory is relatively inactive and we usually try to assign it to new salesmen. Sales have dropped from the time that Joe took over and he is very apologetic about the situation. I've told him that he would have to expect some tough moments and I think his determination to "make a go of it" will be realized because of his conscientiousness. He's always receptive to any help that is offered and tries hard to put suggestions to use. That territory has always been a "dog."

Jim Davey is in his third year and I'd say he's a good salesman. Jim always dresses impeccably in Ivy League fashion and he has good bearing. He responds well to any suggestion that I make to him. It's a funny thing, but whenever I travel with Jim the sales in the territory increase for the next several months. After that, right back to the previous level. Accounts within the territory are scattered, which keeps Jim on the road most of the time.

Aside from the morale problem, Bill King had other reasons for wanting to change the territories. "We expect continued growth," he said, "and at least for the time being I plan to add no new people. I'm positive that by redistributing the sales territories we can get more sales effort from the sales force as a group and thus handle our growth."

Exhibit 1 presents a detailed breakdown of performance by salesman for the years 1968 and 1969 (projected) and Exhibit 2 lists the number of customers for each salesman by dollar volume.

EXHIBIT 1. Performance of Salesmen, 1968–1969*

Salesman	Territory	Terr. No.	Sales Record 1968	Sales Record 1969*	Accounts Metro	Accounts Non-Metro	Accounts Total	1969* Compensation	Selling Cost % to Sales 1969*	Planned Sales 1970†	Planned Accounts 1970	Est. Share of Market 1969*	Est. Share of Market 1970	Selling Cost % to Planned Sales
Ives	Me. N.H. Ver.	1	not covered under present territory arrangement							$ 41	$ 7	....	26.0%	
	Mass.		$ 486	$ 408	54	13	67			324	54	24.0%	18.6	
	R.I.		120	80	13		13			41	7	39.7	49.6	
	Conn.		120	120	13	7	20			80	13	21.2	19.9	
	Total Terr.		726	608	80	20	100	$ 12,600	2.1%	486	81	23.2	19.9	2.6%
Gordon	N.Y. State	2	244	204	27	7	34	6,600	3.2	162	27	50.2	50.3	4.1
Haney	Manhattan	3	2,028	1,944	162		162	18,600	0.96	1,704	142	18.7	18.6	1.1
Richards	Other N.Y. City & L.I.	4	726	804	61	7	68	14,400	1.8	892	74	25.3	25.2	1.6
Whalen	New Jersey	5	162	203	27	7	34			244	40	10.6	16.5	
	Pennsylvania		1,296	1,212	88	13	101			1,056	88	18.2	17.0	
	Total Terr.		1,458	1,415	115	20	135	15,000	1.1	1,300	128	16.9	17.0	1.2
Ericson	Del. Md. Wash D.C.	6	not covered under present territory arrangement							80	13		20.0	
	Va. W. Va.		120	162	13	13	26			162	27	19.9	16.2	
	N. Carolina		120	162	20	7	27			204	34	16.5	16.3	
	S. Carolina		41	80	7	7	14			162	27	11.0	16.5	
	Georgia		120	120	7	13	20			120	20	18.5	14.9	
	Florida		80	162	27	0	27			204	34	20.2	16.1	
	Total Terr.		481	686	74	40	114	10,200	1.5	932	155	16.3	16.4	1.1
Davey	Mississippi	7	41	80	7	7	14			80	13	16.7	16.6	
	Alabama		120	162	13	13	26			162	27	18.3	18.3	
	Kty. & Tenn.			41	7	....	7			41	7	16.5	16.5	
	Total Terr.		161	283	27	20	47	8,400	3.0	283	47	17.4	17.4	3.0
Owens	Ohio & Ind.	8	not covered under present territory arrangement							80	13		14.1	
	Illinois		767	685	51	7	58			607	51	16.2	16.2	
	Michigan		282	282	40	7	47			240	40	15.1	15.1	
	Wisconsin		not covered under present territory arrangement							41	7		16.6	
	Total Terr.		1,049	967	91	14	105	13,800	1.4	968	111	15.1	15.7	1.4
Billings	Minn., Iowa, N. Dak.	9	not covered under present territory arrangement							120	20		18.6	
	S. Dak., Nebraska		not covered under present territory arrangement							365	61		15.1	
	Missouri		80	282	40	7	47			80	13	11.4	16.6	
	Kansas			41	7	...	7			80	13	8.3	16.7	
	Ark. La. Okla.		not covered under present territory arrangement							408	67		14.6	
	Texas		80	162	20	7	27					6.6	15.5	
	Total Terr.		160	485	67	14	81	9,000	1.9	1,053	174	7.9	15.5	.85
Sharp	Mont. Wyo. Idaho	10	not covered under present territory arrangement							120	20		18.7	
	Utah, Col, Ariz., N.M.		not covered under present territory arrangement							162	27		16.6	
	Wash., Ore.		80	120	7	13	20			408	67	18.9	16.6	
	California		282	324	38	7	45					11.3	14.3	
	Nevada		not covered under present territory arrangement											
	Total Terr.		362	444	45	20	65	9,000	2.0	690	114	15.2	15.4	1.3
GRAND TOTAL	United States		$7,395	$7,840	749	162	910	$117,600	1.5	$8,470	$1,053	16.6	17.8	1.4

EXHIBIT 2

Number of Customers by $ Volume
(for the year 1969)

SALESMAN	0 to 999	1,000 to 2,499	2,500 to 4,999	5,000 to 9,999	10,000 to 14,999	15,000 to 24,999	25,000 to 49,999	50,000 to 99,999	TOTAL
Ives..........	32	30	15	10	5	5	2	1	100
Gordon........	10	5	4	12	1	2	—	—	34
Haney.........	26	30	20	31	22	20	10	3	162
Richards......	9	3	13	15	15	8	4	—	67
Whalen........	16	40	30	10	10	21	6	2	135
Ericson.......	34	32	21	8	8	7	4	—	114
Davey.........	14	10	6	7	9	—	2	—	48
Owens.........	33	11	19	13	15	9	3	2	105
Billings......	30	6	13	14	16	2	—	—	81
Sharp.........	10	12	24	8	10	—	—	1	65
TOTAL.........	214	179	165	128	111	74	31	9	911
$ VOLUME TOTALS (000)......	128	365	744	1,152	1,664	1,776	1,350	810	7,989
CUMULATIVE $ TOTAL (000).....		493	1,237	2,389	4,053	5,829	7,179	7,989	
CUMULATIVE % VOLUME......	1.6	6.2	15.5	29.9	50.7	73.0	89.8	100	100
CUMULATIVE % ACCOUNTS......	23.5	43.2	61.3	75.4	87.6	95.7	99.0	100	100

Foremost Dairies, Inc.

Mr. Fred Fornia, Product Manager—Frozen Desserts of Foremost Dairies, Inc., was considering what advertising strategy to use in order to increase the company's sales of ice cream, sherbet and other frozen desserts in 1962.

In the past, the company had followed the practice of introducing new flavors, one at a time during the year, and promoting them for periods of about three months. In 1961, for example, 80% of the company's appropriation of more than $1,000,000[1] for all frozen dessert advertising was devoted to promoting special ice cream flavors as follows:

Cherry Cherie—packed in specially designed packages and promoted from January through March. $340,000[1] was spent on the promotion consisting of one ad run in the February issue of *Reader's Digest* and *Saturday Evening Post*, ads in newspapers, point-of-purchase material distributed to retail stores, and a consumer "name the slogan" contest. In addition, a contest was run for company salesmen to encourage them to promote the sale of special flavors.

Wild Mountain Blackberry—packed in a specially designed ice cream carton. $245,000[1] was spent for point-of-purchase material and newspaper ads to promote the flavor during May and June.

Milk Chocolate Chip—promoted during September, October and November in a specially designed ice cream package. $240,000[1] was spent for point-of-purchase material and newspaper ads.

Candy Cane—promoted in a specially designed ice cream carton during November and December. A $155,000[1] promotional budget was allocated to newspaper advertising and point-of-purchase material.

The remaining 20% of the advertising budget was used throughout the year to promote sherbet, ice milk, imitation ice cream, and novelty frozen desserts.

---

[1] Figures disguised.

In the past, regional sales managers had the responsibility for selecting media, frequency of advertising, and, in some cases, the ad content. The corporate marketing staff was to assume this responsibility in 1962. The product manager believed that frozen dessert advertising over television and radio was more effective than advertising in newspapers. Preliminary plans were to allocate the advertising appropriation primarily to television, using radio to communicate to people not reached by the television advertising.

The special flavors were offered in the top two of five grades of frozen desserts. The grades differed in butterfat content and the amount of "overrun," a term which referred to the amount of air pumped into the product during processing. A brief description of the five grades follows:

1. Catering Grade. Butterfat content approximately 18%, low overrun. The highest quality produced. Sold at a premium price.
2. Regular Grade. Butterfat content approximately 10%. This grade was the "standard" ice cream in the United States and was subject to heavy price competition. Retail grocery store brands usually were of this quality. Foremost produced two brands in this category, one with a 10% to 12% butterfat content called "first label" and a second with a minimum of 10% butterfat content called "second label."
3. Sherbet. Butterfat content less than 1%. Sold at slightly lower price than regular grade ice cream.
4. Ice Milk Grade. Butterfat content 4%. Sold at roughly two-thirds the price of regular grade ice cream.
5. Imitation Grade (Mellorine). Contained vegetable oil instead of butterfat. Sold at the lowest price of any grade of frozen dessert. Due to legal restrictions, imitation ice cream could be sold in 1962 in only 13 states, of which California was one.

The International Association of Ice Cream Manufacturers reported that 1961 industry frozen dessert sales were 71% ice cream, 16% ice milk, 5% mellorine, 4% sherbet, 3% water ices, and 1% other frozen dairy products. The percentage breakdown of Foremost's frozen dessert sales had been similar to that of the industry. Of Foremost's ice cream sales, approximately 10% was of the premium grade and 90% of the regular grade.

A number of flavors were offered in each grade. Mr. Fornia said that the ice cream industry had produced over 300 flavors or flavor combinations in the past, but that vanilla, chocolate and strawberry, or combinations of these three flavors, accounted for about 80% of the volume sold.

Mr. Fornia explained that Foremost typically offered eight or nine flavors in the regular and premium grades of ice cream continuously during the year. The flavors were selected by Mr. Fornia on the basis of past experience and popularity, competitive offerings and his judgment. The company also offered four or five flavors considered appropriate to the season of the year. Heavy bodied flavors like rum were featured in early fall. Flavors such as eggnog, candy cane and holiday pudding were offered in the late fall and cherry and cherry heart ice cream were featured in February in connection with Washington's birthday and Valentine's day. Light flavors containing fruit were marketed in the spring and summer. In addition, a new special flavor was introduced about every three months.

During the fall of 1961, Foremost marketed on the San Francisco Peninsula 14 flavors of regular grade ice cream packaged in half gallon containers. Seven were offered throughout the year. They were vanilla, chocolate, strawberry, marble fudge, rocky road, Neapolitan and maple nut. Five were seasonal flavors offered only that fall. They were strawberry parfait, black walnut, spumoni, butter brickle, and banana and coffee combination. Two were special promotion flavors—Milk Chocolate Chip and Candy Cane.

THE COMPANY

Foremost Dairies had grown substantially in recent years. The company, headquartered in San Francisco, had sales of $33,000,000 in 1947. The next 13 years were marked by more than 80 acquisitions and the company's sales reached $438,000,000 in 1960. In 1961, the company produced and marketed fortified dairy products, baking goods, antibiotics, pharmaceuticals, plastics, chemicals, diet foods, confections, cereals and infant foods in the United States, the Far East, Southeast Asia, Mediterranean countries, South America, and Canada.

Approximately 75% of Foremost's total sales were of consumer products produced and marketed in the United States by the company's Domestic Dairy Division headed by Mr. John L. Bricker, Vice-President and General Manager.

THE PRODUCT MANAGER

Much of the marketing responsibility for consumer products rested with product managers. Ice creams and other frozen desserts, for example, were handled by Mr. Fornia who was one of three product managers who reported to a group product manager for fresh products. The latter executive, in turn, reported to the vice-president and general manager.

The product manager concept was implemented at Foremost in 1961 in order to achieve greater control over the company's marketing efforts. Formerly the responsibility for control of product quality, packaging, procurement and advertising was decentralized by geographic sections of the country.

The introduction of new ice cream flavors was one of Mr. Fornia's major responsibilities. He determined how and when special flavors should be promoted. He recommended grades of Foremost ice cream to be sold in each region and established regional sales objectives for each grade. He allocated the frozen dessert advertising appropriation to specific grades of ice cream offered within each region and recommended advertising media. He standardized ice cream container specifications for all production points, assured that identical product quality standards were being used at all plants and coordinated centralized purchasing of cartons and ice cream ingredients for all grades and flavors to achieve economies of scale and to assure adequate supplies for special promotion flavors.

In the future, it was expected that the company would keep profit and loss records by product line. Thus far the profit centers were plants which produced a number of different products which were not costed separately.

The gross margin and before tax net profit on premium grade ice cream were estimated to be about 37% and 13% respectively for large dairy companies. The corresponding percentages for regular grade first labels were believed to be about 36% and 7% and for the regular grade second labels, 38% and 8%. (See Exhibit 1.)

Mr. Fornia worked closely with the production research manager who developed and checked ice cream flavors. In the course of his work, he consulted informally with the group product manager, the marketing research manager and representatives of the company's advertising agency.

THE INDUSTRY

Historically the dairy industry had been characterized by a large number of small, independent producers serving local markets, high distribution costs, and inefficient plants. Large dairy companies typically had started out with decentralized operations and plants or geographic divisions rather than product lines served as profit centers.

While the gallonage of ice cream sold in the United States had increased with the population, the number of ice cream plants had decreased in recent years. U.S. per capita consumption of ice cream in 1961 was 4.5 gallons, up from 2.9 gallons in 1940. Per capita consumption of frozen dessert products in Foremost sales regions is listed in Exhibits 2 and 3. The number of ice cream plants in the U.S. rose to a peak of nearly 20,-000 in 1955, then decreased to approximately 16,000 in 1961.

It was felt by some observers that the dairy industry in 1961 could be categorized into three groups: (1) national dairy chains and large independent ice cream manufacturers which sold and advertised their brands; (2) supermarkets which retailed (and perhaps manufactured) their own brands usually at prices lower than those of the first category; and (3) specialty frozen dessert manufacturers who sold at retail or wholesale or both.

With recent emergence of large supermarket chains as the leading volume outlets for ice cream, the chain managements had an improved bargaining position for purchasing ice cream for sale under their own brands.

FOREMOST ICE CREAM DISTRIBUTION

Foremost Dairies sold ice cream in 32 states in five major regions as follows: Pacific Region—Washington, Oregon, California and Arizona; Southwest Region—Texas, New Mexico and Louisiana; North Central Region—Arkansas, Kansas, Missouri, Oklahoma, Minnesota, North Dakota and South Dakota; Northeast Region—Connecticut, Delaware, Maryland, Massachusetts, Michigan, New Jersey, New York, Pennsylvania, Vermont and Virginia; and Southeast Region—Alabama, Florida, Georgia, Kentucky, North Carolina, South Carolina, Tennessee and West Virginia.

By 1961, the Foremost brand was sold in an average 20% of the ice cream retail outlets in these states. Foremost Dairies' share of the ice cream market in these regions ranged from 11% to 14% except in the northeast where it was less than 5%. In some markets Foremost had only one or two competitors. In others, like the San Francisco Peninsula, the company competed with six major dairy brands (Arden, Borden, Carnation, Challenge, Meadow Gold and Spreckles) and retailer brands (such as Safeway's Lucerne and Lucky Stores' Lady Lee Brand). The number of Foremost flavors an individual store could carry varied with space limitations and the number of brands and grades stocked. A small grocery store might carry only one brand while a large supermarket might carry two or three brands. If the supermarket was a member of a chain which had its own label (usually in the regular grade which provided the largest sales volume) it might stock a dairy company brand in grades and flavors not carried under the chain's label. The store might stock, for example, six flavors of the dairy company brand's ice milk and four flavors of its premium grade to add to five or six flavors of regular grade sold under its own label. The outside brand stocked often was manufactured by the same company that produced the chain's own label ice cream.

Along with other ice cream producers, Foremost had experienced in the past 15 years a trend in demand from pint and quart sizes to half gallons and from the hand packed bulk ice cream to half gallon containers filled by machines at the plant. Mr. Fornia attributed the trends to growth in the number of home freezers which permitted home storage of frozen products. He did not believe that brand preference in ice creams was strong enough to lead consumers to go to another store in search of a brand they failed to find at their first stop. He believed that most consumers selected ice cream on the basis of type, flavor and price.

(See Appendix A for information on the market for ice cream from a study of "Public Attitudes and Uses of Dairy Products" conducted for the International Association of Ice Cream Manufacturers, the Milk Industry Foundation, and the American Dairy Association by Alfred Politz Research, Inc., in 1959.)

SPECIAL FLAVOR PROMOTIONS

Total sales in 1961 for special flavors was 1,400,000 gallons.[2] Regional breakdowns by flavor were not available to Mr. Fornia. He estimated, however, that Cherry Cherie comprised about 40% of special flavor sales for the year and Wild Mountain Blackberry 25%. The remaining 35% consisted of the combined sales of Milk Chocolate Chip and Candy Cane. These percentages were difficult to interpret because of regional variations in the number of Foremost retail outlets and the promotional effort. Records for 1961 on both factors were kept at Foremost's 31 ice cream plants.

Mr. Fornia gave the following reasons for Foremost's practice of running special flavor promotions:

1. It was difficult to promote a standard flavor such as vanilla.
2. Market studies had indicated that heavy ice cream buyers tended to purchase a variety of new and different flavors that were considered unique and exciting.
3. Television and radio commercials were easier to develop for one new flavor and they were considered to be more effective in increasing ice cream sales than advertising devoted to regular flavors.
4. Special flavor promotions could be used as a sales aid for expanding distribution into retail outlets which had not carried the Foremost brand.

Mr. Fornia regarded special flavor promotions as a means of stimulating sales of all Foremost flavors as well as the special flavor which received the promotional emphasis. Special flavors had accounted for approximately 5% of Foremost's packaged regular grade ice cream sales volume in 1961. An eastern company which relied heavily on special flavor promotion reported that special flavors accounted for up to 25% of its ice cream sales. (See Appendix B.)

Flavor preferences varied somewhat by geographic regions, and, in the past, not all regions promoted the same special flavor at the same time. For 1962, however, Foremost planned to implement the policy of running the same special flavor promotions in all of its markets at the same time. This was easier and more economical to do than varying the special flavors by region.

In the past, the ideas for new Foremost flavors had come either from the company's production department or from suppliers which offered flavors on a franchise basis. The product manager selected those flavors which he regarded to have a promising sales outlook by exercising his

---

[2] Figure disguised.

judgment based on knowledge of historical sales activity. The names of flavors and special promotional plans for the coming year was approved by the group product manager and by the vice-president and general manager, usually by October of the previous year and in no case later than four months prior to the promotion. The main considerations in selecting a flavor were the estimated consumer appeal of the name, the availability of ingredients, the number of suppliers producing that ingredient, and price. When names of flavors had been previously trademarked by a supplier, Foremost contracted for franchise use of the name as in the case of Wild Mountain Blackberry. New names of flavors were trademarked by Foremost when the product was distributed for sale.

RECOMMENDATION TO MANAGEMENT

In looking ahead, Mr. Fornia was considering what advertising recommendations he should make for 1962. Should the special flavor promotions be continued as the company's main advertising strategy? If not, what should be the strategy?

EXHIBIT 1

Estimated Average Income per Gallon of Large Dairy Companies for Premium and Regular Grades of Ice Cream (1961)

	Premium	Regular (1st Label)	Regular (2nd Label)
Manufacturer's price*	$1.90	$1.40	$1.20
Cost of goods sold*	1.20	0.90	0.75
Gross margin	0.70	0.50	0.45
Selling, advertising, delivery & administration expense	0.45	0.40	0.35
Net profit before taxes	$0.25	$0.10	$0.10

* It was estimated that price and cost figures often varied between regions by 25%.

EXHIBIT 2

U.S. Per Capita Consumption of Frozen Desserts in the Regions in Which the Foremost Brand Was Sold (1961) (gallons)

Region	Ice Cream	Ice Milk	Sherbet
North Central	4.92	0.526	0.201
Northeast	4.30	0.229	0.183
Northwest	3.74	0.671	0.221
South Pacific	3.31	0.841	0.316
South Central	2.76	0.724	0.158
Southeast	2.62	0.996	0.182
Southwest	2.08	0.326	0.190

EXHIBIT 3

U.S. Per Capita Consumption of Mellorine (Imitation Ice Cream) in Seven States in Which the Foremost Brand Was Sold (1961)
(gallons)

State	Foremost Region	Consumption
Texas.....................	Southwest	1.998
Oklahoma.................	South Central	1.148
California................	South Pacific	0.772
Missouri.................	South Central	0.692
Oregon...................	Northwest	0.405
Arizona..................	South Pacific	0.350
Louisiana................	Southwest	0.281

Source: Foremost Dairies, Inc.

APPENDIX A: THE ICE CREAM MARKET AND ICE CREAM FLAVORS

(A digest of characteristics of the market for ice cream extracted from "Public Attitudes and Uses of Dairy Products," Highlights Study No. 10, Alfred Politz Research, Inc., Fall, 1959)

Ice Cream Market

One out of three homes had ice cream on hand, i.e., 17,000,000 U.S. households could serve ice cream every day. Home supply was highest in the North Central United States (40%), lowest in the South (28%), but generally good in all areas.

Ice cream was popular at all income levels, although the percentage of families with ice cream on hand increased with income. Fifty-seven per cent of the upper income group had ice cream on hand, 38% of the middle income group, and 23% of the lower income group. The average supply on hand was 3.7 pints per household, or 31,500,000 quarts available in all U.S. homes.

Ice cream eating was popular with all ages. About one out of two children between 6 and 14 years of age ate ice cream on an average day. Ice cream eating dropped with age, but not as much as milk drinking declined. Forty-seven million Americans six years and older ate ice cream every day.

Ice cream generally was popular on all occasions, although most was eaten plain, as a dish by itself, and at home during or after supper. It was popular in great volume at lunch, between lunch and supper, and away from home. Ice cream in cones, in cups and with toppings was more popular away from home than at home.

Most ice cream was eaten in the home and women ate somewhat more ice cream at home than did men. As children became older, they ate more ice cream away from home. The pattern of ice cream eating at home during the day (lunch, snack, supper, etc.) was about the same for men and women. Away from home, men ate ice cream more often for lunch and during the afternoon than did women.

Major occasions for adults eating ice cream were at, or after, supper. For children, lunch, afternoon, supper, and after supper were all popular occasions, and, as children became older, these occasions were about equally popular.

Only 8% of adults (15 years and older) did not eat ice cream as compared to 25% who did not drink milk. Only 3% said they did not like frozen desserts and 2% avoided frozen desserts in dieting, although 9% were dieters.

Estimated servings from half-gallon containers, were slightly larger than servings from pint containers, which probably reflected different family needs rather than differences due to the containers themselves.

Ice cream served by itself averaged an estimated one ounce more than ice cream served with pie or cake.

A "heavy ice cream user" was considered one who ate four quarts or more every two weeks. A "medium user" ate two to three quarts every two weeks, and a "light user" ate two or less quarts every two weeks.

Ice Cream Flavors

Vanilla was the big favorite. Twenty per cent of households had vanilla on hand. Half of those who ate frozen desserts rated vanilla as their favorite. Vanilla on hand in the home was highest in the North Central United States, lowest in the Northeast, but generally popular throughout the country. Although generally parallel, vanilla on hand and vanilla as the most favored flavor had somewhat different patterns of variation from region to region.

Chocolate and strawberry followed vanilla in popularity. Chocolate was on hand in 5% of households (2,500,000 U.S. households). Chocolate on hand was highest in the Northeastern United States and in the South. Chocolate rated higher as a favorite flavor than it did in home supply. Chocolate tended to be a flavor for individual tastes. With some, chocolate tended to be strongly liked or strongly disliked. Strawberry on hand was highest in the South and West. Strawberry appeared to be a "special occasion" flavor, popular for serving to guests.

Flavors other than the big three were not as important in home supply and preference. Single flavors, besides vanilla, chocolate, and strawberry were on hand in 8% of U.S. households (4,000,000). Combinations of flavors (primarily vanilla combinations) were on hand in 5% of U.S. households (2,500,000). Eight per cent of households had more than one flavor (single or combination) on hand, reflecting some demand for variety.

Single flavors were the most popular. Eighty-two per cent of flavors consumed were single flavors of which 49% was vanilla, 11% chocolate, 6% strawberry and 16% other single flavors. The remaining 18% of flavors consumed consisted of 13% vanilla combinations and 5% non-vanilla combinations. Single flavor preference was highest in the Southern United States, lowest in the Northeast. Preference for combined flavors was highest in the Northeast, which probably reflected availability.

Two flavor combinations in total were more popular than three flavor combinations. Two out of three families occasionally served combinations of flavors. The three major flavors were preferred for combinations: vanilla, chocolate, and strawberry; vanilla and chocolate; vanilla and strawberry. These same combinations rated highest among those households interested in trying flavor combinations.

Seventy-five per cent of those who served ice cream served the same size portions in all flavors. Among those who varied the size of servings, vanilla was most often served in larger portions. Chocolate was first among the smaller servings (richer, sharper flavor, etc.).

Ice cream was usually served plain. Vanilla and other flavors and combinations of flavors were usually eaten plain without sauces or toppings, without cake, pie, or cookies. When sauces, toppings, etc. were served on ice cream, vanilla was used more often than other flavors which emphasized that vanilla was more compatible with other items than the more distinctive flavors.

APPENDIX B: SPECIAL FLAVOR PROMOTIONS

(Excerpts from LaBorie, G. W., "Make an Impact with Special Flavor Promotions," *The Ice Cream Review*, December, 1961, p. 24.)

. . . today, the featured flavor has become a permanent weapon in the marketing arsenal, ranging in volume importance from 5% to 25% and something less than this in ledger sheet profit importance. However, the intangible asset of the promotional impetus that featured flavors give to an entire line is just as important a profit contribution as the revenue dollar. This is particularly true in a product line which has traditionally lacked truly imaginative merchandising and has unfortunately succumbed in too many cases to ridiculous price cuts demanded by the trade, rather than preselling the customer with thoughtful and service-oriented promotion. The principal gains, therefore, in featured flavor promotions can be these:

1. Excitement and change of pace in all of the marketing-mix action for the purpose of stimulating continuing interest, not only in the featured product per se, but, importantly to you, in your particular brand . . . an excite-

ment which should permeate all levels—management, sales organization, trade and consumer.

2. Brand switching. If your featured flavor promotion carries enough imagination and weight, it will draw attention away from competition.

3. A distributive wedge. Featured flavors provide an excellent opportunity to expand distribution to new accounts and to increase facings in current accounts.

4. Sampling. Getting customers to try your brand via featured flavors opens the door for higher consumer acceptance of the regular line.

5. It upgrades the flavor image. The unusual featured flavor carries with it the suggestion of higher quality and greater variety of standard flavor.

6. A possible profit opportunity in premium pricing. Generally speaking, featured flavors cost more to make and promote. Because they are unique, they can justify a more favorable price structure, although in many markets, competitors have made featured flavors just another price football. This would appear to be one answer to shrinking margins on standard flavors.

7. An opportunity to extend package identity. Of course, this is an advantage only to those who package featured flavors in cartons identical to those carrying standard flavors. There is the other school of thought that special packaging of the featured flavor dramatizes the very difference which creates many of the gains I've mentioned earlier.

8. It provides a means of replacing at least some secondary or "private label" facings at higher profitability.

9. Continuity of promotion. Because the effective promotional life of a featured flavor varies with its uniqueness, weight of exposure, timeliness, seasonality, etc., the life cycle ranges from three to five weeks. Therefore, an effective featured flavor rotation program should consist of about six to eight special flavors in order to retain continuity of the marketing pluses I've been listing here.

On the other side of the coin, when six to eight featured flavors per year are introduced, costs of laboratory research increase, both in the technical field and in the area of market research. Production costs increase from experimentation and the adjustments necessary to mass-produce special flavor combinations without jeopardizing standard flavor availability. Packaging costs are increased due to the development of special containers and/or carton designs for relatively short production runs. Other sales of standard flavors may suffer and, generally speaking, featured flavor margins are usually slimmer.

Varian Associates, Incorporated

Early in April, 1966, the marketing research director of the Tube Division of Varian Associates, Inc., was faced with the problem of responding to a request made by the manager of the Operations Research Unit to specify exactly what types of decisions could and would be made using data obtained from the media survey now in the field. The media study had been initiated in the fall of 1965 by the advertising manager of the tube division to obtain needed information on the readership of selected magazines and journals. At one time or another a variety of interested parties, including the division's advertising agency, the Corporate Public Relations officer, the Corporate Director of Research, and the division's marketing manager had participated in formulating the study of design.

Varian Associates, with headquarters in Palo Alto, California, is one of the largest electronics companies in the world. Founded as an outgrowth of the pioneering work done before and during World War II on the klystron tube the company grew in some twenty years from 6 people and $22,000 in sales to 6,400 employees and annual sales of $100 million in 1965. The company is organized into three major groups as follows:

1. Microwave Tube Group

This group is comprised of the Palo Alto tube division; the Eimac Division of San Carlos, California; the Bomac Division of Beverly, Massachusetts, S-F-D Laboratories, Inc., of Union, New Jersey; Varian Associates of Canada, Ltd., Georgetown, Ontario; and Semicon Associates, Inc., Lexington, Kentucky. Major products of the group consist of klystron tubes, traveling wave tubes, magnetron tubes, gas switching tubes, microwave components, solid state devices, crossed-field devices, backward wave oscillators, and klystron amplifiers. The basic applications for these products include early warning radar, radar astronomy, satellite communications, missile guidance, air traffic control, weather radar, UHF television, microwave relay systems, beacons, microwave test equipment, navigation aids, and navigation.

2. Instrument Group

This group is comprised of the Analytical Instrument Division of Palo Alto, the Recorder Division also in Palo Alto, and the Quantum Electronics Division of Beverly, Massachusetts and Palo Alto. The major products of the group include spectrometers, laboratory electromagnetics and superconducting magnets, recorders, frequency standards, and magnetometers. The basic applications for these products include quantitative and qualitative nondestructive analysis of chemical compounds, isotope identification, laboratory research, studies of the behavior of matter under the influence of precise magnetic fields, navigation, timekeeping, communications, geophysical exploration, magnetic search, deep space probes, and oceanographic research.

3. Equipment Group

This group produced such products as ultra-high vacuum pumps and systems, vacuum instrumentation, and linear accelerators. The basic applications of these products include appendage pumping, vacuum tube processing, mass spectometers, physics experiments, evaporation and deposition, environmental testing, study of services, metallurgical studies, physical and biological studies, clinical radiation therapy, food irradiation, high energy physics studies, and radiation chemistry studies.

*   *   *   *   *

The Tube Group was the largest in sales of the three groups. It sold its products to both military and industrial companies typically on a contract-bid basis. In 1965 the group employed a total of 40 salesmen and servicemen. In addition, a substantial number of men at the various headquarters offices assisted the field men when the occasion arose. The Tube Group spent several hundred thousands each year in advertising and promotion including media advertising, trade shows, workshops, publicity, direct mail, and catalogs.

The advertising manager of the Tube Group summed up his request for a media study by saying, "I want to know what magazines and journals are the most efficient to use to cover audiences that I specify as needing to receive certain messages." He also indicated that in preparation for a media study of some sort he was revising his master mailing list by omitting individuals who were not influential in the purchase of products produced by the tube group. This master list had been compiled over the years through sales reports, inquiries, trade shows, direct mail, and workshops. In order to bring it up to date all tube sales and service people were asked to indicate the names, titles, and addresses of all those people whom they thought were influential in deciding what supplier to use. The specific request read, "We would like to ask that you prepare a list of the ten most influential people in each of your major accounts; these should be people that you feel we should be reaching with our advertising."

After receiving the names from the field force and further culling, the master list contained approximately 3,500 names of which 600 were indicated as being "prime influentials." It was decided to conduct the survey among all 3,500, but to identify the 600 separately so as to be able to follow up either by phone or mail on them where necessary.

The group's advertising agency was asked what information should be obtained in the media study. The agency's response is shown in Exhibit 1. After evaluating the agency's reply as well as requests from other individuals, a final questionnaire was prepared (see Exhibit 2). Follow-ups were planned on the entire sample to obtain a high rate of returns. The questionnaire was mailed together with a stamped first-class return envelope in February and March, 1966.

At one of the several conferences held to implement the survey the responsibility for analyzing the returns was given to the Operations Research Unit. Since the same survey approach would likely be used by other Varian groups, the OR Unit was anxious to develop a standardized set of procedures for computerizing and analyzing the data. To do this they had to know *exactly* what decisions the advertising manager planned to make using the survey data, what additional information he wished to correlate with the survey data, and what "operational" measures he wanted to use. As an example of the latter the word "coverage" represented a problem. The term could be used in a variety of ways including the number of people reached by the average issue of a given magazine or journal, or it could mean the cumulative audience reached by a given number of issues of a magazine or journal.

The OR Unit requested that the Tube Group marketing research manager get together with the division's advertising manager to respond to numerous suggestions pertaining to the development of a simple media model which could, it was thought, be made operational through the use of the survey data. The proposed model is described in Exhibit 3.

How should the Marketing Research Manager and Advertising Manager of the Tube Group respond to the request from the OR Unit?

EXHIBIT 1

Hoefer, Dieterich & Brown, Inc. Advertising and Public Relations
414 Jackson Square, San Francisco, California 94111—Yukon 1–1811

November 5, 1965

Mr. Dick Barck
Marketing Department
Varian Associates
611 Hansen Way
Palo Alto, California

Dear Dick:

I enclose an outline of the kinds of information that we would find useful when the media preference survey is completed for the Tube Group.

Taking the groupings in order, we're interested in a breakdown of the company's primary areas of interest because different kinds of products should, obviously, be advertised to different kinds of systems manufacturers. You may be able to provide this information within Varian on most of the companies.

We want some sort of a breakdown on job function, because the new Business Publication Association (BPA) figures on circulation by member publication will be broken down in this manner. The functions that I have suggested are those used by Microwaves magazine in their own circulation analysis.

We would like to break the surveys into groupings by (1) specifying function and (2) approving function. In addition, if possible, we would like to have a "rating" as to degree of actual influence in the actual purchase.

As to the publications themselves, I have listed the magazines now under consideration for Tube Group promotion, plus two amateur-oriented publications being used by Eimac. The list should probably be checked with Bob Landon to make sure that we are covering his market adequately. I have consciously excluded questions dealing with the "most useful" editorial or "do you read the advertisements," because I frankly don't know what to do with this type of information after I have it. We don't care, in my opinion, whether he reads the magazine because it contains information pertinent to his job, or because it contributes interdisciplinary information in which he is interested, or because it provides general news about his industry. We do care whether or not he reads it regularly, and whether or not he considers it "must" reading. As to the advertising readership, it's our job to make the ads sufficiently interesting so that he *will* read them.

After the results are in, we will provide cost information which can be related to publication preferences and market coverage. It should be fairly simple to

EXHIBIT 1 (Continued)

determine a "cost efficiency" rating by comparing the weighted percentage of regular readers to the absolute cost of a single advertising page.

Please call me if you have any questions.

Very truly yours,

HOEFER, DIETERICH & BROWN, INC.

/s/ Hal

Hal H. Marquis

sh

Enclosure
cc: Mr. Paul Warner
      Mr. Bill Engel
      Mr. Jim Kirby

(1)   Company's primary areas of interest:

  Communications systems manufacturers
  Telemetering & data systems manufacturers
  Electronic countermeasures systems manufacturers
  Navigation & guidance systems manufacturers
  Air traffic control & landing systems manufacturers
  Weapon control systems manufacturers
  Miscellaneous radar systems manufacturers
  Research & development laboratories
  U.S. Government & military
  Microwave test equipment manufacturers
  Miscellaneous microwave components manufacturers
  General: materials, plasma, nuclear, magnetics, etc.

(2)   Job function of individual answering questionnaire:

  Application engineering
  Development engineering
  Design engineering
  Research
  Engineering management
  Purchasing
  Administrative management
  Production management

(3)   Individual's influence in buying decision:

  a.   Specify components: (rate 1 to 10)
  b.   Review purchase decision: (rate 1 to 10)

(4)   Readership of the following publications (rated "read occasionally," "read regularly," and "consider *must* reading"):

EXHIBIT 1 (Concluded)

PRODUCT: Electronic Design, Electronics, EDN (Electrical Design News), E.E.E., Electro-Technology, Electronic Industries, Signal, Space Aeronautics, Solid State Design, IEEE Proceedings, IEEE Spectrum

PURCHASING: Electronic Procurement, Electronic Specifying and Procurement

MILITARY: Air Force & Space Digest, Armed Forces Management, Army, Ordnance, Data, Journal of the Armed Forces, Naval Institute Proceedings

AMATEUR: CQ and QST

HORIZONTAL: Aviation Week, Astronautics & Aeronautics, Electronic News, Industrial Research, International Science & Technology, Missiles & Rockets, Research/Development, Scientific American

(5) Agency will provide information on circulation, cost-per-thousand-readers, and cost-per-page. Final figures should relate cost-per-page to weighted percentage of regular readers in Varian study.

EXHIBIT 2

Varian Associates Executive Offices

Palo Alto, California

Robert T. Davis
Vice President, Marketing
Dear Sir:

Would you please help us in solving one of our marketing problems?

We're trying to improve our communications programs. During the next eighteen months, we will, with your permission, be calling on you for your personal advice on the subject of magazine ads.

This survey is the first of the series and asks for your reading preference; the second will follow in about six months and will deal with the effectiveness of our ads; the third questionnaire, later in the year, will give you the opportunity to help us actually write our ads.

We hope you will take a few minutes to answer this questionnaire. Your response will be very meaningful and greatly appreciated.

Very truly yours,

Robert T. Davis

RTD/bb

Inside are photographs of 28 magazines serving our industry. In the spaces provided, please check how often you read each of these magazines. If you do not read a magazine, simply leave the spaces blank. (Note: This part of the questionnaire is not contained in the case.)

EXHIBIT 2 (Continued)

Questionnaire*

Which of the 28 mentioned magazines do you find most helpful in your work? (Please list in order of importance)

1. _____   4. _____
2. _____   5. _____
3. _____   6. _____

In addition, we ask you to indicate your job function and the primary area(s) of your work.

My work is primarily concerned with the following:
(Check one only)

MANAGEMENT   ENGINEERING
☐ Administrative   ☐ Design/Application
☐ Engineering Program   ☐ Manufacturing/Production

RESEARCH & DEVELOPMENT   ☐ OTHER _____
☐ Basic (No specific end product)   (Specify)
☐ Applied (Product development)

The primary technical area(s) of my work is (are) concerned with:

☐ RADAR   ☐ TEST MEASUREMENT
☐ NAVIGATION, GUIDANCE   ☐ INDUSTRIAL HEATING
   & CONTROL   PROCESS & CONTROL
☐ ECM/PEN AIDS   ☐ SCIENTIFIC & MEDICAL
☐ TELEMETRY   ☐ OTHER _____
   COMMUNICATIONS   (Specify)
   ☐ Broadcast
   ☐ Military
   ☐ Other _____
      (Specify)

Thank you for taking the time to answer these questions. Your assistance in this phase of our over-all marketing program is sincerely appreciated. All that remains is to fold the questionnaire and return it to me in the enclosed self-addressed envelope.

EXHIBIT 3

Excerpts from the Proposal by the OR Unit to Set up a Media Model

The proposed model (called MISER) has as its objective among selected audience groups the generation of a weighted readership scale *and* a readership distribution. The former provides a score based on reach and frequency of exposure within specified time periods while the latter consists of two distributions, the first of which yields the percentage of readers exposed once, twice, etc. The second distribution is cumulative. By comparing the weighted scores

---

* These questions were asked in addition to those pertaining to the readership (if any) of the 28 magazines.

EXHIBIT 3 (Continued)

and the readership distribution of two or more alternative media schedules the user can decide which schedule best suits his objectives.

The media vehicle data which is being obtained by individuals from the survey will be collapsed into the following question—"what is the probability of prospect X being exposed to the *average* issue of each of a variety of print media vehicles?" No attempt will be made to measure the extent or degree of exposure. Thus, exposure is defined operationally as whether a respondent reports reading "something" within a particular vehicle.

The probability statement is used because of the problem of time. Assume a quarterly journal. If one knew that a prospect is exposed on the average to three out of four issues then the probability of exposure to the *average* issue would be .75; if the exposure is two out of four it would be .50; and so on. Obviously, if the prospect is exposed to all four issues then it would be certain (1.0) that he read the average issue.

The problem of how to treat additional exposures (either within a specific vehicle through time or between media vehicles) is not easily solved. The problem is complex because of the need to ascertain at the margin the effect of each additional exposure given certain time intervals between exposures. Naturally the effect of repetition has to be evaluated differently for different products. In the case at hand it is proposed that the first exposure be rated at .9, the second at 1.0, the third at .9,—all within a two months' interval on the assumption that your advertising will be centered on products which are relatively new and complex; therefore, the "reader" will need exposure to two ads in order to obtain "full" information. A special feature of the model calls for providing you with the opportunity of inserting the "current" media schedule to inoculate individual prospects following which the schedule to be tested can be better evaluated through the weighting of additional exposures.

We estimate the total cost of building MISER at about $4,000 and that each schedule can be "tested" at a cost not to exceed $40.

Playskool Manufacturing Company

The advertising manager of the Playskool Manufacturing Company was reviewing past advertising expenditures in connection with the preparation of next year's budget. The company produced toys for children between the ages of two and ten, but concentrated on a complete line of preschool wood educational toys. The annual advertising budget was approximately $200,000. Most of these funds were used to purchase space in toy catalogues distributed by wholesalers and department stores. About $35,000 was spent for package inserts that showed the entire line and that were included with each toy; $15,000 was used for trade advertising; $10,000 was used for direct mail to school officials and teachers; and $5,000 for booths at school conventions.

Playskool, with an average annual sales increase of about 10 per cent per year since 1939, had become the leader in sales of preschool wood educational toys. The company had about forty competitors, but only one of these made wood and educational toys exclusively. Educational toys for preschool children accounted for approximately 7 per cent of the toy industry's $1.5 billion annual sales volume. Out of this total, Playskool's share was somewhat better than 5 per cent. Pretax net profit margins were generally between 15 and 20 per cent of sales.

Playskool's line generally retailed from 79 cents to $9.00 per toy, with the typical sale in the $1.00–$3.00 category. Included in the line were push toys, pull toys, co-ordination toys, play materials (such as blocks), construction toys, puzzle plaques, and pounding toys. About 90 per cent of all sales were made in toys designed for preschool children. In general, the company's toys were priced slightly higher than other toys of a comparable nature.

Since the company's inception, the management had endeavored to secure consumer brand loyalty through the establishment of a favorable corporate image. To support this policy, the company had undertaken consumer advertising for many years. It was one of only four or five toy manufacturers who advertised to consumers. Playskool, however, typically promoted its entire line of toys, while competitors generally carried out one-item campaigns. Approximately 80 per cent of the Playskool budget had been spent for advertisements in such magazines as *Good Housekeeping, Woman's Day*, and *Parent's Magazine*. Management believed that such magazines had good consumer reputations, which would support the image they desired for their line. In addition, they found that these magazines obtained the best consumer inquiry and response.

In the late 1950's the toy industry became heavily involved in co-operative advertising. At that time, a catalogue printing firm sold a group of wholesalers on the idea that a catalogue, paid for principally by toy manufacturers, would be a good promotional device. Wholesaler salesmen could use the catalogue to sell the retailer by offering large quantities, either free or for a nominal sum, for redistribution under the store's name to its customers. Wholesalers were generally enthusiastic about the idea and placed heavy pressure upon manufacturers to subscribe to catalogues in order to have their toys represented. Playskool executives thought that they had no other alternative but to follow this trend. Now, some several years later, the company's products were represented in some forty catalogues, thirty of which were produced by department stores and the remainder by toy wholesalers. The large expenditures that this required forced the company to drop its consumer advertising entirely. During the past year this co-operative advertising cost approximately 5 per cent of sales to department stores and 2.5 per cent of sales to jobbers. No co-operative advertising funds had as yet been given to chain stores and mail-order accounts, which represented slightly more than one-third of the company's total volume.

The educational toy market varied somewhat from that of the rest of the toy industry. First, its sales did not vary as much seasonally as did those of the industry. Some 70–75 per cent of the toy industry's sales were made during the Christmas season. Second, people tended to shop for specific types of educational toys, whereas the greater share of most other toys were bought on impulse.

Since the move to catalogues, Playskool executives had become increasingly disturbed lest the abandonment of consumer advertising result in a reduction in consumer loyalty and a loss of corporate image. Toy catalogues, they believed, were not adequate for this purpose. As a consequence, the firm began a school advertising campaign on a limited basis. The purpose of this campaign was to acquaint school principals, administrators, teachers, nurses, counselors, and other people dealing with preschool children with Playskool toys. Executives believed that these individuals would be in a very good position to recommend toys, particularly when parents visited the classrooms to observe their children.

Playskool's management thought that teachers were generally responsible for the purchase of new toys for the classroom each year. Funds were obtained from petty cash or from the principal, and purchases were made from one or more school supply wholesalers. When new schools were built, distributors were usually asked to make bids for the total initial requirements.

To reach the school market, Playskool developed a two-part program, each part of which cost about $5,000. The first was directed toward school supply wholesalers and consisted of the preparation of about 1.5 million inserts for placement in the catalogues distributed to schools by the wholesaler salesmen. Playskool inserts appeared in about sixty toy catalogues of this type printed by major wholesalers. Playskool also sent representatives to the school supply wholesaler conventions.

The second part of the program was directed toward school officials and consisted of display booths at five of the major annual school conventions. These conventions, such as the one held by the National Education Association and its various subgroups, were attended primarily by school administrators and elementary school principals. Playskool representatives also attended the convention of the National Kindergarten Association. Various school supply distributors also took booths at these conventions.

The advertising manager was concerned about the effectiveness of these campaigns and whether they were achieving the goals the company sought. Sales to schools had increased from $25,000 to approximately $150,000 over the past five years. It was anticipated that next year sales to this segment would increase by about $20,000. The advertising manager was not certain whether this growth represented a greater share of the market or simply growth of the entire market. He also was not sure whether the campaign had produced any awareness of the Playskool name with either teacher or child or whether any of the information about the educational value of the toys filtered back to parents or retail store owners.

One fault in the program, the advertising manager speculated, was that it might not be adequate. There were about forty school supply distributors who used no co-operative advertising. There were also hundreds of local school conventions that could be attended. Lists of kindergarten schoolteachers' names and addresses were probably available, and there was a trade school publication, *Our Schools,* which covered all elementary grades and which accepted advertising. On the other hand, it was possible that some or all of the funds used in this way were being wasted and could be spent elsewhere to better advantage. While the company was currently appearing in most group catalogues outside the school field, the advertising manager thought that a number of individual store and wholesaler catalogues were still not showing Playskool toys. The manager was somewhat restricted by a general management policy that advertising costs should not exceed 3 per cent of sales.

What changes, if any, should Playskool make in its advertising program?

Hatfield versus Duncan[1]

In early 1966, Oregon's Republican governor, Mark O. Hatfield, appeared to be the winner in the race for the seat in the U.S. Senate that had been vacated by Democrat Maurine Neuberger. Hatfield's Democratic opponent, Representative Robert B. Duncan, was largely unknown to voters outside his own Congressional District in southwest Oregon. Moreover, Hatfield had a record as one of the strongest vote-getters in Oregon's political history. Then one issue—Viet Nam with all its personal and political ramifications—began to change the character of the race.

In late July Hatfield's key staff planners and his advertising agency met to consolidate and to alter the direction of the campaign for the final election in November. At this time it was clear that Hatfield, and not Duncan, was the candidate in trouble.

Hatfield's trouble began in April and May. Although he had previously made statements opposing the administration's policy in Viet Nam, his comments began to attract national attention during a speaking tour in Arizona and Texas early in the year. At that point, Hatfield's position did not seem out of line, because his most likely opponent, Representative Edith Green, was even more of a "dove." The May Democratic primary, however, made Hatfield's position on Viet Nam look unsound politically. Representative Duncan, not Green, ran against Howard Morgan, another "dove" on Viet Nam, who was strongly supported in his campaign by Senator Wayne Morse, one of the most vitriolic critics of the administration with respect to Viet Nam. Duncan won with a vote of 130,478, while Hatfield totaled only 131,025, running against several relatively unknown candidates in the Republican primary. Duncan gave un-

---

[1] This case was prepared by Assistant Professor Michael L. Ray of Stanford and Professor John D. Phillips, a Vice President of Lewis and Clark College, Portland, Oregon. Although the entire case is based on actual events, confidential figures and dates have been changed. The case is merely a description of events and is not meant to be critical of administrative action or political tactics.

mistakable evidence of the kind of campaign he would run against Hatfield. His successful primary effort was laced with statements on Viet Nam like:

If we don't stop the Communists on the Mekong, we'll have to fight them on the banks of the Columbia River.

Communism can't be contained by debate and argument.

There is no road to peaceful settlement which we have not explored. It cannot help our cause to negotiate with each other while Hanoi refuses to negotiate.

Hatfield himself gave Duncan's "hawkish" emphasis further fuel and meaning in the first week of July at the National Governors' Conference in Los Angeles. There Hatfield's views again stirred local and national comment when he refused to sign a resolution supporting the administration's position on Viet Nam—the "military defense of South Viet Nam against aggression." In casting the only negative vote (49 to 1), Hatfield said he did not support escalation of the war.

It was evident that Duncan had an issue that could coalesce any negative feeling that might have existed against Hatfield in Oregon before the Viet Nam problem. The attitude of many Oregonians after the Governors' Conference was:

We're not sure we want two people representing us back there in the Senate who stand alone.

The statement linked Hatfield's lone dissent with Senator Wayne Morse's stand on Viet Nam. Many Democrats saw Hatfield as another Morse—somebody who would regard himself as "his own man" rather than as a man who would be "loyal" to the administration or the party or Oregon. At the same time, many Republicans recalled that Morse was once a Republican and bolted to the Democrats on the basis of a "position" which they naturally regarded as highly unsatisfactory.

All of these events strongly affected the senatorial contest. In July, a survey conducted by pollster John Kraft for the Oregon AFL-CIO showed the following:

	Percent
Duncan	46
Hatfield	40
Uncommitted	14

The Hatfield planners now had an uphill battle on their hands.

THE OREGON POLITICAL ENVIRONMENT

Oregon is a relatively small state in population (about 2 million in 1966), but its political importance is relatively great. Oregon's primaries were quite crucial, for example, in the fortunes of several presidential candidates (e.g., Governor Rockefeller's victory in Oregon in 1964 gave a substantial boost to his campaign), and its senators often had great visibility.

The state could be characterized as Democratic and reasonably "liberal" on most issues. Lumber is the major industry with food and paper products following. The defense industry was showing some growth in Oregon in 1965 and 1966.

Oregonians personally could be classed as rugged outdoor types. Hunting and fishing are very popular. One of the few "liberal" issues that failed to gain substantial support in Oregon was gun control. This failure obviously reflected Oregon's outdoor and "individualistic" style of living.

The Kraft poll taken in July also asked Oregon voters what issues they thought were the most important, and more of them mentioned taxes than anything else. Next came inflation, then "big government," while the fourth ranked area of concern was Viet Nam with about 25 percent.

Oregon was essentially a one-party state until 1954, when Democrat Richard Neuberger was elected to the Senate, and Edith Green launched her career as congressman from the Third District by defeating Republican Tom McCall. In fact, the 1954 elections merely recorded the turning point in a long-term trend of voter registrations toward the Democratic Party. This trend continued during the next ten years, as follows:

Year	Democrats	%	Republicans	%	Others	%	Total
1954	402,283	49.1	404,694	49.4	12,562	1.5	819,539
1956	451,179	51.4	413,659	47.1	13,114	1.5	877,952
1958	447,195	52.3	395,090	46.2	12,759	1.5	855,044
1960	480,588	53.4	405,195	45.0	14,833	1.6	900,616
1962	473,561	53.6	395,351	44.7	14,778	1.7	883,690
1964	511,973	54.9	402,336	43.2	18,152	1.9	932,461

These statistics show that registered Republicans were actually *fewer* in 1964 than in 1954, while the Democrats had registered an increase of 109,690, or 27 percent. In view of this continuing trend, it is somewhat surprising that Oregon politics had remained intensely competitive throughout the five elections.

Three major factors may be cited to help in explaining the continued competitiveness of Oregon politics:

1. The new Democratic registrations were composed largely of recent immigrants from Southern and Midwestern states. Their party preferences arose from the force of habit rather than ideological conviction, and, in the context of Oregon politics, they formed a rather "conservative" bloc of voters.

2. Both party organizations were traditionally very weak in Oregon,

dating from the historical commitment to "popular democracy" of the Progressive Era, and reflecting the continuing popular commitment to (*a*) an open primary system of candidate selection and (*b*) a system of state administration which is virtually devoid of patronage. (For example, despite fairly uniform support for Sig Unander among GOP leaders in 1958, Mark Hatfield defeated him in the gubernatorial primary. But when he became governor, Hatfield had only two positions on his own office staff to dispense to his loyal supporters.)

3. It may be fairly stated that the Republicans had been remarkably fortunate in developing attractive statewide candidates who contrasted favorably with their Democratic counterparts.

Yet despite all of these factors which tended to neutralize the impact of the Democratic registration advantage, it still exercised a critical influence upon Oregon politics. *The Democratic cross-over vote is the pivotal factor in almost every major race;* the Republican candidate strives to maximize it, and the Democratic candidate struggles to minimize it.

Although final figures would not be available from the Elections Division until October 25, it appeared that total voter registrations for the 1966 General Election would approach 960,000—including 528,000 Democrats, 413,000 Republicans, and 19,000 "others." Past experience with similar off-year elections suggested that Republican turnout in this General Election would be about 75 percent to 78 percent. This would give the Democrats a numerical advantage of 396,000 to 322,000, or about 74,000 actual votes. Assuming that the small "other" vote was equally divided, this meant that *in order to win, a statewide Republican candidate had to net at least 37,000 Democratic votes* over and above those required to offset Republican cross-over votes. Or to state the same point another way, even if he could draw 100 percent of the Republican vote, he would also need to attract one out of every ten voting Democrats in order to win.

Any strategy for victory in Oregon also had to consider the geographic composition of voters. Oregon has 36 counties which were organized into four congressional districts in 1966. The biggest plum in any election was the Portland area composed of Multnomah, Clackamas, and Washington counties. This area alone constituted 41 percent of the population and 45 percent of the registered voters. The concentration of Oregon's population was such that if just seven more counties (Lane, Marion, Jackson, Douglas, Linn, Coos, and Klamath) were added to the Portland counties, over 76 percent of Oregon's registered voters could be accounted for. The bulk of the populous counties were in the western part of the state, moving down the Willamette Valley from Portland.

Although Mark Hatfield had always done well throughout the state, Portland was considered to be a relatively strong area for Duncan because of its strong Democratic composition. Duncan's congressional district was the Fourth which was not in the heavily populated Portland area but was composed of seven counties in the southwestern portion of the state.

MARK O. HATFIELD

Despite the extreme problems of the 1966 campaign, the Hatfield planners still had an impressive candidate to work with. In his previous political outing for governor in 1962, Hatfield rolled up a plurality of 80,000 votes over Robert Thornton by securing an estimated *net* cross-over of 21 percent of the voting Democrats. Hatfield's personal attractiveness, his well-advertised church activities, his moderate political posture, and his ten-year exposure as an elected state official gave him a large stock of basic political assets.

Hatfield, born in Dallas, Oregon on July 12, 1922, was often called the "boy wonder" or the "golden boy" because he was the youngest Oregon governor (36) in 1959 and was reelected in 1962.

A former associate professor of political science and dean of students (Willamette U., 1950–1956), Hatfield was a state representative from 1950 to 1954, a state senator from 1954 to 1956 and Oregon's secretary of state from 1957 to 1959.

A lifelong Republican, Hatfield started his political career at 10, carrying literature for Herbert Hoover. By 1960, it was Hatfield who placed Richard M. Nixon in nomination for President at the GOP National Convention and, at the Republican National Convention in 1964 he was Temporary Chairman and Keynoter. In his keynote address, he urged the party to rid itself of extremists, specifically mentioning the Ku Klux Klan, the John Birch Society, and the Communist Party. Later, in a characteristic move for a strong party man, he campaigned actively in Oregon for Barry Goldwater, despite their obvious differences of opinion. This move and others like it led some to charge that Hatfield was a political opportunist who was "wishy-washy" in his views.

A "liberal" of the same ilk as New York's Governor Rockefeller Hatfield prefers calling himself a "moderate" or an exponent of "western Progressivism." Nevertheless, his public record reveals that as a legislator, he took an active role in Oregon's civil rights legislation, one of the most enlightened in the nation, supported strong legislation for the protection of migrant labor, and co-authored the legislation creating Oregon's presidential primary system.

As governor, he supported programs in welfare, education, recreation, and economic development. When he faced an economic crisis (as a result of the legislature refusing to raise the state income tax), he slashed the budget, but refused to institute a sales tax believing such a tax to be "regressive."

Hatfield worked hard to bring industry to Oregon. He advocated "orderly development and growth" and particularly emphasized five areas of growth—wood products, tourism, agriculture, services (auxiliary to transportation and distribution of goods), and industry related to the sciences. Despite his efforts, however, the lumber industry was still of dangerous predominance in the Oregon economy.

Hatfield felt strongly that it was the "challenge of the states to revitalize and retain a powerful position in our federal system," and that reorganization, reform, and consolidation within the states are essential. He contended that there was too much local and too much federal government.

On water-power resources, Hatfield was a "middle-of-the-roader," favoring public or private ownership depending on the circumstances. He did find a need for the states to get together on such matters as the protection of water rights.

Hatfield favored foreign aid for economic development but was against aid to the communist bloc.

The issue about which Hatfield had been most outspoken, of course, was Viet Nam. He continually attempted to make his view clear. He disagreed with Morse's stance in that he did not consider the U.S. position "illegal" nor did he want the withdrawal of troops. But he said that the President's policy was "contradictory" and "unclear," that the administration was not being "candid and truthful" and that he would not give Johnson a "blank check" on the issues of peace or escalation.

Hatfield wanted Johnson to give "guidelines, goals and objectives with regard to the war." Furthermore, he contended that the U.S. should not "go it alone." Alone, he said, the U.S. is "moment by moment in a position of confrontation with Red China." Hatfield believed that the Vietnamese "common man" wanted, above all, to be left alone and to have enough to eat. Judging that a "free" election in the U.S. sense was out of the question, he anticipated that a consensus was the best to be expected at the present in Viet Nam.

Hatfield advocated: "frank and open discussion" on "overall objectives and goals," allied support as well as a halt in their trade with China and North Viet Nam; a look into "every alternative to bloody conflict"; persistence in getting U.N. action; and a reopening of the Geneva Conference.

As a result of his views, Hatfield was dubbed a "duck"—halfway between a "dove" and a "hawk."

Personally, Hatfield is handsome, conservative in dress, and a "cool, competent speaker." This coolness had been turned against him as evidence of his difficulty in dealing with the Oregon legislature. Some critics said he was not competent in the political infighting that would be necessary in the senate. Deeply religious, he neither drinks nor smokes. He is married and has four children. The oldest was seven at the time of the election in 1966.

ROBERT B. DUNCAN

In contrast to Hatfield, Duncan had never been a candidate for state-wide office, although he obtained a certain amount of general exposure as Speaker of the Oregon House of Representatives. His vote-pulling power among Republicans was unknown, and among Democrats it was subject to considerable doubt. In the balloting for Delegates-at-Large to the 1964 Democratic Convention, Duncan finished seventh with 115,000 votes, while Wayne Morse rolled up almost 196,000 votes to finish first. In the primary election of 1966, Duncan raised his total to 131,000 votes and won the senatorial nomination, but his two competitors still drew a total of almost 98,000.

Duncan was born in Normal, Illinois on December 4, 1920 and had practiced law in Oregon since 1948. Before being elected to the House of Representatives he served three terms in the Oregon legislature (1956–1962) and was the only two-term speaker of the Oregon House. He was a delegate to the Democratic National Convention in 1956, 1960, and 1964.

In 1962, President Kennedy appointed Duncan to the advisory committee on intergovernmental relations.

In 1963, as a freshman congressman, he was chosen one of the "ten most promising new faces in the Congress" by the Washington Press Corps. In the same year, Duncan was congressional advisor to the U.S. delegation to the World Food Conference in Rome.

Duncan was a member of the House Appropriations Committee and since May, 1966 had been serving on the United States–Canadian Parliamentary Council.

On the major issue of Viet Nam, Duncan's support of the Administration's policy was part of his belief that "we are now in a critical stage for the free world. This is a period of overall strife. Although some people describe Viet Nam as an isolated incident, it is not. It is just part of the whole."

Otherwise, internationally, he supported the Peace Corps, Food for Peace, and aid to "underdeveloped" countries. He was critical of the slowness of coming to grips with the world's food and population problems as well as the balance of payments and international liquidity.

In trying to underline his bent toward thrift and as a part of his habitual pointing to his Scots ancestry, Duncan boasted that by his one vote on the House Appropriations Committee, he had often saved more money than the general fund budget of Oregon. Also, although some key projects were sometimes not approved, the appropriations committee had allocated more to Oregon than would have been expected on the basis of population alone.

Duncan favored health-improvement measures, aid to education, air and water anti-pollution measures, full-employment programs, and fiscal stability. He also was for suspending investment tax credit to ease inflation.

A former merchant seaman and U.S. Navy fighter pilot, Duncan is a colorful figure, who enjoys chewing "snoose" (a moist snuff), writes reminders to himself on his hand and arm, and delights in wearing Duncan tartan ties. The father of seven children, Duncan worked in the gold fields of Alaska while attending college and has played semi-professional baseball.

THE JULY DECISIONS

On Tuesday, July 26, the Hatfield planning group received the results of a state-wide political study that confirmed the grave nature of their position. The study was based on 1,067 personal interviews with a random sample of registered voters, 55 percent Democratic, 45 percent Republican (excluding "other"). Field work for the study was conducted during the last week in June and the first ten days in July. Inasmuch as the Hanoi-Haiphong bombing commenced midway in the survey period, it was possible to do a "before-after" analysis. It was not possible, however, to gauge the precise effect of Hatfield's lone stand on Viet Nam at the Governors' Conference.

Some of the survey results appear in Exhibit 2. In general, they supported and clarified the views that the planners already had about the election. Preferences were closer than the 46–40 split indicated by the Kraft survey, but Hatfield was slightly behind, especially in certain areas, with certain questioning techniques, and among certain groups. The survey gave additional information on what seemed to cause the preferences, and although the Viet Nam issue was important, other issues and candidate characteristics seemed to be important in planning the campaign.

The most important strategy decisions facing the Hatfield group had to do with what their advertising and campaign workers and candidate should say, how it should be said, and when it would be said. Beyond these decisions were certain questions of implementation, many of which had already been answered and others which would have to be answered later. For instance, some of the media time and space had been scheduled and the rest would be purchased when sufficient funds had been raised.

A variety of approaches to content were supported within the group. For instance:

How much emphasis on Viet Nam?

The opinion varied from those who thought that Viet Nam should be mentioned prominently to those who felt that every piece of campaign material (including the candidate's statements) should exclude all mention of Viet Nam.

An example of the former position was a letter that Hatfield received early in the campaign saying: "Your position expressing concern reflects the innermost feelings of many Oregonians . . . it supports our men in an awful struggle, while questioning this policy that involves them there. . . ." The writer went on to suggest that the issue of Viet Nam could become the center of many crucial statements of concern that Hatfield might make.

Others within the Hatfield group suggested various other emphases. They asserted that Hatfield would be seen as inconsistent and wishy-washy if he completely dropped the issue (the *Oregon Journal* called Hatfield "The Dove that Ducks" because he refused to debate with Duncan on Viet Nam) but would stand to lose much if he continued to be vocal about it. Something clearly had to be done because Hatfield was losing the support of contributors and political names within the party in addition to the support of many voters. (Background on the Hatfield Viet Nam position is in Exhibit 3.)

What other issues should be emphasized?

A general dissatisfaction existed in the U.S. and in Oregon. The extent to which Hatfield could take advantage of this dissatisfaction was in some sense negatively related to his identification with the causes of the dissatisfaction. For instance, with respect to Oregon's economic health, it was apparent that the lumber industry was feeling the pinch of LBJ's "tight-money" policies. Consumers were bothered by inflation. But Hatfield would have to be careful in dealing with these issues, because he bore much of the responsibility for Oregon's economic health since 1959.

What stress should be placed on "gut" versus "intellectual" or future issues?

Hatfield had many concerns that were general and did not strike directly at present-day problems. For instance, he was concerned about world peace and the quality of international relations beyond Viet Nam and beyond Oregonians' present money problems. Some planners felt that he would be best advised to emphasize these statesmanlike stands rather than get involved in everyday problems of Oregon. Others said that, although Hatfield achieved senatorial proportions by emphasizing statesmanship, too much concern with future global and intellectual matters would label him as an "egghead" who cared less about Oregon than about the world and his own career. These advisors suggested that Hatfield should concentrate entirely on "gut" issues that were of immediate relevance to Oregonians.

Should Duncan be answered or even attacked?

Duncan's campaign appeared to be shaping up as a negative one in which he would continually attack Hatfield as indecisive, confused on Viet Nam, even "soft on Communism." The question here was how much Hatfield should respond. Should he meet Duncan's constant challenge to debate? Should he answer carefully all of Duncan's charges? And to what extent should advertising, speeches, campaign workers, public relations releases, etc., actually attack Duncan and his position? Some felt that Duncan should be connected directly to the negative aspects of the Administration's policies and attacked in Hatfield communications. These people wanted to brand Duncan as a "rubber stamp" and to circulate political cartoons showing him, for instance, sitting on LBJ's knee. Others felt that Duncan and his position should be almost totally ignored. They felt that strong attacking tactics might be ethically unsound and practically inept because they might give Duncan added exposure.

Should the Hatfield campaign concentrate on his past record or on what he planned to do as senator?

Hatfield could make many claims about his administration in education, labor and industry, budget, conservation, agriculture, highway development, and social advancement (see Exhibit 4 for details). On the other hand, this approach presented some dangers because his administration had not been completely successful, because this emphasis might remind voters of negative attitudes which they might have had about Hatfield, and because the job of governor might not be regarded as the best preparation for a senatorial post. Further, Hatfield had to indicate, to some extent, his goals in the Senate.

What effort should be expended in dealing with Hatfield's personal image?

Hatfield had a tendency to come over as a "cold fish," as too polished, too intellectual, humorless, and as not ruggedly masculine enough in the context of the "Oregon personality." This was in direct contrast to Duncan's folksy "masculine" approach that was effective on a person-to-person basis. Some of Hatfield's planners felt that his personal appearance and style might reinforce the contention that he was a political opportunist and that he might be a decent administrator but would not fare well in the personal infighting that was necessary in the Senate. These planners felt that Hatfield's personal appearances should be kept to a minimum, that he should be counseled closely as to what to wear, etc., that the bulk of the campaign should be concentrated on mass media advertising, and that maximum advertising attention should be paid to the issues and the candidate's performance rather than to Hatfield himself. The argument here was that voters liked to read an acceptable image into the candidate. Some evidence indicated that personal appearances by the candidate (or any candidate) are less effective and, in fact, might have a zero or negative effect when compared with the effect of the mass media. This might be especially true of Hatfield because he was always asked questions about Viet Nam when he made personal appearances, and his answers tended to remind people of this negative aspect. On the other hand, some argued that Hatfield, while receptive to suggestions from his advisors, could hardly be forced to hold back from personal appearances, despite the demands of his position as governor. And it was hard to imagine Hatfield dramatically changing his personal appearance, even if the ethical aspects of such artificial direction of the candidate's image were dismissed.

The problem of "how to say it" was really two interrelated problems: the question of ad format and the question of advertising media.

The Hatfield planners had a broad array of media open to them, but their problem was that Hatfield's position and his weak early showing limited the extent to which they could use those media. For instance, it was felt that Hatfield would need at least 3,000 campaign workers during the campaign. These would range from precinct workers to office help to well-known people who would be used to make speeches and to lead discussion groups for Hatfield. But, instead of 3,000, the Hatfield staff felt that they were lucky if they had 1,000 committed to the campaign in July. Some evidence suggested that Hatfield's position on Viet Nam, especially his dissenting vote at the Governors' Conference, was something with which campaign workers did not want to be associated. In some quarters, an aura of treason was actually connected with Hatfield, and his planners guessed that many people who normally would have worked for Hatfield were committing themselves to other campaigns (e.g., the Republican gubernatorial campaign) in order to have an excuse for not working for Hatfield. This kind of dropping-out was obviously greater among the more conservative workers, but the situation made the content and form of Hatfield's campaign very important. It would have to meet objections and attract workers who now seemed to be avoiding Hatfield.

The campaign would also have to stimulate contributions in order to utilize the media effectively. It was estimated that the campaign had about $50,000 *pledged* in July and that six times more than this would be necessary to carry out a complete campaign. The candidate, public relations, and the media would have to be used creatively.

Political campaigns used two types of "media"—collateral material and general advertising media. The typical campaign in Oregon used about 50,000 each of a variety of collateral pieces including bumper stickers, campaign buttons, handbills, direct-mail pieces, and door hangers. These ranged in cost from one to 5 cents apiece. Some of the items, such as major brochures and direct-mail pieces, might receive longer press runs (perhaps 150–200,000) and cost 4 or 5 cents apiece. There were also items that could be sold such as hats (25 cents), aprons ($1), and campaign seals ($1 for a sheet of 100 envelope seals). Collateral material would be used in mailings, precinct work and in connection with special events such as key organization meetings, state and county fairs, campaign headquarters openings, and candidate appearances.

All mass media were available in Oregon (see Exhibit 4 for media data). There were about 70 daily and local newspapers headed by *The Oregonian* and the *Oregon Journal*. These two papers were most important in Portland but had coverage and influence throughout the state. The nine key papers and their rates are below. Sunday rates and circulation were approximately 15 percent higher. A Sunday supplement could be run in newspapers throughout the state with a circulation of 600,000 for a cost of $26,000.

Newspaper	Location	Circulation* (000)	Basic B&W 1 Page Rate*
Oregonian...................	Portland-NW	240	$2,000
Oregon Journal...............	Portland-NW	150	1,500
Eugene Register Guard.........	Central-West	50	580
Salem Statesman (Morn.)........			
Capital Journal (Even.).........	Salem-NW	53 (N&E)	731 (M&E)
Medford Mail Tribune..........	Southwest	20	423
Coos Bay World..............	South Coast	15	352
Bend Bulletin................	Central	9	235
Pendleton East Oregonian.......	East	10	330

* There are slight extra charges for color (about 12 percent for 1-color extra). These are approximate rates and circulations.

Portland had four major television stations which reached a large proportion of the state's electorate. One television idea being considered by Hatfield planners was morning and afternoon "coffee with Mark" half-hours that could be combined with neighborhood women's coffees. These would cost about $250 apiece for time and $1,500 for production if, in fact, money could be found. If Hatfield was able to raise sufficient funds, it might also be possible to run an "eleventh-hour" telethon or a two-hour prime time program. This would cost about $30–50,000.

The Portland television stations, rates, and reach are below. There were also stations in Coos Bay, Eugene, Medford, Pendleton, and Salem.

	Spot Rates*		
	60-sec. Daytime	20-sec. Prime Evenings	Average Homes Reached in Prime ¼ Hour*
KATU–TV (ABC).........	150	320	75,000
KGW–TV (NBC).........	110	350	90,000
KOIN–TV (CBS).........	125	325	80,000
KPTV..................	80	250	60,000

* Data are approximate and for case purposes only.

Radio spots and programs could be purchased on all kinds of radio stations (rock, classical, news, talk, etc.) for about $10–20 a minute spot. Fifteen-minute radio shows would cost about $100 for time only. Finally, billboard and transit advertising had already been committed throughout the state. The Hatfield campaign had maximum coverage and was spending approximately $40–50,000 on this phase of the effort.

The campaign was already underway to a limited extent in some media. Exhibit 5 gives some idea of some of the media appeals and formats being used. The present billboards showed a picture of Hatfield in

EXHIBIT 1

Statement of Registration by Congressional Districts, General Election 1966
(prepared by secretary of state, elections division, November 1, 1966)

County*	Precincts	Population†	Democratic	Republican	Other	Total
FIRST DISTRICT						
Benton	50	45,800	8,279	11,046	700	20,025
Clackamas	97	134,000	37,633	31,243	1,007	69,883
Clatsop	46	27,700	7,880	6,178	223	14,281
Columbia	40	24,300	7,775	3,911	176	11,862
Lincoln	44	23,200	6,988	4,896	396	12,280
Multnomah†	164	92,000	21,064	24,863	1,125	47,052
Polk	51	34,200	6,723	7,530	399	14,652
Tillamook	35	16,100	5,030	3,652	112	8,794
Washington	180	122,000	29,154	31,673	1,292	62,119
Yamhill	42	39,900	8,638	8,856	393	17,887
TOTALS	749	559,200	139,164	133,848	5,823	278,835
SECOND DISTRICT						
Baker	27	15,600	4,760	2,989	128	7,877
Crook	16	8,900	2,409	1,451	68	3,928
Deschutes	29	27,000	6,878	5,185	142	12,205
Gilliam	6	3,200	759	610	15	1,384
Grant	15	7,600	1,588	1,691	38	3,317
Harney	18	7,100	1,894	1,326	79	3,299
Hood River	22	14,200	3,309	2,618	230	6,157
Jefferson	14	10,000	2,082	1,565	45	3,692
Klamath	92	48,100	10,814	7,619	531	18,964
Lake	19	6,200	1,455	1,412	30	2,897
Linn	105	65,000	15,585	11,718	497	27,800
Malheur	33	25,400	4,295	4,583	210	9,088
Marion	116	145,000	29,013	32,188	1,079	62,280

Morrow	9	4,750	1,062	991	36	2,089
Sherman	5	3,250	676	578	36	1,290
Umatilla	56	43,100	10,141	8,524	437	19,102
Union	30	17,800	5,072	3,497	126	8,695
Wallowa	14	6,050	1,899	1,191	22	3,112
Wasco	39	23,300	5,485	4,142	145	9,772
Wheeler	6	1,800	515	514	3	1,032
TOTALS	671	483,350	109,691	94,392	3,897	207,980
THIRD DISTRICT						
Multnomah	854	463,000	149,017	93,354	4,254	246,625
FOURTH DISTRICT						
Coos	82	52,400	16,445	8,014	441	24,900
Curry	21	13,000	3,304	2,504	122	5,930
Douglas	105	76,000	18,442	12,856	645	31,943
Jackson	125	92,100	22,041	19,976	1,571	43,588
Josephine	56	35,100	8,662	8,062	260	16,984
Lane	236	198,000	51,983	39,878	2,013	93,874
TOTALS	625	466,600	120,877	91,290	5,052	217,219
COMBINED TOTALS	2,899	1,972,150	518,749	412,884	19,026	950,659

* The counties listed herein are those which were in the new congressional districts as provided in Chapter 1, Oregon Laws 1965, Special Session.
† The 1965 estimates furnished by the Oregon Bureau of Census.
‡ That portion of Multnomah west of the Willamette River and west of the Stadium Freeway.

front of the U.S. flag with one-word messages like "Courage," "Integrity," etc.

The key question now was how much effort would be put against the more geographically specific media like precinct workers and direct mail as opposed to the mass media like television, radio, and newspapers. And, within the media, the question was how and how much should Hatfield himself be used in illustrations and in actual appearances. The planning group wanted also to pull the campaign together with a slogan that would typify their general approach, but they were not certain if this was possible—given the existing multiplicity of goals and approaches.

On top of all these problems was the issue of timing. Of first consideration, of course, was the expected timing of the Duncan campaign. Hatfield's team knew that Duncan planned to make a big push toward the end of the campaign. He had scheduled a large TV telethon. He expected to receive supportive visits toward the end of the campaign from Vice-President Humphrey, Senator Robert Kennedy, and even President Johnson. Duncan himself would not be able to campaign aggressively until after mid-September when Congress was scheduled to adjourn. He was getting support from the labor unions, several of which were organizing a get-out-the-vote campaign for election day. Duncan's campaign timing also had to be considered from a qualitative standpoint. He might well change campaign emphasis midstream with less emphasis on Viet Nam and more on Oregon's problems—the work that he had done and the work that Hatfield had not been able to do. Some of his campaign material is shown in Exhibit 5.

In addition to Duncan's campaign, the Hatfield planners had to consider the possibility of several events occurring. It was unclear what effect victories in Viet Nam for the U.S. and South Viet Nam might have on Oregonian attitudes toward the war. Political analysts expected President Johnson to make some sort of dramatic move in relation to the war before election time. A new "peace offensive" was rumored. There was also the problem of student disturbances and peace demonstrations. To what extent would they occur? To what extent would Hatfield become identified with these disruptions that were increasingly disturbing to the majority of Oregon voters?

Aside from the war issue, the planners had to consider what changes in the economy were likely to occur and of what significance they would be to Oregon voters. Inflation was a continuing problem and Oregon housewives were organizing "Food Price Wars" with boycotts and picketing. The "tight-money" policy was beginning to affect new housing starts, and the Oregon lumber industry was beginning to feel the pinch. Two thousand workers in the lumber industry had been laid off. Further layoffs were being predicted.

Hatfield had to have a campaign that was flexible enough to meet these changing conditions while strong enough to appeal to important segments of the state. Much depended on a strong early campaign as well as the crucial strong finish. Several important pressure groups and state political figures had not indicated where their support lay, but it was clear that Hatfield was at a disadvantage among the more conservative. Newspaper endorsements were likely to appear in early October and, although Duncan appeared to have the "inside track" in this area, the Hatfield media and press campaign clearly would have to work hard to court these endorsements. An early Hatfield campaign, if successful, would have an important effect on obtaining money for the total effort. There was a strong bandwagon effect in campaign contributions and Hatfield had to show early strength in order to reach the campaign goal of over $300,000 and 3,000 workers. The problem was somewhat circular in that he did not now have adequate monies or workers to conduct a large total campaign at the early stage. Since Hatfield had not shown strength in public preference in either the primary or post-primary periods, the campaign now had to be dramatic enough to turn the tide of opinion optimistically in his direction.

What campaign strategy would you recommend for Hatfield? Specifically, what should be his target segments? His message? His message format? The timing of his campaign? The media?

EXHIBIT 2

July Hatfield Survey

Question: "As you know, we're going to have another election this fall where Oregon will elect a new U.S. Senator. Do you happen to know the name of the (Democratic) (Republican) candidate for U.S. Senator?"

(Read across) Group:	(R) Hatfield Correct	(D) Duncan Correct
Total Sample	59%	45%
Democrats	55	45
Republicans	75	54
Not registered or other	36	27

Question: "The two candidates for U.S. Senator from Oregon are Mark Hatfield, Republican, and Robert Duncan, Democrat. If the election were being held today, would you probably vote for Duncan or Hatfield?" (Note: A split-sample approach was used, where the above question was asked of one cross-section, while a comparable cross-section was asked to mark a secret ballot.)

EXHIBIT 2 (Continued)

Group:	Hatfield	Duncan	Undecided	Total
Total Sample....................	45.8%	46.6	7.6	100.0%
By Questioning Technique:				
Oral.........................	46%	43	11	100%
Secret.......................	45%	51	4	100%
By Political Party:				
Democrats....................	21%	73	6	100%
Republicans..................	77%	16	7	100%
Not registered or other..........	44%	43	13	100%
By Hanoi Bombing:				
Before.......................	46%	47	7	100%
After........................	45%	47	8	100%
By Congressional District:				
No. 1........................	51%	41	8	100%
No. 2........................	47%	44	9	100%
No. 3........................	43%	49	8	100%
No. 4........................	40%	54	6	100%
Total Sample....................	45.8%	46.6	7.6	100.0%
By Education:				
College—complete..............	67%	27	6	100%
College—partial................	53%	41	6	100%
High school...................	41%	50	9	100%
Grade or no schooling...........	34%	61	5	100%
By Occupation:				
Professional—managerial.........	63%	33	4	100%
White collar workers...........	51%	41	8	100%
Blue collar workers.............	36%	55	9	100%
Agricultural...................	47%	47	6	100%
By Union Membership:				
Union........................	36%	54	10	100%
Non-union....................	52%	42	6	100%
By Sex:				
Male.........................	45%	49	6	100%
Female.......................	47%	44	9	100%
By Age:				
21–39 years..................	47%	44	9	100%
40–59........................	44%	49	7	100%
60 or over....................	47%	46	7	100%
By Income Level:				
Upper........................	57%	40	3	100%
Middle.......................	44%	47	9	100%
Lower........................	38%	53	9	100%

Question: "On this card are a list of words. Will you please read over the words quickly and tell me, offhand, which words you think describe (Mr. Hatfield) (Mr. Duncan)? Choose as many as you like."

EXHIBIT 2 (Continued)

Words:	Hatfield	Duncan
Intelligent	55%	43%
Politician	48	31
Religious	38	4
Honest	34	31
Friendly	32	26
Polished	31	7
Works for people	31	33
Leader	31	19
Sincere	31	31
Dignified	30	7
Statesman	27	16
Glory-seeker	23	4
Courageous	19	13
Fence-straddler	14	2
Decisive	13	15
Yes-man	7	6
Stuck-up	6	1
Cocky	6	2
Fresh	6	5
Regular guy	5	9
Stuffy	4	1
Irresponsible	2	1
Rugged	2	5
Stale	1	1
Undecided—No Opinion	4	25

Questions: "Now, will you please look at this list. Which two of these specific problems do you feel your U.S. Senator should work the hardest on?"

"Which do you feel is the next most important problem?"

"Now, which two on the list do you think are the least important problems?"

Problems:	Most	Next	Least
Solve the Viet Nam crisis	25%	10%	5%
Attract new industry to Oregon	24	8	5
Cut down on federal spending	19	9	5
Lower property taxes in Oregon	19	8	7
Keep Oregon water from going to other states	16	7	8
Stop the increase in cost of living	14	8	4
Keep Russians out of Oregon fishing waters	11	8	7
Protect Oregon interests in federal timber	11	6	3
Better representation for Oregon in U.S. Senate	11	6	4
Reduce air and water pollution	11	6	7
Reduce federal interference in state affairs	9	5	15
Increase social security benefits	7	4	12
Obtain federal aid for education	6	5	10
War on poverty	5	4	19
Keep Red China out of the U.N.	4	2	17
Do something about Castro and the spread of communism	4	3	18
Expand recreational areas in Oregon	1	3	26
Undecided or other	2	3	13

EXHIBIT 2 (Continued)

Question: "From what you know or have heard, how do you feel about Robert Duncan's stand on Viet Nam . . . ?"

Group:	Strongly Approve	Approve	Dis-approve	Strongly Disapprove	Undecided
Total Sample.................	10%	30	13	5	42
Democrats.................	15%	34	9	3	39
Republicans................	7%	25	20	7	41
Not registered or other.......	7%	27	10	5	51

Question: "Which one of the alternatives best describes how you feel about Mr. Hatfield's stand on Viet Nam?"

Group:	Strongly Approve	Approve	Dis-approve	Strongly Disapprove	Undecided
Total Sample.................	6%	24	33	10	27
Democrats.................	4%	15	43	12	26
Republicans...............	10%	36	25	7	22
Not registered or other......	4%	21	24	11	40

Question: "How do you feel about Wayne Morse's stand on Viet Nam?"

Group:	Strongly Approve	Approve	Dis-approve	Strongly Disapprove	Undecided
Total Sample.................	8%	20	28	27	17
Democrats.................	6%	17	33	31	13
Republicans.................	9%	27	26	25	13
Not registered or other.......	9%	14	22	22	33

Table 4: Reasons for Favoring MR. HATFIELD for U.S. Senator.

	Hatfield Supporters
Experience, Records, Accomplishments: Experience gained as governor; loyalty to Oregon; record in office; industrial accomplishments; Duncan lacks experience	47%
Party Loyalty: I'm a Republican; he's a member of my party; back party's candidates	20
Professional Qualifications: Leader; professional abilities; statesman; better qualified than opponent; job capabilities	20
Viet Nam Views: Agree with Hatfield on Viet Nam; the Viet Nam mess; opposed to Administration's Viet Nam policies; war in Viet Nam	18

EXHIBIT 2 (Continued)

Awareness, Knowledge of Candidates: Know more about Hatfield; familiar with his stands; know little or nothing about Duncan .. 15

Personal Qualifications: Conscientious; hard working; high principles; good family man; dignified; interested in youth 13

Religious 8

Policies, Platform: Agree with his political stands; conservative; like his policies, political beliefs 8

Honest, Sincere 5

Dislike Duncan: Dislike, disagree with Duncan 3

Appearance: Handsome; erect; trim, appeal to women 3

Intelligence, Education 3

Courage of Convictions: Decisive; strong; says what he thinks 2

Speaking Ability 1

Supports Working Man; Pro-Labor 1

Undecided—Just Prefer Him 5

    Total 172%*

* Totals more than 100%, due to multiple response.

Table 5. Reasons for Preferring MR. DUNCAN for U.S. Senator.

	Duncan Supporters
Party Loyalty: Vote party ticket; I'm a Democrat; Duncan's our candidate	30%
Dislike Hatfield: Would not vote for Hatfield; disagree with Hatfield; Duncan is lesser of two evils	29
Viet Nam Views: Agree with Duncan's Viet Nam views; Duncan backs President on Viet Nam; Duncan supports Viet Nam war effort	17
Experience, Record, Accomplishments: Record as Congressman; experience in Oregon Legislature; accomplishments in office; has the experience to do the job	12
Professional Qualifications: A leader; capable of carrying out job; better qualified than Hatfield; legal background	10
General Policies, Platform: Supports Dunes Park; his platform appeals to me; agree with his policies, political beliefs	9
Personal Qualifications: Down-to-earth; good family man; tough; young and aggressive; "Scotsman"	7
Supports Working Man	5
Decisiveness: Strong; makes decisions and sticks to them; more decisive than Hatfield	3
Honest, Sincere	2
Awareness: Know more about Duncan, Duncan's views	2
Need a Change: New political blood; change in political scenery ..	1
Intelligence, Education	1
Miscellaneous: Hard campaigner; religious; dignified; reserved	1
Undecided—Just Prefer Him	10
	139%

EXHIBIT 2 (Continued)

Table 6.   Reasons for NOT Preferring MR. HATFIELD.

	Non-Hatfield Voters
Party Conflict: He's a Republican—I'm a Democrat	20%
Viet Nam Stand: Disagree with Viet Nam views; Hatfield opposed to Viet Nam war; not supporting U.S. forces in Viet Nam; unpatriotic	14
Indecisive: Fence-straddler; afraid to take a firm stand; wishy-washy; beats around the bush; says one thing, does another; no mind of his own	12
Political Ambitions: Places self above state; only interested in himself; wants to be President instead of Oregon senator; uses office to further personal ambitions	9
Gubernatorial Administration: Mediocre record as governor; inefficient administration of office; poor record of running state ...	6
Lack of Accomplishment for State: Has done little, nothing for state; state has not advanced during his administration; lack of results	6
Disagree with Political Policies, Stands: Daylight savings time; Boardman deal; welfare out of Portland; not conservative-minded	5
Personal Characteristics: Stuck-up; arrogant; never has a hair out of place	5
Travels: Out of state too much; too many trips	5
Lack of Support of Working Man: Has done little,.nothing for common man; anti-labor	4
Just Don't Like Him	4
Lack of Professional Capabilities	3
Forces Issues Over Public Vote	2
Like Duncan Better—No Feelings Toward Hatfield	2
Resented Mrs. Hatfield's Remarks on TV	2
Raised Taxes	2
Miscellaneous: Copying Morse (1%); economic views (1%); need a change (1%); too religious (1%)	4
Undecided—No Particular Reason	4
	109%

Table 7.   Reasons for NOT Preferring MR. DUNCAN.

	Non-Duncan Supporters
Lack of Knowledge of Duncan: Not familiar with Duncan, Duncan's stands; know nothing about him; new name	30%
Party Conflict: He's a Democrat—I'm a Republican	20
"Rubber Stamp" Obedience: Blindly backing Administration's	

EXHIBIT 2 (Continued)

policies; LBJ "Yes" man	11
Disagree with Viet Nam Views: Too strongly for Viet Nam war; can't go along with his Viet Nam stand; we shouldn't be in Viet Nam	9
Prefer Hatfield: Hatfield's record is better; can't vote for both candidates; Hatfield is my man	6
Lack of Experience: Insufficient experience for job; Hatfield more experienced	4
Lack of Professional Qualifications: Lacks qualifications for U.S. Senator; lacks leadership qualities of Hatfield	3
Just Don't Like Duncan	1
Too Liberal	1
Congress too Heavily Weighted with Democrats	1
Lacks Statesmanship Qualities: Hatfield more of a statesman; Duncan wouldn't get along with UN officials	1
Indecisive	1
Smooth Talker	1
Disagree with Political Stands	1
He's in Favor of Dunes Park	1
Morse Favors Duncan	1
Undecided—No Particular Reason	10
Total	102%

Table 13a. FAVORABLE Facets of MR. HATFIELD'S Image.

	Total
Personal Characteristics: Clean; forthright; charming; dynamic; friendly; humble; unselfish; considerate; conscientious; patriotic; polished	47%
Professional Capabilities: Capable and dedicated; leader; shrewd judge of people, situations; influential	38
Experienced, Successful Governor: Put Oregon on map; expanded Oregon's industry; outstanding job as Governor; highly experienced executive	23
Honest, Sincere, Truthful	16
Ambitious: Ambitious to carry out goals of office; drives himself; aggressive in actions, accomplishments; energetic	14
Intelligent, Well Educated, Keen Mind	11
Strong, Decisive: Has courage of his convictions; not afraid to speak out; confident, independent thinker	8
Pleasing Appearance: Handsome; well dressed; immaculate; appeals to women; clean-cut	7
Religious	7
Good Politician; Astute Political Stands	4
Good Speaker	3
Well Known, Prominent Figure	2
Has Right Idea on Viet Nam	2

EXHIBIT 2 (Continued)

Dignified, Respected	2
Interested in Working Class	1
Miscellaneous	2
No response	*
Total	187%†

* Less than 0.5 percent.
† Results total more than 100 percent, due to multiple response.

Table 13b. UNFAVORABLE Facets of MR. HATFIELD'S Image.

Total

Overriding Political Ambitions: Everything subordinated to political ambitions; wants to be President; political opportunist; using office as stepping stone; Senate is next political step; shooting for big game 30%

Vacillating: Wishy-washy; evasive on issues; afraid to show how he feels; hedges; hasn't courage of his convictions; won't take a firm stand 21

Self-Centered: Publicity seeker; stuck-up; arrogant; everything revolves around himself; social climber; big-headed; cocky 15

Unsuccessful Governor: Accomplished little as Governor; hasn't carried out promises; been a so-so Governor; others could have done better 10

Immature, Unqualified: Man with school-boy ideas; not ready for the job; too young for Senate; too sissified to work; not qualified for job at this time 10

Traveler: Would rather travel than stay home; away from job half the time; trips cost money; who pays for his wife's travel expenses; absenteeism 8

Appearance: Too well-groomed; don't trust handsome man; fashion plate 6

Has Wrong Idea on Viet Nam 5

Pawn of Special Interest Groups: Works for big business; not interested in "little people" 4

Weak Fiscal Policies: Raised taxes; advocated state tax on federal tax 2

Miscellaneous: Stand on daylight time didn't appeal to me; don't like his wife; poor advisors; shady politician; has some far-fetched ideas; just don't like him 9

No Response .... *

Total .... 120%†

* Less than 0.5 percent.
† Results total more than 100 percent, due to multiple response.

EXHIBIT 2 (Continued)

Table 13c.   FAVORABLE Facets of MR. DUNCAN'S Image.

	Total
Personal Characteristics: Regular guy; down-to-earth; good family man; unselfish; nice fellow; conscientious; clean-cut; patriotic; crew-cut	32%
Professionally Qualified: Dedicated; has sound ideas; has Oregonians' interests at heart; good lawyer; good judgment	30
Honest, Sincere, Truthful	13
Decisive: Strong; not easily swayed; willing to commit himself on issues; means what he says	12
Experienced, Successful Office-Holder: Experienced through service in Congress and Legislature; done a lot for the state; always present to vote in Congress; good record	10
Ambitious: Hard worker; energetic; drives himself to get things done	10
Intelligent, Well Educated, Keen Mind	7
Loyal Democrat: Supports the Administration; behind LBJ; hard worker for party's cause	6
Supports, Helps Workingman	6
Sound Political Stands: Good politician; well versed in political areas	6
Has the Right Idea on Viet Nam	4
Good Speaker	4
Pleasing Appearance	1
Dignified, Respected	1
Miscellaneous	1
No Response	*
Total	143%†

* Less than 0.5 percent.
† Results total more than 100 percent, due to multiple response.

Table 13d. UNFAVORABLE Facets of MR. DUNCAN'S Image.

	Total
Rubber Stamp, Follower: Rubber stamp for the great society; LBJ "Yes" man; Democratic follower; blindly follows party lines ...	26%
Self-Centered: Stuffy; acts like a banty rooster; rash; opinionated; egotistical	17
Inexperienced, Unsuccessful: Hasn't any experience to speak of; all talk, no action; can't think of any accomplishments; do-nothing record; junior politician; can't hold a candle to Hatfield	14
Politically Motivated: Political show-off; politics come first, unscrupulous politician; latches on to the thing of the moment; actions dictated by political expediency	10
Immature, Unqualified: Not serious enough; lesser of two evils; not big enough for the Senate; capabilities not up to the job	10

EXHIBIT 2 (Concluded)

Has Wrong Idea on Viet Nam	8
Vacillating: Goes along with the majority; straddles the fence; indecisive	5
Poor Fiscal Policies: Has fat hand in the taxpayer's pocket; no experience in public money matters	2
Poor Appearance	1
Miscellaneous: Disagree with his educational views; prejudiced against him; just don't like him; poor political stands; failed to help war veterans	6
No Response	3
Total	102%*

* Results total more than 100 percent, due to multiple response.

EXHIBIT 3

EXCLUSIVE INTERVIEW: Oregon Voter, April 2, 1966.

Hatfield's Vietnam Position

When asked: "What do you consider is Gov. Hatfield's position on Vietnam, most people reply, *Oregon Voter* has found, "I'm not sure, but I think he's against the war and favors withdrawal of our troops."

After criticizing both Gov. Hatfield and the press (March 5) for their failure to adequately and clearly set forth Gov. Hatfield's views, *Oregon Voter* was invited to meet privately with the Governor for a "briefing" of his position on the Vietnam war.

The Governor began: "I do not agree with Sen. (Wayne) Morse's position . . . we cannot do less than give full support to our men in Vietnam." Hence, the Governor's support of the $4.8 billion emergency appropriation bill approved by congress last month.

America Committed To Vietnam

Gov. Hatfield continued: "America cannot pull out of Vietnam. We are there, and we cannot turn our back even if things were wrong at the onset. We must stay there until an honorable settlement is reached."

Commenting on Sen. Morse's charges of "illegal" and "unconstitutional" U.S. involvement, Hatfield rose to his feet stating, "It's too late to even discuss legalities—we've 215,000 men there. We're committed."

"Furthermore," he declared, "When you start arguing legalities, you automatically advocate withdrawal." Withdrawal now, he implied, would be defeat in every sense of the word.

Gov. Hatfield, therefore, does not support Sen. Morse's position, nor does he advocate withdrawal of American troops from Vietnam.

Critical of LBJ Policy

The Governor, however, is highly critical of President Johnson's Vietnam war policy. He refused to back the administration last summer at the Governors' conference in Minneapolis, and following a White House briefing last

EXHIBIT 3 (Continued)

fall, he publicly criticized the president for what he termed "contradictory" and "unclear policy."

He said he could not support giving the president a "blank check" on the issue of making peace or escalating the war when the president had not spelled out to this country his "guidelines, goals and objectives with regard to the war."

And last month he abstained from voting with other governors on a resolution endorsing the president's policy, a resolution unanimously adopted by the 38 governors who attended another White House briefing. Although he had planned to attend the briefing, Gov. Hatfield was forced to change his plans when he came down with influenza.

He later announced he would not sign the resolution, because he had not attended the briefing, and had no evidence the administration had changed its policies on matters with which he (Hatfield) disagrees.

Gov. Hatfield's Criticisms

What are Gov. Hatfield's criticisms? Essentially they appear two-fold: (1) failure on the part of the administration to be "candid and truthful" with the American people in spelling out exactly what are its goals and objectives in Vietnam; and (2) the administration's "contradictory foreign policy," particularly with regard to communism.

In the first instance, Gov. Hatfield said we have been bombarded with "illusions, myths and secrecy about our goals and objectives in Vietnam . . . we have been told many things and many so-called facts, most of which have not been borne out or correct.

Outlining specifics, Gov. Hatfield displayed quotes from Sec. of Defense Robert McNamara:

In May, 1963, McNamara said: "The corner has been definitely turned toward victory." In Dec., 1963, he said: "We have every reason to believe that plans will be successful in 1964." In Feb., 1964, McNamara declared: "The U.S. hopes to withdraw most of its troops from South Vietnam before the end of 1965." In Oct., 1965: "The major part of the U.S. military task can be completed by the end of 1965." And in early Dec., 1965, he said: "We have stopped losing the war."

Oregon's Chief Executive again quoted McNamara who said at a press conference on April 24, 1964: "I still believe we can win . . . following the current program, and I don't believe that anyone in the government of South Vietnam or our government believes that the addition of U.S. ground combat troops in South Vietnam, or the introduction of such troops in South Vietnam, would favorably affect the situation there."

Consequences of Buildup

The Governor then quoted U.S. Ambassador to Vietnam Henry Cabot Lodge, who, before returning to Saigon, told reporters in Washington (June 30, 1964) what he thought the consequences of massive American military involvement in Vietnam would be:

"Well," quoting Lodge, "that means we become a colonial power, and I think it's been pretty well established that colonialism is over. I believe that if you start doing that, you will get all kinds of unfortunate results; you'll stir

EXHIBIT 3 (Continued)

up anti-foreign feelings; there'll be a tendency to lay back and let the Americans do it, and all that. I can't think that that's a good thing to do."

Of this Oregon's Governor asked, "Does this indicate the administration has clearly spelled out its goals to the American people?"

Answering his own question, he said "No!" Despite what Sec. McNamara and Ambassador Lodge have said, we now have the "American nation fully committed to a land war in Vietnam."

"The president," the Governor continued, "says we are committed to guaranteeing the right of self determination for the Vietnamese people—through free elections."

"Just what would happen," asked Gov. Hatfield, "if a hard-core communist were to win a free election? What will we have accomplished? Will our boys have died in vain—for nothing?"

He said. "No one sees any person in South Vietnam capable of winning a free election." Our first task, suggested Gov. Hatfield, is to help build Vietnamese support for a friendly candidate who could win such an election.

He continued: "The Vietnam struggle started as a civil war. Peiping later took advantage of the situation and moved in supplies and equipment to the Viet Cong and the National Liberation Front."

Ho-Chi-Minh A Symbol

"What we must realize is that Ho-Chi-Minh is a symbol to the Vietnamese of liberation from the French Colonialists prior to and after World War II, and from the Japanese Imperialists during the War.

"Furthermore," said Gov. Hatfield, "the Vietnamese are concerned with only two things: Being left alone and having a full stomach. They do not understand what freedom is, and no people can be expected to fight for freedom if they don't understand it . . . they could care less about the philosophical debate over democracy vs communism."

Gov. Hatfield suggested this is one of the key reasons we have seen so many changes of government and numerous defections in South Vietnamese military ranks.

"Under these circumstances," he asked, "just what are our guidelines, goals and objectives? How can we expect the American people to know what they are when the administration has yet to be candid with us about the war?"

Moving to the subject of American foreign policy, Gov. Hatfield said he is deeply concerned about the universal threat of communism.

He said he has personally seen communism—Chinese communism. European communism and American communism. "It is a deadly enemy and not purely a philosophical ideal. It is a hard-core committed system, antagonistic to anything free or dear to this country."

If Vietnam is the spot where America is making its stand against Chinese communist expansion in Southeast Asia, Gov. Hatfield asked: "Can the containment of Red China be unilaterally successful—can America do it alone?"

He suggested that if the Vietnam war is a containment of Red China, then it must be a "multi-nation containment."

Singly, he fears, we are "moment by moment in a position of confrontation with Red China."

EDHIBIT 3 (Continued)

No Allied Support

"But where are our allies?" he asked. "South Korea and Australia (to a limited degree) are the only countries which are supporting us. The rest of the free world, in the words of Ambassador Lodge, 'stir up anti-foreign feelings . . .' and '. . . lay back and let the Americans do it.' "

Our allies, he said, are indirectly supporting North Vietnam and Red China with goods and materials with which to build factories and feed their people. This helps give Red China and North Vietnam the means to wage war and weakens the American position, he declared.

Position on Escalation

Gov. Hatfield said he doesn't want to see the U.S. "go it alone," and this is one key reason why he has opposed escalation of the war.

He said, if it is the administration's policy to contain, and possibly confront Red China at Vietnam, "we must have the support of the free world in our pocket." He said the Johnson administration has achieved no such support, to his knowledge, and he doubted if any "one country is willing at this point to confront Peiping—Moscow."

Oregon's Governor continued: "And what is so contradictory about our foreign policy against communist expansion is that 7,000 miles from home we are trying to avert its expansion when in Cuba, 90 miles from our shores, the greatest spawning ground for communist subversion and revolution is building stronger every day."

"What has this administration done," he asked, "to strengthen, support and defend our allies in the western hemisphere against the red plot in our own back yard?"

Referring to the Hungarian revolution in 1956 (Eisenhower era) the Governor asked, "Where was this country's pledge to help?" He said the Hungarians "were people who understood freedom and were willing to fight for it." Instead, he declared, we're fighting off communism in an area where the people don't understand freedom, and "don't appear too determined to fight for it."

Alternatives Offered

Gov. Hatfield offered what he thought are now the alternatives to escalating the war any further:

"There has to be a frank and open discussion with the American people on the administration's over-all objectives and goals.

"We must develop a Get-America-off-the-Spot program by gaining a multi-nation approach to a military and political solution. We've got to persuade our allies to stop supplying our enemy and unite behind us.

"And we must exhaust every alternative to bloody conflict. Escalation hasn't worked yet."

He said we should not be discouraged by the United Nations Security Council's "apparent lack of interest . . . we must be persistent in making the U.N. more effective; and we must insist on re-convening the Geneva Conference where the opportunity of Red China's participation exists. We have to meet them face-to-face."

EXHIBIT 3 (Concluded)

Asked could not the rich natural resources of all Southeast Asia be a deciding factor of whether China will be a "have" or a "have not" country in the future, Gov. Hatfield answered: "Perhaps."

"But," he concluded, "if we are to stop its expansion—as I believe we should —the American people should know that every alternative has been fully explored and that this country has the full support of its allies."

EXHIBIT 4

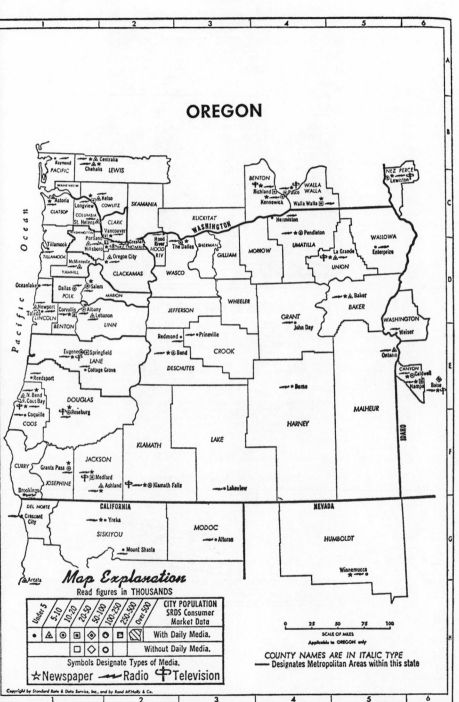

EXHIBIT 5

QUALIFIED APPOINTMENTS

(A Mark of Leadership)

". . . choosing the right individual for the right job at the right time constitutes one of the most important functions of your Governor . . ."
                                                        —Inaugural Address
                                                        January 12, 1959

Mark Hatfield undertook his job as Governor convinced that teamwork is absolutely essential to effective state government. Throughout his term of office, his impartial appointments have been applauded for their competence.

No Governor in this century has been called upon to fill so many high statewide elective offices including the U. S. Senate (Hall S. Lusk), Secretary of State (Howell Appling, Jr.), Supreme Court (A. "Ted" Goodwin), State Treasurer (Howard Belton), Superintendent of Public Instruction (Leon Minear), Multnomah Circuit Court (James M. Burns).

Citizens for Mark Hatfield

Henry A. Carey, Jr.	Bert S. Gooding	James B. O'Hanlon
Edw. L. Casey	John J. Higgins	Frank G. Perri
Don Chapman	Robert A. Leipzig	Frank J. Stark
Albert D. Corrado	James F. Lonergan	Michael J. Walsh
Eugene E. Feltz	Robert W. McMenamin	Charles W. Wentworth

FOR UNITED STATES SENATOR

Hatfield for Senator Committee, Gerald W. Frank, Chairman, 285 Church St., N.E., Salem.

EXHIBIT 5 (Continued)

**MARK ☒ HATFIELD
FOR U.S. SENATOR
MAKE OREGON'S VOTE
COUNT ON CAPITOL HILL**

HE KNOWS OREGON...
OREGON KNOWS HIM
AND HE IS RESPECTED BY THE NATION

Hatfield for U. S. Senator Committee, Gerald W. Frank, Chairman, 285 Church N. E., Salem, Oregon. Phone: 585-6275

Hatfield leadership launched a Decade of Development

Hatfield immediately rallied citizens throughout the state and launched a Decade of Development. Oregon again became a state on the move with these significant achievements:

1) **EDUCATION**—The statewide community college system, established and burgeoned during the Hatfield years, now includes 17,909 students in ten institutions; a state scholarship commission was established; services to the mentally retarded have multiplied ten times; the annual school dropout rate has decreased from 11.3% in 1959 to only 2.9% in 1965.

2) **HIGHWAY CONSTRUCTION AND BEAUTIFICATION**—Oregon has led the nation in the percentage of interstate highways completed to acceptable standards during the Hatfield Years—with the dollar value surpassing the corresponding figure for the last 40 years; highway beautification was a reality in Oregon long before it became a national goal—over $3 million has been expended on state-sponsored beautification programs.

MARK ☒ HATFIELD

YEARS OF GROWTH FOR OREGON

3) **SOCIAL ADVANCEMENT**—Community mental health clinics have been established throughout the state; welfare administration has been greatly improved and work projects have been initiated for welfare recipients; civil rights programs in Oregon have become a model for the entire nation.

4) **AGRICULTURAL DEVELOPMENT**—The State Department of Agriculture has been reorganized for greater service to farmer producers, allied industries and consumers; a new Agriculture Building has been built on the Capitol Mall; Oregon recognized the importance of the consumer in food marketing by the creation of the Consumer Advisory Committee; a vigorous Agri-Business Council was established to improve market relations.

5) **NATURAL RESOURCES**—Oregon's state park system, largest in the nation, has continued to expand, with 24 new parks. Stronger anti-pollution control and enforcement was initiated. Governor Hatfield won legislative approval for a comprehensive water study to show Oregon needs for decades to come and as chairman of the Western Governors he won their support in establishing a water council for the west. Off-shore oil exploration, already an important contributor to the Oregon economy, holds dramatic promise for the future; oceanography research is tapping the vast potential of our state's lengthy shoreline; and space scientists are using Central Oregon as a key testground.

6) **HOLDING THE TAX LINE**—During the Hatfield Years, Oregon had no income tax rate increase—the result of responsible and efficient administration. In 1958, Oregon was eighth highest in the nation in state and local taxes per $1,000 of personal income. By 1964, Oregon had dropped to 23rd. Only Oregon and Louisiana have been able to avoid major tax increases since 1959. Today, per capita taxes in our state are lowest of all Pacific Coast states.

7) **PAYROLLS AND PROGRESS**—During Oregon's Years of Progress the most dynamic growth period in our state's history, per capita personal income has climbed more than 26%—from below the national average to well above average; more than $3 billion in new construction has been started; 180,000 new jobs (non-agricultural), the equivalent of two cities the size of Salem, have been added; over 313 new plants have been constructed and 327 others have been expanded since 1960 alone.

FOR PAYROLLS AND PROGRESS

EXHIBIT 5 (Continued)

THE OREGONIAN, THURSDAY, OCTOBER 20, 1966

Neuberger Supports Duncan Candidacy

WASHINGTON (Special) — What does Sen. Maurine Neuberger think of the two men who are fighting for the privilege of succeeding her in the U.S. Senate?

She knows both of them personally, having served with Gov. Mark Hatfield when she and Hatfield were members of the Oregon Legislature, and having served with Rep. Robert B. Duncan in Congress for the past four years.

Sen. Neuberger favors Duncan. She plans to make a few speeches in his behalf, mainly in Medford Oct. 28 and Eugene Oct. 29, despite her admitted dislike of election campaigning.

Is her preference for Duncan simply because she and he are both Democrats and Hatfield is a Republican and after all, the party expects her to do the proper thing and campaign for Duncan? Or is it to offset the expressed preference of Sen. Wayne Morse for Hatfield?

Not at all, says the senator. Her preference has to do with the different natures of the two senatorial candidates.

Duncan, Called Fighter

"Ever since I've known Bob Duncan," she said in an interview, "I've seen a person completely engrossed in the legislative process. He's not an administrator, and he would have been out of his depth as governor for that reason. But he's cut out to be a fighter for legislation. He knows how to maneuver, how to work with his colleagues, how to get legislation passed. He's a fighting cock."

"Hatfield's nature is entirely different," Sen. Neuberger continued.

"Hatfield looks like a governor. He presides well at meetings. He tries to please all groups. I don't know when we've had a governor who has pleased more groups. He has labor support. The utilities are for him. He has support from liberals and conservatives. He plays a very cautious middle-of-the-road role," said the senator.

"I don't think you get real leadership that way," she added. "You've got to get one side to say, 'I won't vote for you.' Then you know you've done something. Instead, he's always juggling things. You never know where he stands. All of these are characteristic of the politician who wants to stay in office. He hasn't been a bad governor and he hasn't been a great governor. He just hasn't shown any leadership."

Also, Sen. Neuberger thinks Duncan would make a better Oregon senator than Hatfield because Duncan would assert more independence, a trait that is difficult to demonstrate in the House where he is now.

"I think Duncan would be a ball of fire," she said. "Why, he'd take on Wayne Morse and the Southern Democrats and all — and I think other senators would like Duncan's outspokenness."

"If Hatfield is elected," she predicted, "he'll just become a regular Republican, operating under Dirksen's direction. I wouldn't expect him to demonstrate the independence of Javits or Case or Margaret Smith or Kuchel, because Hatfield's ambitions are so very great for a place on the national Republican ticket. Defiance of Dirksen would hurt his prospects. The Republicans are much better at whipping party members into line than the Democrats are. With the exception of two or three mavericks, they stay in line."

Finally, Sen. Neuberger observed that Oregon benefits greatly by various federal programs and projects, some of which depend on the effectiveness of members of the Oregon congressional delegation.

"You can't minimize he fact that a Democratic administration is in power," she asserted, "and there is no doubt that Duncan can do more for Oregon."

"I think Duncan would be a ball of fire"

"Duncan's cut out to be a fighter for legislation... he knows how to get legislation passed. He's a fighting cock."

—Senator Neuberger

KEEP BOB DUNCAN working for Oregon

EXHIBIT 5 (Concluded)

Bob and Marijane Duncan

Meet **BOB DUNCAN**
Democrat for U.S. SENATOR

Visiting with
the Green Beret
soldier

The
Duncan
Clan
at home
in Medford

Bob with the youngest,
Jeannie Beth

...experienced, realistic statesman whom
AP lists as "one of the HARDEST WORKING
Congressmen on Capitol Hill." DUNCAN—the only
man to serve two consecutive terms as speaker
of Oregon House of Representatives. DUNCAN—
the kind of diligent, decisive "shirtsleeve"
senator Oregonians can depend upon for intelligent
leadership in the U. S. Senate. DUNCAN—father
of 7, an Oregon lawyer, WW II Navy pilot and
member of the Navy Reserve—a man you can
trust to make up his mind, stand and be counted.

Bob commuting
between
Washington, D.C.
and Oregon

Duncan for Senate
Committee, Sid Leiken,
Chm., 2230 W. Harvard,
Roseburg, Oregon.

SECTION VII

ORGANIZATION

Bank of California

On the afternoon of January 26, 1966, Mr. Glenn K. Mowry, the Executive Vice President of the Bank of California, was going over a report referred to him by the bank's Corporate Planning Division. According to Mr. Paul Erickson, Director of Corporate Planning, the report had been written by a recent business school graduate who had been working as a trainee under Mr. Erickson. This report (reproduced in Appendix A) was concerned with the organizational implications of the adoption of a marketing concept in commercial banking. Mr. Mowry had scheduled a meeting for the next morning with Mr. Erickson and Mr. Herbert Foedisch, Senior Vice President and head of the Marketing Division, to discuss the report and to determine what action, if any, should be taken concerning Mr. Cunningham's suggestions. Mr. Mowry wanted to assess the report's value in light of the bank's present strategy and organization.

BACKGROUND OF THE BANK OF CALIFORNIA

The Bank of California was founded in San Francisco in 1864 by Mr. D. O. Mills and Mr. William C. Ralson. The bank grew steadily and played an important role in the early economic growth of Northern California. The early financing activities of the bank included the granting of loans to mining companies in the Comstock Lode and to the Central Pacific Railroad for its drive eastward to meet the Union Pacific. With the acquisition of the London & San Francisco Bank, Ltd. in 1905, the Bank of California acquired offices in Portland, Tacoma, and Seattle. Five years later, the bank received a unique national charter allowing it to continue its operations in California, Oregon, and Washington. It still has the distinction of being the only bank in the country chartered by the federal government to do business in more than one state.

During the first half of this century the bank continued to place primary emphasis on traditional banking services to commercial customers. In late 1954, however, the Bank of California acquired the Bank of Martinez and entered the retail banking field. This initial move was followed by other acquisitions and by the establishment of regional-type branch banks. The charter of the bank did not permit branching in Oregon or Washington, and, in the 1950's, all new offices were located in Northern California.

In 1962 Charles de Bretteville, who had been a director of the bank and the president of Spreckles Sugar Company, became president of the Bank of California. Under Mr. de Bretteville's direction a number of changes were introduced. A new organization was developed with added emphasis on personnel development, corporate planning, and marketing. (An organization chart is shown in Exhibit 1.) Increased emphasis was placed on developing international business. International offices were opened in nearly all of the bank's port city locations, and in 1964 a branch was established in Manila. Also, in the same year the bank opened an Edge Act subsidiary, which would permit the bank to make foreign investments of a more risky nature. Prior to 1963, the bank had not had offices in Southern California. In 1963, a major office was opened in Los Angeles. In 1964, the bank expanded its operations in Southern California with the acquisition of the 9-branch American National Bank of San Bernardino. During the 1960's the policy of the Bank of California would be characterized as: maintaining the position as a strong wholesale bank while continuing to develop a competitive position in the retail banking industry. Comparative financial data for 1955 and 1965 are shown in Exhibit 2, and a breakdown of loans by types for the 1965 year-end is given in Exhibit 3.

Marketing Responsibilities in the Bank's Organization

The responsibility for marketing the bank's services was given to several units within its organization.

There were several staff groups which were concerned with business development problems. The Marketing Division, whose organization is shown in Exhibit 4, developed advertising and promotional programs. Their work included both coordination of branch marketing programs and planning of bank-wide promotions. For example, this group had recently arranged for the Bank of California to sponsor the televised broadcasts of San Francisco Giants' games during the coming season. Another promotion program that had been developed by "Marketing" was the Customer-Call Plan. This was a centrally-controlled program by which officers and managers called on present and potential commercial customers to promote the bank's services. In planning these promotions, some marketing research was done by this division.

Mr. Foedisch also headed the bank's National Division, which handled the development of national accounts. As shown in Exhibit 5, the National Division was organized on a geographic basis. The efforts of this group were oriented toward promoting the bank's wholesale services to national companies.

The Corporate Planning Division's work included projects concerned with the bank's marketing policies, especially when the program under study had strategic implications. These studies often involved marketing research activities. The activities and specializations of the seven men in this group are shown in Exhibit 6. Recently the group was trying to determine the primary factors which influence branch growth, and to develop a mathematical model to estimate size of deposits and loans for prospective branch locations. (The actual selection of new branch sites is done by the Branch Expansion Division.) The Corporate Planning Division also worked with the EDP Operations Department in developing new EDP services to attract and hold customers for other bank services. However, as one officer in Corporate Planning said, "Bank of California does not want to become a (computer) service bureau."

The direct business development efforts are the responsibility of the officers and managers of the branches within the bank's system. These men are expected to develop business within their respective areas, using the aid of staff specialists when needed.

EXHIBIT 1

The Bank of California, National Association—Organization Nomenclature Chart

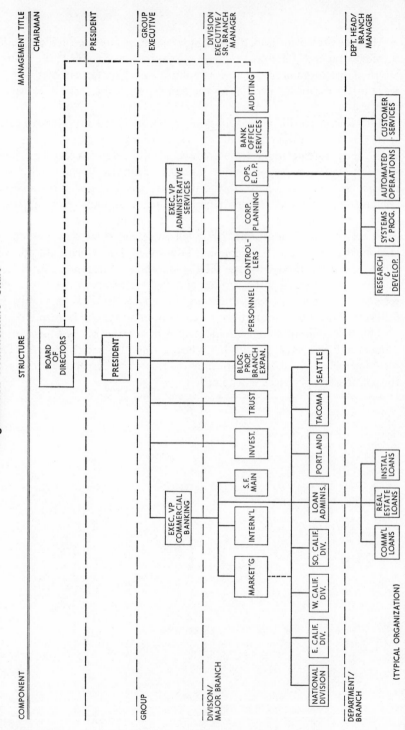

EXHIBIT 2

Comparative Balance Sheet

	December 31	
	1965	*1955*
Assets		
Cash and due from banks.........................	$ 188,091,496	$104,823,007
U.S. Government securities.......................	195,435,908	149,547,587
State and municipal securities....................	132,256,553	31,718,650
Other securities................................	16,429,988	4,630,000
Loans and discounts, less reserve for possible loan		
losses, 1965–$12,329,917......................	763,766,763	215,050,267
Customers' liability on acceptances................	14,536,464	13,452,478
Bank premises and equipment, at cost, less accumulated		
depreciation and amortization, 1965–$8,081,549.....	25,693,532	4,934,260
Accrued interest...............................	7,193,262	1,240,201
Other assets...................................	3,348,547	163,401
Total Assets.............................	$1,346,752,513	$525,559,851
Liabilities and Capital Funds		
Demand deposits...............................	$ 581,798,782	$310,663,570
Savings and other time deposits...................	616,838,280	104,646,795
U.S. Government & other public..................	—	59,106,626
Total Deposits.............................	1,198,637,062	474,416,991
Funds borrowed...............................	5,000,000	—
Accrued taxes and other expenses..................	8,565,975	2,883,792
Dividends payable..............................	836,631	344,520
Acceptances outstanding.........................	14,761,928	13,614,155
Other liabilities...............................	9,353,755	1,296,274
First mortgage notes (4.6% due 1993).............	20,000,000	—
Total Liabilities..........................	1,257,155,351	492,555,732
Capital funds		
Capital notes (4.55% due 1989)................	20,000,000	—
Shareholders' equity:		
Capital stock, authorized 1,959,180 shares $10 per		
value—shares outstanding 1,859,180.............	18,591,800	11,484,000
Surplus..	38,408,200	18,516,000
Undivided profits...............................	12,597,162	3,004,119
Total Shareholders' Equity..................	69,597,162	33,004,119
Total Capital Funds........................	89,597,162	33,004,119
Total Liabilities and Capital Funds.............	$1,346,752,513	$525,559,851

EXHIBIT 3

By Type of Loans

December 31, 1965
(Percent)

Real estate loans..................................	23.6
Loans to banks and financial institutions................	13.0
Loans for purchasing or carrying securities.............	4.9
Loans to farmers....................................	1.1
Commercial and industrial loans......................	34.8
Loans to individuals for personal expenditures..........	21.5
All other loans.....................................	1.1
	100.0

EXHIBIT 4

Marketing Division

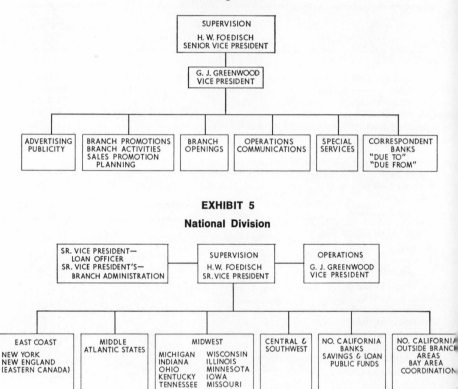

EXHIBIT 5

National Division

EXHIBIT 6

Organization Planning
Manpower Planning

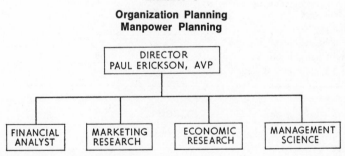

APPENDIX A: THE MARKETING CONCEPT
IN COMMERCIAL BANKING

Introduction

Commercial banking is currently facing strong competitive pressure. It is facing this pressure because it has failed to adapt to the changing needs of its market. The failure to find and implement new and better ways to fill consumers' needs for financial services reflects a shortcoming in the commercial banking industry: the lack of *the marketing concept*. It is the purpose of this report to show the broad implications of the marketing concept for commercial banking. Specifically, we will concentrate on the implications for organizational structure.

The first step will be to identify the major elements of the marketing concept. We will then apply this concept to commercial banking, showing its implications for the proper conduct of this business. Finally, we will describe the organizational structure of a hypothetical bank which has adopted the marketing concept.

The Marketing Concept

Under the marketing concept, the principal task of management is "not so much to be skillful in making the customer do what suits the interest of the business, as to be skillful in conceiving and then making the business do what suits the interests of the customer."[1] Essentially, the business becomes an organization to fill customer needs, not an organization to produce and sell its products and services to whichever customer it can convince to buy them. A business which adopts this concept—one which becomes oriented towards the customer rather than towards its products, focuses its major efforts on introducing new products and services, and seeks out new classes of customers who heretofore have not used the existing products—will be the business which will compete successfully in today's highly competitive markets.

The marketing concept implies working backward from consumer's needs, not forward from the company's product or service. It implies developing an organization which will thrive on continual change. It stresses the firm's distinctive competence in developing products and services which meet the needs of specific market segments.

The Marketing Concept as It Relates to Commercial Banking

The commercial banking industry is one which can benefit greatly from adoption of the marketing concept. Commercial banks *sell financial service*. Lending is a means to meet consumers' need for financing. Trust administration is a means for meeting consumers' needs for financial security and investment. Financial counseling is a means for meeting consumers' needs for proper financial planning. Automated services are a means to meet consumers' needs for financial record keeping. In short, it is financial service that a commercial bank offers to the market place.

What is the true criterion for success in this industry? The answer

---

[1] J. B. McKitterick, "What Is the Marketing Management Concept," *American Marketing Association*, 1957.

lies in the ability of a bank to determine consumers' needs for financial services, to determine how these needs may be segmented, and to determine the ways in which it may organize to most effectively meet these needs. The answer lies in the adoption of the marketing concept. What are the implications of the marketing concept for the commercial bank?

1. The commercial bank should thrive on accepting change, rather than resisting it. It should implement new technological developments and continually strive to develop new and better ways of meeting consumers' needs.

2. The main focus of the creative search for improved performance should be on optimizing the financial service provided to customers, rather than defending against competition.

3. The overall marketing effort should add "consumable value," not merely cost, to the bank's financial services. The commercial bank should use the tools of marketing to improve the "need-satisfying ability" of its products. New products (services) should be developed which will better serve consumer needs. They should be packaged in a way which will further improve their ability to fill consumer demands (repayment flexibility, justifiable deviation from financial restrictions, compensating balance flexibility, etc.), they should be promoted in such a way as to inform a customer of the ways in which they can fill his needs. They should be distributed in a manner (personal call, mail, telephone, or a branch office), and at the time (when he needs it) most optimal to him. If this is done, the marketing effort will add value to the product, further increasing the bank's competitive advantage.

4. The commercial bank should recognize and meet the needs of market segments in order to maximize its ability to solve their unique problems. Commercial banks face many segments. The financial needs of individuals are different from the financial needs of corporations, the needs of domestic corporations are different from the needs of international corporations, the needs of electronic firms are different from the needs of chemical firms, the needs of the wealthy are different from the needs of the poor. A commercial bank should decide which of these segments it wishes to serve, and then develop products which will do this optimally. It must ignore the desire to suppress the differences between these market segments, a desire which is often couched in the philosophy that a dollar is a dollar, no matter who uses it. Instead, recognize that the needs for financial service (which is really its product) will be vastly different for each market segment. It must choose the segments it wishes to deal with, and then tailor its facilities, services, and policies to meet the needs of those segments. If this is done, no competitor who tries to compete by straddling one of these segments will ever be successful. If it is not done, the bank in question will be perpetually vulnerable to any

competitor who sets out specifically to serve the segment it was trying to straddle.

5. The employees of a commercial bank should be "customer's men"
    rather than "company men." Every employee of a commercial bank
    who meets the public is a salesman. Tellers, platform officers and
    callmen are all salesmen. As such they should direct their efforts
    towards serving the customer, not the company. Their sole concern
    should be with mobilizing the total resources of the bank towards
    filling their customer's financial needs. Its efforts should be directed
    towards discovering customer needs ("Could we set up an automatic
    savings account for you, sir, in order to save you trips to the bank?"),
    towards informing management of new ways to solve these needs
    ("Perhaps we should seriously investigate the establishment of an
    Edge Act corporation so we can meet the equity needs of our foreign
    customers?"), and towards tailoring the resources of the bank to
    meet the particular financial needs of its customers.

6. The commercial bank should focus on its distinctive competence,
    using its distinctive resources and skills to optimize its ability to serve
    specific segments of consumer needs. This competence may be in
    the areas of wholesale banking, or retail banking, or international
    banking, or trust, and the like. The bank should focus on a limited
    number of areas, ignoring the temptation to enter into every possible
    market segment. The bank which focuses on its areas of distinctive
    competence succeeds because it is more capable of serving the needs
    of its customers. The bank which does not do so—the bank which
    straddles all markets—remains vulnerable because it does not opti-
    mally serve any specific customer.

In summary, adoption of the marketing concept by commercial banks
would require a great change in present attitudes, procedures, and policies. It would require that the bank thrive on the dynamic change which
its market has undergone, rather than resist or refuse to recognize it. It
would demand that the bank orient itself totally toward consumers'
financial needs, rather than simply meeting its competition and selling its
traditional products. It would place the marketing function in a position
of overriding importance in the bank's power structure. It would mean
that the bank would have to segment its markets, spinning off those which
it could not serve in an optimal manner, and keeping those which it is
uniquely capable of serving.

The author does not mean to imply that nowhere in the field of commercial banking are elements of the marketing concept to be found.
Many enlightened bank officials have been able to "sell" certain elements
of this concept to their policy makers. The results have been significant.
Bank of America's concept of retail banking has resulted in a level of
performance that is unmatched across the country and around the world.
Morgan Guaranty's market segmentation (wholesale banking only) has

been most successful, giving Morgan a distinct advantage over its market-straddling competitors in this area (Chase, City Bank, Manufacturers' Hanover).

Implications of the Marketing Concept for the Bank's Organizational Structure

An organizational structure may be defined as the vehicle for implementing corporate strategy. It is the set of relationships, the allocation of responsibility and authority, which will carry the stated corporate strategy into effect, thus enabling the corporation to achieve its objectives. From this standpoint, each organizational structure must be unique, for it will reflect the particular objectives and strategic choices of each firm. Thus there is no "right" or "wrong" structure for any firm. On the contrary, the correct structure will be that which will enable the firm to implement its unique strategy and achieve its individual objectives.

Because I do not wish to assume the bank's own area of distinctive competence and its own concept of consumers' needs, I cannot recommend the best organizational structure for the Bank of California. However, we can examine some of the implications of the adoption of this concept for the organizational structure of the bank, whatever choices it makes. And we can show what form organizational structure might take, given a hypothetical set of these choices.

Selling Financial Service. The author feels that the first requirement of the adoption of the marketing concept is that individuals throughout all levels of the organization realize that the bank sells financial service, not money, trust, automated services, or the like. It sells specialized financial services to its customers, providing them with a means to satisfy their financial needs. It is particularly because of "marketing myopia" that some commercial banks have been less progressive than other financial intermediaries. Once bank management accepts the general premise that they are selling financial service to meet specific consumers' needs, they may seriously question certain aspects of the bank's organizational structure.

Marketing and Top Management. Another crucial implication of the marketing concept for the organizational structure of this bank is the fact that the marketing function must assume a commanding role in the organizational hierarchy. Top management must have a marketing orientation and must perceive the total market for financial services, so that the bank can foresee and creatively adapt to change. The adoption of the marketing concept means that the marketing function—sales, research, new product analysis, planning, service, and sales training—will assume a role of primary importance in the organizational structure.

The Marketing Function: Management, Services, Operations. The adoption of the marketing concept requires that the marketing function be broken down into three basic segments: management, service, and operations. This is done so that marketing management, divorced from the details of operations, and the specifics of service, devotes its time to the broader implications of new product analysis, organizational planning, management training, and marketing policy. Marketing services—such as advertising, promotion, research, forecasting, and public relations—are indirect selling tools and require a special expertise for their proper utilization. Marketing operations—such as field sales, sales training, customer service, product service, and sales administration—are direct selling tools. The separation of the three functions, therefore, insures that each is handled most capably, that each is evaluated in light of its own responsibility, and that each contributes to overall marketing effort.

Segmentation.   Inherent in the marketing concept is the belief in segmentation. Segmentation is the division of the total market into certain *need* categories, categories which can be identified by some sort of empirical measure. If it adopts the marketing concept, a bank must engage in some sort of market segmentation and structure its organization to reflect the market segments on which it is concentrating. It makes no difference whether it segments by product, by customer type, by geography, or by size of checking account. The important thing is that the method of segmentation give recognition to *differing consumer needs* for financial services.

But ever more important is the fact that the bank cannot properly serve all segments. It cannot force its package of financial services to straddle every part of the market. The bank must choose these segments which it can serve better than anyone else and organize to serve them better.

We emphasize the importance of segmentation in the marketing concept without specifying a procedure by which a bank can determine its "optimal" segments of the market. In general, we urge that bankers examine their total market for financial services, that they try to segment it in the best way possible, and that they then utilize this information to build up a service package which will optimally satisfy those segments which they choose to serve. Finally, they must organize in such a way that this package will be most effectively presented to the segment for which it was produced.

Market Research.   The adoption of the marketing concept implies that the firm will focus its efforts on a creative search for new and better ways to meet their market's needs for financial services. The tool for this effort is market research. Thus market research must play an important role in the organizational structure of this bank. It must be staffed by a professional who is well versed in the techniques of the field. It must be given proper recognition in all marketing analysis and planning. It must be directed towards continually evaluating the effectiveness of the bank's current package of financial services and towards the complete analysis of creative proposals to improve this package. It must be directed towards determining new and better ways to segment markets, and new and better ways to serve them. Its findings will be the cornerstones for the dynamic development of the marketing concept.

Sales Training: Creating Customers' Men. We have seen the importance of salesmen for the implementation of the marketing concept. We have seen that these men must be customers' men, capable of mobilizing the total resources of the bank towards meeting a customer's financial needs. Thus, the adoption of the marketing concept requires that the commercial bank train and develop its employees so that they may have this capability. Training must assume an important position in the organizational structure. It must be centralized, so that the program will focus on the total resources of the bank, not just on particular functions or products. It must be complete, so that no man will leave the program without the total picture of the bank in his mind. It must be continual, as the bank aggressively adapts to its changing market.

Planning: Insurance for Success. The adoption of the marketing concept implies that the planning function assume a great deal of importance in the organizational structure. Planning insures that the organization is continually equipped to meet the dynamic needs of its market, that the firm goes where it wants to go, and that the total organization and its objectives are the guiding principles, not the fragmented objectives of each department or function. Thus the marketing concept, which implies adaptability to change, market innovation, selective segmentation, and corporate direction dictates that the planning function be placed in a position of great influence and recognition; the very functions which planning fulfills are the means to the successful adoption of this concept. Thus the commercial bank which adopts the marketing concept must place the planning function in a commanding position within the organization.

We have touched on a few of the more important implications of the marketing concept, showing how the commercial bank which adopts it must, in determining its organizational structure, give proper recognition to these facts: that the bank is selling financial service; that marketing is a three-pronged tool consisting of management, service, and operations; that the marketing function must assume a commanding role in the organizational power hierarchy, while operations moves into the background; that segmentation must be practiced; that market research will be the key to success; that salesmen must be trained to sell the total package of the bank's financial services; and that planning should be given all the respect and authority due the importance of its responsibility.

Organizational Structure: An Example

We will describe briefly the organizational structure of a hypothetical bank. This example incorporates the organizational implications of the marketing concept described above. Our primary assumption is that the bank has decided to concentrate on two primary areas: retail banking and wholesale banking.

The following comments apply to the organization chart shown in Exhibit 7.

Groups. Two major operating groups, Retail and Wholesale, correspond to the two primary market segments on which the bank will concentrate. The major group managers have total responsibility for development of their respective markets, including "sales" of financial assets (gaining new deposits) and "sales" of financing services (gaining new loans).

Divisions. The Retail and Wholesale groups each have three divisions: Sales, Business Development, and Planning.

Sales division is segmented geographically for purposes of decentralized control. In the Retail group, district executives supervise branch managers. The Wholesale group also is organized with the goal of specialization, with specific-industry departments and geographical segmentation (U.S., Metropolitan, International).

Business Development division includes two departments: Service Managers and Marketing Services. Marketing Services include staff coordination of advertisement, public relations, etc.—sometimes called "indirect selling." Note that so-called "direct selling" is done through the Sales divisions. Service Managers are similar to product managers in manufacturing companies; each Service Manager is responsible for marketing coordination of a specific service, such as installment credit. Service Managers ensure that each "product" or service that the bank sells receives coordinated emphasis in direct and indirect selling operations, e.g., provides service and information on installment credit to all branches.

Planning division includes Training, Market Research, New Service Analysis and Organizational Planning departments. Each of these departments works closely with the Corporate Planning staff function. Each is directly responsible to the Retail or Wholesale operating group, so that the special requirements of that segment of the market can be satisfied.

Corporate Staff Functions. Five staff functions assist in corporate-level operations and decision-making but are separate from the line groups that sell the services of the bank. These staff functions are Legal, Bank Investments, Corporate Planning, Control and Operations. The head of Corporate Planning, for example, will have as assistants his counterparts in the Planning Divisions of the Retail and Wholesale groups.

Conclusion

It has been the hope of the author to present to the reader the organizational implications of the marketing concepts for banking, analyzing them in light of banking's present attitudes and concepts. Specifically, I examined the implications of the marketing concept for the organizational

EXHIBIT 7

Bank Organization Chart with Marketing Concept

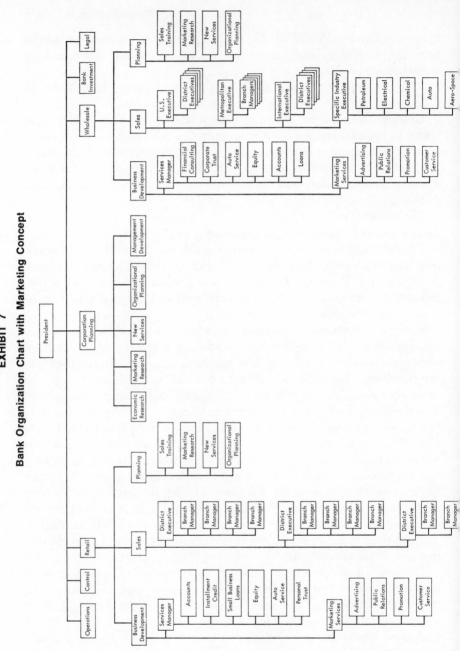

structure of a bank like the Bank of California. I was, of course, unable to present any "organizational truths" or platitudes, for each organizational structure must reflect the unique objectives and strategy of the firm. But I was able to raise the relevant considerations which the bank would have to recognize if it desired to adopt the marketing concept.

I showed how the elements of customer orientation, marketing management, market segmentation, creative innovation, marketing planning, and the like would be reflected in the organizational structure. I also introduced the concept of the Product Manager in an effort to separate the vested influence of products from the primary purpose of customer service. In short, I showed how the bank might organize to reflect the commanding implications of the fully adopted marketing concept.

Above all, the reader must realize that this paper is but a rough beginning to a very complex problem. It handled but a few of the relevant issues, in a manner which barely did them justice. But this does not deny the importance of the marketing concept. Commercial banks have hidden behind their cloaks of conservatism and traditionalism for far too long. Their market has changed. Their customers' demands have changed. Their competitors have changed. For the commercial bank of the future to be successful, it must adopt the marketing concept in its entirety. The nature of its market dictates it, the nature of its product dictates it, the nature of its competition dictates it.

Henry Research Corporation

The Henry Research Corporation produced an extensive line of nondestructive magnetic testing equipment for use in a wide variety of manufacturing, maintenance, and repair functions in industry. The expressed policy of the company was not to sell a testing instrument as such but to sell a means whereby a customer could solve a problem. It had always been difficult to co-ordinate the company's marketing department and its research and engineering department because of the technical nature of the testing instruments and the necessity of constantly developing new instruments and modifying existing ones to suit individual customers' needs. The importance of proper co-ordination between these departments was emphasized by a problem brought about by the introduction by Henry Research several years earlier of a completely new line of testing equipment—generally described as "electronic" —which had not lived up to sales expectations. Research, engineering, and sales expenses devoted to the line in the most recent year alone amounted to $420,000, while total sales of electronic equipment were only $358,000 in the same year. Sales of all electronic testing equipment were approximately 3 percent of the company's total sales. Despite the poor results to date, management was convinced that their line of electronic equipment had a large potential.

Henry Research Corporation was founded in 1929 by Mr. V. M. Danby, a physicist and consulting engineer who developed a magnetic dust inspection method that conclusively located cracks in oil well pipe. The company grew rapidly, and company officials pointed with pride to the fact that it furnished testing instruments to practically every manufacturing industry. Many products, ranging from aircraft to shotguns, had to be tested during manufacture and overhaul to locate any breaks or weak points that might endanger the life or property of the purchaser.

Henry Research furnished a nondestructive, economical test for this purpose. Other inspection processes were developed for use with newer metals, such as aluminum, magnesium, bronze, tungsten carbide, and even certain ceramics and glass.

Through the years, as the company had grown, the sales personnel or field engineers had had the responsibility for recognizing their customers' needs for inspection as their customers developed new products. It was the responsibility of the sales engineers to advise their respective branch and regional sales managers of new problems existing in customers' plants. These needs were discussed with the marketing vice-president and the technical co-ordinator, who appraised the needs and passed them on to the research and engineering department. When a problem was thus passed on from the field, it was often difficult for the marketing vice-president to appraise the importance of the new development on which a customer might be working. Many times a customer's enthusiasm for a new or modified type of testing instrument would have no relationship to possible future demands for such an instrument, even though the research and engineering department could develop a satisfactory answer for the particular customer's problem.

A typically difficult field was that of aircraft manufacturing. As air speeds became greater, the need for testing engines and airframe parts became more critical. Often the Henry Research field engineers were urged by their customers to develop testing methods and instruments for assemblies or parts that might be in only the developmental stage, and at such a stage even aircraft manufacturers could not tell whether contracts would be obtained in a volume sufficient to support development of new testing instruments.

As a result of the difficulty of estimating sales potential for possible new testing methods, the amount of emphasis given to new projects by the marketing department in passing them to research and engineering depended to a large degree on the judgment of the marketing vice-president or the technical co-ordinator. This in turn was influenced by the ability of the sales engineers to "sell" the idea to their superiors.

Another difficulty often encountered in co-ordination between the marketing and the research and engineering departments was that, after a problem had been passed to research and engineering, priority might be determined by that department's interest in the problem or by whether it thought that it would have a reasonable chance of coming up with a solution quickly and easily. In other situations it might approach a problem "on its own," without having received any specific indication from the marketing department as to the potential market for such a product or testing method.

The company's research department was attracted to the new electronic testing equipment as a potentially profitable related field. This method of testing, known as "eddy current testing," had been developed by a German physicist, Dr. Foerster, and was relatively unknown in the United States. According to Dr. Foerster, the method had been researched for a period of some twenty years and was in use commercially in numerous industrial plants in Germany. The principles of this electronic type of testing were based upon the measurement of the impedance and phase relationships of electric current passing through coils. The amount of impedance depended upon the physical properties of the material being tested. Such testing instruments, it was claimed, not only could easily locate defects, both surface and subsurface, but could detect variations in diameter, grade, tensile strength, and hardness. The obvious relationship of eddy current testing to the company's line and the description of its potential led the company to enter into a patent and licensing agreement with Dr. Foerster whereby his equipment would be distributed by Henry Research in the United States.

The company dominated the magnetic testing field; as a result, there was little competitive pressure on the development of new testing methods. The electronic testing field was different—there were more competitors and Henry Research was less well established. If the company delayed in developing an electronic testing method for a new product, there was a real risk that a competitor would beat them to it.

Initially, numerous types of Dr. Foerster's instruments were imported, and a research team was set up to determine what products could be

EXHIBIT 1

Henry Research Organization during Introduction and Development of Edatest Line of Electronic Testing Instruments

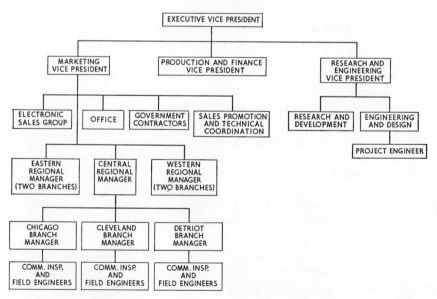

tested by the new instruments and what modifications would have to be made so that they would be commercially applicable for use by industrial plants in the United States. It was not long before the conclusion was reached that, although basic theoretical work had progressed in Europe for over twenty years, most of the testing instruments as imported were not suitable for commercial distribution to any of the company's present customers.

Modifications were made, and much field work was done by the research and Edatest engineering department, which proceeded energetically with the problems of making the Edatest line, which included all eddy current types of instruments applicable to customers' needs. The problems involved were so complex that about three-fourths of all research and engineering personnel were devoting full time to the Edatest line, leaving only about one-fourth to work on other company problems. In addition, a special electronic sales group of three men was organized to work with customers in adapting Edatest testing methods to their problems.

Henry Research was organized in three principal departments, namely, marketing; production and finance; and research and engineering. An abbreviated organization chart as of the time of the introduction and development of the Edatest line is shown in Exhibit 1.

The marketing department was responsible for all sales and was divided into three regions: eastern, central, and western. Each region was in charge of a regional sales manager. Under each region were two or three branches out of which the salesmen, called "field engineers," worked. A total of twenty-seven field engineers worked out of the seven branches. Each branch manager was responsible for the field engineers in his branch and for at least one, and in some cases for as many as four, commercial laboratories that tested products brought in from the field.

A field engineer was typically a well-trained technical man, whose salary ranged from $12,000 to $18,000 per year. He necessarily had to have a great deal of technical knowledge to appraise a particular customer's problem and determine whether Henry Research had a type of testing equipment that would suitably solve the problem or whether he should call on the research and engineering department for help in developing a new or modified type of equipment to solve the customer's problem.

Officials of Henry Research believed that the problem confronting the company concerning the large expenditure for sales and for research and development and the relatively small sales of Edatest equipment not only was important in itself but was indicative of the fact that better coordination between marketing and research and development was needed. The company, by the very nature of its products, had always been heavily research oriented, and the history of its new products had been that a great deal of money had to be expended in developing a new or modified method of testing to suit a customer's need before sales volume of any magnitude could be developed.

It was felt that, in the case of the development of the electronic line of testing instruments, too much of the impetus had come from the research and development department and not enough from the marketing department. The special electronics sales group, which had been set up to survey customers' needs for electronic testing equipment, had worked in a slightly "ivory-tower" atmosphere and had not sought the opinions of the field engineers (general salesmen) or kept them advised of details of developments. This situation apparently had tended to make the field engineers less interested in the new line of electronic equipment. The salesmen concentrated on the older lines of equipment, for which a demand was established and with which they were acquainted.

It was decided that organizational changes were necessary to correct the situation that had been highlighted by the electronic equipment experience. Exhibit 2 shows an abbreviated organization chart incorporating the principal changes that management decided were needed to develop better co-ordination between the marketing and the research and engineering departments. Principal changes in the marketing department

EXHIBIT 2

Henry Research Organization, Reflecting Principal Changes to Effect Better Co-ordination between Marketing and Research and Engineering

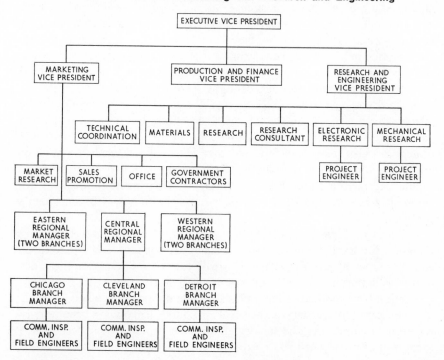

were the establishment of a market research department, the transferring of electronic technical co-ordination from sales promotion to a separate section under research and engineering, and the elimination of the special electronics sales group.

Special provision was made for better liaison between the marketing and the research and engineering departments concerning the new electronic lines by the creation of three new positions known as "regional electronic specialists." Their position in the organizational setup is indicated in Exhibit 3.

EXHIBIT 3

Sales-Engineering Liaison—Electronics

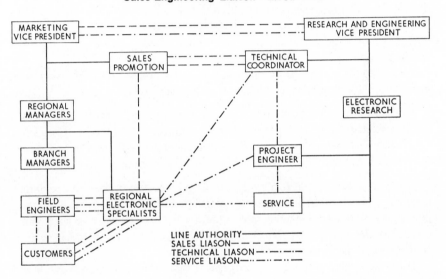

The duties of the technical co-ordinator did not change in the reorganization but were made into a full-time job and transferred to the research and engineering department. The technical co-ordinator was to maintain records of all applications, successful and unsuccessful, of the company's electronic testing methods; to furnish information on these applications and all other pertinent technical data to the field engineers, the regional electronic specialists, the sales promotion manager, and the regional and branch managers; to pass information from the field on customer problems and testing applications to the technical departments in the research and engineering department; and to pass requests for research from the field to the proper technical department, following research developments, and pass results back to the field.

Regional electronic specialists would set up testing laboratories in each sales region to work on customer problems. If they developed a successful testing method for a given problem, they were to report this to the technical co-ordinator, who would inform both the marketing and the research and the engineering departments.

It was expected that the new organization would function as follows: if a field engineer (salesman) found a testing problem that Henry Research had solved before, he would attempt to sell the company's testing method to the potential customer. If the field engineer did not know the proper testing method and if he thought the problem required magnetic testing methods, he would report it to his branch manager. If the field engineer thought electronic testing methods were appropriate, he would report the problem to the regional electronic specialist, who would attempt to solve it by work in his laboratory or at the customer's plant. If the field electronic specialist could not solve the problem, he and the field engineer would report the problem to the branch manager, from where it would be handled in the same manner as were magnetic testing problems.

Problems forwarded to branch managers were passed on to the regional managers, who would attempt to estimate the following:

1. Were Henry Research testing methods applicable to the problem?
2. How large was the potential sales volume for Henry Research?
3. What was the probability of technical success in solving the problem?
4. What was the probable cost of technical development?

If his estimates of the foregoing questions were favorable, the regional manager passed the problem to the marketing research department for a more formal estimate of the sales potential. This report was then submitted to the marketing vice-president, who sent it to the research and engineering department.

Would the new organization improve co-ordination between the marketing and the research and engineering departments?

Funston & Green, Inc.

PROBLEMS OF OPERATING AN ADVERTISING AGENCY

In late 1966, George Funston and Carter Green, two seasoned advertising executives, began to re-evaluate the position of their agency in the advertising industry. Although Funston & Green, Inc. (F & G), had done well in the past, they began to question just where it was headed. Carter had said, "We're doing well right now, George, but we can't afford to just sit by and let things happen. The industry's changing and we've got to change with it if we expect to keep our share."

Background

F & G, headquartered in Chicago, was one of the 50 largest advertising agencies in the United States. In 1966, U.S. advertising agencies made and placed for clients well over $7 billion of advertising, up over 12% from the preceding year. Of this total, the agencies collected, in commissions and fees,[1] in excess of $1 billion.

There were many agencies in the U.S., ranging in volume of billing from $550,000,000 down to $200,000, or even less. Of the 500 accredited agencies[2] reporting their billings annually to *Advertising Age*, the industry's "bible," and to the U.S. Census Bureau every five years, fewer than 100 U.S. based agencies placed 90% of the $7 billion of annual commissionable billing.

In 1966, 12 U.S. agencies billed in excess of $150 million. In the table below, these are listed by both worldwide and domestic volume to indicate the relative importance of international billing. In addition, com-

[1] About 90% of the agencies' billion dollar income comes from commissions paid by the advertising media—TV, radio, newspapers, magazines, etc.

[2] Those recognized by the media as legitimately entitled to collect the standard 15% agency commission.

parative 1966 and 1965 figures are shown to indicate the shift in volume that can occur from one year to the next.

The next 38 agencies ranged in size from $23 to $140 million, with only 7 of the 38 billing $100 million or more. While all top 12 agencies showed a satisfactory growth pattern from 1965 to 1966, growth for the

Agency Billing*
(000,000)

	1966		1965	
Agency	World Total	U.S. Only	World Total	U.S. Only
J. Walter Thompson.................	$557.7	$356.7	$508.1	$317.0
McCann-Erickson, Inc...............	445.0	275.0	420.0	259.0
Young & Rubicam...................	376.3	298.5	347.9	276.0
Batten, Barton, Durstine & Osborne.....	312.0	294.6	292.2	277.1
Ted Bates & Company...............	272.5	176.0	237.5	169.2
Foote, Cone & Belding..............	255.5	199.0	228.0	178.6
Leo Burnett Company...............	220.7	209.9	185.1	174.8
Doyle Dane Bernbach...............	202.9	185.6	141.6	130.0
Benton & Boyles...................	177.5	156.1	138.0	93.8
Grey Advertising...................	168.0	148.0	131.1	116.9
Ogilby & Mather, Inc...............	165.0	95.0	148.5	80.7
Dancer-Fitzgerald-Sample............	151.6	148.7	137.0	134.6

* From the annual report of *Advertising Age*, February 20, 1967.

top 38 as a whole was relatively small. The remaining 50 of the top 100 U.S. agencies ranged in size from $9–$22 million, a substantial drop-off from the "Big 12." With few exceptions, the 50 agencies in this group showed little growth from 1965 to 1966.

F & G billed over $31 million in 1966, of which $5 million was billed through F & G's one branch office in Los Angeles. The Chicago operation accounted for 87% of the agency's net profit; Los Angeles accounted for the remaining 13%. (See Exhibits 1 and 2 for comparative financial data for F & G and the average agency its size.) According to *Advertising Age* figures, only four Chicago-based agencies billed more than F & G.

Management of the Agency

George Funston, 57, and Carter Green, 52, were Chairman of the Board and President, respectively. Together they owned 38% of the company's stock, with the remaining 62% held by other employees.

George and Carter seldom referred to their formal titles. They considered themselves partners which, in the fullest sense, they were. From the beginning of their association in 1954, they had been very good friends, and they had understood each other. This had had an important bearing on the agency's operation, particularly in recent years.

Both George and Carter had, of course, the management responsibility of the agency. This took relatively little time: they employed top people on the financial and administrative side of the business, and they knew how to use them. But George and Carter made policies and enforced them; their philosophy of operation and their attitudes toward the advertising business were so alike that they might have been twins.

Both had been raised in the business as "working" admen and, in their own company, they continued to be that. They called themselves "Management Supervisors," and they split the accounts down the middle. Each accepted final responsibility for his particular half of the billing, and using each other as sounding boards, they had developed a profitable working relationship. They had even become, over the years, interchangeable on accounts.

F & G Organization and Services

Funston & Green had nine departments, each with specific functions and specially trained people. (See Exhibit 3 for a brief description of the functions, operations, and responsibilities of each department.) The nine departments of the agency and the number of people in each department were:

	Chicago	Los Angeles
Management	2	1
Finance and administration	7	1
Account service and marketing (combined)	24	6
Creative services (copy art, television, and radio)	39	9
Merchandising including promotions and premiums	10	2
Research—Advertising, marketing, product	14	3
Media—Analysis, buying	24	4
Mechanical production (advertising and collateral)	9	2
Accounting—Billing, all other financial matters, including use of computers (both offices)	14	—
Clerical	27	6
	170	34

The Chicago Office

Funston & Green's Chicago office had 19 clients at the end of 1966. Eleven were in packaged goods sold through grocery, drug, and liquor stores; 2 were in the appliance field; 3 in finance; 2 in transportation; and 1 in the fashion /fabric business. The office did not handle, and never had handled, an industrial account or a purely corporate campaign. Their list of clients and their relative billing was:

Account Category by Product or Service	Billing
Beer	$5,000,000
Beauty aids	4,000,000
Pet foods	2,500,000
Flour and cereals	1,800,000
Liquor	1,300,000
Proprietary drugs	1,100,000
Canned meats	1,000,000
Dairy foods	900,000
Potato chips/snacks (regional)	800,000
Coffee	600,000
Soft drink line	500,000
Large appliances	2,000,000
Small appliances	1,500,000
"Feeder" airline	600,000
Railroad	500,000
Chicago bank	700,000
Insurance company	500,000
Downstate savings & loan	400,000
Fashion/fabric	300,000

From the above, it was easy to see why Funston & Green, Chicago, was known as a "packaged goods" agency. While they had a few accounts that could qualify them as a "diversified" agency, the figures belied that. The two transportation, three financial, and one fashion account billed in total about $3 million. The 11 packaged goods and two appliance accounts accounted for $23 million in billing.

The Chicago office's largest account billed $5 million; its smallest, $300,000. It had several very important "name" clients, most of whom had grown with the economy, but it was shy on the so-called "growth, speculative-type" accounts.

Because of its professional reputation and its acknowledged capabilities in the fields of advertising *and* marketing, Funston & Green had been approached many times by ambitious, "growth-type" firms whose budgets were, at the moment, small. Naturally, the management people in the companies which offered their business to F & G sincerely believed that the products they planned to advertise and market had great potential. The partners had discussed these opportunities and had decided that such accounts were not worth the gamble. Their judgment had turned out to be right in most cases.

George and Carter recognized that if their judgment happened to be wrong and they turned down an account that became "big time," the agency could suffer in a number of ways above and beyond the loss of larger volume and profit; for example, by being considered too conservative and, therefore, not attractive to promotional-type prospects; by having the staff morale hurt, because its management refused to "gamble";

and by not growing fast enough to be considered a "hot" agency, not getting enough publicity, and not being one of the "talked-about" agencies.

Back in 1962, which had been an especially busy and profitable year for Funston & Green, the agency principals had turned down two accounts for what they then thought were excellent reasons. Thinking back over the circumstances and what happened caused them to wonder if they had been right.

The two opportunities they had considered were these:

An electronics company which spent about $400,000 in scientific trade publications asked Funston & Green to take on its account. As an incentive they told the agency that they might have an interesting consumer product to market within a year, but that it also might never get off the drawing board. The agency told the prospect that accounts of this type were not ones in which it specialized and that the company would undoubtedly get a better job from one of the industrial agencies. It turned out that the consumer product, something of a breakthrough in the low-priced camera field, did get off the drawing board and became an almost instant success. In 1965, the account billed approximately $3,000,000 through the agency it selected.

The second account that Funston & Green declined in 1962 was a candy company which already had two agencies. It had recently developed two new candy bars which it felt were competitive with its existing products. It wanted to test market these new items and the business was offered to F & G. Quite properly, the agency told the client that it would be delighted to handle the business provided the agency was paid a fee to cover its test market costs. The candy people thought differently; they were big spenders and knew that plenty of agencies, perhaps "hungrier" than Funston & Green, would absorb all agency costs. They were right, of course, and one of the better Chicago agencies took on the job, without fee.

One of the candy bars never did come to market but the other did well in test. In 1965, the advertising budget on the successful candy bar was just under $2,000,000. Before the billing reached that figure, the agency which accepted the test market assignment estimated that it had invested close to $250,000 in the product.

The Los Angeles Office

Funston & Green's Los Angeles office was opened in the spring of 1963 with one account billing about $1,000,000. A large regional beer brand had been an important F & G account for nine years. The brewery marketed its brand in two large areas: 10 states in the Midwest and in California. For many years they had had a separate Western agency, headquartered in Los Angeles. For a long time the brand had done very well in both areas of the country, but in 1962, sales and share had slipped in California.

Early in 1963, the brewery management offered the California billing to Funston & Green, provided that they would open a Los Angeles office with a small staff and a good man to head it up.

The brewery made it eminently clear that the decision was entirely up to F & G. If the partners thought that with a million dollar account they could build, in time, a profitable office in fast-growing L.A., fine, then the billing was theirs. If not, the brewery wanted it understood that the main account, the part F & G now handled, would in no way be jeopardized. With this assurance, George Funston and Carter Green were free to make an objective and independent decision.

Over the years both men had spent considerable time in Southern California on client business. They knew it was a difficult advertising market and they knew that opening a branch office there meant taking some risks. There were three risks areas that concerned them most and which they discussed at length:

First, from an agency standpoint, competition for business in Los Angeles had been especially keen since the end of World War II. Most seasoned agency people knew well that there were too few substantial accounts for the number of agencies in operation, which created a dog-eat-dog situation. In 1962, there were approximately 900 "Advertising Agencies and Counsellors" listed in the yellow pages of the L.A. phone book. In San Francisco, there were only 325 agencies listed in the yellow pages. Yet, in terms of volume of agency-placed business, the two markets were identical in size. Getting new business would be difficult and expensive.

Secondly, hiring a good manager and staff was essential. Without that their chances of getting worthwhile accounts would be slim and, furthermore, according to Carter, "we would be pretty stupid to try to palm off mediocre people on the beer account. There are lots of good advertising people in Los Angeles, but they aren't easy to come by and would have to be paid well to get them to switch."

Thirdly, at the $1,000,000 level, F & G would lose money. As closely as George and Carter could figure, the office might break even with $3 million in billing, and it would do well if billings reached $4–$5 million which at a minimum would require three to four years.

With the agency's reputation and with an outstanding manager who had strong local connections, it seemed possible to turn the corner in a couple of years. Naturally, they took into consideration that about half of any losses would be taken care of by Chicago-earned tax dollars. With the last point in mind they did not think the loss could be very great— maybe $30 or $40 thousand at most over a two-year period.

Even though George and Carter thought that opening the branch would be a gamble, they decided to try it. Their client was delighted when they told him of their decision.

George went out to the West Coast a few days later, after putting out some lines to find the right manager. The agency had its first piece of luck in finding and hiring Winston Cooke. He seemed to have a great reputation and first-rate local connections.

Winston Cooke, 37 years old, was a top-flight ad man, hard-driving and ambitious. He had gone to work in the Los Angeles branch of a big New York agency right out of school. He was a learner and he had progressed well: when Funston & Green had wooed him away, he was a vice president and account supervisor on the largest food account in the agency he had always been with.

After several dinner and evening meetings, George decided that Win had it and, what's more, he liked him. After checking Win's references carefully, George offered him the job and he accepted. Win knew his advertising market, he asked for autonomy, and it was, more or less, granted.

A month later, on May 1, 1963, the Funston & Green branch office was opened in a new building on Wilshire Boulevard, with a hand-picked staff of eight people, plus Winston Cooke as Vice President and Manager.

"In Los Angeles, you scramble like crazy," Win Cooke had told his Chicago associates from the beginning. "You have to take chances, and a good many agencies 'wheel and deal.' By that I mean cut corners, give away services that should be paid for."

"But let me tell you at the start," Win added, "that if you run an agency that way, you're just asking to lose your shirt, which is not for you *or* me. I'm not saying I won't use some spot judgments from time to time to stay competitive, but I won't give away the store. I'll work with a sharp pencil because you have to do that. It seems to me, though, that there's business to be had in L.A. and that we can pick up our share. After all, we've got a million in billing, a reputation as a good agency, and a lot of very good friends around town. It's my guess we'll make it just fine, with luck and time on our side."

By 1966, in the toughly competitive L.A. advertising market, Win Cooke had built his office's billing up to $5,000,000 with a highly diversified list of 14 clients as follows:

Account Category by Product or Service	*Billing**
Beer......................................	$1,500,000
Automotive dealer association.................	600,000
Potato chips, snacks (regional)................	500,000
Electronics...............................	400,000
Land development.........................	300,000
Jams and jellies............................	300,000
Savings and loan (regional)...................	250,000
Grocery chain.............................	250,000
Furniture manufacturer......................	200,000
Barbeque equipment.........................	200,000
Bread.....................................	150,000
Cookies and crackers........................	150,000
Industrial saws.............................	100,000
Resort hotel...............................	100,000

* A number of these accounts had been very small at the start but quite a few of them had shown steady growth in both sales and billings through the agency.

Win's progress had been appreciated by Chicago management. He was, they believed, running a first-rate show in the country's fastest growing market. After a couple of years he had been named Executive Vice President, put on the Board, and given sizable stock option opportunities which he had exercised. Since the office Cooke ran was growing and making money, Messrs. Funston and Green did not give it too much thought or attention. They knew that he had worked hard on new business and that his efforts had paid off. They did not really know how Win had managed to do so well, but they were pleased that he had.

In the beginning, Win Cooke realized that, after a period of time, his principal job would be to get new business for Funston & Green's Los Angeles office, but his most immediate assignment was to develop a marketing plan and an advertising and promotional program that would reverse the downward sales trend of the beer account.

He and his hand-picked group lost no time tackling the problem, working in harmony with the client. Together, they came up with what appeared to be a first-rate marketing plan, completely tailored to the California beer situation.

Research had shown that the brand's image had slipped—that, in effect, the heavy and medium beer drinkers considered the brand as old-hat. The agency group figured they had better put together a beer campaign that combined good product "sell" and a different, interesting advertising execution.

Win selected as his key creative men the swinging type—young, bold contemporary.[3] Given a sound sales concept, they were good at develop-

---

[3]This type of creative man was in great demand. To get them you had to pay a premium. Good, solid copy and art creative people could be hired in the $15 to $18,000 range; the "swingers" were getting $20 to $25,000. Win hired the latter and paid the premium.

ing exciting, unusual, attention-getting advertising copy. With nothing else to worry about, everybody in the shop concentrated on the beer campaign—and they were successful. The client thought the new advertising was great and brought it virtually without change. The field sales force also greeted the new program with enthusiasm.

The first Southern California air-date for the new TV campaign was July 15. Within a few days the campaign was being described in Los Angeles advertising circles in such glowing terms as "one of the brightest campaigns to come along in ages," "highly creative," "unusual, different," "entertaining, yet solid brand sell." Best of all as everyone was to learn later, the advertising sold beer and, in just three months' time, the down curve in sales had been sharply reversed.

Almost overnight, Funston & Green had established a strong beachhead on the L.A. scene, in about the best way possible—as a "hot," creative office of a substantial, marketing-oriented "national" agency. And it provided Win Cooke with the very kind of springboard he needed to launch a hard-hitting drive for new accounts.

Win was not a haphazard operator. On the contrary, he was a systematic planner, unwilling to waste his time pushing doorbells at random or indiscriminately following the endless rumors that plagued the ad business. A short time after the beer campaign got underway, he said to his small staff:

"The sales guys at the brewery tell me our beer campaign looks like a sure winner with the trade and the consumer. Anyway, the beer's moving well at retail. Whether it'll hold up remains to be seen, but all the signs are good. So we've got to be off and running on another and, I guess, faster track—new business.

"I'll front it, of course, but I'll need all the help I can get. We all get around and we all do our share of visiting with other people in the business. Before anybody starts chasing will-o'-the-wisps, be sure and check with me. I've got enough friends in the business that I think I can get the straight dope on what's gossip and what's fact in the area of client/agency relationships. If I can't, I wouldn't hesitate to call most ad managers to find out what's what.

"I guess you all know," Win went on, "that I've been pretty active in our industry for the last few years. I know a lot of people, just as all of you do. Between us, we've been on AAAA[4] committees, made speeches, taken Ad Club assignments and the like. That gives us lots of contacts and now is our chance to use them."

In systematic fashion Win Cooke began to cultivate what he considered the agency's most natural prospects—the ad managers or marketing managers whom he knew. He had a good story to tell about Funston & Green, about his reasons for joining them, about the people he had hired,

---

[4] American Association of Advertising Agencies.

about his plans for growth. He was pleased at the number of people who seemed interested in listening—whether out of friendship, respect, or just plain curiosity. He had a sneaking suspicion that the beer campaign had a lot to do with that interest.

Apparently, Win told his story well because the agency began to get more and more favorable "word-of-mouth" comments in the L.A. advertising community. Before long, Funston & Green, along with a lot of other agencies, was invited to solicit three accounts in the fall.

The first was a potato chip and snack account which had billed $300,-000 the preceding year and which was expanding. Management people of the brewery and of the prospective account were close friends, had a lot in common, and had worked together on several promotions. When Win learned that his agency and two others were in the "finals," he asked the brewery management if he could use them as a reference, and, of course, they said "yes." They took the initiative and voluntarily gave Win and the agency a tremendous send-off. Win learned just how important his client's phone call had been shortly after Funston & Green was appointed the agency for the snack company.

The ice had been broken, but the agency had two more solicitations to make in the next month. Both were done professionally, with the proper amount of "theatre" and flair, but without slickness or tricks. It missed on the first of these, which was disappointing. The third presentation of the year was made to a regional winery with a $250,000 budget. The agency's experience with the beer business, while short, had been intense; it had set about learning the beer, wine, and liquor picture in California and had gained practical know-how in the industry. The wine people recognized how well F & G understood the market and what an outstanding advertising job had been done on the beer account. F & G won the wine account, in competition with five other agencies, principally because it had showed such expertise in marketing and advertising a product closely allied to wine.

Two out of three winners for a new agency caused a stir among Los Angeles advertising people. It was to become apparent in succeeding years that the fast start "creatively" and in the area of new business presentations had made an impression on a lot of people on Win's top prospect list.

In F & G's three years in the L.A. market, its branch experienced a much faster growth rate than its Chicago counterpart. Although Win Cooke knew he was appreciated and that he had been well taken care of financially by the "Partners," he sometimes wondered just where he was headed.

Year of Decision

1966 marked a turning point for Funston & Green as an advertising agency. It was, to say the least, a somewhat dramatic "year of decision" for the two men who had run the agency for so many years.

By virtually all standards of measurement Funston & Green had been a highly successful agency. It had had an exceptional profit record; it had fine clients and had very good relations with them. The one "venture" it had undertaken, the opening of the Los Angeles office, had turned out to be a first-rate gamble. George and Carter had, however, turned down several accounts which had turned out to be very lucrative, and they, thus, began to seriously question their conservatism. Nevertheless, the growth of the agency as a whole had been solid. Its principals were satisfied with their progress. The staff seemed happy in their jobs.

But George Funston and Carter Green had sensed that the agency business seemed, somehow, to be changing. This feeling (and that's all it was) had come about more through a series of four happenings in 1966 than through some special sensitivity or some brilliant insight. These "happenings" disturbed George and Carter and made them move, at least mentally, out of their complacency. They had to face some complicated problems which took thought and required specific and sharp solutions. The two men, who had run the agency so well for so long, had to make some difficult decisions and, to their credit, they neither compromised them nor came up with namby-pamby answers.

The First Happening—January, 1966

George Funston and Carter Green had just started eating lunch at Chicago's International Club (which they did almost every Monday) when they had heard someone in the next booth say:

"That George Funston and Carter Green have to be about the biggest agency 'fat cats' in the Midwest. I'm not calling them that in a mean way but what a sweet business; the bigger accounts growing steadily—so up goes the billing and up go the profits. Funny thing, though—for such a sound, solid shop, how come no important new accounts for the Chicago office in a couple of years?"

His companion answered quickly: "When you said 'fat cats' you just weren't a-kiddin'. They've got it made, for now at least. But ask yourself: who's hot in the ad business these days? Easy—the razzle-dazzle creative shops—the Mary Wells', the Doyle Dane's, the Jack Tinker's, the Carl Ally's—not the square agencies, not the solid but sort of dull outfits like Funston & Green. By contrast, look at their Los Angeles office—not too big yet—but plenty aggressive, pretty jumping, turning out 'talked-about' advertising, wouldn't you say? Man, what a job that Win Cooke has done in a short time!" The conversation ended abruptly, as someone appeared to join them.

George Funston put up two fingers signalling the waiter to bring a second round of drinks. Then he said quietly:

"Carter, that gossiping burns me up; you, too, from the look on your face. The trouble is, they've got a point, maybe two or three."

"Yes, I'm afraid they may be more than half right." Carter added, "Like no new business lately—and quite a few strike-outs on new business presentations. Like very few big-time creative awards the last couple of years. But, we are solid and sound and we're certainly sales and marketing oriented. Isn't that what big business really looks for from its agencies? Or is it, these days?"

"Carter, what those fellows behind us were talking about are things you and I talk about all the time," George said. "We're running a good outfit and our clients are happy, particularly with their sales and the market shares of their brands. But maybe, just maybe, mind you, we've been a little set in our ways. A little too conservative—not young enough in our thinking, not 'swinging' as today's creative kid-geniuses put it! Anyway, I guess you and I better think very seriously about maybe buying some hot creative-type guys, and upgrading, at least in execution, our creative product. That's sure the trend, and maybe we'd better get with it."[5]

"And while we're getting with it," Carter concluded, "I think we better get that bright young man of ours in L.A. over here for a week or so. Now that I think of it, just how long is it since we have spent any time with Win Cooke?"

The Second Happening—April, 1966

Win Cooke had joined Funston & Green for one reason, and it wasn't money. He wanted to get into the management side of the agency business and this was his chance. He took it, knowing, of course, that it was a gamble. At F & G, he had an excellent record, particularly on new business, and he had been well-rewarded, at least financially.

Win liked his job and all that went with it. He had a nice wife, two fine children, an attractive house in Brentwood with the usual pool and built-in barbecue. But, as he was driving his foreign car out Wilshire Boulevard toward home on a hot, smoggy Friday afternoon, he was thinking:

"I've got to figure out what's been bothering me lately. I'm restless, jumpy, and, for the first time since I've been running the F & G office out here, I'm bored. Everything's sort of routine . . ."

Later in the evening, by just talking things out with Mary, Win finally knew what was wrong.

"Mary," he said, "the principals in Chicago are taking me and the op-

---

[5] See Appendix A for a discussion and examples of the new "creative" advertising.

eration out here for granted. Maybe I'm wrong but I'm ready for the next step up. Somebody's going to move in directly back of George and Carter and I want to be the one."

"Seems to me, I've proved it here; now I'd like a chance at the big time, which to me means Funston & Green, Chicago. If they'd only give me some indication, show an interest beyond a bigger bonus or paycheck, give me and the L.A. office a little more attention, I'd feel better," Win added.

Mary interrupted, "I know you pretty well, Win. You're hurt and I don't blame you a bit. It gets down to the fact that you feel neglected and sort of unwanted, except maybe by the clients in your own little bailiwick. Maybe you should try and see the Chicago guys soon."

On the following Monday Win received a call from George Funston, asking him to come to Chicago for a week or so and to bring Mary along. He made a special point of asking Win to bring along his billing and profit projections for the balance of 1966 and all of 1967.

The call and the specific request for long-term projections made Win Cooke wonder if George and Carter weren't maybe thinking along the same lines he was. Right then, he began to take a hard look at the whole picture in L.A. He had known right along that his two "seniors" were interested in his ambitions, his progress and such. But he didn't kid himself that their basic concern would be to the welfare of the total agency that bore their names.

Win figured he'd better be ready to answer some tough questions about what might happen to the agency's Los Angeles operation if *he* wasn't running it full time. He knew very well there were pros and cons and that George and Carter would weigh them carefully before making the kind of move that he, Win, wanted.

Win Cooke did his best thinking on paper. Early the next morning he was in his office writing, in longhand, what he chose to call "a memo to myself." It wound up serving *his* purpose, which was all it was intended to do. He typed it himself; he never showed it to anybody, not even his wife, Mary. He kept it, however, in his personal file and he reread it from time to time. Win's memo follows:

Tuesday, April 6, 1966

MEMO FROM: Win Cooke
TO: Win Cooke

Let's first take the LA operation from the top. The Funston & Green office was opened on May 1, 1963 with one account billing $1 million. With hard work and a lot of luck the office had by year end, 3 clients billing at the rate of a million seven. There was a loss but it wasn't astronomical.

Now let's examine the *trend* of growth by comparing 1964 actual billings and profit; 1965 projected billings and profit (with approved budgets and known expenses these projections should be quite accurate); 1966 projected billings and profit (when treated conservatively, not as blue sky as one might think):

Billings

1964 Actual	1965 Projectable	1966 Predictable
$2,800,000	$3,900,000	$5,000,000

Profits

Actual	Projectable	Predictable
−$12,000	+$22,000	+$54,000

So much for the record in terms of numbers. Everybody at F&G, including me, has been happy with both the volume and profit growth pattern. No stockholder would want to jeopardize this profitable billing through an unsound operational change in LA.

Let's take a cold look at the pros and cons, if I were to move up in F&G and no longer run LA. (I'll be objective as possible; I know George and Carter will be completely so.)

Growth Rate. Likely to continue, not likely to accelerate. Reasons: First, the agency has some 30 clients in its 2 offices; thus LA, in particular, could be shut out of many major categories for competitive reasons. Second, to my certain knowledge, most of the relatively big budget accounts are quite solidly locked into their agencies. Third, from a practical standpoint, our new business targets will continue to be the $250M to $500M accounts. The view I'm presenting here is neither optimistic nor pessimistic; it is, I believe, totally realistic.

Successor. You've got to have someone entirely capable of filling your shoes before you can move into a bigger and better job. If things break my way I've got to have a guy who can handle my job. I have him; his name is Bert O'Malley and he was the first man I hired after I went to work at Funston & Green. What makes me so sure? /// Well, let's take a hard look at Bert's record—that's what George and Carter will do."

At Bert's and My Former Agency. Bert started as a research assistant, moved into media, then into account work. When I became a VP and Acct. Supervisor, Bert moved into the Acct. Exec. spot I'd just vacated. It was a big client in the packaged goods field and Bert did a great job. Admittedly, I pirated him but I figured that one of these days the end would justify the means.

At Funston & Green: Started as Account Exec. on the beer acct. and did well. Moved up to Supervisor and spread his wings. Made VP a year ago because he was a top handler of clients, a hard-working, very bright, well-trained "pro," if I do say so myself. Right now, he's my Number 1 back-up in client Service and Marketing. He runs the office when I'm away; the people in the shop like and respect him; so do all the clients. That's Bert and I'd make book that he could handle my job.

The Clients and Win Cooke. It's pretty common in the tricky LA ad market to protect what you've got. Maybe it's cocky to say, but I'd figured, from year one in F&G, that I was going to be first in line for succession to the throne.

Maybe I wasn't quite so sure of myself until I was made Executive VP, a year and a half after the office was opened. Whatever the reason, I decided *not* to overprotect. By that, I mean one thing: there's very little doubt that if owning the accounts had been what I wanted, I coud have owned them. It wasn't, so I did everything I knew how to have the clients agency owned. Not altruistically, believe me, but in all honesty, so that when, as and if the time came, I could move along—to Chicago, that is. Messrs. Funston & Green will have to make the ultimate judgment of whether I'm ready for Chicago, whether I'm the guy they want, whether I'm "expendable" in LA.

Finally, they have to make the judgment on where I can serve the agency best—in Chicago or in L.A. Most important of all, do they need and want a third man and, if they do, just what would my job be and how well would I earn my keep?

The Third Happening—September, 1966

The third of the "1966 incidents" as George and Carter began to call them, was not, on the surface at least, a gamble in any sense (in fact, many agencies would have considered it a real windfall). Carter Green had a neighbor in Winnetka by the name of Jack Spruance, who was the marketing vice president of a very major beauty preparations manufacturer. The company (Raquel Rogers) had been spending about $15 million a year, through its agency, in advertising its various brands of shampoos, hair sprays, hair colorings, nail polishes and other beauty aids. It was the over-all leader in its industry—aggressive, big time, and an innovator of new products. In addition, it was a very tough-minded company (*ruthless* might have been a more accurate description).

Carter Green and his neighbor were very good friends. Their families socialized, the two men often played golf in the same foursome at Exmoor, and they frequently went together to see their Alma Mater, Northwestern, play one of the other teams in the Big 10.

Carter Green and Jack Spruance rarely talked business and when they did it was ever so casually. There had been a reason: one of Funston & Green's oldest and best accounts was Janet Lee, Inc., a strong competitor of the company Jack worked for. Carter's client had an annual budget of $4,000,000; it had far fewer products than the Raquel Rogers line; the ones it had did very well against tough competition. The Nielsen Audit showed that one of Janet Lee's lead items was number 1 nationally in share of market (substantially ahead of the Raquel Rogers product) and that two of their other items were strong seconds in share of market. The beauty aid industry had great respect for Janet Lee, Inc., and for the job its advertising agency had done over the years.

One Monday afternoon, Green's phone rang and when he picked it up, the voice on the other end of the line said, "Carter, this is Jack Spruance. I've got a matter I'd like to discuss with you and I was wondering if we could have lunch together in the next couple of days. Either

Wednesday or Thursday would be fine with me. How are you fixed?"

"I'm okay either day. Why not make it Wednesday," Carter had said. "Where and what time?"

"Let's make it 12:15 at the Chicago Club where it's quiet and not too many advertising-marketing type guys like us are apt to have lunch. See you Wednesday, Carter," and Jack rang off.

When he hung up, Carter walked into George Funston's office, hoping he was alone. He was, so Carter started talking: "George, I just had a phone call from Jack Spruance; you know, that friend of mine who's marketing head of Raquel Rogers. He wanted to get together with me this week and we're having lunch on Wednesday. I may be wrong but I have a hunch he wants to talk about offering us a part of his account."

*   *   *   *

After the waiter had taken their order for lunch, Jack Spruance opened the conversation:

"Carter, I'm going to make a kind of long speech, so will you hear me all the way through before you comment? We're going to have a second agency on the Raquel Rogers account. I know you've got a conflict in the Janet Lee account which, I understand, bills about 4 million a year through you. Funston & Green has done a great job for them; we take Nielsen, too, so we know the figures."

"We've been friends for a long time," Jack continued, "so there's no use beating around the bush or me worrying about the ethics of going after a competitor's agency. The short and straight of it is that we want you to resign the Janet Lee account and handle about half our billing— $7 million to be exact. This may sound abrupt or as though we'd made some sort of a snap decision which I guess you know we sometimes do over at our place. But not this time, believe me!"

"We were months reaching the decision to split the business," Jack added. "Our agency folks have done a good job lately but we know, just as you do, that we've actually got a lot of products in our line that compete with each other; different names, and different packaging, sure, but they're really the same products."

"As a marketing and advertising man, you know that competing products, even though they're made and marketed by the same outfit, should have separate strategies, separate and highly competitive handling. If each is going to succeed, they've got to keep trying to knock each other's brains out—both in advertising and promotion. Ergo, two agencies, right?"

Jack said, "We've reached a decision—the President, our Ad Director and myself—and you're elected! There's nothing fuzzy around the edges —we've even told our agency that we're hiring a second shop to handle about half of our business. In other words, I'm officially offering Funston & Green $7 million in billing with no strings attached. It may seem strange that we're neither asking for a presentation nor talking to other agencies. With your record on the Lee account and your know-how in the beauty aid field, why should we waste time with other agencies if we can pick you up?"

"We'd like to get going as soon as possible," Jack Spruance concluded, "but naturally you'll want to give Janet Lee, Inc., enough time to pick up another agency and get them on the rails. Meanwhile, let's keep this hush-hush, except for George Funston, of course. All I'll tell our people is that we've talked and that I've offered you the business and that you'll get back to me on timing, etc., by early next week."

On his return to the office, Carter went directly to George Funston's office. He opened the conversation by saying:

"My hunch was right; Spruance was authorized by his top management to offer us $7 million in Raquel Rogers' billing, provided, of course, that we kick out our $4 million Janet Lee account. A $3 million increase in billing, dished up on a silver platter."

"The way Jack handled it makes me mad," Carter continued. "He knows well that Janet Lee, Inc., has been an absolutely wonderful client of ours for almost 10 years. And yet he assumes that we'll dump 'em at the drop of a hat—or maybe I should say at the drop of $3 million in plus billing."

"Calm down, Carter," George interrupted, "any guy, friend or otherwise, who has a $7 million piece of business to dangle in front of an agency figures they'll jump into his lap—and no questions asked. An extra $450,000 a year in commissions from the added billing, starting the minute we kick the Lee crowd out our door. From where Spruance sits, at least, any agency would be a sucker not to take his proposition."

George walked over to Carter, put his hand on his shoulder, and said, "If it's any comfort I'm resentful too. Suppose we forget it for now and talk about it tomorrow."

* * * * *

"You know, Carter," George said the next day, "there's more to this matter than the moral issue and the $3 million, although God knows they're both important. Since you got the phone call from Jack Spruance I've done some thinking about both the Raquel Rogers and Janet Lee accounts and I'm sure you have, too."

"Sure I have," Carter agreed, "no matter how hard you try to avoid it, you can't help speculating, particularly at night. You're so right in what you just said about the morality of the question. We know the Janet Lee account intimately and we know a good deal about the Rogers outfit. Let's see if we can tick off the pluses and minuses on them both. Maybe that'll help us come to a sound business decision, instead of an emotional one."

"Take the Lee account first," Carter continued, "a wonderful account by almost every standard. But it does have one notable weakness—a conservative management in a dynamic business that more or less lives off innovations and new products. Maybe that's great in some ways but you have to wonder about its growth potential as a client. But, still and all, a wonderful client to work for. I don't know . . ."

"Let me talk about the Raquel Rogers account," George interrupted. "Big, aggressive, tough-minded in, a big volatile business. Taking gambles on new product intros. Big billing now and with what looks like bigger advertising budgets coming up. That's the *good* side, and very good it is!

"Naturally, the temptation to pick up three million in added volume just has to be attractive. But before we seriously consider whether to stay with what we've got or make a jump, let's remember a couple of things about the Rogers crowd," George continued.

"First, there's a sour side to their new product intros, from the agency point of view. The Product Development geniuses come up with a new idea or a new packaging concept or something and the client decides to test market it. The trouble is that less than one in 10 makes the grade. And an agency drops money on the losers. You spend the same time, you use your best talent, and you work like the devil to build a complete advertising, marketing, and promotion program. Then WHAM—poor sales and poor share in test. So, what does the client say? 'So sorry, agency, better luck next time.'

"Second, the Rogers company hasn't got the best record in the country when it comes to sticking with their agencies. It was only two years ago that they fired one of their shops and consolidated all their billings with our competitor. Now, back to two agencies again; makes you wonder how stable they are when it comes to agency relations."

George concluded, "I'm not saying these two things would happen to us, but they could, you know. All I am saying, Carter, is that before we give Jack our answer we've got to look at all sides of the problem. In net, our decision has to be based on the good as well as the bad."

The Fourth Happening—November, 1966

Harlow MacDonald, Senior Vice President and Treasurer of Funston & Green, was an outstanding financial man. He was, in reality, the third man in the agency. He kept a tight rein on the money, but even so was well liked by the people at F & G.

George and Carter had almost always talked frankly with Harlow about their plans, particularly if spending money was involved. One Monday morning in early November, George had dialed Harlow on the intercom and said: "Harlow, I know it's short notice, but I wonder if you could have lunch with Carter and me today. We've got something we want to talk over with you, and we'd just as soon do it away from the office." The answer was "yes" and, as Harlow hung up, he had thought:

"It's got to be something important because those two guys eat together practically every Monday noon and it's rare for someone else to be asked along. It doesn't sound like trouble; if it was an account loss or something like that they wouldn't be 'talking it over at lunch.' "

MacDonald was curious and wondered if they were thinking merger or with the idea of going public. Anyway, he knew one thing for sure: those two were on the verge of making an important policy decision and it had to do with money.

As the three men were seated in a quiet corner booth in one of Chicago's better restaurants, George ordered cocktails and started the conversation.

"You know, Harlow, we've been doing quite a few new things in the agency this year that have cost a lot of money. Our payroll and operating expenses have been inching up, which has probably concerned you more than it has us. It's been a good volume year and we think the extra money's been well spent, at least in terms of the future."

"What I'm leading up to," George continued, "is whether we shouldn't take a big chunk of the 'Bonus Pool' money we dish out every year and invest it in the agency. If we don't, our profits are going to suffer. Carter and I can't seem to be objective about the 'Pool,' and we'd like you to give us a frank opinion about this rather vague idea we have."

Harlow MacDonald knew every detail of Funston & Green's special Incentive Bonus Plan like the back of his hand. The pool had been in operation for many years and it had always been pretty sacrosanct. It was large, about 30% of the company's profits before taxes, and it would amount to around $400,000 in 1966.

He also knew why George Funston and Carter Green weren't able to be objective about it. They considered that the allocation and distribution of those monies, around Christmas-time each year, was a management prerogative, almost solely their own. Naturally they had elicited the recommendations of each department head as well as certain other key people, including, of course, Winston Cooke in Los Angeles. But it was really their baby, and he knew how much they enjoyed playing Santa Claus.

Harlow knew perfectly well that his two associates must have thought this one over plenty before coming to him. He had also known that they would expect him to level with them, which, of course, he did.

"I know very well that you guys have sometimes wondered if you've fallen into a habit-pattern," Harlow started. "At times, I'm sure you have seriously discussed the idea of allocating at least part of this substantial amount of money to what might, in the long run, be put to better use than simply extra compensation for the agency's people including, of course, yourselves. You surely must have wondered whether you, or any of us, have applied any creative thinking to the use of this money."

"Well, let me tell you both something you may not know and maybe don't want to hear. In trade circles, people say: 'Nobody ever seems to get fired at F & G and practically nobody ever quits.' That happens to be pretty true and I, for one, think it's an unhealthy sort of thing."

"You've asked my opinion and you know I'll give it to you straight," Harlow continued. "Those big bonuses tend to make all of us sort of complacent, kind of self-satisfied. I'm no exception and I don't figure you are either. We've had it good, so why rock the boat? I think it's about time somebody did just that—so I'd say, 'Whack the bonus and put those dollars into a continuing program of building up the agency!'

"I've had my say," Harlow concluded. "It nets down to the fact that, for everybody's sake, you two guys ought to seriously consider cutting back the immediate returns to the individual and make a sizeable investment in the agency's future growth and progress. Opening L.A. sure turned out to be a good gamble; maybe you should take some other 'gambles' about now. End of speech!"

"You know, Carter," George Funston said when they were alone together later that day, "Harlow has got to be right; we hadn't expressed it as flatly as he did at lunch, but we sure knew the 'investment' idea was right for the agency. The trouble is there are a dozen ways we could invest money in building up or even changing the agency but nobody, and I mean nobody, tells us how much to spend on what, or when to do this investing, or which ideas would make the best gambles, and what the chances of 'pay-out' might be . . ."

Carter stopped him by saying, "George, you know perfectly well there are only two men in the agency who should even be expected to come up with the answers to the questions you're raising! And that's you and me!"

EXHIBIT 1

A Comparative Analysis of 1965 Agency Costs as a Percentage of Sales

	*Average Agency Costs**	*F & G*
Agency advertising	0.21	0.04
Depreciation	0.67	0.80
Donations	0.29	0.06
Operating insurance	0.21	0.32
Employee insurance	0.79	1.20
Interest	0.03	—
Legal fees	0.36	0.34
CPA	0.21	0.07
Dues & subscriptions	1.28	1.26
Postage	0.31	0.37
Rent & maintenance	5.72	3.61
Stationery & supplies	1.37	1.42
Taxes (excl. F.I.T.)	2.78	2.37
Tel. & tel.	1.60	1.19
Travel	2.41	1.65
Entertainment	1.01	0.82
Unbillable television	0.31)	—)
Unbillable visual	0.29)	0.28)
Unbillable research	1.01)	1.33)
Unbillable other	0.46)	—)
Unbillable total	2.07	1.61
Miscellaneous	2.71	3.02
TOTAL EXPENSES	24.04	20.15
Payroll	59.54	61.77
Profit sharing trust	2.52	2.53
GRAND TOTAL EXPENSES	86.10	84.45
Profit before F.I.T.†	13.90	15.55
F.I.T.	6.89	7.49
NET PROFIT	7.01	8.06

* Average agency costs are based on the American Association of Advertising Agencies' (the 4A's) Interquartile Average of agencies in the $20–$40 million bracket.

† Were it not for the very large incentive bonus payments made annually to the company's employees (over and above the agency's contribution to its Profit Sharing Trust), Funston & Green's net profit would have been far greater.

EXHIBIT 2

A Comparative Analysis of 1965 Payroll
Costs as a Percentage of Total Payroll by Function

	*Average Agency Costs**	*F & G*
PAYROLL BREAKDOWN BY FUNCTION		
New business	3.14	1.79
Contact, plans & marketing	33.14	35.56
Research	4.29	3.05
Media	8.91	11.15
Copy	13.37	13.86
Visualization	11.89	9.18
Print production	3.13	3.16
TV & radio production	4.69	4.56
Publicity & PR	0.78	—
Accounting	4.65	4.14
General office & executive overhead	12.01	13.55
NET PAYROLL	100.00	100.00

* Average agency costs are based on the American Association of Advertising Agencies' (the 4A's) Interquartile Average of agencies in the $20–$40 million bracket.

EXHIBIT 3

Description of Departmental Functions, Operations, and Responsibilities

MANAGEMENT: Top responsibility for management of the over-all agency and for the ultimate operation of its Chicago accounts rested with the President and the Chairman of the Board. The Los Angeles office was managed, in the same general way, by the agency's Executive Vice-President.

ACCOUNT SERVICE & MARKETING: Funston & Green's account service people were all-around advertising men. They were the direct link between agency and client, and it was their responsibility to interpret and communicate all of the client's problems, viewpoints and opportunities to the agency. It was their job to utilize the agency's varied talents for the clients they served.

Virtually all Funston & Green account men were marketing oriented and marketing trained.

CREATIVE SERVICES: In each office, creative services were provided by an integrated department, responsible for ideas and execution in all print and broadcast media, as well as in sales promotion.

The creative directors on any given Funston & Green account utilized as many as 5 or 6 different copywriters and art directors on creative projects—for ideas and approaches, for specializations (like music), for hard-boiled copy or soft sell.

In addition, each office did a good deal of "experimentation," sometimes for the purpose of testing new approaches and a "new look," sometimes simply to see if they could come up with an entirely different kind of advertising than a client had used in the past.

The Creative Staff in Chicago was headed by a creative director and 5 associate creative directors; in Los Angeles, by a creative director.

EXHIBIT 3 (Continued)

Copy: The work of this group ranged from the rough original idea to finished advertising and sales promotion copy.

Art: The art directors were responsible for layouts, direction of finished art and photography, storyboards for TV, package design, and development of collateral material.

TV-Radio: The direction, execution and production of all commercials— live, film, and tape—were the responsibility of this creative group.

MERCHANDISING: The merchandising department was an "eyes, ears, and think" group, responsible for the development of ideas and programs for use at the point where goods were sold. Its people went into the market place to watch the action of clients' and competitors' products. They kept abreast of the constantly changing market, checked clients' and competitors' retail activities, and kept aware of what was new. This was also the premium development department of the agency.

RESEARCH: The research department conducted advertising, marketing and product research, from image studies and advertising penetration and communications research to straight head counting and involved motivational studies. It was responsible for the analysis of each research study and, in part, for recommendation of "indicated action" evolving from the research.

MEDIA: Creative media planning, complete media analysis and research, space and time buying, scheduling and checking.

MECHANICAL PRODUCTION: Purchasing, supervising, producing, and invoicing of all print advertising and sales promotional material.

FINANCIAL: Accounting, billing, all other financial matters, including use and operation of computer equipment. A senior vice president and treasurer directed the department and worked very closely with management.

CLERICAL: Office management, personnel, secretarial, typing, mail.

APPENDIX A: "CREATIVE" ADVERTISING

In August, 1966, a *Fortune* article on the new Wells, Rich, & Greene Agency made the following observations on the new trend in advertising:

A small group of advertising men have become disenamored with the tactics and techniques of their peers. In some cases, this rebellion has led them to found new agencies distinguished as "creative." The word "creative" has become a bit of a fad in the advertising business and especially when it is self-applied, there is often a touch of pretentiousness in it. The label sometimes serves as a refuge from the blunt economic fact that only a big firm can afford big teams of marketing experts. And some "creative" ads attract attention on Madison Avenue but nowhere else. There are several agencies, however, that deserve the adjective.

APPENDIX A—(Continued)

Among the so-called "creative shops," Doyle Dane Bernbach has been easily the most influential. Its "Think small" campaign for Volkswagen and "We try harder" promotion for Avis register firmly and pleasantly on consumers' minds. Doyle Dane's work is usually humorous and, though often colloquial, consistently literate. Much of its work is characterized by an approach that could be called "understated hyperbole." Yet the agency rarely forgets that the purpose of advertising is to sell its clients' products. Says one of its many admirers: "They make things happen to consumers."

*   *   *   *   *

In style, Wells, Rich, and Greene are beginning to change. (So, for that matter, is Doyle Dane.) The simple, direct, sometimes stark Alka-Seltzer commercials contrast sharply with more recently produced Braniff ads, which are theatrical productions full of movement, color, people, and exotic props. The whole airline promotion is marked by controlled exaggeration and what Mary Wells calls "show-biz ideas."

By changing in this way, the trio is following a shift in the climate of mind of the middle generations in America. Camp art, huge sculpture, visually and emotionally lavish theatrical productions, the rediscovery of convoluted curves in interior decoration, and the use of opulent color in men's as well as women's fashions seem to indicate that American taste is moving toward what might be called *the new baroque*. There is a baroque quality in Detroit's style leaders such as the Riviera and the Mustang Fastback, in the Batman television series, in James Bond movies, in the submergence of the rock-'n'-roll beat to provide a background for playful counterpoint and variation. Parents of teen-age children, as much as anybody, are well aware of the shift in taste—although they may have other words for it.

Wells, Rich, and Greene are "with it," and that may help a lot. In the end, however, regardless of what's in or out, what's lovable or not, they will be judged by the criteria implied in Mary Wells's own definition of advertising: "The art of persuading somebody to buy something. . . ."

In addition to Doyle Dane Bernbach and Wells, Rich & Greene, a number of other agencies have produced so-called "creative" advertising copy. The following reproductions are illustrative of some very effective and creative advertising campaigns.

APPENDIX A (Continued)

Alka-Seltzer—Jack Tinker & Partners

The famous "Blahs!" campaign which was widely used in television and magazines. Helped take a flat sales curve and move it sharply upward —with humorous but hard-selling copy.

Alka-Seltzer.®
When you and your stomach don't agree.

Picture, if you will, a salami-pepper-and-onion sandwich entering your stomach.

It arrives, un-announced, and upsets your stomach.

Blindly striking back, your stomach upsets you and you get heartburn.

That's his way of saying "*Watch it*, Mac."

It's a pity you can't get together with your stomach, and decide what foods you can both agree on.

There *is* a communications problem.

Therefore, you must speak to your stomach in a language he understands, like Alka-Seltzer.

Alka-Seltzer is your way of saying "Forgive me."

It has alkalizers which will soothe your upset stomach and reduce excess acidity.

You take care of your stomach.

Your stomach won't bother you.

Jamaica Tourist Board—Doyle Dane Bernbach Inc.

One of the great ads in a great tourism campaign. Strong identification for Jamaica but, additionally, this and the other ads in the campaign tell a warm and compelling story. Testing showed this ad to be one of the best read magazine ads of the year.

Ella Mae and Lascelles Ormsby, married January 9, 1967, St. James Anglican Church, Burnam Wood. They honeymooned in Jamaica.

The bride carried a bouquet of jasmine.

(But from her garden, not a florist.)

The groom wore a white flower in his hatband.

(Instead of his buttonhole.)

150 guests came in ruffled, brocaded and tulle-y yellows, pinks, blues. And black suits.

(Like at weddings anywhere.)

Leaving church, the couple walked under palm bowers.

(Instead of ducking rice.)

At the reception, they were toasted with rum, then feasted on curried goat, green banana, and hard dough bread, which is chewy like pumpernickel, but white.

(No champagne, no chicken, no chopped liver.)

Instead of *sleeping* on the wedding cake that night, everyone *bet* on it that afternoon. This is how we give gifts of money. We bet on whether the draped wedding cake should be uncovered or not, putting the money in "betting" saucers.

(Instead of envelopes.)

In the evening, dancing. The ska. The rudy. The quadrille.

(Our frug, lindy, waltz.)

Then the happy pair went on their honeymoon. They stepped inside their little Jamaican house.

(No plans for sailing, snorkeling, skin-diving, water-skiing, golfing, or going nightclubbing.)

That's marriage, Jamaican-style.

Not radically unlike yours.

Except—we never have to come home from our Jamaican honeymoons.

For all about the kind you come home from, see your local travel agent or Jamaica Tourist Board in New York, Chicago, Los Angeles, San Francisco, Miami, or Toronto.

APPENDIX A—(Continued)

Benson & Hedges—Wells, Rich & Greene, Inc.

This outstanding creative campaign, humorous but to the point—a long, long cigarette—has kept sales growing steadily for this premium-priced product. Television and print work remarkably well together.

APPENDIX A (Continued)

Volkswagen—Doyle Dane Bernbach Inc.

Clever, clever advertising in virtually all media keeps Volkswagen the leading imported car year after year. In spite of its brightness, Volkswagen advertising always makes a sales point as the ad at right demonstrates by showing the wide variety of models.

Volkswagen builds strong bodies 8 ways.

The following stories are true:

A 1949 VW is still running around on its original engine.

A VW owner went 135,384 miles on his original set of tires.

Another owner went 308,700 miles before trade-in time.

Conclusion: Volkswagens are tough.

For instance, look underneath any VW and you'll see our famous sealed bottom. This ingenious device protects a VW's insides against everything on the outside. Including time. (No other car has anything quite like it.)

A Volkswagen convertible is made so well, so airtight, it helps to open the window a crack to close the door. (No wonder it takes two men one day just to make two convertible tops.)

Like all VWs, the Squareback and Fastback sedans are both painted 3 times over. To make what you see look nicer. And to make what you don't see last longer.

Then there's the VW Karmann Ghia. Its body is practically hand-made.

The Ghia is hand-shaped, hand-welded, hand-smoothed, hand-polished, hand-fitted, hand-stitched, hand-painted and would you believe, hand-sanded. (Whew.)

The VW Station Wagon and Camper are different too. They don't have frames like other wagons. And they're not bolted together either. Each one is a solid hunk of unitized steel, welded together 12,598 times.

Finally, we make trucks. (And, if we make cars as strong as we do, you can imagine how we make trucks.)

So next time you look at a Volkswagen, look at it this way.

It's not the most beautiful body in the world, but it's one of the healthiest.

APPENDIX A (Continued)

Hertz Corporation—Carl Ally, Inc.

This campaign, imaginative yet very hard selling, has helped keep Hertz in a dominant sales position. In spite of vastly increased competition and lower price by rival, Hertz continues to be Number One.

APPENDIX A—(Continued)

Lindsay for Mayor of New York—Young & Rubicam

Although television has been the leading medium in political campaigns, these ads illustrate a remarkably strong print campaign, making *one* selling point at a time. Mayor Lindsay, running as an independent, was behind two candidates in the polls; these ads helped him to win by a good majority.

APPENDIX A (Continued)

Polaroid—Doyle Dane Bernbach Inc.

There are so many great television commercials (and so many terrible ones) that it's hard to pick just one in a campaign. But for a short spot that's right on the product and that's packed with interest, you have to consider the Polaroid series as tops.

1. (Music)

2. (Music)

3. If you're not taking pictures with a Polaroid Color Pack Camera

4. there is something left out of your life.

Barney Corporation

Barney Corporation was founded in 1958 to develop an entirely new field of technology based on the control of the crystalline structure of metals and alloys to a degree not thought possible prior to this development. A whole new product line had been developed from this technology.

Between 1956 and 1967 company sales had grown to about $42 million, and the average growth rate during the past five years had been in excess of 20%. In 1958, Barney stock was offered to the public at a price of $12.50 per share. In 1960, Barney obtained listing on the American Stock Exchange and, in 1967, the stock was trading in the range of $98–$142 after splitting two for one in 1966. The management of Barney felt that this impressive growth rate was due to two factors. Firstly, the vigorous research and development program undertaken by the company, and secondly, a dynamic and aggressive organization which prided itself on modeling its unique technical capabilities to the needs of the market place.

However, conflicts had started to develop within Barney's marketing organization as a result of the rapid expansion experienced by the company. To illustrate some of the problems, the following are excerpts taken from a recent meeting of product managers:

So for the second time in a month I had to ring St. Francis[1] to ask for more time on their order, because you guys in manufacturing don't know the meaning of the word "priority." You also remember the trouble I had persuading R & D to work on this problem in the first place. Now we get a $150,000 order just as a starter, and we can't deliver on time!"

Why do you ask me to spend my time trying to sell tubing when the time given up could be spent on chain, for which I have profit responsibility?

All I do all day long is put out fires. I have no time left to perform my other functions, especially long-range planning.

[1] St. Francis Roller Bearing Company was a major customer of Barney.

I wish you guys would wake up and see that we must move away from product management. Market orientation, that's what we need.

Look, we sell metal products; sure it's high-grade stuff, but it's all based on our product technology. A specialized, single-line sales force under these circumstances doesn't make sense to me.

Comments such as these worried the management of Barney, and they wondered what changes, if any, should be made in Barney's marketing organization, to maintain the expected rapid growth rate in the future.

Company History

In 1955, while working for the Great Western Steel Company's R & D Division as metallurgists, Ken Barrington and George Whitney made an important discovery. Using various metals or alloys and subjecting them to a variety of physical and chemical treatments, they were able to produce compounds with extraordinary properties. These included an extreme degree of hardness, lightweight, elasticity and an ability to change the electrical conductivity of the metal.

Toward the end of 1955, Barrington and Whitney resigned from their positions with Great Western Steel, and started their own company, which they called The Barney Corporation. After a great deal of discussing, it was decided that Barney Corporation would manufacture the finished products resulting from the new technological development, rather than license other companies to use the technology, or to manufacture the metal raw materials only. The Company became a supplier to the electronics, aircraft and aerospace industries almost immediately, although some time had to be spent with the engineers of each customer to acquaint them with the attributes and performance of these new materials.

The Company grew rapidly between 1956 and 1960. Barney continued to concentrate on furthering research and development in the whole field of metal technology. Many patents were applied for and new product development was taking place at an extremely rapid rate. Whitney commented that "hardly a day went by without someone calling us up, with the 'greatest' new idea ever! We received a lot of good ideas in this way."

Marketing of the product line also received a good deal of attention. In order to build for long-range growth, management decided upon the following strategies:

1. Manufacturers representatives were to be used initially, in order to gain national distribution and rapid customer acceptance, until a competent internal marketing organization consisting of metallurgical engineers could be developed.
2. Commercialization of new products would initially be restricted to those with only limited sales potential.

These strategies proved successful and by the early 1960's, Barney had developed to the point where it was able to launch a major expansion program. Existing product lines were greatly expanded, and several new high volume product groups were introduced. The Cincinnati Chain and Cable Company located in Cincinnati, Ohio, was acquired, which opened up markets not served by Barney prior to the acquisition. Barney also purchased the Curtis-Conway Manufacturing Company located in Chicago. Although under the financial direction and control of Barney, this wholly owned subsidiary continued to operate as a separate and autonomous company under the direction of Mr. John Curtis.

At the same time, Barney began the transition to an in-house technically-trained marketing team through the establishment of the product management group and a direct sales force. The marketing group increased from only 10 people in 1960 to 104 in early 1968; in addition, 22 field sales offices were opened. Barney also began a major domestic plant expansion to supplement its leased facilities in an industrial park south of Cleveland. The company purchased 100 acres of land in an industrial park nearby, on which some 420,000 square feet of manufacturing, research and office facilities were constructed. Present facilities had the capacity to handle up to $80 million of business a year. Much of this expansion and construction was financed from the sale of some $7 million of convertible debentures.

Barney also began to expand internationally. In conjunction with Uni-Metals Ltd., Barney set up a subsidiary in England, which had research, manufacturing and marketing facilities, to exploit potential markets in the United Kingdom. Complete control of this British affiliate was acquired in 1966. As overseas marketing efforts were extended to Western Europe, a second manufacturing facility was established in West Germany. Most of the requirements of the European market could be produced by the English and West German facilities.

Although Barney's record had been highly successful to date, management was anxious to maintain the company's impressive growth rate. As such, management's stated financial objectives were to obtain *at least* a 20% increase in sales per year, a 40% annual return on invested capital, and an after-tax profit on sales of 7–9%. Management considered three courses of action prerequisite to fulfilling these objectives: continued technological innovation, adequate patent coverage and vertical integration.

PRODUCT LINE

Technology

Nearly all of Barney's products were based on the science of metal crystallography. The company had developed over 100 different metals and alloys, which, when changed by several chemical and physical processes had desired chemical, physical and electrical properties. Barney utilized these properties to develop novel products and applications ranging from ball bearings to top secret materials for defense contracts, and had over 8,000 different types and sizes of products.

Research and Development

In early 1968, Barney's R & D staff totalled 170, nearly double that of the previous year. Approximately half of the staff were degreed personnel, including 31 with doctorates in metallurgy, engineering and chemistry. Research was carried out in new facilities which included a materials processing area, product development laboratories, and technical service laboratories. England and West Germany had a separate development and technical service group which supplemented the U.S. activity for service to these Western European subsidiaries.

Many of the research projects were initiated by the product management group based on market research or on information from the field sales force. In order to supplement the market research and product development efforts of the product managers, a venture analysis group, which consisted of three men, was set up in early 1967 to explore whole new areas within the technical competence of the company. This group originally reported directly to the President, but was later transferred to the R & D area under Vice President Greenhalgh.

All Barney products were developed through its own research efforts. Over 60% of 1967 company sales were comprised of products introduced in the preceding three years. In addition to patent protection on substantially all of its significant patentable developments, the company had many trade secrets and a large body of confidential technical information and skill. Barney also adopted and used many trademarks. A description of the major product lines follows.

Electrical Wiring

Prior to the development of special alloys for high-performance electrical wiring by Barney, electrical wiring could be made to withstand only quite narrow extremes of physical conditions. For example, there was high-temperature wire and low-temperature wire, each being suitable for applications only in a fairly narrow temperature range. The alloys developed by Barney allowed one wire to be used under all temperature conditions. Up to 1964, the wire insulating step in the manufacturing process had been subcontracted out, but in 1964, Barney purchased the Wells Insulating Corporation in Toledo, Ohio, and thus acquired its own insulating capability. Many coating materials were used including teflon, rubber, polyethylene, PVC and several other special compounds. This coated wire was sold in many forms including hook-up wire, single and multi-conductor cable, and various configurations of coaxial cables. The line had wide acceptance in the electronics, aircraft, missile, and aerospace industries because of its unique properties. It was also used extensively in uncoated form, in the wiring of special purpose electric motors.

About 50% of the sales of electrical wiring went into government products such as the F-111, the Lockheed C-5A and Poseidon missile.

Tubing

Another major property, which could be conferred upon alloys by a variety of treatments, was extremely high tensile strength. Coupling this property with the ability to withstand temperature extremes had led to the development of tubing for fuel lines of aircraft and missiles. It had been determined that this particular tubing would not rupture when it was subjected to five times the pressure expected under normal applications. Barney tubing was now specified in government contracts, for a number of aircraft and missiles, as well as for commercial aircraft such as the Boeing and Douglas range of jetliners.

Despite this widespread acceptance in the missile and aircraft industries, tubing sales were only moderate because the number of units (missiles and aircraft) produced and the amount of tubing required per unit were only quite small. Barney was, therefore, actively exploring other outlets for this product line. Barney had recently been successful in switching over the country's major manufacturer of pressure gauges to its own tubing line. Barney was also actively working closely with such other potential major customers, such as boiler manufacturers, and contractors involved in the installation of commercial nuclear reactors. However, since extensive testing of all new products was required by these customers, progress in these applications had been rather slow.

One contractor, Pittsburg-Nuclear Corporation had indicated to the Company recently that it had almost completed testing of Barney tubing, and that the results to date had been extremely promising. The sales engineer handling the account had been given to understand, that Pittsburg-Nuclear could make a complete switch to Barney tubing in about six months time. A major question confronting the Product Manager for this product group was how to capitalize upon this development, once the change became official.

Ball and Roller Bearings[2]

Barney had made a major breakthrough with this product line recently. For a number of years, Barney had been working in close co-operation with the St. Francis Roller Bearing Company, one of the major

---

[2] The company did not produce finished bearings. It produced only spherical or cylindrical shaped alloy ball and roller bearings, ground and polished to the required tolerances. These "ball bearings" were then sold to bearing manufacturers who made a final polish and then manufactured the bearings.

producers of ball and roller bearings in the U.S.A. In the past, St. Francis had manufactured over 300 different types of bearings, in many different sizes and shapes, depending upon the application, required life, load carrying capacity and many other factors. Many different alloys were used, to produce this large product range. After several years of testing, St. Francis had recently decided to standardize on ball and roller bearings manufactured by Barney. As a result of this change, St. Francis was able to reduce its line of bearings to about 35 basic types, with great savings in manufacturing and inventory costs.

The first commercial order had been received about six months ago, and it would appear that potential business for this application would reach at least $10 million within a very short space of time.

Barney was now actively soliciting business with other bearing manufacturers, and had initiated a study project to determine whether it should begin to manufacture finished bearings. Barney had been approached recently by one of the major motor car manufacturers, regarding the supply of finished bearings manufactured from Barney alloys.

Chain and Cable

These products were sold to a wide variety of industrial users. The major product advantages over competing lines was a high degree of hardness and high tensile strength. Chain was sold to automobile companies and other engine manufacturers for timing chain, to bicycle and motor bicycle manufacturers as driving chain and to other industrial users for a variety of applications. Another line of chain was manufactured for cutting purposes and found a major outlet in power saw manufacturers either as chain or band saws.

Mechanical cable was also manufactured in a wide variety of alloys depending upon the required application. Some cable went into aircraft, and to automobile manufacturers. Other high tension cable was sold to contractors involved in the construction of bridges and commercial office buildings. One major customer was the Langsford Elevator Corporation, one of the major manufacturers of elevators in the U.S.A. Both the main cable and the safety cable of lifts manufactured by Langsford were made from Barney cable.

Castings

Barney had developed many alloys for use in a wide variety of castings. In addition to a wide variety of castings manufactured in its own foundries, Barney sold metal to other foundries for casting purposes. This was the only purpose for which Barney sold raw metal or alloy.

Barney owned several foundries in different parts of the U.S.A. located close to major customers. Major use for casting was in a wide variety of precision items. Automobile manufacturers were major customers and others included manufacturers of earthmoving and agricultural equipment. The leading edges of bulldozer blades, power shovels, plows and harrows were major outlets for Barney castings.

Another group of important, potential customers for castings was the nation's railways. Rails are laid in 100-foot lengths but cannot be welded together, since expansion during hot weather would lead to buckling. A gap of about one to one and one-half inches has to be left between these lengths to allow for expansion. This means that the wear at the end of the rail is about three times as great as that on the rest of the rail, leading to costly maintenance problems. Barney had conducted tests for some years with a variety of alloys, whose special attribute was extreme hardness, to combat this problem. It currently had a cast sleeve in the final stages of testing which looked very promising. It appeared that it would need replacement only once during the life of a rail rather than three or four times. If this product proved acceptable to the railways, a market of some $20–25 million annually was projected by the Product Manager responsible for casting products.

Welding and Soldering Devices

Because of the special nature of Barney alloys, they could not be welded or soldered with ordinary equipment. Barney, therefore, produced a line of welding equipment and soldering guns, as well as special welding and soldering rods for use with its product line. These devices accounted for less than 3% of Barney sales.

Manufacturing

Manufacturing at Barney took place in two distinct phases:

i. Firstly, a smelting and treatment plant, where metals and alloys were melted, mixed and treated in batch quantities, depending upon the use to which the metal was to be put.

ii. Product lines for wire, bearings, cable, tubing, etc. where the products in question were manufactured from the alloys produced in the smelting and treatment plant.

Conflicts between product groups could, therefore, take place at both of these phases of the manufacturing process. About 80–85% of the time, the conflict occurred in the smelting and treatment plant. Two or more product managers might, for example, ask the plant, at the same time, to produce alloy on an urgent basis for orders which they had obtained and for which manufacture had not been planned.

The remaining 15–20% of conflicts occurred on the product lines, where, for example, two urgent orders for cable might arrive at the same time, and some means of setting priorities had to be arrived at.

MARKETING

Barney attributed much of its success to its desire and ability to respond quickly and effectively to the needs of the marketplace. If a customer wanted an item at a given time which manufacturing could not fit into the production schedule, then manufacturing would be asked to work overtime to complete the order. Likewise, if a product manager wanted R & D to design a new application for a customer with a significant potential, then R & D would set aside less pressing projects in order to satisfy the customer's requirements.

Markets and Customers

Barney's sales were concentrated in a relatively small number of accounts and industries. In 1967, the three largest customers accounted for approximately 21% of sales, and the 10 largest customers accounted for 41%. The industry breakdown for 1967 sales was approximately as follows: aircraft (principally military), 29%; missiles and space, 14%; electronics, telecommunications and computers, 26%; automobiles, 18%; other 15%. The profitability of sales to all the industries was roughly comparable.

Sales for United States Government end use (estimated at approximately 48% of sales during fiscal 1967, including approximately 3% direct sales to the United States Government) were dependent upon continuance of appropriations and requirements for national defense and aerospace programs and were subject to renegotiation. Most of Barney's sales for governmental end use were to customers operating under government prime contracts and subcontracts which contained standard provisions for termination or curtailment at the convenience of the government. Sales for commercial use had expanded to approximately 60% in the first six months of fiscal 1968, primarily due to increased commercial aircraft business and to the addition of the ball bearing business, plus much higher sales to the automotive market.

Competition

Although Barney's products were sold in highly competitive markets, there were few directly comparable products. Barney competed with many companies and divisions of companies both larger and smaller than Barney, but only a few of these companies supplied competitive products that provided similar technical solutions to the functional problems of customers. Barney competed primarily on the basis of its unique technical capabilities and the advantages thereof—high reliability, labor cost savings, less repair work.

Sales Organization

Barney sales were originally handled primarily through manufacturer's representatives who sold both Barney's entire product line and other related products. These representatives were used to set up a national sales network at a low cost (average $4\frac{1}{2}\%$ commission). Barney utilized some distributors for casting products and a small direct sales force which handled sales in some eastern states, missionary sales, and contacts with the manufacturer's representatives.

When Barney's rapid expansion made a direct sales force expedient, the manufacturer's representatives were phased out. Barney found it advantageous, however, to retain its distributors for casting sales, even though it built up its own direct sales force. The nature of the casting market lent itself to mass distribution because approximately 80% was sold in small quantities. Furthermore, only the distributors could effectively provide the necessary local service to this diverse market. Because Barney was able to offer its distributors a high markup (45–55%), the distributors pushed Barney casting products, so that Barney became a major line with most of them. And even though castings became more price competitive, the distributor, rather than Barney, absorbed the price erosion; yet the line's volume still commanded a great deal of his time and effort. Moreover, the distributor presently had an added incentive to find new applications for Barney products, in that he was in direct competition with Barney; only if the distributor found a new market or application was he allowed to sell it; otherwise, Barney handled the new accounts directly.

As Barney expanded its direct sales force and district offices were opened throughout the United States, the current sales organization took shape (see Figure 1).

The general sales manager's position was established in December, 1966, to coordinate the activities of the three regional managers who had previously reported directly to Vice President Ron McOnie. Peter Joyner, the current field sales manager, defined his job as mostly administrative at the outset; however, in the long run, he expected to spend about half of his time selling and half on administrative detail.

The regional sales managers were responsible for all accounts within their respective regions. They worked with the salesmen and Branch managers to set priorities and to sell to major or difficult accounts. According to Joyner, "the regional manager should spend at least 80% of his time actually selling."

The Barney sales force in the U.S. consisted of 58 men, of whom 24 were managers of Branch sales offices. The Branch managers had anywhere from one to seven salesmen working out of their individual offices. Much of the sales effort was directed toward project selling. Of the 24

FIGURE 1

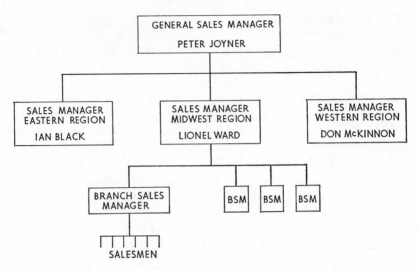

branch sales offices in the United States, most were established in response to the needs of specific projects or accounts. For example, an office was set up in St. Louis, Missouri, to gain and service the St. Francis account.

The Barney sales force ranged in age from 23 to 52 and averaged eight years of sales experience. Sales compensation consisted of a salary (ranging from $12–18,000 per year) plus a bonus based on each salesman's performance. The basis for evaluating performance was the quarterly sales forecast, which was a combination of

1. The forecast made by the salesmen in conjunction with their branch and regional managers, based on key accounts, distributor sales, and new projects
2. The forecast made by the product managers based on their work in the field and new product developments.

Sales performance was reviewed monthly by the sales managers. Of the 58 sophisticated and technically trained salesmen in the U.S., three-quarters had scientific or engineering backgrounds and 12 held MBA degrees. They attempted to create the image of being "consultants" to their accounts based on their high technical competence. Primary emphasis was placed upon working with the engineering and manufacturing departments of customers and potential customers.

Barney had another 31 salesmen working out of its 11 sales offices in Europe and Canada. These offices, staffed with engineering personnel, provided a full range of marketing services and maintained inventories to meet customer requirements. Foreign sales accounted for about 14% of the company total in 1967.

All of the salesmen went through a rigorous three-month training program which emphasized company philosophy, product knowledge, and company capabilities. Nearly two-thirds of the program was devoted to detailed technical information and applications of the company's products and processes. The other third of the time was spent on sales training, including role playing, information on customers and markets, and field experience. Upon completion of the training course, a salesman was assigned to the field either as a multi-line salesman covering a given geographical area, or as a specialized salesman selling a given line of products to specific markets. Although each salesman had originally handled all products, the demands of the marketplace had recently made expedient the use of a specialized sales force, oriented to specific products and markets.

Product Management

According to one of Barney's six product managers, "The product manager has the best job in the company. The whole structure here is such that things get funnelled to the product manager, and then he crosses whatever lines he needs to get things done. It's where the action is." Each of Barney's major product lines was under the direct control and responsibility of a product manager who coordinated and directed the entire marketing program for his particular product line.

Barney's product managers ranged in age from 29 to 38. All but one had both sales experience and a scientific or engineering background; in addition, all of them held MBA degrees. Their compensation consisted of a salary (ranging from $14–22,000) plus a bonus (based on management's estimates of each man's relative contribution to profitability and sales growth). The organization of the product management group, under the direction of Terry Westwood is shown in Figure 2.

According to Westwood, "the product manager should operate much as a general manager of his own business with P & L responsibility, but without his own sales force or manufacturing facilities." One of the product managers described the role in more detail:

The product manager is responsible for the profitability and growth of his product line, and a major part of that responsibility should be the long-range planning for that line. He is essentially a coordinating function between sales, manufacturing, and R & D. He is responsible for training and equipping the sales force to sell the existing product line, which boils down to training new men, retraining existing people, promotional material, literature, and sales aids. He's also in charge of advertising—where, what media, how much. He is responsible for guiding R & D in the design of new products to meet whatever requirements he finds. The product manager is also directly involved with

FIGURE 2

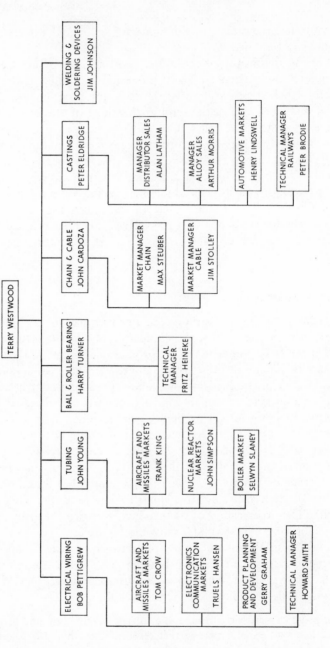

field sales problems. Often he will go to specific areas where there are major problems, or major sales efforts or programs and will assist the local guy in whatever way he can.

The product manager also had pricing responsibility. Since Barney had little direct competition because of the unique properties and applications of its products, customers were often willing to pay a premium for Barney products which offered such advantages as high reliability, or savings in labor and repair costs. Prices were usually based on value to the customer, rather than cost plus a fixed percentage. As such, most of Barney's products were very profitable.

Although the product manager was responsible for the profitability of his product line, he was technically in a staff position with no direct authority. He had to deal directly with the people in manufacturing, R & D, and sales and "sell" them on his projects and ideas. According to another of the product managers, "the basic philosophy at Barney essentially promotes a nonorganizational type of function. In other words, each guy is pretty much on his own to accomplish what has to be done to fulfill his job function without a lot of mickey mouse organization stuff. If I want R & D to work on something, I talk to the guy who knows the most about what I want done, and I get it done."

Occasionally, however, conflicts would arise between product areas, and these conflicts were becoming increasingly difficult to resolve within the growing company framework. The unique characteristics of each product line presented different requirements and marketing problems for each product manager, as the following examples show.

Welding and Soldering Devices. This product line, under the direction of Jim Johnson, crossed all other product lines except ball bearings because of its essentially supportive nature. Johnson did not look to the marketplace itself to ascertain the need for his type of product as the other product managers did. He had to deal with the needs of the other product managers and field sales people since his devices provided them with a great deal of leverage to generate sales in other product lines.

Although Johnson theoretically had the same profit and loss responsibility as the other product managers, he did not have the same pricing authority that they did—they could "give away" one of his devices in order to close a sale. Furthermore, his line was characterized by low volume and high unit cost and, thus, he could not be evaluated on the same basis as the other product managers.

Castings. This line also differed from the other product lines in several respects. First, most of the casting products were marketed through a series of distributors who took title to the products. Secondly, castings were subject to more direct competition than the other product lines.

Eldridge had three staff marketing assistants to cover the four major markets for his products, and the fourth of Eldridge's assistants was in charge of distributor sales.

Electrical Wiring. Bob Pettigrew, who was responsible for the large electrical wiring line, had four men working with him. Howard Smith was primarily involved in the technical aspects of the line including technical problems both in the plant and in the field, writing product specifications, and preparing sales literature. Because of the nature of the product line, electrical wiring experienced far more technical problems than the other lines.

Pettigrew also had one man aiding him with product planning and development. Gerry Graham had recently been transferred to the product management group from his position as Midwestern Regional Sales Manager. Pettigrew himself was very involved with the selling function, and he estimated that 75% of his time was spent dealing directly with the sales force.

Barney's electrical wiring line had significant competition from the many other producers of coated wire products. Since Barney's products were often quite different, the salesmen sometimes had difficulty getting their products specified by the customers, because Barney would then become their sole source of supply.

Tubing. John Young was responsible for the tubing product line. Since this product line differed from the others somewhat in that a larger portion of his orders were manufactured on a custom basis, he spent a good deal of his time on new product strategy—determining which had the greatest potential, establishing prices, etc. Recently, two men had been hired to work with him on the nuclear reactor and boiler markets.

John Simpson was in charge of tubing for the nuclear reactor market, and had responsibility for sales development to contractors and industries where the major potential for high pressure tubing was. These included the electric utilities companies, shipyards involved in the nuclear submarine program, and companies working on a variety of other projects, utilizing nuclear reactors, such as desalination. It was anticipated that once all these markets became fully developed, the regular sales force would have to be supplemented with a group of six to seven specialists. The reason for this expansion was the fact that the potential was expected to be very large, and secondly, that the construction work would be carried out by a large number of subcontractors, all of whom would have to be familiarized with the special properties of Barney tubing.

Selwyn Slaney was responsible for the development of sales to the boiler and steam generator markets. Included in his list of potential customers were public and private electric utilities and equipment manufacturers. It was Slaney's job also to identify other possible major markets for high pressure tubing, and to ensure that such products were developed to add to the present line.

There was some duplication in terms of product responsibility between Simpson and Slaney. Often contractors were quoting on both nuclear and conventional power generators so that two sales engineers might be working with the same contractor at the same time. The characteristics of the tubing used in nuclear and conventional power generators were quite different, but Young wondered whether the present system was the best way to utilize very high cost sales resources.

In addition, this line of tubing shared production facilities with tubing required for use in aircraft and missiles. Occasionally a conflict would arise in manufacturing. For example, Simpson recently ordered a considerable quantity of specialized tubing for extensive testing purposes by one of his potential customers, at the same time as Frank King received a large tubing order for an aircraft application. Terry Westwood had to resolve the conflict by authorizing the use of both overtime and subcontracting to complete the two projects in time.

Product Manager's Meeting

The following dialogue concerning Barney's marketing operations took place at a recent meeting of the product management group.

CARDOZA: One of the basic defects in our present product management setup is that we're too concerned with day-to-day problems, and we're unable to spend as much time as we should looking ahead and planning what direction the product line should be taking. Basically, there's just too much to do, and we've really got to skim the top.

TURNER: Yeah! Day-to-day ticky-tack gobbles up a fierce amount of time. It's easy to put off formal long-range planning and sales forecasting in favor of more pressing immediate needs.

JOHNSON: True. With so many men in the field now, I sometimes never get the phone off my shoulder all day long. But, after all, the open phone-open door policy is our real strength. We've maintained our growth record by being able to react quickly to the customer's needs rather than by sitting down and figuring out by market research what area we really want to shoot at, then designing a product to meet that need, and then going out and promoting it.

YOUNG: But one of the biggest problems ahead is going to be to keep developing new products and new potentials, so that we can sustain that growth rate.

KING: John's right. And the product management concept was set up at Barney to create new products and new markets.

YOUNG: Long-range planning may not be the panacea, but I think you'll agree with me, John, that as the field sales organization grows, product management has got to grow to support the activities of the product in the field.

PETTIGREW: I have to disagree with you, John. This may be a sacrilegious statement in this group, but I think we're going to have to get away from the product management concept toward that of market management, which I've already done to a certain extent in my line. I have two staff marketing assistants in charge of the big potential wiring markets. I've come to the conclusion that if we intend to turn an almost job shop kind of business into a high volume operation, we need market development and emphasis.

SIMPSON: I agree, Bob. After all, I'm basically a market manager myself. I think it's inevitable that we ultimately organize on a market basis, because our products and markets are not clearly and exclusively defined. I say that we should be oriented on a market basis—including the sales force. We've got to fit our company capabilities to the needs of an industry.

JOHNSON: Your product areas may need market specialists, but that doesn't hold for me. We all need more time for planning, etc., but what I need is an applications engineer to do some of my leg-work. I suspect that more technical support might be valid for electrical wiring, too.

SMITH: Well, that's pretty much how Bob and I have things divided now, anyway. I'm taking care of most of the technical problems, but we need a larger technical back-up staff to keep up with them.

TURNER: As I see it, we have a couple of alternatives for evolution. First, if the company organized itself into product divisions—when we're big enough to afford the luxury of it—the product management concept would make some sense, because one guy would have real control and responsibility for manufacturing, marketing, sales, and new product development for his line. Then Terry's definition of a product manager as a mini-general manager with his own business would be realistic. Right now we don't really have that flexibility, because we're single-sourced by manufacturing and R & D, and we always have to work within the framework of the whole company.

An alternative to the division manager would be to have market managers, which probably makes more sense from a growth and marketing standpoint. We already have some market specialists under the product managers, but since they sometimes have to cross product lines, we find ourselves in competition with each other, or the wrong guy gets the credit for making things happen, and so on.

KING: I can vouch for that. The markets I deal with buy tubing, but I'm sure they could use some electrical wire, too. But there's no incentive for me to spend my time trying to sell them wire if it takes time away from the products where I have authority and profit responsibility.

TURNER: Yeah, we keep saying we're marketing oriented, but boy, the whole concept of product management is a very unmarketing oriented way to do things. It's a manufacturing approach. I mean, I will sell bearings to anyone who wants to buy them. But what if my customer needs some castings or cable? I'm not really going to get credit for it on a formal basis unless we install a halfway decent profit-compensation plan which gives credit where it's due.

HANSEN: Isn't that what you guys from Biz School would label the authority/responsibility syndrome? It's inevitable that a conflict will come up now and then, where there's an authority/responsibility gap, but if you can persuade people, it really isn't that much of a problem.

CARDOZA: Right. We're recognized as the guiding group and our requests are respected by the various functions. It may take a certain amount of salesmanship to sell a point, but if the project's any good. . . .

In spite of some problems inherent in the product management system, Terry Westwood felt that it had operated effectively at Barney. He was, however, concerned that additional problems might arise as the company continued its rapid expansion. One of his current concerns was how to allocate R & D time among the various projects recommended by the product managers. The relative importance of each project was not always clear cut, since the product managers frequently did not have enough time to devote to market research.

Current crises generally commanded most of the product manager's time, and the results of the time so expended were often more measurable than that spent on long-range plans or new product development. As a result, Westwood felt that the company might unintentionally exclude itself from new markets or applications. Active evaluation and pursuit of new markets and applications were essential if Barney expected to maintain its ambitious growth rate.

Companhia Gaucha

Companhia Gaucha was a large distributor of agricultural and industrial materials and equipment in southern Brazil. In November 1965, Sr. Santos, the president, was reviewing the company's sales organization with his sales manager, Sr. Genovatti. Earlier that year, one of Companhia Gaucha's major competitors had opened a series of eight showrooms to display its products throughout southern Brazil, and was making strong

FIGURE 1

Marketing Area

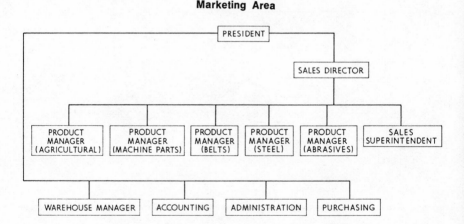

inroads into Companhia Gaucha's sales of abrasives and industrial belts. To meet this challenge, both Sr. Santos and Sr. Genovatti agreed that Gaucha needed to increase its sales effectiveness beyond the present sales force of seven men, representing the full range of products in different geographic areas (see Figure 1). Each, however, supported a different program for this improvement.

Sr. Santos was in favor of expanding Gaucha's sales branches (the company was currently operating one branch in Bage). He believed that Gaucha should meet this new competition "head on."

"Putting sales branches out there would show our customers that we're really a part of their neighborhood," he said. "When they had a problem, they could come to our branch and get it solved immediately. When a customer needed a rush order he could pick it up right there at the branch, instead of trying to reach us through our cumbersome communication network. As for salesman morale," Sr. Santos continued, "if our salesmen were operating out of a branch office, they would feel much more a part of their territory while still being an integral part of our company."

Sr. Genovatti, on the other hand, was in favor of specialized salesmen for each product group, covering the whole market area. He asserted that setting up a sales force specialized in this manner was the only way in which the salesman could truly serve the customers and stated: "Salesmen can't possibly know very much about any one product if obliged to represent such a diverse group of products to so many different kinds of customers."

THE COMPANY

Companhia Gaucha was organized in 1940 as a distributor of agricultural equipment, belt conveyors, and industrial hoses, in the states of Rio Grande do Sul and Santa Catarina. By 1965 the company was handling over 300 classes of products, including a wide range of steel products, industrial machines, spare parts, and abrasive wheels, as well as a full line of agricultural equipment and belts for both industrial and agricultural machinery. Growing steadily, sales reached over Cr$482,720,000.00 in 1965 and returned a profit of Cr$69,350,000.00.[1] Table 1 outlines part of the company's sales and financial history, from 1961 through 1965.

In its early history, Companhia Gaucha had utilized exclusive dealer arrangements throughout most of its sales area and had employed a few direct salesmen to reach the end users. In the early 1950's, however, as national production began to develop and import restrictions came into force, the dealers turned directly to the Brazilian manufacturers, although they maintained Gaucha as one of their suppliers. At that time, Companhia Gaucha dropped its exclusive arrangements and turned to depending on its own sales force to call on independent dealers and end users.

The market area was divided into territories which had about 600 customers each (both end users and dealers). Even though every salesman represented the full line of products, each developed some product specialization. Sales by salesmen and product lines are presented in Table 2.

---

[1] The free rate of exchange in Brazil was 620.0 cruzeiros (designated Cr$620.0) to the U.S. dollar.

TABLE 1

Departmental Sales and Gross Margins, 1959–1963
(sales in millions of cruzeiros)
(gross margin as percentage of sales)

Department	1961 Jan.–Dec.	1962 Jan.–Dec.	1963 Jan.–Dec.	1964 Jan.–Dec.	Oct. 1964– Sept. 1965
Agriculture					
Sales.............	18.7	23.3	39.4	67.8	47.2
Gross margin........	29.8	29.1	31.1	34.8	38.3
Belts					
Sales.............	16.5	27.6	37.6	59.9	103.1
Gross margin........	33.2	30.4	30.0	34.8	35.7
Steel					
Sales.............	33.9	39.1	54.8	94.2	217.3
Gross margin........	27.4	22.7	24.7	29.7	30.1
Machines					
Sales.............	11.6	20.4	24.0	52.7	52.1
Gross margin........	33.0	27.6	30.0	34.2	37.2
Abrasives					
Sales.............	—	3.2	7.3	11.2	47.4
Gross margin........	—	32.0	30.2	29.5	34.1
Parts*					
Sales.............	5.1	6.8	9.9	9.9	15.6
Gross margin........	56.3	52.1	47.7	67.4	55.6

* The sale of parts for the agriculture and machinery department was mentioned separately, although responsibility for these sales was shared by the product managers.
SOURCE: Company records.

Credit was a key tool in selling Gaucha products, and 90% of the company's sales were made on terms ranging from 30 to 90 days. To encourage cash payment, Gaucha offered a 7.5% cash discount, but found this had little effect.

For promotion of their products, Companhia Gaucha relied on bi-weekly ads in newspapers, which circulated through the interior as well as in Porto Alegre. These ads, generally featuring agricultural and industrial equipment, were prepared by an advertising agency. For more extensive coverage, Gaucha mailed copies of these ads to interior customers not covered by the newspapers.

The Agricultural Equipment Market

The chief market for agricultural equipment was among the large farmers. Due to their efficient management, they tended to be good credit risks. Because the tractors and heavy implements which they demanded were difficult to procure in southern Brazil, Companhia Gaucha could easily sell any of this equipment which it could obtain. The small farmers, constituting the bulk of the market, were generally high-risk customers, primarily because of their dependence on one major agricultural product such as wheat or rice. These farmers purchased relatively small equip-

TABLE 2

Salesmen Sales by Product Class*
October 1, 1964–September 30, 1965
(in thousands of cruzeiros)

	PRODUCTS (%)						*Cruzeiro Sales* (*'000*)
Salesman	*Agricultural*	*Belts*	*Steel*	*Machinery*	*Abrasives*	*Total*	
1............	7.8	26.9	54.8	6.5	4.3	100.0	53,600
2............	33.0	16.6	35.8	12.2	3.4	100.0	74,210
3............	5.7	25.1	38.3	27.2	3.9	100.0	46,200
4............	9.2	26.0	37.2	12.0	15.3	100.0	42,820
5............	2.0	10.3	64.3	9.2	14.2	100.0	60,400
6............	1.2	20.4	69.9	5.5	2.8	100.0	40,830
7............	2.4	9.0	49.0	10.7	28.7	100.0	50,500
8............	20.0	28.9	37.8	11.6	2.6	100.0	70,640
Sales branch........	6.4	32.6	22.1	19.0	19.8	100.0	43,520
							482,720

* Sales of parts are included in the agricultural and machinery product groups.

ment, which was sold on a highly competitive basis. The salesmen for Companhia Gaucha called on most of the agricultural equipment dealers in their areas, but they made the bulk of their sales to the farmer by establishing direct contact through the local co-ops and commercial associations.

The Market for Abrasives

The most important market for abrasives was in the industrialized area around Porto Alegre. The second concentration existed just north of Porto Alegre near Caxias and Novo Hamburg, among shoe and appliance manufacturers. In addition, the company sold to small equipment manufacturers and repair shops, which were scattered through the whole market area.

Although most abrasive distributors handled a wide range of products similar to Companhia Gaucha, the strongest competition came from specialized distributors selling directly to end users, through their own showrooms. The executives of Companhia Gaucha had taken on the abrasive line in 1961 but had not been able to obtain an exclusive distributorship for their market area. In fact, Companhia Gaucha operated on an annual quota system with the abrasive manufacturer. Under these arrangements, Gaucha was granted a 20% discount from the suggested retail price.

The Market for Industrial and Agricultural Belts

The market for industrial and agricultural belts was similar to that for abrasive wheels. While users were to be found throughout the market area, they were concentrated in the industrial centers. Companhia Gaucha served as the exclusive distributor for a well-known Brazilian belt manufacturer. Gaucha salesmen called on a wide range of end users as well as dealers, although management believed that dealers probably sold over three-fourths of the total.

Four major belt manufacturers provided Companhia Gaucha with keen competition for this market. One manufacturer was represented by a local distributor, another utilized his own sales force calling directly on end users, while the remaining two distributed through independent dealers. All of these manufacturers undersold Companhia Gaucha with a lower quality product. The superior quality of the Gaucha belt was apparent, however, only when the belts were used properly. Since most of the smaller users (about two-thirds of Gaucha's belt users) seldom exercised appropriate care in their employment of the belts, the difference in quality was generally unrecognized.

Machinery Market

Companhia Gaucha carried a wide assortment of small industrial tools and equipment, such as small electric and gasoline motors, grinders, conveyors, and tools for machinists. Occasionally, they were able to import and sell heavier equipment, such as turbines. The management suspected that a large share of these sales (probably 80%) were made directly to end users, while the remainder moved through many of the same dealers who sold Gaucha belts and abrasives. Inasmuch as these products were generally more expensive than abrasive wheels or belts, the brand, quality, and reputation of Companhia Gaucha played a more important role in their sales.

Industrial and Construction Steel

The steel market was the most favorable one for Companhia Gaucha which stocked a full range of products, from rolled sheets to steel construction beams. Buying most of its steel from one large Brazilian producer, the characteristically short supply of steel in Brazil obliged the Gaucha buying office to make supplementary purchases from a number of smaller mills. Although the margins on these products tended to be low, Gaucha found a ready market for all of the steel which it was able to obtain. These products were sold by the sales force directly to the contractors, canners, and other steel-using industries.

Product Managers

Product managers were responsible for controlling the inventories and prices of their respective product groups. In these activities, the product managers worked closely with the president as well as with the sales manager, especially in forecasting future sales. Each product manager had one assistant to aid him in these functions. Based on sales forecasts and the current inventory level, the product managers filed buying requests with the purchasing department. When the materials were received by Companhia Gaucha, the product managers, after consulting the president and the sales manager, set the retail price. This price determination was largely based on desired gross margins (a minimum of 30% for imported items and 20% for Brazilian goods) and competitive prices. The established retail prices were firm to end users, although for large orders (except on steel items and belts) the salesmen could request the granting of small discounts.

The product managers had little sales contact with Companhia Gaucha customers. They acted as inside salesmen for customers, but these sales were strictly cash and usually represented less than 10% of total Gaucha sales. In addition to sales contacts, however, the product managers had the responsibility of informing customers of shipment delays or stock shortages. This brought them into frequent mail or cable contact with customers in the interior.

All but the abrasives manager, who joined the company in 1963, had been with the company for a number of years. They were all paid salaries which averaged Cr$250,000.00 in 1965.

The Sales Force

As indicated earlier, each Companhia Gaucha salesman (with the exception of the sales office in Bage) was responsible for the sale of all Gaucha products in their territories. Sr. Santos was convinced that each customer should be called on at least once every two months. Generally, each salesman spent a total of 50 days in calling on customers in the field, and 10 days in the home office every two months. The salesmen typically covered half of their territories between visits to the home office. The Gaucha executives had attempted to keep the territories reasonably well balanced, to minimize friction between salesmen because of the greater potential in some territories than in others.[2]

In the field, salesmen called on all past and potential customers, checked their inventories, wrote up any orders (mailed to the home office daily), and generated good will for sales between the bimonthly calls. Most of the orders were received at the time of the salesman's call, although some were made by mail.

Sr. Genovatti relied on the careful routing of the salesmen as his primary means of sales control. While in the office, each salesman prepared a

---

[2] Under Brazilian law, a company could not take any customers away from a salesman nor make any other modifications in sales territories *if* it would mean a loss in income (based on the average income over the last 6 months) to the salesman.

detailed list of all customers whom he planned to visit during his next trip and submitted the list to Sr. Genovatti. Having submitted travel plans, the salesmen met with the product managers to discuss the product problems experienced or the equipment desired by their customers. In the course of this meeting, the product managers brought the salesmen's price lists up to date. After talking to the product managers, the salesmen met with the credit manager and turned in their financial reports on the customers visited on the last trip. At this time, they received whatever credit information had been developed in the home office. During these home office visits of the salesmen, Sr. Santos was frequently involved in the discussions with the product and credit managers. He generally handled the salesmen's personal or administrative problems himself.

Once he had returned to the field, the salesman had little contact with the home office. This was due to the poor communications which prevailed in most of Companhia Gaucha's sales territory. Telephone communications were virtually impossible, and telegrams were frequently delayed. In addition, each salesman was empowered to adjust his travel plan according to the situation that he found in his territory. Although the salesmen were instructed to notify the home office of each change, the poor communications sometimes caused the home office to lose complete track of salesmen during their trips into the interior.

The salesmen submitted daily reports which specified the customers visited and the orders received. These reports were reviewed every day by Sr. Santos, Sr. Genovatti, and the sales supervisor. They were then forwarded to the product manager to ensure that the orders were in stock. Afterwards they were sent to the credit department for approval of shipment, and finally to the administrative department, to compute compensation and to check the call against the customer list, in order to make certain that each customer was visited every 60 days.

Companhia Gaucha depended on the salesmen as the primary source of information about the market, although Sr. Santos believed that recording specific customer information, beyond the listing of daily calls and what credit information the salesmen could obtain, would prove an undue hardship to them. Further, individual records on all customers would become very complicated in view of the large number of customers and wide range of products.

The direct supervision of the sales force, the review of daily sales reports, and the approval of salesmen's field trips, as well as the coordination of the product managers and salesmen, had proved to be a heavy load for Sr. Genovatti. Therefore, in 1961, Companhia Gaucha had hired a sales supervisor to assist him in directing the sales force and obtaining cooperation with the product managers for salesman briefings.

THE BAGE SALES BRANCH

The Bage sales branch had proved to be a successful undertaking. In 1963 Sr. Santos and Sr. Genovatti had decided that one sales territory offered an unusually favorable potential, and they had established a sales office to serve the customers in that area. Since opening the branch, sales of abrasives, belts, and light industrial and agricultural machinery products had more than quadrupled in that territory. The direct cost of the sales office was approximately 5% of sales in the area, which compared favorably with the 4% cost of traveling salesmen (2% commission plus 2% transportation allowances).[3] Inasmuch as the facilities were rented, the only significant investment was in the inventory which the branch carried. The Gaucha executives anticipated that any new showrooms would require at least this much additional inventory. (See Table 3.)

Sr. Santos was convinced that new sales branches could operate on the same cost basis as the one recently established. The main problem that he foresaw was one of staffing. In the recent case, the salesman with that territorial responsibility before 1963 had proved to be a sound administrator, and he had ably taken over the management of the sales branch, with the help of one stock clerk. Most of the other Gaucha salesmen, however, were "old line" salesmen who had been with Companhia Gaucha for years and were not interested in any administrative responsibilities. As for bringing in new personnel, Companhia Gaucha had experienced great difficulty in finding capable salesmen or product managers who would work at the present levels of compensation. Therefore, Sr. Genovatti argued, Companhia Gaucha could only attract good managers for the new sales branches by paying more than 50% above the present level of compensation.

---

[3] In the event that an order was received directly from a customer who had not been visited the preceding 60 days, the salesman would lose his commission on that sale.

SECTION VIII

CONTROL AND REAPPRAISAL

Maxwell House Coffee

The product manager for ground Maxwell House Coffee was at work in his office preparing his budget for the next fiscal year. Unexpectedly, he was interrupted by a long distance telephone call from Stockton, California. One of the company's salesmen called to report that the J. A. Folger Company had just introduced a new keyless one-pound can for its brand of ground coffee in Stockton supermarkets, apparently on a test market basis. He was forwarding samples of the can to headquarters in White Plains, New York by air mail.

The product manager reported the news to his immediate superior, the Advertising and Merchandising Manager, who in turn notified the General Manager of the Maxwell House Division of General Foods Corporation. All three executives would be intimately involved in considering the development because of the large potential impact of a packaging change on the profits of the Maxwell House Division.

POTENTIAL IMPLICATIONS OF A CHANGE

Maxwell House was the leading brand of ground coffee (drip, regular and fine grind) in the United States, selling about 300,000,000 pounds annually. The brand accounted for about 21% of all ground coffee sold and was followed by Folger's with about 15%. Because of the large volume, a cost reduction of as much as 1 cent per can could save Maxwell House about $3,000,000 a year. If a packaging change should cause the brand to either lose or gain a 1% share of market, factory sales would be affected by about $9,000,000, assuming a selling price of 63 cents per pound, and gross margin would be affected by about $1,000,000.[1]

Approximately 60% of the 300,000,000 pounds of ground Maxwell House Coffee sold annually were packed in one-pound cans; 40% in two-pound cans.

[1] Gross margin figure disguised.

The Maxwell House Division also roasted and marketed ground coffee under the Yuban brand and a decaffeinated ground coffee under the Sanka label. Yuban had about 1.9% and Sanka had 1.5% of the ground coffee market. (See Exhibit 1.) The Maxwell House Division had maintained a position of leadership in the coffee industry for many years. Sales of its three brands in both ground and soluble form had grown to account for 35% of all coffee sold in the United States in 1962.

While Maxwell House led other brands of ground coffee on a nationwide basis, its market position was much stronger in the East than the West. The opposite was true for Folger's. For example, 50% of the sales of Maxwell House were made in the eastern and mideastern sales districts which accounted for only 5% of Folger's sales. In 1962, Folger's was not sold in markets which accounted for about 40% of the sales of ground Maxwell House coffee. They included Boston, New York, Philadelphia, Syracuse, Washington, D.C., Youngstown, Charlotte and Atlanta. The west central and western regions contributed only 15% of the total sales of Maxwell House ground coffee compared to 71% for Folger's. (See Exhibit 2.) In Northern California, Folger's sold about four times as much ground coffee as did Maxwell House.

Maxwell House enjoyed 36.2% of the vacuum packed ground coffee market in its mideastern sales region where Folger's share was 6.1%. In its west central region, Maxwell House had a share of 8.5% compared to 29.1% for Folger's. (See Exhibit 3.)

Matters of packaging and labeling were of concern to the product manager because of his responsibility for the domestic marketing of ground Maxwell House Coffee. Aided by a group of assistants, he established annual sales objectives, worked with the advertising agency to develop and implement advertising and promotional programs, evaluated possible changes in the product, determined what price changes should be recommended, and maintained programs of market testing and consumer research.

GROUND COFFEE PACKAGING

The packaging of ground coffee in the United States had undergone no major change since the late 1920's when a can developed for shortening products was adopted for coffee. At that time the large can suppliers tooled to produce a key opening can 5⅛ inches in diameter and 3⅝ inches in height. Such a can had been used since then by most brands except during World War II when glass jars were substituted to save metal. After the war, electrolytic tinning replaced the old hot-dip process and a lighter weight "tin plate" (Steel plate coated with tin) was used to reduce costs and improve appearance and resistance to rust. The can companies' tooling did not change, however. Use of a key opening can of the same dimensions continued.

The Folger test in Stockton which prompted the phone call to the Product Manager late in October, 1962, was not the first indication of that company's interest in a keyless can. In August, 1962, Folger's had introduced a three-pound keyless can in Stockton. The move was of no unusual concern to Maxwell House executives who viewed it as a test of the three-pound size which they earlier had decided not to market. They saw no manufacturing economies in it and they believed the number of families who could use three pounds of coffee in two weeks was very limited. Coffee tended to become stale about two weeks after the can was first opened.

After receiving the new keyless, one-pound can from Stockton, the Product Manager sent the following memorandum to the Advertising and Merchandising Manager on October 26, 1962:

Forwarded with this memorandum is the new Folger can. Its principal features are a smaller diameter, a taller shape, and its opening device (regular can opener vs. key strip). The can was picked up in Stockton, California, by our sales force. There is a research questionnaire enclosed in the cap and our intelligence indicates that Folger is testing it only in the Stockton area. The sales force also reports that Folger will be introducing a similar two-pound can in Stockton in the near future.

The new can is made by the American Can Company and it costs (including plastic lid) considerably more than the Maxwell House can (about 15¢ per unit of 12 pounds). To mass produce this can, it would be necessary to invest in molds for the plastic lid and in line conversion parts (estimated total cost for Maxwell House, about $600,000).

We have findings from consumer research on can shapes similar to this one. An American Can Company test conducted by Forbes Research in July, 1962, indicated that consumers preferred a smaller diameter, taller can to the standard shape. Their preference was not great enough, however, to influence them to purchase a brand not normally used just because of the can. Although the can used in this research had a conventional key strip opening device, we still believe the research conclusion is valid as far as preference for the shape is concerned.

With regard to the opening device, we feel this may offer an important consumer appeal. Maxwell House had investigated cans that could be opened with a regular home can opener before, but it was decided not to pursue this further.

Now that the Folger Company has indicated interest in this type of can, we will have to stay on top of the development. Accordingly, we plan to conduct consumer interviews in Stockton to learn of consumer reaction to the Folger can. A research proposal for this study will be available early next week, and either a member of the product group or a representative from the Market Research Department will go to Stockton next week to observe Folger's sales activity.

We have alerted the sales force to be looking for this can in all areas and will keep you advised of any new developments.

The Product Manager approved proposals for consumer interviews and store audits of retail sales of ground coffee in Stockton.

STOCKTON CONSUMER INTERVIEWS

The Marketing Research Department of the Maxwell House Division planned a survey of women purchasers of Folger's coffee in the new no-key can and by October 29, 1962, it had employed Survey Research Services, Inc., of San Francisco, California, to do the interviewing.

During the weekends starting November 8 and 15, interviewers were stationed in Stockton supermarkets. They introduced themselves to women who had purchased Folger's in the new can. In order to guard against bias, a series of three questions were asked about each of five different product categories, one of which was ground coffee. The questions were aimed at ascertaining the respondent's usual brand; the brand she bought the last time she purchased the given type of product, not counting purchases made on the day of the interview; and the brand purchased on the day of the interview. If Folger's was not the respondent's usual brand of coffee, she was asked why she happened to buy Folger's on the day of the interview. The interviewer also obtained the respondent's name, address and telephone number and noted the name and location of the store in which the interview was conducted. (See Exhibit 4 for questionnaire.)

Ten days to two weeks later, telephone interviews were conducted with 125 women who had been interviewed in the supermarkets.[2] Respondents first were asked open questions about what they thought of the Folger's coffee they bought in the new type of can and how they felt about the container itself. Several more specific questions then were asked. (See Exhibit 5 for questionnaire.)

Eighty-six per cent of the respondents reinterviewed considered the new Folger's container better than the usual kind of coffee can. The corresponding figure for women whose usual brand was not Folger's was 80%. (See Exhibit 6.) The main reasons given were ease of opening, slimmer shape which made for ease of handling, reusability of the can as a cannister, and the plastic lid for resealing which was thought to keep the coffee "better and fresher."

Ninety-three per cent of the spontaneous comments on the new can were favorable. When asked to rate the new container and its contents on each of several points, 86% said it was easier to open and 80% said it was easier to reclose than the key can. Coffee purchased in the new can was seen as superior in flavor, aroma and freshness to that bought in the conventional can.

---

[2] Eighty-eight women interviewed in supermarkets were not represented in the telephone survey results. Forty-five refused reinterview, 27 could not be reached and 16 interviews were completed after the established deadline.

Sixty-one per cent of the women reinterviewed had purchased ground coffee in the two weeks between the in-store interview and the telephone follow-up. In so doing, 56% of the women reinterviewed had selected Folger's. The corresponding figures for women who usually bought a brand other than Folger's were 53% and 47%. Thirty per cent of the non-regular users of Folger's and 53% of the regular users had purchased Folger's in the new can more than once. (See Exhibit 7.)

Ninety-six per cent of the regular users and 70% of the non-regular users of Folger's stated that their next purchase of ground coffee would be Folger's in the new can. When asked why, 59% referred to the coffee and 48% referred to the container in some way. (See Exhibit 8.)

When women who regularly used a brand other than Folger's were asked in the in-store interview why they had selected Folger's, 57% (17 of 30 women) said they did so because it was on sale and 33% replied by referring to the container. (See Exhibit 9.)

The Marketing Research Department reported as follows on the results of the Stockton interviews:

The available data are extremely favorable to the new Folger's can type. Attempts to generalize from the data, however, must be read within the limitations of one fairly small sample in one city with three quarters of the respondents buyers of a single brand—Folger's.

It is suggested, therefore that further research be carried out to check the favorable reaction indicated here among a larger, more diversified sample. Resultant data might then be collated with comparable data for the several new can prototypes now under development by the Division.

RETAIL SALES AUDIT

Arrangements were made to have the Burgoyne Index, Inc., of Cincinnati, Ohio, audit retail sales of Folger's, Maxwell House and other selected brands of ground coffee in 21 Stockton stores during the weeks beginning November 5, 12, and 19.

Results of the audits showed that Folger's in one-pound and three-pound no-key cans accounted for 10.1% of the total pounds of ground coffee sold in the first week, 14.7% in the second week, and 10.6% in the third week. (See Exhibit 10.) The larger share in the second week was due to an increase in sales of the three-pound size which did not continue into the third week. The Burgoyne staff reported that special merchandising promotions in Stockton stores during the three-week period were limited to a floor display of Folger's one-pound size in the new can and to "the usual shelf strips." Retail prices were not affected by the change in cans.

During the three-week period of the store audits, the three-pound size accounted for 8.1% of the ground coffee sold in Stockton. The corresponding figure for the Maxwell House San Francisco sales district was

0.6%. Folger's share of ground coffee sales (all sizes and both the key and the keyless containers) during each of the three weeks was 23.9%, 28.5%, and 24.7%. Maxwell House's shares of ground coffee sales in Stockton for the same three weeks were 18.7%, 15.3%, and 18.5%. Folger's accounted for 28.5% of the sales of ground coffee in the San Francisco sales district during the three-week period compared with 7.8% for Maxwell House. (See Exhibit 11.)

The costs to Maxwell House of the research conducted in Stockton and described on the preceding pages were about $2,800 for the retail sales audits and about $2,200 for the consumer interviews.

CUSTOMER ACCEPTANCE

During November and December, 1962, members of the Maxwell House management engaged in many discussions as they considered what to do about the no-key can.

In studying the question of consumer acceptance, they reviewed available studies made by other organizations of consumer likes and dislikes in packaging. The results contained evidence of dissatisfaction with cans that required a key to open and one survey made in 1960 found that 5% of the women regarded coffee packages as "poor." (See Exhibit 12.)

The finding that Stockton women who tried the keyless can preferred it highlighted questions as to what the effects would be if Folger's converted to that can and Maxwell House did not. Would Folger's thereby gain an advantage in the 20 Maxwell House sales districts in which Maxwell House and Folger's competed? Would Folger's be able to use the new can as a merchandising lever to successfully introduce its brand into the eastern sales districts in which Folger's was not now represented and to increase its share in the eastern and mideastern regions which accounted for half of Maxwell House's sales? Folger's might elect to use any increase in gross margin resulting from lower can costs for additional promotion in an effort to increase market position. Maxwell House executives believed they would have to match such an increase in order to hold position for Maxwell House ground coffee.

In considering what the effects would be if Maxwell House converted to the keyless can, Maxwell House executives noted that the three-week audit of retail sales in Stockton provided no evidence that Folger's sales and share of market had increased. They were unwilling to take action which might lead to a decrease in market share. They feared that a decline in share, once started, could not be contained. Because of the large volume involved, a drop in share for the Maxwell House brand could have a significant adverse effect on General Foods corporate sales figures at a time when great emphasis was being placed on growth and a decline in share was regarded as a red flag signaling possible deterioration of a brand's consumer franchise.

ADEQUACY OF NO-KEY CAN

The Production Services Manager and the Packaging Development Manager reported that they had investigated possible use of a no-key can in 1956 and again in 1959. On those occasions, decisions were made against the no-key can because of technical problems affecting the strength of the metal, the high cost of polyethylene lids and the feeling of the marketing group that its appearance was not of high quality. At the same time, however, it was found that the no-key can was easier to make than the key can. If the cost of the polyethylene lid were excluded, it also was less expensive to manufacture.

The Folger's no-key can was $4\frac{1}{16}$ inches in diameter (called a 401 can) as compared to the standard key can of $5\frac{2}{16}$ inches in diameter (called the 502 can). The cylindrical portion of the Folger's no-key can was made from 60-pound tin plate which was less expensive than the 90-pound tin plate used in the conventional key can. After studying no-key can packaging alternatives in 1962, Maxwell House's researchers concluded that a can made from 90-pound tin plate for the sides and 75-pound tin plate for the ends would be necessary to satisfactorily withstand the pressures which characteristically built up inside a coffee can a few days after it was packed. The Maxwell House production manager believed that a can made with 60-pound tin plate would be vulnerable to bulging and structural failure.

COST CONSIDERATIONS

Maxwell House production personnel investigated what the costs of a keyless can would be both if Maxwell House should manufacture it and if the can were purchased from suppliers. While the make or buy study was under way, several large United States oil companies switched from steel tin plate cans $4\frac{1}{16}$ inches in diameter (401 cans) to plastic coated paper containers for packaging oil. Their move left some of the machines of the American Can Company and the Continental Can Company available for other uses. While the can companies no doubt would prefer to continue producing coffee cans from their key can machines, the General Foods Purchasing Manager reasoned that they nevertheless recognized that the coffee industry was interested in a packaging change and now might be willing to quote an attractive price on the 401 can.

The following cost figures were compiled from prices quoted by can companies and from the manufacturing cost study made by Maxwell House purchasing, accounting and engineering personnel:

| | Cost per Thousand Cans with Lithographed Labels | | | |
| | One-Pound Size | | Two-Pound Size | |
	If Make	If Buy	If Make	If Buy
No-key can.....................	$46.00	$55.00	$67.00	$ 78.00
Polyethylene lid...............	6.50	8.00	7.75	9.50
Total..................	$52.50	$63.00	$74.75	$ 87.50
Key can currently in use..........	$60.00	$75.00	$87.00	$120.00

In the past, Maxwell House had purchased its cans. The $46.00 and the $67.00 figures in the above table included both variable and fixed costs for the Hoboken, N.J. plant production of about 75,000,000 one-pound cans and about 25,000,000 two-pound cans a year. Plant and equipment needed if the Hoboken plant were to make the no-key can would cost an estimated $2,800,000. The comparable figure for the key can was $4,000,000. It was the company's practice to write off machinery over a 15-year period and buildings over a 40-year period. Cans for the other Maxwell House plants in Jacksonville, Florida; Houston, Texas; and San Leandro, California, would continue to be purchased because of their lower volume requirements.

The cost estimates for the 401 can assumed the use of 90-pound tin plate for the sides and 75-pound plate for the ends. Producers of polyethylene lids had quoted $12 per thousand for initial orders filled while they would be expanding their capacity. The Purchasing Manager estimated $8.00 as the future price after mass production techniques had been perfected and capacity had been expanded.

The "buy" figures in the above table did not include the costs of converting the 10 Maxwell House production lines for handling the keyless can. These costs were estimated at $600,000 for capital equipment and $800,000 for labor and expense for a total of about $1,400,000. The costs pertained almost entirely to the one-pound size because the two-pound keyless can had the same dimensions as the two-pound key can.

Another factor which the Maxwell House management attempted to weigh was the probable drop in plant efficiency which would result during plant conversion and continue for some time thereafter. Use of the same methods of packing for many years had resulted in high levels of productivity. Maxwell House executives did not wish to unnecessarily take on new problems which would add to costs. They noted that can company representatives had expressed the opinion that Folger's no-key can was merely an experiment that would not develop into anything beyond a test.

WAIT FOR A NEW QUICK STRIP CAN?

A further important consideration was that Maxwell House was working with the American Can Company in the development of another major innovation in can design which would use neither a key nor a plastic lid. Its metal cover would be sealed on the side just below the top with a flexible aluminum coated plastic strip one-half inch wide. The can would be reclosed with its own cover which would have deeper side wells than the lid of the key can, providing a tighter fit which would help keep contents fresher.

Maxwell House executives were convinced that the can being developed, which they called "quick strip," would be superior to both the traditional key can and the new keyless can, combining their advantages. Its cost was expected to be comparable to that of the key can. The American Can Company had applied for several patents covering the tear-strip opening principle. While there was no exclusivity arrangement, Maxwell House executives were confident that they would obtain first rights to receive the can for their needs until such time as American Can had developed sufficient capacity to supply the total industry. Since the cost and time necessary for developing such capacity were expected to be great, Maxwell House executives felt that from a practical standpoint they would enjoy lead time ranging from three or four months in all areas and up to 12 months in many areas of the United States before the quick strip can would be available to competition.

In January 1963, the American Can Company representatives estimated that with a reasonable amount of luck, the developmental work on the quick strip would proceed so that 100,000 units could be supplied for test marketing by May or June; and that one production line capable of producing 1,000,000 cans a week could be in operation by September or October, 1963. Full scale production which would permit Maxwell House to use the can for its total output of ground coffee was expected to be possible three or four months after the first production line was put in operation or by January, 1964, in accordance with the above schedule.

Maxwell House executives were inclined to be less optimistic. They thought that there was only about a 50% chance that 100,000 cans would be available by October, 1963, and they believed it would be unrealistic to assume that tests on the first 100,000 units would find the can technically perfect. They recognized the possibility that technical problems might arise which would delay introduction of the quick strip can indefinitely. Once test results permitted a decision to go ahead, about six months would be required before the can company could achieve a production rate which would satisfy the total container needs of ground Maxwell House Coffee.[3]

In reviewing the situation, the Maxwell House executives wondered

---

[3] In response to questioning a year later, the Advertising and Merchandising Manager said that in January, 1963, Maxwell House executives probably would have given the following estimates of probabilities as to when the American Can Company's first production line would be turning out 1,000,000 cans a week: by December, 1963, 50%; by March, 1964, 75%; by June, 1964, 85%; and never, 10%. They expected that full production for Maxwell House's total needs could be attained about four months after the first production line had started operations.

whether it would be better to wait and make one large move from the 502
to the quick strip can or convert in the near future to the keyless can
which they regarded as an interim step in coffee packaging. Costs of converting production lines from the keyless to the quick strip can would be
minor because the cans were of the same size.

A NEW STOCKTON SURVEY

On December 12, 1962, a Maxwell House production manager received by telephone findings of research done for the Continental Can
Company on the acceptance of Folger's keyless can in Stockton. While
details about the study were lacking, the notes made during the phone
conversation contained the information that 186 telephone calls had been
completed to Stockton homes. One hundred of the 186 respondents said
they were aware of Folger's keyless can and 55 had bought it. Of the 55,
69% said they usually bought Folger's; 31% said they normally bought
other brands although only 25% reported doing so the last time they
bought coffee prior to the telephone interview. Of the 55 people who
had tried Folger's in the keyless can, 51% had repurchased it at least
once; 16% had repurchased it three times; and 16% had repurchased it
more than three times. Forty-nine percent of the 55 people who had
tried the keyless can either had not repurchased it or said they did not
intend to do so.

Of the regular Folger's users who had purchased Folger's in the keyless
can, 17% mentioned the container when asked for reasons. Among respondents who said they usually bought brands other than Folger's, 64%
said they purchased Folger's in the keyless can because they "were curious." Explanations of their purchases by respondents who did not buy
Folger's in the keyless can when they had the opportunity to do so did
not reveal much in the way of negative feelings about the can itself. (See
Exhibit 13.)

FOLGER ADDS THREE MARKETS

Folger had introduced its one-pound no-key can in Sacramento, California; St. Louis, Missouri; and Muncie, Indiana, by mid-January, 1963.
While Folger's plans for the future were not known to Maxwell House,
rumors were abundant and had been reported by all levels of Maxwell
House Division management and by General Foods corporate executives
as well.

Contributing to the tension of the situation was the fact that the rumors
often were conflicting. One day, for example, a Maxwell House manager
heard that Folger's was dropping all distribution of the no-key can. The
next day, he received word from a source regarded "equally as reliable"
that Folger's would have the no-key can in national distribution within a

few weeks. A variety of rumors circulated in the trade and were being relayed to headquarters by the company's sales force. The situation led one executive to remark that the rumor factory was working overtime and that the Maxwell House ground coffee group was receiving much phony intelligence.

PRESSURE FOR DECISION

The consensus in late January was that no outside party really knew how far Folger had committed itself to national distribution of the keyless can. At the same time, however, there were strong pressures on Maxwell House executives to decide what to do. One Maxwell House manager commented that the speed at which decisions had to be made did not allow anyone to have a comfortable grasp of the situation and it did not permit normal test market procedures.

Although store audits had not been continued in Stockton, the Maxwell House sales force reported in January their observations that the sales of Folger's ground coffee had remained about the same there as they had been before the introduction of the no-key can. Folger's recently had switched from 60-pound to 90-pound tin plate for the sides of the can.

Consideration was being given to converting only the San Leandro plant in order to gain both manufacturing and marketing experience with the keyless can. A majority of the families which purchased coffee in the one-pound size did so at least once every two weeks. In view of this fact, the market research manager estimated that observation of a minimum of two months of sales results from retail store audits in selected markets would be required to ascertain whether the change to the keyless can would not adversely affect Maxwell House's share of market.

By converting the San Leandro plant, Maxwell House might be able to supply the keyless can to sales districts in which Folger had introduced the new can. Following a policy of matching Folger's packaging on a market to market basis, however, could create inventory and transportation problems. While the San Leandro plant could conveniently supply western sales districts, it would have difficulty in supplying a market like St. Louis which normally was served by the Houston plant.

Investigation revealed that suppliers with injection molding equipment capable of producing plastic tops for the no-key can badly lacked capacity sufficient to fill Maxwell House's needs should the brand convert to the keyless can. No single supplier could produce as much as 2,000,000 lids a year. Time would be required to increase lid capacity and to acquire and install can closing machines and new parts needed for packing lines.

None of the four plants in which Maxwell House Coffee was roasted and packed had unused capacity. The San Leandro plant accounted for about 15% of the company's production for domestic sales and the Hoboken plant about 40%. The remaining 45% was split about evenly between Jacksonville and Houston.[4] Conversion could be accomplished one production line at a time. It would have to be carried out on a rotational basis in order to keep retail stores supplied with Maxwell House Coffee. The Hoboken plant had four lines, the other plants two each.

It was estimated that once a decision was made to convert to the keyless can nationally, four months would be required for conversion before the keyless can output could start. Volume could be expected to build up smoothly from that time until six months later when the full output of Maxwell House ground coffee would be in keyless cans. In other words, the equivalent of five full months of output in the keyless can could be achieved during the first year after a decision had been made to convert.

In late January, the General Manager was attempting to determine what course of action the Maxwell House Division should follow in regard to the keyless can.

EXHIBIT 1

Estimated Percentage Share of Ground Coffee Sales for Maxwell House, Folger's, Sanka and Yuban Brands, in the United States, 1953–1962

	1953	1954	1955	1956	1957
Maxwell House	15.6	16.5	16.3	17.3	16.7
Folger's	—	—	—	—	—
Sanka	1.1	1.0	0.8	0.9	1.0
Yuban	—	—	—	0.5	0.7

	1958	1959	1960	1961	1962
Maxwell House	17.3	19.1	20.8	21.6	21.4
Folger's	—	—	14.6	14.8	14.7
Sanka	1.1	1.1	1.2	1.3	1.5
Yuban	0.8	0.8	1.0	1.8	1.9

SOURCE: Maxwell House Division, Market Research Department.

---

[4] Figures disguised.

EXHIBIT 2

Estimated Percentage Distribution of Sales of Vacuum Packed Ground Coffee and Sales of Selected Brands by Maxwell House Sales Regions, 1962

Region (and Sales Districts in Each)	All Brands	Maxwell House	Yuban	Folger's	Chase & Sanborn	Hills
Eastern.................... (Boston, New York, Phil- adelphia, Syracuse)	18.7	29.0	24.1	0	26.7	0.7
Mideastern................. (Washington, Youngs- town, Cincinnati, Louis- ville)	13.2	22.4	8.6	5.0	22.4	5.0
Southern................... (Charlotte, Atlanta, Jack- sonville, Memphis, New Orleans)	13.0	19.9	5.3	9.3	13.9	0.5
Central.................... (Detroit, Indianapolis, Chicago, Milwaukee, St. Louis)	18.4	13.9	5.0	14.2	21.2	48.3
West Central............... (Minneapolis, Omaha, Kansas City, Dallas, Houston)	16.4	6.2	1.0	34.6	4.1	10.3
Western................... (Portland, San Francisco, Los Angeles, Denver, Phoenix)	20.3	8.6	56.0	36.9	11.7	35.2
	100.0	100.0	100.0	100.0	100.0	100.0

SOURCE: Maxwell House Division, Market Research Department.

EXHIBIT 3

Estimated Percentage of Vacuum Packed Ground Coffee Sales for Selected Brands by Maxwell House Sales Regions, Late in 1962

Region (and Sales Districts in Each)	Maxwell House	Yuban	Folger's	Chase & Sanborn	Hills
Eastern............................ (Boston, New York, Philadelphia, Syracuse)	32.1	1.8	—	6.4	0.4
Mideastern......................... (Washington, Youngstown, Cincinnati, Louisville)	36.2	1.2	6.1	10.1	4.4
Southern........................... (Charlotte, Atlanta, Jacksonville, Memphis, New Orleans)	32.8	0.7	9.5	7.0	0.5
Central............................ (Detroit, Indianapolis, Chicago, Milwaukee, St. Louis)	14.9	0.5	12.1	7.1	27.1
West Central....................... (Minneapolis, Omaha, Kansas City, Dallas, Houston)	8.5	0.1	29.1	1.7	7.4
Western............................ (Portland, San Francisco, Los Angeles, Denver, Phoenix)	8.5	5.3	26.3	4.4	17.4

SOURCE: Maxwell House Division, Market Research Department.

EXHIBIT 4

Questionnaire for the Stockton In-Store Consumer Interviews

We are doing a study of the different products people buy. (IF NECESSARY, EXPLAIN THAT YOU ARE WITH SURVEY RESEARCH SERVICES, AN INDEPENDENT MARKET RESEARCH COMPANY AND THAT YOU ARE NOT SELLING ANYTHING) (INTERVIEW ONLY PEOPLE WHO ARE BUYING THE NEW FOLGER CAN WHICH CAN BE OPENED WITH A CAN OPENER)

Ques. 1a: What brand do you usually buy of each of the following products . . . detergent? toothpaste? regular ground coffee? paper toweling? margarine? WRITE IN BRAND BELOW.

Ques. 1b: (ASK FOR EACH PRODUCT)   The last time you bought_____, not counting today, what brand did you buy?

Ques. 1c: (ASK FOR EACH PRODUCT)   If you bought any _____ today, would you tell me which brand you bought?

	Ques. 1a	*Ques. 1b*	*Ques. 1c*
	Usual brand	Last brand	Brand today
Detergent			
Toothpaste			
Ground coffee (regular coffee)			
Paper toweling			
Margarine			

IF FOLGER'S NOT USUAL BRAND (QUES. 1a) ASK:

Ques. 2:   Why did you happen to buy Folger's coffee today?

BE SURE TO OBTAIN THE FOLLOWING INFORMATION:

Name _____   Telephone no. _____

Address _____   Interviewer's initials_____

Store name_____

Location _____

EXHIBIT 5

Questionnaire for Telephone Interviews of Consumers in Stockton

Hello, my name is _____ from Survey Research Services. We're conducting a survey in this area . . . about two weeks ago you bought some Folger's coffee in a new type of can . . .

1a.   What did you think of the Folger's coffee you bought in the new type of can? (PROBE: Why is that?)

1b.   How about the new container itself, how did you feel about that?

2a.   Would you say that the new type of coffee can was,   SAME............. 1
generally speaking, better or worse or about the same   BETTER.......... 2
as the usual kind of coffee can?   WORSE........... 3

2b.   Why is that?

3.   Now, for each of the following, would you tell me whether the Folger's coffee in the new type of can was as good as what you used to get in the usual kind of can, or better or worse.

	As good	Better	Worse
The freshness of the coffee	1	2	3
The aroma of the coffee	4	5	6
The flavor of the coffee	1	2	3
Ease of opening the can	4	5	6
Ease of reclosing the can	7	8	9

4a.   Have you bought any ground coffee since the time   YES........ 1
you were interviewed in the store about two weeks ago?   NO........ X
       (IF YES):   What brand?_____

4b.   The next time you buy ground coffee   FOLGER'S IN THE NEW CAN.... 1
do you think it will be Folger's in the   SOME OTHER KIND............. 2
new can or some other kind?

4c.   Why is that?

5.   Have you bought this Folger's brand of   HAVE BOUGHT BEFORE........ 1
coffee in this new can before, or is this   FIRST TIME.................... 2
the first time?

EXHIBIT 5 (Continued)

CLASSIFICATION

A.	Which of the following groups comes closest to your own age? (READ LETTER AND GROUP)	A. UNDER 25	1
		B. 25—34	2
		C. 35—44	3
		D. 45 AND OVER	4
		REFUSED	0

B. Would you tell me the last grade you completed in school?

8th GRADE OR LESS 1
1–3 YEARS HIGH SCHOOL 2
4 YEARS HIGH SCHOOL 3
ANY COLLEGE 4
REFUSED 0

C. What is the occupation of the head of the household?

_____

D. Which of the following comes closest to your family's total annual income? (READ LETTER AND GROUP)

A. UNDER $3,000 1
B. $3,000—$4,999 2
C. $5,000—$7,499 3
D. $7,500—$9,999 4
E. $10,000 and over 5
REFUSED 0

NAME_____   PHONE NO._____
ADDRESS_____
CITY_____   STATE_____
INTERVIEWER'S NAME_____   DATE_____

EXHIBIT 6

Percentages of Respondents Who Considered Folger's No-Key Can Better Than, Same As, or Worse Than Conventional Key Can

	All Respondents	Respondents by Usual Brand of Ground Coffee	
		Folger's	*Other*
(Number of Respondents)	(125)	(95)	(30)*
	100%	100%	100%
Consider New Container			
Better than the usual coffee can	86	88	80
About the *same* as the usual coffee can	12	10	17
Worse than the usual coffee can	2	2	3

* Percentages should be interpreted with caution because of the small base.

Question asked: Would you say that the new type of coffee can was, generally speaking, better or worse or about the same as the usual kind of coffee can?
Respondents were women who had purchased Folger's ground coffee in the no-key can in Stockton, California, during the weekends of November 8 and 15, 1962.

EXHIBIT 7

Ground Coffee Purchasing by Respondents since and before First Interview

	All Respondents	Respondents by Usual Brand of Ground Coffee	
		Folger's	Other
(Number of Respondents)	(125)	(95)	(30)
	100%	100%	100%
Purchases of Coffee since Initial Interview			
Have Bought Ground Coffee in Past Two Weeks (since Initial Interview)	61%	63%	53%
Folger's	56	59	47
Hills Brothers	2	1	3
Maxwell House	1	1	—
Chase & Sanborn	1	1	—
Edwards	1	—	3
Sanka	1	—	3
Don't remember	1	1	—
Have Not Bought Ground Coffee Since Initial Interview	39	37	47
Purchases of Folger's in New Can before Initial Interview			
Had Bought Folger's in New Can Before Day of In-Store Interview	47%	53%	30%
Purchase on Day of In-Store Interview Was the First	53	47	70

Questions: Have you bought any ground coffee since the time you were interviewed in the store about two weeks ago? What brand?

Have you bought this Folger's brand of coffee in this new can before, or is this the first time?

Respondents were women who had purchased Folger's ground coffee in the no-key can in Stockton, California, during the weekends of November 8 and 15, 1962.

EXHIBIT 8

Percentages of Respondents Who Said Their Next Ground Coffee Purchase Would Be Folger's in the New Can and Reasons Why

	All Respondents	*Respondents by Usual Brand of Ground Coffee*	
		Folger's	*Other*
(Number of Respondents).....	(125)	(95)	(30)
	100%	100%	100%
Next Purchase of Ground Coffee Will Be:			
Folger's in new can............	90	96	70
Some other kind..............	2	1	7
Will buy what is on sale........	6	2	20
Don't know..................	2	1	3

	Totals
(Number of Respondents Who Said Next Ground Coffee Purchase Would Be Folger's in New Can)........................	(112)
	100%
Percent Referring to Coffee in Explaining Why...........	59
Always buy Folger's; like it better; never use any other brand...............................	48
Like the coffee...................................	11
Percent Referring to Container in Explaining Why........	48
Like the new can (unspecified)...................	30
Like the top.....................................	2
Can is easier to open.............................	1
Can keeps coffee fresher........................	1
Can is reusable................................	16
Can is handy; easier to handle...................	2
Easy to store; doesn't take up so much room........	2
No answer.....................................	6

Question asked: The next time you buy ground coffee do you think it will be Folger's in the new can or some other kind? Why is that?

Respondents were women who had purchased Folger's ground coffee in the no-key can in Stockton, California, during the weekends of November 8 and 15, 1962.

EXHIBIT 9

Percentages of Respondents Who Usually Bought Ground Coffee Other Than Folger's by Reasons Given for Buying Folger's in the No-Key Can

	Totals
(Number of Respondents)...............................	(30)
	100%
Bought Folger's because It Was on Sale........................	57
Referred to Container in Explaining Why.......................	33
Can use container for other purposes: cookie jar, puddings, fruitcakes, freezer container...........................	13
Wanted to try new can; liked it.........................	10
New can looked easy to open...........................	7
Liked the new lid.......................................	7
Can looked easier to handle.............................	3
Can looked easy to empty into canister...................	3
Don't know; no answer................................	10

Question asked: Why did you happen to buy Folger's coffee today? (Day of in-store interview)

Respondents were women who had purchased Folger's ground coffee in the no-key can in Stockton, California, during the weekends of November 8 and 15, 1962, but who said they usually bought another brand.

EXHIBIT 10

Percentage Shares of Total Pounds of Ground Coffee Sold in 21 Stockton, California Stores during Weeks of November 5, 12 and 19, 1962

Brand and Type of Container	Size of Can (lbs.)	Nov. 5– Nov. 11	Nov. 12– Nov. 18	Nov. 19– Nov. 26	Number of Stores Stocking
Folgers: New (no-key)	1	7.0	6.9	8.6	21
New (no-key)	3	3.1	7.8	2.0	5
Total New Can		10.1	14.7	10.6	21
Old (key)	½	0.7	1.6	0.7	18
Old (key)	1	0.1	—	0.2	4
Old (key)	2	12.9	12.1	12.6	21
Old (key)	4	0.1	0.1	0.6	3
Total Old Cans		13.8	13.8	14.1	21
Total Folger's		23.9	28.5	24.7	21
Maxwell House: Old	1	6.5	3.4	4.5	21
Old (5 cents off)	1	0.1	0.2	—	6
Old	2	12.1	11.7	13.7	21
Old (12 cents off)	2	—	—	0.3	3
Total Maxwell House		18.7	15.3	18.5	21
Yuban: Old	1	2.2	2.3	3.1	21
Old	2	1.0	1.6	1.1	9
Total Yuban		3.2	3.9	4.2	21
Sanka: Old	1	3.4	1.5	1.3	21
Old (6 cents off)	1	—	—	—	1
Total Sanka		3.4	1.5	1.3	21
Total General Foods		25.3	20.7	24.0	21
MJB	all	14.7	14.0	21.4	21
Hills	all	17.9	23.9	15.1	21
Butternut	all	3.9	1.8	2.2	9
Chase and Sanborn	all	4.9	4.2	4.7	7
All Others	all	9.4	6.9	7.9	19
Total All Brands		100.0	100.0	100.0	—

Source: Store audits made for Maxwell House Division.

EXHIBIT 11

Ground Coffee Sold in Stockton and San Francisco by Brand and Size of Container During Weeks of November 5, 12 and 19, 1962 (in per cent of total pounds)

Size of Can; Brand	San Francisco* (3-week period)	Stockton, Calif.†		
		Week of Nov. 5	Week of Nov. 12	Week of Nov. 19
1 Lb. and Under				
All Brands	42.6	40.5	37.0	36.1
Folger's	13.2	7.0	8.5	9.5
Maxwell House	2.7	6.6	3.6	4.5
2 Lbs.				
All Brands	56.8	56.3	54.9	61.3
Folger's	14.9	12.9	12.1	12.6
Maxwell House	5.1	12.1	11.7	14.0
3 Lbs.				
All Brands	0.6	3.2	8.1	2.6
Folger's	0.4	3.2	7.9	2.6
Maxwell House	—	—	—	—
All Sizes Combined				
Folger's	28.5	23.9	28.5	24.7
Maxwell House	7.8	18.7	15.3	18.5

* Maxwell House's San Francisco sales district.
† In sample of 21 Stockton stores.
SOURCE: Store audits conducted for Maxwell House Division.

EXHIBIT 12

(Excerpts from a Maxwell House Division Interdepartmental Memorandum)

CONSUMER DISSATISFACTION WITH PACKAGING

In line with emphasis on maintaining and improving a brand's competitive position with consumer-accepted packaging innovations, it is advantageous to identify available documented consumer dissatisfactions with current packages. This is the purpose of this memorandum.

Unfortunately, documented information, i.e., research findings on this subject are sparse and much of the material is biased by the vested interests of the disseminators.

Packaging per se may in many instances be only a contributing factor in a brand purchase decision. Yet it may be the pivot point in this decision if product and merchandising (both advertising and promotion) do not strongly differentiate between brands. In examining past trade articles, it is apparent that innovations in coffee packaging have been lagging behind many other product categories. One available study on the subject indicated that packaging ranked fifth in what the consumer thought influenced her purchase decision, outranked by the shopper's own experience, recommendation of friends, price and advertising.

Two studies, a 1960 study by *Sales Management* utilizing a National Family Opinion panel of 1,000 respondents and a 1962 study conducted for the Chicago Printed String Company by Market Facts, Inc., will be used to demonstrate consumer packaging dissatisfactions and preferences.

First, consumers are vocal about packaging because at every turn they are confronted with a package of some type. Ninety-four percent of male heads-of-households, when asked if their wives ever asked them to assist in opening a package, answered "yes." Certainly this is manifest proof that there are areas for improvement. The most frequent type of container the husband is asked to open is the "jar" (76%), followed by the bottles (40%), containers with keys (27%), and plastic containers (8%). Yet 68% of the women open most of the packages in the family.

At the time of the 1960 survey, the women interviewed felt these packages were "poor:"

EXHIBIT 12 (Continued)

Item	% of Women
Frozen foods	15
Paper flour sacks	8
Rice	6
Cereals	6
Bread	6
Coffee	5
Packaged lunch meats	4
Crackers	3
Cheese	2

What package gave the housewife the most trouble?

Item	% of Women
Cartons which are stapled	52
Cartons which are glued shut	43
Plastic bags or coverings	41
Cardboard box	37
Cartons which need to be closed again	35
Packages with metal binding (required key to open)	35
Pry-open lids	32
Screw top jars	27
Tied packages (string or wire)	22
Vacuum sealed containers	14
Cartons which are taped shut	14
Paper wrapped packages	8
Containers with opening tear tapes	7
Other	4

To judge the magnitude of the package opening problem, the findings showed that 70% of the women found most packages fairly easy to open and 14% found most packages fairly difficult to open. Only 3% mentioned coffee as a product with which they had specific difficulty. Three percent said coffee was a "really good package."

Consumers when asked their likes and dislikes about different closures and containers, responded as indicated below:

Container or Closure	Like	Dislike	Don't Care
Package with spout	87	4	7
Inner wrap of foil	85	3	10
Packages that reveal product	85	1	12
Containers usable for other purposes	85	1	16
Pull tab openings	76	8	13
Aluminum screw tops	71	7	19
¼ Twist off lid	69	11	17
Other metal screw tops	63	10	22
Tuck in top on cardboard package	68	17	14
Square glass bottle or jar	63	12	22
Inner wrap of paper	61	19	16
Large economy size container	59	18	20
Plastic screw tops	53	18	25
Plastic flip caps	52	10	33
Plastic squeeze containers	52	22	22
Individual serving container	49	12	37
Stretched tops on bags	38	42	15
CANS THAT OPEN WITH A KEY	*35*	*48*	*15*
Metal lids on cardboard containers	27	35	36
Tear open cylindrical containers	26	33	36

EXHIBIT 12 (Continued)

Available data clearly point out that consumer oriented packaging improvements which have added to ease of opening and resealing have been well accepted in recent years and that they still represent a major target area for future functional packaging improvements. The value of the material available is that it has largely excluded product and design elements while concentrating on a very manifest level of dissatisfaction.

There are two other areas of concern in the adaptation of functional packaging improvements to varying food categories, i.e., how these relate to frequency of usage, expectations for product freshness, in-home storage and previous dissatisfaction within the product category, just to mention a few. This does not try to include the functional attributes of size and shape.

One note of caution is pointed out in these studies. "The best liked features are relatively recent innovations. The least liked are those that have been around the longest."

(In 1951, for example, 54% liked cans that opened with a key. Today (1962) 35% like them and 48% do not.)

EXHIBIT 13

Notes on December 1962 Telephone Report of Findings of Continental Can Company Study of Acceptance of Folger's Keyless Can in Stockton

186 telephone calls were made to people in Stockton, California. 100 people were aware of the new containers. Of those who were aware of the new can, 55 had tried it and 45 had not. Of the 55 people who had tried the new container:

    69% were Folger's users
    31% were users of brands other than Folger's
    100%

The reasons for purchasing the new container among:
Respondents who usually bought Folger's:

    52% always used it
    20   were curious
    10   thought the container was attractive and cute
    7   thought they could use the container for other things
    11   had various other reasons
    100%

Respondents who usually bought brands other than Folger's:

    64% were curious
    36   other
    100%

Of the 45 people who did not purchase the new container originally:

    2% thought the flavor would not be as good
    36   (reason not available)
    33   always bought another brand
    7   did not because another brand was on sale
    10   bought Folger's in the 2-lb. size (key can)
    12   other
    100%

Of those who had tried the new container:

    49% normally purchased the 1-lb. size
    44   normally purchased the 2-lb. size
    5   normally purchased the 3-lb. size
    2   varied the size of container normally purchased
    100%

Of the 55 respondents who had tried Folger's in the no-key can:

    51% had repurchased it at least once
    44   had not repurchased it
    5   did not intend to repurchase
    100%

    20% had repurchased it twice
    16   had repurchased it three times
    16   had repurchased it more than three times

What brand did you buy the last time?

    75% bought Folger's
    25   bought brands other than Folger's
    100%

Ninety-five per cent normally purchased their coffee in a can.

General Foods—Birds-Eye Division

The end of the calendar year was always a critical time for Riley Smith, product manager of Birds-Eye frozen regular vegetables, who at that time had to prepare the annual forecast of the demand for each of the 35 different regular vegetables that were his responsibility. This forecast largely determined the extent of the Birds-Eye Division's commitment to buy the acceptable vegetable production of scores of farmers during the coming 12 to 18 months. There was little room for error in the preparation. A forecast that was too high would lead ultimately to large inventories, price reductions to move the excess, and a reduction in profits and return on funds employed. On the other hand, a forecast that was short of demand meant a possible irreversible loss of franchise, or a reduction in profits if the resulting price increases, designed to slow product movement and conserve inventories, were not successful. Another factor was that the realization of the forecast could always be confused by unexpectedly large or small crop yields, which automatically led to unbalanced inventories; although this generally did not happen to the whole product line, but rather to individual vegetables.

The forecast to be made at the end of 1966 presented special problems. For the previous seven years the volume demand for Birds-Eye regular vegetables had been declining between 5% and 10% each year as private and controlled labels increasingly dominated the market. However, there was some evidence that the growth of these brands had stabilized during 1966. A potentially greater influence on the forecast was a test which was being conducted by the Birds-Eye Division to determine possible changes in the pricing and promotion strategy for regular vegetables. Because these tests had been initiated in April of 1966, Riley Smith had only limited evidence on their probable impact available to him by November, 1966. Yet he knew that he had to use this evidence in making at least some tentative judgments on the pricing and promotion strategy that would be used during 1967, before he could meaningfully work on the details of the related volume forecast.

In addition to regular vegetables, the Birds-Eye Division also marketed: (a) frozen vegetable combinations, a premium line of vegetables, pre-prepared through the addition of a sauce or another vegetable, such as, peas with pearl onions and French green beans with almonds; (b) vacuum sealed or boil-in-bag vegetables, which were frozen in a vacuum sealed pliofilm pouch along with a butter and seasoning sauce; and (c) southern vegetables, such as black-eyed peas, which had a regional and/or ethnic appeal. To a considerable, although undefined, extent these specialty lines competed with regular vegetables, so that their prospects also had to be weighed for any adverse impact on the forecast for regular vegetables.

ELEMENTS OF FORECASTING FOR VEGETABLES

The major factor which Riley Smith had to take into account in making the year-end forecast were: (1) once a commitment for a certain volume had been made there was virtually no way of getting more product if demand was greater than expected other than the fortuitous circumstance of unusually high crop yields; and (2) the forecast period started in May of the coming year and might extend to September of the following year. In effect, he must estimate demand for periods up to 20 months in the future.

The actual forecast period for each vegetable embraced the twelve months between annual National Distribution Dates (this was the date by which the harvest was usually in, frozen, packaged, distributed to regional warehouses and ready to supply going sales or existing stock shortages). This key date varied according to the vegetable—from late May for asparagus to September for corn—and by the length of the pack period, which might last from three weeks to three months. Most of the high volume items had short pack periods, which insured consistently high quality.

Despite the extreme length of the forecast, and the accuracy with which it had to be made, there was no way of delaying the final decision on the forecast much past the end of the year. The item-by-item volume forecasts determined the course of negotiations with growers, and the extent of the contracts of acreage which were made for all vegetables on the same day in March. Each grower contracted to sell all the production of a certain crop from his acreage, and Birds-Eye, or any packer, agreed to buy everything from that acreage as long as it met agreed upon quality specifications. Each party to the contract had a good idea as to the usual yield to be expected. A high percentage of growers always contracted for the same packer. However, in recent years, a number of growers had given up certain risky crops, which meant considerable competition for the remaining growers of that crop.

BACKGROUND TO THE MARKET

Frozen foods were first sold to retail stores in 1930. Initial acceptance was very slow because of formidable technical problems. The major problems to be overcome were: (a) achieving distribution in retail stores, which meant developing small inexpensive freezer units that could be rented to retailers; (b) supplying these freezers meant providing insulated facilities for storing and transporting frozen foods at a constant temperature of 0°; (c) there was a serious capacity bottleneck because of the lack of efficient portable quick freeze units for handling large harvests.

In addition, a major educational campaign was necessary to teach consumers the difference between quick freezing and the existing "cold storage" method. Consumers needed to be convinced that quick freezing was a vastly superior means of preserving the qualities of the food product, whereas slow freezing was uncertain, uncontrolled and often caused quality deterioration. In many products quick freezing formed small ice crystals, readily absorbed without damage to the product. The existing slow freezing or cold storage method formed large ice crystals which damaged the cells of the tissue structure.

The marketing strategy followed in the mid-1930's emphasized exposure of the product and technological improvements. The war assisted greatly in expanding the distribution of frozen foods. The industry was judged essential to the war effort, for among other advantages, it required less steel than cans. The growing demand from the 24% of all housewives who were war workers and appreciated the convenience of frozen foods was magnified by the needs of the armed services. This set the stage for uninterrupted postwar growth in consumption:

Per Capita Consumption of Frozen Foods
(In edible pounds)

1940	1945	1950	1955	1956	1957
0.58	1.88	3.38	6.64	7.26	7.48

The attraction of explosive growth, plus low initial capital requirements, crowded over 1,500 separate producers into the freezing business by the early 1950's. Most of these producers were oriented toward serving a particular region, crop, or group of farmers. The growing need to deal with the expanding regional and national supermarket chains led to considerable consolidation of these individual producers. Because growth prospects continued excellent, each consolidation resulted in an expansion of capacity which cumulated into a temporary over-capacity situation by 1955.

To gain market volume, many of the consolidated processors went directly to the food chains with offers of regionally controlled labels or special private label packs. By selling direct, the processors were able to keep their margins down. This enabled the retailers to price items from 15% to 20% below comparable national brand items without reducing their high margins on frozen foods. The availability of these lower product prices coincided with a period of growing retailer interest in having private brands throughout the store. By 1954, frozen vegetables were the second largest frozen food item (see Exhibit 1), and between 1955 and 1961 became one of the most successful private brand items.

Frozen Vegetables—Annual Share Trends
(pound volume basis—percent)

Fiscal Year	National Brands	Private Label	Others*	Total
1955	59	14	27	100
1956	57	20	23	100
1957	47	28	25	100
1961	31	39	30	100
1962	30	39	31	100
1963	29	40	31	100
1964	28	39	33	100
1965 (Mar. 1965 to Feb. 1966)	29	40	31	100

* Controlled and regional packer brands.
SOURCE: Birds-Eye Market Research Group.

The apparent leveling out of the sharp decline in national brand market share by the early 1960's was a welcome trend to Birds-Eye and other national brand manufacturers. There was no obvious single reason for the stability of the market shares at the 1963 level. One possibility was that private and controlled labels could not effectively penetrate a hard core of buyers who were "more national brand loyal than private label interested." Also the remaining national brands had learned to live with the situation by adjusting their price and trade promotion strategies. Another factor was the recognition by retailers that variety of choice was important to their customers, and that familiar national brand names had a drawing power that should not be ignored. Finally, some national brand manufacturers had succeeded in bringing out new frozen vegetable items such as vegetable combinations and boil-in-bag vegetables that were often not immediately copied by the private labels.

In the 1960's the frozen vegetable market continued to grow, but at a considerably reduced rate. Average annual growth between 1961 and 1966 was 2.75% on a volume basis, with population growth accounting for an increase of 1.5% per year. The growth of frozen vegetables was entirely at the expense of fresh vegetables:

Total Vegetable Consumption by Process Type
(percent)

Year	Frozen	Canned	Fresh	Total
1954	6.2	39.2	54.6	100
1955	6.6	40.5	52.9	100
1956	6.8	40.3	52.9	100
1957	7.0	40.3	52.7	100
1958	7.6	41.0	51.4	100
1959	7.7	41.1	51.2	100
1960	7.7	40.7	51.6	100
1961	7.9	40.8	51.3	100
1962	8.6	41.7	49.7	100
1963	8.3	42.4	49.3	100
1964	9.0	42.7	48.3	100
1965	9.1	43.0	47.9	100

Source: Vegetable Situation (USDA; TVS-104).

Specialty vegetables were introduced in 1962 and accounted for much of the growth of frozen vegetables.

Retail—Frozen Vegetable Market Growth
(volume in millions of dozens)

Fiscal Year	Frozen Vegetables	Specialty Vegetables	Regular Vegetables
1960	123.6	—	123.6
1961	130.0	—	130.0
1962	131.8	0.6	131.2
1963	137.9	3.0	134.9
1964	144.6	4.3	140.3
1965	144.1	8.5	136.1
1966 (est.)	148.0	13.5	134.5

Source: Birds-Eye Market Research Group.

One reason for the difference in growth of regular versus specialty frozen vegetables was the extent of promotional support each received. Trade sources stated that virtually nothing was spent on media advertising (exclusive of supermarket flyers and other local media) for all regular vegetables in 1966. This was approximately ⅓ of 1% of total industry sales of $325 million. Another reason for the success of specialty vegetables was that they offered a means for overcoming the general feeling of consumers that vegetables were dull, uninteresting, and difficult to make interesting. (See summary of consumer survey, Exhibit 2.)

Those housewives who did not use frozen vegetables were bound by habit, and either a strong preference for the freshness and economy of fresh vegetables or the long shelf life, softer texture, and quick, foolproof preparation of canned vegetables. The fact that frozen vegetables were approximately the same price per edible ounce as canned vegetables while delivering more nutritional value (by not precooking nutritional value out of the solid to the same extent) seemed to have little influence on the preferences for each type. Thus, a study of consumer menus in 1956 (see Exhibit 3) showed that frozen vegetables were more popular among high income families, who apparently were willing to pay for the convenience plus flavor benefits of frozen vegetables and were relatively less concerned over differences in value between canned and frozen.

BIRDS-EYE REGULAR VEGETABLE MARKETING STRATEGIES (TO DECEMBER 1965)

The most enduring features of the regular vegetable marketing strategies were: high product quality, national distribution, wide product line and high individual product prices. Between 1955 and 1965 a variety of advertising and price dealing plans had been used to take advantage of these basic elements.

(A) *Product quality* first received significant emphasis by Birds-Eye during the widespread introduction of private label frozen vegetables. To maintain a consistent superiority over private label quality, Birds-Eye kept upgrading its product standards and exerting closer control over the growers of its vegetables. Through such control it was possible to ensure that the best seeds were used, growing conditions were uniform among all growers, and the latest agricultural technology was properly used.

Disposal of that portion of the product that did not quite meet these new high product standards was relieved by the growth of institutional business, as well as the establishment of a number of Birds-Eye house brands. These house brands were generally offered to local food chains on an exclusive basis and served the same function as a private label for that chain. This business was not profitable in itself, but did provide some contribution to fixed plant costs.

(B) The ability to maintain *national distribution* was a major factor in the relative success of Birds-Eye regular vegetables compared to the other national brand competitors. (See Exhibit 4.)

Most of the difficulties of gaining and/or maintaining distribution were a direct consequence of an almost uniform policy practiced by retailers of displaying only their private or controlled brand and one national brand of any frozen food item. Such a policy was made necessary by the proliferation of frozen food products and brands, plus the high unit handling costs and the lack of freezer display space (see Appendix A).

Birds-Eye had enough frozen food volume to support company salesmen in very large metropolitan areas such as New York. However, about 80% of the area of the country was covered by food brokers who received a fixed commission. Other large competitors used brokers to the same or even greater extent.

The claim of national distribution for Birds-Eye regular vegetables was subject to the qualification that the degree of success within a specific region was highly variable. For example, a high volume item in the Birds-Eye line, such as French green beans, might be stocked by 77% of the stores in one marketing district and 10% in another (see Exhibit 5 for details). As a result of these disparities, 80% of the Birds-Eye regular vegetable sales came from areas that accounted for only 50% of the total sales of frozen vegetables in the country.

Some of the extreme differences between districts could be accounted for by regional preferences, or unusual national or private label competitive strength. In other cases the Birds-Eye brand had been historically weak or strong. During the period of retrenchment in the face of private label advances, these long-term differences were magnified by a policy of concentrating company resources to protect strong products in the strongest districts. One result was that large districts which were already weak, lost so much ground that they could no longer justify the use of company salesmen. Sales experience between 1964 and 1966 showed that the switch to brokers had improved the situation in these weak districts. However, much of the improvement was thought to be the result of the extra effort a broker usually put into a new line in the first year, so there was little expectation that it would continue.

(C) The depth of the sales coverage helped to support one of the *widest lines* of regular and specialty vegetables (over and above southern vegetables) in the industry. Having a wide line was regarded as a significant advantage, even though it tended to diffuse the time the salesman could devote to regular vegetables. Firstly, it meant that Birds-Eye could maximize its share of freezer cabinet space by getting more items into the freezer. Secondly, freezing and packing facilities were already available for high volume items but only used during short harvest seasons. A new vegetable that could be packed and frozen during a different harvest season became a profit contributor even if sales were low. The distribution penetration of the small volume items depended on regional preferences, degree of sales push, and the private label orientation of the retailer. Generally when the retailer had his own brand of a small volume item, he was not willing to stock a national brand.

(D) *Pricing* was one of the most contentious issues in the marketing of Birds-Eye regular vegetables. Birds-Eye had always been premium priced, but how much premium should be required was a pervading question. Until 1964 the governing feature had been the necessity of meeting unit profit goals, generally at the expense of volume. By late 1964 this approach was being increasingly questioned, and evidence was being gathered in the hope of demonstrating that excessive retail price spreads were damaging to total profit performance. A complicating feature was the product line price structure which had evolved into a separate price for each item in the line. However, the following is representative of the price structure in a district with low private label prices (District A), and other districts with high private label prices resulting from an umbrella of very high national brand prices (District B).

	Wholesale Price/Dozen			Retail Price/Package			Retail Profit Margins	
	Birds-Eye	Private Label	Spread	Birds-Eye	Private Label	Spread	Birds-Eye	Private Label
District A								
Peas...............	$2.08	$1.65	$0.43	22.5¢	18.3¢	4.2¢	21.5%	23.5%
Corn..............	1.95	1.35	0.50	22.5	16.5	6.0	25.6	29.3
District B								
Peas...............	$2.08	$1.65	$0.43	24.5¢	21.5¢	3.0¢	28.5%	35.9%
Corn..............	1.95	1.35	0.50	24.5	21.5	3.0	32.2	47.4

(E) The role of *advertising* in the regular vegetable promotion mix had varied widely since the upsurge of private brand competition. Up to 1964 most of the effort had been concerned with strengthening the Birds-Eye premium quality image. However, the impact of private labels had caused volume and profit declines in most of the company's staple frozen food lines by the end of 1964. Since there was no prospect of an immediate end to these declines it was decided that the company should: (1) concentrate its resources on new products with prospects for long-term distinction from private label competition, and (2) use defensive strategies to slow and if possible halt sales and profit declines.

These considerations, plus the judgment that advertising effectiveness was reduced by the fact that Birds-Eye and certain varieties of private label regular vegetables were sometimes not perceptibly different in quality, led to the decision to stop all media advertising at the end of calendar 1964. The monies saved were largely invested in the new specialty vegetable lines. It was expected there would be some carry-over benefit to regular vegetables from this move, since the Birds-Eye name itself would be constantly associated with quality vegetables. By the end of calendar 1965 the specialty vegetables were 20% of total Birds-Eye vegetable dollar sales and 13% of the weight volume.

(F) *Trade dealing* was chosen as the main tool with which to defend current authorizations by stores to stock Birds-Eye regular vegetables. During calendar 1965 and 1966 trade dealing took the place of all media advertising and most of the consumer promotional activity such as coupons, contests and refund offers for regular vegetables. Two different approaches were used during this period: (1) *Buying allowances* were offered to chain headquarters or wholesaler distributors acting for independent stores or buying chains. Depending on the size of the allowance, the retailer might receive a 10 to 30 cent reduction in the per dozen invoice price. The offer applied to all purchases during a given month, but might only be made two or three times a year to a specific chain or wholesaler. This type of promotion was only regarded as effective if the trade became over-loaded with stock and had to cut retail prices to move the excess inventory. Thus, the stated objective was, "creating the impression of value to the consumer." (2) *Direct account performance offers* were intended to serve a different purpose in that they demanded some specific promotional performance by the retailer or wholesaler before any payment was made. One unfortunate feature of this incentive was the legal requirement that payment had to be made to the wholesaler or chain headquarters. Thus a distributor could qualify by placing a small ad in a catalogue and the payment from Birds-Eye would not reach the retailer as intended. Nor was it necessary for the distributor to pass on to the retailer any payment made for an advertisement or promotion of Birds-Eye regular vegetables run locally by the retailer.

(G) *Consumer Dealing.* The cents-off promotion which was independent of retailer cooperation and always benefited the customer was used sparingly, and usually only when there was a particularly heavy inventory to move. One of the reasons for this was that the trade objected to the duplication of inventory extra bookkeeping and freezer space demands and the confusion of regular and special packs. The cost to Birds-Eye of gaining cooperation through extended terms and trade allowances was high. Secondly, there was little of the flexibility usually associated with cents-off promotions because all the packaging and over-wrapping was done once per year. Packaging at some date after freezing cost between 12 and 20 cents per dozen. Finally, experience had shown that cents-off did not help low volume items, apparently because of consumer reluctance to devote valuable freezer space to something that might not be wanted by the family.

Other forms of consumer dealing, such as coupons and contests, were seldom used (see below) because it was felt that they did not address the key problem of protecting distribution.

Per Dozen Advertising and Deal Expenditures

Fiscal Year	Trade Deals	Consumer Deals	Advertising	Total
1958	Nil	.012	.105	.117
1959	.008	.015	.085	.108
1960	.018	.032	.099	.149
1961	.025	.012	.096	.133
1962	.060	.004	.110	.174
1963	.029	.018	.084	.131
1964	.119	.027	.095	.241
1965	.094	.079	.061	.234
1966 (est.)	.169	.021	.009	.199

However, in early 1965, frustration over the dependence on trade deals led to an attempt to combine trade and consumer deals. The offer consisted of payment to the trade of heavy allowances, amounting in total to $500,000 during the March quarter. These allowances were to be used to cut prices on all Birds-Eye products to a specific level. Seven to sixteen weeks' normal volume (depending on the vegetable) had earlier been packed with an overwrap on the package which left room for the retailer to mark in the reduced price. It was expected that the volume packed would suffice for a two-week feature period.

The majority of the trade took advantage of the promotion to stock up. But the unexpected element was the willingness of most of the trade to treat the specially labelled merchandise as regular—sometimes without bothering to reduce the price at all. In few instances was the allowance reflected in reduced retail prices for more than a week. Many consumers were confused or irritated at the pronouncement of a non-existent saving.

THE SEARCH FOR A NEW STRATEGY

By the close of fiscal 1966,[1] it was clear that the strategy of high price, heavy dealing and no advertising had not succeeded in halting the deterioration in volume and profits.

Birds-Eye Regular Vegetables—Volume and Profits

Fiscal	Regular Vegetable Volume (millions of dozens)	Gross Profits (millions of dollars)	Profits before Taxes (millions of dollars)
1955	16.9	8.0	3.3
1961	16.8	9.2	4.0
1962	16.2	11.4	5.3
1963	15.1	9.1	4.0
1964	13.8	8.9	2.9
1965	11.4	7.5	2.4

Nor had two years of promotional emphasis on specialty vegetables contributed profits that could offset the above decline. The unexpectedly long pay-back period was attributed largely to problems in achieving distribution and the strong franchise of the competitors who had entered the market first. The effect on the return on funds employed was even

---

[1] Fiscal year 1966 started April 1, 1965 and ended March 31, 1966.

more drastic since both inventory and allocated plant investment had actually increased.

The skepticism toward the existing strategy gained impetus from disquieting evidence on the inefficiency of trade deals. During calendar 1965 and 1966, over 40% of Birds-Eye regular vegetables were sold to the trade on a buying allowance price and 25% of the total movement was linked to some kind of performance offer. Yet a study of the actual prices paid by the buyer revealed that only 30% to 50% of the buying allowance expenditure had any effect on the retail price.

At this time, evidence on possible alternative strategies were accumulated in a series of *pricing* tests. In addition, a number of potentially useful suggestions about possible shifts in consumer buying behavior were made. Management requested a series of research studies to be completed by early 1967, and it was expected that the results of the studies would be used as the basis for any long-term shifts in strategy.

NEW IDEAS ABOUT VEGETABLE BUYING BEHAVIOR

The following is a review of some hypotheses which were brought to the attention of Birds-Eye management about possible ways of encouraging more interest and usage of vegetables, frozen vegetables, and Birds-Eye frozen vegetables in particular. Many of these ideas had some basis on fact, gathered through various research studies or analyses of specific problems. The problem for management lay in the contradictory nature of some hypotheses and the lack of evidence on their relative importance.

(A) *Overcoming Birds-Eye Regular Vegetable Problems.* The traditional superiority of Birds-Eye regular vegetables was based largely on the consistency of the quality across the entire product line which led to a strong and durable consumer image of reliability. It was probable that the slowly improving image of private-label vegetables was eroding the Birds-Eye position, although the extent of the erosion was difficult to appraise. Some Birds-Eye executives thought that the extent could be appraised by the degree to which Birds-Eye was only thought of in connection with special occasions, rather than as regular everyday frozen vegetables. Others in the division, who agreed with this approach, also questioned what effect the lack of promotion was having on the perceived quality gap between Birds-Eye and private label frozen vegetables. These questions were not easy to answer because of variability in the consumer's criteria of quality. Past experience showed that richness and consistency of color, price level, and evenness of cut and size were all influential to some degree.

One attractive, although hard to accept, hypothesis argued that the strength of the Birds-Eye line should be capitalized on through an advertising approach that linked regular and specialty vegetables. The big unanswered question, that made the hypotheses hard to accept, concerned the degree to which regular and specialty vegetables competed.

The notion of a central theme was somewhat at variance with another hypothesis about a possible quality continuum. According to one researcher:

The consumer perceives three different points: the high point typified by brands like Birds-Eye (the most "carefully selected" and highest price) and the low point by what she describes as "off" brands (brands other than private label or advertised brands *and* low priced). In the middle, housewives position private label brands. The private label user therefore feels she is being a "good shopper" when she selects private label—rejecting both the low priced brand and the high-priced, self-indulgent brand."

If this is true, it suggests that perhaps one way to get some of the private label business is to push private label's "middle of the road" image off center. In other words, if there were brands added *on top*, in terms of the perceived quality continuum, private label brands could no longer be plunk in the middle. This might cause some consumers to upscale their buying.

(B) Possible Shifts in the Relationship of Types of Vegetables. Throughout the industry there was a growing conviction that the heavy users of fresh vegetables were more likely to partially or wholly convert to frozen, than were heavy users of canned. This hypothesis was largely based on observations of a growing dissatisfaction with fresh vegetables— *as they were found in the supermarket.* Examples of consumer's complaints were: the time which elapsed between picking and purchasing actually rendered the vegetables less fresh than frozen; the price was too high and didn't seem to go down during the picking season; the waste added to the final cost; and fresh vegetables were often not uniform in quality. Support for the hypothesis came from company research which showed that canned users would be hard to shift because of: (1) a general lack of interest in the flavors and appearance of food or food preparation and serving; (2) a firm attachment to the traditional flavors and textures of canned vegetables; (3) a lack of confidence in their ability to cook well, and a reliance on canned vegetables as the "safest" to prepare; and (4) a strong budget orientation with "low cost" being a significant factor in the choice of the canned type.

(C) Identification of Market Segments for Frozen Vegetables. There was a constant need for information on the size and characteristics of various market groups which might offer opportunities for increased Birds-Eye usage. Among the groups suggested were: (1) present users; (2) multiple vegetable type users; (3) weight watchers who desired a sensible nutritious eating plan; (4) young mothers—particularly because children who become used to the texture and taste of canned vegetables are hard to switch to fresh; (5) working women who desire quick and easy preparation without sacrifice of quality and appearance, and have the additional money to contribute to the family budget; (6) young and old couples—representing the two periods in the life cycle with maximum interest in self-satisfaction and no diversion from family demands. Some evidence on the size of these market targets was available from existing knowledge about family characteristics (see Exhibit 6).

Other questions concerned the potential in each of the above groups if some of the problems of frozen vegetable usage could be overcome in new ways. Two notable problems were the need to watch frozen vegetables closely while they were being cooked, and the inability of a standard 10 ounce package to exactly satisfy most family needs.

The problem of package size was borne out by the growing popularity of the 20 or 32 ounce see-through economy size plastic bags.

Frozen Vegetables Annual Volume Trend by Package Size (percent)

	1962	1963	1965	1966
20–32 ounce size	11	14	16	20 ↑
Other sizes	89	86	84	80 ↓

SOURCE: Birds-Eye Market Research Group.

Not only did these bags offer a free flowing product so the housewife could use as much as necessary, but the package apparently also enhanced the appearance of the vegetables. As of late 1966 Birds-Eye had not been able to discover how to take advantage of the demand for the large package. There was a feeling that retailers would not permit two different economy size bags in the freezer at the same time, and it would be very hard to differentiate the bags because of lack of space for advertising.

RESULTS OF PRICING TESTS

During calendar year 1964 and 1965 three low price tests were in effect in different parts of the country—one by design and two in response to peculiarities of the market. Meanwhile, the rest of the country conformed to the company policy of a single national price to all distributors.

From these price tests came the first evidence of the effect of lower list prices and reduced deal rates on volume and profitability. The evidence, while encouraging, was very tentative since product movement results were not based on store audits and thus were subject to inaccuracies, as well as to inflation, by transshipments to neighboring districts where higher prices prevailed.

Test 1 (Washington-Oregon). For reasons relating to freight costs, Birds-Eye peas sold in this area were historically priced 20 cents a dozen (about 10%), below the national price. Deal rates were adjusted downward to partly compensate for the reduced gross profit. The effect of this long run price reduction on sales is shown below for a six months period in 1964.

	District Sales as % of National Birds-Eye Sales		Birds-Eye Share of Market within District	
	All Vegetables	*Peas*	*All Vegetables*	*Peas*
Seattle...................	5.1%	6.5%	10.1%	10.8%
Portland.................	3.0	5.1	5.0	9.1

Test 2 (Buffalo-Syracuse). During the spring, summer and fall quarters of 1965, prices and deal rates on beans and spinach were reduced together to a level where the net price after deals in the area approximated the national net price. Birds-Eye sales of these products decreased 9.5%, over the same period of the year before in the test area, compared to a decline of 20% in the adjacent areas.

Test 3 (San Francisco-Los Angeles). By December, 1964, the combination of high Birds-Eye regular vegetable prices and low private label margins and retail prices in the San Francisco district caused: (1) unusually wide price spreads with Birds-Eye prices from 15% to 40% higher than typical private label prices on the same item, (2) an acceleration in the decline of consumer demand for Birds-Eye vegetables, and (3) loss of authorization in the Apex grocery chain, which represented 15.6% of that district's volume. The Apex business was taken over by a competitor, who offered lower retail prices and higher margins.

To protect the San Francisco market from further deterioration an immediate price cut was made. The amount of the cut per item varied, but generally put Birds-Eye close to the new national brand competitive prices (see Exhibit 7). This move, however, caused a negative reaction in the Los Angeles market where price spreads were also large. Existing authorizations in Los Angeles were under attack as national brand competitors tried to lower their prices. The disparity in wholesale price between San Francisco and Los Angeles led to considerable bootlegging (reshipping) and prospects of legal problems. The move to equalize San Francisco and Los Angeles prices in July, 1965 was unavoidable. To protect profit margins the new equalized price structure was somewhat higher than that put into effect in San Francisco in January, 1965 (see Exhibit 7 and below).

Product	Existing San Francisco Price	Existing Los Angeles Price	New San Francisco— Los Angeles Price
French beans............	$2.07	$2.52	$2.31
Broccoli................	2.36	2.90	2.42
Cut corn................	1.78	2.01	1.92
Peas...................	1.98	2.12	1.98
Leaf spinach............	1.68	1.98	1.74

A break-even analysis showed that the new prices in the two districts would have to result in a volume performance 7% better than the balance of the country, to maintain the existing contribution less deals margin:

Break-Even Analysis (June 1965)
(rate per dozen)

	National Price	San Francisco— Los Angeles Current Price
Gross sales.....................	$2.52	$2.30
Net sales.......................	2.06	1.90
Contribution margin..............	1.09	0.97
Promotions.....................	0.25	0.18
Contributions (less promotions)......	$0.84	$0.79

Interim results showed that the price cut did improve the over-all contribution less deals margin. Whereas national regular vegetable sales (excluding San Francisco and Los Angeles) were down 8.7% between September, 1964 and September, 1965, San Francisco sales were up 7.6% for the same period and Los Angeles was up 0.2%.

FISCAL 1967 MARKETING STRATEGY

The results of the pricing tests were sufficiently convincing that Birds-Eye management permitted the regular vegetables manager to move gradually toward a structure of lower everyday pricing for regular vegetables. Experience was to be gained by offering several alternative plans in three areas which varied in competitive conditions, price levels and price spreads. (See Exhibit 8 for a description of areas chosen.) The results of these tests would be used to specify the new established prices on regular vegetables. The plan called for one of the new low-price structures to be extended to the whole country by March, 1967, *IF* results were satisfactory.

The alternative plans had the following features in common:

(A)   Reduced price spreads between Birds-Eye and private label on most products—but maintaining some premium for Birds-Eye.

(B)   Elimination of the existing structure of individual item wholesale prices, in favor of grouped wholesale prices. It was felt that having three prices rather than 20 would: make it easier for the sales force to gain acceptance of the new prices; increase consumer acceptance and awareness through product grouping in the retail cabinet by price level; mask wide price spreads where they still existed; and encourage multiple consumer purchases of Birds-Eye products.

(C)   Psychological pricing which basically meant pricing within the same decile as private label. It was well known that it was more attractive for a higher priced product to have a 2 cent difference at 2/39 cents and 2/37 cents than at 2/41 cents and 2/39 cents.

(D)   Wholesale prices set to give the trade a maximum 25% margin. No product was to be priced at a level that didn't yield some contribution at the merchandising margin level unless the inventory position was long.

(E)   Trade deals were to be accommodated to each plan by the requirement that the net price, after the allowance was taken, be the same under both new and old price plans. It was hoped that this would reduce the volume increase needed to break even. The effect of such a requirement was difficult to appraise, but it was clear that fewer goods would move at deal prices, since there was less incentive for the dealer to maintain stocks that would last from one quarterly deal period to the next.

(F)   Price cuts would be directed at high volume items, which were particularly price sensitive.

The request to proceed with these three price tests, and ultimately a lower everyday price structure, was accompanied by a request for newspaper and radio advertising in support of the reductions. The request was based on: (1) the general lack of buyer awareness of specific prices, because of the multitude of prices that have to be considered, and the likelihood that the price decrease would not be perceived by private label buyers; (2) the need to justify the price decrease and assure the buyer that there would be no decrease in Birds-Eye quality; and (3) the need for additional leverage on the trade to ensure that the wholesale price reduction was reflected adequately in lower retail prices. Past experience indicated that obtaining the price reduction would be the most difficult aspect of the plan. Company management agreed on the extent of the latter problem, but felt that the execution of the plan was entirely a sales department responsibility, and that local advertising would have little useful effect.

DESCRIPTION OF ALTERNATIVE PLANS BY MARKET

1. Cleveland Market.   Pricing was aimed at specific group retail prices, 1 cent per selling unit below the decile break, i.e., 2/39 cents,

2/49 cents, 29 cents. The buying allowance was reduced from an average 20 cents per dozen to 10 cents per dozen. The following sample of items shows the extent of the cuts:

		Current Price (Dozen)	New Price (Dozen)	Retail Price Objective
Group 1:	Peas....................	$2.12	$1.80	2/39¢
	Cut beans...............	2.52	1.80	2/39¢
	French beans............	2.52	1.80	2/39¢
	Cut corn................	2.01	1.80	2/39¢
	Leaf spinach............	1.98	1.80	2/39¢
Group 2:	Broccoli................	2.90	2.30	2/49¢
	Italian beans............	2.67	2.30	2/49¢
	Wax beans..............	2.45	2.30	2/49¢

2. *Washington Market.* Pricing was aimed at the above retail price objectives, but with 10 cents per dozen higher wholesale price across the board (see Exhibit 8 for the reason for the difference in approach to this market).

3. *Dallas Market.* Differed by applying the lower retail and wholesale prices to only 60% of the line, and sharply reducing deal rates to totally offset the amount of gross profit loss due to the price reductions.

4. *Metropolitan Boston Market.* Only two products, French beans and cut beans, were adjusted to the new Cleveland price structure. According to the manager, ". . . the purpose of this move was to test trade reactions to reductions, which if reflected at retail at a 25% margin, would have Birds-Eye and private label at approximately the same price. In short, we are walking cautiously in this market where high margins are taken on both private label and Birds-Eye rather than gambling on a full line approach which, if the trade reacted unfavorably, could cost us our vegetable franchise via de-authorization. The equally unattractive alternate result could be our pouring money down the drain if the trade did not reflect reductions at all."

INFLUENCE OF NEW PRICES ON VOLUME— APPRAISAL OF TEST RESULTS

The first real need for an appraisal of the effectiveness of the price tests, developed from the annual demand forecast which was due at the end of 1966. In the past, forecasts had been strongly influenced by a seemingly inevitable 6% to 8% annual decline in sales. If a new national price structure were put into effect in April, 1967, this would no longer be true. But the product manager realized that the extent to which the historical decline in *volume* (not necessarily profits) was reduced or eliminated would depend on: (*a*) the price alternative chosen (whether Cleveland or Washington test levels, or something higher, and whether applicable to the full line or merely selected items as in Dallas); (*b*) the extent of reduction in deal rates; and (*c*) the projection of the volume increase in the test district to the national market.

The projection to national volume required the manager to recognize and balance: (1) the peculiarities of the test areas (see Exhibit 8); (2) the possibility that the sales force in the test district might have executed the new prices more aggressively than normal because of the test situation; (3) the possibility that retail prices might not stay at the lower level; and (4) the likelihood that 20% to 25% of the country would reject the new prices. Areas where low prices would find disfavor with the trade were usually those dominated by strong private label retailers, who used the high Birds-Eye prices as an umbrella over their relatively high private label prices and very high (35% to 40%) gross margins.

By November, the manager had in a sense decided on the "Cleveland" pricing approach since he had already recommended that the prices tested in this market be extended to Los Angeles and San Francisco as part of the national roll-out of new low prices. This would be a very significant extension since the Los Angeles district accounted for 14% of the sales of Birds-Eye regular vegetables and the San Francisco district accounted for another 5%. However, the price reduction recommendation was still in the discussion stage with company management, having been delayed by requests for more substantive estimates of the volume and profit improvement to be expected. The pressure for more accurate forecasting data in a specific market was added to the existing problem of the annual volume forecast.

By early November, 1966, Riley Smith had the following data to consider in the two forecasts he had to make:

(*A*) *Sales Results: Los Angeles and San Francisco.* The financial analyst reported, "There is evidence that we reversed a consistently declining volume trend immediately upon reducing prices. There is also some indication that the non-price reduced items tended to level off at the same time (see Exhibit 9—giving 12 month rolling total volume) in San Francisco, where reduced prices have been in effect for one and one-half years. There may be some evidence of another downward trend . . ." However, Riley Smith did not feel that the evidence was adequate to establish a definite price-volume relationship.

The volume performance of the Los Angeles–San Francisco market (up 2.9% between fiscal 1965 and 1966) compared to a decline of 7.6% in the rest of the country meant that the price cut had surpassed the 7% volume required to break even. However, a recommended price cut, to the "Cleveland" level, would require a further 6% volume increase in the coming year:

	National Prices Los Angeles San Francisco	San Francisco— Los Angeles Price (as of June 1965)	Recommended "Cleveland" Level Prices
Gross sales....................	$2.52	$2.30	$2.15
Net sales......................	2.06	1.90	1.79
Contribution margin.............	1.09	0.97	0.86
Promotions.....................	0.25	0.18	0.11
Contributions less promotions......	$0.84	$0.79	$0.75
Required volume increase to break at new price level.............	+7%	+6%	

(B) The analyst reported in the same memo, that, "In the *Buffalo-Syracuse* test, little change in the downward trend has been observed. The price reduced products continue to decline at rates equal to those for non-price-reduced products."

(C) *Store Audit Results: Cleveland-Washington.* A total of 40 stores had been audited in these two test areas between April and August of 1966. The overall results were very favorable. The Birds-Eye share of total frozen vegetables sales of 20 test items was up 34 percent and 26 percent in Cleveland and Washington, respectively. Most of the improvement was at the expense of private label regular vegetables. However, interpretation of the results was complicated by: (1) a sharp increase in the number of times Birds-Eye prices were featured in store advertising material; (2) Birds-Eye did not have a direct competitor in a specific vegetable item more than 40% of the time; and (3) in the remaining competitive situations Birds-Eye was out of stock or not stocked 35% of the time and prices were not reduced in a further 25% of the possible occasions. At the same time, factory shipments were up 29% in Cleveland and down 0.6% in Washington over the same period in the previous year. Without considering these two markets, the national shipments were down 8.8% from the year before.

(D) *Boston Market.* The only useful result was an object lesson in the difficulties of getting trade cooperation in the toughest markets. Even six months after the 72 cent per dozen reduction on the two vegetables went into effect, there was no effect to be seen on retail prices. Nor was there any promotion by the trade. District sales of Birds-Eye cut beans were up 3% in the six months, while sales of French beans were up 6%. These increases, however, only paralleled a 4% increase in district sales of all Birds-Eye regular vegetables.

LONG RUN MARKETING STRATEGY

There was a keen awareness among Birds-Eye management that pricing could only achieve short run success in reversing the regular vegetable sales and profit declines. It was felt that true long run success would

EXHIBIT 1 →

Annual Sales Trends—Major Frozen Categories—(Retail Prices)

	Vegetables*		Fruits		Fruit Juices		Seafoods		Meat		Poultry		Prepared Foods	
	MM$	% Change	MM$	% Change	MM$	% Change	MM$	% Change	MM$	% Change	MM$	% Change	MM$	% Change
1955	217		53		211		106		57		371		151	
1956	235	+9	56	+7	230	+9	111	+5	72	+26	400	+8	261	+73
1957	257	+9	60	+7	255	+11	114	+3	83	+15	439	+10	339	+30
1958	254	−1	57	−4	273	+7	120	+5	87	+5	481	+10	431	+27
1959	280	+10	56	−3	317	+16	126	+5	84	−4	499	+4	475	+10
1960	300	+7	56	+1	304	−4	118	−6	78	−7	512	+3	537	+13
1961	311	+4	58	+3	317	+4	119	+1	75	−3	512	—	565	+5
1962	345	+11	63	+9	348	+10	126	+6	78	+3	498	−3	631	+12
1963	364	+6	68	+7	330	−5	132	+5	78	+1	522	+5	654	+4
1964	385	+6	60	−12	341	+3	129	−2	75	−4	533	+2	707	+8

* Includes potatoes.
SOURCE: *Frozen Food Review.*

come from a significant differentiation of Birds-Eye products from private label and other competition. Such an achievement would permit improved margins, a return to consumer advertising and hopefully less dependence on commodity marketing techniques.

EXHIBIT 2

Consumer Survey—Attitudes toward Vegetables
(excerpts only)

Vegetables are the dullest—most "difficult" type of food to make more appetizing, according to almost half the women interviewed.

	% Selecting as Most Dull Food 1,034 = 100%	% Selecting as Most Difficult to Make More Appetizing 1,034 = 100%
Vegetables........................	42	53
Meat.............................	5	9
Salad............................	7	8
Bread/rolls.......................	21	3
Dessert..........................	7	3
None............................	16	24
All..............................	1	—
No answer.......................	1	—
	100	100

SOURCE: USDA Survey.

College educated women, more than any other group, are likely to regard vegetables as the type of food hardest to make appetizing.

The most frequently cited reasons for selecting vegetables as a difficult type of food include . . .

Narrow range of vegetable recipes	39%
("Only a few ways to fix . . .")	
Personal and/or family disliking of vegetables	21%
Tendency to "stick to only a few kinds of vegetables"	19%

Additional evidence of women's frustration with vegetables is the large majority of women agreeing with these two statements:

"It's hard to think up new ways of serving vegetables." (79% agree)

and

"I often wish there were some ways to make vegetables more interesting." (81% agree)

Difficulty in Getting Children to Eat Vegetables

Almost three-fifths of the mothers in the sample claimed to have difficulty in getting their children to eat vegetables. Of these mothers, about half said they prepare vegetables in special ways, the most popular preparations being:

EXHIBIT 2 (Continued)

cream sauce (46% of responses), cheese sauce (16%), butter (12%), casseroles (18%), sauces in general (9%) and several vegetables together (7%).

Receptiveness to a New Product Designed to Make Vegetables More Appetizing

Women were asked which type of new product they would prefer, one designed to make vegetables more appetizing, another to make meat more appetizing, and the other to make desserts more appetizing. The resulting vote on this question gave a slight edge to the meat product over the one for vegetables.

New Product For	%
Meat	42
Vegetables	39
Desserts	15
None	3
All	1

Only half of the women who originally said vegetables were "most difficult to make appetizing" indicated a preference for the new vegetable product. Most of the "defectors" decided that a meat product would be more important to them. Basically, the appeal for the meat product was attributable to the perceived importance of meat, relative to other foods, in the overall success of a meal.

The most frequently noted reason for preferring the vegetable product was its possible use as a means of inducing family members (particularly children) to eat more vegetables. The other major reasons centered on the women's own frustrations in their search for new ways of preparing vegetables.

Women who preferred the vegetable product tended to be somewhat better educated and of higher income than the women who preferred the meat product.

EXHIBIT 3

Results of 1956 Menu Study

(based on one week's consumption by 4,000 families)

Vegetable	Form	Income Class		
		$7,000+	*$4,000 to $6,999*	*Under $4,000*
1. Green beans	Fresh	700	791	1,327
	Frozen (% of total)	221 (15%)	157 (10.2%)	72 (3.8%)
	Canned	558	593	520
		1,479	1,541	1,919
2. Corn	Fresh	231	313	500
	Frozen (% of total)	139 (11%)	126 (9.5%)	77 (5.9%)
	Canned	806	881	732
		1,176	1,320	1,309
3. Peas	Fresh	187	268	605
	Frozen	503 (31%)	365 (21.8%)	287 (15.9%)
	Canned	932	1,044	910
		1,622	1,677	1,802

Number of families/income class:

$7,000+ .... 11 million
$4,000 to 6,999 .... 22.6 million
Under $4,000 .... 17.6 million

NOTE: All figures are expressed in servings per 1000 people.

EXHIBIT 4

Share of Market Trends—By Brand
(percent)

	FY 1956	FY 1957	FY 1958	FY 1961	FY 1962	FY 1963	FY 1964	FY 1965	FY 1966	Calendar 1966			
										Feb.–Mar.	April–May	June–July	Aug.–Sept.
Birds-Eye................	19.6	18.9	16.8	13.3	13.2	12.5	11.1	10.6	9.2	12.1	11.5	12.1	12.2 (AVG) 12.1
Four largest competitive brands................	39.4	38.1	32.2	17.7	16.8	16.5	16.9	18.4	18.8				
Private, controlled house labels and insignificant regional labels..........	41	43	53	69	70	71	72	71	73				(AVG) 75.7

Sources: Birds-Eye Market Research Department; consumer panel data until February 1966 when store audit data substituted.

EXHIBIT 5

Distribution Analysis
(based on % of store's stocking)

	Chopped Spinach	Green Beans (French)	Green Peas
National (Metropolitan).............	41	50	67
New York District..................	74	65	76
Boston District.....................	31	30	42
Youngstown District...............	77	77	81
Philadelphia District...............	43	65	80
Detroit District.....................	74	65	76
Atlanta District.....................	35	48	61
Chicago District....................	31	41	82
St. Louis District...................	31	41	82
Dallas District......................	15	26	42
Los Angeles District...............	31	53	75
San Francisco District..............	20	26	42

SOURCE: Birds-Eye Market Research Department.

EXHIBIT 6

Regular Vegetables, Family Characteristics, April 1965–March 1966

	% of Total U.S. Families	Total Households Buying		% of Total Pound Volume	
		Total	Birds-Eye	Total	Birds-Eye
Housewife Employment					
Employed...............	35	35	35	34	33
Unemployed............	65	65	64	66	67
Occupation					
Blue Collar.............	42	35	44	34	35
White Collar............	33	43	28	50	48
Farmer, Unclassified......	25	22	28	16	17
Age of Housewife					
Under 35...............	29	28	26	30	26
35–54..................	42	42	43	46	46
55 & over..............	29	30	31	24	28
Household Size					
1 or 2..................	41	36	40	31	41
3......................	19	17	14	21	19
4 or more..............	40	47	46	49	40
Income					
$8,000 or over...........	23	39	50	44	50
$4,000–$7,999............	44	39	32	39	37
Under $4,000...........	33	22	18	17	13
City Size					
Urban over 500 M.........	18	20	25	26	27
Urban 50M–500M........	15	17	16	16	14
Suburban over 500M.......	15	19	22	22	26
Suburban 50M–500M......	12	15	16	14	18
Under 50M.............	40	29	21	22	15

SOURCE: Birds-Eye Market Research Department.

EXHIBIT 7

Price and Deal Schedule—January 1965,
San Francisco District

Item*	1964 Retail Prices (per 10 Ounce Package)		Wholesale Prices (Per Dozen)				Promotional Offer‡	
	Birds-Eye	Private Label	Birds-Eye† (Dec. '64)	Birds-Eye (Jan. '65)	National Competitor	Private Label	Birds-Eye Deals and Allowances (Effective Jan. '65)	Net Variance Birds-Eye versus Private Label
French beans........	29.0¢	20–21.5¢	$2.52	$2.07	$2.15	$1.82	$.18	$(.08)
Cut corn...........	23	17–19.5	2.01	1.78	1.79	1.48	.30	—
Peas..............	21.5	18.5–20	2.12	1.98	1.99	1.76	.23	.01
Chopped spinach....	23	14–15	1.98	1.59	1.56	1.24	.15	(.20)
Wax beans.........	—	—	2.45	2.45	2.40	2.01	—	—

* This is a partial list only.
† This was the national price.
‡ Offered once per quarter.

EXHIBIT 8

Manager's Memo on Areas Selected for Price Tests Nov. 2, 1965

"The markets selected for expansion of low pricing should be representative of probable extremes in trade reaction or in extremes in facility of accomplishing objectives.

1. Washington is judged as a relatively easy market to accomplish the stated objectives because trade margins on Birds-Eye are low, and the current spreads with Private Label high. Therefore, it is judged the trade, in general, will not resent the low price approach.

2. Cleveland, because of high margins on Private Label and Birds-Eye, will be a tougher market to crack, since the accomplishment of our retail price objectives will, in many instances, leave the trade the alternates of having Birds-Eye and Private Label at the same price or reducing the margins on Private Label to maintain a price differential.

3. The metropolitan Boston area, where Regular Vegetables have been declining at a faster pace than national, is also a market where the trade takes high margins, particularly on Private Label. Because of the importance of the market (and the risk involved with reducing the complete line), it is judged that extreme reductions on two products may answer the question of trade reaction as well as pinpointing volume increases we could expect in major areas with pricing close to Private Label.

4. The Dallas District contains market extremes within the district. The Fort Worth trade is accustomed to high margins, and Birds-Eye has competition from two "national" competitors which are priced considerably under Birds-Eye. The solution to this problem is an additional reason for price action. Dallas is a market where the trade works on close margins on Birds-Eye, and it could be expected that reductions in wholesale prices will be reflected to a lower level than the 27% margin objective while reducing spreads with Private Label."

EXHIBIT 9

San Francisco–Los Angeles Pricing

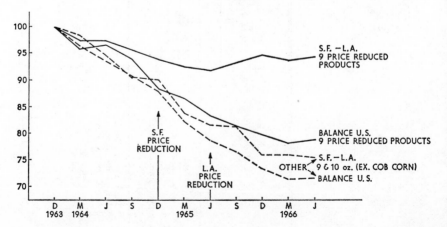

Appendix A: The Economics of Frozen Foods at the Retail Level

Using the concept of direct product profit or DPP (equal to gross profit less direct product costs of warehousing, delivery to stores, shelving and frozen food space) McKinsey found frozen food departments to be consistently more profitable than other departments. At the same time they found considerable ignorance and confusion regarding the true profitability of frozen foods.

The favorable profit picture was largely due to: (1) a high ratio of sales unit of space, from 1.5 to 3 times that of groceries, coupled with (2) high gross margins to cover higher handling and space costs; while overall handling costs were not as high as was generally believed. As a consequence the leverage on profits from volume changes were found to be very high. That is, when volume was sufficient to cover space costs each additional unit of volume contributed importantly to profits.

Thus, in a typical store it was found:

	(Percent)	
	Retail Sales	D.P.P.
Grocery	61	57
Meat	22	17
Produce	10	12
Total frozen foods	7	14
	100	100

SOURCE: Abstracts of a study by McKinsey and Co., published in March 1964.

Implications for Manufacturers of Specific Items

1. Frozen food profits were found to be heavily concentrated in the fast moving items, i.e., top 10% of items accounted for the following percentages of:

	(Percent)	
	Dry Groceries	Frozen Foods
Sales	42	48
Gross profits	35	48
Direct prod. profits (before space costs)	29	48

SOURCE: Abstracts of a study by McKinsey and Co., published in March 1964.

2. Despite wide variations in movement of various items (leading to absorption of gross profit by direct product costs that varied from 24%

to 120%) there was no relationship between movement and gross margin for frozen foods:

Items	Percentage of Total Retail Sales	Average Frozen Food Gross Margin	Average Dry Grocery Gross Margin
Top 20%.....................	62	28.1%	16.0%
Next 20%....................	19	28.4	20.9
Next 20%....................	11	28.0	22.1
Next 20%....................	6	29.5	23.9
Bottom 20%.................	2	27.4	31.8
	100	28.3%	18.2%

3. There was nothing very consistent—or factual—about the basis on which most retailers decided on the number of items to stock. For example, three chains with 50 to 80 stores, stocked 392, 379 and 275 items of comparable product categories.

4. The complexity of the item selection problem is compounded by: (1) the large numbers of sizes, brands and types available in each frozen food category (according to the Nielsen Researcher, Vol. 3, 1964, there were 639 sizes, brands and types of vegetables available) and (2) new product activity. One distributor estimated he was offered roughly 200 new items each year.

5. The prevailing price structure of most groceries didn't encourage the use of significant price cuts. Even substantial gains in volume would not offset the revenue loss due to small price cuts. However, the high margins for frozen foods meant a much higher percentage of sales income could be profitably spent on features, displays, etc. In many stores this opportunity was not being put to use to build volume.

6. Evidence showed that it was often profitable to use promotional efforts to shift volume from dry groceries, meat or produce to frozen foods, despite many opinions to the contrary.

7. Much of the variation in frozen food sales between stores, other than related to the size of the operation, was accounted for by the level of income in the trading area."

Tasty Foods Company

AUDITING A SALES REGION

Mr. Charles Magnes, the Vice-President of Marketing for Tasty Foods Company (TFC), a large national manufacturer of packaged grocery products, was concerned about the Boston Region because its sales had been considerably below the Company's market share objectives. Mr. Magnes wanted to explore the forces influencing TFC's market position in the Boston Region by auditing the region, but he wondered what the best way was to go about making such an audit.

During the summer of 1966, Montgomery Joy, an MBA student between his first and second year in Business School, participated in a special summer program at Tasty Foods Company. The dual objectives of the program were to allow the student to take a good look at the Company and the industry, and to allow the Company to reciprocate with a good look at the student. To effect these objectives, a great deal of flexibility was incorporated into the program.

Since Monty's interest was in marketing, Mr. Charles Magnes assigned the study of the Boston market area to Monty and provided him with the latitude to approach this investigation as he wished. Essentially, Monty's task was to: "Find out why Tasty Foods Company is not the Number One company in share of the Boston market and recommend a course of action which will help Tasty Foods Company attain that position."

Background

The Tasty Foods Company processed and sold a wide product line including cereals, baking mix products, snacks, coffee, salad dressings, margarine, mayonnaise, pancakes, and dehydrated potatoes. Company sales of consumer products had increased substantially over the past several years due primarily to new product introductions. Sales in 1966 reached $397 million. In that year, the Company successfully introduced 26 new consumer products. About three-quarters of the total sales dollar volume was generated by eight product categories: cereals, cake mixes, puddings, pancake mixes, coffee, mayonnaise, salad dressings, and dehydrated potatoes. (See Exhibit 1 for a per capita consumption index of these products in Boston.) Because of its wide range of products, TFC was in competition with many of the larger companies in the food processing industry. TFC's products competed with those of Corn Products Company, General Foods, General Mills, National Biscuit Company, Pillsbury, Procter and Gamble (Duncan Hines' and Folger's Divisions), Quaker Oats, Standard Brands, and others.

Tasty Foods Company subscribed to industry market data from an outside market research organization which provided statistics on total consumer sales by brand within product class within sales region over time. Although these statistics indicated that TFC had improved its market position in Boston in many products over the past five years, Mr. Magnes expressed concern that some of the major product categories not only failed to meet share objectives but also had shown a decline in market share in 1966: cake mixes (-5.5 share points), pancakes (-1.0), cereals (-1.3), coffee (-3.7), and mayonnaise (-1.0). At the same time, other lines that were not meeting share objectives did show some improvement: puddings ($+0.7$), dehydrated potatoes ($+3.0$), and salad dressings ($+2.1$). (See Exhibit 2 for graphs of market size and of TFC's share of market in the Boston Region.)

The Boston Market

After first familiarizing himself with Tasty Foods' relative market position, Monty examined the characteristics of the Boston market. The Boston Region, including all of metropolitan Boston, the North Shore, Worcester, and Rhode Island, had a population of about 5.5 million. Monty found that the demographic profile of this segment appeared to differ markedly from what might be called an American "norm." One out of two persons in the region was Roman Catholic, compared to one out of four nationally. Immigrant groups were strong: 42% of metropolitan Boston's 1960 population were either immigrants or born of immigrant parents, compared to 19% for the U.S. as a whole. The major ethnic groups were Canadian, Italian, Irish, Russian, English, and Polish. Three percent of the SMSA[1] population was Negro compared to 10.5% in the U.S. as a whole; 9% of the Boston City population was Negro. Coexisting with the immigrant population in Boston was an older, higher-income, and more established group—the Back Bay Brahmins—which tended to inhabit the suburban areas. (See Exhibit 3.)

---

[1] Standard Metropolitan Statistical Area.

When Monty tried to view the Boston Region as a socioeconomic entity, he found some interesting contrasts. Across the nation, 46% of family incomes exceeded $6,000 in 1960 while 58% of Boston's families exceeded that figure. The median family income in Boston was $6,687. Bostonians annually spent more per person ($103 each in 1963) on dining out than consumers in most other major cities; similarly, Bostonians spent more for retail bakery goods than did consumers of other major cities. (See Exhibit 4.) In addition, the lower per capita consumption of flour (see Exhibit 5) indicated that baking from "scratch" was not popular in Boston.

Age and social class characteristics provided further insights into the Boston area. The median age in Boston was 32 years; the median age for women was 33.7 years; 38.1% of all women over 14 were in the labor force in Boston compared to only 34.5% nationally.

In the Boston Region there were approximately 6,000 retail food stores. The major chains were Stop & Shop (S & S), First National, and A & P; smaller chains included Elm Farm, Buy Rite, and Star. According to a newspaper report, leadership in retail sales dollar volume had recently passed from First National to Stop & Shop because of the latter's discount operations; however, profits of all three major chains were said to be hurt by S & S's move. Some of the principal wholesalers were New England, Cressy-Dockham, Roger Williams, Almacs, C & S Wholesale, and A.G. The top 12 retail and wholesale accounts accounted for 75% of the TFC's branch retail dollar volume.

While the retail chain stores constituted the single largest distribution network for consumer food products in the Boston Region as a whole, their influence varied markedly in the different cities. For example, independents and voluntary cooperatives accounted for 34% of sales in metropolitan Boston, 67% in Worcester, and 20% in Providence [according to *Supermarket News*]. The corresponding figure for independents and voluntary cooperatives in the U.S. in 1965 was 58.6%.

Marketing Organization

Monty also studied the operation of the marketing department at Tasty Foods. The TFC Marketing Managers, under the general guidance of the Vice-President of Marketing, were responsible and accountable for the sales and profits of their products. The functions of the Marketing Manager were defined in a memo regarding organizational structure.

The Marketing Manager . . . ties together all company activities connected with his product(s) to build volume and profits. He plans, implements, maintains administrative control, and evaluates results for replanning.

To do this he must have the proven ability to motivate people of diverse interests and functions.

Planning. The Marketing Manager shapes a broad 5-year plan for his products and prepares a comprehensive annual plan within that framework. Plans are written, specific, and contain supporting detail; they are both a plan for action and a standard for measurement. They contain,

a statement of current positions, strengths, and weaknesses of a product, and assumptions of expected market trends.

a statement of objectives, to include share, volume, revenue, spending and contribution and subobjectives such as geographical penetration and distribution penetration.

a recommended marketing program based on evaluation of alternatives, and experimentation to achieve objectives set forth.

Implementing. The ongoing activity of the Marketing Manager is directed largely to implementation of the programs outlined in the annual plan. His participation in the decision making that this involves is shown in . . . advertising, promotion, product improvement, and pricing.

The Marketing Managers focused their attention on the 25 major population centers which accounted for well over half of Company sales. The sales effort within each area was allocated to the key wholesale and retail accounts by a weighting of present and potential sales. Actual allocation of the sales effort was the responsibility of each Regional Sales Manager. (See Exhibit 6 for an organizational chart.)

Monty talked with some of the Marketing Managers in an attempt to determine the nature of the problem in Boston. He first contacted the pancake manager, Harry Bremmer:

HARRY: I don't know whether you can say there's a "corporate" problem in Boston. I think you ought to tackle your assignment in terms of the various categories of products we market there. The problem for pancakes, I would say, is considerably different from that for coffee. Our share in two-pound pancakes (#2) increased steadily for five years until this year when we tried to stop offering deals on our products. This attempt to eliminate price cutting hurt us across the nation. But that doesn't tell you anything about brownies or cereals. Regular cereals declined, for example, because of the introduction of Instant Breakfast. My chief concern right now in Boston is the loss of distribution for one-pound pancakes (#1) in the S & S chain which accounts for over 20% of the Boston Region retail dollar volume. S & S even turned us down recently when we offered them a big promotional allowance. Maybe *you* can tell *me* the problem after you've been in Boston a while.

Monty next called on the cereal manager, Arthur Gordon, and asked him if he could offer any suggestions as to the problems in Boston.

ART: I don't know how much I can help you, Monty. Although I've personally never been in Boston, I don't think that Boston's problems are any different from those in any other key marketing area. All our cereal products have the same trouble; the "franchise," or brand loyalty, is weak.

MONTY: You make it *sound* really bad, but the record shows you've increased your share of cereal sales in Boston over the past five years. Isn't that your chief objective in any city?

ART: Well, we've isolated some variables which we think will increase long run sales, and we have the salesmen working on them. For example, the more shelf fronts we get, the more visual impact the product should have on the buying consumer. Also, getting products positioned next to the leading brands provides a higher probability of the consumer seeing and buying them.

The increase in the number of trade and consumer promotions offered has probably contributed to our share increase, too. When a consumer buys our product at a reduced price, we hope she will buy it again later at full price. But where we don't have strong brand loyalty, we *have* to deal to keep the product moving off the retailer's shelves. For example, when we adopted a policy to stop dealing for awhile, some sales dropped off. The consumer may be buying our products on price rather than on brand preference.

The big questions, Monty, are, of course, where to deal and what type of deal to offer. We can promote either nationally or in selected areas. If the latter, should it be in strong or weak areas? Should we offer trade money or consumer money?

Frankly, I don't know what type of deal would go best in Boston or whether there is some sort of general promotion we could use. What makes Bostonians tick? Maybe they're different from people in the rest of the country. Should we try a green St. Patrick's Day cereal—you let me know. . . .

Monty also talked briefly to the Marketing Manager for puddings who attributed his brand problems to the allocation of the sales effort. He complained to Monty that the Boston sales manager, Parris Shaw, was "always pushing cakes."

Sales Organization

The TFC sales organization, headed by the Vice President of Sales, consisted of 6 Divisional Sales Managers in charge of the 6 geographical divisions, 45 Regional Sales Managers, and approximately 700 salesmen. The chief responsibility of the sales organization was to obtain and maintain distribution of the Company's brands, and to reach the sales goals set in the annual marketing plans. The sales executive groups also advised the Marketing Managers about certain elements of the marketing plans, particularly the use of various types of trade and consumer promotions. All planning and coordinating of plans at the local level were based on discussions between the Divisional Sales Managers and the Marketing Managers, although some informal contact existed between the Marketing Managers and the Regional Sales Managers.

Parris Shaw had been the Regional Sales Manager in Boston for six years, having risen from the ranks of the salesmen. There were 20 full-time salesmen under his direction: 6 were assigned to the key accounts (the largest retail chains); 3 were "sales merchandisers" for these salesmen; 11 covered the smaller chains and independents. The sales force was unique in the Eastern Division because no salesman had left the force in over two years; this record was attributed to the morale established under Parris Shaw.

When Monty arrived at Branch Headquarters in Boston, he introduced himself to Parris.

PARRIS: You picked a good day to arrive! Take a look at this letter I got this morning. It confirms the rumors that have been flying for the past week. First National has decided to cut out what they call "slow moving" products. Some of our competitors have lost up to ten pounds apiece, but it looks like we're going to lose more than that. Most of these products don't account for a lot of sales, but. . . .

MONTY: How come they're so anxious to trim the shelves?

PARRIS: Personally, I think it's a belated reaction to the profit squeeze created when Stop & Shop turned to discount supermarketing. Instead of dropping prices when S & S adopted "mini-pricing" and discontinued trading stamps, First National increased the number of trading stamps given. According to a newspaper report, both stores have been hurt; First National's sales and profits dropped and S & S's sales didn't increase enough to offset its lower margins.

MONTY: What about offering more deals? Would that help to keep things on the shelves?

PARRIS: We've tried trade money, Monty, and it doesn't seem to hit home. Take the buyer from S & S—he probably wouldn't take our salad dressings even if we gave them away. I'm not sure trade money is the answer: last month we offered a deal on cake mixes, and one of the chains just kept the money. We could go for some consumer packs maybe, but there are other problems there. The independents won't take the price-off packs because they can't make anything on them. They'll take trade money, but that doesn't solve the problem with the chains. And since the independents are pretty strong in the branch— especially in Worcester—we often suggest trade promotions when regional management asks for recommendations on the type of deals to offer. The trade always asks us for deals on dehydrated potatoes because they sell well, but it doesn't do *us* any good because the consumers of those products are relatively price insensitive. I think advertising's the answer on something like that. On the other hand, I thought we should offer a deal on mayonnaise to meet our competition, but the head office doesn't agree, I guess.

MONTY: Which product categories do you think should be pushed in Boston to improve TFC's position?

PARRIS: Well, we usually can tell which products the head office feels are most important by the number of salesman bonus points assigned to each product category. This list ranks products according to sales bonus points: cake mix, pancakes, dehydrated potatoes, salad dressing, cereal, coffee, mayonnaise, pudding. I have another list which ranks the product categories by quantity consumed per capita in Boston: cereal, coffee, cake mix, mayonnaise, puddings, dehydrated potatoes, salad dressings, and pancakes. By consolidating these two, I came up with a list of specific products I think we ought to push: pancakes (#2), instant coffee, chocolate and butterscotch pudding, Berry Bran, and Yellow Cake. Since Bostonians consume more of these specific products than people almost anywhere in the country, I think they ought to be pushed the hardest.

Parris discussed new product introductions with Monty since "Raisin Custard Puddin'," a new pudding mix, was scheduled for introduction the following week.

PARRIS: I'm not sure how the men should present "Raisin Custard Puddin'." Three weeks ago, when we presented the deal on one-pound pancakes to S & S, they did a total "movement" analysis of the whole pancake section and discovered that our buttermilk pancakes were the slowest moving; not only did they reject the offer to reintroduce one-pound, but they threw out buttermilk as well! I'm afraid with "Raisin Custard Puddin' " that they'll analyze our whole pudding and pie filling section. . . .

I don't really understand it, Monty. The deal we offered on one-pound pancakes would have earned them a $50,000 profit if it sold as predicted. And, that's not peanuts, even for S & S! But since margins on pancakes are relatively low, they want to use the space for other products. I can see their point, I guess, but it sure hurts.

MONTY: That doesn't sound too promising. How are you going to present "Raisin Custard Puddin' " to minimize the possibility of that happening to puddings?

PARRIS: Well, I've thought of presenting it first to the independents outside Boston. If it goes, the track record and consumer pull might help us gain distribution in Stop & Shop. Our brand image just isn't strong enough to get our new products in easily.

After spending several weeks in the Boston Region attempting to clearly visualize and understand its operations and problems, Monty concluded that he would have to limit the scope of his investigation; thus, he did not attempt to evaluate the effectiveness of the salesforce. He felt, however, that TFC's sales effort was not always directed toward the apparent wants of the trade because the Boston retail trade judged TFC's quality food products as *discount items:* buyers who were once food men had become businessmen who based their purchases on IBM stock sheets.

Monty also concluded that TFC's franchise, or brand loyalty, in the Boston area appeared to be relatively weak; there was a direct correlation between total sales and the number of deals offered on products. To strengthen TFC's franchise, the salesmen had been instructed to concentrate on getting both more shelf fronts for TFC products and better placement of TFC products next to the leading brand to increase the consumer's exposure to the product. In addition, TFC normally allocated about 60% of its advertising budget to national advertising (including print, radio, and TV) and about 40% for deals and other promotions.[2] The cost of the sales force was roughly half of that budgeted for advertising.

Monty also learned that, since 1960, three major events had revolu-

---

[2] Grocery products were often promoted by offering "deals" to either the consumer or the trade. A consumer deal might be a "cents-off" package; a trade deal might consist of a discount to the retailer of, say, $1/case.

tionized the market for packaged grocery products: first, the introduction of private label brands in leading supermarket chains across the nation; second, the trend toward committee buying; and third, the advent of discount supermarketing.

The growth of private label brands increased rapidly in New England in the early sixties. Private labels existed for cakes, bread, coffee, cheese, canned fruits and vegetables, frozen vegetables and juices, mayonnaise, and salad dressing. They were usually given the shelf position nearest the leading brand; thus, as the number of products and brands increased and floor space remained constant, the number three and four brands (in relative sales volume) in each product category were often eliminated when computerized stock sheets indicated they were not "moving."

The trend toward committee buying greatly influenced the purchasing function of many supermarkets. In evaluating new products, a supermarket's buying committee considered profitability, market factors, advertising, packaging, product characteristics, merchandising; no product could gain admission to a store's product line without the express consent of the buying committee.

The Boston grocery market was becoming increasingly discount oriented, especially with the advent of Stop & Shop's conversion to "mini-pricing." Discounting in supermarkets had effectively diminished the number of baking mix products which were carried. When Stop & Shop decided to allot space according to contribution to store profit, the areas of the baking mix departments generally were reduced. With less space available, S & S used "case movement from the warehouse" as the criterion for allotting space to the major brands—thus assuming that its margins on major brands were identical. As a consequence, TFC had lost its distribution of one-pound pancakes in the S & S stores. In addition to the new criterion for space allotment, increasing competition and the proliferation of new products were also squeezing out the slower moving items.

The trend toward discount supermarketing had placed the nondiscount supermarkets in a profit squeeze; thus, these markets were accepting TFC's trade money without reflecting it in consumer prices. There were actually two separate attitudes held by discount supermarkets in Boston: one favored high-powered promotional programs; the other favored consistently low prices on the leading brand. The independents and smaller chains generally adopted the high-powered promotional approach to discounting. They were amenable to trade money and often featured TFC products on mass displays as loss leaders. They did not like cents-off packs because of the additional warehousing space required for the special product and because the cents-off packs were factory marked and had to be sold at the reduced price.

The larger discount supermarkets such as Stop & Shop favored consistently low prices on the leading brand. These supermarkets tended to stock only that portion of TFC's product line which were already best sellers. The aim of these markets was to increase profitability by a high turnover of goods and by reduced labor charges for stocking.

The small independent stores which practiced full pricing constituted about one-third of the metropolitan Boston retail trade. Many of these stores were in the tenement areas of Boston, and they usually carried only the leading brand of any product category. Eastern Division management felt it would be almost impossible to displace the leading brand and take over the business in these stores because they had either a brand conscious clientele or a pre-established relationship with the wholesaler.

When Monty returned to TFC headquarters near the end of summer, he had a massive amount of information on the industry, the Boston Market, and TFC's position in the Boston Market, which he had to consolidate into a meaningful report to Mr. Magnes. He concluded that the most critical general problems in Boston resulted from a lack of communication between the Marketing Managers and the Regional Sales Managers regarding the priorities which should be placed on the various products. He wanted to write a report to management which not only would show how TFC's position in Boston could be improved, but also would be helpful to him in approaching future studies in other marketing areas. Monty's final report to management follows.

September 1, 1966

TO: Charles Magnes
FROM: Montgomery Joy
RE: *A Study of the Boston Revenue Opportunity*

My assignment was to make an analysis of the Boston market which would result in recommendations for improving TFC's corporate position in that market. The analysis was to serve both as an aid to decision-making for TFC, and as a meaningful learning experience about TFC and the food industry for me. This report centers on what I consider the first and most important step in improving TFC's market position—the establishment of priorities for TFC products. Hopefully, by providing the means for setting priorities, the different functions of TFC management will be able to arrive more easily at a consensus on the allocation of resources for any given branch.

The importance of good communications to the effective cooperation of sales and marketing organizations should not be underestimated. Although it is not intuitively obvious that "communications" is the answer to the general question of "How can TFC improve its position in Boston?," the effective solution of marketing problems *presupposes* that a system of priorities has been set up and agreed upon by the Regional and Marketing managers. I have thus tackled the strategic question, "Where do we go?," rather than the more operational question, "How do we get there?"

This report thus has a dual purpose: to establish a priority list for incremental investment of TFC's money and effort in Boston and, more generally, to provide a method for structuring the problems in any given region. On the basis of my analysis, I recommend that the "revenue reward" approach to setting priorities for incremental investment at regional level be used, and that the following product categories be emphasized for incremental investment in

Boston (in order of magnitude): cake mix, cereal, pudding, pancakes, dehydrated potatoes, mayonnaise, coffee, salad dressing.

I have chosen the concept of "revenue reward" as a foundation for approaching the question of how and where TFC should allocate its marketing resources. This concept is a composite of the two elements which are necessary to maximize the return on each investment dollar. The first element is "revenue after fixed." I measured TFC's opportunities in Boston with gross margin revenue dollars rather than sales dollars or tonnage because it provides an approximation of the dollar amount we can expect on our investment. For example, if the long run average return on product "A" is $50,000 per year, we would not want to spend more than $50,000 per year to get it. Revenue also measures the efficiency with which TFC uses its investment capital. For maximum efficiency, TFC should invest where the revenue return per case is the greatest. Based on this criterion alone, the product categories would be ranked in the following order: coffee, cereal, cake mix, pancakes, mayonnaise, dehydrated potatoes, salad dressing, pudding.

The second element in investment consideration is the absolute size of the potential market gain. As a measure of this, I have used the size of the gap between TFC and the chief competitor. Essentially, I take the competitor's level of retail distribution and case movement for each product as standards of what is possible for TFC in Boston and compute how much it would be worth to gain that sales level. The maximum reward for each product is calculated by measuring the gap in terms of the number of cases and then multiplying that figure by the revenue per case.[3]

The "revenue reward" is thus a composite which weights the absolute size of the potential market gain for a product by the revenue per case it returns to TFC. The list of such rewards provides a rough idea of the priorities for incremental investment in any given market. These rewards, in addition to trend and distribution analyses, and information about the Boston retail trade and consumer, should provide the Marketing Managers and Divisional or Regional Sales Managers with a solid basis for decisions on the allocation of resources. Moreover, although the Marketing Managers may have only limited use for the priority list of a given branch, the revenue reward concept applied to a whole region would enable them to spotlight their opportunities on a national scale.

If the revenue reward concept is adopted, it will provide a means of communication between the Marketing and Divisional Sales Managers. Since the Divisional Sales Manager must formulate and defend a division-wide strategy, this concept offers him a basis for planning and for discussing divisional differences. In thus facilitating consensus on priorities for incremental investment or for allocation of sales effort, TFC's over-all position in the market would be improved.

---

[3] A more rigorous financial analysis would probably disregard the absolute size of the reward (which might favor new products) for the relative contribution return each product makes. But if TFC were to disregard the absolute size of the gap for certain products (particularly where the gap was considerable), the Boston retail trade might discontinue additional products. TFC must, therefore, consider the hidden financial cost of discontinuance and reintroduction when deciding on incremental investment.

SECTION I

Boston Branch

In this study, I concentrated on the major product lines which had not met the Company's sales objectives. I measured each product against similar (in price and quality) products among the major brands because these competitors possessed roughly the same tools as TFC for generating marketing impact.

The revenue reward approach may be illustrated by taking Wheat Flakes cereal as an example. The two variables in this approach are the average number of distribution points (DP)[4] per product and the movement or number of cases sold through each distribution point (C/pt.). The top competitor for Wheat Flakes had 98 distribution points in the region with an average yearly movement of 498 cases per point. TFC, on the other hand, had only 73 DP's averaging only 371 cases per point. If TFC gained 25 DP's (to reach the level of the competitor) without increasing its movement, the gain would be worth $15,026, or 9,275 cases. Similarly, if TFC increased movement by 127 C/pt., the value of the gain (holding DP constant) would be $15,019, or 9,271 cases. Calculating the rewards for movement and distribution improvement separately provides a means to determine whether the Boston share problem is one of movement or distribution or both.

The total revenue reward to be gained from increasing both movement and distribution to the major competitor's level is greater than the sum of the revenues for improving each separately. Thus, to obtain the total revenue reward for Wheat Flakes (the competitor's current volume less TFC's current volume), TFC would have to sell 21,721 additional cases by increasing distribution and movement simultaneously. This would be worth $35,188.

The following matrix of the revenue opportunities for the Boston Region market by product shows how much revenue[5] TFC could generate by increasing either distribution or movement to the level of its chief competitor in Boston, or by increasing both distribution and movement to its chief competitor's level. (See Exhibit 7 of this report.) Based on these results, the product categories should be emphasized for incremental investment in Boston in the following order:

Cake Mix
Cereal
Pudding
Pancakes
Dehydrated Potatoes
Mayonnaise
Coffee
Salad Dressing

---

[4] DP (Distribution Point) is a measurement established by an outside marketing research organization for comparing market penetration. The total number of DP's for a given product is computed by weighting the actual number of outlets for that product by the sales volumes of the outlets.

[5] Revenue after fixed, but before advertising, sales promotion, and general administrative expenses.

The "revenue reward" method can also be used to spotlight and compare opportunities between regions. To illustrate this, I have compared the revenue opportunities for pancakes *within* the Eastern Division and *between* the Eastern Division as a whole and the Los Angeles Region. By this method, the Los Angeles revenue opportunity exceeds that of the whole Eastern Division. (See Exhibit 8 of this report.) These results suggest that TFC *consider* taking some action in the Los Angeles market.

Should the proposed revenue reward be accepted?

EXHIBIT 1

Boston Per Capita Consumption Index
(U.S. = 100)

Cereals		112	*Pancakes*		63
Wheat Flakes	102		1 Pound (#1)	54	
Corn Puffs	98		2 Pound (#2)	212	
Choc-Bits	113		Buttermilk	59	
Rice Crunchies	96		*Mayonnaise*		102
Toasted Oats	112				
Sugar Snaks	107		*Coffee*		111
Berry Bran	131		Regular	89	
Cake Mixes		110	Instant	127	
White	85		*Puddings and Pie Fillings*		100
Yellow	125		Vanilla	99	
Chocolate	113		Chocolate	136	
Spice	113		Butterscotch	114	
Angel Food	103		Lemon	74	
Salad Dressings		89	*Potato Products*		93
Italian	62		Instant Mashed	47	
Garlic	73		Au Gratin.	98	
Blue Cheese	97				

EXHIBIT 2

**Graphical Presentation of Size of Total Market
and TFC's Share of Market in the Boston Region
for Eight Product Categories**

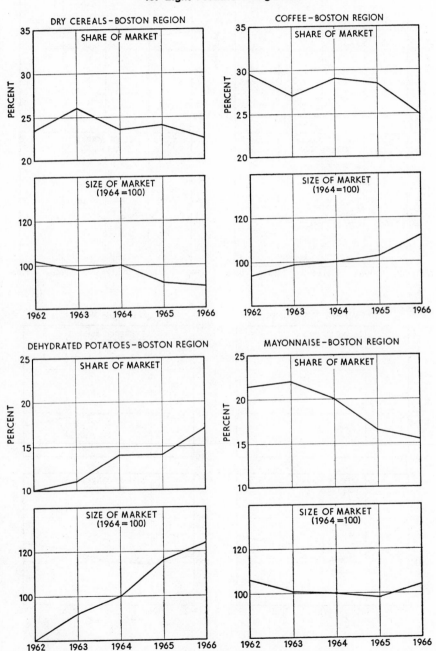

EXHIBIT 2 (Continued)

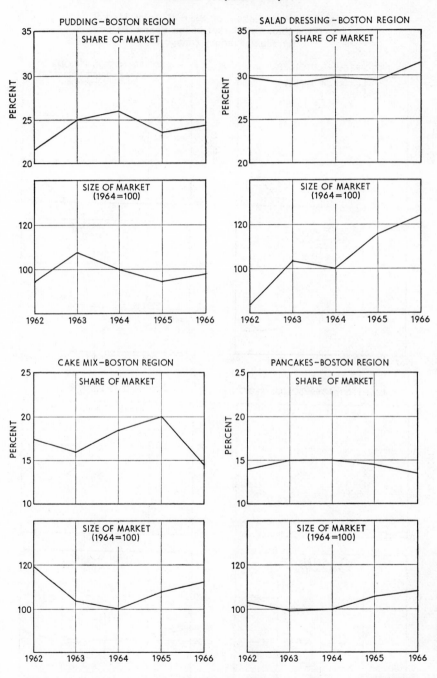

EXHIBIT 3

Socioeconomic Data on Selected SMSA's*

SMSA	Population of SMSA	Age				Annual Family Income			Women over 14 in Labor Force	Foreign Stock	
		Median Age	<18	>65	Median Age —Women—	<$6,000	>$10,000	Median		Foreign Born	Second Generation
Boston.........	2,595,481	32.0 yrs.	32.5%	10.9%	33.7 yrs.	41.7%	21.3%	$6,687	38.1%	12.4%	29.4%
Buffalo.........	1,306,957	30.9	35.0	9.0	31.4	43.8	17.3	6,455	33.3	8.8	23.7
Chicago.........	6,220,913	31.3	33.8	8.6	31.8	34.9	25.9	7,342	39.0	9.7	22.7
Cleveland.........	1,909,483	31.4	34.3	8.9	31.9	37.8	22.4	6,962	36.3	9.7	23.0
Dallas.........	1,083,601	28.2	36.1	7.1	28.8	50.8	17.7	5,925	41.2	1.5	4.3
Detroit.........	3,762,360	29.3	37.3	7.2	29.5	40.1	22.0	6,825	32.9	9.7	20.4
Los Angeles.........	10,687,367	30.9	33.8	8.9	31.8	37.9	24.6	7,066	37.6	9.1	17.4
Milwaukee.........	1,706,994	30.0	34.9	8.8	30.5	35.6	20.7	6,995	37.2	6.7	21.5
New Orleans.........	1,123,033	26.1	37.1	7.3	29.4	59.6	13.4	5,195	33.8	2.1	6.0
New York.........	15,646,307	34.0	30.2	9.7	34.8	43.9	22.2	6,548	37.9	17.4	28.4
Philadelphia.........	5,737,442	31.5	33.5	9.1	32.6	44.8	19.2	6,433	35.8	6.8	18.2
Pittsburgh.........	2,878,235	32.1	33.9	9.5	32.5	50.7	15.8	5,954	28.4	6.5	22.3
St. Louis.........	2,104,669	30.5	35.3	9.3	31.3	46.6	16.9	6,275	34.7	2.8	10.0
San Francisco.........	2,648,762	31.8	32.6	9.0	32.5	37.0	24.3	7,092	38.9	10.8	19.6
Seattle.........	1,107,213	30.2	35.3	9.6	30.5	38.6	21.9	6,896	36.9	8.1	18.7
Washington, D.C......	2,001,897	28.9	34.9	6.2	30.2	35.0	30.5	7,577	44.5	4.2	9.3
U.S..........	179,272,920	29.5	38.5	9.0	30.4	54.2	14.1	5,660	34.5	5.4	13.6

* Data based on Standard Metropolitan Statistical Areas (SMSA) designated by the U.S. Bureau of the Budget.

SOURCE: *1960 U.S. Census.*

EXHIBIT 4

Per Capita Expenditures on Bakery Goods and Dining out in Selected Areas

SMSA*	Per Capita Expenditures on Bakery Goods	Per Capita Expenditures on Dining out
Boston........................	$9.12	$103.12
Buffalo........................	5.99	71.75
Chicago.......................	7.66	102.11
Cleveland......................	4.99	84.88
Dallas.........................	1.92	97.70
Detroit........................	4.57	70.49
Los Angeles....................	3.34	71.93
Milwaukee.....................	5.50	51.90
New Orleans...................	3.41	64.59
New York......................	8.66	97.72
Philadelphia...................	4.18	62.94
Pittsburgh.....................	6.08	47.18
St. Louis......................	5.36	72.65
San Francisco..................	7.56	132.05
Seattle........................	3.68	98.32
Washington, D.C...............	3.48	128.38
U.S...........................	4.64	77.64

* Data based on Standard Metropolitan Statistical Areas (SMSA) designated by the U.S. Bureau of the Budget.

SOURCE: *1963 Census of Business.*

EXHIBIT 5

Flour Consumption Index for TFC's Eastern Division and Selected Regions (U.S. = 100)

Eastern Division....................	49
Boston Region......................	40
Buffalo Region.....................	76
Chicago Region.....................	60
Jacksonville Region.................	91
Minneapolis Region.................	81
New York Region..................	32
Philadelphia Region.................	44
Portland Region....................	71

EXHIBIT 6

Organizational Chart

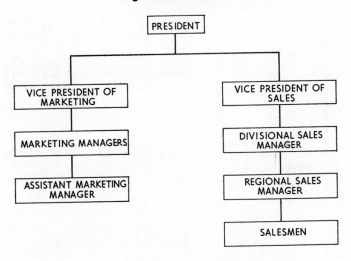

EXHIBIT 7

Boston Region Revenue Opportunity for Selected Products

	TFC's Average Level of Distribution (DP)*	Chief Competitor's Average Level of Distribution (DP)	TFC's Average Annual Movement (C/pt.)†	Chief Competitor's Average Annual Movement (C/pt.)	Revenue Reward for Increasing Distribution (DP) to Chief Competitor's Level	Revenue Reward for Increasing Movement (C/pt.) to Chief Competitor's Level	Total Revenue Reward for Increasing Both Distribution and Movement to Chief Competitor's Level
Cereals†							
Wheat Flakes	73	98	371	498	15,026	15,019	35,188
Corn Puffs	66	81	213	386	5,176	18,497	27,877
Choc-Bits	31	78	43	116	3,395	3,802	12,961
Rice Crunchies	74	89	176	244	4,250	8,102	13,994
Toasted Oats	47	42	84	88	...	301	...
Sugar Snaks	79	84	254	196	2,108	1,764	...
Berry Bran	75	76	79	93	133	...	1,920
TOTAL					30,088	47,485	91,940
Cake Mixes							
White	68	97	214	273	8,564	5,537	16,462
Yellow	79	98	296	532	8,099	26,847	41,403
Chocolate	72	86	138	391	2,724	25,685	33,403
Spice	44	79	176	198	8,870	1,394	11,373
Angel Food	69	98	250	316	10,150	6,376	19,205
TOTAL					38,407	65,839	121,846

Salad Dressings							
Italian	87	95	86	128	482	2,558	3,275
Garlic	79	79	51	101	. . .	2,765	2,765
Blue Cheese	23	63	36	84	1,008	773	3,125
TOTAL					1,490	6,096	9,165
Pancakes							
#1 (one pound)	42	87	177	211	8,363	1,499	11,469
#2 (two pound)	64	88	605	719	14,084	7,077	23,815
Buttermilk	23	25	154	154	339	. . .	339
TOTAL					22,786	8,576	35,623
Mayonnaise	73	86	636	754	7,110	7,408	15,838
Coffee							
Regular	98	99	531	593	1,062	12,152	13,338
Instant	98	98	476	505	. . .	5,997	5,997
TOTAL					1,062	18,149	19,335
Puddings & Pie Fillings							
Vanilla	77	88	76	243	510	7,844	9,475
Chocolate	77	93	88	297	831	9,495	12,299
Butterscotch	39	81	36	201	922	3,925	9,075
Lemon	42	75	84	193	1,663	2,747	6,568
TOTAL					3,926	24,011	37,417
Potato Products							
Mashed	77	88	714	832	5,262	6,088	12,219
Au Gratin	65	69	56	298	199	14,000	15,061
TOTAL					5,461	20,088	27,280

* Distribution point.
† Cases per DP.
‡ Each cereal is measured against comparable ones, e.g., Choc-Bits with other chocolate flavored dry cereals.

EXHIBIT 8

Pancake Revenue Opportunity
Eastern Division vs. Los Angeles Region

	TFC's Average Level of Distribution (DP)	Chief Competitor's Average Level of Distribution (DP)	TFC's Average Annual Movement (C/pt.)	Chief Competitor's Average Annual Movement (C/pt.)	Revenue Reward for Increasing Distribution (DP) to Chief Competitor's Level	Revenue Reward for Increasing Movement (C/pt.) to Chief Competitor's Level	Total Revenue Reward for Increasing Both Distribution and Movement to Chief Competitor's Level
Eastern Division							
Boston Region							
One pound (#1)	42	87	177	211	8,363	1,499	11,469
Two pound (#2)	64	88	605	719	14,084	7,077	23,815
Buttermilk	23	25	154	154	339	....	339
Total					22,786	8,576	35,623
Buffalo Region							
#1	66	77	158	184	1,825	1,801	3,927
#2	85	85	1,076	1,294	....	17,974	17,974
Buttermilk	51	59	343	417	3,018	4,151	7,821
Total					4,843	23,926	29,722
Philadelphia Region							
#1	75	90	209	458	3,292	19,609	26,822
#2	77	91	509	1,153	6,912	48,100	63,758
Buttermilk	40	41	146	250	161	4,576	4,851
Total					10,365	72,285	95,431

Portland Region							
#1	66	77	221	250	2,553	2,010	4,897
#2	83	85	1,104	1,173	2,142	5,555	7,831
Buttermilk	38	37	407	448	....	1,714	1,221
Total					4,695	9,279	13,949
New York Region							
#1	69	89	400	737	8,400	24,416	39,893
#2	73	86	833	1,489	10,504	46,451	65,228
Buttermilk	28	49	252	436	5,821	5,667	15,739
Total					24,725	76,534	120,860
Total Eastern Division					67,414	190,600	295,585
Los Angeles Region							
#1	37	89	224	757	12,230	20,707	62,039
#2	78	92	1,242	3,271	16,866	153,514	197,934
Buttermilk	29	86	278	666	17,431	12,377	54,135
Total Los Angeles Region					46,527	186,598	314,108

Litz Instrument Corporation

In January, 1968, the Director of Marketing for Litz Instrument Corporation, a U.S. manufacturer of analytical instruments, was wondering what changes should be made in the company's new sales forecasting system. When the system was instituted in mid-1967, he had decided that he would make a major evaluation of the program after about six months' experience to determine whether it should be continued as originally conceived, altered, or abandoned.

BACKGROUND

The Litz Instrument Corporation, with sales of approximately $20 million in 1967, produced a specialized line of sophisticated scientific instruments. Prices for these instruments ranged from $2,000 to $25,000 although the majority of the sales were in the $3,000–$15,000 range. The products had an established worldwide reputation, and the company was currently growing faster than the analytical instrument industry in general.

Litz instruments were sold to three major markets: (1) to universities for research and teaching laboratories; (2) to industrial concerns for research labs and for quality and process control; and (3) to government agencies and nonprofit institutions for use in research labs.

Litz and nine other U.S. based companies produced about 90% of the instruments in this product class sold in the United States. The remaining market share was spread among a number of small U.S. producers and two foreign competitors. Since most of the companies had products with nearly identical specifications—particularly in the largest volume items—competition was based primarily on price, delivery, and service.

THE BUYING PROCESS

The purchase of a Litz scientific instrument often involved a lengthy process because the actual user of the instrument seldom had complete authority to make the buying decision. The following sequence, which frequently took from one to six months or longer, was typical of the buying process. First, the scientist or engineer who would be using the instrument would identify a need for such a product and make preliminary inquiries for general product information. Second, he would submit a request for funding either to the buying committee in his organization (if it was to be funded by the organization itself) or to an external organization (if it was to be funded by an outside source such as a government grant). Third, when the funds were authorized, he would solicit quotes and specific product information on specifications, delivery time, etc., from company salesmen and/or individuals at the supplier's home office. In evaluating the various products and brands in relation to his specific needs, the prospective buyer would often check with recognized leaders in the field with respect to product and company reputation. After assimilating word-of-mouth recommendations and information from competitive suppliers the prospective buyer would place an order with a company salesman for a specific instrument.

MARKETING

Product Line. Litz produced 45 different instruments, six of which accounted for over 50% of dollar volume. Although most Litz products were of equal quality to those of competitors, Litz was regarded in most instances as the "Chevy" rather than the "Cadillac" of the industry.

Sales Organization. The complete line of instruments was sold by twenty-one salesmen who covered the entire U.S. Most of the salesmen had engineering or scientific backgrounds and were typically well-informed about the activity and prospects in their respective territories. They were paid a salary plus commission. The sales organization had a back-up technical service staff which had a reputation for fast and efficient warranty service.

Advertising and Promotion. Litz did very little advertising in trade publications. The product line was promoted primarily by regularly mailed catalogues and specification sheets and by occasional direct mail promotions. In addition, special workshops on specific instruments and end uses were frequently held for potential customers. Litz also showed its products at all of the major trade shows.

Pricing. The division had a general policy of being price competitive; however, its prices were not always as low as the lowest priced competitors'.

THE SALES FORECASTING MODEL

In the Spring of 1967, the Director of Marketing, the Production Manager, and the Sales Manager met to discuss means of improving short-term sales forecasting for the company. It was becoming increasingly important to have more accurate sales forecasts because of growing inventory costs and increasing competition. For example, several sales had been lost recently because Litz was unable to deliver the instrument as rapidly as a competitor. The current method of basing forecasts on past sales had proved to be unsatisfactory since sales of individual products fluctuated widely from month to month.

A major concern of the Director of Marketing, Jim Clay, was that the salesmen were not being utilized effectively as a source of market information. He estimated that each salesman probably knew of about 90% of the prospects in his territory and had a great deal of information about the kinds of customers and their end use applications, and so on, but this information was rarely made available to managers in the home office. In addition, he felt that when Litz lost a sale, the salesman generally knew which company got it and the reason "why." Clay felt that this information could be collected and used effectively for forecasting and analyzing sales performance in various market segments. In addition, he felt that such information would help him and his product managers improve other planning.

The Sales Manager, Robert Taylor, was also concerned about utilizing his salesmen more efficiently. At the present time the salesmen kept call records, but there was no formal procedure for accumulating this information and using it to help salesmen allocate their time and efforts more effectively. Although he thought salesmen could provide information which could be used in forecasting and he desired a better way of keeping track of their activities, he did not want his salesmen to be diverted from their primary function—making sales.

Nick Egen, the Production Manager, felt that both Manufacturing and Sales could benefit greatly from better sales forecasting. Egen wanted to know both the *expected number* and *range* of orders likely to be received in the next 30, 60, 90 days even if the forecast had to be made on a subjective basis. If he had forecasts of this type, he could shift production from one product to another to minimize delivery delays and reduce inventory carrying costs.

As a result of this meeting, Clay decided to call in a consultant, George Williams, who had done work for Litz in the past in the areas of marketing and operations research. After hearing the concerns of Clay, Taylor, and Harper, Williams indicated that he thought their respective problems might be solved by a relatively simple sales forecasting and information system. Two weeks after the initial meeting Williams described the system shown in Exhibit 1 to the individuals at Litz and, after lengthy discussions, a decision was made to implement it as soon as possible.

The heart of the system proposed by Williams was the Prospect Report (PR1). This report (Exhibit 2) was to be filled out by every salesman and sent to the home office once each month. Each salesman was to record the following information for each prospective customer: the prospect's name; the type of organization (e.g., government, university, etc.); end use (e.g., chemical analysis); the quote number (if one had been made); the instrument number; the quantity; and prospect status (e.g., pending, sold, or lost). If the prospect was still in the market for the instrument, i.e., "pending," the salesman was to record his subjective probability estimates of getting the sale in 30, 60, and 90 days. If the prospect had been sold by the salesmen in the past month, he was to record the order number for the sale. If the prospect had been sold by a competitor in the past month, i.e., "lost," the salesman was to record the competitor's name, the instrument number, and the reason for losing the sale.

As the prospect reports came into the home office each month, an IBM card was punched for each prospect and the cards were then run through a computer program which produced the following reports:

1. A New Prospect Report which listed all of the information on pending prospects except the probabilities of making the sale which were reported in the past month.
2. A Salesman Summary Report (SS1) which summarized each salesman's pending, sold, and lost information by product (see Exhibit 3).
3. A Product Summary Report (PS1) which summarized pending, sold, and lost information for each product (see Exhibit 4).
4. A Sales Forecast (SF1) which gave the expected unit sales and the cumulative probability curve for each product for 30, 60, and 90 days (see Exhibit 5).

After the above reports were generated, they were to be distributed as follows: The new prospect reports were sent back to the salesman so that he could record new information for the current month; the SS1, PS1, and SF1 reports were sent to the sales manager and the product manager; the SF1 report was sent to the production manager. After processing, the IBM cards were retained in the company's computation facility so that they could be used as a data bank for possible future analyses.

DEVELOPMENT OF THE SALES FORECAST

Mr. Williams explained how the subjective probability estimates of selling a given instrument to a specific prospect could be used to generate the expected sales and cumulative probability curve in the following way.

Let,

$N_{i,j,k,t}$ = Number of units of instrument i, which might be sold to prospect j, by salesman k, in month t.

$P_{i,j,k,t}$ = Subjective probability estimate of making the sale.

$C_{k,t}$ = A correction factor for salesman k's bias in estimation.

$P^*_{i,j,k,t}$ = Corrected probability estimate.

$\qquad = P_{i,j,k,t} \cdot C_{k,t}$

$E[N]^*_{i,t}$ = Expected unit sales of instrument i, in month t.

$$= \sum_k \sum_j P^*_{i,j,k,t} \cdot N_{i,j,k,t}$$

$V_{i,t}$ = The variance of the expected sales distribution.

$$= \sum_k \sum_j [P^*_{i,j,k,t}) (1 - P_{i,j,k,t}) \cdot N^2_{i,j,k,t}].$$

The cumulative probability distribution could then be calculated using $E[N]^*_{i,t}$, $V_{i,t}$, and an assumption of normality. Mr. Williams explained that he expected salesmen to be consistently optimistic about their ability to get a sale.[1] Hence, it would be necessary to correct each probability estimate to avoid overstating the expected value and to calculate the correct variance of the sales forecast. He also pointed out that initially he would set the correction factor equal to one, but as data on actual and expected sales were accumulated the computer program would automatically calculate new values for each salesman using exponential smoothing.

EVALUATION OF THE FORECAST SYSTEM

As a part of his evaluation, Clay asked Bob Taylor, Nick Egen, and individual product managers for their opinions about the accuracy and usefulness of the new forecasting system and whether they thought it should be continued, altered or abandoned.[2] Clay was somewhat surprised by the uniformity of response—almost everyone involved was pleased with the system and thought that it should be continued. However, several persons voiced concern about certain aspects of the program.

For example, Egen was delighted with the probabilistic sales forecasts the system provided. Although he had not made a detailed analysis of the average forecast error for the new system as compared to the old, he felt sure that the new approach produced more accurate estimates. He was, however, concerned about the fact that the expected value—even when

---

[1] The actual data provided evidence to support this hypothesis. For example, ratios of actual sales to the unadjusted thirty day forecast of expected sales for all instruments in the first three months were: .47, .49, and .50.

[2] Exhibit 6 shows actual and forecast sales for the first six months the system was in operation and forecasts for the seventh month.

corrected for salesman bias—typically overstated the actual sales for a given month. He told Clay that he planned to take this matter up with Williams to determine whether it was a result of the way in which the computer program calculated the expected value, the choice of the alpha value, or simply a characteristic of the approach.

Bob Taylor was pleased with the system for two reasons. First, it was much easier for him to keep track of salesmen activity. He could, by analyzing the Salesman Summary Report for a given salesman over time, quickly assess the trend in pending prospects, as well as lost business. Second, Taylor was pleased with the system because his salesmen liked it. Nearly all of the salesmen had reported that the Prospect Report Form simplified their own record keeping and provided them with a quick method of reviewing the "pending" prospects in their territory each month. However, Taylor noted that several salesmen had voiced some concern about reporting a prospect even though they felt they had a very small chance of getting the sale. They were concerned that many of these prospects would be lost to competitors and that Taylor would ride them about a high lost sales ratio.

The product managers also told Clay that they liked the idea of the system. However, when he questioned them about how they were using the information provided by it, there was a great deal of hemming and hawing and few explicit answers.

After assimilating the above information and finding out that the operating costs for computer time, paper, key punching, etc. were approximately $100/month, Clay tentatively concluded that the system should be continued, but he was uncertain about what changes should be made. He felt, however, that the system should be expanded to provide a marketing information system which would have the capability of doing far more than merely forecasting sales. Thus, for example, he thought that if the proper data bank could be set up the marketing group could better schedule individual salesmen, determine whether additional salesmen were needed as well as where they should be located, determine the efficiency of the firm's alternative promotional efforts, ascertain the product features most wanted by different market segments, and so on.

In his thinking about a marketing information system he considered the use of statistical models which would "process" the raw data in such ways as to facilitate the analysis of the data. In particular, he felt that such models would be essential if only to summarize the micro data. He was also undecided about the role of decision models in the information system.

After several months of intermittent study about the design and implementation of an M.I.S. he finally concluded that he should attempt, first, to get his most senior product manager to specify what problems he had to solve of a continuous nature, what relative weight he placed on each, what specific information he needed to either diagnose or help "solve" each problem, the source of such information, its currency, and how it should be "summarized" (if at all) or "treated" statistically. He did not think he should ask the product manager to indicate a value on each piece of information at this time.

Assume you are the Product Manager. How would you answer this request?

EXHIBIT 1

Sales Forecasting System

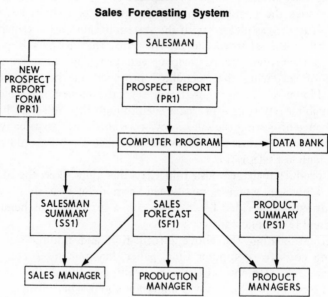

EXHIBIT 2
Prospect Report Form (Form PR1)

Date		Prospect					Probability of Sale				Sold		Lost		
	Instrument	Name	Type	Quote	Quantity	30	60	90	Instrument	Quantity	Competitor	Instrument	Reason		

EXHIBIT 3

Salesman Summary (Form SS1)

PENDING

| | | | Prospect | | | | Probability | | | 30 days | | Total 60 days | | 90 days | |
Date	Instrument	Salesman	Name	Type	Quote	Quantity	30	60	90	Exp. Units	Exp. $	Exp. Units	Exp. $	Exp. Units	Exp. $

SOLD

Date	Instrument	Salesman	Prospect	Quantity	Total Units	Total $

LOST

Competitor	Reason	Total Units

EXHIBIT 4

Product Summary (Form PS1)

					Probability			PENDING 30 days		Total 60 days		90 days	
Date	Instr.	Prospect	Type	Quantity	30	60	90	Expected Units	Expected $	Expected Units	Expected $	Expected Units	Expected $

SOLD

Date	Instrument	Prospect	Quantity

LOST

Date	Instrument	Prospect	Quantity	Competitor	Reason

EXHIBIT 5

Sales Forecast (SF1)

INSTRUMENT NO. _____   DATE _____

EXPECTED UNITS   30 DAYS   60 DAYS   90 DAYS

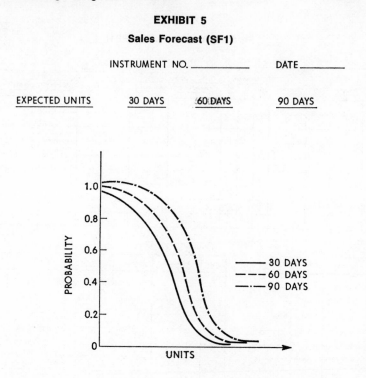

EXHIBIT 6

**Actual and Forecast Sales for Selected Instruments
as of January 31, 1968**

	Month	Actual Sales in Month t	Forecast Made in		
			$t-1$	$t-2$	$t-3$
INSTRUMENT #1	August..............	11	20	—	—
	September...........	9	17	18	—
	October.............	9	14	19	18
	November...........	13	20	19	20
	December...........	13	19	24	23
	January.............	12	12	20	19
	February............		13	12	22
INSTRUMENT #2	August..............	6	8	—	—
	September...........	5	8	8	—
	October.............	5	7	9	8
	November...........	3	6	6	7
	December...........	10	11	10	9
	January.............	2	8	14	9
	February............		9	9	15
INSTRUMENT #3	August..............	11	17	—	—
	September...........	13	22	20	—
	October.............	4	11	19	15
	November...........	11	15	17	19
	December...........	11	15	15	20
	January.............	10	13	21	12
	February............		13	13	23
INSTRUMENT #4	August..............	1	8	—	—
	September...........	3	9	10	—
	October.............	5	10	12	9
	November...........	3	5	9	10
	December...........	2	6	6	7
	January.............	4	8	8	7
	February............		8	9	11
INSTRUMENT #5	August..............	3	12	—	—
	September...........	4	10	11	—
	October.............	6	8	9	10
	November...........	2	6	7	9
	December...........	5	7	7	8
	January.............	2	7	10	5
	February............		5	7	12

INDEX OF CASES

Index of Cases